General Motors J-cars Automotive Repair Manual

by Larry Warren and John H Haynes
Member of the Guild of Motoring Writers

Models covered:

Chevrolet Cavalier, Pontiac J2000 & Sunbird
Buick Skyhawk, Oldsmobile Firenza and
Cadillac Cimarron

1982 through 1994

(2E11 - 38015)

(766)

ABCDE
FGH

2

Haynes Publishing Group
Sparkford Nr Yeovil
Somerset BA22 7JJ England

Haynes North America, Inc
861 Lawrence Drive
Newbury Park
California 91320 USA

Acknowledgements

This book was written with the gracious help and cooperation of Tomco Industries, 1435 Woodson Road, St. Louis, Missouri 63132. Wiring diagrams originated exclusively for Haynes North America, Inc. by Valley Forge Technical Information Services. Technical writers who contributed to this project include Rob Maddox, Mark Ryan, Jeff Killingsworth and Mike Stubblefield.

A book in the Haynes Automotive Repair Manual Series

Printed in the U.S.A.

ISBN 1 56392 121 9

Library of Congress Catalog Card Number 94-77761

98-288

Contents

Haynes mechanic, author and photographer with Buick Skyhawk

About this manual

Its purpose

The purpose of this manual is to help you get the best value from your vehicle. It can do so in several ways. It can help you decide what work must be done, even if you choose to have it done by a dealer service department or a repair shop; it provides information and procedures for routine maintenance and servicing; and it offers diagnostic and repair procedures to follow when trouble occurs.

We hope you use the manual to tackle the work yourself. For many simpler jobs, doing it yourself may be quicker than arranging an appointment to get the vehicle into a shop and making the trips to leave it and pick it up. More importantly, a lot of money can be saved by avoiding the expense the shop must pass on to you to cover its labor and overhead costs. An added benefit is the sense of satisfaction and accomplishment that you feel after doing the job yourself.

Using the manual

The manual is divided into Chapters. Each Chapter is divided into numbered Sections, which are headed in bold type between horizontal lines. Each Section consists of consecutively numbered paragraphs.

At the beginning of each numbered Section you will be referred to any illustrations which apply to the procedures in that Section. The reference numbers used in illustration captions pinpoint the pertinent Section and the Step within that Section. That is, illustration 3.2 means the illustration refers to Section 3 and Step (or paragraph) 2 within that Section.

Procedures, once described in the text, are not normally repeated. When it's necessary to refer to another Chapter, the reference will be given as Chapter and Section number. Cross references given without use of the word "Chapter" apply to Sections and/or paragraphs in the same Chapter. For example, "see Section 8" means in the same Chapter.

References to the left or right side of the vehicle assume you are sitting in the driver's seat, facing forward.

Even though we have prepared this manual with extreme care, neither the publisher nor the author can accept responsibility for any errors in, or omissions from, the information given.

NOTE

A **Note** provides information necessary to properly complete a procedure or information which will make the procedure easier to understand.

CAUTION

A **Caution** provides a special procedure or special steps which must be taken while completing the procedure where the Caution is found. Not heeding a Caution can result in damage to the assembly being worked on.

WARNING

A **Warning** provides a special procedure or special steps which must be taken while completing the procedure where the Warning is found. Not heeding a Warning can result in personal injury.

Introduction to the General Motors J-cars

These models are available in convertible, 2-door coupe or liftback, 4-door sedan and station wagon body styles. All are front-wheel drive.

Since its introduction in 1982, the popular GM J-body design has gone through many changes. Although the basic chassis design has changed little, several engines, fuel systems and ignition systems have been offered.

Four cylinder models are equipped with the 1.8 and 2.0 liter overhead cam (OHC) or 1.8, 2.0 and 2.2 liter overhead valve (OHV) engine.

The 60-degree (angle between cylinder banks) OHV V6 engine used in these models is of either 2.8 liter or 3.1 liter displacement.

Most models use a Throttle Body Injection (TBI) or multi-port fuel injection (MPFI) system, although some earlier models are carbureted.

The engine drives the front wheels through either a manual or automatic transaxle via unequal-length driveaxles. The power assisted rack-and-pinion steering gear assembly is mounted behind the engine.

The front suspension is composed of MacPherson struts, three-point control arms and a stabilizer bar. The rear suspension consists of a solid axle with integral trailing arms, coil springs and shock absorbers.

The brakes are disc at the front and drum at the rear, with power assist standard. Some later models are equipped with an Anti-lock Brake System (ABS).

Vehicle identification numbers

Modifications are a continuing and unpublicized process in vehicle manufacturing. Since spare parts manuals and lists are compiled on a numerical basis, the individual vehicle numbers are essential to correctly identify the component required.

Vehicle identification number (VIN)

This very important identification number is located on a plate attached to the top left corner of the dashboard of the vehicle (see illustration). The VIN also appears on the Vehicle Certificate of Title and Registration. It contains valuable information such as where and when the vehicle was manufactured, the model year and the body style.

VIN engine code

One particularly important piece of information found in the VIN is the engine code. Counting from the left, this letter is the 8th digit (see illustration). The code varies by year:

1982
G - 1.8L OHV

1983
O - 1.8L OHC
P - 2.0L OHV

1984 through 1986
J - 1.8L OHC turbo
O - 1.8L OHC
P - 2.0L OHV
W - 2.8L V6

1987 through 1989
K - 2.0L OHC
M - 2.0L OHC turbo
1 - 2.0L OHV
W - 2.8L V6

1990
K - 2.0L OHC
M - 2.0L OHC turbo
G - 2.2L OHV
T - 3.1L V6

1991
K - 2.0L OHC
G - 2.2L OHV
T - 3.1L V6

1992 through 1994
4 - 2.2L OHV
T - 3.1L V6
H - 2.0L OHC

Model year code

Counting from the left, this letter is the 10th digit. On the models covered by this manual the model years codes are:

C = 1982
D = 1983
E = 1984
F = 1985
G = 1986
H = 1987
J = 1988
K = 1989
L = 1990
M = 1991
N = 1992
P = 1993
R = 1994

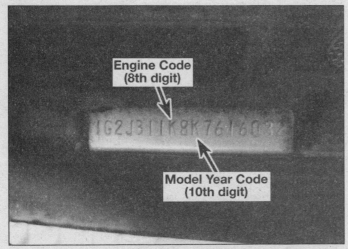

Counting from the left, the engine code is the eighth digit in the Vehicle Identification Number

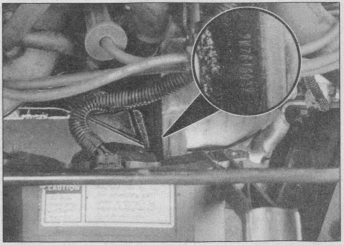

Location of the identification number on the OHC engine

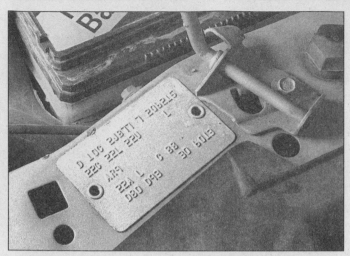

Location of the engine code number on the OHV engine

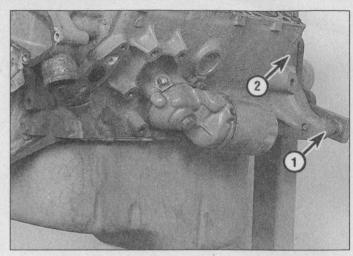

Location of the identification number on the V6 engine

1   VIN number   2   Engine code

Body identification plate

This metal plate is normally located on or near the top side of the radiator support. Like the VIN, it contains valuable information concerning the production of the vehicle, as well as information about the way in which the vehicle is equipped. This plate is especially useful for matching the color and type of paint during repair work.

Engine identification numbers

On 1.8L liter four-cylinder OHC engines, the engine number is stamped onto a machined pad, adjacent to the transaxle **(see illustration)**.

The engine number on the OHV four-cylinder engine is either stamped on a pad at the front of the cylinder block, above the timing cover **(see illustration)**, or at the rear of the block, adjacent to the transaxle.

On 2.8 and 3.1 liter V6 engines, the number is found below the left cylinder head, near the rear of the timing cover **(see illustration)** or on the vertical web at the rear of the engine, near the starter motor **(see illustration)**.

Manual transaxle number

The manual transaxle ID number is located on a pad on the forward side of the transaxle case **(see illustration)**.

Automatic transaxle numbers

The VIN number is located on a flange pad at either the lower front edge, near the dipstick or the top of the transaxle case **(see illustration)**. The model code is located at the top of the case.

Alternator numbers

The alternator ID number is located on top of the drive end frame.

Vehicle Emissions Control Information label

The Emissions Control Information label is usually attached to the front of the suspension strut tower.

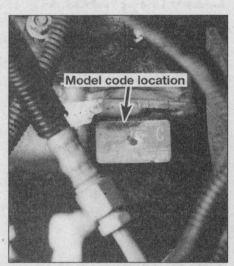

Automatic transaxle identification number locations

Buying parts

Replacement parts are available from many sources, which generally fall into one of two categories - authorized dealer parts departments and independent retail auto parts stores. Our advice concerning these parts is as follows:

Retail auto parts stores: Good auto parts stores will stock frequently needed components which wear out relatively fast, such as clutch components, exhaust systems, brake parts, tune-up parts, etc. These stores often supply new or reconditioned parts on an exchange basis, which can save a considerable amount of money. Discount auto parts stores are often very good places to buy materials and parts needed for general vehicle maintenance such as oil, grease, filters, spark plugs, belts, touch-up paint, bulbs, etc. They also usually sell tools and general accessories, have convenient hours, charge lower prices and can often be found not far from home.

Authorized dealer parts department: This is the best source for parts which are unique to the vehicle and not generally available elsewhere (such as major engine parts, transmission parts, trim pieces, etc.).

Warranty information: If the vehicle is still covered under warranty, be sure that any replacement parts purchased - regardless of the source - do not invalidate the warranty!

To be sure of obtaining the correct parts, have engine and chassis numbers available and, if possible, take the old parts along for positive identification.

Maintenance techniques, tools and working facilities

Maintenance techniques

There are a number of techniques involved in maintenance and repair that will be referred to throughout this manual. Application of these techniques will enable the home mechanic to be more efficient, better organized and capable of performing the various tasks properly, which will ensure that the repair job is thorough and complete.

Fasteners

Fasteners are nuts, bolts, studs and screws used to hold two or more parts together. There are a few things to keep in mind when working with fasteners. Almost all of them use a locking device of some type, either a lockwasher, locknut, locking tab or thread adhesive. All threaded fasteners should be clean and straight, with undamaged threads and undamaged corners on the hex head where the wrench fits. Develop the habit of replacing all damaged nuts and bolts with new ones. Special locknuts with nylon or fiber inserts can only be used once. If they are removed, they lose their locking ability and must be replaced with new ones.

Rusted nuts and bolts should be treated with a penetrating fluid to ease removal and prevent breakage. Some mechanics use turpentine in a spout-type oil can, which works quite well. After applying the rust penetrant, let it work for a few minutes before trying to loosen the nut or bolt. Badly rusted fasteners may have to be chiseled or sawed off or removed with a special nut breaker, available at tool stores.

If a bolt or stud breaks off in an assembly, it can be drilled and removed with a special tool commonly available for this purpose. Most automotive machine shops can perform this task, as well as other repair procedures, such as the repair of threaded holes that have been stripped out.

Flat washers and lockwashers, when removed from an assembly, should always be replaced exactly as removed. Replace any damaged washers with new ones. Never use a lockwasher on any soft metal surface (such as aluminum), thin sheet metal or plastic.

Fastener sizes

For a number of reasons, automobile manufacturers are making wider and wider use of metric fasteners. Therefore, it is important to be able to tell the difference between standard (sometimes called U.S. or SAE) and metric hardware, since they cannot be interchanged.

All bolts, whether standard or metric, are sized according to diameter, thread pitch and length. For example, a standard 1/2 - 13 x 1 bolt is 1/2 inch in diameter, has 13 threads per inch and is 1 inch long. An M12 - 1.75 x 25 metric bolt is 12 mm in diameter, has a thread pitch of 1.75 mm (the distance between threads) and is 25 mm long. The two bolts are nearly identical, and easily confused, but they are not interchangeable.

In addition to the differences in diameter, thread pitch and length, metric and standard bolts can also be distinguished by examining the bolt heads. To begin with, the distance across the flats on a standard bolt head is measured in inches, while the same dimension on a metric bolt is sized in millimeters (the same is true for nuts). As a result, a standard wrench should not be used on a metric bolt and a metric wrench should not be used on a standard bolt. Also, most standard bolts have slashes radiating out from the center of the head to denote the grade or strength of the bolt, which is an indication of the amount of torque that can be applied to it. The greater the number of slashes, the greater the strength of the bolt. Grades 0 through 5 are commonly used on automobiles. Metric bolts have a property class (grade) number, rather than a slash, molded into their heads to indicate bolt strength. In this case, the higher the number, the stronger the bolt. Property class numbers 8.8, 9.8 and 10.9 are commonly used on automobiles.

Strength markings can also be used to distinguish standard hex nuts from metric hex nuts. Many standard nuts have dots stamped into one side, while metric nuts are marked with a number. The greater the number of dots, or the higher the number, the greater the strength of the nut.

Metric studs are also marked on their ends according to property class (grade). Larger studs are numbered (the same as metric bolts), while smaller studs carry a geometric code to denote grade.

It should be noted that many fasteners, especially Grades 0 through 2, have no distinguishing marks on them. When such is the case, the only way to determine whether it is standard or metric is to measure the thread pitch or compare it to a known fastener of the same size.

Standard fasteners are often referred to as SAE, as opposed to metric. However, it should be noted that SAE technically refers to a non-metric fine thread fastener only. Coarse thread non-metric fasteners are referred to as USS sizes.

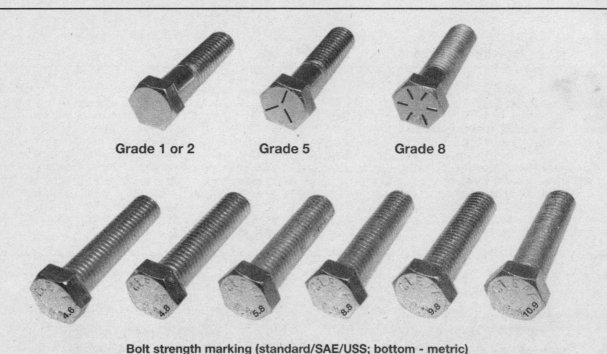

Grade 1 or 2   Grade 5   Grade 8

Bolt strength marking (standard/SAE/USS; bottom - metric)

Grade	Identification
Hex Nut Grade 5	3 Dots
Hex Nut Grade 8	6 Dots

Grade	Identification
Hex Nut Property Class 9	Arabic 9
Hex Nut Property Class 10	Arabic 10

Standard hex nut strength markings

Metric hex nut strength markings

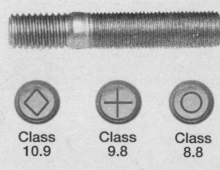

Class 10.9   Class 9.8   Class 8.8

Metric stud strength markings

00-1 HAYNES

Since fasteners of the same size (both standard and metric) may have different strength ratings, be sure to reinstall any bolts, studs or nuts removed from your vehicle in their original locations. Also, when replacing a fastener with a new one, make sure that the new one has a strength rating equal to or greater than the original.

Tightening sequences and procedures

Most threaded fasteners should be tightened to a specific torque value (torque is the twisting force applied to a threaded component such as a nut or bolt). Overtightening the fastener can weaken it and cause it to break, while undertightening can cause it to eventually come loose. Bolts, screws and studs, depending on the material they are made of and their thread diameters, have specific torque values, many of which are noted in the Specifications at the beginning of each Chapter. Be sure to follow the torque recommendations closely. For fasteners not assigned a specific torque, a general torque value chart is presented here as a guide. These torque values are for dry (unlubricated) fasteners threaded into steel or cast iron (not aluminum). As was previously mentioned, the size and grade of a fastener determine the amount of torque that can safely be applied to it. The figures listed here are approximate for Grade 2 and Grade 3 fasteners. Higher grades can tolerate higher torque values.

Fasteners laid out in a pattern, such as cylinder head bolts, oil pan bolts, differential cover bolts, etc., must be loosened or tightened in sequence to avoid warping the component. This sequence will normally be shown in the appropriate Chapter. If a specific pattern is not given, the following procedures can be used to prevent warping.

Metric thread sizes	Ft-lbs	Nm
M-6	6 to 9	9 to 12
M-8	14 to 21	19 to 28
M-10	28 to 40	38 to 54
M-12	50 to 71	68 to 96
M-14	80 to 140	109 to 154
Pipe thread sizes		
1/8	5 to 8	7 to 10
1/4	12 to 18	17 to 24
3/8	22 to 33	30 to 44
1/2	25 to 35	34 to 47
U.S. thread sizes		
1/4 - 20	6 to 9	9 to 12
5/16 - 18	12 to 18	17 to 24
5/16 - 24	14 to 20	19 to 27
3/8 - 16	22 to 32	30 to 43
3/8 - 24	27 to 38	37 to 51
7/16 - 14	40 to 55	55 to 74
7/16 - 20	40 to 60	55 to 81
1/2 - 13	55 to 80	75 to 108

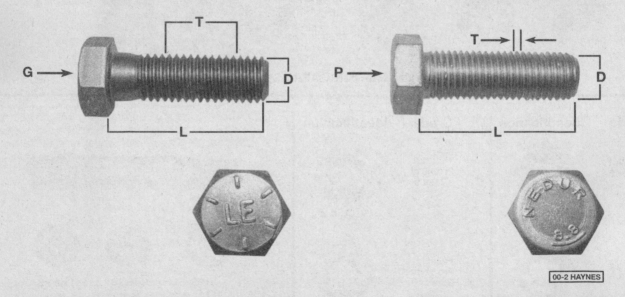

00-2 HAYNES

Standard (SAE and USS) bolt dimensions/grade marks

G   Grade marks (bolt strength)
L   Length (in inches)
T   Thread pitch (number of threads per inch)
D   Nominal diameter (in inches)

Metric bolt dimensions/grade marks

P   Property class (bolt strength)
L   Length (in millimeters)
T   Thread pitch (distance between threads in millimeters)
D   Diameter

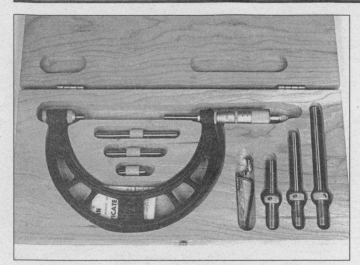

Micrometer set

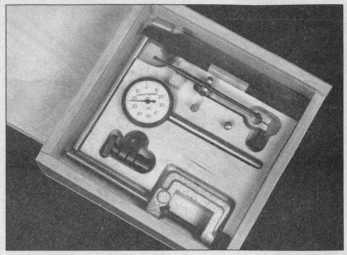

Dial indicator set

Initially, the bolts or nuts should be assembled finger-tight only. Next, they should be tightened one full turn each, in a criss-cross or diagonal pattern. After each one has been tightened one full turn, return to the first one and tighten them all one-half turn, following the same pattern. Finally, tighten each of them one-quarter turn at a time until each fastener has been tightened to the proper torque. To loosen and remove the fasteners, the procedure would be reversed.

Component disassembly

Component disassembly should be done with care and purpose to help ensure that the parts go back together properly. Always keep track of the sequence in which parts are removed. Make note of special characteristics or marks on parts that can be installed more than one way, such as a grooved thrust washer on a shaft. It is a good idea to lay the disassembled parts out on a clean surface in the order that they were removed. It may also be helpful to make sketches or take instant photos of components before removal.

When removing fasteners from a component, keep track of their locations. Sometimes threading a bolt back in a part, or putting the washers and nut back on a stud, can prevent mix-ups later. If nuts and bolts cannot be returned to their original locations, they should be kept in a compartmented box or a series of small boxes. A cupcake or muffin tin is ideal for this purpose, since each cavity can hold the bolts and nuts from a particular area (i.e. oil pan bolts, valve cover bolts, engine mount bolts, etc.). A pan of this type is especially helpful when working on assemblies with very small parts, such as the carburetor, alternator, valve train or interior dash and trim pieces. The cavities can be marked with paint or tape to identify the contents.

Whenever wiring looms, harnesses or connectors are separated, it is a good idea to identify the two halves with numbered pieces of masking tape so they can be easily reconnected.

Gasket sealing surfaces

Throughout any vehicle, gaskets are used to seal the mating surfaces between two parts and keep lubricants, fluids, vacuum or pressure contained in an assembly.

Many times these gaskets are coated with a liquid or paste-type gasket sealing compound before assembly. Age, heat and pressure can sometimes cause the two parts to stick together so tightly that they are very difficult to separate. Often, the assembly can be loosened by striking it with a soft-face hammer near the mating surfaces. A regular hammer can be used if a block of wood is placed between the hammer and the part. Do not hammer on cast parts or parts that could be easily damaged. With any particularly stubborn part, always recheck to make sure that every fastener has been removed.

Avoid using a screwdriver or bar to pry apart an assembly, as they can easily mar the gasket sealing surfaces of the parts, which must remain smooth. If prying is absolutely necessary, use an old broom handle, but keep in mind that extra clean up will be necessary if the wood splinters.

After the parts are separated, the old gasket must be carefully scraped off and the gasket surfaces cleaned. Stubborn gasket material can be soaked with rust penetrant or treated with a special chemical to soften it so it can be easily scraped off. A scraper can be fashioned from a piece of copper tubing by flattening and sharpening one end. Copper is recommended because it is usually softer than the surfaces to be scraped, which reduces the chance of gouging the part. Some gaskets can be removed with a wire brush, but regardless of the method used, the mating surfaces must be left clean and smooth. If for some reason the gasket surface is gouged, then a gasket sealer thick enough to fill scratches will have to be used during reassembly of the components. For most applications, a non-drying (or semi-drying) gasket sealer should be used.

Hose removal tips

Warning: *If the vehicle is equipped with air conditioning, do not disconnect any of the A/C hoses without first having the system depressurized by a dealer service department or a service station.*

Hose removal precautions closely parallel gasket removal precautions. Avoid scratching or gouging the surface that the hose mates against or the connection may leak. This is especially true for radiator hoses. Because of various chemical reactions, the rubber in hoses can bond itself to the metal spigot that the hose fits over. To remove a hose, first loosen the hose clamps that secure it to the spigot. Then, with slip-joint pliers, grab the hose at the clamp and rotate it around the spigot. Work it back and forth until it is completely free, then pull it off. Silicone or other lubricants will ease removal if they can be applied between the hose and the outside of the spigot. Apply the same lubricant to the inside of the hose and the outside of the spigot to simplify installation.

As a last resort (and if the hose is to be replaced with a new one anyway), the rubber can be slit with a knife and the hose peeled from the spigot. If this must be done, be careful that the metal connection is not damaged.

If a hose clamp is broken or damaged, do not reuse it. Wire-type clamps usually weaken with age, so it is a good idea to replace them with screw-type clamps whenever a hose is removed.

Tools

A selection of good tools is a basic requirement for anyone who plans to maintain and repair his or her own vehicle. For the owner who has few tools, the initial investment might seem high, but when compared to the spiraling costs of professional auto maintenance and repair, it is a wise one.

To help the owner decide which tools are needed to perform the tasks detailed in this manual, the following tool lists are offered: *Maintenance and minor repair,*

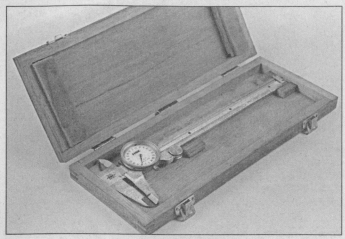

Dial caliper

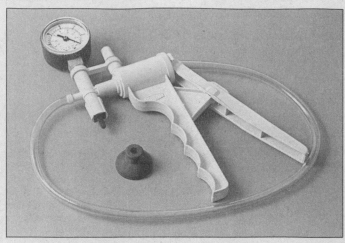

Hand-operated vacuum pump

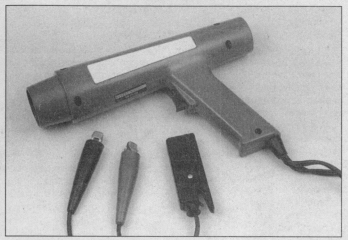

Timing light

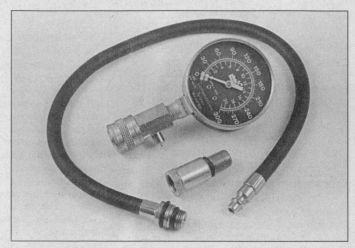

Compression gauge with spark plug hole adapter

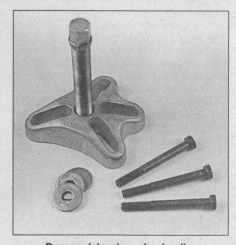

Damper/steering wheel puller

General purpose puller

Hydraulic lifter removal tool

Repair/overhaul and *Special.*

The newcomer to practical mechanics should start off with the *maintenance and minor repair* tool kit, which is adequate for the simpler jobs performed on a vehicle. Then, as confidence and experience grow, the owner can tackle more difficult tasks, buying additional tools as they are needed.

Eventually the basic kit will be expanded into the *repair and overhaul* tool set. Over a period of time, the experienced do-it-yourselfer will assemble a tool set complete enough for most repair and overhaul procedures and will add tools from the special category when it is felt that the expense is justified by the frequency of use.

Maintenance and minor repair tool kit

The tools in this list should be considered the minimum required for performance of routine maintenance, servicing and minor repair work. We recommend the purchase of combination wrenches (box-end and open-

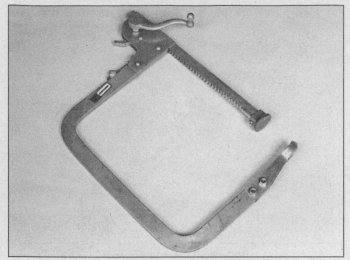

Valve spring compressor

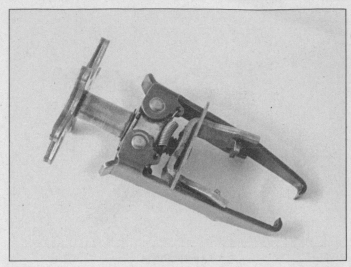

Valve spring compressor

Ridge reamer

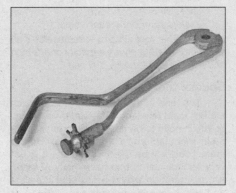

Piston ring groove cleaning tool

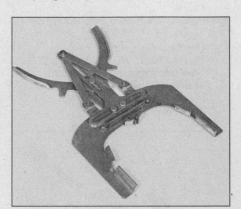

Ring removal/installation tool

Ring compressor

end combined in one wrench). While more expensive than open end wrenches, they offer the advantages of both types of wrench.

Combination wrench set (1/4-inch to 1 inch or 6 mm to 19 mm)
Adjustable wrench, 8 inch
Spark plug wrench with rubber insert
Spark plug gap adjusting tool
Feeler gauge set
Brake bleeder wrench
Standard screwdriver (5/16-inch x 6 inch)
Phillips screwdriver (No. 2 x 6 inch)
Combination pliers - 6 inch
Hacksaw and assortment of blades
Tire pressure gauge
Grease gun
Oil can
Fine emery cloth
Wire brush
Battery post and cable cleaning tool
Oil filter wrench
Funnel (medium size)
Safety goggles
Jackstands (2)
Drain pan

Note: *If basic tune-ups are going to be part of routine maintenance, it will be necessary to purchase a good quality stroboscopic timing light and combination tachometer/dwell meter. Although they are included in the list of special tools, it is mentioned here because they are absolutely necessary for tuning most vehicles properly.*

Repair and overhaul tool set

These tools are essential for anyone who plans to perform major repairs and are in addition to those in the maintenance and minor repair tool kit. Included is a comprehensive set of sockets which, though expensive, are invaluable because of their versatility, especially when various extensions and drives are available. We recommend the 1/2-inch drive over the 3/8-inch drive. Although the larger drive is bulky and more expensive, it has the capacity of accepting a very wide range of large sockets. Ideally, however, the mechanic should have a 3/8-inch drive set and a 1/2-inch drive set.

Socket set(s)
Reversible ratchet
Extension - 10 inch
Universal joint
Torque wrench (same size drive as sockets)
Ball peen hammer - 8 ounce
Soft-face hammer (plastic/rubber)

Standard screwdriver (1/4-inch x 6 inch)
Standard screwdriver (stubby - 5/16-inch)
Phillips screwdriver (No. 3 x 8 inch)
Phillips screwdriver (stubby - No. 2)
Pliers - vise grip
Pliers - lineman's
Pliers - needle nose
Pliers - snap-ring (internal and external)
Cold chisel - 1/2-inch

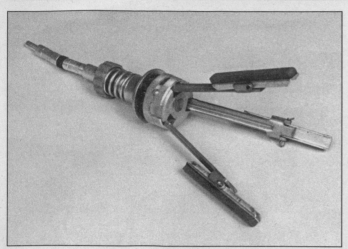

Cylinder hone

Brake hold-down spring tool

Scribe
Scraper (made from flattened copper tubing)
Centerpunch
Pin punches (1/16, 1/8, 3/16-inch)
Steel rule/straightedge - 12 inch
Allen wrench set (1/8 to 3/8-inch or 4 mm to 10 mm)
A selection of files

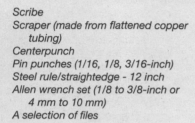

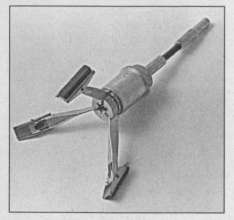

Brake cylinder hone

Wire brush (large)
Jackstands (second set)
Jack (scissor or hydraulic type)

Note: *Another tool which is often useful is an electric drill with a chuck capacity of 3/8-inch and a set of good quality drill bits.*

Special tools

The tools in this list include those which are not used regularly, are expensive to buy, or which need to be used in accordance with their manufacturer's instructions. Unless these tools will be used frequently, it is not very economical to purchase many of them. A consideration would be to split the cost and use between yourself and a friend or friends. In addition, most of these tools can be obtained from a tool rental shop on a temporary basis.

This list primarily contains only those tools and instruments widely available to the public, and not those special tools produced by the vehicle manufacturer for distribution to dealer service departments. Occasionally, references to the manufacturer's special tools are included in the text of this manual. Generally, an alternative method of doing the job without the special tool is offered. How-ever, sometimes there is no alternative to their use. Where this is the case, and the tool cannot be purchased or borrowed, the work should be turned over to the dealer service department or an automotive repair shop.

Valve spring compressor
Piston ring groove cleaning tool
Piston ring compressor
Piston ring installation tool
Cylinder compression gauge
Cylinder ridge reamer
Cylinder surfacing hone
Cylinder bore gauge
Micrometers and/or dial calipers
Hydraulic lifter removal tool
Balljoint separator
Universal-type puller
Impact screwdriver
Dial indicator set
Stroboscopic timing light (inductive pick-up)
Hand operated vacuum/pressure pump
Tachometer/dwell meter
Universal electrical multimeter
Cable hoist
Brake spring removal and installation tools
Floor jack

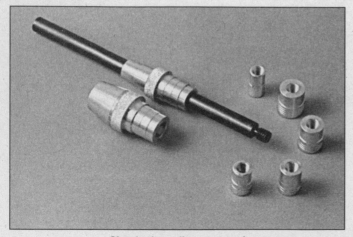

Clutch plate alignment tool

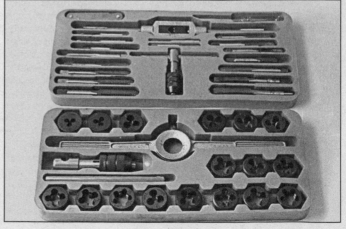

Tap and die set

Buying tools

For the do-it-yourselfer who is just starting to get involved in vehicle maintenance and repair, there are a number of options available when purchasing tools. If maintenance and minor repair is the extent of the work to be done, the purchase of individual tools is satisfactory. If, on the other hand, extensive work is planned, it would be a good idea to purchase a modest tool set from one of the large retail chain stores. A set can usually be bought at a substantial savings over the individual tool prices, and they often come with a tool box. As additional tools are needed, add-on sets, individual tools and a larger tool box can be purchased to expand the tool selection. Building a tool set gradually allows the cost of the tools to be spread over a longer period of time and gives the mechanic the freedom to choose only those tools that will actually be used.

Tool stores will often be the only source of some of the special tools that are needed, but regardless of where tools are bought, try to avoid cheap ones, especially when buying screwdrivers and sockets, because they won't last very long. The expense involved in replacing cheap tools will eventually be greater than the initial cost of quality tools.

Care and maintenance of tools

Good tools are expensive, so it makes sense to treat them with respect. Keep them clean and in usable condition and store them properly when not in use. Always wipe off any dirt, grease or metal chips before putting them away. Never leave tools lying around in the work area. Upon completion of a job, always check closely under the hood for tools that may have been left there so they won't get lost during a test drive.

Some tools, such as screwdrivers, pliers, wrenches and sockets, can be hung on a panel mounted on the garage or workshop wall, while others should be kept in a tool box or tray. Measuring instruments, gauges, meters, etc. must be carefully stored where they cannot be damaged by weather or impact from other tools.

When tools are used with care and stored properly, they will last a very long time. Even with the best of care, though, tools will wear out if used frequently. When a tool is damaged or worn out, replace it. Subsequent jobs will be safer and more enjoyable if you do.

How to repair damaged threads

Sometimes, the internal threads of a nut or bolt hole can become stripped, usually from overtightening. Stripping threads is an all-too-common occurrence, especially when working with aluminum parts, because aluminum is so soft that it easily strips out.

Usually, external or internal threads are only partially stripped. After they've been cleaned up with a tap or die, they'll still work. Sometimes, however, threads are badly damaged. When this happens, you've got three choices:

1) Drill and tap the hole to the next suitable oversize and install a larger diameter bolt, screw or stud.

2) Drill and tap the hole to accept a threaded plug, then drill and tap the plug to the original screw size. You can also buy a plug already threaded to the original size. Then you simply drill a hole to the specified size, then run the threaded plug into the hole with a bolt and jam nut. Once the plug is fully seated, remove the jam nut and bolt.

3) The third method uses a patented thread repair kit like Heli-Coil or Slimsert. These easy-to-use kits are designed to repair damaged threads in straight-through holes and blind holes. Both are available as kits which can handle a variety of sizes and thread patterns. Drill the hole, then tap it with the special included tap. Install the Heli-Coil and the hole is back to its original diameter and thread pitch.

Regardless of which method you use, be sure to proceed calmly and carefully. A little impatience or carelessness during one of these relatively simple procedures can ruin your whole day's work and cost you a bundle if you wreck an expensive part.

Working facilities

Not to be overlooked when discussing tools is the workshop. If anything more than routine maintenance is to be carried out, some sort of suitable work area is essential.

It is understood, and appreciated, that many home mechanics do not have a good workshop or garage available, and end up removing an engine or doing major repairs outside. It is recommended, however, that the overhaul or repair be completed under the cover of a roof.

A clean, flat workbench or table of comfortable working height is an absolute necessity. The workbench should be equipped with a vise that has a jaw opening of at least four inches.

As mentioned previously, some clean, dry storage space is also required for tools, as well as the lubricants, fluids, cleaning solvents, etc. which soon become necessary.

Sometimes waste oil and fluids, drained from the engine or cooling system during normal maintenance or repairs, present a disposal problem. To avoid pouring them on the ground or into a sewage system, pour the used fluids into large containers, seal them with caps and take them to an authorized disposal site or recycling center. Plastic jugs, such as old antifreeze containers, are ideal for this purpose.

Always keep a supply of old newspapers and clean rags available. Old towels are excellent for mopping up spills. Many mechanics use rolls of paper towels for most work because they are readily available and disposable. To help keep the area under the vehicle clean, a large cardboard box can be cut open and flattened to protect the garage or shop floor.

Whenever working over a painted surface, such as when leaning over a fender to service something under the hood, always cover it with an old blanket or bedspread to protect the finish. Vinyl covered pads, made especially for this purpose, are available at auto parts stores.

Delco-Loc II anti-theft audio system

General information

1   Some 1992 and later models are equipped with the Delco Loc II audio system, which includes an anti-theft feature that will render the stereo inoperative if stolen. If the power source to the stereo is cut with the anti-theft feature activated, the stereo will be inoperative. Even if the power source is immediately re-connected, the stereo will not function. If your vehicle is equipped with this anti-theft system, do not disconnect the battery, remove the stereo or disconnect related components unless you have either turned off the feature or have the individual ID (code) number for the stereo.

2   Refer to your vehicle's owner's manual for more complete information on this audio system and its anti-theft feature.

Disabling the anti-theft feature

3   Press the stereo's 1 and 4 buttons at the same time for five seconds with the ignition on and the radio power off. The display will show SEC, indicating the unit is in the secure mode (anti-theft feature enabled).

4   Press the SET button. The display will show "000."

5   Press the SEEK button to make the first number appear.

6   Rotate the TUNE knob right or left to make the last two numbers agree with your code. The numbers will be displayed as entered.

7   Press the lower BAND knob. "000" will be displayed.

8   Enter the second three digits of the code.

9   Press the lower BAND knob. If the display shows "_ _," you have successfully disabled the anti-theft feature. If SEC is displayed, the code you entered was incorrect and the anti-theft feature is still enabled.

Unlocking the stereo after a power loss

10   When power is restored to the stereo, the stereo won't turn on and LOC will appear on the display. Enter your ID code as follows; pause no more than 15 seconds between Steps.

11   Turn the ignition switch to ON, but leave the stereo off.

12   Press the SET button. "000" should display.

13   Press the SEEK button to make the first number appear.

14   Rotate the TUNE knob right or left to make the last two numbers agree with your code.

15   Repeat Steps 2 through 4 for the last three digits of your code.

16   Press the lower BAND knob. The time should appear, indicating the stereo is unlocked. If SEC appears, the numbers you entered were not correct and the stereo is still inoperative.

Jacking and towing

Jacking

The jack supplied with the vehicle should only be used for raising the vehicle when changing a tire or placing jackstands under the frame. **Warning:** *Never work under the vehicle or start the engine while this jack is being used as the only means of support.*

The vehicle should be on level ground with the wheels blocked and the transmission in Park (automatic) or Reverse (manual). Pry off the hub cap (if equipped) using the tapered end of the lug wrench. Loosen the wheel nuts one-half turn and leave them in place until the wheel is raised off the ground.

Place the jack under the side of the vehicle in the indicated position and place the jack lever in the "up" position. Raise the jack until the jack head groove fits into the rocker panel flange notch **(see illustration)**. Operate the jack with a slow, smooth motion, using your hand or foot to pump the handle until the wheel is raised off the ground. Remove the wheel nuts, pull off the wheel and replace it with the spare. (If you have a stowaway spare, refer to the instructions accompanying the supplied inflator.)

With the beveled side in, replace the wheel nuts and tighten them until snug. Place the jack lever in the "down" position and lower the vehicle. Remove the jack and tighten the nuts in a criss-cross sequence by turning the wrench clockwise. Replace the hub cap (if equipped) by placing it into position and using the heel of your hand or a rubber mallet to seat it.

Towing

The vehicle can be towed with all four wheels on the ground, provided that speeds do not exceed 35 mph and the distance is not over 50 miles, otherwise transmission damage can result.

Towing equipment specifically designed for this purpose should be used and should be attached to the main structural members of the vehicle and not the bumper or brackets.

Safety is a major consideration when towing and all applicable state and local laws must be obeyed. A safety chain system must be used for all towing.

While towing, the parking brake should be released and the transmission should be in Neutral. The steering must be unlocked (ignition switch in the Off position). Remember that power steering and power brakes will not work with the engine off.

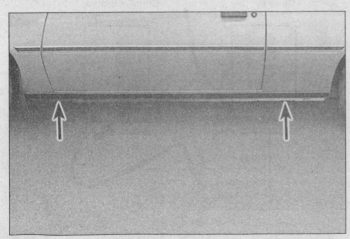

Location of the rocker panel flange notches used for jack placement

Placement and operation of the jack for tire changing (left) and details of matching the jack head groove-to-rocker panel flange notch (right)

Booster battery (jump) starting

Booster battery (jump) starting

Observe the following precautions when using a booster battery to start a vehicle:

a) *Before connecting the booster battery, make sure the ignition switch is in the Off position.*

b) *Ensure that all electrical equipment (lights, heater, wipers etc.) are switched off.*

c) *Make sure that the booster battery is the same voltage as the discharged battery in the vehicle.*

d) *If the battery is being jump started from the battery in another vehicle, the two vehicles MUST NOT TOUCH each other.*

e) *Make sure the transaxle is in Neutral (manual transaxle) or Park (automatic transaxle).*

f) *Wear eye protection when jump starting a vehicle.*

Connect one jumper lead between the positive (+) terminals of the two batteries. Connect the other jumper lead first to the negative (-) terminal of the booster battery, then to a good engine ground on the vehicle to be started **(see illustration)**. Attach the lead at least 18 inches from the battery, if possible. Make sure that the jumper leads will not contact the fan, drivebelt of other moving parts of the engine.

Start the engine using the booster battery and allow the engine idle speed to stabilize. Disconnect the jumper leads in the reverse order of connection.

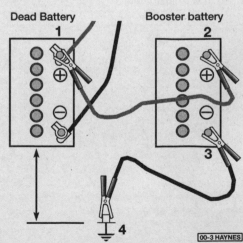

Make the booster battery cable connections in the numerical order shown (note that the negative cable of the booster battery is NOT attached to the negative terminal of the dead battery)

Automotive chemicals and lubricants

A number of automotive chemicals and lubricants are available for use during vehicle maintenance and repair. They include a wide variety of products ranging from cleaning solvents and degreasers to lubricants and protective sprays for rubber, plastic and vinyl.

Cleaners

Carburetor cleaner and choke cleaner is a strong solvent for gum, varnish and carbon. Most carburetor cleaners leave a dry-type lubricant film which will not harden or gum up. Because of this film it is not recommended for use on electrical components.

Brake system cleaner is used to remove grease and brake fluid from the brake system, where clean surfaces are absolutely necessary. It leaves no residue and often eliminates brake squeal caused by contaminants.

Electrical cleaner removes oxidation, corrosion and carbon deposits from electrical contacts, restoring full current flow. It can also be used to clean spark plugs, carburetor jets, voltage regulators and other parts where an oil-free surface is desired.

Demoisturants remove water and moisture from electrical components such as alternators, voltage regulators, electrical connectors and fuse blocks. They are non-conductive, non-corrosive and non-flammable.

Degreasers are heavy-duty solvents used to remove grease from the outside of the engine and from chassis components. They can be sprayed or brushed on and, depending on the type, are rinsed off either with water or solvent.

Lubricants

Motor oil is the lubricant formulated for use in engines. It normally contains a wide variety of additives to prevent corrosion and reduce foaming and wear. Motor oil comes in various weights (viscosity ratings) from 0 to 50. The recommended weight of the oil depends on the season, temperature and the demands on the engine. Light oil is used in cold climates and under light load conditions. Heavy oil is used in hot climates and where high loads are encountered. Multi-viscosity oils are designed to have characteristics of both light and heavy oils and are available in a number of weights from 5W-20 to 20W-50.

Gear oil is designed to be used in differentials, manual transmissions and other areas where high-temperature lubrication is required.

Chassis and wheel bearing grease is a heavy grease used where increased loads and friction are encountered, such as for wheel bearings, balljoints, tie-rod ends and universal joints.

High-temperature wheel bearing grease is designed to withstand the extreme temperatures encountered by wheel bearings in disc brake equipped vehicles. It usually contains molybdenum disulfide (moly), which is a dry-type lubricant.

White grease is a heavy grease for metal-to-metal applications where water is a problem. White grease stays soft under both low and high temperatures (usually from -100 to +190-degrees F), and will not wash off or dilute in the presence of water.

Assembly lube is a special extreme pressure lubricant, usually containing moly, used to lubricate high-load parts (such as main and rod bearings and cam lobes) for initial start-up of a new engine. The assembly lube lubricates the parts without being squeezed out or washed away until the engine oiling system begins to function.

Silicone lubricants are used to protect rubber, plastic, vinyl and nylon parts.

Graphite lubricants are used where oils cannot be used due to contamination problems, such as in locks. The dry graphite will lubricate metal parts while remaining uncontaminated by dirt, water, oil or acids. It is electrically conductive and will not foul electrical contacts in locks such as the ignition switch.

Moly penetrants loosen and lubricate frozen, rusted and corroded fasteners and prevent future rusting or freezing.

Heat-sink grease is a special electrically non-conductive grease that is used for mounting electronic ignition modules where it is essential that heat is transferred away from the module.

Sealants

RTV sealant is one of the most widely used gasket compounds. Made from silicone, RTV is air curing, it seals, bonds, waterproofs, fills surface irregularities, remains flexible, doesn't shrink, is relatively easy to remove, and is used as a supplementary sealer with almost all low and medium temperature gaskets.

Anaerobic sealant is much like RTV in that it can be used either to seal gaskets or to form gaskets by itself. It remains flexible, is solvent resistant and fills surface imperfections. The difference between an anaerobic sealant and an RTV-type sealant is in the curing. RTV cures when exposed to air, while an anaerobic sealant cures only in the absence of air. This means that an anaerobic sealant cures only after the assembly of parts, sealing them together.

Thread and pipe sealant is used for sealing hydraulic and pneumatic fittings and vacuum lines. It is usually made from a Teflon compound, and comes in a spray, a paint-on liquid and as a wrap-around tape.

Chemicals

Anti-seize compound prevents seizing, galling, cold welding, rust and corrosion in fasteners. High-temperature ant-seize, usually made with copper and graphite lubricants, is used for exhaust system and exhaust manifold bolts.

Anaerobic locking compounds are used to keep fasteners from vibrating or working loose and cure only after installation, in the absence of air. Medium strength locking compound is used for small nuts, bolts and screws that may be removed later. High-strength locking compound is for large nuts, bolts and studs which aren't removed on a regular basis.

Oil additives range from viscosity index improvers to chemical treatments that claim to reduce internal engine friction. It should be noted that most oil manufacturers caution against using additives with their oils.

Gas additives perform several functions, depending on their chemical makeup. They usually contain solvents that help dissolve gum and varnish that build up on carburetor, fuel injection and intake parts. They also serve to break down carbon deposits that form on the inside surfaces of the combustion chambers. Some additives contain upper cylinder lubricants for valves and piston rings, and others contain chemicals to remove condensation from the gas tank.

Miscellaneous

Brake fluid is specially formulated hydraulic fluid that can withstand the heat and pressure encountered in brake systems. Care must be taken so this fluid does not come in contact with painted surfaces or plastics. An opened container should always be resealed to prevent contamination by water or dirt.

Weatherstrip adhesive is used to bond weatherstripping around doors, windows and trunk lids. It is sometimes used to attach trim pieces.

Undercoating is a petroleum-based, tar-like substance that is designed to protect metal surfaces on the underside of the vehicle from corrosion. It also acts as a sound-deadening agent by insulating the bottom of the vehicle.

Waxes and polishes are used to help protect painted and plated surfaces from the weather. Different types of paint may require the use of different types of wax and polish. Some polishes utilize a chemical or abrasive cleaner to help remove the top layer of oxidized (dull) paint on older vehicles. In recent years many non-wax polishes that contain a wide variety of chemicals such as polymers and silicones have been introduced. These non-wax polishes are usually easier to apply and last longer than conventional waxes and polishes.

Conversion factors

Length (distance)
Inches (in)	X	25.4	= Millimetres (mm)	X 0.0394	= Inches (in)
Feet (ft)	X	0.305	= Metres (m)	X 3.281	= Feet (ft)
Miles	X	1.609	= Kilometres (km)	X 0.621	= Miles

Volume (capacity)
Cubic inches (cu in; in^3)	X	16.387	= Cubic centimetres (cc; cm^3)	X 0.061	= Cubic inches (cu in; in^3)
Imperial pints (Imp pt)	X	0.568	= Litres (l)	X 1.76	= Imperial pints (Imp pt)
Imperial quarts (Imp qt)	X	1.137	= Litres (l)	X 0.88	= Imperial quarts (Imp qt)
Imperial quarts (Imp qt)	X	1.201	= US quarts (US qt)	X 0.833	= Imperial quarts (Imp qt)
US quarts (US qt)	X	0.946	= Litres (l)	X 1.057	= US quarts (US qt)
Imperial gallons (Imp gal)	X	4.546	= Litres (l)	X 0.22	= Imperial gallons (Imp gal)
Imperial gallons (Imp gal)	X	1.201	= US gallons (US gal)	X 0.833	= Imperial gallons (Imp gal)
US gallons (US gal)	X	3.785	= Litres (l)	X 0.264	= US gallons (US gal)

Mass (weight)
Ounces (oz)	X	28.35	= Grams (g)	X 0.035	= Ounces (oz)
Pounds (lb)	X	0.454	= Kilograms (kg)	X 2.205	= Pounds (lb)

Force
Ounces-force (ozf; oz)	X	0.278	= Newtons (N)	X 3.6	= Ounces-force (ozf; oz)
Pounds-force (lbf; lb)	X	4.448	= Newtons (N)	X 0.225	= Pounds-force (lbf; lb)
Newtons (N)	X	0.1	= Kilograms-force (kgf; kg)	X 9.81	= Newtons (N)

Pressure
Pounds-force per square inch (psi; lbf/in^2; lb/in^2)	X	0.070	= Kilograms-force per square centimetre (kgf/cm^2; kg/cm^2)	X 14.223	= Pounds-force per square inch (psi; lbf/in^2; lb/in^2)
Pounds-force per square inch (psi; lbf/in^2; lb/in^2)	X	0.068	= Atmospheres (atm)	X 14.696	= Pounds-force per square inch (psi; lbf/in^2; lb/in^2)
Pounds-force per square inch (psi; lbf/in^2; lb/in^2)	X	0.069	= Bars	X 14.5	= Pounds-force per square inch (psi; lbf/in^2; lb/in^2)
Pounds-force per square inch (psi; lbf/in^2; lb/in^2)	X	6.895	= Kilopascals (kPa)	X 0.145	= Pounds-force per square inch (psi; lbf/in^2; lb/in^2)
Kilopascals (kPa)	X	0.01	= Kilograms-force per square centimetre (kgf/cm^2; kg/cm^2)	X 98.1	= Kilopascals (kPa)

Torque (moment of force)
Pounds-force inches (lbf in; lb in)	X	1.152	= Kilograms-force centimetre (kgf cm; kg cm)	X 0.868	= Pounds-force inches (lbf in; lb in)
Pounds-force inches (lbf in; lb in)	X	0.113	= Newton metres (Nm)	X 8.85	= Pounds-force inches (lbf in; lb in)
Pounds-force inches (lbf in; lb in)	X	0.083	= Pounds-force feet (lbf ft; lb ft)	X 12	= Pounds-force inches (lbf in; lb in)
Pounds-force feet (lbf ft; lb ft)	X	0.138	= Kilograms-force metres (kgf m; kg m)	X 7.233	= Pounds-force feet (lbf ft; lb ft)
Pounds-force feet (lbf ft; lb ft)	X	1.356	= Newton metres (Nm)	X 0.738	= Pounds-force feet (lbf ft; lb ft)
Newton metres (Nm)	X	0.102	= Kilograms-force metres (kgf m; kg m)	X 9.804	= Newton metres (Nm)

Vacuum
Inches mercury (in. Hg)	X	3.377	= Kilopascals (kPa)	X 0.2961	= Inches mercury
Inches mercury (in. Hg)	X	25.4	= Millimeters mercury (mm Hg)	X 0.0394	= Inches mercury

Power
Horsepower (hp)	X	745.7	= Watts (W)	X 0.0013	= Horsepower (hp)

Velocity (speed)
Miles per hour (miles/hr; mph)	X	1.609	= Kilometres per hour (km/hr; kph)	X 0.621	= Miles per hour (miles/hr; mph)

Fuel consumption*
Miles per gallon, Imperial (mpg)	X	0.354	= Kilometres per litre (km/l)	X 2.825	= Miles per gallon, Imperial (mpg)
Miles per gallon, US (mpg)	X	0.425	= Kilometres per litre (km/l)	X 2.352	= Miles per gallon, US (mpg)

Temperature
Degrees Fahrenheit = (°C x 1.8) + 32   Degrees Celsius (Degrees Centigrade; °C) = (°F - 32) x 0.56

*It is common practice to convert from miles per gallon (mpg) to litres/100 kilometres (l/100km), where mpg (Imperial) x l/100 km = 282 and mpg (US) x l/100 km = 235

Safety first!

Regardless of how enthusiastic you may be about getting on with the job at hand, take the time to ensure that your safety is not jeopardized. A moment's lack of attention can result in an accident, as can failure to observe certain simple safety precautions. The possibility of an accident will always exist, and the following points should not be considered a comprehensive list of all dangers. Rather, they are intended to make you aware of the risks and to encourage a safety conscious approach to all work you carry out on your vehicle.

Essential DOs and DON'Ts

DON'T rely on a jack when working under the vehicle. Always use approved jackstands to support the weight of the vehicle and place them under the recommended lift or support points.

DON'T attempt to loosen extremely tight fasteners (i.e. wheel lug nuts) while the vehicle is on a jack - it may fall.

DON'T start the engine without first making sure that the transmission is in Neutral (or Park where applicable) and the parking brake is set.

DON'T remove the radiator cap from a hot cooling system - let it cool or cover it with a cloth and release the pressure gradually.

DON'T attempt to drain the engine oil until you are sure it has cooled to the point that it will not burn you.

DON'T touch any part of the engine or exhaust system until it has cooled sufficiently to avoid burns.

DON'T siphon toxic liquids such as gasoline, antifreeze and brake fluid by mouth, or allow them to remain on your skin.

DON'T inhale brake lining dust - it is potentially hazardous (see *Asbestos* below).

DON'T allow spilled oil or grease to remain on the floor - wipe it up before someone slips on it.

DON'T use loose fitting wrenches or other tools which may slip and cause injury.

DON'T push on wrenches when loosening or tightening nuts or bolts. Always try to pull the wrench toward you. If the situation calls for pushing the wrench away, push with an open hand to avoid scraped knuckles if the wrench should slip.

DON'T attempt to lift a heavy component alone - get someone to help you.

DON'T rush or take unsafe shortcuts to finish a job.

DON'T allow children or animals in or around the vehicle while you are working on it.

DO wear eye protection when using power tools such as a drill, sander, bench grinder, etc. and when working under a vehicle.

DO keep loose clothing and long hair well out of the way of moving parts.

DO make sure that any hoist used has a safe working load rating adequate for the job.

DO get someone to check on you periodically when working alone on a vehicle.

DO carry out work in a logical sequence and make sure that everything is correctly assembled and tightened.

DO keep chemicals and fluids tightly capped and out of the reach of children and pets.

DO remember that your vehicle's safety affects that of yourself and others. If in doubt on any point, get professional advice.

Asbestos

Certain friction, insulating, sealing, and other products - such as brake linings, brake bands, clutch linings, torque converters, gaskets, etc. - may contain asbestos. Extreme care must be taken to avoid inhalation of dust from such products, since it is hazardous to health. If in doubt, assume that they do contain asbestos.

Fire

Remember at all times that gasoline is highly flammable. Never smoke or have any kind of open flame around when working on a vehicle. But the risk does not end there. A spark caused by an electrical short circuit, by two metal surfaces contacting each other, or even by static electricity built up in your body under certain conditions, can ignite gasoline vapors, which in a confined space are highly explosive. Do not, under any circumstances, use gasoline for cleaning parts. Use an approved safety solvent.

Always disconnect the battery ground (-) cable at the battery before working on any part of the fuel system or electrical system. Never risk spilling fuel on a hot engine or exhaust component. It is strongly recommended that a fire extinguisher suitable for use on fuel and electrical fires be kept handy in the garage or workshop at all times. Never try to extinguish a fuel or electrical fire with water.

Fumes

Certain fumes are highly toxic and can quickly cause unconsciousness and even death if inhaled to any extent. Gasoline vapor falls into this category, as do the vapors from some cleaning solvents. Any draining or pouring of such volatile fluids should be done in a well ventilated area.

When using cleaning fluids and solvents, read the instructions on the container carefully. Never use materials from unmarked containers.

Never run the engine in an enclosed space, such as a garage. Exhaust fumes contain carbon monoxide, which is extremely poisonous. If you need to run the engine, always do so in the open air, or at least have the rear of the vehicle outside the work area.

If you are fortunate enough to have the use of an inspection pit, never drain or pour gasoline and never run the engine while the vehicle is over the pit. The fumes, being heavier than air, will concentrate in the pit with possibly lethal results.

The battery

Never create a spark or allow a bare light bulb near a battery. They normally give off a certain amount of hydrogen gas, which is highly explosive.

Always disconnect the battery ground (-) cable at the battery before working on the fuel or electrical systems.

If possible, loosen the filler caps or cover when charging the battery from an external source (this does not apply to sealed or maintenance-free batteries). Do not charge at an excessive rate or the battery may burst.

Take care when adding water to a non maintenance-free battery and when carrying a battery. The electrolyte, even when diluted, is very corrosive and should not be allowed to contact clothing or skin.

Always wear eye protection when cleaning the battery to prevent the caustic deposits from entering your eyes.

Household current

When using an electric power tool, inspection light, etc., which operates on household current, always make sure that the tool is correctly connected to its plug and that, where necessary, it is properly grounded. Do not use such items in damp conditions and, again, do not create a spark or apply excessive heat in the vicinity of fuel or fuel vapor.

Secondary ignition system voltage

A severe electric shock can result from touching certain parts of the ignition system (such as the spark plug wires) when the engine is running or being cranked, particularly if components are damp or the insulation is defective. In the case of an electronic ignition system, the secondary system voltage is much higher and could prove fatal.

Troubleshooting

Contents

This Section provides an easy reference guide to the more common problems which may occur during the operation of your vehicle. These problems and possible causes are grouped under various components or systems; i.e. Engine, Cooling system, etc., and also refer to the Chapter and/or Section which deals with the problem.

Remember that successful troubleshooting is not a mysterious ''black art'' practiced only by professional mechanics; it's simply the result of a bit of knowledge combined with an intelligent, systematic approach to the problem. Always work by a process of elimination, starting with the simplest solution and working through to the most complex - and never overlook the obvious. Anyone can forget to fill the gas tank or leave the lights on overnight, so don't assume that you are above such oversights.

Finally, always get clear in your mind why a problem has occurred and take steps to ensure that it doesn't happen again. If the electrical system fails because of a poor connection, check all other connections in the system to make sure that they don't fail as well; if a particular fuse continues to blow, find out why - don't just go on replacing fuses. Remember, failure of a small component can often be indicative of potential failure or incorrect functioning of a more important component or system.

Engine and engine performance

1 Engine will not rotate when attempting to start

1 Battery terminal connections loose or corroded. Check the cable terminals at the battery; tighten the cable or remove corrosion as necessary .
2 Battery discharged or faulty. If the cable connections are clean and tight on the battery posts, turn the key to the On position and switch on the headlights and/or windshield wipers. If they fail to function, the battery is discharged.
3 Automatic transaxle not completely engaged in Park or clutch not completely depressed.
4 Broken, loose or disconnected wiring in the starting circuit. Inspect all wiring and connectors at the battery, starter solenoid, neutral start switch and ignition switch.
5 Starter motor pinion jammed in flywheel ring gear. If manual transaxle, place transaxle in gear and rock the vehicle to manually turn the engine. Remove starter and inspect pinion and flywheel at earliest convenience.
6 Starter solenoid faulty (Chapter 5).
7 Starter motor faulty (Chapter 5).
8 Ignition switch faulty (Chapter 12).

2 Engine rotates but will not start

1 Fuel tank empty.
2 Battery discharged (engine rotates slowly). Check the operation of electrical components as described in previous Section.
3 Battery terminal connections loose or corroded. See previous Section .
4 Carburetor flooded and/or fuel level in carburetor incorrect. This will usually be accompanied by a strong fuel odor from under the hood. Wait a few minutes, depress the accelerator pedal all the way to the floor and attempt to start the engine.
5 Choke control inoperative - carbureted models (Chapter 1).
6 Fuel not reaching carburetor or fuel-injection system (Chapter 4).
7 Fuel injector or fuel pump faulty (fuel-injected vehicles) (Chapter 4).
8 Excessive moisture on, or damage to, ignition components (Chapter 5).
9 Worn, faulty or incorrectly gapped spark plugs (Chapter 1).
10 Broken, loose or disconnected wiring in the starting circuit (see previous Section).
11 Distributor loose, causing ignition timing to change (HEI ignition systems only). Turn the distributor as necessary to start engine, then set ignition timing as soon as possible (Chapter 1).
12 Broken, loose or disconnected wires at the ignition coil(s) or faulty coil(s) (Chapter 5).
13 Broken or stripped timing belt (OHC engines only) (Chapter 2).

3 Starter motor operates without rotating engine

1 Starter pinion sticking. Remove the starter (Chapter 5) and inspect.
2 Starter pinion or flywheel teeth worn or broken. Remove the cover at the rear of the engine and inspect.

4 Engine hard to start when cold

1 Battery discharged or low. Check as described in Section 1.
2 Choke control inoperative or out of adjustment - carbureted models (Chapter 4).
3 Carburetor flooded (see Section 2).
4 Insufficient fuel supply reaching the carburetor of fuel-injection system - check fuel pressure (Chapter 4).
5 Leaky fuel injectors, fuel lines or fuel pump outlet check valve, causing fuel pressure to bleed down while the vehicle is sitting (multi-port fuel injection systems) (Chapter 4).
6 Carburetor/fuel injection system malfunctioning (Chapter 4).
7 Distributor rotor carbon tracked (Chapter 1).

5 Engine hard to start when hot

1 Choke sticking in the closed position - carbureted models - (Chapter 1).
2 Carburetor flooded (see Section 2).
3 Air filter clogged (Chapter 1).
4 Malfunction in the carburetor or fuel injection system (Chapter 4).
5 Insufficient fuel supply reaching the carburetor or fuel injection system. Check the fuel pressure (Chapter 4).
6 Leaky fuel injectors, fuel lines or fuel pump outlet check valve, causing fuel pressure to bleed down while the vehicle is sitting (multi-port fuel injection systems) (Chapter 4).

6 Starter motor noisy or excessively rough in engagement

1 Pinion or flywheel gear teeth worn or broken. Remove the cover at the rear of the engine (if so equipped) and inspect.
2 Starter motor mounting bolts loose or missing.

7 Engine starts but stops immediately

1 Loose or faulty electrical connections at distributor, coil or alternator.
2 Insufficient fuel reaching the carburetor/fuel injector(s) - check the fuel pressure (Chapter 4).
3 Vacuum leak at the gasket surfaces of the intake manifold and/or carburetor/throttle body. Make sure that all mounting bolts (nuts) are re-tightened securely and that all vacuum hoses connected to the carburetor/fuel injection unit(s) and manifold are positioned properly and in good condition.

8 Engine "lopes" while idling or idles erratically

1 Vacuum leakage. Check mounting bolts (nuts) at the carburetor/throttle body and intake manifold for tightness. Make sure that all vacuum hoses are connected and in good condition. Use a length of fuel hose held against your ear to listen for vacuum leaks while the engine is running. A hissing sound will be heard. A soapy water solution will also detect leaks. Check the carburetor/throttle body and intake manifold gasket surfaces. Also check the points where the injectors are attached to the intake ports (multi-port fuel injection).
2 Leaking EGR valve or plugged PCV valve (see Chapters 1 and 6).
3 Air filter clogged (Chapter 1).
4 Fuel pump not delivering sufficient fuel to the carburetor/fuel injector(s) - check the fuel pressure (Chapter 4).
5 Carburetor out of adjustment (Chapter 4) or clogged fuel injectors.
6 Leaking head gasket. If this is suspected,

take the vehicle to a repair shop or dealer where the engine can be pressure checked.

7   Timing chain and/or gears worn (Chapter 2).

8   Camshaft lobes worn (Chapter 2).

9   Engine misses at idle speed

1   All the causes listed in the previous Section, plus:

2   Spark plugs worn or not gapped properly (Chapter 1).

3   Faulty spark plug wires (Chapter 1).

4   Choke not operating properly - carbureted models (Chapter 1).

10   Engine misses throughout the driving speed range

1   Fuel filter clogged and/or impurities in the fuel system (Chapter 1). Also check the fuel pressure (Chapter 4).

2   Clogged fuel injectors.

3   Faulty or incorrectly gapped spark plugs (Chapter 1).

4   Incorrect ignition timing (Chapter 1).

5   On early models with HEI ignition, check for cracked distributor cap, disconnected distributor wires and damaged distributor components (Chapter 1).

6   Leaking spark plug wires (Chapter 1).

7   Faulty emissions system components (Chapter 6).

8   Low or uneven cylinder compression pressures. Remove spark plugs and test compression with gauge (Chapter 1).

9   Weak or faulty ignition system (Chapter 5).

10   Vacuum leaks at carburetor/throttle body, intake manifold or vacuum hoses (see Section 8).

11   Engine stalls

1   Idle speed incorrect (Chapter 1) or automatic idle speed control circuit malfunctioning.

2   Fuel filter clogged and/or water and impurities in the fuel system (Chapter 1).

3   Choke improperly adjusted or sticking - carbureted models - (Chapter 1).

4   Distributor components damp or damaged - early models with HEI ignition systems (Chapter 5).

5   Faulty emissions system components (Chapter 6).

6   Faulty or incorrectly gapped spark plugs (Chapter 1). Also check spark plug wires (Chapter 1).

7   Vacuum leak at the carburetor/throttle body, intake manifold or vacuum hoses. Check as described in Section 8.

8   If the engine stalls after cruising (where the torque converter clutch [TCC] engages), but then re-starts, the problem could be a faulty TCC solenoid. If the solenoid sticks closed, the clutch will remain engaged when the vehicle is coming to a stop, which will stall

the engine. Refer to the *Haynes Automatic Transmission and Transaxle Overhaul Manual* for details on this relatively simple repair.

12   Engine lacks power

1   Incorrect ignition timing - early models with HEI ignition systems - (Chapter 1).

2   Excessive play in distributor shaft (early models with HEI). At the same time, check for worn rotor, faulty distributor cap, wires, etc. (Chapters 1 and 5).

3   Faulty or incorrectly gapped spark plugs (Chapter 1).

4   Carburetor/fuel injection system excessively worn (Chapter 4).

5   Faulty ignition coil(s) (Chapter 5).

6   Brakes binding (Chapter 1).

7   Automatic transaxle fluid level incorrect (Chapter 1).

8   Clutch slipping (Chapter 8).

9   Fuel filter clogged and/or impurities in the fuel system (Chapter 1).

10   Emissions control system not functioning properly (Chapter 6).

11   Use of substandard fuel. Fill tank with proper octane fuel.

12   Low or uneven cylinder compression pressures. Test with compression tester, which will detect leaking valves and/or blown head gasket (Chapter 1).

13   Engine backfires

1   Emissions system not functioning properly (Chapter 6).

2   Ignition timing incorrect - early models with HEI ignition systems (Chapter 1).

3   Faulty secondary ignition system (cracked spark plug insulator, faulty plug wires, distributor cap and/or rotor) (Chapters 1 and 5).

4   Carburetor/fuel injection system in need of adjustment or worn excessively (Chapter 4). A clogged fuel injector may also cause this problem.

5   Vacuum leak at carburetor/throttle body, intake manifold or vacuum hoses. Check as described in Section 8.

6   Valves sticking or burned (Chapter 2).

14   Pinging or knocking engine sounds during acceleration or uphill

1   Incorrect grade of fuel. Fill tank with fuel of the proper octane rating .

2   Ignition timing incorrect (Chapter 1).

3   Carburetor/fuel injection system excessively worn (Chapter 4).

4   Improper spark plugs. Check plug type against *Emissions Control Information* label located in engine compartment. Also check plugs and wires for damage (Chapter 1).

5   Worn or damaged distributor components (Chapter 5).

6   Faulty emissions system (Chapter 6).

7   Vacuum leak. Check as described in Section 8.

15   Engine diesels (continues to run) after switching off

1   Vacuum leaks. Check as described in Section 8.

2   Idle speed too high (Chapter 1).

3   Ignition timing incorrectly adjusted (Chapter 1).

4   Thermo-controlled air cleaner heat valve not operating properly (Chapter 6).

5   Excessive engine operating temperature. Probable causes of this are malfunctioning thermostat, clogged radiator, faulty water pump (Chapter 3).

Engine electrical system

16   Battery will not hold a charge

1   Alternator drivebelt defective or not adjusted properly (Chapter 1).

2   Electrolyte level low or battery discharged (Chapter 1).

3   Battery terminals loose or corroded (Chapter 1).

4   Alternator not charging properly (Chapter 5).

5   Loose, broken or faulty wiring in the charging circuit (Chapter 5).

6   Short in vehicle wiring causing a continual drain on battery

7   Battery defective internally.

17   Alternator light fails to go out

1   Fault in alternator or charging circuit (Chapter 5).

2   Alternator drivebelt defective or not properly adjusted (Chapter 1).

18   Ignition light fails to come on when key is turned on

1   Warning light bulb defective (Chapter 12).

2   Alternator faulty (Chapter 5).

3   Fault in the printed circuit, dash wiring or bulb holder (Chapter 12).

19   "CHECK ENGINE" light comes on

Check for trouble codes stored in the ECM (see Chapter 6).

Fuel system

20   Excessive fuel consumption

1   Dirty or clogged air filter element (Chap-

ter 1).

2   Incorrectly set ignition timing - early models with HEI ignition system (Chapter 1).

3   Choke sticking or improperly adjusted - carbureted models (Chapter 1).

4   Emissions system not functioning properly (Chapter 6).

5   Carburetor/fuel injection internal parts excessively worn or damaged (Chapter 4).

6   Low tire pressure or incorrect tire size (Chapter 1).

21 Fuel leakage and/or fuel odor

1   Leak in a fuel feed or vent line (Chapter 4).

2   Tank overfilled. Fill only to automatic shut-off.

3   Emissions system filter clogged (Chapter 1).

4   Vapor leaks from system lines (Chapter 4).

5   Carburetor/fuel injection internal parts excessively worn (Chapter 4).

Cooling system

22 Overheating

1   Insufficient coolant in system (Chapter 1).

2   Water pump drivebelt defective or not adjusted properly (Chapter 1).

3   Radiator core blocked or radiator grille dirty and restricted (Chapter 3).

4   Thermostat faulty (Chapter 3).

5   Fan blades broken or cracked.

6   Radiator cap not maintaining proper pressure. Have cap pressure tested by a gas station.

7   Ignition timing incorrect - models with a distributor (Chapter 1).

23 Overcooling

1   Thermostat faulty (Chapter 3).

2   Inaccurate temperature gauge or sending unit (Chapter 12).

24 External coolant leakage

1   Deteriorated or damaged hoses or loose clamps. Replace hoses and/or tighten clamps at hose connections (Chapter 11).

2   Water pump seals defective. If this is the case, water will drip from the "weep" hole in the water pump body (Chapter 3).

3   Leakage from radiator core or header tank. This will require the radiator to be pro-

fessionally repaired (see Chapter 3 for removal procedures).

4   Engine drain plugs or water jacket core plugs leaking (see Chapter 2).

25 Internal coolant leakage

Note: *Internal coolant leaks can usually be detected by examining the oil. Check the dipstick and inside of the valve cover for water deposits and an oil consistency like that of a milkshake.*

1   Leaking cylinder head gasket. Have the cooling system pressure tested.

2   Cracked cylinder bore or cylinder head. Dismantle engine and inspect (Chapter 2).

26 Coolant loss

1   Too much coolant in system (Chapter 1).

2   Coolant boiling away due to overheating (see Section 24).

3   Internal or external leakage (see Sections 26 and 27).

4   Faulty radiator cap. Have the cap pressure tested.

27 Poor coolant circulation

1   Inoperative water pump. A quick test is to pinch the top radiator hose closed with your hand while the engine is idling, then let it loose. You should feel the surge of coolant if the pump is working properly (Chapter 3).

2   Restriction in cooling system. Drain, flush and refill the system (Chapter 1). If necessary, remove the radiator (Chapter 3) and have it reverse flushed.

3   Water pump drivebelt defective or not adjusted properly (Chapter 1).

4   Thermostat sticking (Chapter 3).

Clutch

28 Fails to release (pedal pressed to the floor - shift lever does not move freely in and out of Reverse)

1   Improper linkage free play adjustment.

2   Clutch cable excessively stretched or damaged (Chapter 8).

3   Air in clutch hydraulic release system (Chapter 8).

4   Leaking clutch hydraulic release system (Chapter 8).

2   Clutch fork off ball stud.

3   Clutch plate warped or damaged (Chapter 8).

29 Clutch slips (engine speed increases with no increase in vehicle speed)

1   Linkage out of adjustment (Chapter 8).

2   Clutch plate oil soaked or lining worn. Remove clutch (Chapter 8) and inspect.

3   Clutch plate not seated. It may take 30 or 40 normal starts for a new one to seat.

30 Grabbing (chattering) as clutch is engaged

1   Oil on clutch plate lining. Remove (Chapter 8) and inspect. Correct any leakage source.

2   Worn or loose engine or transaxle mounts. These units move slightly when clutch is released. Inspect mounts and bolts.

3   Worn splines on clutch plate hub. Remove clutch components (Chapter 8) and inspect.

4   Warped pressure plate or flywheel. Remove clutch components and inspect.

31 Squeal or rumble with clutch fully engaged (pedal released)

1   Improper adjustment; no freeplay (Chapter 1).

2   Release bearing binding on transaxle bearing retainer. Remove clutch components (Chapter 8) and check bearing. Remove any burrs or nicks, clean and relubricate before reinstallation.

3   Weak linkage return spring. Replace the spring.

32 Squeal or rumble with clutch fully disengaged (pedal depressed)

1   Worn, defective or broken release bearing (Chapter 8).

2   Worn or broken pressure plate springs (or diaphragm fingers) (Chapter 8).

33 Clutch pedal travels to floor - no pressure or very little resistance

1   Clutch cable damaged or linkage binding.

2   Clutch hydraulic release system leaking or faulty (Chapter 8)

3   No fluid in clutch hydraulic release system reservoir (Chapter 1).

4   Broken release bearing or fork (Chapter 8).

5   Sticking clutch release diaphragm fingers (Chapter 8).

Manual transaxle

34   Noisy in Neutral with engine running

1   Input shaft bearing worn.
2   Damaged main drive gear bearing.
3   Worn countershaft bearings.
4   Worn or damaged countershaft endplay shims.

35   Noisy in all gears

1   Any of the above causes, and/or:
2   Insufficient lubricant (see checking procedures in Chapter 1).

36   Noisy in one particular gear

1   Worn, damaged or chipped gear teeth for that particular gear.
2   Worn or damaged synchronizer for that particular gear.

37   Slips out of high gear

1   Transaxle loose on clutch housing (Chapter 7).
2   Shift rods interfering with engine mounts or clutch lever (Chapter 7).
3   Shift rods not working freely (Chapter 7).
4   Damaged mainshaft pilot bearing.
5   Dirt between transaxle case and engine or misalignment of transaxle (Chapter 7).
6   Worn or improperly adjusted linkage (Chapter 7).

38   Difficulty in engaging gears

1   Clutch not releasing completely (see clutch adjustment in Chap-ter 8).
2   Loose, damaged or out of adjustment shift linkage. Make a thorough inspection, replacing parts as necessary Chapter 7).

39   Oil leakage

1   Excessive amount of lubricant in transaxle (see Chapter 1 for correct checking procedures). Drain lubricant as required.
2   Driveaxle oil seal(s) leaking (Chapter 7).
3   Speedometer oil seal in need of replacement (Chapter 7).

Automatic transaxle

Note: *Due to the complexity of the automatic transaxle, it is difficult for the home mechanic to properly diagnose and service this component. For problems other than the following, the vehicle should be taken to a dealer service department or reputable mechanic.*

40   General shift mechanism problems

1   Chapter 7 deals with checking and adjusting the shift linkage on automatic transaxles. Common problems which may be attributed to poorly adjusted linkage are:

    Engine starting in gears other than Park or Neutral.
    Indicator on shifter pointing to a gear other than the one actually being used.
    Vehicle moves when in Park.
2   Refer to Chapter 7 to adjust the linkage.

41   Transaxle will not downshift with accelerator pedal pressed to the floor

    Chapter 7 deals with adjusting the throttle valve (TV) cable to enable the transaxle to downshift properly.

42   Transaxle slips, shifts rough, is noisy or has no drive in forward or reverse gears

1   There are many probable causes for the above problems, but the home mechanic should be concerned with only one possibility - fluid level.
2   Before taking the vehicle to a repair shop, check the level and condition of the fluid, as described in Chapter 1. Correct fluid level as necessary or change the fluid and filter if needed. If the problem persists, have a professional diagnose the probable cause.

43   Fluid leakage

1   Automatic transaxle fluid is a deep red color. Fluid leaks should not be confused with engine oil, which can easily be blown by air flow to the transaxle.
2   To pinpoint a leak, first remove all built-up dirt and grime from around the transaxle Degreasing agents and/or steam cleaning will achieve this. With the underside clean, drive the vehicle at low speeds so air flow will not blow the leak far from its source. Raise the vehicle and determine where the leak is coming from. Common areas of leakage are:

a)   *Pan:* Tighten mounting bolts and/or replace pan gasket as necessary (see Chapters 1 and 7).
b)   *Filler pipe:* Replace the rubber seal where pipe enters transaxle case.
c)   *Transaxle oil lines:* Tighten connectors where lines enter transaxle case and/or rep)ace lines.
d)   *Vent pipe:* Transaxle overfilled and/or water in fluid (see checking procedures, Chapter 1).

e)   *Speedometer connector: Replace the O-ring where speedometer cable enters transaxle case (Chapter 7).*
f)   *Driveaxle oil seal: Replace the driveaxle oil seal(s) (Chapter 7).*

Driveaxles

44   Clicking noise in turns

    Worn or damaged outer CV joint. Check for cut or damaged CV joint boots. Repair as necessary (Chapter 8).

45   Knock or clunk when accelerating from coasting

    Worn or damaged inner CV joint. Check for cut or damaged CV joint boots. Repair as necessary (Chapter 8)

46   Shudder or vibration during acceleration

1   Worn or damaged inner or outer CV joints. Repair or replace as necessary (Chapter 8).
2   Sticking inner CV joint assembly. Correct or replace as necessary (Chapter 8).

Rear axle

47   Noise

1   Road noise. No corrective procedures available.
2   Tire noise. Inspect tires and check tire pressures (Chapter 1).
3   Rear wheel bearings loose, worn or damaged (Chapter 10).

Brakes

Note: *Before assuming that a brake problem exists, make sure that the tires are in good condition and inflated properly (see Chapter 1), that the front end alignment is correct and that the vehicle is not loaded with weight in an unequal manner.*

48   Vehicle pulls to one side during braking

1   Defective, damaged or oil contaminated disc brake pads on one side. Inspect as described in Chapter 9.

2   Excessive wear of brake pad material or disc on one side. Inspect and correct as necessary.
3   Loose or disconnected front suspension components. Inspect and tighten all bolts to the specified torque (Chapter 10).
4   Defective caliper assembly. Remove caliper and inspect for stuck piston or other damage (Chapter 9).

49   Noise (high-pitched squeal when the brakes are applied)

Disc brake pads worn out. The noise comes from the wear sensor rubbing against the disc (does not apply to all vehicles). Replace pads with new ones immediately (Chapter 9).

50   Excessive brake pedal travel

1   Partial brake system failure. Inspect entire system (Chapter 9) and correct as required.
2   Insufficient fluid in master cylinder. Check (Chapter 1), add fluid and bleed system if necessary (Chapter 9).
3   Rear brakes not adjusting properly. Make a series of starts and stops while the vehicle is in Reverse. If this does not correct the situation, remove drums and inspect self adjusters (Chapter 9).

51   Brake pedal feels spongy when depressed

1   Air in hydraulic lines. Bleed the brake system (Chapter 9).
2   Faulty flexible hoses. Inspect all system hoses and lines. Replace parts as necessary.
3   Master cylinder mounting bolts/nuts loose.
4   Master cylinder defective (Chapter 9).

52   Excessive effort required to stop vehicle

1   Power brake booster not operating properly (Chapter 9).
2   Excessively worn linings or pads. Inspect and replace if necessary (Chapter 9).
3   One or more caliper pistons or wheel cylinders seized or sticking. Inspect and rebuild as required (Chapter 9).
4   Brake linings or pads contaminated with oil or grease. Inspect and replace as required (Chapter 9).
5   New pads or shoes installed and not yet seated. It will take a while for the new material to seat against the drum (or rotor).

53   Pedal travels to the floor with little resistance

Little or no fluid in the master cylinder reservoir caused by leaking wheel cylinder(s), leaking caliper piston(s), loose, damaged or disconnected brake lines. Inspect entire system and correct as necessary.

54   Brake pedal pulsates during brake application

1   Wheel bearings not adjusted properly or in need of replacement (Chapter 1).
2   Caliper not sliding properly due to improper installation or obstructions. Remove and inspect (Chapter 9).
3   Disc defective. Remove the disc (Chapter 9) and check for excessive lateral runout and parallelism. Have the disc resurfaced or replace it with a new one.

Suspension and steering systems

55   Vehicle pulls to one side

1   Tire pressures uneven (Chapter 1).
2   Defective tire (Chapter 1).
3   Excessive wear in suspension or steering components (Chapter 10).
4   Front end in need of alignment.
5   Front brakes dragging. Inspect brakes as described in Chapter 9.

56   Shimmy, shake or vibration

1   Tire or wheel out-of-balance or out-of-round. Have professionally balanced.
2   Worn wheel bearings (Chapter 10).
3   Shock absorbers and/or suspension components worn or damaged (Chapter 10).

57   Excessive pitching and/or rolling around corners or during braking

1.   Defective struts/shock absorbers. Replace as a set (Chapter 10).
2   Broken or weak springs and/or suspension components. Inspect as described in Chapter 10.

58   Excessively stiff steering

1   Lack of fluid in power steering fluid reservoir (Chapter 1).
2   Incorrect tire pressures (Chapter 1).
3   Lack of lubrication at steering joints (Chapter 1).
4   Front end out of alignment.
5   See also section titled *Lack of power assistance*.

59   Excessive play in steering

1   Worn front wheel bearings (Chapter 10).
2   Excessive wear in suspension or steering components (Chapter 10).
3   Steering gearbox worn or damaged (Chapter 10).

60   Lack of power assistance

1   Steering pump drivebelt faulty or not adjusted properly (Chapter 1).
2   Fluid level low (Chapter 1).
3   Hoses or lines restricted. Inspect and replace parts as necessary.
4   Air in power steering system. Bleed system (Chapter 10).

61   Excessive tire wear (not specific to one area)

1   Incorrect tire pressures (Chapter 1).
2   Tires out of balance. Have professionally balanced.
3   Wheels damaged. Inspect and replace as necessary.
4   Suspension or steering components excessively worn (Chapter 10).

62   Excessive tire wear on outside edge

1   Inflation pressures incorrect (Chapter 1).
2   Excessive speed in turns.
3   Front end alignment incorrect (excessive toe in). Have professionally aligned.
4   Suspension arm bent or twisted (Chapter 10).

63   Excessive tire wear on inside edge

1   Inflation pressures incorrect (Chapter 1).
2   Front end alignment incorrect (toe-out). Have professionally aligned.
3   Loose or damaged steering components (Chapter 10).

64   Tire tread worn in one place

1   Tires out of balance.
2   Damaged or buckled wheel. Inspect and replace if necessary.
3   Defective tire (Chapter 10).

Notes

Chapter 1
Tune-up and routine maintenance

Contents

Specifications

Recommended lubricants and fluids

Note: *The fluids and lubricants listed here are those recommended by the manufacturer at the time this manual was printed. Vehicle manufacturers occasionally upgrade their fluid and lubricant specifications. Check with your local auto parts store for the most current fluid and lubricant recommendations for your vehicle.*

Engine oil type	API grade SG or SG/CD multigrade and fuel efficient oil
Engine oil viscosity	See accompanying chart

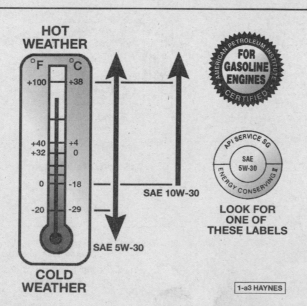

Engine oil viscosity chart - for best fuel economy and cold starting, select the lowest SAE viscosity grade for the expected temperature range

Recommended lubricants and fluids (continued)

Coolant type	50/50 mixture of ethylene glycol-based antifreeze and water
Automatic transaxle fluid type	DEXRON II
Manual transaxle lubricant type	
1982	DEXRON II
1983 through 1987	5W-30 engine oil
1988 on	GM transaxle lubricant (part no. 1235349) or equivalent
Brake fluid type...	DOT 3 brake fluid
Power steering fluid type	
1985 and earlier models..	GM power steering fluid (part no. 1050017) or equivalent
1986 and later models...	GM power steering fluid (part no. 1052884) or equivalent
Hydraulic clutch fluid type	DOT 3 brake fluid

Capacities*

Engine oil (**Note:** *When changing the oil filter,1/2 to one additional quart* *of oil may be needed*)	4 qts
Automatic transaxle fluid (initial refill - see Section 34) for the filling procedure)	4 qts
Manual transaxle lubricant...	2 qts
Cooling system	
Four-cylinder engine	10 quarts
V6 engine..	14 quarts

* All capacities approximate. Add as necessary to bring to the appropriate level.

General engine

Radiator cap opening pressure	15 psi
Thermostat	
Starts to open...	188 to 193-degrees F
Fully open...	212-degrees F
Engine idle speed*	
Automatic transaxle	700 rpm
Manual transaxle	750 rpm
Drivebelt deflection..	1/4 to 1/2 inch
Serpentine drivebelt tension	Automatically adjusted

* Refer to the Vehicle Emission Control Information label in the engine compartment and follow the information on the label if it differs from that shown here.

Ignition system

Distributor direction of rotation...................................	Clockwise
Firing order	
Four-cylinder engines..	1-3-4-2
V6 engines...	1-2-3-4-5-6

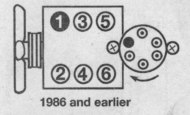
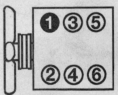
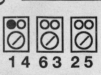

1986 and earlier   **1987 and later**

766-2a-specs HAYNES

1.8, 2.0 and 2.2 liter overhead valve (OHV) four-cylinder engines

1986 and earlier

2.8L and 3.1L V6 engines   **1 4 6 3 2 5**

1987 and later

766-2c-specs HAYNES

766-2b-specs HAYNES

1.8 and 2.0 overhead cam (OHC) four-cylinder engines

The blackened terminal shown on the distributor cap or coil pack indicates the Number One spark plug wire position

Cylinder location and distributor rotation (or coil terminal location)

Ignition system (continued)

Spark plug type and gap*

	Type	Gap
Four-cylinder engines..		
1982 through 1986		
1.8L OHV carbureted...	AC R42TS or equivalent	0.035 inch
2.0L OHV carbureted...	AC R42TS or equivalent	0.035 inch
1.8L OHC fuel injected	AC R44XLS or equivalent	0.035 inch
2.0L OHV fuel injected..	AC R42TS or equivalent	0.035 inch
1.8L OHC turbo	AC R42XLS or equivalent	0.035 inch
1987 and 1988		
2.0L OHV...	AC R44LTSM or equivalent	0.035 inch
2.0 OHC...	AC R44XLS6 or equivalent	0.060 inch
2.0L OHC turbo	AC R42XLS or equivalent	0.035 inch
1989		
2.0 OHC	AC R45XLS or equivalent	0.045 inch
2.0L OHC turbo...	AC R42XLS or equivalent	0.035 inch
2.0L OHV	AC R44LTSM or equivalent	0.035 inch
1990 and 1991		
2.0 OHC...	AC R45XLS or equivalent	0.045 inch
2.0L OHC turbo	AC R42XLS or equivalent	0.035 inch
2.2L OHV	AC R44LTSM or equivalent	0.045 inch
1992 and 1993		
2.0 OHC	AC R43XLS or equivalent	0.045 inch
2.2L OHV...	AC R44LTSMA or equivalent	0.045 inch
1994		
2.0 OHC	AC R43XLS or equivalent	0.045 inch
2.2L OHV...	AC 41-908 or equivalent	0.060 inch
V6 engines		
1985 through 1986		
2.8L...	AC R42TS or equivalent	0.045 inch
1987 through 1990		
2.8L and 3.1L..	AC R43LTSE/R44LTSM or equivalent	0.045 inch
1991 and later		
2.8L and 3.1L..	AC R44LTSM or equivalent	0.045 inch

Ignition timing*
Four-cylinder engine .... 8-degrees BTDC
V6 engines
  2.8L.. 10-degrees BTDC

Refer to the Vehicle Emission Control Information label in the engine compartment and follow the information on the label if it differs from that shown here.

Brakes

Disc brake pad minimum thickness. .... 1/8 inch
Drum brake shoe minimum thickness. .... 1/16 inch

Torque specifications   Ft-lbs (unless otherwise indicated)

Spark plugs
  1.8L and 2.0L OHC 15
  2.2L OHV 11
  1.8L OHV.. 7 to 15
  2.0L OHV.. 7 to 20
  V6 .... 10 to 25
Automatic transaxle fluid pan bolts .... 120 in-lbs
Carburetor mounting nuts/bolts .... 120 in-lbs
TBI mounting nuts/bolts .... 156 in-lbs
Wheel lug nuts 100
Oxygen sensor.. 30

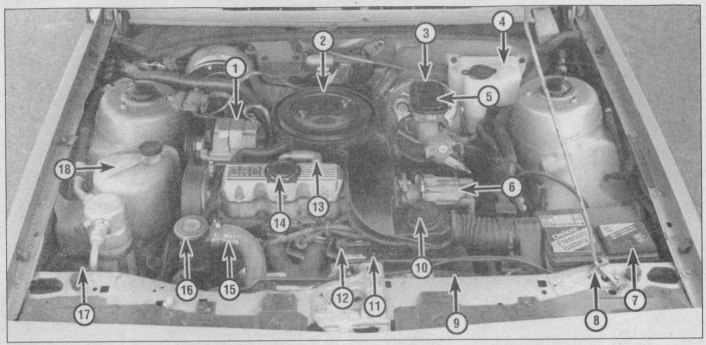

Typical engine compartment component layout (OHC four-cylinder engine)

1	Alternator (Chapter 5)	10	Thermostatic air cleaner motor (Section 25)
2	Air cleaner assembly (Section 33)	11	Engine oil dipstick (Section 4)
3	Power brake booster (Chapter 9)	12	Spark plug (Section 38)
4	Windshield washer reservoir (Section 4)	13	PCV valve (Section 36)
5	Brake master cylinder fluid reservoir (Section 4)	14	Engine oil filler cap (Section 4)
6	Distributor (Chapter 5)	15	Radiator hose (Section 12)
7	Battery (Section 9)	16	Thermostat/cooling system filler cap (Section 32)
8	Hood prop	17	Evaporative emissions system canister (Section 37)
9	Radiator reservoir (Section 4)	18	Coolant reservoir (Section 4)

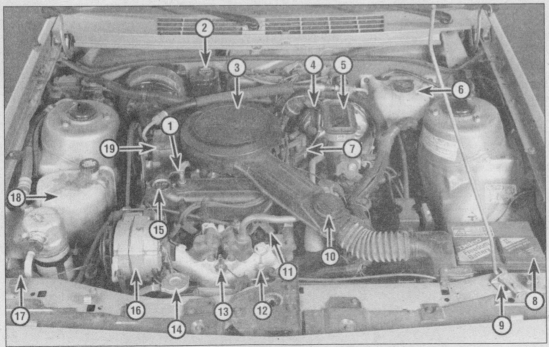

1   PCV valve (Section 36)
2   Power steering fluid reservoir (Section 6)
3   Air cleaner (Section 33)
4   Power brake booster (Chapter 9)
5   Brake master cylinder fluid reservoir (Section 4)
6   Windshield washer fluid reservoir (Section 4)
7   Distributor (Chapter 5)
8   Battery (Section 9)
9   Hood prop
10   Thermostatic air cleaner motor (Section 25)
11   Spark plug (Section 38)
12   Engine oil dipstick (Section 4)
13   Oxygen sensor (Section 40)
14   Radiator cap (Section 32)
15   Engine oil fill cap (Section 4)
16   Alternator (Chapter 5)
17   Evaporative emissions control system canister location (Section 37)
18   Coolant reservoir (Section 4)
19   Power steering pump (Chapter 10)

Typical engine compartment component layout (OHV four-cylinder engine)

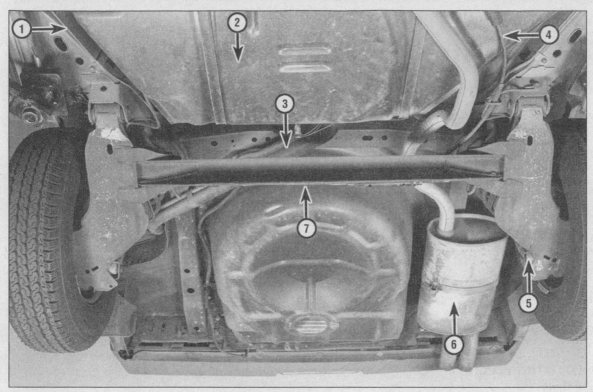

Typical rear underside component layout

1   Brake line (Section 17)
2   Fuel tank (Chapter 4)
3   Fuel filler tube (Section 21)
4   Parking brake cable (Chapter 9)
5   Shock absorber (Chapter 10)
6   Muffler (Section 15)
7   Rear axle (Chapter 10)

FRONT

Typical engine compartment underside layout

1   Drivebelt (Section 10)
2   Air conditioning compressor (Chapter 3)
3   Oxygen sensor (Section 40)
4   Cooling fan (Chapter 3)
5   Brake hose (Chapter 9)
6   Disc brake caliper (Section 17)
7   Grease fitting (Section 14)
8   Manual transaxle drain plug (Section 28)
9   Transaxle case
10 Rack-and-pinion steering boot (Section 16)
11 Inner CV joint (Section 26)
12 CV joint boot (Section 26)
13 Stabilizer bar (Section 16)
14 Engine oil drain plug (Section 4)

1 Routine maintenance schedule

The following recommendations are given with the assumption that the vehicle owner will be doing the maintenance or service work, as opposed to having it done by a dealer service department. The following are factory maintenance recommendations. The owner interested in keeping his or her vehicle in peak conditions at all times may wish to perform these operations more often. This can also enhance the resale value of the vehicle, and we encourage such owner initiative.

When the vehicle is new it should be serviced by a factory authorized dealer service department to protect the factory warranty. In many cases the initial maintenance check is done at no cost to the owner. **Note:** *The following maintenance intervals are based on recommendations by the manufacturer. In the interest of vehicle longevity, we recommend shorter intervals on certain operations, such as fluid and filter replacement.*

Every 250 miles or weekly, whichever comes first

Check the engine oil level (Section 4)
Check the engine coolant level (Section 4)
Check the windshield washer fluid level (Section 4)
Check the brake fluid level (Section 4)
Check the tires and tire pressures (Section 5)

Every 3,000 miles or 3 months, whichever comes first

Check the power steering fluid level (Section 6)
Check the automatic transaxle fluid level (Section 7)
Change the engine oil and oil filter (Section 8)

Every 5,000 miles or 5 months, whichever comes first

Adjust the clutch pedal (1984 and earlier models only) (Section 20)

Every 6,000 miles or 6 months, whichever comes first

Check and service the battery (Section 9)
Check and adjust if necessary, the engine drivebelts (Section 10)
Check the cooling system (Section 11)
Check and replace (if necessary) the underhood hoses (Section 12)
Check and replace (if necessary) the windshield wiper blades (Section 13)
Check and lubricate the chassis components (Section 14)
Check the exhaust system (Section 15)
Check the steering and suspension components (Section 16)
Check the brake system (Section 17)
Check the operation of the choke (Section 18)
Check the engine idle speed (Section 19)
Adjust the clutch pedal (1984 and earlier models only) (Section 20)

Every 12,000 miles or 12 months, whichever comes first

Check the fuel system components (Section 21)
Replace the fuel filter (Section 22)
Check the throttle linkage (Section 23)
Check the carburetor/Throttle Body Injection (TBI) mounting nut/bolt torque (Section 24)
Check the thermostatically-controlled air cleaner (THERMAC) for proper operation (Section 25)
Check the driveaxle oil seals and driveaxle boots (Section 26)
Rotate the tires (Section 27)
Check the manual transaxle fluid level (Section 28)

Every 24,000 miles or 24 months, whichever comes first

Check the wheel bearings (Section 29)
Check the EGR system (Section 30)
Check and adjust (if necessary) the ignition timing (Section 31)

Every 30,000 miles or 30 months, whichever comes first

Drain, flush and refill the cooling system (Section 32)
Replace the air filter and PCV valve filter (Section 33)
Change the automatic transaxle fluid and filter (Section 34)
Change the manual transaxle lubricant (Section 35)
Inspect and replace (if necessary) the PCV valve (Section 36)
Check the EECS emissions system and replace the canister filter (Section 37)
Check the engine compression (Chapter 2D)
Replace the spark plugs (Section 38)
Inspect and replace (if necessary) the spark plug wires, distributor cap and rotor (Section 39)

Every 48000 miles or 48 months, whichever comes first

Check the oxygen sensor (Chapter 6) and replace if necessary (Section 40)

2   Introduction

This Chapter was designed to help the home mechanic maintain his or her vehicle for peak performance, economy, safety and long life.

On the following pages you will find a maintenance schedule, along with Sections which deal specifically with each item on the schedule. Included are visual checks, adjustments and component replacement procedures.

Servicing your vehicle using the time/mileage maintenance schedule and the sequenced Sections will give you a planned program of maintenance. Keep in mind that it is a full plan, and maintaining only a few items at the specified intervals will not give you the same results.

As you service your vehicle you will find that many of the procedures can, and should, be grouped together, due to the nature of the job at hand. Examples of this are as follows:

If the vehicle is raised for chassis lubrication, for example, it is an ideal time to check the exhaust system, suspension, steering and fuel system.

If the tires and wheels are removed, as during a routine tire rotation, check the brakes and wheel bearings at the same time.

If you must borrow or rent a torque wrench it is a good idea to service the spark plugs and check the carburetor or TBI mounting nut/bolt torque all in the same day to save time and money.

The first step of the maintenance plan is to prepare yourself before the actual work begins. Read through the appropriate Sections for all work that is to be performed. Gather together all the necessary parts and tools. If it appears that you could have a problem during a particular job, don't hesitate to seek advice from your local parts man or dealer service department.

3   Tune-up general information

The term tune-up is loosely used for any general operation that puts the engine back in its proper running condition. A tune-up is not a specific operation, but rather a combination of individual operations, such as replacing the spark plugs, adjusting the idle speed, setting the ignition timing, etc.

If, from the time the vehicle is new, the routine maintenance schedule (Section 2) is followed closely and frequent checks are made of fluid levels and high wear items, as suggested throughout this manual, the engine will be kept in relatively good running condition and the need for additional tune-ups will be minimized.

More likely than not, however, there will be times when the engine is running poorly due to lack of regular maintenance. This is even more likely if a used vehicle, which has not received regular and frequent maintenance checks, is purchased. In such cases

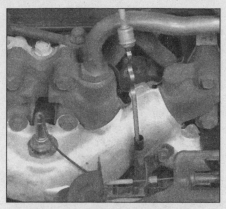

4.4a The engine oil dipstick is located on the front side of the engine, behind the radiator

an engine tune-up will be needed outside of the regular routine maintenance intervals.

The following series of operations are those most often needed to bring a poor running engine back into a proper state of tune.

Minor tune-up

Clean, inspect and test the battery (Section 9)
Check all engine-related fluids (Section 4)
Check the engine compression (Chapter 2D)
Check and adjust the drivebelts (Section 10)
Replace the spark plugs (Section 38)
Inspect the distributor cap and rotor (Section 39)
Inspect the spark plug wires and coil wire (Section 39)
Check and adjust the idle speed (Section 19)
Check and adjust the timing (Section 31)
Replace the fuel filter (Section 22)
Check the PCV valve (Section 36)
Check the cooling system (Section 11)

Major tune-up

All items listed under Minor tune-up plus . . .
Check the EGR system (Chapter 6)
Check the ignition system (Chapter 5)
Check the charging system (Chapter 5)
Check the fuel system (Section 21)

4   Fluid level checks (every 250 miles or weekly)

1   There are a number of components on a vehicle which rely on the use of fluids to perform their job. During normal operation of the vehicle these fluids are used up and must be replenished before damage occurs. See *Recommended lubricants and fluids* at the beginning of this Chapter for the specific fluid to be used when addition is required. When checking fluid levels it is important to have the vehicle on a level surface.

Engine oil

Refer to illustrations 4.4a, 4.4b and 4.6
2   The engine oil level is checked with a

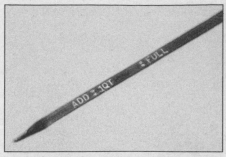

4.4b The oil level should be between the Add and Full marks - if it's below the ADD line, add enough oil to bring the level near the upper line (it takes one quart of oil to raise the level from the lower to upper mark)

dipstick, which is located at the front (radiator) side of the engine block. The dipstick travels through a tube and into the oil pan.
3   Preferably the oil level should be checked before the vehicle has been driven, or about 15 minutes after the engine has been shut off. If the oil is checked immediately after driving the vehicle, some of the oil will remain in the upper engine components, producing an inaccurate reading on the dipstick.
4   Pull the dipstick from the tube and wipe the oil from the end with a clean rag. Insert the clean dipstick all the way back into the oil pan and pull it out again **(see illustration)**. Observe the oil at the end of the dipstick. At its highest point, the level should be between the Add and Full marks **(see illustration)**.
5   It takes one quart of oil to raise the level from the Add mark to the Full mark on the dipstick. Do not allow the level to drop below the add mark as engine damage due to oil starvation may occur. On the other hand, do not overfill the engine by adding oil above the full mark, since this may result in oil-fouled spark plugs, oil leaks or oil seal failures.
6   Oil is added to the engine after removing a twist-off cap located on the valve cover or through a raised tube near the front of the

4.6 The oil filler cap is located on the valve cover - always make sure the area around the opening is clean before unscrewing the cap to prevent dirt from contaminating the engine

4.9 The engine coolant level should appear near the Full Hot mark with the engine at normal operating temperature

4.10 The radiator cap is removed by pushing down and rotating (arrows), but never remove the radiator cap while the engine is hot

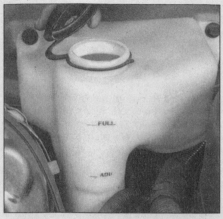

4.15 The windshield washer fluid level should be kept between the Full and Add marks

engine **(see illustration)**. The cap should be marked *Engine Oil* or *Oil*. An oil can spout or funnel will help reduce spills.

7   Checking the oil level can also be an important preventative maintenance step. If you find the oil level dropping abnormally, it is an indication of oil leakage or internal engine wear which should be corrected. The condition of the oil can also be checked along with the level. If there are water droplets in the oil, or if the oil looks like chocolate milk, component failure is indicated and the engine should be checked immediately. With the dipstick removed from the engine, take your thumb and index finger and wipe the oil up the dipstick, looking for small dirt or metal particles which will cling to the dipstick. This is an indication that the oil should be drained and fresh oil added (see Section 8).

Engine coolant

Refer to illustrations 4.9 and 4.10
Warning: *Do not allow antifreeze to come in contact with your skin or painted surfaces of the vehicle. Rinse off spills immediately with plenty of water. Antifreeze is highly toxic if ingested. Never leave antifreeze lying around in an open container or in puddles on the floor; children and pets are attracted by it's sweet smell and may drink it. Check with local authorities about disposing of used antifreeze. Many communities have collection centers which will see that antifreeze is disposed of safely.*

8   All vehicles covered by this manual are equipped with a pressurized coolant recovery system. A white coolant reservoir or expansion tank located in the engine compartment is connected by a hose to the radiator. If the engine overheats, coolant escapes from the radiator and travels through the hose into the reservoir or tank. As the engine cools, the coolant is automatically drawn back into the cooling system to maintain the correct level.

9   The coolant level in the tank should be checked regularly. **Warning:** *Do not remove the radiator cap or expansion tank cap to check the coolant level when the engine is warm! The level in the tank varies with the*

temperature of the engine. When the engine is cold, the coolant level should be at or slightly above the FULL COLD mark on the reservoir. Once the engine has warmed up, the level should be at or near the FULL HOT mark. If it isn't, allow the engine to cool, then remove the cap from the tank and add a 50/50 mixture of ethylene glycol based antifreeze and water **(see illustration)**. If the system is completely cool you can also check the level in the radiator or expansion tank by removing the cap.

10   **Warning:** *Under no circumstances should the radiator or expansion tank cap be removed when the system is hot. Escaping steam and scalding liquid could cause serious personal injury.* In the case of the radiator, wait until the system has cooled completely, then wrap a thick cloth around the cap and turn it to the first stop **(see illustration)**. If any steam escapes, wait until the system has cooled further, then remove the cap. The coolant recovery cap may be removed after it is apparent that no further boiling is occurring in the expansion tank.

11   If only a small amount of coolant is required to bring the system up to the proper level, regular water can be used. However, to maintain the proper antifreeze/water mixture in the system, both should be mixed together to replenish a low level. High-quality antifreeze offering protection to -20-degrees F should be mixed with water in the proportion specified on the container. Do not allow antifreeze to come in contact with your skin or painted surfaces of the vehicle. Flush contacted areas immediately with plenty of water.

12   Coolant should be added to the reservoir or expansion tank until it reaches the FULL COLD mark.

13   As the coolant level is checked, note the condition of the coolant. It should be relatively clear. If it is brown or a rust color, the system should be drained, flushed and refilled (see Section 32).

14   If the cooling system requires repeated additions to maintain the proper level, have

the radiator or expansion tank cap checked for proper sealing. Also check for leaks in the system (cracked hoses, loose hose connections, leaking gaskets, etc.).

Windshield washer fluid

Refer to illustration 4.15
15   Fluid for the windshield washer system is located in a plastic reservoir in the left (drivers side) side of the engine compartment **(see illustration)**. The reservoir should be kept no more than two-thirds full to allow for expansion should the fluid freeze. The use of a windshield washer fluid additive, available at auto parts stores, will help lower the freezing point of the fluid and will result in better cleaning of the windshield surface. Do not use antifreeze because it will cause damage to the vehicle's paint.

16   To prevent icing in cold weather, warm the windshield with the defroster before using the washer.

Battery electrolyte

Refer to illustration 4.17
17   All vehicles with which this manual is concerned are equipped with a maintenance-free battery which is permanently sealed (except for vent holes) and has no filler caps. Water does not have to be added to these batteries. If, however, the battery has been replaced with a traditional-style battery, remove the filler caps and check the level **(see illustration)**. It must be at or near the split ring. If the level is low, add distilled water. Install and securely retighten the caps. **Caution:** *Overfilling the cells may cause electrolyte to spill over during periods of heavy charging, causing corrosion or damage.*

Brake fluid

Refer to illustrations 4.19 and 4.21
18   The brake master cylinder is mounted on the firewall (non-power brake models) or on the front of the power booster unit (power brake models) in the engine compartment.

19   The master cylinder reservoir incorporates a window which allows checking the fluid level without removal of the reservoir

4.17 Remove the cell caps to check the water level in a conventional battery - if the level is low, add distilled water only

4.19 The brake fluid level can be checked without removing the cap

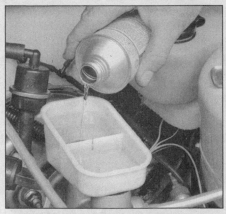

4.21 Clean around the cap to keep from getting dirt in the reservoir, then add the brake fluid - be careful not to get it on painted surfaces

cover. The level should be maintained at 1/4-inch below the lowest edge of each reservoir **(see illustration)**.

20 If a low level is indicated, be sure to wipe the top of the reservoir cover with a clean rag to prevent contamination of the brake system before removing the cover.

21 When adding fluid, pour it carefully into the reservoir, taking care not to spill any onto surrounding painted surfaces **(see illustration)**. Be sure the specified fluid is used, since mixing different types of brake fluid can cause damage to the system. See *Recommended lubricants and fluids* or your owner's manual.

22 At this time the fluid and cylinder can be inspected for contamination. Normally the brake system will not need periodic draining and refilling, but if rust deposits, dirt particles or water droplets are seen in the fluid the system should be disassembled, drained and refilled with fresh fluid.

23 After filling the reservoir to the proper level, make sure the lid is properly seated to prevent fluid leakage and/or system pressure loss.

24 The brake fluid in the master cylinder will drop slightly as the brake shoes or pads

at each wheel wear down during normal operation. If the master cylinder requires repeated replenishing to keep it at the proper level, this is an indication of leakage in the brake system, which should be corrected immediately. Check all brake lines and connections, along with the wheel cylinders and booster (see Section 17 for more information).

25 If, upon checking the master cylinder fluid level, you discover one or both reservoirs empty or nearly empty, the brake system should be bled (see Chapter 9).

Hydraulic clutch fluid

26 The hydraulic clutch fluid is located in a reservoir next to the brake master cylinder. Check the fluid level in the reservoir at least once every month and add more fluid as required. The proper level is indicated by a step on the reservoir. **Caution:** *Be sure to clean the top and sides of the reservoir before removing the cover.*

5   Tire and tire pressure checks (every 250 miles or weekly)

Refer to illustrations 5.2, 5.3, 5.4a, 5.4b and 5.8

1   Periodic inspection of the tires may save you the inconvenience of being stranded with a flat tire. It can also provide you with vital information regarding possible problems in the steering and suspension systems before major damage occurs.

2   Tires are equipped with 1/2-inch wide bands that will appear when tread depth reaches 1/16-inch, at which time the tires can be considered worn out. Tread wear can be monitored with a simple, inexpensive device known as a tread depth indicator **(see illustration)**.

3   Note any abnormal tire wear **(see illus-**

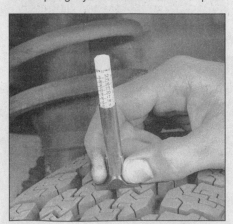

5.2 Use a tire tread depth indicator to monitor tire wear - they are available at auto parts stores and service stations and cost very little

UNDERINFLATION   CUPPING   OVERINFLATION

Cupping may be caused by:
- Underinflation and/or mechanical irregularities such as out-of-balance condition of wheel and/or tire, and bent or damaged wheel.
- Loose or worn steering tie-rod or steering idler arm.
- Loose, damaged or worn front suspension parts.

INCORRECT TOE-IN OR EXTREME CAMBER   FEATHERING DUE TO MISALIGNMENT

5.3 This chart will help you determine the condition of the tires, the probable cause(s) of abnormal wear and the corrective action necessary

5.4a If a tire loses air on a steady basis, check the valve stem core first to make sure it's snug (special inexpensive wrenches are commonly available at auto parts stores

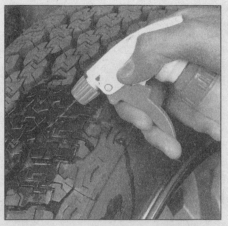

5.4b If the valve stem core is tight, raise the corner of the vehicle with the low tire and spray a soapy water solution onto the tread as the tire is turned slowly - leaks will cause small bubbles to appear

5.8 To extend the life of the tires, check the air pressure at least once a week with an accurate gauge (don't forget the spare)

tration). Tread pattern irregularities such as cupping, flat spots and more wear on one side that the other are indications of front end alignment and/or balance problems. If any of these conditions are noted, take the vehicle to a tire shop or service station to correct the problem.

4   Look closely for cuts, punctures and embedded nails or tacks. Sometimes a tire will hold air pressure for a short time or leak down very slowly after a nail has embedded itself in the tread. If a slow leak persists, check the valve stem core to make sure it is tight **(see illustration)**. Examine the tread for an object that may have embedded itself in the tire or for a "plug" that may have begun to leak (radial tire punctures are repaired with a plug that is installed in the puncture). If a puncture is suspected, it can be easily verified by spraying a solution of soapy water onto the puncture **(see illustration)**. The soapy solution will bubble if there is a leak. Unless the puncture is unusually large, a tire shop or service station can usually repair the tire.

5   Carefully inspect the inner sidewall of each tire for evidence of brake fluid leakage. If you see any, inspect the brakes immediately.

6   Correct air pressure adds miles to the lifespan of the tires, improves mileage and enhances overall ride quality. Tire pressure cannot be accurately estimated by looking at a tire, especially if it's a radial. A tire pressure gauge is essential. Keep an accurate gauge in the glove compartment. The pressure gauges attached to the nozzles of air hoses at gas stations are often inaccurate.

7   Always check tire pressure when the tires are cold. Cold, in this case, means the vehicle has not been driven over a mile in the three hours preceding a tire pressure check. A pressure rise of four to eight pounds is not uncommon once the tires are warm.

8   Unscrew the valve cap protruding from the wheel or hubcap and push the gauge

firmly onto the valve stem **(see illustration)**. Note the reading on the gauge and compare the figure to the recommended tire pressure shown in your owner's manual or on the tire placard on the passenger side door or door pillar. Be sure to reinstall the valve cap to keep dirt and moisture out of the valve stem mechanism. Check all four tires and, if necessary, add enough air to bring them to the recommended pressure.

9   Don't forget to keep the spare tire inflated to the specified pressure (refer to your owner's manual or the placard attached to the door pillar). Note that the pressure recommended for temporary (mini) spare tires is higher than for the tires on the vehicle.

---

6   Power steering fluid steering fluid level check (every 3,000 or 3 months)

Refer to illustrations 6.2 and 6.6
1   Unlike manual steering, the power steer-

6.2 The power steering reservoir is located on the firewall or the front of the engine

ing system relies on fluid which may, over a period of time, require replenishing.

2   The fluid reservoir for the power steering pump will either be located near the front of the engine or on the engine compartment firewall **(see illustration)**.

3   For the check, the front wheels should be pointed straight ahead and the engine should be off.

4   Use a clean rag to wipe off the reservoir cap and the area around the cap. This will help prevent any foreign matter from entering the reservoir during the check.

5   Warm the engine to normal operating temperature.

6   Remove the dipstick, wipe it off with a clean rag, reinsert it, then withdraw it and read the fluid level **(see illustration)**. The level should be between the Add and Full Hot marks.

7   If additional fluid is required, pour the specified type directly into the reservoir, using a funnel to prevent spills.

8   If the reservoir requires frequent fluid additions, all power steering hoses, hose connections and the power steering pump should be checked for leaks.

6.6 Checking of the power steering fluid level is done with the engine at normal operating temperature (the level should be near the Full Hot mark)

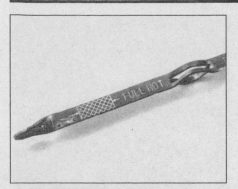

7.7 The automatic transaxle level should be kept within the marked areas, depending on whether the fluid is hot or cool when checked

7.10 Use a funnel to add fluid to the automatic transaxle through the dipstick tube

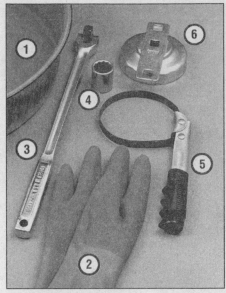

8.3 These tools are required when changing the engine oil and filter

1   *Drain pan* - It should be fairly shallow in depth, but wide to prevent spills
2   *Rubber gloves* - When removing the drain plug and filter, you will get oil on your hands (the gloves will prevent burns)
3   *Breaker bar* - Sometimes the oil drain plug is tight, and a long breaker bar is needed to loosen it
4   *Socket* - To be used with the breaker bar or a ratchet (must be the correct size to fit the drain plug - six-point preferred)
5   *Filter wrench* - This is a metal band-type wrench, which requires clearance around the filter to be effective
6   *Filter wrench* - This type fits on the bottom of the filter and can be turned with a ratchet or breaker bar (different-size wrenches are available for different types of filters)

7   Automatic transaxle fluid check (every 3,000 miles or 3 months)

Refer to illustrations 7.7 and 7.10

1   The level of the automatic transaxle fluid should be carefully maintained. Low fluid level can lead to slipping or loss of drive, while overfilling can cause foaming and loss of fluid.
2   With the parking brake set, start the engine, then move the shift lever through all the gear ranges, ending in Park. The fluid level must be checked with the vehicle level and the engine running at idle. **Note:** *Incorrect fluid level readings will result if the vehicle has just been driven at high speeds for an extended period, in hot weather in city traffic, or if it's been pulling a trailer. If any of these conditions apply, wait until the fluid has cooled (about 30 minutes).*
3   With the transaxle at normal operating temperature, remove the dipstick, located on the left side of the engine compartment.
4   Wipe the fluid from the dipstick with a clean rag and push it back into the filler tube until the cap seats.
5   Carefully touch the end of the dipstick to determine the temperature of the fluid. It may be cool, warm or hot.
6   Wipe the fluid from the dipstick with a clean rag and push the dipstick back into the filler tube until the cap seats.
7   Pull the dipstick out and note the fluid level **(see illustration)**.
8   If the fluid felt cool or warm, the level should be between the dimples above the Full mark.
9   If the fluid felt hot, the level should be in the cross-hatched area near the Full mark.
10   Add just enough of the recommended fluid to fill the transaxle to the proper level **(see illustration)**. It takes about one pint to raise the level from the Add mark to the Full mark with a hot transaxle, so add the fluid a little at a time and keep checking the level until it is correct.
11   The condition of the fluid should also be checked. If the fluid is a dark reddish-brown color, or if the fluid has a burned smell, the

transaxle fluid should be changed. If you are in doubt about the condition of the fluid, purchase some new fluid and compare the two for color and smell.

8   Engine oil and filter change (every 3,000 miles or 3 months)

Refer to illustrations 8.3, 8.14 and 8.19

1   Frequent oil changes may be the best form of preventative maintenance available to the home mechanic. When engine oil ages, it becomes diluted and contaminated, which leads to premature engine wear.
2   Although some sources recommend oil filter changes every other oil change, we feel that the minimal cost of an oil filter and the relative ease with which it is installed dictate that a new filter be used whenever the oil is changed.
3   The tools necessary for a oil and filter change are a wrench to fit the drain plug at the bottom of the oil pan, an oil filter wrench to remove the old filter, a container with at least a six-quart capacity to drain the old oil into and a funnel to help pour fresh oil into the engine **(see illustration)**.
4   In addition, you should have plenty of clean rags and newspapers handy to mop up any spills. Access to the underside of the vehicle is greatly improved if the vehicle can be lifted on a hoist, driven onto ramps or supported by jackstands. **Warning:** *Do not work under a vehicle which is supported only by a jack.*
5   If this is your first oil change on the vehicle, it is a good idea to crawl underneath and familiarize yourself with the locations of the oil drain plug and the oil filter. The engine and exhaust components will be hot during the actual work, so it is a good idea to figure out any potential problems before becoming involved with the procedure.
6   Allow the engine to warm up to normal operating temperature. If the new oil or any tools are needed, use this warm-up time to

gather everything necessary for the job. The correct type of oil to buy for your application can be found in *Recommended lubricants and fluids* at the beginning of this manual.
7   With the engine oil warm (warm engine oil will drain better and more built-up sludge will be removed with the oil), raise and support the vehicle. Make sure it is firmly supported.
8   Move all necessary tools, rags and newspapers under the vehicle. Position the drain pan under the drain plug. Keep in mind that the oil will initially flow from the pan with some force, so place the pan accordingly.
9   Being careful not to touch any of the hot exhaust components, use the wrench to remove the drain plug near the bottom of the oil pan. Depending on how hot the oil has become, you may want to wear gloves while unscrewing the plug the final few turns.
10   Allow the old oil to drain into the pan. It may be necessary to reposition the pan as

8.14 A strap-type oil filter wrench works well in hard-to-reach locations

8.19 Lubricate the oil filter gasket with clean engine oil before installing it on the engine

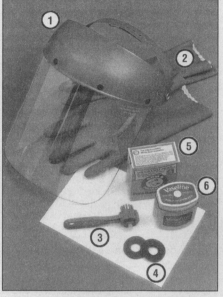

9.1 Tools and materials required for battery maintenance

1   *Face shield/safety goggles - When removing corrosion with a brush, the acidic particles can easily fly up into your eyes*
2   *Rubber gloves - Another safety item to consider when servicing the battery - remember that's acid inside the battery!*
3   *Battery terminal/cable cleaner - This wire brush cleaning tool will remove all traces of corrosion from the battery and cable*
4   *Treated felt washers - Placing one of these on each terminal, directly under the cable end, will help prevent corrosion (be sure to get the correct type for side-terminal batteries)*
5   *Baking soda - A solution of baking soda and water can be used to neutralize corrosion*
6   *Petroleum jelly - A layer of this on the battery terminal bolts will help prevent corrosion*

the oil flow slows to a trickle.

11   After all the oil has drained wipe off the drain plug with a clean rag. Small metal particles may cling to the plug and would immediately contaminate the new oil.

12   Clean the area around the drain plug opening and reinstall the plug. Tighten the plug securely with the wrench.

13   Move the drain pan into position under the oil filter.

14   Use the filter wrench to loosen the oil filter. Chain or metal band-type filter wrenches may distort the filter canister, but this is of no concern as the filter will be discarded **(see illustration)**.

15   Sometimes the oil filter is on so tight it cannot be loosened, or is positioned in an area which is inaccessible with a filter wrench. As a last resort you can punch a metal bar or long screwdriver directly through the sides of the canister and use it as a T-handle to turn the filter. If this becomes necessary be prepared for oil to spurt out of the canister as it is punctured.

16   Completely unscrew the old filter. Be careful, it is full of oil. Empty the filter into the drain pan.

17   Compare the old filter with the new one to make sure they are the same type.

18   Use a clean rag to remove all oil, dirt and sludge from the area where the oil filter mounts to the engine. Check the old filter to make sure the rubber gasket is not stuck to the engine mounting surface. If the gasket is stuck to the engine remove it.

19   Open one of the containers of oil and fill the filter half-full. Apply a light coat of oil around the full circumference of the rubber gasket of the oil filter **(see illustration)**.

20   Attach the filter to the engine following the tightening directions printed on the filter canister or packing box. Most filter manufacturers recommend against using a filter wrench due to the possibility of overtightening and damage to the seal.

21   Remove all tools, rags, etc. from under the vehicle, being careful not to spill the oil in the drain pan, then lower the vehicle.

22   Move to the engine compartment and locate the oil filler cap on the engine. Remove the cap.

23   Pour the new oil through the filler opening.

24   Pour three quarts of fresh oil into the engine. Wait a few minutes to allow the oil to drain into the pan, then check the level on the oil dipstick (see Section 4 if necessary). If the oil level is at or near the lower Add mark, start the engine and allow the new oil to circulate.

25   Run the engine for one minute then shut it off. Immediately look under the vehicle and check for leaks at the oil pan drain plug and around the oil filter. If either is leaking, tighten with a bit more force.

26   With the new oil circulated and the filter now completely full, recheck the level on the dipstick and add enough oil to bring the level to the Full mark on the dipstick.

27   During the first few trips after an oil change, make it a point to check frequently for leaks and proper oil level.

28   The old oil drained from the engine cannot be reused in its present state and should be disposed of. Oil reclamation centers, auto repair shops and gas stations will normally accept the oil, which can be refined and used again. After the oil has cooled. it can be drained into a suitable container (capped plastic jugs, topped bottles, milk cartons, etc.) for transport to one of these disposal sites.

---

9   Battery check, maintenance and charging (every 6,000 miles or 6 months)

Check and maintenance

Refer to illustrations 9.1, 9.7a, 9.7b and 9.9

Warning: *Certain precautions must be followed when checking and servicing the battery. Hydrogen gas, which is highly flammable, is always present in the battery cells, so keep lighted tobacco and all other flames and sparks away from it. The electrolyte*

inside the battery is actually dilute sulfuric acid, which will cause injury if splashed on your skin or in your eyes. It will also ruin clothes and painted surfaces. When removing the battery cables, always detach the negative cable first and hook it up last!

1   Battery maintenance is an important procedure which will help ensure that you are not stranded because of a dead battery. Several tools are required for this procedure **(see illustration)**.

2   Before servicing the battery, always turn the engine and all accessories off and disconnect the cable from the negative terminal of the battery.

3   A sealed (sometimes called maintenance free) battery is standard equipment. The cell caps cannot be removed, no electrolyte checks are required and water cannot be added to the cells. However, if an after-

9.7a On these models, the cable terminals are located on the side of the battery

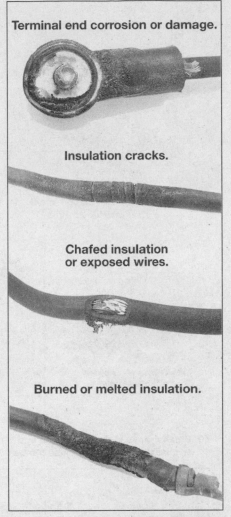

Terminal end corrosion or damage.

Insulation cracks.

Chafed insulation or exposed wires.

Burned or melted insulation.

9.7b Typical battery cable problems

9.9 Use a socket and extension to reach the battery hold-down bolt

market battery has been installed and it is a type that requires regular maintenance, the following procedures can be used.

4   Check the electrolyte level in each of the battery cells (see Section 4). It must be above the plates. There's usually a split-ring indicator in each cell to indicate the correct level. If the level is low, add distilled water only, then install the cell caps. **Caution:** *Overfilling the cells may cause electrolyte to spill over during periods of heavy charging, causing corrosion and damage to nearby components.*

5   If the positive terminal and cable clamp on your vehicle's battery is equipped with a rubber or plastic protector, make sure that it's not torn or damaged. It should completely cover the terminal.

6   The external condition of the battery should be checked periodically. Look for damage such as a cracked case.

7   Check the tightness of the battery cable terminals to ensure good electrical connections and inspect the entire length of each cable, looking for cracked or abraded insulation and frayed conductors **(see illustrations)**.

8   If corrosion (visible as white, fluffy deposits) is evident, remove the cables from the terminals, clean them with a battery brush and reinstall them. Corrosion can be kept to a minimum by installing specially treated washers available at auto parts stores or by applying a layer of petroleum jelly or grease to the terminals and cable clamps after they are assembled.

9   Make sure the battery carrier is in good condition and that the hold-down clamp bolt is tight **(see illustration)**. If the battery is removed (see Chapter 5 for the removal and installation procedure), make sure that no parts remain in the bottom of the carrier when it's reinstalled. When reinstalling the hold-down clamp, don't overtighten the bolt.

10   Corrosion on the carrier, battery case and surrounding areas can be removed with a solution of water and baking soda. Apply the mixture with a small brush, let it work, then rinse it off with plenty of clean water.

11   Any metal parts of the vehicle damaged by corrosion should be coated with a zinc-

based primer, then painted.

12   Additional information on the battery and jump starting can be found in Chapter 5 and at the front of this manual.

Charging

13   Remove all of the cell caps (if equipped) and cover the holes with a clean cloth to prevent spattering electrolyte. Disconnect the negative battery cable and hook the battery charger leads to the battery posts (positive to positive, negative to negative), then plug in the charger. Make sure it is set at 12-volts if it has a selector switch.

14   If you're using a charger with a rate higher than two amps, check the battery regularly during charging to make sure it doesn't overheat. If you're using a trickle charger, you can safely let the battery charge overnight after you've checked it regularly for the first couple of hours.

15   If the battery has removable cell caps, measure the specific gravity with a hydrometer every hour during the last few hours of the charging cycle. Hydrometers are available inexpensively from auto parts stores - follow

the instructions that come with the hydrometer. Consider the battery charged when there's no change in the specific gravity reading for two hours and the electrolyte in the cells is gassing (bubbling) freely. The specific gravity reading from each cell should be very close to the others. If not, the battery probably has a bad cell(s).

16   Some batteries with sealed tops have built-in hydrometers on the top that indicate the state of charge by the color displayed in the hydrometer window. Normally, a bright-colored hydrometer indicates a full charge and a dark hydrometer indicates the battery still needs charging. Check the battery manufacturer's instructions to be sure you know what the colors mean.

17   If the battery has a sealed top and no built-in hydrometer, you can hook up a voltmeter across the battery terminals to check the charge. A fully charged battery should read 12.6-volts or higher.

18   Further information on the battery and jump starting can be found in Chapter 5 and at the front of this manual.

10   Drivebelt check and adjustment (every 6,000 miles or 6 months)

Refer to illustrations 10.3, 10.4, 10.6, 10.9 and 10.10

1   The drivebelts, or V-belts as they are often called, are located at the front of the engine and play an important role in the overall operation of the vehicle and its components. Due to their function and material make-up, the belts are prone to failure after a period of time and should be inspected and adjusted periodically to prevent major engine damage.

2   The number of belts used on a particular vehicle depends on the accessories installed. Drivebelts are used to turn the generator/alternator, power steering pump, water pump and air-conditioning compressor. Depending on the pulley arrangement, more than one of these components may be driven by a single belt.

3   With the engine off, open the hood and

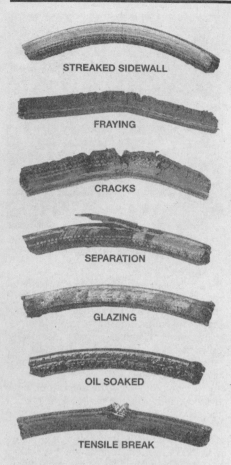

STREAKED SIDEWALL

FRAYING

CRACKS

SEPARATION

GLAZING

OIL SOAKED

TENSILE BREAK

10.3 Here are some of the more common problems associated with drivebelts (check the belts carefully to prevent an untimely breakdown)

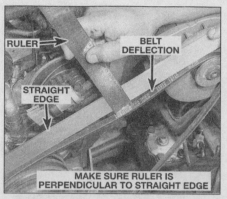

10.4 Drivebelt tension can be checked with a straightedge and ruler

ACCEPTABLE

Cracks Running Across "V" Portions of Belt

UNACCEPTABLE

1/2"

Missing Two or More Adjacent Ribs 1/2" or longer

Cracks Running Parallel to "V" Portions of Belt

10.9 Small cracks in the under side of a V-ribbed belt are acceptable -lengthwise cracks, or missing pieces that cause the belt to make noise, are cause for replacement

10.6 Typical alternator drivebelt adjustment components (arrows)

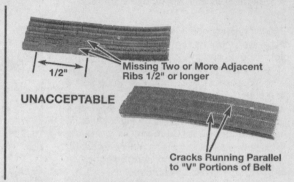

locate the various belts at the front of the engine. Using your fingers (and a flashlight, if necessary) , move along the belts checking for cracks and separation of the belt plies **(see illustration)**. Also check for fraying and glazing, which gives the belt a shiny appearance. Both sides of the belt should be inspected, which means you will have to twist the belt to check the underside.

4   The tension of each belt is checked by pushing on the belt at a distance halfway between the pulleys. Push firmly with your thumb and see how much the belt moves (deflects). A rule of thumb is that if the distance from pulley center to pulley center is between 7 and 11 inches, the belt should deflect 1/4-inch. If the belt travels between pulleys spaced 12 to 16 inches apart, the belt should deflect 1/2-inch**(see illustration)**.

5   If it is necessary to adjust the belt tension, either to make the belt tighter or looser, it is done by moving the belt-driven accessory on the bracket.

6   For each component there will be an adjusting bolt and a pivot bolt. Both bolts must be loosened slightly to enable you to move the component **(see illustration)**.

7   After the two bolts have been loosened,

move the component away from the engine to tighten the belt or toward the engine to loosen the belt. Hold the accessory in position and check the belt tension. If it is correct, tighten the two bolts until just snug, then recheck the tension. If the tension is all right, tighten the bolts.

8   It will often be necessary to use some sort of prybar to move the accessory while the belt is adjusted. If this must be done to gain the proper leverage, be very careful not to damage the component being moved or the part being pried against.

9   Later models are equipped with a single "serpentine" drivebelt, which powers all engine accessories. Some of these belts require no adjustment; it is handled by a spring-loaded tensioner pulley. Others do require manual adjustment. The belt should be inspected regularly for missing ribs and frayed plies. Cracks in the belt ribs do not necessarily indicate a faulty or damaged belt, since they will not impair belt performance **(see illustration)**.

10   To replace the belt on models with an automatic tensioner, insert a half-inch drive breaker bar (some models require a 15 mm socket) into the tensioner and rotate the pulley to release belt tension **(see illustration)**.

11   To replace a serpentine belt on models with a manual adjuster, loosen the adjustment and pivot bolts on the tensioner, insert

a torque wrench into the square-drive hole in the tensioner, then apply 90-ft-lbs (new belt) or 65 ft-lbs (used belt) to the tensioner. Tighten the adjustment and pivot bolts.

12   Remove the drivebelt from the pulleys.

13   Install the new belt, starting with the bottom pulleys, then release the tensioner. Make sure the belt is properly centered on each pulley.

10.10 Use a breaker bar to lift the tensioner (1) and release the tension from the belt (2)

Check for a chafed area that could fail prematurely.

Check for a soft area indicating the hose has deteriorated inside.

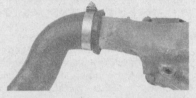

Overtightening the clamp on a hardened hose will damage the hose and cause a leak.

Check each hose for swelling and oil-soaked ends. Cracks and breaks can be located by squeezing the hose.

11.4a Hoses, like drivebelts, have a habit of failing at the worst possible time - to prevent the inconvenience of a blown radiator or heater hose, inspect them carefully as shown here

11   Cooling system check (every 6,000 miles or 6 months)

Refer to illustrations 11.4a and 11.4b

1   Many major engine failures can be attributed to a faulty cooling system. If the vehicle is equipped with an automatic transaxle, the cooling system also plays an important role in prolonging transaxle life.

2   The cooling system should be checked with the engine cold. Do this before the vehicle is driven for the day or after it has been shut off for at least three hours.

3   Remove the radiator cap and thoroughly clean the cap, inside and out, with clean water. Also clean the filler neck on the radiator. All traces of corrosion should be removed.

4   Carefully check the upper and lower radiator hoses and the smaller diameter heater hoses. Inspect each hose along its entire length, replacing any hose which is cracked, swollen or shows signs of deteriora-

11.4b Although this radiator hose appears to be in good condition, it should be periodically checked for cracks (more easily revealed when squeezed)

tion. Cracks may become more apparent if the hose is squeezed **(see illustrations).**

5   Make sure that all hose connections are tight. A leak in the cooling system will usually show up as white or rust colored deposits on the areas near the leak.

6   Use compressed air or a soft brush to remove bugs, leaves, etc. from the front of the radiator or air-conditioning condenser. Be careful not to damage the delicate cooling fins or cut yourself on them.

7   Finally, have the cap and system pressure tested. If you do not have a pressure tester, most gas stations and repair shops will do this for a minimal change.

12   Underhood hose check and replacement (every 6,000 miles or 6 months)

Warning: *Replacement of air-conditioning hoses must be left to a dealer or air-conditioning specialist who can depressurize the system and perform the work safely. Never disconnect air conditioning hoses or components until the system has been depressurized.*

1   The high temperatures present under the hood can cause deterioration of rubber and plastic hoses.

2   Periodic inspection should be made for cracks, loose clamps and leaks. Some of the hoses are part of the emissions control systems and can affect the engine's performance.

3   Remove the air cleaner if necessary and trace the entire length of each hose. Squeeze each hose to check for cracks and look for swelling, discoloration and leaks.

4   If the vehicle has considerable mileage or if one or more of the hoses is suspect, it is a good idea to replace all of the hoses at one time.

5   Measure the length and inside diameter of each hose and obtain and cut the replacement to size. Since original equipment hose clamps are often good for only one use it is a

good idea to replace them with screw-type clamps.

6   Replace each hose one at a time to eliminate the possibility of confusion. Hoses attached to the heater and radiator contain coolant, so newspapers or rags should be kept handy to catch the spills when they are disconnected.

7   After installation, run the engine until it reaches operating temperature, shut it off and check for leaks. After the engine has cooled, retighten all of the screw-type clamps.

13   Wiper blade inspection and replacement (every 6,000 miles or 6 months)

Refer to illustrations 13.6 and 13.9

1   The windshield wiper and blade assembly should be inspected periodically for damage, loose components and cracked or worn blade elements.

2   Road film can build up on the wiper blades and affect their efficiency, so they should be washed regularly with a mild detergent solution.

3   The action of the wiping mechanism can loosen the bolts, nuts and fasteners so they should be checked and tightened. as necessary, at the same time the wiper blades are checked.

4   If the wiper blade elements are cracked, worn or warped, they should be replaced with new ones.

5   These models are equipped with three types of wipers.

6   Remove the Type 1 wiper blade element by raising the wiper arm and pushing the blade off the pin on the arm **(see illustration).**

7   Remove the element by inserting a screwdriver under the spring loaded retainer at each metal tab, rotating it, then sliding the element up and out of the tabs. Install the element by sliding it into the retaining tabs, lining up the slot in the element with the tabs and snapping it into place.

8   Detach the Type 2 blade from the arm

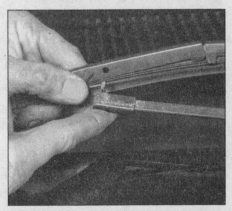

13.6   Remove the Type 1 wiper by lifting the release lever

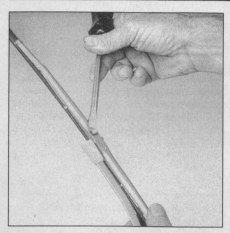

13.9 Insert a screwdriver under the release spring - pry up and pull the wiper blade off of the arm

14.1 Materials required for chassis and body lubrication

1   **Engine oil** - *Light engine oil in a can like this can be used for door and hood hinges*
2   **Graphite spray** - *Used to lubricate lock cylinders*
3   **Grease** - *Grease, in a variety of types and weights, is available for use in a grease gun. Check the Specification for your requirements*
4   **Grease gun** - *A common grease gun, shown here with a detachable hose and nozzle, is needed for chassis lubrication. After use, clean it thoroughly!*

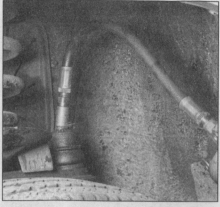

14.6a The steering arm grease fitting can be reached through the wheel opening

by pressing the release spring. Replace the element by bending the top of the housing down, while pulling the element up and twisting it out with the housing tab and element release notches lined up. Slide the element down until all the tabs are removed through the notch.

9   The Type 3 wiper is removed by inserting a screwdriver under the release spring **(see illustration)**. The element is retained by tabs on the blade housing. Disengage these tabs by pulling the housing back until the element can be pulled out of the assembly.

10   Install the blade by inserting the pronged end of the arm into the blade slots and pulling the bottom of the blade towards the arm to lock it in place.

14   Chassis lubrication (every 6,000 miles or 6 months)

Refer to illustrations 14.1, 14.6a, 14.6b and 14.10

1   A grease gun and a cartridge filled with the proper grease (see *Recommended fluids and lubricants*) are usually the only equipment necessary to lubricate the chassis components. In some chassis locations plugs may be installed rather than grease fittings, in which case grease fittings will have to be installed **(see illustration)**.

2   The grease fittings are located at steering arm tie-rod ends and front control arm lower balljoints. Look under the vehicle to find these components and determine if grease fittings or solid plugs are installed. If there are plugs, remove them and thread grease fittings into the component. A dealer service department or auto parts store will be able to supply replacement fittings. Straight, as well as angled, fittings are available.

3   For easier access under the vehicle raise it with a jack and place jackstands under the frame. Make sure the vehicle is securely supported by the stands.

4   Before proceeding, pump a little of the grease out of the nozzle of the grease gun to

remove any dirt from the end of the gun. Wipe the nozzle clean with a rag.

5   With the grease gun, plenty of clean rags and the diagram, crawl under the vehicle and begin lubricating the components.

6   Wipe the grease fitting clean and push the nozzle firmly over the fitting. Pump the trigger on the grease gun to force grease into the component. **Note**: *The tie-rod ends should be lubricated until the rubber boot is firm to the touch. Do not pump too much grease into these fittings as it could rupture the boot* **(see illustration)**. On the control

14.6b The control arm balljoint grease fitting is accessible from under the vehicle

arm balljoint fittings, continue pumping grease into the fitting until grease seeps out of the joint between the two components **(see illustration)**. If the grease seeps out around the grease gun nozzle, the fitting is clogged or the nozzle is not seated on the fitting. Re-secure the gun nozzle to the fitting and try again. If necessary, replace the fitting.

7   Wipe the excess grease from the components and the grease fitting. Follow the same procedures for the remaining fittings.

8   While you are under the vehicle clean and lubricate the parking brake cable, the cable guides and levers. This can be done by smearing some of the chassis grease onto the cable and its related parts with your fingers. Place a few drops of light engine oil on the transaxle shift linkage rods and swivels.

9   Lower the vehicle for the remaining lubrication procedures.

10   Open the hood and apply chassis grease to the hood latch mechanism **(see illustration)**. If the hood has an inside release, have an assistant pull the release knob as you lubricate the cable at the latch.

11   Lubricate all the hinges (door, hood, liftgate) with a few drops of light engine oil.

12   The key lock cylinders should be lubricated with spray-on graphite dry lubricant, which is available at auto parts stores.

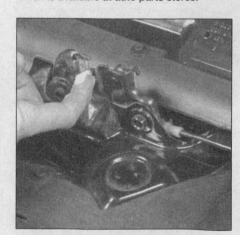

14.10 Multi-purpose grease is used to lubricate the hood latch mechanism

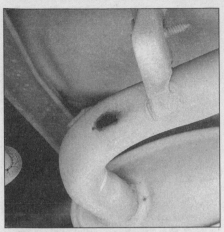

15.2 Check the pipes and connections for signs of leakage - this stain around a small hole is indicative of a tailpipe needing replacement

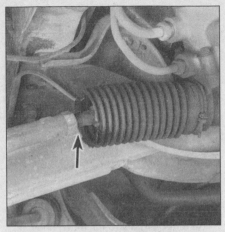

16.6 Check the steering gear for ripped or torn boots which could cause the steering gear to fail prematurely

cumstances, use petroleum-based solvents to clean brake parts. Use brake system cleaner only!

Note: For detailed photographs of the brake system, see Chapter 9.

1   The brakes should be inspected every time the wheels are removed or whenever a defect is suspected. Indications of a potential brake system defect are:

a) The vehicle pulls to one side when the brake pedal is depressed.
b) Noises coming from the brakes when they are applied.
c) Excessive brake pedal travel.
d) Pulsating pedal.
e) Leakage of fluid, usually seen on the inside of the tire or wheel.

Disc brakes

2   Disc brakes can be visually checked without removing any parts except the wheels.

3   Raise the vehicle and place it securely on jackstands. Remove the wheels (see *Jacking and towing* at the front of the manual, if necessary).

4   The disc brake calipers, which contain the pads, are now visible. There is an outer pad and an inner pad in each caliper. All pads should be inspected.

5   The outer pads on the front wheels are equipped with a wear sensor. This is a small, bent piece of metal which is visible from the inboard side of the brake caliper. When the pads wear to the danger limit the metal sensor rubs against the disc and makes a screeching sound.

6   Check the pad thickness by looking at each end of the caliper and through the inspection hole in the caliper body **(see illustrations)**. If the wear sensor clip is very close to the disc, or if the lining material is 1/8-inch or less in thickness, the pads should be replaced. Keep in mind that the lining material is riveted or bonded to a metal backing shoe and the metal portion is not included in this measurement.

15   Exhaust system check (every 6,000 miles or 6 months)

Refer to illustration 15.2

1   With the engine cold (at least three hours after the vehicle has been driven) , check the complete exhaust system from its starting point at the engine to the end of the tailpipe. This should be done on a hoist where unrestricted access is available.

2   Check the pipes and connections for signs of leakage and corrosion, indicating a potential failure **(see illustration)**. Make sure that all brackets and hangers are in good condition and tight.

3   Inspect the underside of the body for holes, corrosion, open seams, etc., which may allow exhaust gases to enter the passenger compartment. Seal all body openings with silicone or body putty.

4   Rattles and other noises can often be traced to the exhaust system, especially the mounts and hangers. Try to move the pipes, muffler and catalytic converter. If the components can come in contact with the body or suspension parts, secure the exhaust system with new mounts.

5   Check the running condition of the engine by inspecting inside the end of the tailpipe. The exhaust deposits here are an indication of engine state-of-tune. If the pipe is black and sooty or coated with white deposits, the engine is in need of a tune-up, including a thorough carburetor inspection and adjustment.

16   Suspension and steering check (every 6,000 miles or 6 months)

Refer to illustration 16.6

1   Whenever the front of the vehicle is raised for service visually check the suspension and steering components for wear.

2   Indications of a fault in these systems

are excessive play in the steering wheel before the front wheels react, excessive sway around corners, body movement over rough roads or binding at some point as the steering wheel is turned.

3   Before the vehicle is raised for inspection, test the shock absorbers by pushing down to rock the vehicle at each corner. If you push down and the vehicle does not come back to a level position within one or two bounces, the shocks/struts are worn and must be replaced. As this is done, check for squeaks and noises coming from the suspension components. Information on suspension components can be found in Chapter 10.

4   Raise the front of the vehicle and support it securely on jackstands placed under the frame rails.

5   Check the wheel bearings (see Section 29).

6   Crawl under the vehicle and check for loose bolts, broken or disconnected parts and deteriorated rubber bushings on all suspension and steering components. Look for grease or fluid leaking from the steering gear **(see illustration)**. Check the power steering hoses and connections for leaks. Check the balljoints for wear.

7   Have an assistant turn the steering wheel from side-to-side and check the steering components for free movement, chafing and binding. If the steering does not react with the movement of the steering wheel, try to determine where the slack is located.

17   Brake check (every 6,000 miles or 6 months)

Refer to illustrations 17.6a, 17.6b and 17.13

Warning: The dust created by the brake system may contain asbestos, which is harmful to your health. Never blow it out with compressed air and don't inhale any of it. An approved filtering mask should be worn when working on the brakes. Do not, under any cir-

17.6a The amount of disc pad material remaining can be checked by looking through the opening in the caliper

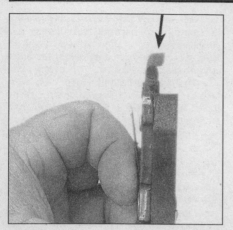

17.6b The disc brake pads have built in wear indicators that contact the rotor and emit a squealing sound when the pads have worn to their limit

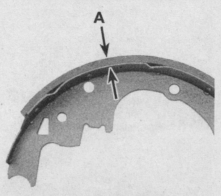

17.13 If the lining is bonded to the brake shoe, measure the lining thickness from the outer surface to the metal shoe, as shown here; if the lining is riveted to the shoe, measure from the lining outer surface to the rivet head

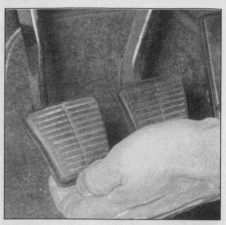

20.2 Pull the clutch pedal back to the stop, then depress it slowly to adjust the freeplay

7   Remove the pads for further inspection or replacement if you are in doubt as to the condition of the pad.

8   Before installing the wheels, check for leakage around the brake hose connections leading to the caliper and damage (cracking, splitting, etc.) to the brake hose. Replace the hose or fittings as necessary, referring to Chapter 9.

9   Check the condition of the disc. Look for scoring, gouging and burned spots. If these conditions exist the disc should be removed for servicing (see Chapter 9).

Drum brakes

10   Using a scribe or chalk, mark the drum and hub so the drum can be reinstalled in the same position on the hub.

11   Remove and discard the retaining clip and pull the brake drum off the axle and brake assembly. If this proves difficult, make sure the parking brake is released, then squirt some penetrating oil around the center hub area. Allow the oil to soak in and try to pull the drum off again. If the drum still can't be pulled off, the brake shoes will have to be retracted. This is done by first removing the lanced knock-out in the backing plate with a hammer and chisel. With the lanced area punched in, pull the self-adjusting lever off the star wheel and use a small screwdriver to turn the wheel, which will move the shoes away from the drum.

12   With the drum removed, clean the assembly with brake system cleaner.

13   Note the thickness of the lining material on the brake shoes **(see illustration)**. If the material is worn to within 1/16-inch of the recessed rivets or metal backing, the shoes should be replaced. If the linings look worn, but you are unable to determine their exact thickness, compare them with a new set at an auto parts store. The shoes should also be replaced if they are cracked, glazed (shiny surface) or contaminated with brake fluid.

14   Check to see that all the brake assembly springs are connected and in good condition.

15   Check the brake components for signs of fluid leakage. Carefully pry back the rubber cups on the wheel cylinder, located at the top of the brake backing plate. Any leakage is an indication that the wheel cylinders should be overhauled immediately (see Chapter 9). Also check the hoses and connections for signs of leakage.

16   Clean the inside of the drum with brake system cleaner. Again, be careful not to breathe the asbestos dust.

17   Check the inside of the drum for cracks, scores, deep scratches and hard spots, which will appear as small discolored areas. If imperfections cannot be removed with fine emery cloth the drum must be taken to a machine shop for resurfacing.

18   After the inspection process, if all parts are found to be in good condition, reinstall the brake drum. Install the wheel and lower the vehicle to the ground.

Parking brake

19   The easiest way to check the operation of the parking brake is to park the vehicle on a steep hill with the parking brake set and the transaxle in Neutral (stay in the car while performing this check). If the parking brake can't prevent the vehicle from rolling, it is in need of adjustment (see Chapter 9).

18   Carburetor choke check (every 6,000 miles or 6 months)

1   The choke operates only when the engine is cold, so this check should be performed before the engine has been started for the day.

2   Open the hood and remove the top plate of the air cleaner assembly. It is held in place by a wing nut. If any vacuum hoses must be disconnected make sure you tag them to insure reinstallation in their original positions. Place the top plate and nut aside, out of the way of moving engine components.

3   Look at the top of the carburetor at the center of the air cleaner housing. You will notice a flat plate at the carburetor opening.

4   Have an assistant press the accelerator pedal to the floor. The plate should close completely. Start the engine while you observe the plate at the carburetor. **Warning:** *Do not position your face directly over the carburetor. The engine could backfire and cause serious burns.* When the engine starts the choke plate should open slightly.

5   Allow the engine to continue running at an idle speed. Every thirty seconds depress the throttle slightly. As the engine warms up to operating temperature the plate should slowly open, allowing more air to enter through the top of the carburetor.

6   After a few minutes the choke plate should be all the way open to the vertical position.

7   You will notice that the engine speed corresponds with the plate opening. With the plate completely closed, the engine should run at a fast idle. As the plate opens, the engine speed will decrease.

8   If a malfunction is detected during the above checks, see Chapter 4 for specific information related to adjusting and servicing choke components.

19   Engine idle speed check and adjustment (every 6,000 miles or 6 months)

1   The engine idle speed is adjustable on some models and should be checked at the scheduled maintenance interval.

2   On those vehicles with provisions for idle speed adjustment, the specifications for such adjustments are shown on the *Vehicle Emissions Control Information* label. However, the adjustments must be made using calibrated test equipment. The adjustments should therefore be made by a dealer service department or other repair facility.

21.5 Make sure the gasket around the fuel tank cap has an even imprint around the entire circumference

20 Clutch pedal adjustment (1984 and earlier models) (every 6,000 miles or 6 months)

Refer to illustration 20.2

1   At the specified interval the clutch pedal must be adjusted to maintain a constant tension on the clutch self-adjusting mechanism cable.

2   Grasp the pedal and pull it up to the rubber stop, then depress the pedal slowly **(see illustration). Note:** *Do not pull up on the pedal after it stops or the clutch linkage could be damaged.*

21 Fuel system check (every 12,000 miles or 12 months)

Refer to illustration 21.5
Warning: *Gasoline is extremely flammable, so take extra precautions when you work on any part of the fuel system. Don't smoke or allow open flames or bare light bulbs near the work area, and don't work in a garage where a natural gas-type appliance (such as a water heater or clothes dryer) with a pilot light is present. If you spill any fuel on your skin, rinse it off immediately with soap and water. When you perform any kind of work on the fuel system, wear safety glasses and have a Class B type fire extinguisher on hand.*

1   If your vehicle is equipped with fuel injection, refer to the fuel pressure relief procedure (see Chapter 4) before servicing any component of the fuel system. Also, remove the fuel tank cap to relieve the pressure in the tank.

2   The fuel system is under a small amount of pressure, so before any fuel lines are disconnected for servicing be prepared to catch the fuel as it spurts out. Plug all disconnected fuel lines immediately after disconnection to prevent the tank from emptying itself.

3   The fuel system is most easily checked with the vehicle raised on a hoist so the components underneath the vehicle are readily visible and accessible.

4   If the smell of gasoline is noticed while driving or after the vehicle has been in the sun, the system should be thoroughly inspected immediately.

5   Remove the gas filler cap and check for damage, corrosion and an unbroken sealing imprint on the gasket **(see illustration)**. Replace the cap with a new one if necessary.

6   With the vehicle raised, inspect the gas tank and filler neck for punctures, cracks or other damage. The connection between the filler neck and the tank is especially critical. Sometimes a rubber filler neck will leak due to loose clamps or deteriorated rubber, problems a home mechanic can usually rectify. **Warning:** *Do not, under any circumstances, try to repair a fuel tank yourself (except rubber components). A torch or even a spark can easily cause the fuel vapors to explode if the proper precautions are not taken.*

7   Check all rubber hoses and metal lines leading away from the fuel tank. Check for loose connections, deteriorated hoses, crimped lines and other damage. Follow the lines to the front of the vehicle, carefully inspecting them all the way. Repair or replace damaged sections as necessary.

8   If a fuel odor is still evident after the inspection, check the evaporative emissions control system (see Section 37).

22 Fuel filter replacement (every 12,000 miles or 12 months)

Refer to illustrations 22.1, 22.17, 22.23 and 22.24
Warning: *Gasoline is extremely flammable, so take extra precautions when you work on any part of the fuel system. Don't smoke or allow open flames or bare light bulbs near the work area, and don't work in a garage where a natural gas-type appliance (such as a water heater or clothes dryer) with a pilot light is present. Since gasoline is carcinogenic, wear latex gloves when there's a possibility of being exposed to fuel, and, if you spill any fuel on your skin, rinse it off immediately with soap and water. Mop up any spills immediately and do not store fuel-soaked rags where they could ignite. The fuel system is under constant pressure, so, if any fuel lines are to*

be disconnected, the fuel pressure in the system must be relieved first (see Chapter 4 for more information). When you perform any kind of work on the fuel system, wear safety glasses and have a Class B type fire extinguisher on hand.*

Carbureted models

1   On these models the fuel filter is located inside the fuel inlet at the carburetor. It is made of pleated paper and cannot be cleaned or reused **(see illustration)**.

2   This job should be done with the engine cold (after sitting at least three hours). The necessary tools include open-end wrenches to fit the fuel line nuts. Flare nut wrenches, which wrap around the nut, should be used, if available, to prevent damage to the fittings, which are generally made of brass or aluminum. In addition, you will have to obtain a replacement filter. Make sure it is for your specific vehicle and engine. You will also need some clean rags.

3   Remove the air cleaner assembly. If vacuum hoses must be disconnected, be sure to note their positions and/or tag them so they can be reinstalled correctly.

4   Follow the fuel line from the fuel pump to the point where it enters the carburetor. The fuel pump is located low on the engine, at the right front. In most cases the fuel line will be metal all the way from the fuel pump to the carburetor.

5   Place some rags under the fuel inlet fittings to catch spilled fuel as the fittings are disconnected. Remove the fuel tank cap to relieve the pressure in the tank.

6   With the proper size wrench, hold the large nut immediately next to the carburetor body. Loosen the fitting at the end of the metal fuel line. A flare nut wrench on this fitting will help prevent slipping and possible damage. Make sure the larger nut next to the carburetor is held securely while the fuel line is disconnected.

7   After the fuel line is disconnected, move it aside for better access to the inlet filter nut. Do not crimp the fuel line.

8   Unscrew the fuel inlet filter nut which was previously held steady. As this fitting is drawn away from the carburetor body, be careful not to lose the thin washer-type gasket or the

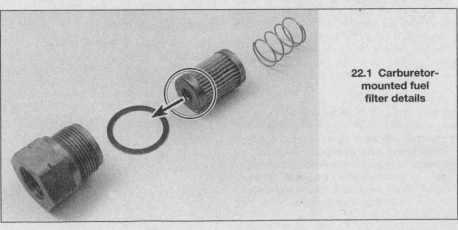

22.1 Carburetor-mounted fuel filter details

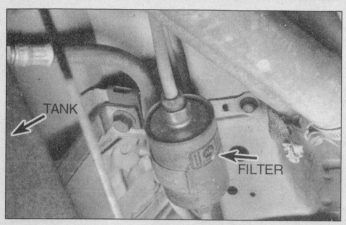

22.17 Multi-Port Fuel Injection fuel filter details

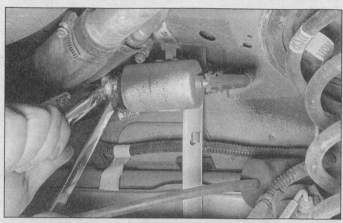

22.23 Use two wrenches, one to steady the fuel filter and the other to unscrew the threaded fitting

spring located behind the fuel filter.

9   Compare the old filter with the new one to make sure they are the same length and design.

10   Reinstall the spring in the carburetor body.

11   Place the new filter in position. The filter will have a rubber gasket and a check valve at one end, which should point away from the carburetor.

12   Install a new washer-type gasket on the fuel inlet filter nut. A gasket is usually supplied with the new filter. Install the nut in the carburetor. Make sure it is not cross-threaded. Tighten it securely, but do not overtighten it, as the hole can strip easily, causing fuel leaks.

13   Hold the fuel inlet nut securely with a wrench while the fuel line is connected. Again, be careful not to cross-thread the fitting. Tighten the fitting securely.

14   Plug the vacuum hose which leads to the air cleaner snorkel motor so the engine can be started.

15   Start the engine and check carefully for

leaks. If the fuel line connector leaks, disconnect it using the above procedures and check for stripped or damaged threads. If the fuel line fitting has stripped threads, remove the entire line and have a repair shop install a new fitting, or replace the line.

16   Reinstall the air cleaner assembly, connecting the hoses in their original positions.

Fuel-injected models

Warning: *Refer to the fuel pressure relief procedure in Chapter 4 before performing this procedure.*

17   Fuel-injected models employ a stainless steel in-line fuel filter. On TBI engines it is located at the left rear of the engine, clamped to the cylinder head. On Multi-Port Fuel Injected (MPFI) models the filter is attached to the frame rail or on the rear crossmember in the engine compartment **(see illustration)**.

18   With the engine cold, place a container under the fuel filter.

TBI models

19   Remove any bolts attaching the fuel filter bracket to the engine.

20   Remove the line from the top of the filter. Use a flare nut wrench, if available.

21   Unclamp and remove the fuel line from the bottom of the filter and remove the filter.

22   Install the new filter by reversing the removal procedure. Do not overtighten the fitting at the top of the fuel filter.

MPFI models

23   Use a backup wrench to steady the filter, unscrew the threaded fittings at each end of the filter (use a flare nut wrench if possible), then remove the clamp bolt and detach the filter **(see illustration)**. Before connecting the fuel lines to the filter, apply a few drops of clean engine oil to the male connectors and fuel lines.

24   On later models, the filter outlet fitting is retained with a quick-disconnect clip instead of a threaded collar. On these models, grasp the fitting with pliers, turn it 1/4-turn in each direction to dislodge any dirt, then use compressed air or aerosol carburetor cleaner to

blow or wash the dirt out. Depress the quick disconnect tabs to release the fuel line from the filter **(see illustration)**.

23 Accelerator cable check and maintenance (every 12,000 miles or 12 months)

1   The accelerator linkage is a cable type and although there are no adjustments to the linkage itself, periodic maintenance is necessary to assure its proper function.

2   Remove the air cleaner so the entire linkage is visible.

3   Check the entire length of the cable to make sure that it is not binding.

4   Check all the nylon bushings for wear, replacing them with new ones as necessary.

5   Lubricate the cable mechanisms with engine oil at the pivot points, but do not lubricate the cable itself.

24 Carburetor/Throttle Body Injection (TBI) mounting nut/bolt torque check (every 12,000 miles or 12 months)

1   The carburetor/TBI unit is attached to the top of the intake manifold by four nuts or bolts. These fasteners can sometimes work loose from vibration and temperature changes during normal engine operation and cause a vacuum leak.

2   To properly tighten the mounting nuts a torque wrench is necessary. If you do not own one, they can usually be rented on a daily basis.

3   Remove the air cleaner assembly, tagging each hose to be disconnected with a piece of numbered tape to make reassembly easier.

4   Locate the mounting nuts/bolts at the base of the carburetor/TBI unit. Decide what special tools or adapters will be necessary, if any, to tighten the fasteners with a socket and the torque wrench.

22.24 On later models, wrap a rag around the fuel line (otherwise the residual pressure in the line will spray out) and use pliers to gently depress the white plastic quick-disconnect tabs, then detach the fuel line from the filter

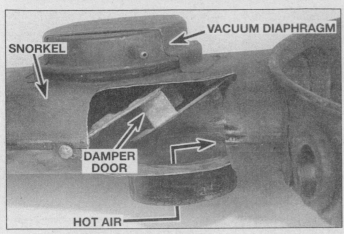

25.3 THERMAC assembly shown with the snorkel passage (damper door) open to heated air

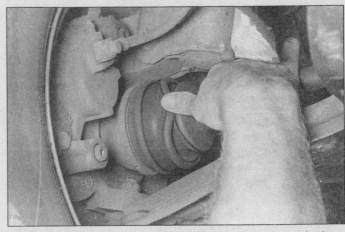

26.4 Check the driveaxle boot to make sure it is not cracked or leaking and the band is not loose

5   Tighten the nuts/bolts to the torque listed in this Chapter's Specifications. Do not overtighten them, as the threads could strip.

6   If you suspect that a vacuum leak exists at the bottom of the carburetor, obtain a length of hose about the diameter of fuel hose. Start the engine and place one end of the hose next to your ear as you probe around the base of the carburetor/TBI unit with the other end. You will hear a hissing sound if a leak exists.

7   If, after the nuts/bolts are properly tightened, a vacuum leak still exists, the carburetor/TBI unit must be removed and a new gasket installed. See Chapter 4 for more information.

8   After tightening the fasteners, reinstall the air cleaner and return all hoses to their original positions.

25   Thermostatically controlled air cleaner (THERMAC) check (every 12,000 miles or 12 months)

Refer to illustration 25.3

Note: *This procedure applies to carbureted and Throttle Body Injected models only.*

1   All carbureted and Throttle Body Injected engines are equipped with a thermostatically controlled air cleaner which draws air to the carburetor from different locations, depending on engine temperature.

2   This is a visual check. If access is limited, a small mirror may have to be used.

3   Open the hood and locate the damper door inside the air cleaner assembly. It will be located inside the long snorkel of the metal air cleaner housing **(see illustration)**.

4   If there is a flexible air duct attached to the end of the snorkel, leading to an area behind the grille, disconnect it at the snorkel. This will enable you to look through the end of the snorkel and see the damper inside.

5   The check should be done when the engine is cold. Start the engine and look through the snorkel at the damper, which should move to a closed position. With the

damper closed. air can't enter through the end of the snorkel, but instead enters the air cleaner through the flexible duct attached to the exhaust manifold and the heat stove passage.

6   As the engine warms up to operating temperature, the damper should open to allow air through the snorkel end. Depending on ambient temperature, this may take 10 to 15 minutes. To speed up this check you can reconnect the snorkel air duct, drive the vehicle, then check to see if the damper is completely open.

7   If the thermo-controlled air cleaner is not operating properly see Chapter 6 for more information.

26   Driveaxle oil seal and driveaxle boot check (every 12,000 miles or 12 months)

Refer to illustration 26.4

1   At the recommended intervals the transaxle output shaft seals and driveaxle boots should be inspected for leaks and damage.

2   Raise the front of the vehicle and support it securely on jackstands.

3   Check the driveaxle oil seals located where the driveaxles exit from the transaxle. It may be necessary to clean this area before inspection. If there is any oil leaking from either of the driveaxle/transaxle junctions, the driveaxle oil seals must be replaced (see Chapter 7).

4   The driveaxle boots prevent dirt, water and other foreign material from entering and damaging the constant velocity (CV) joints. Inspect the condition of all four boots (two on each driveaxle) **(see illustration)**. Clean the boots using soap and water, as oil or grease will cause the boot material to deteriorate prematurely. If there is any damage or evidence of leaking lubricant they must be replaced as described in Chapter 8. Check the tightness of the boot clamps. If they are loose and can't be tightened, the clamp must be replaced.

27   Tire rotation (every 12,000 miles or 12 months)

Refer to illustration 27.2

1   The tires should be rotated at the specified intervals and whenever uneven wear is noticed. With the vehicle raised and the tires removed, you can also check the brakes (see Section 17) and the wheel bearings (see Section 29).

2   Refer to the accompanying illustration of the preferred tire rotation patterns **(see illustration)**.

3   Refer to the information in *Jacking and towing* at the front of this manual for the proper procedures to follow when raising the vehicle and changing a tire. If the brakes are to be checked, do not apply the parking brake as stated. Make sure the tires are blocked to prevent the vehicle from rolling.

4   Preferably, the entire vehicle should be raised at the same time. This can be done on a hoist or by jacking up each corner and then lowering the vehicle onto jackstands placed under the frame rails. Always use four jack-

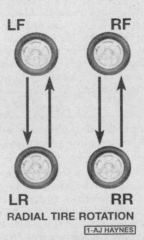

RADIAL TIRE ROTATION

1-AJ HAYNES

27.2 The recommended tire rotation diagram for these vehicles

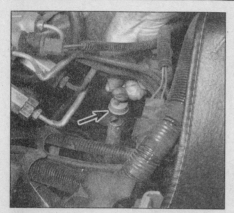

28.1 The lubricant level on manual transaxles is checked with a dipstick

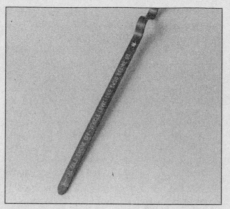

28.3 Follow the manual transaxle checking procedure and lubricant type instructions on the dipstick

30.2 The diaphragm on most vehicles, located under the EGR valve, should be checked for free movement

stands and make sure the vehicle is securely supported.
5   After rotation, check and adjust the tire pressures as necessary and be sure to check the lug nut tightness.

28   Manual transaxle fluid level check (every 12,000 or 12 months)

Refer to illustrations 28.1 and 28.3
1   All transaxles are equipped with a dipstick for checking the lubricant level **(see illustration)**.
2   Check the lubricant level only when the engine is off, the vehicle is on a level surface and the transaxle is cool enough to touch without burning your fingers.
3   Remove the dipstick and wipe it off with a rag, then reinsert it and remove it again. Read the indicated level **(see illustration)**.
   a) *If the dipstick indicates FULL, and the transaxle is warm, the lubricant level is correct.*
   b) *If the dipstick indicates C (cold) and the transaxle is cold, the lubricant level is correct.*
   c) *If the dipstick indicates ADD, or below, add the proper type of lubricant (see Recommended lubricants and fluids at the front of this Chapter) to fill the transaxle. Be sure the lubricant level is between the FULL and C (cold) marks on the dipstick.*

29   Wheel bearing check (every 15,000 miles or 15 months)

1   With the vehicle securely supported on jackstands, spin the wheels and check for noise, rolling resistance and freeplay. Grasp the top of the tire with one hand and the bottom of the tire with the other. Move the tire in and out. If you can feel any play, the bearings should be checked and, if necessary, replaced.
2   The wheel bearings on these models are

of the sealed type which cannot be serviced and must be replaced with new ones if a fault develops. See Chapter 10 for the proper procedure.

30   Exhaust Gas Recirculation (EGR) valve check (every 24,000 miles or 24 months)

Refer to illustration 30.2
1   The EGR valve is located on the intake manifold. Most problems in the emissions control system are due to a stuck or corroded EGR valve.
2   With the engine cold to prevent burns, reach under the EGR valve and manually push on the diaphragm. Using moderate pressure, you should be able to press the diaphragm up and down inside the housing **(see illustration)**.
3   If the diaphragm does not move or moves only with much effort, replace the EGR valve with a new one. If in doubt about the condition of the valve, compare the free movement of your EGR valve with a new valve.
4   See Chapter 6 for more information on the EGR system.

31   Ignition timing check and adjustment (every 24,000 miles or 24 months)

Refer to illustrations 31.1 and 31.2
Note: *It is imperative that the procedures included on the Vehicle Emissions Control Information label be followed when adjusting the ignition timing. The label will include all information concerning preliminary steps to be performed before adjusting the timing as well as the timing specifications. Two different methods of timing are used. The conventional method and, on some early model four-cylinder models, the averaging method. The VECI label will tell you which method is used with your engine.*
1   Locate the VECI label under the hood

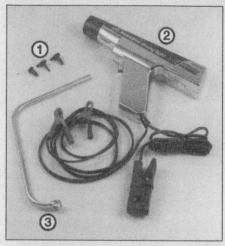

31.1 Tools needed to check and adjust the ignition timing

1   *Vacuum plugs - Vacuum hoses will, in most cases, have to be disconnected and plugged. Molded plugs in various shapes and sizes are available for this*
2   *Inductive pick-up timing light - Flashes a bright concentrated beam of light whenever the number one spark plug fires. Connect the leads according to the instructions supplied with the light*
3   *Distributor wrench - On some models, the hold-down bolt for the distributor are difficult to reach and turn with a conventional wrenches or sockets. A special wrench like this must be used*

and read through and perform all preliminary instructions concerning ignition timing. Tools required for this procedure include an inductive pick-up timing light, a tachometer and a distributor wrench **(see illustration)**.
2   Locate the timing scale located beside the crankshaft pulley. The O mark represents Top Dead Center (TDC). The pointer plate will be marked in either one or two-degree increments and should have the proper timing mark for your particular vehicle noted. If not,

31.2 Location of a typical timing scale

count back from the O mark the correct number of degrees BTDC (*Before* Top Dead Center), as noted on the VECI label, and mark the scale **(see illustration)**.

3   Locate the notch on the crankshaft balancer or pulley and mark it with chalk or a dab of paint so it will be visible under the timing light.

4   Start the engine, warm it up to the normal operating temperature and shut it off. Turn off all lights and other electrical loads.

5   With the ignition off, connect the pick-up lead of the timing light to the number one spark plug wire. Connect the timing light power leads according to the manufacturer's instructions.

6   Start the engine, aim the timing light at the timing mark by the crankshaft pulley and note which timing mark the notch on the pulley is lining up with.

7   If the notch is not lining up with the correct mark. loosen the distributor hold-down bolt and rotate the distributor until the notch is lined up with the correct timing mark.

8   Retighten the hold-down bolt and recheck the timing.

9   Turn off the engine and disconnect the timing light. Reconnect the number one spark plug wire, if removed, and any other components which were disconnected.

Averaging method

10   The averaging method is used to bring the timing of each cylinder into alignment with the base timing specification. Models using the averaging method have a double-notched crankshaft pulley with the notch for the number one cylinder scribed across all three edges of the pulley. Another notch, scribed across only the center section of the pulley, is located 180-degrees away. The coil wire, instead of the number one spark plug wire, is used to trigger the timing light. Because the trigger signal is picked up at the coil wire, each spark firing causes a flash from the timing light. This makes the timing notch appear to jiggle since each firing is indicated. Adjustment is accomplished by centering the total apparent notch width over the specified timing mark.

11   On electronic spark timing equipped

models disconnect the four terminal EST plug at the distributor so the engine will operate in the bypass timing mode.

12   Connect the timing light, following the manufacturer's instructions. Be very careful not to tangle the wires in moving engine parts.

13   Clamp the timing light inductive pick-up around the high tension coil wire. Peel back the protective plastic sheath on the wire when installing the timing light inductive pick-up.

14   Loosen the distributor clamp nut sufficiently to allow the distributor to be rotated for adjustment.

15   Start the engine, aim the timing light at the timing tab and, if necessary, rotate the distributor to center the notch width over the specified mark. Remember that a slight jiggling of the pulley notch is normal.

16   Shut the engine off and tighten the distributor clamp nut, taking care not to move the distributor.

17   Recheck the timing and repeat the adjustment if necessary.

18   Plug in the EST connector, replace the plastic cover on the coil wire and remove the timing light. **Note:** *On some models it will be necessary to remove and replace the ECM 1 fuse to clear the trouble code memory.*

32   Cooling system servicing (draining, flushing and refilling) (every 30,000 miles or 30 months)

Warning: *Do not allow antifreeze to come in contact with your skin or painted surfaces of the vehicle. Rinse off spills immediately with plenty of water. Antifreeze is highly toxic if ingested. Never leave antifreeze lying around in an open container or in puddles on the floor; children and pets are attracted by it's sweet smell and may drink it. Check with local authorities about disposing of used antifreeze. Many communities have collection centers which will see that antifreeze is disposed of safely.*

1   Periodically the cooling system should be drained, flushed and refilled to replenish the antifreeze mixture and prevent formation of rust and corrosion, which can impair the performance of the cooling system and cause engine damage.

2   At the same time the cooling system is serviced, all hoses and the radiator cap should be inspected and, if necessary, replaced (see Section 11).

3   Since antifreeze is a corrosive and poisonous solution, be careful not to spill any of the coolant mixture on the vehicle's paint or your skin. If this happens, rinse immediately with plenty of clean water. Consult your local authorities about the dumping of antifreeze before draining the cooling system. In many areas reclamation centers have been set up to collect automobile oil and drained antifreeze/water mixtures, rather than allowing them to be added to the sewage system.

4   With the engine cold, remove the radiator cap. On models with a thermostat in a housing with a removable cap, remove the cap and thermostat.

5   Move a large container under the radiator to catch the coolant as it is drained.

6   Drain the radiator. Most models are equipped with a drain plug at the bottom. If this drain has excessive corrosion and cannot be turned easily, or if the radiator is not equipped with a drain, disconnect the lower radiator hose to allow the coolant to drain. Be careful that none of the solution is splashed on your skin or into your eyes.

7   If accessible, remove the engine block drain plug(s). There is usually one plug on each side of the engine about halfway back, on the lower edge near the oil pan rail. These will allow the coolant to drain from the engine itself.

8   Disconnect the hose from the coolant reservoir and remove the reservoir. Flush it out with clean water.

9   Place a garden hose in the radiator filler neck and flush the system until the water runs clear at all drain points.

10   In severe cases of contamination or clogging of the radiator, remove it (see Chapter 3) and reverse flush it. This involves inserting the hose in the bottom radiator outlet to allow the clear water to run against the normal flow, draining through the top. A radiator repair shop should be consulted if further cleaning or repair is necessary.

11   When the coolant is regularly drained and the system refilled with the correct antifreeze/water mixture, there should be no need to use chemical cleaners or descalers.

12   To refill the system reconnect the radiator hoses and install the drain plugs securely in the engine. Special thread-sealing tape, available at auto parts stores, should be used on the drain plugs. Install the reservoir and the overflow hose where applicable.

13   Fill the radiator to the base of the filler neck and then add more coolant to the reservoir until it reaches the Full Cold mark. On models with a thermostat that has a removable cap, install the radiator cap and refill the system through the thermostat housing. Install the thermostat and cap.

14   Run the engine until normal operating temperature is reached and, with the engine idling, add coolant to the Full Hot level. Install the radiator and reservoir caps.

15   Always refill the system with a mixture of high quality antifreeze and water in the proportion called for on the antifreeze container or in your owner's manual. Chapter 3 also contains information on antifreeze mixtures.

16   Keep a close watch on the coolant level and the various cooling system hoses during the first few miles of driving. Tighten the hose clamps and add more coolant as necessary.

33   Air filter and PCV filter replacement (every 30,000 miles or 30 months)

Refer to illustrations 33.2, 33.4a, 33.4b, 33.8a and 33.8b

1   At the specified intervals, the air filter

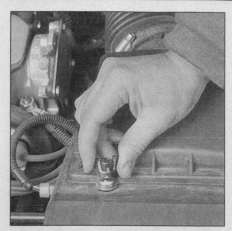

33.2 Remove the plastic wingnuts on port fuel-injected models and lift the cover and hose up for access to the element

33.4a Removing the air filter element on carbureted or TBI models

33.4b On models with port fuel injection, the air filter is located in a housing in the left side of the engine compartment

and (if equipped) PCV filter should be replaced with new ones. A thorough program of preventative maintenance would call for the two filters to be inspected between changes.

2   On some models, the air filter is located inside the air cleaner housing on the top of the engine. On other models the air cleaner housing is located on the left side of the engine compartment. On some models the filter is replaced by removing the wing nut at the top of the air cleaner assembly and lifting off the top plate. On other models, spring clips or wingnuts must be released to lift the cover off of the housing **(see illustration)**.

3   While the top plate is off, be careful not to drop anything down into the carburetor or TBI unit.

4   Lift the air filter element out of the housing **(see illustrations)**. On models with a flat, pleated paper filter element, be sure to note which way the filter is installed.

5   Wipe out the inside of the air cleaner housing with a clean rag.

6   Place the new filter into the air cleaner housing. Make sure it seats properly in the bottom of the housing.

7   On some models, the PCV filter is also

located inside the air cleaner housing. Remove the top plate and air filter as described previously, then locate the PCV filter on the side of the housing.

8   Remove the PCV filter housing clip and remove the PCV filter **(see illustrations)**.

9   Install a new PCV filter and the air filter.

10   Install the top plate and any hoses which were disconnected.

34   Automatic transaxle fluid and filter change (every 30,000 miles or 30 months)

Refer to illustrations 34.7, 34.9, 34.11 and 34.17

1   At the specified time intervals the automatic transaxle fluid should be changed and the filter replaced.

2   Since there is no drain plug, the transaxle oil pan must be removed to drain the fluid. Before beginning work, purchase the specified transaxle fluid (see *Recommended lubricants and fluids* at the front of this Chapter) , and a new filter.

3   Other tools necessary for this job

include jackstands to support the vehicle in a raised position, a drain pan capable of holding at least eight pints, newspapers and clean rags.

4   The fluid should be drained immediately after the vehicle has been driven. This will remove any built-up sediment better than if the fluid were cold. Because of this, it is wise to wear protective gloves. Fluid temperature can exceed 350-degrees in a hot transaxle.

5   After the vehicle has been driven to warm up the fluid. raise it and place it on jackstands for access underneath.

6   Move the necessary equipment under the vehicle, being careful not to touch any of the hot exhaust components.

7   Place the drain pan under the transaxle fluid pan and loosen, but do not remove, the bolts at one end of the pan **(see illustration)**.

8   Moving around the pan, loosen all the bolts a little at a time. Be sure the drain pan is in position, as fluid will begin dripping out. Continue in this manner until all of the bolts are removed except for one at each of the corners.

9   While supporting the pan, remove the remaining bolts and lower the pan **(see illustration)**. If necessary, use a screwdriver to

33.8a Removing the PCV filter housing retaining clip

33.8b Pull the PCV filter out of the housing

34.7 Begin the automatic transaxle drain pan removal by loosening the bolts at one end

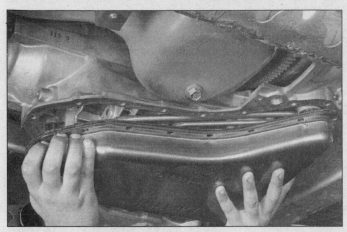

34.9 Lower the fluid pan carefully because it still contains fluid

34.11 Detach the filter from the transaxle body

break the gasket seal, but be careful not to damage the pan or transaxle gasket surfaces. Drain the remaining fluid into the drain pan. As this is done check the fluid for metal particles, which may be an indication of internal failure.

10   Now visible at the bottom of the transaxle is the filter/strainer.

11   Remove the filter and O-ring seal **(see illustration).**

12   Thoroughly clean the transaxle fluid pan with solvent. Check for metal filings or foreign material. Dry with compressed air if available. It is important that all remaining gasket material be removed from the pan mounting flange. Use a gasket scraper or putty knife for this.

13   Clean the filter mounting surface on the valve body. Again, this surface should be smooth and free of any leftover gasket material.

14   Install the new filter with a new O-ring seal.

15   Press the new gasket into place on the pan, making sure all bolt holes line up.

16   Lift the pan up to the bottom of the transaxle and install the mounting bolts. Tighten the bolts in a diagonal pattern working around the pan. Using a torque wrench, tighten the bolts in a criss-cross pattern to the torque listed in this Chapter's Specifications.

17   When reinstalling the pan on a 1989 and later 3-speed transaxle, you must apply thread locking compound to the threads of bolt A **(see illustration)** to prevent fluid leaks.

18   Lower the vehicle.

19   Open the hood and remove the transaxle fluid dipstick.

20   Add the specified amount and type of fluid to the transaxle through the filler tube. Use a funnel to prevent spills. It is best to add a little fluid at a time, continually checking the level with the dipstick. Allow the fluid time to drain into the pan.

21   With the selector lever in Park, apply the parking brake and start the engine without depressing the accelerator pedal (if possible). Do not race the engine - run it at idle only.

22   With the engine idling, check the level on the dipstick. Look under the vehicle for leaks around the transaxle oil pan mating surface.

23   Check the fluid level to make sure it is just below the Add mark on the dipstick. Do not allow the fluid level to go above this point as the transaxle would then be overfilled, necessitating the removal of the pan to drain excess fluid.

24   Push the dipstick firmly back into its

tube and let the engine idle, with the transaxle in Park, for three minutes. Check the fluid level again and add as necessary to bring the level to just above the add mark. Now drive the vehicle far enough to reach normal operating temperature in the transaxle. This should take just a few miles of highway driving, slightly less in the city. Park the vehicle on a level surface and check the fluid level on the dipstick with the engine idling and the transaxle in Park. The level should now be at the F mark on the dipstick. If not, add more fluid, a little at a time, to bring the level up to this point. Again, do not overfill.

35   Manual transaxle lubricant change (every 30,000 miles or 30 months)

Refer to illustration 35.3

1   Remove the dipstick. Raise the vehicle and support it securely on jackstands.

2   Move a drain pan, rags, newspapers and wrenches under the transaxle.

3   Remove the transaxle drain plug at the bottom of the case and allow the oil to drain

34.17 Begin the automatic transaxle drain pan removal by loosening the bolts at one end

35.3 Manual transaxle drain plug location

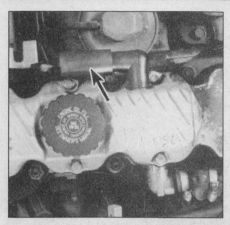

36.1a Typical PCV on a TBI unit

36.1b On some models the PCV valve plugs into the intake manifold

36.2 Pull the PCV valve from the valve cover and detach it from the hose

into the pan **(see illustration)**.
4   After the oil has drained completely, reinstall the plug and tighten it securely.
5   Lower the vehicle.
6   Using a funnel, fill the transaxle with the correct amount of the specified lubricant. Reinstall the dipstick and check the lubricant level (Section 28).

36   Positive Crankcase Ventilation (PCV) valve check and replacement (every 30,000 miles or 30 months)

Refer to illustrations 36.1a, 36.1b and 36.2
1   On some models the PCV valve is located in the valve cover. A hose runs from the valve to the carburetor base plate, TBI unit or intake manifold **(see illustration)**. On other models, the valve plugs into the intake manifold and is connected to the valve cover by a hose **(see illustration)**.
2   Pull the valve (with hose attached) from the rubber grommet in the valve cover **(see illustration)** or, on models with the valve mounted in the intake manifold, detach the PCV hose from its fitting on the valve cover.
3   Start the engine and bring it to normal operating temperature.
4   Place your finger over the end of the valve or hose. If the engine speed drops, the valve is working properly. If the speed does-n't drop the valve is faulty and should be replaced with a new one.
5   To replace the valve, pull it from the end of the hose or out of the manifold, noting its installed position and direction.
6   When purchasing a replacement PCV valve, make sure it is for your particular vehi-cle, model year and engine size. Compare the old valve with the new one to make sure they are the same. Push the valve into the end of the hose until it is seated.
7   Inspect the rubber grommet for damage and replace it with a new one if necessary.
8   Push the PCV valve and hose securely into position.
9   More information on the PCV system can be found in Chapter 6.

37.2 The evaporative emissions canister is located at the right front corner of the engine compartment

37   Evaporative Emissions Control System (EECS) check (every 30,000 miles or 30 months)

Refer to illustration 37.2
1   The function of the Evaporative Emis-sions Control System is to capture fuel vapors from the fuel tank and carburetor and intake manifold before they can escape into the atmosphere, store them in a charcoal canister and then burn them during normal engine operation.
2   The most common symptom of a fault in the evaporative emissions system is a strong fuel odor in the engine compartment. If a fuel odor is detected, inspect the charcoal canis-ter, located at the right front corner of the engine compartment, and system hoses **(see illustration)**.
3   A simple check of system operation is to place your hand under the canister with the engine at normal operating temperature and slowly increase engine speed. If air can be felt being sucked into the bottom of the can-ister the system is operating properly.
4   The evaporative emissions control sys-tem is explained in more detail in Chapter 6.

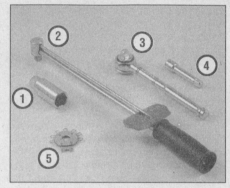

38.1 Tools required for changing spark plugs

1   **Spark plug socket** - *This will have special padding inside to protect the spark plug's porcelain insulator*
2   **Torque wrench** - *Although not mandatory, using this tool is the best way to ensure the plugs are tightened properly*
3   **Ratchet** - *Standard hand tool to fit the spark plug socket*
4   **Extension** - *Depending on model and accessories, you may need special extensions and universal joints to reach one or more of the plugs*
5   **Spark plug gap gauge** - *This gauge for checking the gap comes in a variety of styles. Make sure the gap for your engine is included*

38   Spark plug replacement (every 30,000 miles or 30 months)

Refer to illustrations 38.1, 38.5a, 38.5b, 38.6, 38.9 and 38.10
1   In most cases, tools necessary for a spark plug replacement include a plug wrench or spark plug socket which fits onto a ratchet wrench (this special socket will be insulated inside to protect the porcelain insu-lator) and a wire-type feeler gauge to check and adjust the spark plug gap **(see illustra-tion)**.

38.5a Spark plug manufacturers recommend using a wire-type gauge when checking the gap - if the wire does not slide between the electrodes with a slight drag, adjustment is required

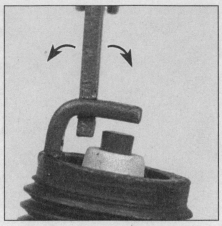

38.5b To change the gap, bend the side electrode only, as indicated by the arrows, and be very careful not to crack or chip the porcelain insulator surrounding the center electrode

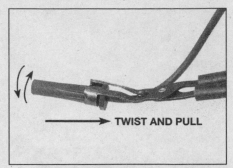

38.6 When removing the spark plug wires, pull only on the boot and twist it back-and-forth

38.9 Apply a coat of anti-seize compound to the spark plug threads

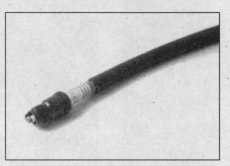

38.10 A length of 3/8-inch I.D. rubber hose eases the job of installing a spark plug in difficult to reach areas

2   The spark plugs are located on each side of V6 engines and on the front (radiator) side of four-cylinder engines.

3   The best procedure to follow when replacing the spark plugs is to purchase the new spark plugs beforehand, adjust them to the proper gap and then replace each plug one at a time. When buying the new spark plugs, it is important to obtain the correct plugs for your specific engine. This information can be found on the *Vehicle Emissions Control Information* label, located under the hood, or in the owner's manual. If differences exist between these sources, purchase the spark plug type specified on the label because the information was printed for your specific engine.

4   With the new spark plugs at hand, allow the engine to cool completely before attempting plug removal. During this time, each of the new spark plugs can be inspected for defects and the gaps can be checked.

5   The gap is checked by inserting the proper thickness gauge between the electrodes at the tip of the plug. The gap between

the electrodes should be the same as that given in this Chapter's Specifications or on the *Vehicle Emissions Control Information* label. The wire should just touch each of the electrodes **(see illustration)**. If the gap is incorrect, use the notched adjuster on the feeler gauge body to bend the curved side electrode slightly until the proper gap is achieved **(see illustration)**. If the side electrode is not exactly over the center electrode, use the notched adjuster to align the two. Check for cracks in the porcelain insulator, indicating the spark plug should not be used.

6   With the engine cool, remove the spark plug wire from one spark plug. Do this by grabbing the boot at the end of the wire, not the wire itself. Sometimes it is necessary to use a twisting motion while the boot and plug wire are pulled free **(see illustration)**.

7   If compressed air is available, use it to blow any dirt or foreign material away from the spark plug area. A common bicycle pump will also work. The idea here is to eliminate the possibility of material falling into the cylinder as the spark plug is removed.

8   Place the spark plug wrench or socket over the plug and remove it from the engine by turning in a counterclockwise direction.

9   Compare the spark plug with those shown in the accompanying photos to get an

indication of the overall running condition of the engine. Prior to installing the new plugs, it is a good idea to coat their threads with anti-seize compound **(see illustration)**.

10   Due to the angle at which the spark plugs must be installed on most engines, installation will be simplified by inserting the end of the new spark plug into a 3/8-inch I.D. rubber hose, a few inches long **(see illustration)**. This procedure serves two purposes. The rubber hose gives you flexibility for establishing the proper angle of plug insertion in the head and, should the threads be improperly aligned, the rubber hose will slip on the spark plug when it meets resistance, preventing cross-threading into the head.

11   After installing the plug to the limit of the hose grip, tighten it with the socket. It is a good idea to use a torque wrench for this to insure that the plug is seated correctly. The correct torque figure is included in this Chapter's Specifications.

12   Before pushing the spark plug wire onto the end of the plug, inspect it following the procedures outlined in Section 39.

13   Attach the plug wire to the new spark plug, again using a twisting motion on the boot until it is firmly seated on the spark plug. Make sure the wire is routed away from the exhaust manifold.

14   Allow the above procedure for the remaining spark plugs, replacing them one at a time to prevent mixing up the spark plug wires.

39   Spark plug wires, distributor cap and rotor check and replacement (every 30,000 miles or 30 months)

Refer to illustrations 39.3a, 39.3b, 39.4, 39.6 and 39.7

1   Begin this procedure by making a visual check of the spark plug wires while the engine is running. In a darkened garage (do this at night with the garage door open) start the engine and observe each plug wire. Be careful not to come into contact with any moving engine parts. If there is a break in the wire, you will see arcing or a small spark at the damaged area. If arcing is noticed, make a note to obtain new wires, then allow the

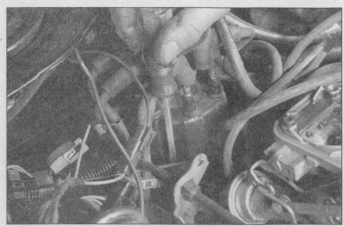

39.3a Use a Phillips head screwdriver to release the distributor cap hold-down latches by pushing down and rotating counterclockwise

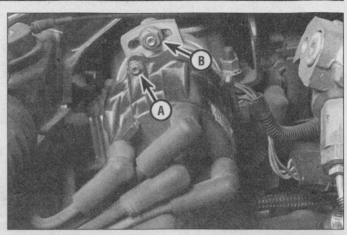

39.3b On some OHC engines, the distributor cap is retained by screws (A) - don't confuse them with the adjusting nut (B)

39.4 Inspect the distributor cap for cracks and carbon tracks and the terminals (arrow) for corrosion and damage

39.6 Remove the screws and lift the rotor off

engine to cool and check the distributor cap and rotor.

2   Disconnect the negative cable from the battery. **Caution**: *If the vehicle is equipped with a Delco Loc II audio system, make sure you have the correct activation code before disconnecting the battery. See the information at the front of this manual for the radio re-activation procedure.* At the distributor, disconnect the ECM connector and the coil connector (coil-in-cap models) or coil wire (models with a separately mounted coil).

3   Remove the distributor cap by placing a screwdriver on the slotted head of each latch. Press down on the latch and turn it 90-degrees to release the hooked end at the bottom **(see illustration)**. On some engines, due to restricted working room, a stubby screwdriver will work best. With all latches disengaged, separate the cap from the distributor with the spark plug wires still attached. **Note**: *Some models may use screws instead of latches* **(see illustration)**.

4   Inspect the cap for cracks and other damage. Closely examine the terminals on the inside of the cap for excessive corrosion **(see illustration)**. Slight pitting is normal. Deposits on the terminals may be removed

with a small file.

5   If the inspection reveals damage to the cap, make a note to obtain a replacement for your particular engine, then examine the rotor.

6   The rotor is visible, with the cap removed, at the top of the distributor shaft. It is held in place by two screws. Remove the screws and the rotor **(see illustration)**.

7   Inspect the rotor for cracks and other damage. Carefully check the condition of the metal contact at the top of the rotor for excessive burning and pitting **(see illustration)**. On coil-in-cap models, also check the top of the rotor for carbon tracks. This is a sign of moisture contamination due to a leaking seal between the distributor cap and the coil. The rotor and seal should be replaced with new ones if carbon tracks are visible.

8   If it is determined that a new rotor is required, make a note to that effect. If the rotor and cap are in good condition, reinstall them at this time. Be sure to apply a small dab of silicone lubricant to the terminals inside the cap before installing it. Note that the rotor has two raised pegs on the bottom and that it has a wide slot and a narrow slot. Make sure that the slots are correctly aligned and that the pegs are firmly seated with the

rotor is installed.

9   If the cap must be replaced, do not reinstall it. Leave it off the distributor with the wires still connected.

10   If the spark plug wires are being replaced, now is the time to obtain a new set, along with a new cap and rotor as determined in the checks above. Purchase a wire set for your particular engine, pre-cut to the proper size, with the rubber boots already installed.

11   If the spark plug wires passed the check in Step 1, they should be checked further as follows.

12   Examine the wires one at a time to avoid mixing them up.

13   Disconnect the plug wire from the spark plug. A removal tool can be used for this, or you can grab the rubber boot, twist slightly and then pull the wire free. Do not pull on the wire itself, only on the rubber boot.

14   Inspect inside the boot for corrosion, which will look like a white crusty powder. Some models use a conductive white silicone lubricant, which should not be mistaken for corrosion.

15   Push the wire and boot back onto the end of the spark plug. It should be a tight fit

39.7 The metal contact on this rotor reveals a normal wear pattern

on the plug end. If not, remove the wire and use pliers to carefully crimp the metal connector inside the wire boot until the fit is snug.

16 Using a clean rag, clean the entire length of the wire. Remove all built-up dirt and grease. As this is done, check for burns, cracks and any other form of damage. Bend the wires in several places to ensure that the conductive wire inside has not hardened.

17 The wires should be checked at the distributor cap (or coils, on models with a distributorless ignition system) in the same manner. On four-cylinder engines and later model V6 engines, remove the wire from the cap by pulling on the boot, again examining the wires one at a time, and reinstalling each one after examination. Apply new silicone lubricant before installation.

18 If the wires appear to be in good condition, reinstall the retaining ring (some models) and make sure that all wires are secure at both ends. If the cap and rotor are also in good condition, the check is finished. Reconnect the wires at the distributor (or coil) and the battery.

19 If it was determined that new wires are required, obtain them at this time, along with a new cap and rotor if so determined by the

checks above.

20 If a new cap is being installed on a coil-in-cap type distributor, the coil and cover from the cap being replaced should be transferred to the new cap.

21 Remove the three coil attaching screws and lift off the cover.

22 Remove the coil attaching screws, disconnect the leads and separate the coil from the distributor.

23 Attach the new coil to the cap by reversing Steps 21 and 22. Use a new seal between the coil and cap and be sure to lubricate the seal with multi-purpose grease.

24 Attach the rotor to the distributor. Make sure that the carbon brush is properly installed in the cap, as a side gap between the carbon brush and the rotor will cause rotor burn-through and/or damage to the distributor cap.

25 If new wires are being installed, replace them one at a time. **Note:** *It is important to replace wires one at a time, noting the routing as each wire is removed and installed, to maintain the correct firing order and to prevent cross-firing.*

26 Attach the cap to the distributor, reconnecting all wires disconnected earlier, then reconnect the battery cable.

40 Oxygen sensor replacement (every 48,000 miles or 48 months)

Refer to illustration 40.1

1 The sensor is located in the exhaust manifold or exhaust pipe and is accessible from under the vehicle or in the engine compartment **(see illustration).**

2 Since the oxygen sensor may be difficult to remove with the engine cold, begin by operating the engine until it has warmed to at least 120-degrees F.

3 Disconnect the oxygen sensor electrical connector.

4 Note the position of the silicone boot and carefully back out the oxygen sensor from the exhaust manifold. Be advised that excessive force may damage the threads. Inspect the oxygen sensor for damage. **Note:**

40.1 The oxygen sensor (arrow) threads into the exhaust manifold

Special care must be taken when handling the oxygen sensor:

a) *The oxygen sensor has a permanently attached pigtail and connector, which should not be removed from the sensor. Damage or removal of the pigtail or connector can adversely affect its operation*

b) *Grease, dirt and other contaminants should be kept away from the electrical connector and the louvered end of the sensor.*

c) *Do not use cleaning solvents of any kind on the oxygen sensor.*

d) *Do not drop or roughly handle the sensor.*

e) *The silicone boot must be installed in the correct position to prevent the boot from being melted and to allow the sensor to operate properly.*

5 A special anti-seize compound must be used on the threads of the oxygen sensor to aid in future removal. New or replacement sensors will have this compound already applied. but if for any reason an oxygen sensor is removed and then reinstalled, the threads must be coated before reinstallation.

6 Install the sensor and tighten it to the torque listed in this Chapter's Specifications.

7 Plug in the electrical connector.

Notes

Chapter 2 Part A
1.8, 2.0 and 2.2 liter overhead valve (OHV) four-cylinder engines

Contents

Specifications

General

Cylinder numbers (drivebelt end-to-transaxle end)	1-2-3-4
Firing order	1-3-4-2

Torque specifications

Ft-lbs (unless otherwise indicated)

Camshaft sprocket bolt	77
Crankshaft pulley-to-hub bolts	37
Crankshaft pulley center bolt	77
Cylinder head bolts	
Cast iron cylinder head	70
Aluminum cylinder head	
Step 1	
Short bolts	43
Long bolts	46
Step 2	tighten all bolts an additional 90-degrees

1986 and earlier

1987 and later

766-2a-specs HAYNES

The blackened terminal shown on the distributor cap indicates the Number One spark plug wire position

Cylinder location and distributor rotation (or coil terminal location)

Torque specifications (continued)   Ft-lbs (unless otherwise indicated)

Exhaust manifold fasteners
   Aluminum cylinder head... 12
   Cast iron cylinder head
      with cast iron manifold... 25
      with tubular steel manifold....................................... 35
Flywheel bolts.. 54
Driveplate bolts... 52
Intake manifold fasteners 22
Oil pan nuts.. 89 in-lbs
Oil pump mounting bolt... 32
Valve cover bolts .... 96 in-lbs
Rocker arm nuts 22
Timing chain cover bolts... 96 in-lbs
Timing chain tensioner bolts... 18
Valve lifter anti-rotational bracket..................................... 96 in-lbs
Front engine mount
   1982 through 1984
      mount-to-engine bracket nuts................................. 30
      mount-to-frame bolts... 40
   1985 and later
      mount-to-engine bracket bolts............................... 50
      mount-to-frame bolts... 50
Rear engine mount
   mount-to-frame nuts.. 18
   mount-to-engine bracket bolts.. 50

1   General information

This Part of Chapter 2 is devoted to in-vehicle repair procedures for the 1.8, 2.0 and 2.2 liter four-cylinder (OHV) overhead valve engines. These engines have cast iron blocks, cast aluminum pistons and either a cast iron or aluminum cylinder head. The aluminum cylinder head has replaceable valve seats and guides. Stamped steel rocker arms and tubular pushrods actuate the valves.

All information concerning engine removal and installation and engine block and cylinder head overhaul can be found in Part D of this Chapter.

The following repair procedures are based on the assumption the engine is in the vehicle. If the engine has been removed from the vehicle and mounted on a stand, many of the steps outlined in this Part of Chapter 2 will not apply.

The Specifications included in this Part of Chapter 2 apply only to the procedures contained in this Part. Part D of Chapter 2 contains the Specifications necessary for cylinder head and engine block rebuilding.

2   Repair operations possible with the engine in the vehicle

Many major repair operations can be accomplished without removing the engine from the vehicle.

Clean the engine compartment and the exterior of the engine with some type of degreaser before any work is started. It'll make the job easier and help keep dirt out of the internal areas of the engine.

Depending on the components involved, it may be helpful to remove the hood to improve access to the engine as repairs are performed (refer to Chapter 11 if necessary). Cover the fenders to prevent damage to the paint. Special pads are available, but an old bedspread or blanket will also work.

If vacuum, exhaust, oil or coolant leaks develop, indicating a need for gasket or seal replacement, the repairs can generally be made with the engine in the vehicle. The intake and exhaust manifold gaskets, timing chain cover gasket, oil pan gasket, crankshaft oil seals and cylinder head gasket are all accessible with the engine in place.

Exterior engine components, such as the intake and exhaust manifolds, the oil pan (and the oil pump), the water pump, the starter motor, the alternator and the fuel system components can be removed for repair with the engine in place.

Since the cylinder head can be removed without pulling the engine, valve component servicing can also be accomplished with the engine in the vehicle. Replacement of the timing chain and sprockets is also possible with the engine in the vehicle.

In extreme cases caused by a lack of necessary equipment, repair or replacement of piston rings, pistons, connecting rods and rod bearings are possible with the engine in the vehicle. However, this practice is not recommended because of the cleaning and preparation work that must be done to the components involved.

3   Top Dead Center (TDC) for number one piston - locating

Refer to illustration 3.6

Note: *The following procedure is based on the assumption that the distributor is correctly installed. If you are trying to locate TDC to install the distributor correctly, piston position must be determined by feeling for compression at the number one spark plug hole, then aligning the ignition timing marks as described in Step 8.*

1   Top Dead Center (TDC) is the highest point in the cylinder that each piston reaches as it travels up-and-down when the crankshaft turns. Each piston reaches TDC on the compression stroke and again on the exhaust stroke, but TDC generally refers to piston position on the compression stroke.

2   Positioning the piston(s) at TDC on the compression stroke is an essential part of many procedures such as valve train component removal and distributor removal.

3   Before beginning this procedure, be sure to place the transaxle in Neutral and apply the parking brake or block the rear wheels. Also, disable the ignition system by detaching the coil wire from the center terminal of the distributor cap and grounding it on the block with a jumper wire (models with a distributor) or disconnecting the small-wire electrical connector from the coil pack (models with direct ignition). Remove the spark plugs (see Chapter 1).

4   When looking at the drivebelt end of the engine, normal crankshaft rotation is clockwise. In order to bring any piston to TDC, the crankshaft must be turned with a socket and ratchet attached to the bolt threaded into the center of the lower drivebelt pulley (vibration damper) on the crankshaft.

5   Have an assistant turn the crankshaft with a socket and ratchet as described above while you hold a finger over the number one spark plug hole. **Note:** *See the Specifications for the engine you are working on for the number one cylinder location.*

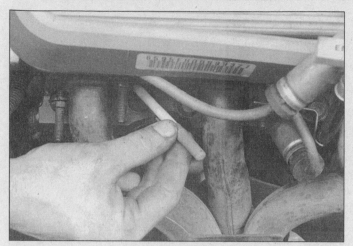

3.6 On engines with direct ignition and no timing marks, a plastic pen inserted into the spark plug hole can be used to find TDC

4.6 Remove the valve cover bolts (arrows) and lift the valve cover from the cylinder head (aluminum head shown)

6   When the piston approaches TDC on the compression stroke, air pressure will be felt exiting the spark plug hole. Have your assistant stop turning the crankshaft when the timing marks at the crankshaft pulley are aligned. **Note:** *On models with no distributor (direct ignition systems), there may be no timing marks.* After you feel pressure, stop turning the crankshaft, then insert a plastic pen into the spark plug hole **(see illustration)**. As the piston rises, the pen will be pushed out. Note the point where the pen stops moving out - this is TDC.

7   If the timing marks are bypassed, turn the crankshaft two complete revolutions clockwise until the timing marks are properly aligned again.

8   After the number one piston has been positioned at TDC on the compression stroke, TDC for any of the remaining pistons can be located by turning the crankshaft one-half turn (180-degrees) on four-cylinder engines or one-third turn (120-degrees) on V6 engines to get to TDC for the next cylinder in the firing order.

4   Valve cover - removal and installation

Refer to illustrations 4.6

Removal

1   Remove the air cleaner assembly, tagging each hose to be disconnected with a piece of numbered tape to simplify installation.

2   Remove the crankcase breather hose or PCV valve and hose from the valve cover.

3   If equipped with a cast iron cylinder head, remove the spark plug wires from the spark plugs and from the valve cover clips. Number the spark plug wires to simplify installation. Remove the distributor cap with the spark plug wires and lay aside.

4   If equipped with a cast iron cylinder head, disconnect the vacuum hoses and pipes. Disconnect the electrical connector to the oxygen sensor and remove the ground wire at the bracket.

5   If equipped with a cast iron cylinder head, remove the throttle linkage bracket.

6   Remove the valve cover bolts **(see illustration)**.

7   Detach the valve cover from the head. **Note:** *If the cover is stuck to the cylinder head, use a block of wood and hammer to dislodge it. If that doesn't work, try to slip a flexible putty knife between the head and cover to break the gasket seal. Don't pry at the cover-to-head joint or damage to the sealing surfaces may occur (leading to oil leaks in the future).*

Installation

8   The mating surfaces of the cylinder head and valve cover must be perfectly clean when the cover is installed. Use a gasket scraper to remove all traces of sealant or old gasket, then clean the mating surfaces with lacquer thinner or acetone (if there's sealant or oil on the mating surfaces when the cover is installed, oil leaks may develop). If the head and cover are made of aluminum, so be extra careful not to nick or gouge the mating surfaces with the scraper.

9   Clean the mounting bolt threads with a die if necessary to remove any corrosion and restore damaged threads. Make sure the threaded holes in the head are clean - run a tap into them if necessary to remove corrosion and restore damaged threads.

10   Apply a 1/8-inch bead of RTV type sealant to the sealing flange on the cover (if equipped with cast iron head) or install a new gasket (if equipped with aluminum head).

11   Place the valve cover on the cylinder head. Install the mounting bolts and tighten the bolts a little at a time to the torque listed in this Chapter's Specifications.

12   The remainder of installation is the reverse of removal procedures. Start the engine and check for leaks.

5   Valve train components - removal, inspection, installation and valve lash adjustment

Rocker arms and pushrods
Removal

Refer to illustrations 5.2, 5.4a and 5.4b

1   Refer to Section 4 and detach the valve cover from the cylinder head.

2   Beginning at the front of the cylinder head, loosen the rocker arm nuts **(see illustration)**. **Note:** *If the pushrods are the only items being removed, rotate the rocker arms to one side so the pushrods can be lifted out.*

3   Remove the nuts, the rocker arms and the pivot balls and store them in marked containers (they must be reinstalled in their original locations).

4   Remove the pushrods and store them separately to make sure they don't get mixed

5.2 Loosen the nuts and pivot the rocker arms to one side if just the pushrods are being removed (otherwise, remove the nuts and lift off the pivot balls and rocker arms)

5.4a The pushrods can be lifted straight out

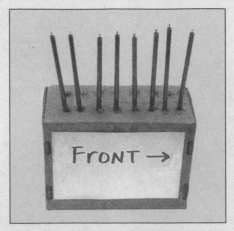

5.4b A perforated cardboard box can be used to store the pushrods to ensure they're reinstalled in their original locations - Note the label indicating the front (drivebelt end) of the engine

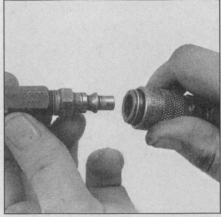

5.15 This is what the air hose adapter that threads into the spark plug hole looks like - they're commonly available at auto parts stores

up during installation **(see illustrations)**.

5   If the pushrod guides must be removed for any reason, make sure they're marked so they can be reinstalled in their original locations.

Inspection

6   Check each rocker arm for wear, cracks and other damage, especially where the pushrods and valve stems contact the rocker arm faces.

7   Make sure the hole at the pushrod end of each rocker arm is open.

8   Check each rocker arm pivot area for wear, cracks and galling. If the rocker arms are worn or damaged, replace them with new ones and use new pivot balls as well.

9   Inspect the pushrods for cracks and excessive wear at the ends. Make sure the oil passage way is un-obstructed. Roll each pushrod across a piece of plate glass to see if it's bent (if it wobbles, it's bent and must be replaced).

Installation

10   Lubricate the lower ends of the pushrods with clean engine oil or moly-base grease and install them in their original locations. Make sure each pushrod seats completely in the lifter socket.

11   Apply moly-base grease to the ends of the valve stems and the upper ends of the pushrods before positioning the rocker arms and installing the nuts.

12   Set the rocker arms in place, then install the pivot balls and nuts. Apply moly-base grease to the pivot balls to prevent damage to the mating surfaces before engine oil pressure builds up. Adjust the valve lash (if equipped with cast iron heads and adjustable rockers) or tighten the nuts to the torque listed in this Chapter's Specifications (if equipped with aluminum heads).

Valve springs, retainers and seals

Replacement

Refer to illustrations 5.15, 5.20 and 5.28
Note: *Broken valve springs and defective*

valve stem seals can be replaced without removing the cylinder head. Two special tools and a compressed air source are normally required to perform this operation, so read through this Section carefully and rent or buy the tools before beginning the job. If compressed air isn't available, a length of nylon rope can be used to keep the valves from falling into the cylinder during this procedure.

13   Remove the spark plug from the cylinder which has the defective component. If all of the valve stem seals are being replaced, all of the spark plugs should be removed.

14   Turn the crankshaft until the piston in the affected cylinder is at top dead center on the compression stroke (see Section 3). If you're replacing all of the valve stem seals, begin with cylinder number one and work on the valves for one cylinder at a time. Move from cylinder-to-cylinder following the firing order sequence (see this Chapter's Specifications).

15   Thread an air hose adapter into the spark plug hole **(see illustration)** and connect an air hose from a compressed air source to it. Most auto parts stores can supply the air hose adapter. **Note:** *Many cylinder compression gauges utilize a screw-in fitting that may work with your air hose quick-disconnect fitting.*

16   Remove the nut, pivot ball and rocker arm for the valve with the defective part and pull out the pushrod. If all of the valve stem seals are being replaced, all of the rocker arms and pushrods should be removed (refer to Section 4).

17   Apply compressed air to the cylinder. **Warning:** *The piston may be forced down by compressed air, causing the crankshaft to turn suddenly. If the wrench used when positioning the number one piston at TDC is still attached to the bolt in the crankshaft nose, it could cause damage or injury when the crankshaft moves.*

18   The valves should be held in place by the air pressure. If the valve faces or seats

are in poor condition, leaks may prevent air pressure from retaining the valves - a "valve job" is necessary to correct this problem.

19   If you don't have access to compressed air, an alternative method can be used. Position the piston at a point approximately 45-degrees (1/8-turn) before TDC on the compression stroke, then feed a long piece of nylon rope through the spark plug hole until it fills the combustion chamber. Be sure to leave the end of the rope hanging out of the engine so it can be removed easily. Use a large ratchet and socket to rotate the crankshaft in the normal direction of rotation (clockwise) until slight resistance is felt.

20   Stuff shop rags into the cylinder head holes above and below the valves to prevent parts and tools from falling into the engine, then use a valve spring compressor to compress the spring. Remove the keepers with small needle-nose pliers or a magnet **(see illustration)**. **Note:** *A couple of different types of tools are available for compressing the valve springs with the head in place. One type utilizes the rocker arm stud and nut for leverage, while the other type grips the lower spring coils and presses on the retainer as the knob is turned. Both types work very well, although the lever type is usually less expensive.*

21   Remove the spring retainer and valve spring, then remove the valve guide seal. **Note:** *If air pressure fails to hold the valve in the closed position during this operation, the valve face or seat is probably damaged. If so, the cylinder head will have to be removed for additional repair operations.*

22   Wrap a rubber band or tape around the top of the valve stem so the valve won't fall into the combustion chamber, then release the air pressure. **Note:** *If a rope was used instead of air pressure, turn the crankshaft slightly in the direction opposite normal rotation.*

23   Inspect the valve stem for damage. Rotate the valve in the guide and check the end for eccentric movement, which would

5.20 Once the spring is compressed, remove the keepers with a magnet or needle-nose pliers

5.28 Keepers don't always stay in place, so apply a small dab of grease to each one, as shown here, before installation - it'll hold them in place on the valve stem as the spring is released

5.35 Determine the point where all lash has been removed by tightening the rocker arm nut while spinning the pushrod

indicate the valve stem is bent.

24   Move the valve up-and-down in the guide and make sure it doesn't bind. If the valve stem binds, either the valve is bent or the guide is damaged. In either case, the head will have to be removed for repair.

25   Reapply air pressure to the cylinder to retain the valve in the closed position, then remove the tape or rubber band from the valve stem. If a rope was used instead of air pressure, rotate the crankshaft in the normal direction of rotation until slight resistance is felt.

26   Lubricate the valve stem with engine oil and install a new valve guide seal. **Note:** *Intake and exhaust valve seals are different.*

27   Install the spring in position over the valve.

28   Install the valve spring retainer. Compress the valve spring and carefully install the keepers in the groove. Apply a small dab of grease to the inside of each keeper to hold it in place if necessary **(see illustration)**. Remove the pressure from the spring tool and make sure the keepers are seated.

29   Disconnect the air hose and remove the adapter from the spark plug hole. If a rope was used in place of air pressure, pull it out of the cylinder.

30   Install the pushrods, rocker arms, balls and nuts. Adjust the valve lash (if equipped with cast iron heads) or tighten the rocker arm nuts to the torque listed in this Chapter's Specifications (if equipped with aluminum heads).

31   The remaining steps are the reverse of the removal procedure.

32   Start and run the engine, then check for oil leaks and unusual sounds coming from the valve cover area.

Valve lash adjustment

Refer to illustration 5.35

Note: *Only early models with cast iron cylinder heads require valve lash adjustment anytime the rocker arms have been removed or the nuts loosened. On later models with aluminum cylinder heads no adjustment is*

required - simply tighten the self-locking rocker arm nut to the torque listed in this Chapters Specifications.

33   Adjust the valve lash when the valve lifters are on the base of the camshaft lobes as follows.

34   Rotate the crankshaft until the number one piston is at Top Dead Center (TDC) on the compression stroke (see Section 3).

35   Starting with number one cylinder intake valve, tighten the rocker arm nut until all lash has been removed ("zero lash"). This can be determined by moving the pushrod up and down and spinning it while tightening the nut. Zero lash is reached when all clearance between the pushrod and rocker arm is eliminated and there's just a slight drag felt while spinning the pushrod **(see illustration)**. Tighten the nut an additional 3/4-turn to center the lifter plunger.

36   While the engine is positioned on number one TDC, also adjust the number one cylinder exhaust valve, number two intake valve and number three exhaust valve using the method described.

37   Rotate the crankshaft 360-degrees (number four cylinder will now be at TDC) and adjust the following valves: number two exhaust, number three intake and number four intake and exhaust.

6   Intake manifold - removal and installation

1   On fuel-injected models, relieve the fuel pressure (see Chapter 4). Then, on all models, disconnect the negative battery cable from the battery. **Caution:** *If the vehicle is equipped with a Delco Loc II audio system, make sure you have the correct activation code before disconnecting the battery. See the information at the front of this manual for the radio activation procedure.*

2   Remove the air cleaner assembly.

3   Drain the coolant (refer to Chapter 1).

4   If necessary for clearance, remove the power steering pump, AIR pump (if equipped), brackets and idler pulley (if equipped). Tie them aside in an upright position.

5   Remove the necessary vacuum lines and disconnect the necessary electrical connectors.

6   Disconnect the fuel line and throttle cable or linkage. Remove the carburetor or TBI unit (see Chapter 4).

7   On early models with cast iron cylinder heads, remove the distributor (see Chapter 5).

8   Raise the front of the vehicle and support it securely on jackstands. Remove the heater hose and coolant line retaining nut near the bottom of the intake manifold.

9   Remove the mounting bolts and nuts from the intake manifold. Separate the intake manifold and gasket from the engine. Scrape all traces of gasket material off the intake manifold and head gasket mating surfaces. When scraping, be careful not to scratch or gouge the delicate aluminum gasket surfaces on the head and manifold. Clean the surfaces with a rag soaked in lacquer thinner or acetone.

10   The remainder of installation is the reverse of removal. Be sure to use a new gasket. Tighten the nuts/bolts to the torque listed in this Chapter's Specifications starting from the center and working out in a spiraling pattern.

11   Add coolant, run the engine and check for leaks and proper operation.

7   Exhaust manifold - removal and installation

Refer to illustrations 7.9

Caution: *Allow the engine to cool completely before beginning this procedure.*

1   Disconnect the negative cable from the battery. **Caution:** *If the vehicle is equipped*

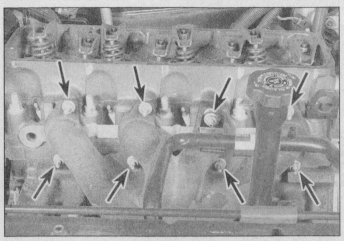

7.9 Remove the exhaust manifold nuts (arrows) from the cylinder head

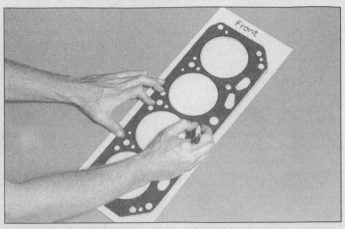

8.11a To avoid mixing up the head bolts, use the new gasket to transfer the bolt hole pattern to a piece of cardboard, then punch holes in the cardboard to accept the bolts

with a Delco Loc II audio system, make sure you have the correct activation code before disconnecting the battery. See the information at the front of this manual for the radio activation procedure.

2   Remove the air cleaner and air duct assembly.

3   Remove the exhaust manifold shield (if equipped) and unplug the oxygen sensor lead.

4   Remove the oil level dipstick and dipstick tube bracket.

5   Remove the air conditioning suction line bracket, if equipped.

6   Remove AIR plumbing, if equipped.

7   Remove the drivebelt, the alternator and the alternator rear support bracket (see Chapters 1 and 5).

8   Raise the front of the vehicle, support it securely on jackstands and apply the parking brake. Block the rear wheels to keep the vehicle from rolling off the jackstands. Unbolt the exhaust pipe from the manifold. Lower the vehicle.

9   Remove the exhaust manifold-to-cylinder head nuts/bolts **(see illustration)**, pull the manifold off the engine and lift it out of the exhaust pipe flange. Remove and discard the gasket.

10   Scrape all traces of gasket material off the exhaust manifold and cylinder head mating surfaces. Be careful not to scratch or gouge the delicate aluminum cylinder head (if equipped) or exhaust leaks will develop. Wipe the surfaces clean with a rag soaked in lacquer thinner or acetone.

11   Clean all bolt and stud threads before installation. A wire brush can be used on the manifold mounting studs, while a tap works well when cleaning the cylinder head bolt holes.

12   If a new manifold is being installed, transfer the oxygen sensor from the old manifold to the new one. Be sure to use anti-seize compound on the threads.

13   Installation is the reverse of removal. Be sure to use a new gasket and tighten the nuts/bolts to the torque listed in this Chap-

ter's Specifications. Work in a spiral pattern from the center out.

8   Cylinder head - removal and installation

Caution: *Allow the engine to cool completely before beginning this procedure.*

Note: *On vehicles with high mileage and during an engine overhaul, camshaft lobe height should be checked prior to cylinder head removal (see Chapter 2, Part D for instructions).*

Removal

Refer to illustrations 8.11a and 8.11b

1   If equipped with EFI, relieve the fuel pressure (see Chapter 4). Disconnect the cable from the negative battery terminal. **Caution:** *If the vehicle is equipped with a Delco Loc II audio system, make sure you have the correct activation code before disconnecting the battery. See the information at the front of this manual for the radio activation procedure.*

2   Remove the drivebelts (see Chapter 1) and remove the alternator and brackets as described in Chapter 5.

3   Remove the intake manifold as described in Section 6.

4   Remove the exhaust manifold as described in Section 7.

5   Unbolt and remove the drivebelt tensioner bracket, if equipped.

6   Unbolt the power steering pump (if equipped) and, if necessary, the air conditioning compressor (if equipped) and set them aside without disconnecting the hoses (see Chapters 3 and 10).

7   Disconnect any remaining wires, hoses, fuel and vacuum lines from the cylinder head. Be sure to label them to simplify reinstallation.

8   Disconnect the spark plug wires and remove the spark plugs. Be sure the plug wires are labeled to simplify reinstallation. Remove the distributor, if equipped (see Chapter 5).

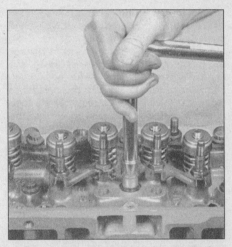

8.11b Loosen the cylinder head bolts in 1/4-turn increments to avoid warping the head

9   Remove the valve cover (see Section 4).

10   Remove the rocker arms and pushrods (see Section 4).

11   Using the new head gasket, outline the cylinders and bolt pattern on a piece of cardboard **(see illustration)**. Be sure to indicate the front of the engine for reference. Punch holes at the bolt locations. Loosen each of the cylinder head mounting bolts 1/4-turn at a time until they can be removed by hand **(see illustration)**. Store the bolts in the cardboard holder as they're removed - this will ensure they are reinstalled in their original locations, which is absolutely essential.

12   Lift the head off the engine. If it's stuck, don't attempt to pry it off - you could damage the sealing surfaces. Instead, use a hammer and block of wood to tap the head and break the gasket seal. Place the head on a block of wood to prevent damage to the gasket surface.

13   Remove the cylinder head gasket.

14   Refer to Chapter 2, Part D, for cylinder head disassembly and valve service procedures.

8.17 A die should be used to remove corrosion and sealant from the head bolt threads prior to installation

8.21a Cylinder head bolt tightening sequence

38015-08.21b HAYNES

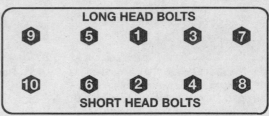

8.21b Typical cylinder head mounting details (aluminum cylinder head shown)

38015-2a-08.21b HAYNES

Installation

Refer to illustrations 8.17, 8.21a and 8.21b

15   If a new cylinder head is being installed, transfer all external parts from the old cylinder head to the new one.

16   If not already done, thoroughly clean the gasket surfaces on the cylinder head and the engine block. Do not gouge or otherwise damage the soft aluminum gasket surfaces.

17   To get the proper torque readings, the threads of the head bolts must be clean **(see illustration)**. This also applies to the threaded holes in the engine block. Run a tap through the holes to ensure they are clean.

18   Place the gasket in position over the engine block dowel pins. Note any marks like **"THIS SIDE UP"** and install the gasket accordingly.

19   Carefully lower the cylinder head onto the engine, over the dowel pins and the gasket.

20   Install the bolts finger tight. Don't tighten any of the bolts at this time.

21   Tighten each of the bolts in 1/4-turn increments in the recommended sequence **(see illustration)**. On aluminum head engines note that the rear bolts have a different torque specification than the front bolts **(see illustration)**. Continue tightening in the rec-

ommended sequence until the torque (and angle of rotation, if applicable) specified in this Chapter is reached. Mark each bolt with a felt-tip marker each time you tighten it to make sure none of the bolts have been left out of the sequence.

22   The remaining installation steps are the reverse of removal. If equipped with a cast iron cylinder head, adjust the valve lash (see Section 5).

23   Be sure to refill the cooling system and change the oil and filter (see Chapter 1).

9   Hydraulic valve lifters - removal, inspection and installation

1993 and earlier models

Refer to illustrations 9.6a, 9.6b, 9.6c and 9.6d

1   A common cause of a noisy valve lifter is a piece of dirt trapped between the plunger and the lifter body. A noisy valve lifter can sometimes be isolated with the engine idling and listening with a stethoscope.

2   Remove the valve cover as described in Section 4.

3   Loosen the rocker arm nuts and rotate the rocker arms away from the pushrods.

4   Remove the pushrods. Label and store the pushrods so they may be installed in their original locations on re-assembly.

5   Using a lifter removal tool, remove the lifters from their bores. Label and store the lifters so they may be installed in their original locations on re-assembly.

6   Inspect each lifter to identify excessive wear and damage **(see illustrations)**. If they are worn, damaged or stuck, replace them as a set, along with a new camshaft (see Section 13). **Caution:** *Never replace only the lifters or only the camshaft, since accelerated wear to the components may result. Reassemble used components only when the original lifters can be replaced in the same*

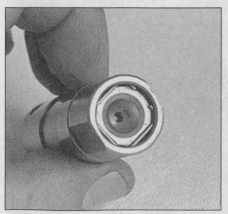

9.6a Check the pushrod seat (arrow) in the top of each lifter for wear

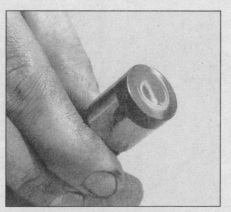

9.6b If the bottom of any lifter is worn concave, scratched or galled, replace the entire set with new lifters

9.6c If the lifters are pitted or rough, they shouldn't be reused

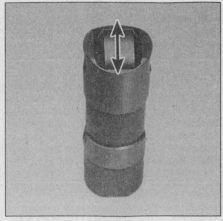

9.6d The foot of each lifter should be slightly convex - the side of another lifter can be used as a straightedge to check it; if it appears flat, it is worn and must not be reused

9.11 Roller valve lifter installation details

1   Anti-rotational bracket

9.13 The roller on roller lifters must turn freely - check for wear and excessive play as well

position on the original camshaft.

7   When installing the lifters, make sure they are replaced in their original bores. Coat them with moly-base grease or engine assembly lube.

8   The remaining installation steps are the reverse of removal. Adjust the valve lash if equipped with a cast iron cylinder head (see Section 5).

1994 models

Refer to illustrations 9.11 and 9.13

9   Roller valve lifters are used on 1994 models. The roller valve lifter anti-rotational brackets cannot be removed with the cylinder head in place.

10   Remove the cylinder head (see Section 8).

11   Remove the bolt and anti-rotational bracket from the engine block **(see illustration).**

12   Using a lifter removal tool, remove the lifters from their bores. Label and store the lifters so they may be installed in their original locations.

13   Inspect each lifter for excessive wear and damage. Inspect the roller for smooth operation and excessive play **(see illustration).**

14   Install the lifters into their original bores. If new roller lifters are being installed, they may be used with the original camshaft as long as there is no damage or wear evident on the camshaft lobes.

15   Install the anti-rotational brackets and tighten the bolts to the torque listed in this Chapter's Specifications.

16   The remainder of installation is the reverse of removal.

---

10   Crankshaft pulley - removal and installation

Refer to illustrations 10.4a, 10.4b and 10.6

Removal

1   Remove the cable from the negative battery terminal. **Caution:** *If the vehicle is equipped with a Delco Loc II audio system, make sure you have the correct activation code before disconnecting the battery. See*

the information at the front of this manual for the radio activation procedure.

2   Remove the drivebelt (see Chapter 1).

3   Raise the front of the vehicle and support it securely on jackstands. Remove the right front wheel and the inner fender splash shield.

4   Remove the crankshaft pulley-to-crankshaft bolt **(see illustration).** A breaker bar will probably be needed, since the bolt is very tight. If necessary, remove the lower bellhousing cover and insert a large screwdriver into the teeth of the flywheel/driveplate ring gear to prevent the crankshaft from turning **(see illustration).**

5   Remove the three bolts that attach the pulley to the hub.

6   Using a puller, remove the crankshaft pulley or hub from the crankshaft **(see illustration).**

Installation

7   Refer to Section 11 for the oil seal replacement procedure.

8   Apply a thin layer of clean multi-purpose grease to the seal contact surface of the hub.

10.4a Use a puller to remove the crankshaft and/or hub

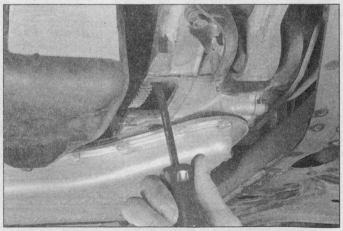

10.4b Have an assistant jam the ring gear with a large screwdriver as the pulley-to-crankshaft bolt is loosened/tightened

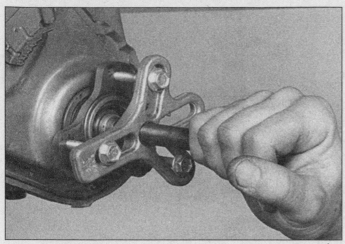

10.6 Use a puller to remove the crankshaft pulley hub

11.5 The timing chain cover is bolted to the front of the engine block and the oil pan

9   Position the hub on the crankshaft and slide it through the seal until it bottoms against the crankshaft gear. Note that the slot (keyway) in the hub must be aligned with the Woodruff key in the end of the crankshaft. The pulley-to-crankshaft bolt can be used to press the hub into position.
10   Tighten the pulley-to-crankshaft bolt to the torque listed in this Chapter's Specifications.
11   The remaining installation steps are the reverse of removal.

11   Timing chain cover - removal and installation

Refer to illustration 11.5
1   Remove the crankshaft pulley and hub as described in Section 10.
2   Remove the oil pan (see Section 14).
3   Remove the bolts holding the power steering pump and position it aside.
4   Remove the alternator bolts and position it aside.
5   Remove the drivebelt tensioner and bracket and the timing chain cover-to-block bolts, then detach the cover **(see illustration)**.
6   Using a scraper and degreaser, remove all old gasket material from the sealing surfaces of the timing chain cover, engine block and oil pan.
7   If necessary, replace the front oil seal by carefully prying it out of the cover with a seal removal tool or a large screwdriver. Don't distort the cover.
8   Install the new seal with the spring side toward the inside of the cover. Drive the seal into place using a seal installation tool or a large socket and hammer. A block of wood will also work.
9   Use a thin coat of RTV sealant to position a new gasket on the timing chain cover.
10   Place the cover in position over the dowel pins on the block.
11   Install the bolts that secure the cover to

the block, then tighten all of them to the torque listed in this Chapter's Specifications. Follow a criss-cross pattern to avoid distorting the cover.
12   Install the oil pan (see Section 14).
13   Complete the installation by reversing the removal procedure.

12   Timing chain and sprockets - inspection, removal and installation

Refer to illustrations 12.9 and 12.14

Inspection
1   Disconnect the cable from the negative battery terminal. **Caution:** *If the vehicle is equipped with a Delco Loc II audio system, make sure you have the correct activation code before disconnecting the battery. See the information at the front of this manual for the radio activation procedure.*
2   Remove the crankshaft pulley (see Section 10).
3   Remove the timing chain cover (see Section 11).
4   Before removing the chain and sprockets, visually inspect the teeth on the sprockets for wear and the chain for excessive slack. Also check the condition of the timing chain tensioner.
5   If either or both sprockets show any signs of wear (edges on the teeth of the camshaft sprocket not "square," bright or blue areas on the teeth of either sprocket, chipping, pitting, etc.), they should be replaced with new ones. Wear in these areas is very common.
6   Failure to replace a worn timing chain may result in erratic engine performance, loss of power and lowered fuel mileage.
7   If any one component requires replacement, all related components, including the tensioner, should be replaced as well.
8   If the chain and sprockets must be replaced, proceed as follows.

12.9 Align the camshaft and crankshaft sprocket marks with the tabs on the timing chain tensioner (arrows)

Removal
9   Temporarily install the bolt in the end of the crankshaft. Turn the engine over using the bolt until the marks on the camshaft and crankshaft line up **(see illustration)**. Note: *Do not attempt to remove the timing chain until this is done and do not turn the crankshaft or camshaft while the sprockets and chain are removed from the engine.*
10   Remove the timing chain tensioner upper bolt. Loosen the timing chain tensioner Torx bolt as far as possible but don't remove it.
11   Remove the camshaft sprocket retaining bolt and detach the camshaft sprocket and timing chain. It may be necessary to tap the sprocket with a soft-face hammer to dislodge it.
12   If the crankshaft sprocket must be removed, it can be drawn off the crankshaft with a puller.

Installation
13   Lubricate the thrust side of the crankshaft sprocket with moly-base grease and install the sprocket on the crankshaft. Be sure the Woodruff key is aligned with the key-

12.14 Press the tensioner in and insert an appropriate size drill bit through the hole to retain the tensioner in the retracted position

14.18 Remove the oil pan mounting bolts (arrows; not all the bolts are visible in this photo)

way as the sprocket is installed. Drive the sprocket into place using a special driver or section of pipe just large enough to fit over the nose of the crankshaft.

14   Compress the timing chain tensioner spring and insert a nail or cotter pin into hole A **(see illustration)** to hold the spring in place during installation. Don't forget to remove the nail or pin after installing the timing chain and sprockets.

15   Slip the timing chain onto the camshaft sprocket and with the timing marks aligned, slip the chain under the crankshaft sprocket. Align the dowel in the camshaft with the dowel hole in the camshaft sprocket and install the sprocket on the camshaft. Draw the camshaft sprocket into place with the retaining bolt and tighten it to the torque listed in this Chapter's Specifications. **Caution:** *Do not hammer or attempt to drive the camshaft sprocket into place - it could dislodge the welch plug at the rear of the engine.*

16   Remove the nail or pin from the timing chain tensioner and tighten the tensioner bolt to the torque listed in this Chapter's Specifications.

17   With the chain and both sprockets in place, check again to make sure the timing marks on the two sprockets are properly aligned **(see illustration 12.9)**. If not, remove the camshaft sprocket and move the chain until they are.

18   Lubricate the chain and sprockets with clean engine oil and install the cover.

19   Install the remaining components in the reverse order of removal.

13   Camshaft and bearings - removal, inspection and installation

Due to the fact the engine is mounted transversely in the vehicle, there isn't enough room to remove the camshaft with the engine in place. Therefore, the procedure is covered in Chapter 2, Part D.

14   Oil pan - removal and installation

Refer to illustration 14.18

1   Warm up the engine, then drain the oil and remove the oil filter (see Chapter 1).

2   Detach the cable from the negative battery terminal. **Caution:** *If the vehicle is equipped with a Delco Loc II audio system, make sure you have the correct activation code before disconnecting the battery. See the information at the front of this manual for the radio activation procedure.*

3   Loosen the right front wheel lug nuts, then raise the vehicle and support it securely on jackstands.

4   Remove the right front wheel.

5   Remove the right-side engine splash shield.

6   Remove the exhaust pipe and catalytic converter.

7   On air conditioned models, remove the air conditioner brace at the starter.

8   Remove the starter and bracket (see Chapter 5).

9   Remove the lower bellhousing cover.

10   On air conditioned models, remove the air conditioning compressor brace.

11   Remove the four right support bolts. Lower the support slightly to gain clearance for oil pan removal.

12   Remove the oil filter extension (automatic transaxle equipped models only).

13   Remove the bolts and nuts securing the oil pan to the engine block.

14   Tap on the pan with a soft-face hammer to break the gasket seal, then detach the oil pan from the engine.

15   Using a gasket scraper, remove all traces of old gasket and/or sealant from the engine block and oil pan. Make sure the threaded bolt holes in the block are clean. Wash the oil pan with solvent and dry it thoroughly.

16   Check the gasket flanges for distortion, particularly around the bolt holes. If necessary, place the pan on a block of wood and use a hammer to flatten and restore the gas-

ket surfaces. Clean the mating surfaces with lacquer thinner or acetone.

17   Place a 2 mm diameter bead of RTV sealant on the oil pan-to-block sealing flanges and the oil pan-to-front cover surface.

18   Apply a thin coat of RTV sealant to the ends of the rear oil pan seal down to the ears. Press the oil pan seal into position **(see illustration)**.

19   Carefully place the oil pan against the block.

20   Install the bolts/nuts and tighten them in 1/4-turn increments to the torque listed in this Chapter's Specifications. Start with the bolts closest to the center of the pan and work out in a spiral pattern. Don't overtighten them or leakage may occur.

21   Reinstall components removed for access to the oil pan.

22   Add oil and install a new filter, run the engine and check for oil leaks.

15   Oil pump - removal and installation

1   Remove the oil pan (see Section 14).

2   Place a large drain pan under the engine.

3   Unbolt the pump from the rear main bearing cap.

4   Lower the pump and extension shaft from the engine.

5   Before installation, prime the pump with engine oil. Pour oil into the pick-up while the pump extension shaft is turned.

6   Attach the pump, extension shaft and retainer to the main bearing cap. While aligning the pump with the dowel pins at the bottom of the main bearing cap, align the top end of the extension shaft with the lower end of the oil pump drive. When aligned properly, it should slip into place easily.

7   Install the pump mounting bolt and tighten it to the torque listed in this Chapter's Specifications.

8   Install the oil pan and add oil (see Section 14).

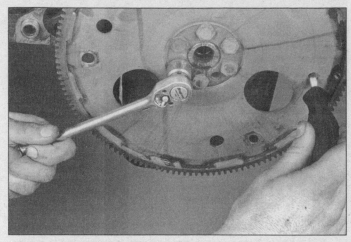

16.3 Most flywheels and driveplates have locating dowels (arrow) - if the one you're working on doesn't, make some marks to ensure correct installation

16.4 A large screwdriver wedged in the starter ring gear teeth or one of the holes in the driveplate can be used to keep the flywheel/driveplate from turning as the mounting bolts are removed

16   Flywheel/driveplate - removal and installation

Refer to illustrations 16.3 and 16.4

1   Raise the vehicle and support it securely on jackstands, then refer to Chapter 7 and remove the transaxle. If it's leaking, now would be a very good time to have the front pump seal and O-ring replaced (automatic transaxle only).

2   Remove the pressure plate and clutch disc (Chapter 8 - manual transaxle equipped vehicles). Now is a good time to check/replace the clutch components and pilot bearing.

3   If there is no dowel pin, make some marks on the flywheel/drive-plate and crankshaft to ensure correct alignment during reinstallation **(see illustration)**.

4   Remove the bolts that secure the flywheel/driveplate to the crankshaft **(see illustration)**. If the crankshaft turns, wedge a screwdriver through the openings in the driveplate (automatic transaxle) or against the flywheel ring gear teeth (manual transaxle). Since the flywheel is fairly heavy, be sure to support it while removing the last bolt.

5   Remove the flywheel/driveplate from the crankshaft.

6   Clean the flywheel to remove grease and oil. Inspect the friction surface for cracks, rivet grooves, burned areas and score marks. Light scoring can be removed with emery cloth. Check for cracked and broken ring gear teeth. Lay the flywheel on a flat surface and use a straightedge to check for warpage.

7   Clean and inspect the mating surfaces of the flywheel/driveplate and the crankshaft. If the crankshaft rear seal is leaking, replace it before reinstalling the flywheel/driveplate.

8   Position the flywheel/driveplate against the crankshaft. Be sure to align the dowel or marks made during removal. Before installing the bolts, apply thread locking compound to the threads.

9   Keep the flywheel/driveplate from turning as described above while you tighten the bolts to the torque listed in this Chapter's Specifications.

10   The remainder of installation is the reverse of the removal procedure.

17   Crankshaft oil seals - replacement

Rear oil seal

1   Remove the flywheel/driveplate (see Section 16).

2   Using a thin screwdriver or seal removal tool, carefully remove the oil seal from the engine block. Be very careful not to damage the crankshaft surface while prying the seal out.

3   Clean the bore in the block and the seal contact surface on the crankshaft. Check the seal contact surface on the crankshaft for scratches and nicks that could damage the new seal lip and cause oil leaks - if the crankshaft is damaged, the only alternative is a new or different crankshaft. Inspect the seal bore for nicks and scratches. Carefully smooth it with a fine file if necessary, but don't nick the crankshaft in the process.

4   A special tool is recommended to install the new oil seal. Lubricate the oil seal lips with clean engine oil. Slide the seal onto the mandril until the dust lip bottoms squarely against the collar of the tool. **Note:** *If the special tool isn't available, carefully work the seal lip over the crankshaft and tap it into place with a hammer and blunt punch.*

5   Align the dowel pin on the tool with the dowel pin hole in the crankshaft and attach the tool to the crankshaft by hand-tightening the bolts.

6   Turn the tool handle until the collar bottoms against the case, seating the seal.

7   Loosen the tool handle and remove the bolts. Remove the tool.

8   Check the seal and make sure it's seated squarely in the bore.

9   Install the flywheel/driveplate (see Section 16).

10   Install the transaxle.

Front oil seal

11   Remove the crankshaft pulley and hub (see Section 10).

12   Pry the old oil seal out with a seal removal tool or a screwdriver. Be very careful not to nick or otherwise damage the crankshaft in the process. Wrap the screwdriver tip with vinyl tape to protect the crankshaft.

13   Apply a thin coat of RTV sealant to the outer edge of the new seal. Lubricate the seal lip with moly-base grease or clean engine oil.

14   Place the seal squarely in position in the bore and drive it into place.

15   If the special tool is not available, carefully tap the seal into place with a large socket or piece of pipe and a hammer. The outer diameter of the socket or pipe should be the same size as the seal outer diameter. Make sure the seal is seated completely in the bore.

16   Install the crankshaft hub and pulley (see Section 10).

17   Reinstall the remaining parts in the reverse order of removal.

18   Start the engine and check for oil leaks at the seal.

18   Engine mounts - check and replacement

Refer to illustrations 18.9a and 18.9b

1   Engine mounts seldom require attention, but broken or deteriorated mounts should be replaced immediately or the added strain placed on the driveline components may cause damage or wear.

Check

2   During the check, the engine must be raised slightly to remove the weight from the mounts.

3   Raise the vehicle and support it securely

18.9a Front engine mount installation details

18.9b Rear engine mount installation details

on jackstands, then position a jack under the engine oil pan. Place a large block of wood between the jack head and the oil pan, then carefully raise the engine just enough to take the weight off the mounts. **Warning:** *DO NOT place any part of your body under the engine when it's supported only by a jack!*

4   Check the mounts to see if the rubber is cracked, hardened or separated from the metal plates. Sometimes the rubber will split right down the center.

5   Check for relative movement between the mount plates and the engine or frame (use a large screwdriver or prybar to attempt to move the mounts). If no movement is noted, lower the engine and tighten the mount fasteners.

6   Rubber preservative should be applied to the mounts to slow deterioration.

Replacement

7   Disconnect the negative battery cable from the battery. **Caution:** *If the vehicle is equipped with a Delco Loc II audio system, make sure you have the correct activation code before disconnecting the battery. See the information at the front of this manual for the radio activation procedure.* Raise the vehicle and support it securely on jackstands (if not already done).

Front mount

8   Raise the engine slightly with a jack or hoist, to remove the weight from the mounts and support the engine securely in this position. Remove the right inner fender splash shield.

9   Remove the upper mount-to-body bracket bolts and remove the upper mount-

to-engine bracket bolts **(see illustrations)**.

10   Remove the lower mount-to-body bracket bolts and remove the lower mount-to-engine bracket bolts. Remove the mount.

11   Installation is the reverse of removal. Clean the threads on all engine mount bolts, apply thread locking compound on the threads and tighten the bolts to the torque listed in this Chapter's Specifications.

Rear mount

12   Remove the engine mount-to-body bracket nuts. Remove the engine mount-to-engine bracket bolts. Remove the mount **(see illustration)**.

13   Installation is the reverse of removal. Clean the threads on all engine mount bolts, apply thread locking compound on the threads and tighten the bolts to the torque listed in this Chapter's Specifications.

Chapter 2 Part B
1.8 and 2.0 liter overhead cam (OHC) four-cylinder engines

Contents

Specifications

General
Cylinder numbering order (timing belt-to-transaxle)	1-2-3-4
Firing order	1-3-4-2

Oil pump
Outer gear-to-body clearance	0.004 to 0.007 inch
Inner gear-to-body clearance	0.007 to 0.010 inch
Gear-to-cover clearance	0.001 to 0.004 inch

Torque Specifications
	Ft-lbs (unless otherwise indicated)
Camshaft carrier cover bolts	72 in-lbs
Camshaft sprocket retaining bolt	34
Camshaft thrust plate bolts	72 in-lbs
Crankshaft pulley-to-sprocket bolts	15
Crankshaft sprocket retaining bolt	115
Cylinder head and camshaft carrier bolts	
Step 1	18
Step 2	tighten an additional 60 degrees
Step 3	tighten an additional 60 degrees
Step 4	tighten an additional 60 degrees
Step 5	tighten an additional 30 to 50 degrees (with the engine hot)
Engine mount bolts	
Front engine mount-to-engine bracket bolts	40
Front engine mount-to-frame bolts	40
Rear engine mount-to-engine bracket bolts	40
Rear engine mount-to-frame bracket nuts	18
Exhaust manifold bolts/nuts	16
Flywheel/driveplate bolts	48
Intake manifold nuts	16
Oil pan bolts	48 in-lbs
Oil pump control valve plug	15
Oil pump cover bolts	72 in-lbs
Oil pump pick-up tube-to-block bolts	72 in-lbs
Oil pump pick-up tube-to-oil pump bolts	72 in-lbs
Oil pump-to-engine block bolts	60 in-lbs
Timing belt cover bolts	60 in-lbs

The blackened terminal shown on the distributor cap indicates the Number One spark plug wire position

Cylinder location and distributor rotation

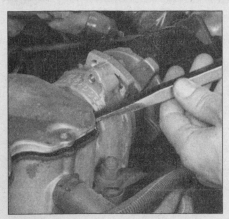

3.3 Breaking the camshaft cover gasket seal with a chisel and hammer - be careful not to damage the sealing surfaces!

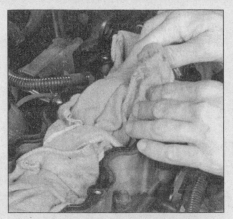

3.4 Rags placed in the camshaft gallery will keep foreign material out

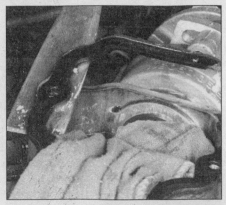

3.5 When removing the camshaft cover gasket with a scraper, be careful not to nick or gouge the carrier (it's made of aluminum and is very soft)

1   General information

The overhead cam (OHC) engine block is made of cast iron with a removable aluminum cylinder head. The camshaft is located in the cylinder head and actuates the valves via rocker arms and hydraulic valve lash compensators.

This Part of Chapter 2 is devoted to "in vehicle" repair procedures for the OHC engine. Information concerning engine block and cylinder head servicing can be found in Part D of this Chapter.

The repair procedures included in this part are based on the assumption that the engine is still installed in the vehicle. Therefore, if this information is being used during a complete engine overhaul, with the engine already out of the vehicle and on a stand, many of the steps included here will not apply.

The specifications included in this part of Chapter 2 apply only to the engine and procedures found here. For specifications regarding OHV engines, see Part A. Part D of Chapter 2 contains the specifications necessary for engine block and cylinder head rebuilding.

2   Repair operations possible with the engine in the vehicle

Many major repair operations can be accomplished without removing the engine from the vehicle.

Clean the engine compartment and the exterior of the engine with some type of degreaser before any work is done. It'll make the job easier and help keep dirt out of the internal areas of the engine.

Depending on the components involved, it may be helpful to remove the hood to improve access to the engine as repairs are performed (refer to Chapter 11 if necessary). Cover the fenders to prevent damage to the paint. Special pads are available, but an old bedspread or blanket will also work.

If vacuum, exhaust, oil or coolant leaks develop, indicating a need for gasket or seal replacement, the repairs can generally be made with the engine in the vehicle. The intake and exhaust manifold gaskets, timing chain cover gasket, oil pan gasket, crankshaft oil seals and cylinder head gasket are all accessible with the engine in place.

Exterior engine components, such as the intake and exhaust manifolds, the oil pan (and the oil pump), the water pump, the starter motor, the alternator and the fuel system components can be removed for repair with the engine in place.

Since the cylinder head can be removed without pulling the engine, valve component servicing can also be accomplished with the engine in the vehicle. Replacement of the timing belt and sprockets is also possible with the engine in the vehicle.

In extreme cases caused by a lack of necessary equipment, repair or replacement of piston rings, pistons, connecting rods and rod bearings is possible with the engine in the vehicle. However, this practice is not recommended because of the cleaning and preparation work that must be done to the components involved.

3   Camshaft cover - removal and installation

Removal

Refer to illustrations 3.3, 3.4 and 3.5

1   Remove the air cleaner assembly.
2   Remove the PVC valve and hose.
3   Remove the retaining bolts and separate the cover from the engine. It may be necessary to break the gasket seal by either tapping the cover with a soft-faced hammer or inserting a very thin-bladed scraper or screwdriver at the corner **(see illustration)**.
4   Place clean rags in the camshaft gallery to keep foreign material from falling into the engine **(see illustration)**.
5   Clean all traces of gasket material from the camshaft cover gasket mating surfaces. Be careful not to nick or gouge the soft aluminum **(see illustration)**.

Installation

6   Place the cover and new gasket in position. Install the attaching bolts and tighten to the torque listed in this Chapter's Specifications.
7   Install the air cleaner and PCV assemblies.

4   Timing belt covers - removal and installation

Refer to illustration 4.11

Removal

1   Disconnect the cable from the negative battery terminal.
2   Remove the alternator and power steering drivebelts or the serpentine drivebelt (see Chapter 1).

Front cover

1986 and earlier

3   Remove the coolant reservoir and disconnect the charcoal canister purge line.
4   Remove the timing belt cover bolts).
5   Raise the vehicle, support it securely on jackstands and remove the right front wheel.
6   Remove the splash shield and the two lower timing belt cover bolts.
7   Lower the vehicle and remove the timing belt cover.

1987 and 1988

8   Loosen the serpentine belt tensioner bolt and swing the tensioner arm down, out of the way.
9   Unsnap the retaining clips and detach the front covers (upper first, then lower) from the rear cover.

1989 and later

10   Loosen the serpentine belt tensioner bolt and swing the tensioner arm down, out of the way.
11   Remove the timing belt cover bolts/nuts and remove the cover **(see illustration)**.

Rear cover

12   Remove the timing belt front cover and the timing belt (see Section 5).

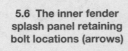

4.11 Remove the timing cover, five retaining bolts and one nut (arrows)

1986 and earlier

13   Remove the bolts and separate the rear cover from the engine.

1987 and 1988

14   Remove the camshaft sprocket (see Section 6).

15   Remove the bolts and rubber grommets securing the cover to the engine and remove the cover.

1989 and later

16   Remove the camshaft and the crankshaft sprockets (see Section 6).

17   Remove the timing belt tensioner assembly.

18   Remove the bolts securing the cover to the engine and remove the cover.

Installation

19   Installation is the reverse of removal for all models.

---

5   Timing belt - removal, inspection and installation

Caution: *Incorrect installation or adjustment of the timing belt could result in engine damage. DO NOT turn the camshaft with a wrench on the sprocket bolt - damage to the cam bearings may result. When necessary, turn the camshaft with an open end wrench on the machined hex above cylinder number four (inside the camshaft cover).*

Removal

Refer to illustrations 5.6, 5.7a, 5.7b, 5.12 and 5.13

1   Remove the timing belt front cover (see Section 4).

2   Drain the coolant (see Chapter 1).

3   Remove the coolant reservoir.

4   Disconnect the cable from the negative battery terminal.

5   Raise the vehicle and support it securely on jackstands.

6   Remove the right front wheel. Remove the bolts and detach the inner splash panel

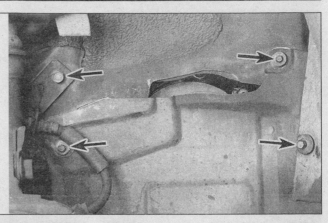

5.6 The inner fender splash panel retaining bolt locations (arrows)

5.7a The crankshaft pulley notch must be aligned with the 10 degree BTDC mark (arrows) before the timing belt is removed

from the wheel well **(see illustration)**.

7   On 1988 and earlier models, rotate the crankshaft until the timing mark on the crankshaft pulley is aligned with the ten degree BTDC mark on the indicator scale and the camshaft sprocket mark is aligned with the mark on the camshaft carrier **(see illustrations)**.

8   On 1989 and later models, rotate the crankshaft and camshaft until the marks on the timing belt sprockets are aligned with the marks on the rear cover.

9   Remove the bolts and detach the pulley from the crankshaft.

10   On 1988 and earlier models, remove the

5.7b The valve timing marks are easy to see grooves cast into the camshaft sprocket and rear cover (arrows)

timing probe for bolt access.

11   On all years, loosen the water pump bolts.

12   Use a large screwdriver to break the water pump gasket seal **(see illustration)**.

13   Grasp the water pump with a pair of pliers and release the tension from the timing belt by rotating the pump toward the engine **(see illustration)**. **Note:** *On 1989 and later models, it may be necessary to use a special tool to rotate the water pump* **(see illustration 5.22)**.

14   Slip the belt off the sprockets. **Caution:** *Don't rotate the crankshaft or camshaft while the belt is off.*

5.12 Carefully pry out on the water pump to break the gasket seal

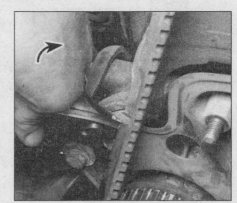

5.13 Rotate the water pump in the direction shown (arrow) to release the timing belt tension

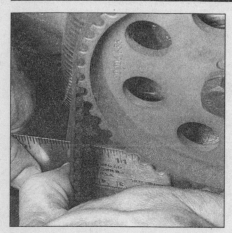

5.17 Using a ruler to check the timing belt tension

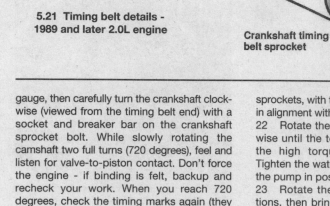

High torque stop

Hole in base

Water pump

Tension pulley/ indicator

Crankshaft timing belt sprocket

5.21 Timing belt details - 1989 and later 2.0L engine

38015-2B-05.21 HAYNES

Installation and adjustment

Refer to illustration 5.17

1988 and earlier models without the factory tools

15   Slip the new belt onto the sprockets, install the crankshaft pulley and make sure the crankshaft and camshaft marks are aligned.

16   Rotate the water pump to apply tension to the timing belt and tighten the water pump bolts.

17   Measure the belt deflection midway between the water pump and the camshaft sprocket with a straightedge and ruler **(see illustration)**. Adjust the belt tension until the deflection is 1/4-inch. **Caution:** *Be sure to have the belt checked and adjusted by a dealer service department or a repair shop before driving the vehicle extensively.*

1988 and earlier models with the factory tools

18   Install the adjusting tool and gauge as described in the instructions accompanying the tools. Adjust the tension until it's within the range on the gauge.

19   After adjusting the tension, remove the gauge, then carefully turn the crankshaft clockwise (viewed from the timing belt end) with a socket and breaker bar on the crankshaft sprocket bolt. While slowly rotating the camshaft two full turns (720 degrees), feel and listen for valve-to-piston contact. Don't force the engine - if binding is felt, backup and recheck your work. When you reach 720 degrees, check the timing marks again (they should be aligned). **Note:** *New belts should be run in several minutes and then rechecked.*

20   Reinstall all components, then refill the cooling system and run the engine. After normal operating temperature is reached, check carefully for leaks.

1989 and later models

Refer to illustrations 5.21 and 5.22

21   Recheck the alignment of the crankshaft and camshaft sprockets. Install the timing belt, routing it properly around the tensioner pulley **(see illustration)**. There should be tension on the belt between the camshaft and crankshaft sprockets, with the marks on the sprockets still in alignment with the marks on the rear cover.

22   Rotate the water pump eccentric clockwise until the tensioner makes contact with the high torque stop **(see illustration)**. Tighten the water pump bolts enough to hold the pump in position.

23   Rotate the crankshaft two full revolutions, then bring the timing marks back into alignment.

24   Loosen the water pump bolts slightly, then turn the pump counterclockwise until the hole in the tensioner arm is aligned with the hole in the tensioner base.

25   Tighten the water pump bolts to the torque specified in Chapter 3, while making sure the tensioner holes are still in alignment.

26   The remainder of installation is the reverse of the removal procedure. Refill the cooling system (see Chapter 1) and check for leaks.

6   Camshaft sprocket - removal and installation

Removal

Refer to illustration 6.4

1   Remove the timing belt front cover (Section 4).

2   Remove the timing belt (make sure the mark on the sprocket is aligned with one on the cover) (Section 5).

3   Remove the camshaft cover (Section 3).

4   Hold the camshaft with a wrench on the flats located between the lobes and remove the sprocket bolt **(see illustration)**. The camshaft must not be allowed to turn.

5   Remove the sprocket and washer.

Installation

6   Place the sprocket in position on the camshaft and align the sprocket and cover marks.

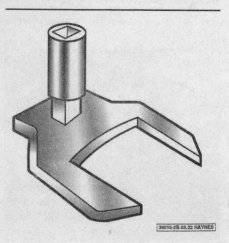

5.22 Special tool for rotating the water pump (available at most auto parts stores)

38015-2B-05.22 HAYNES

6.4 Hold the camshaft with a large wrench at the flats provided and remove the sprocket bolt

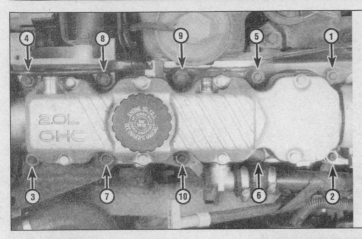

7.4 Camshaft carrier/cylinder head bolt LOOSENING sequence

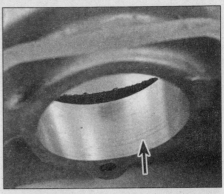

7.9 Check the camshaft carrier bearing surfaces (arrow) for wear and damage

7.10 Check the camshaft retainer contact surface (arrow) for wear

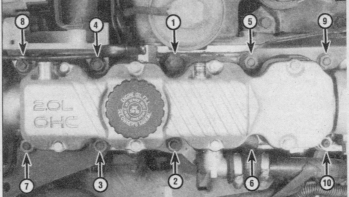

7.16 Camshaft carrier/cylinder head bolt TIGHTENING sequence

7   Hold the camshaft with the wrench and install the bolt and washer. Tighten the bolt to the torque listed in this Chapter's specifications.
8   Install the timing belt, cover and any other components which were removed.

7   Camshaft carrier - removal and installation

Note: *Whenever the camshaft carrier/cylinder head bolts are loosened or removed, the engine must be cold and the cylinder head gasket must be replaced with a new one.*

Removal

Refer to illustration 7.4

1   Disconnect the PCV hose from the camshaft cover.
2   Drain the engine oil and coolant (Chapter 1), then remove the distributor (Chapter 5).
3   Remove the camshaft sprocket (Section 6).
4   Loosen the camshaft carrier/cylinder head bolts 1/4-turn at a time in the prescribed order (see illustration). As the bolts are loosened, the force exerted by the valve springs will tend to separate the carrier from the cylinder head. Remove the bolts and discard them - new ones must be used when installing the cylinder head!
5   Detach the camshaft carrier assembly from the cylinder head.

6   Refer to Section 3 and separate the cover from the carrier, then remove the camshaft from the carrier (Section 8).

Inspection

Refer to illustrations 7.9 and 7.10

7   Carefully remove the oil seal out of the front of the carrier.
8   Clean all parts with solvent and dry them with compressed air (if available).
9   Check the bearing surfaces in the carrier for score marks and other damage (see illustration). Use a telescoping gauge and micrometer to measure the camshaft bearing bores in the carrier. Measure the camshaft journal diameters with a micrometer, then subtract each journal diameter from the corresponding bore diameter to determine the oil clearances. If they're excessive, a new carrier may be required. Refer to Part D of this Chapter for additional camshaft inspection procedures.
10   Check the camshaft retainer surface for wear, score marks and other damage. Replace it with a new one if necessary (see illustration).

Installation

Refer to illustrations 7.16 and 7.17

11   Using your fingers, install a new oil seal in the front of the carrier.
12   Install the camshaft in the carrier as described in Section 8.
13   Install a new cylinder head gasket (Section 12).
14   Clean the mating surfaces of the

camshaft carrier and the cylinder head with lacquer thinner or acetone, then apply a thin (3 mm) bead of anaerobic sealant to the carrier-to-head mating surfaces.
15   Make sure the valve lash compensators and rocker arms are in place. Position the carrier on the cylinder head and install the new bolts.
16   Tighten the bolts to 18 ft-lbs in 1/4-turn increments. Work from the center of the head to the ends in the prescribed order (see illustration). **Caution:** *If the bolts are tightened in increments greater than 1/4-turn, the carrier may be distorted.*
17   Tighten each bolt another 60-degrees,

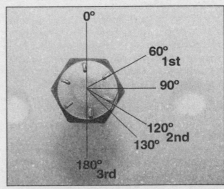

7.17 After the camshaft carrier/cylinder head bolt initial torque is reached, the bolts must be turned an additional 180-degrees in three increments

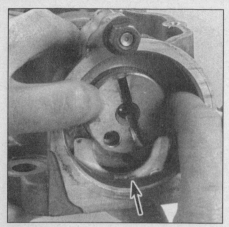

8.3 Push down on the ends of the retainer (arrow) to release it from the groove in the camshaft

8.4 Carefully slide the camshaft out of the carrier to prevent damage to the bearing surfaces

9.5a Lift the rocker arms off and keep them in order - they must be reinstalled in their original locations!

following the same sequence. This must be done three times, until each bolt has been turned an additional 180-degrees (1/2-turn) **(see illustration)**.

18   Reinstall all components that were removed.

19   Refill the cooling system (Chapter 1).

20   Start the engine and run it until normal operating temperature is reached, then check for oil and coolant leaks.

21   Shut the engine off and tighten all of the head bolts, in sequence, an additional 30-to-50 degrees.

22   Change the engine oil and install a new filter (see Chapter 1).

8   Camshaft - removal and installation

Refer to illustrations 8.3 and 8.4

Note: *GM recommends special tools for this procedure (no. J22794 and J33302-25). If they aren't used, the camshaft carrier must be removed first, then the camshaft can be withdrawn from the carrier. When the carrier is removed, the head gasket seal is broken, which means the cylinder head must be completely removed in order to install a new head gasket and bolts. The cost of the special tools is quite high, so, in spite of the extra work and time involved, the procedure outlined here was devised to avoid using them. Before removing the camshaft, refer to Chapter 2, Part D, and check the lobe lift.*

Removal

1   Refer to Section 7 and remove the camshaft carrier.

2   Remove the retainer mounting bolts (at the distributor end of the carrier). If the bolts have hex heads, a special driver will be required for removal and installation.

3   Remove the retainer **(see illustration)**.

4   Support the camshaft at both ends and carefully withdraw it from the distributor end of the carrier (don't damage the bearing sur-

faces with the lobes) **(see illustration)**. Refer to Chapter 2 Part D for the camshaft inspection procedure and Section 7 for the retainer and carrier inspection procedures.

Installation

Note: *If a new camshaft is installed, replace all rocker arms as well- don't install used rocker arms with a new camshaft.*

5   Apply moly-base grease or engine assembly lube to the lip of the front camshaft seal, the camshaft lobes and the bearing surfaces, then carefully insert the camshaft into the carrier.

6   Install the retainer and bolts. Tighten the bolts to the torque listed in this Chapter's specifications.

7   Check the camshaft endplay with a dial indicator and compare it to the Specifications in Chapter 2 Part D.

8   Install the camshaft being careful not to damage the seal.

9   Install the camshaft carrier assembly as described in Section 7.

9   Rocker arms and valve lash compensators - removal and installation

Refer to illustrations 9.5a and 9.5b

Removal

1   Disconnect the battery cable from the negative battery terminal.

2   Disconnect the PCV valve hose from the camshaft cover.

3   Remove the camshaft cover (see Section 3).

4   Remove the camshaft carrier assembly (see Section 7).

5   Remove the rocker arms, rocker arm guides and valve lash compensators and store them in order in a numbered container **(see illustrations)**. Inspection procedures are included in Chapter 2 Part D.

9.5b The rocker arm guides and lash compensators (arrows) can be removed with a magnet (keep them in order as well)

Installation

6   Install a new cylinder head gasket (Section 12).

7   Install the valve lash compensators and rocker arm guides, followed by the rocker arms, in their original locations. Valve adjustment is not required on these models.

8   Install the camshaft carrier and cover.

9   Connect the PCV hose.

10   Connect the battery cable to the negative battery terminal.

10   Intake manifold - removal and installation

Refer to illustration 10.6

Removal

1   Disconnect the battery cable from the negative battery terminal.

2   Remove the air cleaner (if equipped), induction, vacuum and PCV hoses connected to the intake system.

3   Drain the coolant (Chapter 1).

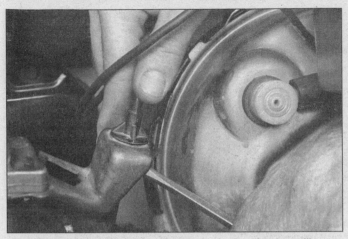

10.6 Disconnect the throttle cable from the bracket by pulling up while pushing in on the snap with a screwdriver

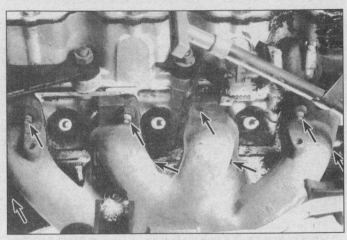

11.7 Remove the exhaust manifold mounting nuts (arrows)

4   Remove the alternator and brackets (Chapter 5).

5   Remove the power steering pump and brackets (Chapter 10). Remove the cruise control cable (if equipped) from the intake manifold bracket.

6   Disconnect the throttle cable, downshift cable and TV cable from the EFI assembly. To remove the cable from the bracket, pull up while using a screwdriver to push the snap in **(see illustration)**.

7   Disconnect and label the wiring to the throttle body, MAP sensor, wastegate (if equipped) and ignition coil. Remove the ignition coil.

8   Relieve the fuel system pressure (Chapter 4).

9   Remove the fuel lines at the fuel rail inlet and regulator outlet.

10   Detach the wires at the fuel injector(s). Remove the fuel rail and injectors on MPFI equipped models (see chapter 4). Remove the EGR valve on MPFI equipped models.

11   Remove the manifold support bracket.

12   Remove the manifold retaining nuts and washers.

13   Detach the intake manifold and gasket.

Installation

Note: *The mating surfaces of the head and manifold must be perfectly clean when the manifold is installed. Gasket removal solvents in aerosol cans are available at most auto parts stores and may be helpful when removing old gasket material that's stuck to the head and manifold (since the components are made of aluminum, aggressive scraping can cause damage). Be sure to follow the directions printed on the container.*

14   Use a gasket scraper to remove all traces of sealant and gasket material, then clean the mating surfaces with lacquer thinner or acetone. If pieces of gasket, sealant or oil are left on the mating surfaces when the manifold is installed, vacuum leaks may develop.

15   Install a new gasket (no sealant is required), place the manifold in position on the studs and install the retaining nuts. Tighten the nuts to the torque listed in this Chapter's Specifications. Work from the center of the manifold out, in a criss-cross pattern to avoid distorting the manifold.

16   Reinstall the components that were removed to gain access to the intake manifold.

17   Start and run the engine and check for fuel and vacuum leaks.

11   Exhaust manifold - removal and installation

Refer to illustration 11.7

Removal

1   Disconnect the battery cable from the negative battery terminal.

2   Remove the air cleaner (if equipped) or air induction tube.

3   Disconnect the spark plug wires from the spark plugs and label them.

4   Disconnect the oxygen sensor electrical connector.

5   Remove the oil dipstick tube.

6   Remove the exhaust pipe at the manifold or the turbo-to-manifold retaining nuts and bolts (if equipped).

7   Remove the exhaust manifold mounting bolts and detach the heat shield **(see illustration)**.

8   Separate the manifold from the engine.

Installation

9   Use a gasket scraper to remove all traces of carbon and old gasket material from the manifold and head mating surfaces, then clean them with lacquer thinner or acetone. Be careful not to nick or gouge the head surface.

10   Install the gasket, manifold and retaining nuts or bolts to the cylinder head. Don't use sealant to hold the gasket in place. **Note:** The expansion joints on the gasket must face out, away from the cylinder head.

11   When tightening the bolts, work from the center of the manifold out to the ends. Using a torque wrench, tighten the bolts in three or four equal steps to the torque listed in this Chapter's Specifications.

12   Install the components that were removed for access and connect the battery cable to the negative battery terminal.

13   Start the engine and check for exhaust leaks.

12   Cylinder head - removal and installation

Note: *The engine must be cold whenever the camshaft carrier/cylinder head bolts are loosened or removed.*

Removal

Refer to illustrations 12.14a, 12.14b, 12.16 and 12.18

1   Relieve the fuel system pressure (see Chapter 4) and disconnect the battery cable from the negative battery terminal.

2   Remove the air cleaner or air induction tubes and PCV hoses/tubes. Drain the cooling system, disconnect the upper radiator hose, unplug the connectors and remove the thermostat housing (Chapters 1 and 3).

3   Remove the alternator and bracket (Chapter 5).

4   Remove the power steering pump and bracket assembly and lay it to one side (Chapter 10).

5   Disconnect the spark plug wires and distributor cap, if equipped, and remove them as an assembly.

6   Remove the ignition coil(s), distributor (if equipped) and wiring (Chapter 5).

7   Disconnect the throttle cable from the intake manifold bracket.

8   Disconnect the throttle, downshift and TV cables from the EFI assembly.

9   Disconnect the ECM connectors from the EFI components.

10   Remove the fuel inlet and return lines. Remove the vacuum hose going to the brake booster.

12.14a The cylinder head bolts will be easier to remove if penetrating oil is applied

12.14b Keep the cylinder head bolts in order in a container or on a marked piece of cardboard

12.16 Use a block of wood and a hammer to break the cylinder head gasket seal - don't strike the head directly with a metal hammer!

11 Remove the heater hose from the intake manifold fitting.

12 Disconnect the exhaust pipe or turbo from the exhaust manifold.

13 Remove the timing belt (Section 5).

14 Refer to Section 7 and remove the camshaft carrier/cylinder head mounting bolts, then detach the carrier from the head. **Note:** *Prior to removal, apply penetrating oil to the cylinder head bolts* **(see illustration)**. *Keep the cylinder head bolts in order in a marked container or piece of cardboard* **(see illustration)**.

15 Remove the rocker arms, rocker arm guides and valve lash compensators (Section 9).

16 Break the gasket seal by tapping the cylinder head with a soft-face hammer or a hammer and wood block **(see illustration)**.

17 Separate the cylinder head from the engine.

18 Remove the gasket from the engine **(see illustration)**.

Installation

19 The mating surfaces of the camshaft carrier, cylinder head and block must be perfectly clean when the head is installed.

20 Use a gasket scraper to remove all traces of carbon and old gasket material, then clean the mating surfaces with lacquer thinner or acetone. If there's oil on the mating surfaces when the head is installed, the gasket may not seal correctly and leaks may develop. Use a vacuum cleaner to remove any debris that falls into the cylinders.

21 Check the carrier, block and head mating surfaces for nicks, deep scratches and other damage. If damage is slight, it can be removed with a file; if it's excessive, machining may be the only alternative. Check the cylinder head gasket mating surface for warpage with a straight edge and feeler gauge, see Chapter 2, Part D for more information and specifications on this procedure.

22 Use a tap of the correct size to chase the threads of the head bolt holes in the block. Dirt, corrosion, sealant and damaged threads will affect torque readings. The bolts

12.18 Use a scraper to remove the old head gasket

should be discarded - new ones must be used when the head is installed.

23 Position the new gasket over the dowel pins in the block. The top of the gasket should be stamped TOP or THIS SIDE UP to ensure correct installation. Don't use sealant on the gasket.

24 Carefully position the head on the block without disturbing the gasket. Make sure it slips over the dowel pins and rests on the gasket.

25 Install the camshaft carrier and new cylinder head bolts. Refer to Section 7 for the head bolt tightening procedures.

26 The remaining installation steps are the reverse of removal.

---

13 Valves, springs and valve stem oil seals - removal and installation

The design of the OHC engine doesn't allow for replacement of the valve stem oil seals or valve springs with the cylinder head in place. To service valve train components, the cylinder head must be removed from the engine and disassembled on a workbench. Refer to the cylinder head removal and instal-

lation procedure in Section 12 and the cylinder head overhaul procedures in Chapter 2, Part D.

---

14 Oil pan - removal and installation

Refer to illustration 14.9

Removal

1 Disconnect the battery cable from the negative battery terminal.

2 Loosen the lug nuts on the right front wheel.

3 Raise the front of the vehicle and support it securely on jackstands.

4 Remove the right front wheel.

5 Remove the right front fender liner (Chapter 11).

6 On Turbo-charged models disconnect the exhaust pipe at the wastegate.

7 Remove the bellhousing dust cover, unbolt the exhaust pipe and disconnect it from the manifold.

8 Drain the engine oil and replace the filter (Chapter 1).

9 Remove the oil pan bolts and separate the oil pan from the engine **(see illustration)**. Use a hammer and block of wood to dislodge

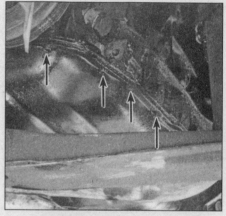

14.9 Remove the oil pan bolts and separate the oil pan from the engine

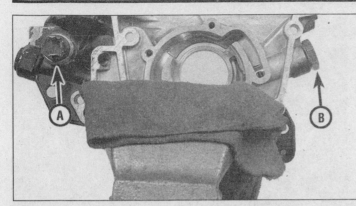

15.9 The oil pump will be easier to work on if mounted in a vise with padded jaws

A Oil pressure sending unit
B Pressure regulator valve plug

it if it's stuck - don't pry between the sealing surfaces as damage that could lead to oil leaks may occur .

10   If equipped, separate the windage tray from the oil pan.

Installation

11   Use a gasket scraper to remove all traces of old gasket material and sealant from the windage tray, oil pan and block, then clean the mating surfaces with lacquer thinner or acetone.

12   Make sure the bolts and the bolt holes in the block are clean. Check the oil pan and windage tray flanges for distortion, particularly around the bolt holes. If necessary, place them on a block of wood and use a hammer to flatten and restore the gasket mating surfaces.

13   Attach the new gasket to the windage tray, then apply RTV-sealant to the oil pan flange and the upper side of the gasket.

14   Attach the oil pan, windage tray and gasket to the engine. Apply thread locking compound to the threads and install the bolts. Tighten the bolts to the torque listed in this Chapter's Specifications in three or four steps. Start at the center of the pan and work out toward the ends in a spiral pattern.

15   The remaining steps are the reverse of removal. **Caution:** *Don't forget to refill the engine with oil before starting it (see Chapter 1).*

16   Start the engine and check carefully for oil leaks at the oil pan-to-block junction.

Oil pump pick-up tube

17   Remove the bolts and detach the pick-up tube from the block.

18   Remove the O-ring from the tube and discard it. Clean the tube and screen assembly with solvent and dry it with compressed air (if available).

19   Attach a new O-ring to the tube and position the tube on the block. Install the bolts and tighten them to the torque listed in this Chapter's Specifications.

20   Install the oil pan.

---

15   Oil pump - removal and installation

Removal

1   The oil pump is mounted low on the timing belt end of the engine and is driven directly off the end of the crankshaft. Remove the timing belt, the rear timing belt cover and the crankshaft sprocket (see Section 5).

2   Unplug the wiring harness from the oil pressure switch, located near the oil filter.

3   Remove the oil pan (Section 14) and the oil filter.

4   Remove the pick-up tube assembly (Section 14).

5   Pry out the crankshaft oil seal - be careful not to damage the shaft or bore in the process (see Section 17).

6   Remove the six bolts and separate the oil pump from the block.

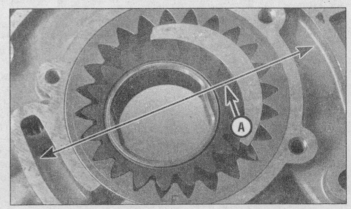

15.12 Checking the outer gear-to-body clearance with a feeler gauge

Disassembly

Refer to illustrations 15.9a and 15.9b

7   Remove the screws and detach the cover from the rear of the pump.

8   Remove the gears from the pump body. It may be necessary to turn the body over to remove the gears by allowing them to fall out.

9   Mount the pump body in a vise equipped with soft jaws and remove the oil pressure sending unit, plug, pressure regulator valve plunger and spring **(see illustrations).**

Inspection

Refer to illustrations 15.12, 15.13 and 15.14

10   Clean the parts with solvent and dry them with compressed air, if available.

11   Inspect the components for wear, cracks and other damage. Replace any damaged or worn parts with new ones.

12   Check the outer gear-to-body clearance **(see illustration).**

13   Check the inner gear-to-body clearance **(see illustration).**

14   Check the gear-to-cover clearance **(see illustration).** Compare your measurements with this Chapter's Specifications, if any are excessive, replace the pump assembly.

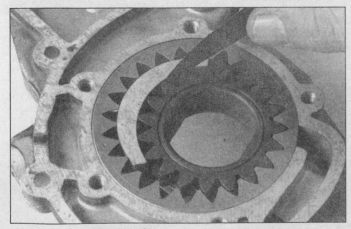

15.13 Checking the drive gear-to-body clearance

15.14 The gear-to-cover clearance is checked by inserting a feeler gauge between the gear and a straightedge laid across the pump body at point A

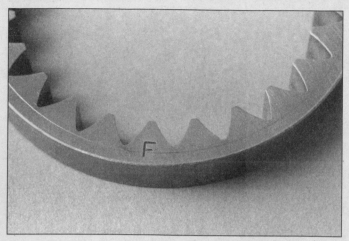

15.17 The mark (F) on the oil pump idler gear MUST face the cover

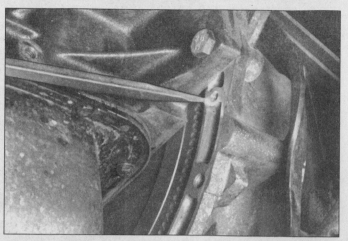

16.4 A screwdriver inserted in the flywheel starter gear teeth will lock the engine so the crankshaft pulley bolt can be loosened

Reassembly

Refer to illustration 15.17

15   Install the valve plunger and spring assembly.

16   Coat the plug threads with Locktite, then install and tighten it to the torque listed in this Chapter's Specifications.

17   Install the gears, noting that the outer gear is identified by a mark. This mark must face the cover **(see illustration)**.

18   Completely pack the pump with petroleum jelly to ensure pump priming. Install the cover and tighten the screws to the torque listed in this Chapter's Specifications.

19   Install the oil pressure sending unit and tighten securely.

Installation

20   Use a gasket scraper to remove all old gasket material from the oil pump and block, then clean the sealing surfaces with lacquer thinner or acetone.

21   Place the pump and a new gasket into position and install the bolts. Tighten the bolts to the torque listed in this Chapter's Specifications. Install a new oil seal (see Section 17).

22   Install the pick-up tube assembly (Section 14).

23   Install the oil pan (Section 14).

24   Install a new oil filter and connect the oil pressure switch harness.

25   Install the crankshaft sprocket, timing belt and covers.

26   Refill the engine with the specified oil (Chapter 1).

27   Start the engine and check for oil leaks.

16   Flywheel/driveplate - removal and installation

Refer to illustrations 16.4

1   Raise the vehicle and support it securely on jackstands, then refer to Chapter 7 and remove the transaxle. If it's leaking, now would be a very good time to have the front

17.4 Removing the front oil seal with a screwdriver

pump seal/O-ring replaced (automatic transaxle only).

2   Remove the pressure plate and clutch disc (Chapter 8 - manual transaxle equipped vehicles). Now is a good time to check/replace the clutch components and pilot bearing.

3   If there is no dowel pin, make some marks on the flywheel/driveplate and crankshaft to ensure correct alignment during reinstallation.

4   Remove the bolts that secure the flywheel/driveplate to the crankshaft. If the crankshaft turns, wedge a screwdriver **(see illustration)** through the openings in the driveplate (automatic transaxle) or against the flywheel ring gear teeth (manual transaxle). Since the flywheel is fairly heavy, be sure to support it while removing the last bolt.

5   Remove the flywheel/driveplate from the crankshaft.

6   Clean the flywheel to remove grease and oil. Inspect the friction surface for cracks, rivet grooves, burned areas and score marks. Light scoring can be removed with emery

cloth. Check for cracked and broken ring gear teeth. Lay the flywheel on a flat surface and use a straightedge to check for warpage.

7   Clean and inspect the mating surfaces of the flywheel/driveplate and the crankshaft. If the crankshaft rear seal is leaking, replace it before reinstalling the flywheel/driveplate.

8   Position the flywheel/driveplate against the crankshaft. Be sure to align the dowel or marks made during removal. Before installing the bolts, apply thread locking compound to the threads.

9   Keep the flywheel/driveplate from turning as described above while you tighten the bolts to the torque listed in this Chapter's Specifications.

10   The remainder of installation is the reverse of the removal procedure.

17   Crankshaft oil seals - replacement

Front oil seal

Removal

Refer to illustration 17.4

1   Remove the serpentine drivebelt (Chapter 1), timing belt front cover (Section 4) and timing belt (Section 5).

2   Remove the flywheel cover and lock the flywheel by wedging a screwdriver in the starter ring gear teeth. The screwdriver must be held against the engine block, not the transaxle case **(see illustration 16.4)**.

3   Remove the bolt and washer and detach the crankshaft sprocket. The bolt is usually very tight, so a 1/2-inch drive breaker bar and a six-point socket should be used.

4   Pry the old oil seal out with a seal removal tool or a screwdriver. Be very careful not to nick or otherwise damage the crankshaft in the process **(see illustration)**.

Installation

Refer to illustrations 17.7a and 17.7b

5   Apply a thin coat of RTV-type sealant to the outer edge of the new seal. Lubricate the

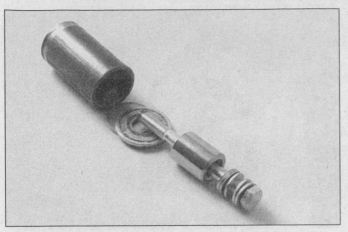

17.7a A tool for installing the front crankshaft oil seal can be made from pieces of pipe, washers and a bolt

17.7b Tighten the tool bolt slowly to push the seal squarely into place

seal lip with moly-base grease or clean engine oil.

6   Place the seal squarely in position in the bore.

7   Push the seal into the bore with a hammer and the factory special tool (GM no. J330831) or a tool made up of a long metric coarse thread bolt, a piece of pipe and washers **(see illustrations)**. Be sure the bolt diameter and thread pitch match the sprocket bolt and the pipe diameter matches the seal to prevent distortion. Make sure the seal is seated completely in the bore.

8   Align the keyway in the sprocket with the key in the end of the crankshaft, then slide the sprocket into place. Install the washer and bolt and tighten the bolt to the torque listed in this Chapter's Specifications.

9   Remove the screwdriver and install the flywheel cover.

10   Install the timing belt, front cover and serpentine drivebelt.

11   Install the rear timing belt cover (if removed), the Woodruff key and the crankshaft sprocket.

12   Check the engine oil and add, if necessary. Start the engine and check for oil leaks at the seal.

Rear seal

Removal

Refer to illustration 17.17

13   Remove the flywheel dust cover.

14   On automatic transaxle models, remove the torque converter retaining bolts.

15   Remove the transaxle from the engine (see Chapter 7). **Note:** *The torque converter should remain in the transaxle when it is removed from the vehicle.*

16   Remove the driveplate (automatic) or flywheel and clutch pressure plate and disc (manual transaxle).

17   Pry the old seal out very carefully with a screwdriver or similar tool **(see illustration)**.

Installation

Refer to illustration 17.20

18   Carefully clean the sealing surfaces of the engine block and crankshaft. Inspect the crankshaft for nicks and scratches.

19   Coat the seal and engine contact surfaces with clean engine oil.

20   Insert the new seal squarely into position and tap it into place until it bottoms in the bore **(see illustration)**.

21   Install the flywheel or driveplate and

clutch assembly, if equipped.

22   Install the transaxle and the flywheel dust cover.

---

18   Engine mounts - check and replacement

Refer to illustration 18.5

Warning: *A special tool is available from most auto part stores to support the engine during repair operations. Similar fixtures are available from rental yards. Improper lifting methods or devices are hazardous and could result in severe injury or death. DO NOT place any part of your body under the engine/transaxle when it's supported only by a jack. Failure of the lifting device could result in serious injury or death.*

1   If the rubber mounts have hardened, cracked or separated from the metal backing plates, they must be replaced. This operation may be carried out with the engine/transaxle still in the vehicle.

2   Disconnect the battery cable from the negative battery terminal.

3   Raise the front of the vehicle and sup-

17.17 Pry out the rear main oil seal very carefully - don't damage the surface of the crankshaft or the new seal will leak

17.20 Tap around the outer edge of the new oil seal with a hammer and a blunt punch to seat it squarely in the bore

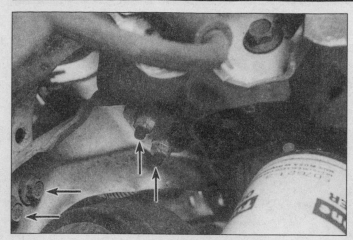 

18.5 Engine mount components - Typical

1   *Front engine mount*   2   *Rear engine mount*

port it securely on jackstands.
4   Support the engine securely with an engine supporting fixture (see **Warning**).

Front mount

5   Remove the two mount-to-engine bracket bolts or nuts **(see illustration)**.
6   Remove the mount-to-frame bolts.
7   Remove the mount from the vehicle. Clean the mount bolts and apply thread locking compound to the threads.

8   Place the new mount into position and install the mount-to-frame bolts.
9   Install the mount-to-engine bracket bolts and tighten all the mount bolts to the torque listed in this Chapter's Specifications.

Rear mount

10   Remove the two mount-to-frame bracket nuts **(see illustration 18.5)**.
11   Remove the mount-to-engine bracket bolts.

12   Remove the mount from the vehicle. Clean the mount bolts and apply thread locking compound to the threads.
13   Place the new mount into position and install the mount-to-engine bracket bolts.
14   Install the mount-to-frame bracket nuts and tighten all the bolts and nuts to the torque listed in this Chapter's Specifications
15   Lower the engine and remove the engine support fixture.
16   The remainder of installation is the reverse of removal.

Chapter 2 Part C
2.8 and 3.1 liter V6 engines

Contents

Specifications

General

Cylinder numbers (drivebelt end-to-transaxle end)
Front bank (radiator side)	2-4-6
Rear bank	1-3-5
Firing order	1-2-3-4-5-6

Torque specifications

Ft-lbs

Camshaft sprocket bolts	20
Rear camshaft cover bolts	7
Cylinder head bolts	
1986 and earlier	68
1987 and later	
Step 1	33
Step 2	Turn an additional 90-degrees
Crankshaft pulley bolts	25
Vibration damper bolt	75
Front engine mount-to-frame bracket bolts	45
Front engine mount-to-engine bracket bolts	50
Rear engine mount-to-frame bracket nuts	18
Rear engine mount-to-engine bracket bolts	45
Exhaust manifold mounting bolts	20
Flywheel/driveplate mounting bolts	50
Front cover mounting bolts	
Small bolts	
1986 and earlier	15
1987 and later	20
Large bolts	
1986 and earlier	25
1987 and later	28

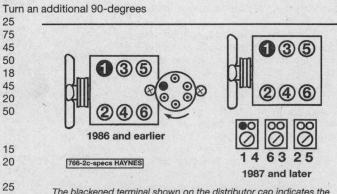

1986 and earlier

766-2c-specs HAYNES

1 4 6 3 2 5

1987 and later

The blackened terminal shown on the distributor cap indicates the Number One spark plug wire position

**Cylinder location and distributor rotation
(or coil terminal location)**

Torque specifications (continued)   Ft-lbs

Intake manifold mounting bolts	
1986 and earlier	23
1987 and later	
Step 1	15
Step 2	24
Oil pan mounting bolts/nuts	
Small bolts	8
Large bolts	18
Nuts (if equipped)	8
Oil pump mounting bolt	30
Oil pump cover bolts	8
Valve cover bolts	8
Rocker arm nuts (1987 and later)	20
Timing chain tensioner bolts	15

1   General information

The following Sections in this Part of Chapter 2 are devoted to in-vehicle repair procedures for the 2.8 liter and 3.1 liter V6 engines. All information concerning engine removal and installation and cylinder block and cylinder head servicing can be found in Part D of this Chapter.

The repair procedures are based on the assumption that the engine is still installed in the vehicle. Therefore, if this information is being used during a complete engine overhaul - with the engine already out of the vehicle and on a stand - many of the Steps included here will not apply.

The Specifications included in this Part of Chapter 2 apply only to the engines and procedures found here. For specifications regarding engines other than the 2.8 liter and 3.1 liter V6, see Part A or B, whichever applies. Part D of Chapter 2 contains the specifications necessary for engine block and cylinder head rebuilding procedures.

2   Repair operations possible with the engine in the vehicle

Many major repair operations can be accomplished without removing the engine from the vehicle.

Clean the engine compartment and the exterior of the engine with some type of degreaser before any work is done. It'll make the job easier and help keep dirt out of the internal areas of the engine.

Depending on the components involved, it may be helpful to remove the hood to improve access to the engine as repairs are performed (refer to Chapter 11 if necessary). Cover the fenders to prevent damage to the paint. Special pads are available, but an old bedspread or blanket will also work.

If vacuum, exhaust, oil or coolant leaks develop, indicating a need for gasket or seal replacement, the repairs can generally be made with the engine in the vehicle. The intake and exhaust manifold gaskets, timing chain cover gasket, oil pan gasket, crankshaft oil seals and cylinder head gasket are all accessible with the engine in place.

Exterior engine components, such as the intake and exhaust manifolds, the oil pan (and the oil pump), the water pump, the starter motor, the alternator and the fuel system components can be removed for repair with the engine in place.

Since the cylinder head can be removed without pulling the engine, valve component servicing can also be accomplished with the engine in the vehicle. Replacement of the timing chain and sprockets is also possible with the engine in the vehicle.

In extreme cases caused by a lack of necessary equipment, repair or replacement of piston rings, pistons, connecting rods and rod bearings is possible with the engine in the vehicle. However, this practice is not recommended because of the cleaning and preparation work that must be done to the components involved.

3   Valve covers - removal and installation

Removal

1   Disconnect the cable from the negative battery terminal. **Caution:** *If the vehicle is equipped with a Delco Loc II audio system, make sure you have the correct activation code before disconnecting the battery. See the information at the front of this manual for the radio re-activation procedure.*

2   Disconnect the hoses at the PCV valve and label them.

3   Disconnect all other wires and hoses that would interfere with the removal of the valve cover, tagging them as they are disconnected.

4   Remove any fuel injection (air induction) parts necessary to gain access to the valve cover bolts and cover.

5   Mark the spark plug wires with tape to facilitate reassembly, then disconnect the wires and lay them out of the way.

Front cover

6   On 1986 and earlier models equipped with a distributor, remove the ignition coil from the bracket.

7   On 1987 and later models, drain the coolant from the radiator (see Chapter 1). Loosen the coolant tube hose clamp below the thermostat housing, then disconnect the other end of the hose at the water pump. Unbolt the coolant tube bracket and move it aside.

8   Remove the vent tube from the valve cover to the air inlet hose.

Rear cover

9   Disconnect the accelerator cable and on automatic transaxle-equipped models, disconnect the throttle valve (TV) cable from the fuel injection throttle body.

10   Remove the bolts retaining the air management valve (if equipped).

11   On 1986 and earlier models, disconnect the EGR pipe at the EGR valve and remove the air intake plenum.

12   On 1987 and later models, detach the brake booster vacuum line from the bracket.

13   Remove the serpentine drivebelt (see Chapter 1).

14   Mark the wires to the alternator with pieces of numbered tape, then disconnect the wires. Remove the rear alternator brace and detach the alternator.

15   Remove the alternator bracket.

Both covers

Refer to illustration 3.16

16   Remove the valve cover bolts **(see illustration)**.

17   Remove the valve cover(s). **Note:** *If the cover sticks to the cylinder head, use a block of wood and a hammer to dislodge it. If the cover still will not come loose, pry on it carefully, but do not distort the sealing flange surface.*

Installation

18   Clean the valve cover and cylinder head mating surfaces with a scraper and solvent or degreaser. Be sure to remove all traces of old gasket material and sealant.

1986 and earlier models

19   Apply a continuous 3/16-inch diameter

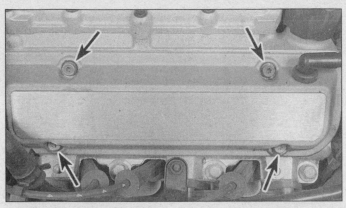

3.16 Valve cover mounting bolt locations on 1987 and later models - note that many of these later valve covers are secured by Torx bolts

4.2 Remove the rocker arm nuts (arrows)

bead of RTV-type sealant to the flange of the cover. Be sure to apply the sealant inner side of the bolt holes.

1987 and later models

20   Apply a 3 mm dab of RTV sealant to the intake manifold-to-cylinder head notch at each end of the engine.
21   Install a new valve cover gasket. It may be helpful to "glue" the gasket to the valve cover using a small amount of sealant. Make sure the bolt holes in the gasket line up with the holes in the cover.

All models

22   Place the valve cover on the cylinder head while the sealant is still wet and install the mounting bolts. Tighten the bolts a little at a time to the torque listed in this Chapter's Specifications.
23   Complete the job by reversing the removal procedure. Run the engine and check for leaks.

---

4   Valve train components - replacement (cylinder head installed)

Rocker arms and pushrods

Refer to illustrations 4.2 and 4.3

Removal

1   Remove the rocker arm covers (see Section 3).
2   Remove the rocker arm nuts and remove the rocker arms and pivot balls **(see illustration)**. Store each set of rocker arm components separately in a marked plastic bag to insure they're reinstalled in their original location. **Note:** *If you only need to remove the pushrods, loosen the rocker arm nuts and turn the rocker arms to allow room for pushrod removal.*
3   Remove the pushrods and store them separately to make sure they don't get mixed up during installation **(see illustration)**. **Note:** *Intake and exhaust pushrods are different lengths with the exhaust pushrod being the*

longer of the two. Intake pushrods are color-coded orange and exhaust pushrods are coded blue.

Inspection

4   Inspect each rocker arm for wear, cracks and other damage, especially where the pushrod and valve stem make contact.
5   Check the pivot seat in each rocker arm and the pivot ball face. Look for galling, stress cracks and unusual wear patterns. If the rocker arms are worn or damaged, replace them with new rocker arms and pivot balls as well.
6   Make sure the hole in each rocker arm is open and the pushrod tube is free of obstructions.
7   Inspect the pushrods for cracks and excessive wear at the ends. Roll each pushrod across a glass plate or mirror to see if it's bent (if it wobbles, it's bent).

Installation

8   Lubricate the lower end of each pushrod with clean engine oil or moly-based grease and install them in their original locations. Make sure each pushrod seats completely in the lifter socket. Apply moly-based grease to the ends of the valve stems, the upper ends of the pushrods and to the pivot balls.
9   Install the rocker arms, pivot balls and nuts, make sure the pushrod is properly seated in the rocker arm. On 1987 and later models, tighten the rocker arm nuts to the torque listed in this Chapter's Specifications. On 1986 and earlier models, adjust the valve lash (see Section 7).

Valve springs, retainers and seals

10   This procedure is essentially the same as for the OHV four-cylinder engines. Follow the procedure in Chapter 2, Part A except note that the valve seals, which are pressed onto the valve guide protrusion on the cylinder head, are removed differently. GM recommends using a special valve seal removal tool to avoid seal damage, although a pair of pliers will work, since the old seal is always discarded. Install the new seal before

4.3 A perforated cardboard box can be use to store the pushrods to ensure they are installed in their original locations - note the label indicating the transaxle end of the engine

installing the spring and retainer, and note that intake and exhaust valve seals are different.

---

5   Intake manifold - removal and installation

Warning: *Gasoline is extremely flammable, so take extra precautions when you work on any part of the fuel system. Don't smoke or allow open flames or bare light bulbs near the work area, and don't work in a garage where a natural gas-type appliance (such as a water heater or clothes dryer) with a pilot light is present. If you spill any fuel on your skin, rinse it off immediately with soap and water. When you perform any kind of work on the fuel system, wear safety glasses and have a Class B type fire extinguisher on hand.*

Removal

Refer to illustrations 5.18 and 5.19

1   Relieve the fuel system pressure (see Chapter 4).
2   Disconnect the cable from the negative

5.18 Remove the manifold mounting bolts

5.19 Pry the manifold loose at a casting boss - don't pry between the gasket surfaces!

battery terminal. **Caution:** *If the vehicle is equipped with a Delco Loc II audio system, make sure you have the correct activation code before disconnecting the battery. See the information at the front of this manual for the radio re-activation procedure.*

3   Drain the coolant from the radiator (Chapter 1).

4   Disconnect the air intake duct at the throttle body. Disconnect the throttle cable and, if equipped, the cruise control cable and automatic transaxle downshift cable from the throttle body. Make careful note of how the cables were installed.

5   Label and disconnect all electrical wires and vacuum hoses at the throttle body.

6   Remove the EGR valve (1987 and later models) or disconnect the EGR pipe at the EGR valve (1986 and earlier models).

7   Remove any vacuum lines, cable brackets and wiring harness connectors attached to the plenum and remove the air intake plenum (upper half of the intake manifold) with the throttle body attached.

8   Remove the fuel inlet and return lines at the fuel rail (see Chapter 4).

9   Remove the serpentine belt (see Chapter 10.

10   Remove the power steering pump without disconnecting the hoses and set it aside,

being careful not to spill any fluid (see Chapter 10).

11   Disconnect the electrical connectors at the alternator and remove the alternator. Remove the alternator bracket, if necessary.

12   Disconnect the electrical connectors at each fuel injector and remove the fuel rail (see Chapter 4).

13   Disconnect the spark plug wires at the spark plugs (label the wires for ease of reassembly). Remove any spark plug wire guides or brackets attached to the intake manifold or valve covers.

14   On 1986 and earlier models, equipped with a distributor, remove the wires at the ignition coil and remove the distributor (see Chapter 5).

15   Remove the upper radiator hose at the thermostat housing. Remove the heater inlet hose or pipe and the coolant by-pass hose or pipe.

16   Remove both valve covers (see Section 3).

17   Disconnect any remaining electrical connectors (coolant sensor, oil sending switch, etc.) that are still attached to the intake manifold. Make sure that all wires, vacuum hoses and coolant hoses that would interfere with manifold removal have been disconnected and moved out of the way.

18   Remove the manifold mounting bolts **(see illustration)**.

19   Separate the manifold from the engine by prying with a suitable bar (do not pry between the mating surfaces) or tap the manifold with a hammer and wooden block to loosen it **(see illustration)**.

Installation

Refer to illustrations 5.23 and 5.28

20   If a new manifold is being installed, transfer the external components from the old manifold to the new one.

21   On 1987 and later models, loosen the rocker arm nuts and remove the pushrods. Store the pushrods separately to ensure reinstallation in the same positions.

22   Before installing the manifold, place clean, lint-free rags in the engine cavity and clean the engine block, cylinder head and manifold gasket surfaces. All gasket material and sealant must be removed prior to installation (a gasket scraper is very helpful). Remove all dirt and gasket remnants from the engine cavity.

23   Clean the gasket sealing surfaces with degreaser, then apply a 3/16-inch diameter bead of RTV-type sealant to the engine block end ridges only **(see illustration)**.

24   Install the new intake gaskets on the

5.23 Apply a 3/16-inch bead of RTV sealant (arrows) to the front and rear ridges of the engine block (1987 and later models shown, but earlier models require sealant at the same locations)

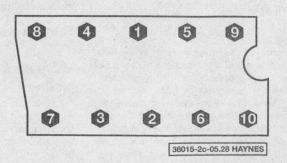

38015-2c-05.28 HAYNES

5.28 Intake manifold installation details and mounting bolt tightening sequence

6.3a A magnetic pick-up tool . . .

6.3b . . . or a scribe can be used to remove the lifters

6.4 Store the lifters in a box like this to ensure installation in their original locations

cylinder heads. Notice that the gaskets are normally marked Right and Left. Be sure to use the correct gasket on each cylinder head.
25   On 1987 and later models, install the pushrods in their original locations and reposition the rocker arms on the pushrods. Tighten the rocker arm nuts to the torque listed in this Chapter's Specifications.
26   Hold the gaskets in place by extending the bead of RTV 1 /4-inch onto the gasket ends. On 1986 and earlier models, the new gaskets will have to be cut, so they can be installed behind the pushrods.
27   Carefully lower the intake manifold into position, making sure that you do not disturb the gaskets.
28   Install the intake manifold mounting bolts and tighten them following the sequence illustrated. Tighten the bolts a little at a time until they are all at the torque listed in this Chapter's Specifications **(see illustration)**.
29   Install the remaining components in the reverse order of removal.
30   Fill the radiator with coolant, start the engine and check for leaks. Adjust the ignition timing and idle speed as necessary (refer to Chap-ter 1).

---

6   Hydraulic lifters - removal, inspection and installation

Refer to illustrations 6.3a, 6.3b, and 6.4

Removal

1   Remove the intake manifold and rocker arm covers (see Sections 3 and 5).
2   Remove the rocker arms and pushrods (see Section 4).
3   There are several ways to extract the lifters from their bores. A special tool designed to grip and remove lifters is manufactured by many tool companies and is widely available. On newer engines without a lot of varnish buildup, the lifters can often be removed with a magnet or machinist's scribe **(see illustrations)**. **Caution:** *Don't use pliers*

to remove the lifters. The pliers may damage the hardened surface of the lifters, rendering them useless.
4   Before removing the lifters, arrange to store them in a clearly labeled box to ensure they're reinstalled in their original locations. Remove the lifters and store them where they won't get dirty **(see illustration)**. **Note:** *Some engine may have both standard and 0.010 inch oversize lifters installed at the factory. If oversized lifters have been installed they will be marked on the block.*

Inspection and installation

5   Refer to Chapter 2, Part A for lifter inspection procedures. If the lifters are worn, they must be replaced with new ones and the camshaft must be replaced as well - never install new lifters with a used camshaft, or used lifters with a new camshaft.
6   When installing used lifters, make sure they're installed in their original bores. Soak the lifters in oil to remove trapped air, and coat the foot of the lifter with moly-based lube prior to installation.
7   The remaining installation steps are the reverse of removal. Run the engine and check for any abnormal noises or leaks.

---

7   Valve lash - adjustment (1986 and earlier models only)

Refer to illustration 7.6

1   **Note:** *1987 and later models have rocker arms that are secured by locking nuts - the valve lash is pre-set and cannot be adjusted.*
2   Disconnect the cable from the negative battery terminal. **Caution:** *If the vehicle is equipped with a Delco Loc II audio system, make sure you have the correct activation code before disconnecting the battery. See the information at the front of this manual for the radio re-activation procedure.*
3   If the valve covers are still on the engine, refer to Section 3 and remove them.
4   If the valve train components have been

7.6 Determining at what point drag is felt on the pushrod by rotating it as the nut is tightened

serviced just prior to this procedure, make sure that the components are completely reassembled.
5   Rotate the crankshaft until the number one piston is at Top Dead Center (TDC) on the compression stroke (see Chapter 2A).
6   Start with the number one cylinder intake valve. Back off the rocker arm nut until play is felt at the pushrod, then turn it back in until all play is removed. This can be determined by rotating the pushrod while tightening the nut. Just when a slight drag is felt when rotating the pushrod, all lash has been removed. Now tighten the nut an additional 3/4 turn **(see illustration)**.
7   Adjust the number one, five and six cylinder intake valves and the number one, two and three cylinder exhaust valves, with the crankshaft in this position, using the method just described.
8   Rotate the crankshaft 360 degrees, the number four piston is now at TDC on the compression stroke, and adjust the number two, three and four cylinder intake valves and the number four, five and six cylinder exhaust valves.

9   Refer to Section 3 and install the valve covers.

8   Exhaust manifolds - removal and installation

Warning: *The engine must be completely cool before beginning this procedure.*
1   Remove the cable from the negative battery terminal. **Caution:** *If the vehicle is equipped with a Delco Loc II audio system, make sure you have the correct activation code before disconnecting the battery. See the information at the front of this manual for the radio re-activation procedure.*
2   Remove the air cleaner assembly, labeling all hoses.

Rear manifold

3   Remove the bolts attaching the crossover pipe to the manifold.
4   Raise the front of the vehicle and support it securely on jackstands. Block the rear wheels to keep the vehicle from rolling.
5   Remove the bolts attaching the exhaust pipe to the exhaust manifold, then separate the pipe from the manifold.
6   Remove the jackstands and lower the vehicle.
7   Disconnect the oxygen sensor pigtail electrical connector.
8   Remove the EGR valve and related parts.
9   Disconnect the spark plug wires from the spark plugs, labeling them as they are disconnected to simplify installation.
10   Remove the exhaust manifold mounting bolts and separate the manifold from the engine.
11   Installation is the reverse of the removal procedure. Before installing the manifold, be sure to thoroughly clean the mating surfaces on the manifold and cylinder head.

Front manifold

12   Disconnect the exhaust crossover pipe. On 1987 and later models, drain the coolant (see Chapter 1) and remove the coolant by-pass pipe.
13   Remove the bolts retaining the exhaust pipe to the manifold, then disconnect the pipe from the manifold.
14   Remove the four bolts and one nut accessible at the rear of the manifold.

15   Disconnect and label any wires that will interfere with the removal of the manifold.
16   Remove the remaining manifold bolts and separate the manifold and heat shield from the engine.
17   Installation is the reverse of the removal procedure. Be sure to thoroughly clean the cylinder head and manifold surfaces before installing the manifold.

9   Cylinder heads - removal and installation

Refer to illustration 9.15
1   Disconnect the cable from the negative battery terminal.
2   Raise the vehicle and place it securely on jackstands.
3   Locate the engine block drain plugs, remove them and drain the coolant (the plug on the left side is just above the oil filter).
4   Disconnect the exhaust pipe from the rear exhaust manifold, then remove the jackstands and lower the vehicle.
5   Remove the alternator and bracket.
6   Remove the oil dipstick tube assembly from the left side of the engine, then remove the cruise control servo bracket (if equipped).
7   Remove the intake manifold (see Section 5) the exhaust crossover pipe and exhaust manifolds (see Section 8).
8   Loosen the rocker arm nuts enough to allow removal of the pushrods, then remove the pushrods (see Section 4).
9   Loosen the head bolts in a sequence opposite to the one used for tightening **(see illustration 9.15).** Remove the head bolts and store them in a cardboard holder in the order they are removed. This will ensure that they will be installed in their original locations.
10   Remove the cylinder heads. To break the gasket seal, using a pry bar, pry each head up at each corner but don't pry between the head and the block as damage to the sealing surface will result.
11   If a new cylinder head is being installed, transfer the various components, such as the manifold, brackets and coolant temperature sensor, from the old head. Before installing the new head, use a gasket scraper to clean the gasket surfaces of both the head and the engine block and make sure they're free of nicks and scratches. Also, the threads in the block and on the head bolts must be completely clean, as any dirt or sealant in the

threads will affect bolt torque. Taps and dies can be used to clean the bolt holes and bolts. Gasket removal solvents are commonly available at auto parts stores and may prove helpful.
12   Place the gaskets in position over the locating dowels, with the note *This Side Up* visible.
13   Position the cylinder heads over the gaskets.
14   Coat the cylinder head bolts with an appropriate sealant and install the bolts.
15   Tighten the bolts in the proper sequence **(see illustration)** to the specified torque. Work up to the final torque in two steps.
16   Install the pushrods, making sure the lower ends are in the lifter seats, place the rocker arm ends over the pushrods and install the rocker arms. On 1986 and earlier models, install the rocker arm nuts loosely. On 1987 and later models, tighten the rocker arm nuts to the torque listed in this Chapter's Specifications.
17   The remaining installation Steps are the reverse of those for removal. On 1986 and earlier models, adjust the valve lash (refer to Section 7) before installing the valve covers.

10   Oil pan - removal and installation

Note: *Most of the Steps in this procedure will not be required if the engine has been removed from the vehicle. The pan can simply be unbolted and removed, cleaned and installed as indicated.*

Removal

1   Disconnect the cable from the negative battery terminal. **Caution:** *If the vehicle is equipped with a Delco Loc II audio system, make sure you have the correct activation code before disconnecting the battery. See the information at the front of this manual for the radio re-activation procedure.*
2   On 1987 and later models, remove the serpentine belt and remove the belt tensioner.
3   Raise the vehicle and support it on jackstands.
4   Drain the engine oil and remove the oil filter (see Chapter 1).
5   Remove the flywheel/driveplate cover.
6   Remove the starter (see Chapter 5).
7   Support the engine from above with a hoist or other suitable engine support fixture.
8   Remove the engine-to-frame mount nuts (see Section 18). Remove the right inner fender splash shield.
9   Remove the oil pan bolts. Note the different sizes used and their locations.
10   Raise the engine slightly and remove the oil pan.
11   Before installing the pan, make sure that the sealing surfaces on the pan, block and front cover are clean and free of oil. If the old pan is being reinstalled, make sure that all sealant has been removed from the pan sealing flange and from the blind attaching holes.

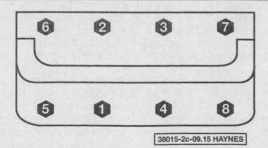

9.15 Cylinder head mounting details and recommended tightening sequence for the cylinder head mounting bolts

38015-2c-09.15 HAYNES

11.2 Oil pump mounting bolt location (arrow)

12.6 Remove the vibration damper-to-crankshaft bolt (arrow) - it's very tight, so use a six-point socket and a breaker bar

12.7 Use a puller to remove the vibration damper

Gasket removal solvents are available at auto parts stores and may prove helpful. Make sure all bolts are clean and that the pan sealing flanges are straight. To straighten a bent pan flange, support the flange from below on a piece of 1-by-4 wood and tap on the top of the pan flange with a hammer.

Installation

1986 and earlier models

12   With all the sealing surfaces clean, place a 1/8-inch bead of RTV-type sealant on the oil pan sealing flange. Make sure you run the bead to the inner side of the bolt holes or oil leaks will develop at the bolt holes.

1987 and later models

13   1987 and later models use a special one-piece neoprene gasket. Apply a bead of RTV sealant to the front of the gasket, where it contacts the front cover, then install the gasket on the pan carefully so it does not fall out of position when installed.

All models

14   Lift the pan into position and install all bolts finger tight. Tighten the bolts, working from the center out, to the torque listed in this Chapter's Specifications. Do not take more than five minutes from the time the sealant is applied to the time the bolts are tightened, otherwise the sealant will not bond properly to the block.

15   Lower the front of the engine onto the mount and install the retaining nuts. Tighten the nuts to the torque listed in this Chapter's Specifications.

16   Follow the removal steps in reverse order. Fill the crankcase with the correct grade and quantity of oil, start the engine and check for leaks.

---

11   Oil pump - removal and installation

Refer to illustration 11.2

1   Remove the oil pan (refer to Section 10).

2   Remove the pump-to-rear main bearing cap bolt and separate the pump and extension shaft from the engine **(see illustration)**.

3   Considering the relatively reasonable cost of a new oil pump compared with the potential of major engine damage if the oil pump malfunctions, we recommend replacing the oil pump any time it's removed. Inspect the extension shaft for any wear in the areas where it fits into the distributor drive gear and oil pump. Also inspect the shaft for twisting damage. Replace it if there's any wear or damage. Again, we recommend replacing the shaft as a matter of course whenever it's removed, since shaft failure means a complete loss in oil pressure.

4   Before installing the pump, prime the pump by lowering the pick-up screen into a container of clean motor oil, turn the pump driveshaft by hand until oil is forced out of the pump outlet port.

5   To install the pump, place it into position and align the top end of the hexagonal extension shaft with the hexagonal socket in the lower end of the distributor drive gear (oil pump drive on DIS models). The distributor drives the oil pump, so it is essential that this alignment is correct.

6   Install the oil pump-to-rear main bearing cap bolt and tighten it to the torque listed in this Chapter's Specifications.

7   Reinstall the oil pan. Start the engine, check for leaks and by observing the gauge or warning light, verify that the oil pressure is correct.

---

12   Vibration damper - removal and installation

Refer to illustrations 12.6 and 12.7

1   Disconnect the negative cable at the battery. **Caution:** *If the vehicle is equipped with a Delco Loc II audio system, make sure you have the correct activation code before disconnecting the battery. See the information at the front of this manual for the radio* re-activation procedure.

2   Remove the serpentine belt (see Chapter 1).

3   Raise the vehicle and support it securely on jackstands.

4   Remove the right inner fender splash shield for access.

5   Remove the flywheel/driveplate cover.

6   Remove the center bolt from the vibration damper **(see illustration)**. The crankshaft will probably rotate, since the bolt is very tight. Wedge a large screwdriver into the ring gear teeth on the flywheel/driveplate to keep the crankshaft from rotating.

7   Attach a puller to the damper. Draw the damper off the crankshaft, being careful not to drop it as it breaks free **(see illustration)**. A common gear puller should not be used to draw the damper off, as it may separate the outer portion of the damper from the hub. Use only a puller which bolts to the hub.

8   Before installing the damper, coat the front cover seal area on the damper with moly-base grease.

9   Place the damper in position over the key on the crankshaft. Make sure the damper keyway lines up with the key.

10   Using a damper installation tool to push the damper onto the crankshaft. The special tool distributes the pressure evenly around the hub.

11   Remove the installation tool and install the damper retaining bolt. Tighten the bolt to the torque listed in this Chapter's Specifications.

12   Follow the removal procedure in the reverse order for the remaining components.

---

13   Timing chain cover - removal and installation

Refer to Illustrations 13.4 and 13.15

1   Disconnect the cable from the negative battery terminal. **Caution:** *If the vehicle is equipped with a Delco Loc II audio system, make sure you have the correct activation code before disconnecting the battery. See*

13.4 On 1987 and later models, the drivebelt tensioner is secured to the timing chain cover by a bolt (arrow)

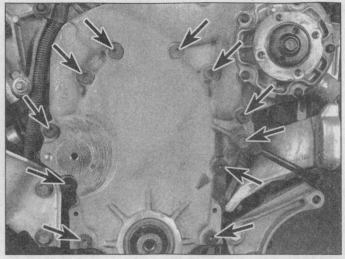

13.15 Front cover bolt locations (1987 and later models)

the information at the front of this manual for the radio re-activation procedure.

2   Drain the cooling system (see Chapter 1).

3   Remove the serpentine belt (see Chapter 1).

4   Remove the serpentine belt tensioner **(see illustration)**. **Note:** *A single bolt is used to secure the tensioner on 1987 and later models; 1986 and earlier models use a manual tensioner.*

5   Unbolt the alternator and position it aside.

6   Unbolt the power steering pump and move it aside. It is not necessary to disconnect the power steering hoses.

7   Raise the vehicle and support it on jackstands.

8   Remove the right inner fender splash shield for access.

9   Remove the vibration damper (refer to Section 12).

10   Drain the engine oil and remove the oil pan (see Section 10).

11   Remove the lower front cover bolts.

12   Lower the vehicle.

13   Disconnect the radiator hose at the water pump. Remove the water pump pulley.

14   Disconnect the heater hose, bypass and overflow hoses, and position them aside.

15   Remove the remaining front cover bolts and separate the cover from the engine block **(see illustration)**. If the cover sticks, break it loose with a soft-face hammer, but do not pry between the sealing surfaces.

16   Clean all traces of old gasket material from the front cover and engine block mating surfaces.

17   Install a new front cover gasket and apply RTV-type sealant to the bottom ends of the gasket.

18   Place the front cover in position and install the upper mounting bolts.

19   Once again, raise the vehicle and support it on jackstands.

20   Install the lower cover mounting bolts and tighten them to the torque listed in this

Chapter's Specifications.

21   Tighten the upper bolts to the torque listed in this Chapter's Specifications.

22   Install the crankshaft damper pulley.

23   Lower the vehicle.

24   Reconnect the heater hose, radiator hose, and bypass and overflow hoses.

25   Install the power steering pump.

26   Install the alternator.

27   Install the belt tensioner and serpentine belt.

28   Fill the cooling system with the proper antifreeze solution (refer to Chapter 1). Do not install the cooling system pressure cap at this time.

29   Reconnect the battery cable and start the engine. Allow it to run until the upper radiator hose becomes warm to the touch, indicating that the thermostat has opened.

30   Stop the engine and check the coolant level. Add coolant as necessary, install the pressure cap and check for leaks.

---

14   Timing chain and sprockets - removal and installation

Refer to illustrations 14.9, 14.10 and 14.13

Removal

1   Disconnect the cable from the negative battery terminal. **Caution:** *If the vehicle is equipped with a Delco Loc II audio system, make sure you have the correct activation code before disconnecting the battery. See the information at the front of this manual for the radio re-activation procedure.*

2   Remove the vibration damper (refer to Section 12).

3   Remove the timing chain cover (refer to Section 13).

4   Before removing the chain and sprockets, visually inspect the teeth on the sprockets for signs of wear and the chain for looseness.

5   If either or both sprockets show any

signs of wear (edges on the teeth of the camshaft sprocket not "square", bright blue areas on the teeth of either sprocket, chipping, pitting, etc.), they should be replaced with new ones. Wear in these areas is very common.

6   Failure to replace a worn timing chain may result in erratic engine performance, loss of power and lowered gas mileage.

7   If any one component requires replacement, all related components should be replaced as well.

8   If it is determined that the timing components require replacement, proceed as follows. **Note:** *Considering how time consuming it is to change the chain and sprockets, we recommend doing so whenever they are removed.*

9   Rotate the crankshaft until the marks on the camshaft and crankshaft are in exact alignment (this can be done by re-installing the vibration damper bolt into the end of the crankshaft and using a socket and breaker bar to turn it). At this point the number one and four pistons will be at top dead center with the number four piston in the firing position (verify by checking the position of the

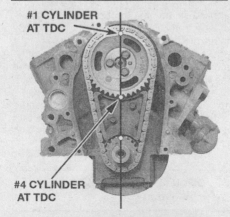

#1 CYLINDER AT TDC

#4 CYLINDER AT TDC

14.9 Proper alignment of the camshaft and crankshaft timing marks

14.10 Timing chain and sprocket installation details

14.13 Lubricate the thrust surface of the camshaft sprocket

rotor in the distributor or, on models with direct ignition, by removing the number four spark plug and feeling for compression at the spark plug hole as the crankshaft is rotated). Do not attempt to remove either sprocket or the timing chain until this is done and do not turn the crankshaft or camshaft after the sprockets and chain are removed **(see illustration)**.

10 Remove the three camshaft sprocket retaining bolts and lift the camshaft sprocket and timing chain off the front of the engine. It may be necessary to tap the sprocket with a soft-face hammer to dislodge it **(see illustration)**.

11 If it is necessary to remove the crankshaft sprocket, it can be withdrawn from the crankshaft with a puller.

Installation

12 Push the crankshaft sprocket onto the nose of the crankshaft, aligning it with the key, until it seats against the shoulder.

13 Lubricate the thrust (rear) surface of the camshaft sprocket with moly-base grease or engine assembly lube **(see illustration)**. Install the timing chain over the camshaft sprocket with slack in the chain hanging down over the crankshaft sprocket.

14 With the timing marks aligned, slip the chain over the crankshaft sprocket and then draw the camshaft sprocket into place with the three retaining bolts. Do not hammer or attempt to drive the camshaft sprocket into place, as it could dislodge the Welch plug at the rear of the engine.

15 With the chain and both sprockets in place, check again to ensure that the timing marks on the two sprockets are properly aligned. If not, remove the timing chain and cam sprocket, turn the camshaft enough to change the chain position on the crankshaft sprocket one tooth, reinstall the chain and camshaft sprocket and check the timing mark alignment. Repeat as necessary until the marks are in alignment.

16 Lubricate the chain with engine oil and install the remaining components in the reverse order of removal.

15 Camshaft - removal and installation

Since the engine must be removed from the vehicle for this procedure, the procedure is covered in Chapter 2, Part D. If your vehicle is a 1986 or earlier model, be sure to adjust the valve lash (Section 7) after the engine is reassembled.

16 Flywheel/driveplate - removal and installation

Removal

1 Disconnect the negative battery cable from the battery.

2 Raise the vehicle and support it securely on jackstands, then refer to Chapter 7 and remove the transmission. If it's leaking, now would be a very good time to have the front pump seal/O-ring replaced (auto-matic transmission only).

3 Remove the pressure plate and clutch disc (see Chapter 8) (manual transmission equipped vehicles). Now is a good time to check/replace the clutch components and pilot bearing.

4 Look for factory paint marks that indicate flywheel-to-crankshaft alignment. If they aren't there, use paint or a center-punch to make alignment marks on the flywheel/driveplate and crankshaft to ensure correct alignment during reinstallation.

5 Remove the bolts that secure the flywheel/driveplate to the crankshaft. If the crankshaft turns, wedge a screwdriver through the starter opening to jam the flywheel.

6 Remove the flywheel/driveplate from the crankshaft. **Caution:** *Since the flywheel is fairly heavy, be sure to support it while removing the last bolt.*

Installation

7 Clean the flywheel to remove grease

and oil. Inspect the surface for cracks, rivet grooves, burned areas and score marks. Light scoring can be removed with emery cloth. Check for cracked and broken ring gear teeth. Lay the flywheel on a flat surface and use a straightedge to check for warpage.

8 Clean and inspect the mating surfaces of the flywheel/driveplate and the crankshaft. If the crankshaft rear seal is leaking, replace it before reinstalling the flywheel/driveplate.

9 Position the flywheel/driveplate against the crankshaft. Be sure to align the marks made during removal. Note that some engines have an alignment dowel or staggered bolt holes to ensure correct installation.

10 Wedge a screwdriver through the starter motor opening to keep the flywheel/driveplate from turning as you tighten the bolts to the torque listed in this Chapter's Specifications.

11 The remainder of installation is the reverse of the removal procedure.

17 Crankshaft oil seals - replacement

Rear main oil seal

Refer to illustration 17.3

1 Remove the transmission (refer to Chapter 7).

2 Remove the flywheel or driveplate.

3 Pry out the old seal, taking care not to mar the crankshaft or seal bore surfaces. Inspect the crankshaft for scratches, burrs and nicks on the sealing surface **(see illustration)**.

4 A special seal installation tool (GM tool J-34686) is required to properly seat the seal in the bore without damaging it. Lubricate the seal bore, seal lip and sealing surface on the crankshaft with engine oil. Slide the seal over the mandrill on the tool until the dust lip on the seal bottoms squarely against the collar on the tool.

17.3 Use a screwdriver to pry the rear main seal from the bore (be careful not to scratch the crankshaft sealing surface or the edge of the bore)

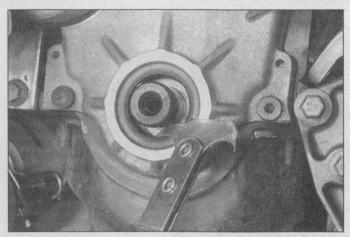

**17.9 Carefully pry the old seal out of the timing chain cover -
don't damage the crankshaft in the process**

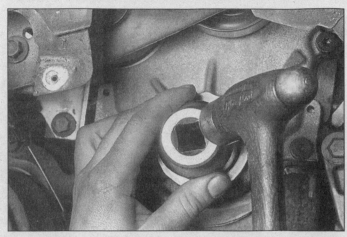

**17.11 Drive the new seal into place with a large
socket and hammer**

5   Position the dowel pin on the tool in the alignment hole in the crankshaft and secure the tool to the crankshaft.
6   Turn the T-handle of the tool until the collar pushes the seal completely into the bore. Make sure the seal is installed squarely.
7   To complete the operation, install the flywheel (or driveplate) and transmission, then start the engine and check for leaks.

Crankshaft front oil seal

Refer to illustrations 17.9 and 17.11
8   Remove the vibration damper (see Section 12). **Note:** *Always inspect the seal contact area on the vibration damper as part of this procedure. If there is a groove on the damper (caused by wear from contacting the seal), the new seal will probably leak. Auto parts stores may stock sleeves to fit over the damaged area, restoring a flat contact surface. If a sleeve is not available, the only alternative is a new vibration damper.*
9   Pry the old seal out of the crankcase front cover with a seal removal tool or screwdriver **(see illustration)**. Be careful not to damage the surface of the crankshaft or the seal bore. If you're using a screwdriver, it's a good idea to wrap the tip in tape to prevent damaging the crankshaft or seal bore.
10   Coat the inside and outside diameter of the new seal with engine oil. Place the new seal in position with the open end of the seal (seal lip) in toward the engine.
11   Drive the seal into the cover until it is seated. If the special tool is not available, a section of large-diameter pipe or a large socket can also be used **(see illustration)**.
12   Install all components previously removed. Run the engine and check for leaks.

18   Engine mounts - check and replacement

1   Mounts seldom require attention, but broken or deteriorated mounts should be replaced immediately or the added strain placed on the driveline components may cause damage or wear.

Check

2   During the check, the engine must be raised slightly to remove the weight from the mounts.
3   Raise the vehicle and support it securely on jackstands, then position a jack under the engine oil pan. Place a large block of wood between the jack head and the oil pan, then carefully raise the engine just enough to take the weight off the mounts. **Warning:** *DO NOT place any part of your body under the engine when it's supported only by a jack!*
4   Check the mounts to see if the rubber is cracked, hardened or separated from the metal plates. Sometimes the rubber will split right down the center.
5   Check for relative movement between the mount plates and the engine or frame (use a large screwdriver or pry bar to attempt to move the mounts). If no movement is noted, lower the engine and tighten the mount fasteners.
6   Rubber preservative should be applied to the mounts to slow deterioration.

Replacement

7   Raise the vehicle and support it securely on jack stands. Remove the right inner fender splash shield.
8   Raise the engine slightly, using a hoist or a jack with a wood block under the oil pan. The engine should be raised only enough to remove the weight of the engine from the mounts. **Warning:** *DO NOT place any part of your body under the engine when it's supported only by a jack!*

Front engine mount

9   Remove the engine mount-to engine bracket bolts.
10   Remove the engine mount-to-frame bracket bolts and remove the mount.
11   Clean all the engine mount bolts and apply thread locking compound to the bolt threads. Install the new mount and install the engine mount-to-frame bolts.
12   Install the engine mount to engine bracket bolts and tighten all the engine mount bolts to the torque listed in this Chapter's Specifications.

Rear engine mount

13   Remove the engine mount-to-frame bracket nuts.
14   Remove the engine mount-to-engine bracket bolts and remove the mount.
15   Clean all the engine mount bolts and apply thread locking compound to the bolt threads. Install the mount and install the engine mount-to-engine bracket bolts.
16   Install the engine mount-to-frame nuts and tighten all the engine mount nuts and bolts to the torque listed in this Chapter's Specifications.
17   Lower the engine, install the slash shield and lower the vehicle.

Chapter 2 Part D
General engine overhaul procedures

Contents

Specifications

1.8 and 2.0 liter OHC four-cylinder engines

General
Cylinder compression
  Minimum ... 100 psi
  Maximum variation between cylinders ... 25 percent
Oil pressure ... 15 psi minimum at 1000 rpm

Cylinder head
Warpage limit ... 0.005 inch

Valves and related components
Valve face angle ... 46 degrees
Valve seat angle ... 45 degrees
Valve margin width ... 0.0312 inch minimum
Stem-to-guide clearance
  Intake ... 0.0006 to 0.0017 inch
  Exhaust ... 0.0012 to 0.0024 inch
Valve spring free length ... 1.89 inch

Crankshaft and connecting rods
Crankshaft endplay ... 0.0028 to 0.012 inch
Connecting rod side clearance ... 0.0028 to 0.0095 inch
Main bearing journal
  Diameter ... 2.2828 to 2.2833 inches
  Taper limit ... 0.0002 inch
  Out-of-round limit ... 0.0002 inch
Main bearing oil clearance ... 0.0006 to 0.0016 inch
Connecting rod bearing journal
  Diameter ... 1.9278 to 1.9286 inches
  Taper limit ... 0.0002 inch
  Out-of-round limit ... 0.0002 inch
Connecting rod bearing oil clearance ... 0.0007 to 0.0024 inch

1.8 and 2.0 liter OHC four-cylinder engines (continued)

Engine block

Cylinder bore

  Diameter

    1.8 liter .... 3.336 to 3.342 inches

    2.0 liter .... 3.385 to 3.387 inches

  Out-of-round limit .... 0.005 inch

  Taper limit .... 0.005 inch

Pistons and rings

Piston-to-bore clearance

  Non-turbo .... 0.0004 to 0.0012 inch

  Turbo .... 0.0012 to 0.0020 inch

Piston ring groove clearance

  Top compression ring .... 0.002 to 0.003 inch

  2nd compression ring .... 0.001 to 0.0024 inch

Piston ring end gap

  Top compression ring .... 0.012 to 0.020 inch

  2nd compression ring .... 0.012 to 0.020 inch

  Oil control ring .... 0.016 to 0.055 inch

Camshaft

Lobe lift

  1988 and earlier .... 0.2409 inch

  1989 through 1991

    Non-turbo

      Intake 0.2366

      Exhaust 0.2515

    Turbo 0.2625

  1992 and later 0.2626

Endplay .... 0.016 to 0.064 inch

Bearing journal diameters

  No. 1

    1988 and earlier .... 1.6720 to 1.6714 inches

    1989 and later .... 1.6712 to 1.6706 inches

  No. 2 .... 1.6818 to 1.6812 inches

  No. 3 .... 1.6917 to 1.6911 inches

  No. 4 .... 1.7015 to 1.7009 inches

  No. 5

    1988 and earlier .... 1.7114 to 1.7108 inches

    1989 and later .... 1.7106 to 1.7100 inches

Bearing oil clearance

  1988 and earlier .... 0.0008 inch

  1989 and later .... 0.0011 to 0.0035 inch

Torque specifications*   **Ft-lbs** (unless otherwise noted)

Main bearing cap bolts

  1.8 liter 57

  2.0 liter

    Step 1 44

    Step 2 .... Turn an additional 40-to-50 degrees

Connecting rod cap nuts**

  1.8 liter 39

  2.0 liter

    Step 1 26

    Step 2 .... Turn an additional 40-to-50 degrees

Crankshaft pulley-to-sprocket bolt 20

Crankshaft sprocket retaining bolt 115

Driveplate-to-crankshaft bolts (automatic transmission) 48

Flywheel-to-crankshaft bolts (manual transmission)***

  1986 and earlier 45

  1987 and later

    Step 1 48

    Step 2 .... Turn an additional 30 degrees

Refer to Part B for additional torque specifications.

*** Discard the bolts each time the nuts are removed and use new ones for installation.*

**** Discard the bolts and use new bolts each time they are removed*

1.8, 2.0 and 2.2 liter OHV four-cylinder engines

General
Cylinder compression pressure	
Minimum	100 psi
Maximum variation between cylinders	30-percent
Oil pressure	15 psi minimum at 1200 rpm

Cylinder head
Warpage limit	0.005 inch

Valves and related components
Valve face angle	45-degrees
Valve seat angle	46-degrees
Valve margin width	0.0312 inch minimum
Valve stem-to-guide clearance	
Intake	0.0011 to 0.0026 inch
Exhaust	0.0014 to 0.0030 inch
Valve spring free length	
1982 through 1988	1.91 inch
1989 through 1991	2.06 inch
1992 and 1993	1.89 inch
1994	1.95 inch
Valve spring installed height	1.60 inch

Crankshaft and connecting rods
Crankshaft endplay	0.002 to 0.008 inch
Connecting rod side clearance	0.004 to 0.015 inch
Main bearing journal	
Diameter	2.4945 to 2.4954 inch
Taper limit	0.0002 inch
Out -of-round limit	0.0002 inch
Main bearing oil clearance	0.0006 to 0.0019 inch
Connecting rod journal	
Diameter	1.9983 to 1.9994 inch
Taper limit	0.0002 inch
Out-of-round limit	0.0002 inch
Connecting rod bearing oil clearance	0.001 to 0.0031 inch

Engine block
Cylinder bore	
Diameter	3.5036 to 3.5043 inch
Out-of-round limit	0.0005 inch
Taper limit	0.0005 inch

Pistons and rings
Piston-to-bore clearance	0.0007 to 0.0017 inch
Piston ring groove clearance	
Compression rings	0.0019 to 0.0027 inch
Oil control ring	0.0019 to 0.0082 inch
Piston ring end gap	
Compression rings	0.010 to 0.020 inch
Oil control ring	0.010 to 0.050 inch

Camshaft
Lobe lift	
1982 through 1988	0.260 inch
1989	0.262 inch
1990 and 1991	0.259 inch
1992 and 1993	
Intake	0.259 inch
Exhaust	0.250 inch
1994	0.288 inch
Bearing journal diameter	1.867 to 1.869 inch
Bearing oil clearance	0.001 to 0.0039 inch

1.8, 2.0 and 2.2 liter OHV four-cylinder engines (continued)

Torque specifications*	Ft-lbs
Main bearing cap bolts	70
Connecting rod cap nuts	38
Camshaft thrust plate-to-block bolts	9
Flywheel/driveplate-to-block bolts	55
Crankshaft pulley center bolt	77

Refer to Part A for additional torque specifications.

2.8 and 3.1 liter V6 engines

General

Cylinder compression	
Minimum	100 psi
Maximum variation between cylinders	30 percent
Oil pressure	15 psi minimum at 1100 rpm

Cylinder head

Cylinder head warpage limit	0.005 inch

Valves and related components

Valve face angle	45-degrees
Valve seat angle	46-degrees
Stem-to-guide clearance	
Intake	0.0011 to 0.0026 inch
Exhaust	0.0014 to 0.0030 inch
Valve margin width	0.0312 inch minimum
Valve spring free length	1.91 inches
Valve spring installed height	
1992 and earlier	1.5748 inch
1993 and later	1.693 inch

Crankshaft and connecting rods

Crankshaft endplay	0.0024 to 0.0083 inch
Connecting rod side clearance	
1987 and earlier	0.006 to 0.017 inch
1988 through 1992	0.014 to 0.027 inch
1993 and later	0.007 to 0.017 inch
Main bearing journal	
Diameter	2.6473 to 2.6483 inches
Taper limit	0.0002 inch
Out-of-round limit	0.0002 inch
Main bearing oil clearance	
1987 and earlier	0.0016 to 0.0032 inch
1988 and 1989	0.0012 to 0.0027 inch
1990 and later	0.0012 to 0.0030 inch
Connecting rod bearing journal	
Diameter	1.9983 to 1.9994 inches
Taper limit	0.0002 inch
Out-of-round limit	0.0002 inch
Connecting rod bearing oil clearance	
1989 and earlier	0.0014 to 0.0036 inch
1990 and later	0.0011 to 0.0034 inch

Engine block

Cylinder bore diameter	
1987 and earlier	3.503 to 3.506 inches
1988 and 1989	3.5033 to 3.5046 inches
1990 and later	3.5046 to 3.5053 inches
Out-of-round limit	0.0005 inch
Taper limit	0.0005 inch

Pistons and rings

Compression ring groove clearance
    Top compression ring

1987 and earlier	0.001 to 0.003 inch
1988 and later	0.002 to 0.0035 inch

    Second compression ring

1987 and earlier	0.001 to 0.003 inch
1988 and later	0.002 to 0.0035 inch
Oil ring groove clearance (maximum)	0.008 inch

Piston ring end gap (compression rings only)

1989 and earlier	0.010 to 0.020 inch

    1990 and later

Top compression ring	0.010 to 0.020 inch
Second compression ring	0.020 to 0.028 inch

Piston-to-bore clearance

1986 and earlier	0.0012 to 0.0022 inch
1987 and 1988	0.0020 to 0.0028 inch
1989 and later	0.0009 to 0.0023 inch

Camshaft

Lobe lift

Intake	0.2626 inch
Exhaust...	0.2732 inch

Bearing journal diameter

1992 and earlier	1.8678 to 1.8815 inch

    1993 and later

No. 1 and 4	2.009 to 2.011 inch
No. 2 and 3	1.999 to 2.001 inch
Bearing oil clearance	0.001 to 0.004 inch

Torque specifications*

	Ft-lbs
Main bearing cap bolts	73
Connecting rod cap nuts	39
Crankshaft balancer bolt	76
Flywheel/driveplate bolts	58

Refer to Part C for additional torque specifications

1   General information

Included in this portion of Chapter 2 are the general overhaul procedures for the cylinder head and internal engine components. The information ranges from advice concerning preparation for an overhaul and the purchase of replacement parts to detailed, step-by-step procedures covering removal and installation of internal engine components and the inspection of parts.

The following Sections have been written based on the assumption that the engine has been removed from the vehicle. For information concerning in-vehicle engine repair, as well as removal and installation of the external components necessary for the overhaul, see Part A, B or C of this Chapter (depending on engine type) and Section 8 of this Part.

The Specifications included here in Part D are only those necessary for the inspection and overhaul procedures which follow. Refer to Part A, B or C for additional specifications related to the various engines covered in this manual.

2   Engine overhaul - general information

Refer to illustration 2.4

It is not always easy to determine when, or if, an engine should be completely overhauled, as a number of factors must be considered.

High mileage is not necessarily an indication that an overhaul is needed, while low mileage does not preclude the need for an overhaul. Frequency of servicing is probably the most important consideration. An engine that has had regular and frequent oil and filter changes, as well as other required maintenance, will most likely give many thousands of miles of reliable service. Conversely, a neglected engine may require an overhaul very early in its life.

Excessive oil consumption is an indication that piston rings and/or valve guides are in need of attention. Make sure, however, that oil leaks are not responsible before deciding that the rings and guides are bad. Have a compression or leak-down test performed by an experienced tune-up mechanic to determine the extent of the work required.

2.4 On 2.8L/3.1L V6 engines, the oil pressure sending unit is located just behind the oil filter adapter (arrow)

If the engine is making obvious knocking or rumbling noises, the connecting rod and/or main bearings are probably at fault. Check the oil pressure with a gauge, installed in place of the oil pressure sending unit, and compare it to the Specifications. **Note:** *The oil pressure sending unit on most models is near the oil filter* **(see illustration)**. If it is

3.4 Use a compression gauge to check cylinder compression

extremely low, the bearings and/or oil pump are probably worn out.

Loss of power, rough running, excessive valve train noise and high fuel consumption rates may also point to the need for an overhaul, especially if they are all present at the same time. If a complete tune-up does not remedy the situation, major mechanical work is the only solution.

An engine overhaul involves restoring the internal parts to the specifications of a new engine. During an overhaul, the piston rings are replaced and the cylinder walls are reconditioned (rebored or honed). If a rebore is done, new pistons are also required. The main and connecting rod bearings are replaced with new ones and, if necessary, the crankshaft may be reground to restore the journals. Generally, the valves are serviced as well, since they are usually in less-than-perfect condition at this point. While the engine is being overhauled, other components, such as the carburetor, distributor, starter and alternator can be rebuilt as well. The end result should be a like-new engine that will give many thousands of trouble-free miles.

Before beginning the engine overhaul, read through the entire procedure to familiarize yourself with the scope and requirements of the job. Overhauling an engine is not difficult, but it is time consuming. Plan on the vehicle being tied up for a minimum of two weeks, especially if parts must be taken to an automotive machine shop for repair or reconditioning. Check on availability of parts and make sure that any necessary special tools and equipment are obtained in advance. Most work can be done with typical hand tools, although a number of precision measuring tools are required for inspecting parts to determine if they must be replaced. Often an automotive machine shop will handle the inspection of parts and offer advice concerning reconditioning and replacement. **Note:** *Always wait until the engine has been completely disassembled and all components, especially the engine block, have been inspected before deciding what service and repair operations must be performed by an*

automotive machine shop. Since the block's condition will be the major factor to consider when determining whether to overhaul the original engine or buy a rebuilt one, never purchase parts or have machine work done on other components until the block has been thoroughly inspected. As a general rule, time is the primary cost of an overhaul, so it does not pay to install worn or sub-standard parts.

As a final note, to ensure maximum life and minimum trouble from a rebuilt engine, everything must be assembled with care in a spotlessly clean environment.

3   Compression check

Refer to illustration 3.4

1   A compression check will tell you what mechanical condition the engine is in. Specifically, it can tell you if the compression is down due to leakage caused by worn piston rings, defective valves and seats or a blown head gasket.
Note: *The engine must be at normal operating temperature and the battery must be fully charged for this check.*
2   Begin by cleaning the area around the spark plugs before you remove them. This will keep dirt from falling into the cylinders while you are performing the compression test.
3   Disconnect the coil wire from the distributor or the small-wire electrical connector from the direct ignition system coil pack. Block the throttle and choke valve (if equipped) open.
4   With the compression gauge in the number one spark plug hole, crank the engine over at least four compression strokes and observe the gauge **(see illustration)**. The compression should build up quickly in a healthy engine. Low compression on the first stroke, which does not build up during successive strokes, indicates leaking valves, a blown head gasket or a cracked head. Record the highest gauge reading obtained.
5   Repeat the procedure for the remaining cylinders. The lowest compression reading should not be less than 70% of the highest reading. No reading should be less than 100 lbs.
6   If the readings are below normal, pour a couple of teaspoons of engine oil (a squirt can works great for this) into each cylinder, through the spark plug hole, and repeat the test.
7   If the compression increases after the oil is added, the piston rings are worn. If the compression does not increase significantly, the leakage is occurring at the valves or head gasket. Leakage past the valves may be caused by burned valve seats or faces or warped, cracked or bent valves.
8   If two adjacent cylinders have equally low compression, there is a strong possibility that the head gasket between them is blown. The appearance of coolant in the combustion

chambers or the crankcase would verify this condition.
9   If the compression is higher than normal, the combustion chambers are probably coated with carbon deposits. If that it the case, the cylinder head(s) should be removed and decarbonized.
10   If compression is down or varies greatly between cylinders, it would be a good idea to have a leak-down test performed by an automotive repair shop. This test will pinpoint exactly where the leakage is occurring and how severe it is.

4   Vacuum gauge diagnostic checks

Refer to illustration 4.5

1   A vacuum gauge provides valuable information about what is going on in the engine at a low cost. You can check for worn rings or cylinder walls, leaking head or intake manifold gaskets, vacuum leaks in the intake manifold, restricted exhaust, stuck or burned valves, weak valve springs, improper valve timing, and ignition problems. Vacuum gauge readings are easy to misinterpret, however, so they should be used in conjunction with other tests to confirm the diagnosis.
2   Both the absolute readings and the rate of needle movement are important for accurate interpretation. Most gauges measure vacuum in inches of mercury (in-Hg). The following references to vacuum assume the diagnosis is being performed at sea level. As elevation increases (or atmospheric pressure decreases), the reading will decrease. For every 1,000 foot increase in elevation above approximately 2000 feet, the gauge readings will decrease about one inch of mercury.
3   Connect the vacuum gauge directly to intake manifold vacuum, not to ported (throttle body) vacuum. Be sure no hoses are left disconnected during the test or false readings will result. **Note:** *Do not disconnect engine sensors or vacuum solenoids to connect the vacuum gauge. Disconnected engine control components can affect engine operation and produce abnormal vacuum gauge readings.*
4   Before you begin the test, warm the engine up completely. Block the wheels and set the parking brake. With the transmission in Park, start the engine and allow it to run at normal idle speed. **Warning:** *Carefully inspect the fan blades for cracks or damage before starting the engine. Keep your hands and the vacuum gauge clear of the fan and do not stand in front of the vehicle or in line with the fan when the engine is running.*
5   Read the vacuum gauge; an average, healthy engine should normally produce about 17 to 22 inches of vacuum with a fairly steady gauge needle at idle. Refer to the following vacuum gauge readings and what they indicate about the engine's condition **(see illustration):**
6   A low steady reading usually indicates a

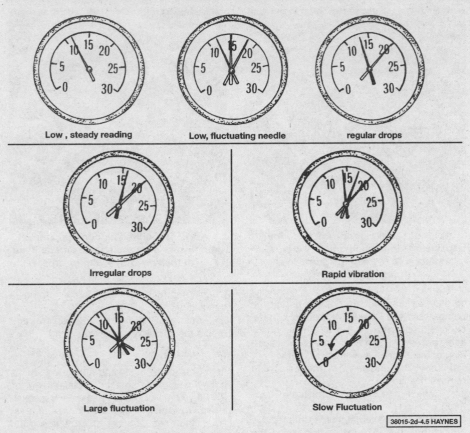

Low , steady reading   Low, fluctuating needle   regular drops

Irregular drops   Rapid vibration

Large fluctuation   Slow Fluctuation

38015-2d-4.5 HAYNES

4.5 Typical vacuum gauge diagnostic readings

leaking intake manifold gasket. this could be at one of the cylinder heads, between the upper and lower manifolds, or at the throttle body. Other possible causes are a leaky vacuum hose or incorrect camshaft timing.

7   If the reading is 3 to 8 inches below normal and it fluctuates at that low reading, suspect an intake manifold gasket leak at an intake port or a faulty fuel injector.

8   If the needle regularly drops about two to four inches at a steady rate, the valves are probably leaking. Perform a compression check or leakdown test to confirm this.

9   An irregular drop or downward flicker of the needle can be caused by a sticking valve or an ignition misfire. Perform a compression check or leakdown test and inspect the spark plugs to identify the faulty cylinder.

10   A rapid needle vibration of about four inches at idle combined with exhaust smoke indicates worn valve guides. Perform a leakdown test to confirm this. If the rapid vibration occurs with an increase in engine speed, check for a leaking intake manifold gasket or head gasket, weak valve springs, burned valves, or ignition misfire.

11   A slight fluctuation - one inch up and down - may mean ignition problems. Check all the usual tune-up items and, if necessary, run the engine on an ignition analyzer.

12   If there is a large fluctuation, perform a compression or leakdown test to look for a weak or dead cylinder or a blown head gasket.

13   If the needle moves slowly through a wide range, check for a clogged PCV system or intake manifold gasket leaks.

14   Check for a slow return of the gauge to a normal idle reading after revving the engine by quickly snapping the throttle open until the engine reaches about 2,500 rpm and let it shut. Normally the reading should drop to near zero, rise about 5 inches above normal idle reading, and then return to the previous idle reading. If the vacuum returns slowly and doesn't peak when the throttle is snapped shut, the rings may be worn. If there is a long delay, look for a restricted exhaust system (often the muffler or catalytic converter). One way to check this is to temporarily disconnect the exhaust ahead of the suspected part and repeat the test.

5   Engine removal - methods and precautions

If it has been decided that an engine must be removed for overhaul or major repair work, certain preliminary steps should be taken.

Locating a suitable work area is extremely important. A shop is, of course, the most desirable place to work. Adequate work space, along with storage space for the vehicle, is very important. If a shop or garage is not available, at the very least a flat, level,

clean work surface made of concrete or asphalt is required.

Cleaning the engine compartment and engine prior to removal will help keep tools clean and organized.

An engine hoist or A-frame will also be necessary. Make sure that the equipment is rated in excess of the combined weight of the engine and its accessories. Safety is of primary importance, considering the potential hazards involved in lifting the engine out of the vehicle.

If the engine is being removed by a novice, a helper should be available. Advice and aid from someone more experienced would also be helpful. There are many instances when one person cannot simultaneously perform all of the operations required when lifting the engine out of the vehicle.

Plan the operation ahead of time. Arrange for or obtain all the tools and equipment you will need prior to beginning the job. Some of the equipment necessary to perform engine removal and installation safely and with relative ease are, in addition to an engine hoist, a heavy-duty floor jack, a complete set of wrenches and sockets as described in the front of this manual, wooden blocks and plenty of rags and cleaning solvent for mopping up the inevitable spills. If the hoist is to be rented, make sure that you arrange for it in advance and perform beforehand all of the operations possible without it. This will save you money and time.

Plan for the vehicle to be out of use for a considerable amount of time. A machine shop will be required to perform some of the work which the do-it-yourselfer cannot accomplish due to a lack of special equipment. These shops often have a busy schedule, so it would be wise to consult them before removing the engine in order to accurately estimate the amount of time required to rebuild or repair components that may need work.

Always use extreme caution when removing and installing the engine. Serious injury can result from careless actions. Plan ahead. Take your time and a job of this nature, although major, can be accomplished successfully.

6   Engine - removal and installation

Warning 1: *Gasoline is extremely flammable, so take extra precautions when you work on any part of the fuel system. don't smoke or allow open flames or bare light bulbs near the work area, and don't work in a garage where a natural gas-type appliance (such as a water heater or clothes dryer) with a pilot light is present. If you spill any fuel on your skin, rinse it off immediately with soap and water. When you perform any kind of work on the fuel system, wear safety glasses and have a Class B type fire extinguisher on hand.*

Warning 2: *The air conditioning system is under high pressure! Have a dealer service department or automotive air conditioning*

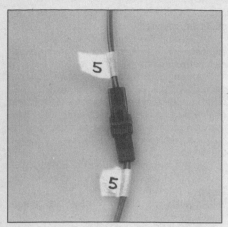

6.5 Label each hose and electrical connection with pieces of numbered tape before disconnecting them

6.11 Use a wire or or rope to tie the power steering pump out of the way - make sure to keep the pump in an upright position

6.12 Unbolt the air conditioning compressor from the engine and tie it out of the way with a wire or rope

shop discharge the system before disconnecting any air conditioning system hoses or fittings.
Note: *Read through the following Steps carefully and familiarize yourself with the procedure before beginning work.*

Removal

Refer to illustrations 6.5, 6.11, 6.12 and 6.19

1   Refer to Chapter 4 and relieve the fuel system pressure (fuel-injected models only), then disconnect the negative cable from the battery.

2   Cover the fenders and cowl and remove the hood (see Chapter 11). Special pads are available to protect the fenders, but an old bedspread or blanket will also work.

3   Remove the air cleaner assembly.

4   Drain the cooling system (see Chapter 1).

5   Label the vacuum lines, emissions system hoses, wiring connectors, ground straps and fuel lines, to ensure correct reinstallation, then detach them. Pieces of masking tape with numbers or letters written on them work well **(see illustration)**. If there's any possibility of confusion, make a sketch of the engine compartment and clearly label the lines, hoses and wires. Photographs may also help.

6   Label and detach all coolant hoses from the engine.

7   Disconnect the engine mounting torque strut from the bracket on the engine (if equipped), loosen the through-bolt at the other end of the strut and rotate the strut out of the way.

8   Remove the drivebelts (see Chapter 1).

9   Disconnect the fuel lines running from the engine to the chassis (see Chapter 4). Plug or cap all open fittings/lines.

10   Disconnect the throttle linkage (and TV linkage/speed control cable, if equipped) from the engine (see Chapter 4).

11   On power-steering-equipped models, unbolt the power steering pump (see Chapter 10). Leave the lines/hoses attached and make sure the pump is kept in an upright position in the engine compartment **(see illustration)**.

12   On air conditioned models, unbolt the compressor (see Chapter 3) and set it aside. Do not disconnect the hoses unless absolutely necessary. See Warning 2 at the beginning of this Section **(see illustration)**.

13   Drain the engine oil (Chapter 1) and remove the filter.

14   Remove the starter motor (see Chapter 5).

15   Remove the alternator (see Chapter 5).

16   Unbolt the exhaust system from the engine (see Chapter 4).

17   If you're working on a vehicle with an automatic transaxle, refer to Chapter 7 and remove the torque converter-to-driveplate fasteners.

18   Support the transaxle with a jack. Position a block of wood between them to prevent damage to the transaxle. Special transmission jacks with safety chains are available - use one if possible.

19   Attach an engine sling or a length of chain to the lifting brackets on the engine **(see illustration)**.

20   Roll the hoist into position and connect the sling to it. Take up the slack in the sling or chain, but don't lift the engine. **Warning:** *DO NOT place any part of your body under the engine when it's supported only by a hoist or other lifting device.*

21   Remove the transaxle-to-engine block bolts.

22   Remove the engine mount-to-frame bolts.

23   Recheck to be sure nothing is still connecting the engine to the transaxle or vehicle. Disconnect anything still remaining.

24   Raise the engine slightly. Carefully separate it from the transaxle. If you're working on a vehicle with an automatic transaxle, be sure the torque converter stays in the transaxle (clamp a pair of vise-grips to the housing to keep the converter from sliding out). If you're working on a vehicle with a manual transaxle, the input shaft must be completely disengaged from the clutch. Slowly raise the engine out of the engine compartment.

Check carefully to make sure nothing is hanging up.

25   Remove the flywheel/driveplate and mount the engine on an engine stand.

Installation

26   Check the engine and transaxle mounts. If they're worn or damaged, replace them.

27   If you're working on a manual transaxle-equipped vehicle, install the clutch and pressure plate (see Chapter 8). Now is a good time to install a new clutch.

28   Carefully lower the engine into the engine compartment - make sure the engine mounts line up.

29   Align the engine with the transaxle bellhousing and carefully slide them together. Make sure the dowel pins line up and the transaxle input shaft (manual transaxle models) slides into the clutch friction disc.

30   Install the transaxle-to-engine bolts and tighten them securely. **Caution:** *DO NOT use the bolts to force the transaxle and engine together!*

31   Reinstall the remaining components in the reverse order of removal.

32   Add coolant, oil, power steering and transmission fluid as needed.

33   Run the engine and check for leaks and proper operation of all accessories, then install the hood and test drive the vehicle.

34   Have the air conditioning system recharged and leak tested.

7   Engine rebuilding alternatives

The do-it-yourselfer is faced with a number of options when performing an engine overhaul. The decision to replace the engine block, piston/connecting rod assemblies and crankshaft depends on a number of factors, with the primary consideration being the condition of the block. Other considerations are cost, access to machine shop facilities, parts availability, time required to complete the project and experience.

6.19 Attach the chain or hoist cable to the engine brackets (arrows) - V6 shown

Some of the rebuilding alternatives include:

Individual parts - If the inspection procedures reveal that the engine block and most engine components are in reusable condition, purchasing individual parts may be the most economical alternative. The block, crankshaft and piston/connecting rod assemblies should all be inspected carefully. Even if the block shows little wear, the cylinder bores should receive a finish hone; a job for an automotive machine shop.

Master kit (crankshaft kit) - This rebuild package usually consists of a re-ground crankshaft and a matched set of pistons, connecting rods and bearings. The pistons will already be installed on the connecting rods. These kits are commonly available for standard cylinder bores, as well as for engine blocks which have been bored to a regular oversize.

Short block - A short block consists of an engine block with a crankshaft, camshaft and piston/connecting rod assemblies already installed. All new bearings are incorporated and all clearances will be correct. Depending on where the short block is purchased, a guarantee may be included. The existing valve train components, cylinder head and external parts can be bolted to the short block with little or no machine shop work necessary.

Long block - A long block consists of a short block plus an oil pump, oil pan, cylinder head and valve train components, timing sprockets and chain and timing chain cover. All components are installed with new bearings, seals and gaskets incorporated throughout. The installation of manifolds and external parts is all that is necessary. Some form of guarantee is usually included with the purchase.

Give careful thought to which alternative is best for you and discuss the situation with local automotive machine shops, auto parts dealers or dealership parts personnel before ordering or purchasing replacement parts.

8 Engine overhaul disassembly sequence

1 It's much easier to disassemble and work on the engine if it's mounted on a portable engine stand. These stands can often be rented quite cheaply from an equipment rental yard. Before the engine is mounted on a stand, the flywheel/driveplate should be removed from the crankshaft.

2 If a stand isn't available, it's possible to disassemble the engine with it blocked up on a sturdy workbench or on the floor. Be extra careful not to tip or drop the engine when working without a stand.

3 If you're going to buy a rebuilt engine, all external components must come off first, to be transferred to the replacement engine, just as they will if you're doing a complete engine overhaul yourself. They include:

Alternator and brackets
Emissions control components
Distributor, spark plug wires and spark plugs
Thermostat and housing cover
Water pump
EFI components
Intake/exhaust manifolds
Oil filter
Engine mounts
Clutch and flywheel or driveplate

Note: *When removing the external/ components from the engine, pay close attention to details that may be helpful or important during reassembly. Note the installed position of gaskets. seals, spacers, pins, washers, bolts and other small items.*

4 If you're installing a short block, which consists of the engine block, crankshaft, pistons and connecting rods all assembled, then the cylinder head(s), oil pan and oil pump will have to be removed as well. See *Engine rebuilding alternatives* for additional information regarding the different possibilities to be considered.

5 If you're planning a complete overhaul, the engine must be disassembled and the internal components removed in the following general order:

OHC four-cylinder engines
Clutch and flywheel or driveplate
Camshaft cover
Intake and exhaust manifolds
Timing belt/sprockets
Camshaft carrier
Camshaft
Cylinder head
Oil pan
Oil pump
Piston/connecting rod assemblies
Crankshaft and main bearings

OHV four-cylinder and V6 engines
Clutch and flywheel or driveplate
Rocker arm covers
Intake and exhaust manifolds
Rocker arms and pushrods
Valve lifters
Cylinder head(s)
Timing cover
Timing chain and sprockets
Camshaft
Oil pan
Oil pump
Piston/connecting rod assemblies
Crankshaft and main bearings

6 Critical cooling system components such as the hoses, drivebelts, thermostat and water pump MUST be replaced with new parts when an engine is overhauled. Also, we don't recommend overhauling the oil pump, always install a new one when an engine is rebuilt.

7 Before beginning the disassembly and overhaul procedures, make sure the following items are available:

Common hand tools
Small cardboard boxes or plastic bags for storing parts
Gasket scraper
Ridge reamer
Vibration damper puller
Micrometers
Telescoping gauges
Dial indicator set
Valve spring compressor
Cylinder surfacing hone
Piston ring groove cleaning tool
Electric drill motor
Tap and die set
Wire brushes
Oil gallery brushes
Cleaning solvent

9 Cylinder head - disassembly

Refer to illustrations 9.4a and 9.4b
Note: *New and rebuilt cylinder heads are commonly available for most engines at dealerships and auto parts stores. Due to the fact that some specialized tools are necessary for the disassembly and inspection procedures, and replacement parts may not be readily available, it may be more practical and economical for the home mechanic to purchase a replacement head rather than taking the time to disassemble, inspect and recondition the original head.*

1 On OHC engines, separate the camshaft carrier from the cylinder head and remove the rocker arms and valve lash compensators.

2 Cylinder head disassembly involves removal of the intake and exhaust valves and their related components. If they are still in place, remove the nuts or bolts and pivot balls, then separate the rocker arms and/or shafts from the cylinder head. Label the parts or store them separately so they can be reinstalled in their original locations.

3 Before the valves are removed, arrange to label and store them, along with their related components, so they can be kept separate and reinstalled in the same valve guides.

4 Compress the valve spring with a spring compressor and remove the keepers **(see**

9.4a Use a valve spring compressor to compress the springs, then remove the keepers from the valve stem with a magnet or small needle-nose pliers

9.4b If you can't pull the valve through the guide, deburr the edge of the stem end and the area around the top of the keeper groove with a file or whetstone

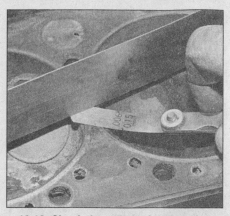

10.12 Check the cylinder head gasket surface for warpage by trying to slip a feeler gauge under the straightedge (see this chapter's Specifications for the maximum warpage allowed and use a feeler gauge of that thickness)

illustration). Carefully release the valve spring compressor and remove the retainer, the shield (if so equipped), exhaust valve rotators (if so equipped), the springs, the valve guide seal and/or O-ring seal, any spring seat shims and the valve from the head. If the valve binds in the guide (won't pull through), push it back into the head and deburr the area around the keeper groove with a fine file or whetstone **(see illustration)**.

5   Repeat the procedure for the remaining valves. Remember to keep together all the parts for each valve so they can be reinstalled in the same locations.

6   Once the valves have been removed and safely stored, the head should be thoroughly cleaned and inspected. If a complete engine overhaul is being done, finish the engine disassembly procedures before beginning the cylinder head cleaning and inspection process.

10 Cylinder head - cleaning and inspection

Cleaning

1   Thorough cleaning of the cylinder head and related valve train components, followed by a detailed inspection, will enable you to decide how much valve service work must be done during the engine overhaul.

2   Scrape away all traces of old gasket material and sealing compound from the head gasket, intake manifold and exhaust manifold sealing surfaces.

3   Remove any built-up scale around the coolant passages.

4   Run a stiff wire brush through the oil holes to remove any deposits that may have formed in them.

5   It is a good idea to run a tap into each of the threaded holes to remove any corrosion and thread sealant that may be present. If compressed air is available, use it to clear the holes of the debris produced by this operation.

6   Clean the exhaust and intake manifold stud threads with a die. Clean the rocker arm pivot bolt or stud threads with a wire brush.

7   Clean the cylinder head with solvent and dry it thoroughly. Compressed air will speed the drying process and ensure that all holes and recessed areas are clean. **Note:** *Decarbonizing chemicals are available and may prove very useful when cleaning cylinder heads and valve train components. They are very caustic and should be used with caution. Be sure to follow the instructions on the container.*

8   Clean the rocker arms, pivot balls and pushrods with solvent and dry them thoroughly. Compressed air will speed the drying process and can be used to clean out the oil passages.

9   Clean all the valve springs, keepers, retainers, shields and spring seat shims with solvent and dry them thoroughly. Work on the components from one valve at a time to avoid mixing up the parts.

10   Scrape off any heavy deposits that may have formed on the valves, then use a motorized wire brush to remove deposits from the valve heads and stems. Again, make sure the valves don't get mixed up.

Inspection
Cylinder head
Refer to illustrations 10.12, 10.14a and 10.14b

11   Inspect the head very carefully for cracks, evidence of coolant leakage or other damage. If cracks are found, a new cylinder head should be obtained.

12   Using a straightedge and feeler gauge, check the head gasket mating surface for warpage **(see illustration)**. If the warpage exceeds 0.005 inch over the length of the head, it can be resurfaced at an automotive machine shop.

13   Examine the valve seats in each of the combustion chambers. If they are pitted, cracked or burned, the head will require valve service that is beyond the scope of the home mechanic.

14   Measure the inside diameter of the valve guides (at both ends and the center of each guide) with a small hole gauge and a 0-to-1-inch micrometer **(see illustration)**. Record the measurements for future reference. These measurements, along with the valve stem

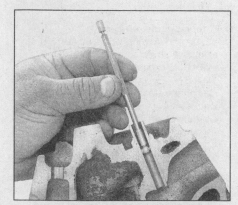

10.14a Use a small-hole gauge to determine the inside diameter of the valve guides (the gauge is then measured with a micrometer)

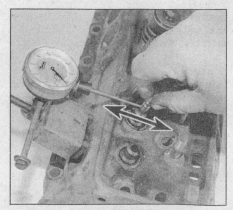

10.14b A dial indicator can also be used to determine the valve stem-to-guide clearance

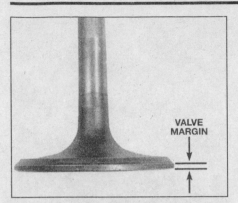

10.19 The margin width on each valve must be no less than specified (if no margin exists, the valve must be replaced)

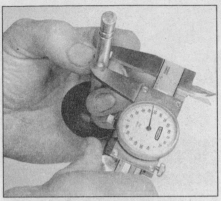

10.20 Measure the valve stem diameter at three points

10.21a Measure the free length of each valve spring with a dial or vernier caliper

10.21b Check each valve spring for squareness

diameter measurements, will enable you to compute the valve stem-to-guide clearance. This clearance, when compared to the Specifications, will be one factor that will determine the extent of valve service work required. The guides are measured at the ends and at the center to determine if they are worn in a bell-mouth pattern (more wear at the ends). If they are, guide reconditioning or replacement is necessary. As an alternative to using a small-hole gauge and micrometer, use a dial indicator to measure the lateral movement of each valve stem with the valve in the guide and approximately 1/16-inch off the seat **(see illustration)**.

Rocker arm components

15   Check the rocker arm faces, where they contact the pushrod ends and valve stems, for pits, wear and rough spots. Check the pivot contact areas as well.
16   Inspect the pushrod ends for scuffing and excessive wear. Roll the pushrod on a flat surface, such as a piece of glass, to determine if it is bent.
17   Any damaged or excessively worn parts must be replaced with new ones.

Valves

Refer to illustrations 10.19 and 10.20
18   Carefully inspect each valve face for cracks, pits and burned spots. Check the valve stem and neck for cracks. Rotate the valve and check for any obvious indication that it is bent. Check the end of the stem for pits and excessive wear. The presence of any of these conditions indicates the need for valve service by a properly equipped shop.
19   Measure the width of the valve margin on each valve and compare it to this Chapter's Specifications. Any valve with a margin narrower than specified will have to be replaced with a new one **(see illustration)**.
20   Measure the valve stem diameter **(see illustration)**. By subtracting the stem diameter from the corresponding valve guide diameter, the valve stem-to-guide clearance is obtained. Compare the results to this Chapter's Specifications. If the stem-to-guide clearance is greater than specified, the

guides will have to be reconditioned and new valves may have to be installed, depending on the condition of the old valves.

Valve components

Refer to illustrations 10.21a and 10.21b
21   Check each valve spring for wear and pits on the ends. Measure the free length and compare it to this Chapter's Specifications **(see illustration)**. Any springs that are shorter than specified have sagged and should not be reused. Stand the spring on a flat surface and check it for squareness **(see illustration)**. Any spring that is out-of-square should be discarded.
22   Check the spring retainers and keepers for obvious wear and cracks. Any questionable parts should be replaced with new ones, as extensive damage will occur in the event of failure during engine operation.
23   If the inspection process indicates that the valve components are in generally poor condition and worn beyond the limits specified, which is usually the case in an engine that is being overhauled, reassemble the valves in the cylinder head and refer to Section 11 for valve servicing recommendations.
24   If the inspection turns up no excessively worn parts, and if the valve faces and seats are in good condition, the valve train components can be reinstalled in the cylinder head without major servicing. Refer to the appropriate Section for cylinder head reassembly procedures.

11   Valves - servicing

1   Because of the complex nature of the job and the special tools and equipment needed, servicing of the valves, the valve seats and the valve guides (commonly known as a valve job) is best left to a professional.
2   The home mechanic can remove and disassemble the head, do the initial cleaning and inspection, then reassemble and deliver the head to a dealer service department or an automotive machine shop for the actual valve servicing.
3   The dealer service department, or automotive machine shop, will remove the valves

and springs, recondition or replace the valves and valve seats, recondition the valve guides, check and replace the valve springs, spring retainers and keepers (as necessary), replace the valve seals with new ones, reassemble the valve components and make sure the installed spring height is correct. The cylinder head gasket surface will also be resurfaced if it is warped.
4   After the valve job has been performed by a professional, the head will be in like-new condition. When the head is returned, be sure to clean it again to remove any metal particles and abrasive grit that may still be present from the valve service or head resurfacing operations. Use compressed air, if available, to blow out all the oil holes and passages.

12   Cylinder head - reassembly

Refer to illustrations 12.12 and 12.13
1   Regardless of whether or not the head was sent to an automotive repair shop for valve servicing, make sure it is clean before beginning reassembly.
2   If the head was sent out for valve servicing, the valves and related components will already be in place.
3   Install new seals on each of the valve guides.

OHC four cylinder engines

4   Coat the first valve stem with clean engine oil then slide the supplied plastic sleeve onto the valve stem.

5   Slide the new valve stem oil seal over the valve stem, seat it over the valve guide using the plastic sleeve and then remove the sleeve. Repeat the procedure for the remaining valves.

6   Install the valve spring and retainers and use a valve spring compressor to install the keepers.

7   Install the valve lash compensators and rocker arms.

8   Install the camshaft into the camshaft carrier (see Part B).

OHV four cylinder and V6 engines

9   Using a hammer and a deep socket, gently tap each seal into place until it is properly seated on the guide. Do not twist or cock the seals during installation or they will not seal properly on the valve stems.

10   Install the valves, taking care not to damage the new valve stem oil seals, drop the valve spring shim(s) and exhaust valve rotators around the valve guide boss and set the valve spring, cap and retainer in place.

11   Compress the spring with a valve compressor tool and install the valve locks. Release the compressor tool, making sure the locks are seated properly in the valve stem upper groove. If necessary, grease can be used to hold the locks in place while the compressor tool is released.

12   Check the valve spring installed height for each valve **(see illustration)**. The top of the retainer should be at the installed height listed in this Chapter's Specifications. If it is not, install an additional valve spring seat shim (available from your dealer) to bring the top of the retainer to the specified height.

13   On models equipped with O-ring-type seals, check the seals with a vacuum pump and adapter **(see illustration)**. A properly installed oil seal should not leak vacuum.

14   Install the rocker arms and tighten the

12.12 Measure the valve spring installed height

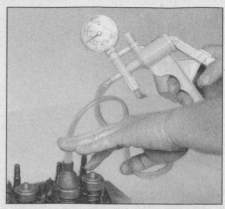

12.13 Check the valve stem seals for leakage (models with O-ring type seals)

nuts to the specified torque. Be sure to lubricate the ball pivots with moly-base grease or engine assembly lube.

13   Camshaft - removal, inspection and installation

Camshaft lobe lift check

Refer to illustration 13.3 and 13.9

1   In order to determine the extent of cam lobe wear, the lobe lift should be checked prior to camshaft removal. Refer to Part A, B or C and remove the valve cover(s) or camshaft cover.

2   Position the number one piston at TDC on the compression stroke (see the appropriate section in Part A, B or C).

3   Beginning with the number one cylinder, mount a dial indicator on the engine and position the plunger against the top surface of the first rocker arm on OHV engines or directly on the cam lobe on OHC engines. The plunger should be directly above and in line with the pushrod or cam lobe **(see illustration)**.

4   Zero the dial indicator, then very slowly turn the crankshaft in the normal direction of rotation (clockwise) until the indicator needle

stops and begins to move in the opposite direction. The point at which it stops indicates maximum cam lobe lift.

5   Record this figure for future reference, then reposition the piston at TDC on the compression stroke.

6   Move the dial indicator to the remaining number one cylinder rocker arm or cam lobe and repeat the check. Be sure to record the results for each valve.

7   Repeat the check for the remaining valves. Since each piston must be at TDC on the compression stroke for this procedure, work from cylinder-to-cylinder, following the firing order sequence.

8   After the check is complete, compare the results to this Chapter's Specifications. If camshaft lobe lift is less than specified, cam lobe wear has occurred and a new camshaft should be installed.

9   If the cylinder heads have already been removed, an alternate method of lobe measurement can be used. Using a micrometer, measure the lobe at its highest point. Then measure the base circle perpendicular (90-degrees) to the lobe **(see illustration)**. Do this for each lobe and record the results.

10   Subtract the base circle measurement from the lobe height. The difference is the lobe lift. See Step 8 above.

13.3 When checking the camshaft lobe lift, the dial indicator plunger must be positioned directly above and in-line with the pushrod (OHV) or camshaft lobe (OHC)

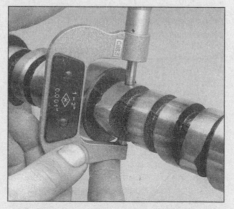

13.9 To verify camshaft lobe lift, measure the base circle as shown and subtract the base circle measurement from the lobe height. The difference is the lobe lift

13.15 Thread long bolts into the sprocket bolt holes to use as a handle when removing and installing the camshaft on OHV engines

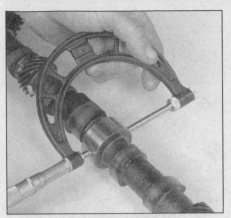

13.19 The camshaft bearing journal diameter is subtracted from the bearing inside diameter to obtain the oil clearance, which must be as listed in this Chapter's Specifications

14.2 A special tool is required to remove the ridge from the top of each cylinder before removing the piston

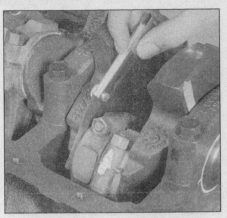

14.6 Check the connecting rod side clearance with a feeler gauge

14.8 To prevent damage to the crankshaft journals and cylinder walls, slip sections of hose over the rod bolts before removing the pistons

Removal

Refer to illustration 13.15

11   Refer to the appropriate Sections in Part A, B or C and remove the timing chain, camshaft gear, rocker arms, hydraulic lifters and pushrods on OHV engines. Remove the camshaft carrier and camshaft sprocket on OHC engines.

12   On carbureted models, remove the fuel pump and pushrod (see Chapter 4).

13   On models so equipped, remove the distributor (see Chapter 5).

14   Remove the camshaft thrust plate-to-block bolts (and the rear cam cover on OHC engines).

15   On OHV engines, thread long bolts into the camshaft sprocket bolt holes to use as a handle when removing the camshaft from the block **(see illustration)**.

16   Carefully pull the camshaft out of the block (from the rear of the carrier on OHC engines). Support the cam near the block or carrier so the lobes Don't nick or gouge the bearings as It's withdrawn.

17   When reinstalling the camshaft, be sure to coat the bearing journals and lobes, as well as the wear surfaces of all other valve train components, with moly-base grease or engine assembly lube. Again, install the camshaft very carefully to avoid damaging the camshaft bearings. The remainder of installation is the reverse of removal.

Inspection

Camshaft

Refer to illustration 13.19

18   After the camshaft has been removed from the engine, cleaned with solvent and dried, inspect the bearing journals for uneven wear, pitting and evidence of seizure. If the journals are damaged, the bearing inserts in the block are probably damaged as well. Both the camshaft and bearings will have to be replaced.

19   Measure the bearing journals with a micrometer **(see illustration)** to determine if

they're excessively worn or out-of-round.

20   Check the camshaft lobes for heat discoloration, score marks, chipped areas, pitting and uneven wear. If the lobes are in good condition, and if the lobe lift measurements are as specified, the camshaft can be reused.

Camshaft bearings

21   Check the bearings in the block for wear and damage. Look for galling, pitting and discolored areas.

22   The inside diameter of each bearing can be determined with a telescoping gauge and outside micrometer or an inside micrometer. Subtract the camshaft bearing journal diameters from the corresponding bearing inside diameters to obtain the bearing oil clearance. If It's excessive, new bearings will be required regardless of the condition of the originals. On OHC engines the bearings are actually part of the camshaft carrier, if wear is indicated the camshaft carrier will have to be replaced.

23   On OHV engines camshaft bearing replacement requires special tools and expertise that place it outside the scope of the home mechanic. Take the block to an automotive machine shop to ensure the job is done correctly.

14   Piston/connecting rod assembly - removal

Refer to illustrations 14.2, 14.6 and 14.8

1   Prior to removal of the piston/connecting rod assemblies, the engine should be positioned upright.

2   Using a ridge reamer, completely remove the ridge at the top of each cylinder. Follow the manufacturer's instructions provided with the ridge reaming tool **(see illustration)**. Failure to remove the ridge before attempting to remove the piston/connecting rod assembly will result in piston breakage.

3   After the cylinder wear ridge have been removed, turn the engine upside-down.

4   Before the connecting rods are removed, check the connecting rod side clearance. Mount a dial indicator with its stem in line with

the crankshaft and touching the side of the number one connecting rod cap.

5   Push the connecting rod backward, as far as possible, and zero the dial indicator. Next, push the connecting rod all the way to the front and check the reading on the dial indicator. The distance that it moves is the side clearance. If the side clearance exceeds the limit listed in this Chapter's Specifications, a new connecting rod will be required. Repeat the procedure for the remaining connecting rods.

6   An alternative method is to slip feeler gauges between the connecting rod and the crankshaft throw until the play is removed **(see illustration)**. The side clearance is then equal to the total thickness of the feeler gauges.

7   Check the connecting rods and connecting rod caps for identification marks. If they are not plainly marked, identify each rod and cap, using a small punch to make the appropriate number of indentations to indicate the cylinders they are associated with.

8   Loosen each of the connecting rod cap nuts approximately 1/2-turn. Remove the number one connecting rod cap and bearing insert. Do not drop the bearing insert out of the cap. Slip a short length of plastic or rub-

15.1 Check the crankshaft endplay with a dial indicator . . .

15.3 . . . or check the crankshaft endplay with a feeler gauge

15.4 Use a center-punch or number stamping dies to mark the main bearing caps to ensure installation in their original locations on the block - make the punch marks near one of the bolt heads

ber hose over each connecting rod cap bolt to protect the crankshaft journal and cylinder wall when the piston is removed **(see illustration)** and push the connecting rod/piston assembly out through the top of the engine. Use a wooden tool to push on the upper bearing insert in the connecting rod. If resistance is felt, double-check to make sure that all of the ridge was removed from the cylinder.

9   Repeat the procedure for the remaining cylinders. After removal, reassemble the connecting rod caps and bearing inserts in their respective connecting rods and install the cap nuts finger-tight. Leaving the old bearing inserts in place until reassembly will help prevent the connecting rod bearing surfaces from being accidentally nicked or gouged.

15   Crankshaft - removal

Refer to illustrations 15.1, 15.3 and 15.4

1   Before the crankshaft is removed check the endplay. Mount a dial indicator with the stem in line with the crankshaft and just touching one of the crank throws **(see illustration)**.

2·   Push the crankshaft all the way to the rear and zero the dial indicator. Next, pry the crankshaft to the front as far as possible and check the reading on the dial indicator. The distance that it moves is the endplay. If it is greater than specified, check the crankshaft thrust surfaces for wear. If no wear is apparent, new main bearings should correct the endplay.

3   If a dial indicator is not available, feeler gauges can be used. Gently pry or push the crankshaft all the way to the front of the engine. Slip feeler gauges between the crankshaft and the front face of the thrust main bearing **(see illustration)** to determine the clearance, which is equivalent to crankshaft endplay.

4   Loosen each of the main bearing cap bolts 1/4-turn at a time, until they can be removed by hand. Check the main bearing caps to see if they are marked as to their locations. They are usually numbered consecutively from the front of the engine to the rear. If

they are not, mark them with number stamping dies or a center-punch **(see illustration)**. Most main bearing caps have a cast-in arrow, which points to the front of the engine.

5   Gently tap the caps with a soft-face hammer, then separate them from the engine block. If necessary, use the main bearing cap bolts as levers to remove the caps. Try not to drop the bearing insert if it comes out with the cap.

6   Carefully lift the crankshaft out of the engine. It is a good idea to have an assistant available, since the crankshaft is quite heavy. With the bearing inserts in place in the engine block and in the main bearing caps, return the caps to their respective locations on the engine block and tighten the bolts finger-tight.

16   Engine block - cleaning

Refer to illustrations 16.1a, 16.1b and 16.10

1   Remove the soft plugs from the engine block. To do this, knock the plugs into the block, using a hammer and punch, then grasp them with large pliers and pull them back through the holes **(see illustrations)**.

2   Using a gasket scraper, remove all traces of gasket material from the engine block. Be very careful not to nick or gouge the gasket sealing surfaces.

16.1a A hammer and large punch can be used to drive the soft plugs into the block

3   Remove the main bearing caps and separate the bearing inserts from the caps and the engine block. Tag the bearings according to which cylinder they are removed from and whether they were in the cap or the block, then set them aside.

4   Remove the threaded oil gallery plugs from the front and back of the block.

5   If the engine is extremely dirty, it should be taken to an automotive machine shop to be steam cleaned or hot tanked. Any bearings left in the block, such as the camshaft bearings, will be damaged by the cleaning process, so plan on having new ones installed while the block is at the machine shop.

6   After the block is returned, clean all oil holes and oil galleries one more time. Brushes for cleaning oil holes and galleries are available at most auto parts stores. Flush the passages with warm water until the water runs clear, dry the block thoroughly and wipe all machined surfaces with a light, rust preventative oil. If you have access to compressed air, use it to speed the drying process and to blow out all the oil holes and galleries.

7   If the block is not extremely dirty or sludged up, you can do an adequate cleaning job with warm soapy water and a stiff brush.

16.1b Use pliers to remove the soft plug from the block

16.10 A large socket on an extension can be used to drive the new soft plugs into their bores

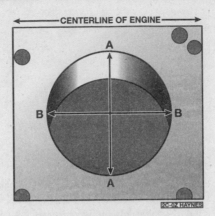

17.4a Measure the diameter of each cylinder at a right angle to the engine center line (A), and parallel to the engine center line (B) - out-of-round is the difference between A and B; taper is the difference between A and B at the top of the cylinder and A and B at the bottom of the cylinder

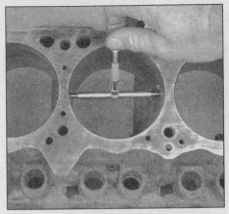

17.4b The ability to feel when the telescoping gauge is at the correct point will be developed over time, so work slowly and repeat the check until you're satisfied the bore measurement is accurate

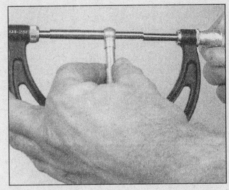

17.4c The gauge is then measured with a micrometer to determine the bore size

Take plenty of time and do a thorough job. Regardless of the cleaning method used, be very sure to thoroughly clean all oil holes and galleries, dry the block completely and coat all machined surfaces with light oil.

8   The threaded holes in the block must be clean to ensure accurate torque readings during reassembly. Run the proper-size tap into each of the holes to remove any rust, corrosion, thread sealant or sludge and to restore any damaged threads. If possible, use compressed air to clear the holes of debris produced by this operation. Now is a good time to thoroughly clean the threads on the head bolts and the main bearing cap bolts as well.

9   Reinstall the main bearing caps and tighten the bolts finger-tight.

10   After coating the sealing surfaces of the new soft plugs with a non-hardening gasket sealant, such as Permatex no. 2, install them in the engine block (see illustration). Make sure they are driven in straight and seated properly or leakage could result. Special tools are available for this purpose, but equally good results can be obtained using a socket with an outside diameter that will just slip into the soft plug and a hammer.

11   If the engine is not going to be reassembled right away, cover it with a large plastic trash bag to keep it clean.

17   Engine block - inspection

Refer to illustrations 17.4a, 17.4b and 17.4c

1   Thoroughly clean the engine block as described in Section 16 and double-check to make sure that the ridge at the top of each cylinder has been completely removed.

2   Visually check the block for cracks, rust and corrosion. Look for stripped threads in the threaded holes. It is also a good idea to have the block checked for hidden cracks by an automotive machine shop that has the special equipment to do this type of work. If defects are found, have the block repaired, if possible, or replaced.

3   Check the cylinder bores for scuffing and scoring.

4   Using an expansion gauge and micrometer, measure each cylinder's diameter at the top (just under the ridge), center and bottom of the cylinder bore, parallel to the crankshaft axis (see illustrations). Next, measure each cylinder's diameter at the same three locations across the crankshaft axis. Compare the results to the Specifications. If the cylinder walls are badly scuffed or scored, or if they are out-of-round or tapered beyond the limits listed in this Chapter's Specifications, have the engine block rebored and honed at an automotive machine shop. If a rebore is done, oversize pistons and rings will be required.

5   If the cylinders are in reasonably good condition and not worn to out of limits, and if the piston-to-cylinder clearance can be maintained properly, then they do not have to be rebored. Honing is all that is necessary.

18   Cylinder honing

Refer to illustrations 18.3a and 18.3b

1   Prior to engine reassembly, the cylinder bores must be honed so the new piston rings will seat correctly and provide the best possible combustion chamber seal. **Note:** *If you do not have the tools or do not want to tackle the honing operation, most automotive machine shops will do it for a reasonable fee.*

2   Before honing the cylinders, install the main bearing caps and tighten the bolts to the torque listed in this Chapter's Specifications.

3   Two types of cylinder hones are commonly available - the flex hone or - "bottle brush" type and the more traditional surfacing hone with spring-loaded stones. Both will do the job, but for the less experienced mechanic the "bottle brush" hone will probably be easier to use. You will also need plenty

of light oil or honing oil, some rags and an electric drill motor. Proceed as follows:

a)   *Mount the hone in the drill motor, compress the stones and slip it into the first cylinder (see illustration).*

b)   *Lubricate the cylinder with plenty of oil, turn on the drill and move the hone up-and-down in the cylinder at a pace*

18.3a Better results are more easily achieved with a bottle-brush type cylinder hone

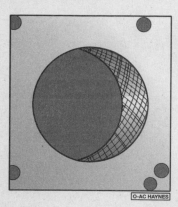

18.3b The cylinder hone should leave a smooth, crosshatch pattern with the lines intersecting at approximately 60-degree angles

19.4 Clean the piston ring grooves with a piston ring groove cleaner, as shown here (a piece of a broken piston ring can also be used)

19.10 Check the piston ring groove clearance with a feeler gauge at several points around the groove

which will produce a fine crosshatch pattern on the cylinder walls. Ideally, the crosshatch lines should intersect at approximately a 60-degree angle (see illustration). *Be sure to use plenty of lubricant and do not take off any more material than is absolutely necessary to produce the desired finish.* **Note:** *Piston ring manufacturers may specify a smaller crosshatch angle than the traditional 60-degrees, typically 45 degrees, so read and follow any instructions printed on the piston ring packages.*

c) *Do not withdraw the hone from the cylinder while it is running. Instead, shut off the drill and continue moving the hone up-and-down in the cylinder until it comes to a complete stop, then compress the stones and withdraw the hone. If you are using a - "bottle brush" type hone, stop the drill motor, then turn the chuck in the normal direction of rotation while withdrawing the hone from the cylinder.*

d) *Wipe the oil out of the cylinder and repeat the procedure for the remaining cylinders.*

4   After the honing job is complete, chamfer the top edges of the cylinder bores with a small file so the rings will not catch when the pistons are installed. Be very careful not to nick the cylinder walls with the end of the file.

5   The entire engine block must be washed again very thoroughly with warm, soapy water to remove all traces of the abrasive grit produced during the honing operation. **Note:** *The bores can be considered clean when a white cloth - dampened with clean engine oil - used to wipe down the bores does not pick-up any more honing residue, which will show up as gray areas on the cloth. Be sure to run a brush through all oil holes and galleries and flush them with running water.*

6   After rinsing, dry the block and apply a coat of light rust preventive oil to all machined surfaces. Wrap the block in a plastic trash bag to keep it clean and set it aside until reassembly.

19   Piston/connecting rod assembly - inspection

Refer to illustrations 19.4, 19.10 and 19.11

1   Before the inspection process can be carried out, the piston/connecting rod assemblies must be cleaned and the original piston rings removed from the pistons. **Note:** *Always use new piston rings when the engine is reassembled.*

2   Using a piston ring installation tool, carefully remove the rings from the pistons. Do not nick or gouge the pistons in the process.

3   Scrape all traces of carbon from the top (or crown) of the piston. A hand-held wire brush or a piece of fine emery cloth can be used once the majority of the deposits have been scraped away. Do not, under any circumstances, use a wire brush mounted in a drill motor to remove deposits from the pistons. The piston material is soft and will be eroded away by the wire brush.

4   Use a piston ring groove cleaning tool to remove any carbon deposits from the ring grooves. If a tool is not available, a piece broken off an old ring will do the job. Be very careful to remove only the carbon deposits. Do not remove any metal and do not nick or scratch the sides of the ring grooves **(see illustration)**.

5   Once the deposits have been removed, clean the piston/rod assemblies with solvent and dry them thoroughly. Make sure that the oil return holes in the back sides of the ring grooves are clear.

6   If the pistons are not damaged or worn excessively, and if the engine block is not rebored, new pistons will not be necessary. Normal piston wear appears as even, vertical wear on the piston thrust surfaces and slight looseness of the top ring in its groove. New piston rings, on the other hand, should always be used when an engine is rebuilt.

7   Carefully inspect each piston for cracks around the skirt, at the pin bosses and at the ring lands.

8   Look for scoring and scuffing on the thrust faces of the skirt, holes in the piston crown and burned areas at the edge of the crown. If the skirt is scored or scuffed, the engine may have been suffering from overheating or abnormal combustion, which caused excessively high operating temperatures. The cooling and lubrication systems should be checked thoroughly. A hole in the piston crown is an indication that abnormal combustion (preignition) was occurring. Burned areas at the edge of the piston crown are usually evidence of spark knock (detonation). If any of the above problems exist, the causes must be corrected or the damage will occur again.

9   Corrosion of the piston (evidenced by pitting) indicates that coolant is leaking into the combustion chamber or the crankcase. Again, the cause must be corrected or the problem may persist in the rebuilt engine.

10   Measure the piston ring groove clearance by laying a new piston ring in each ring groove and slipping a feeler gauge between the ring and the edge of the ring groove **(see illustration)**. Check the clearance at four locations around each groove. Be sure to use the correct ring for each groove; they are different. If the groove clearance is greater than that listed in this Chapter's Specifications, new pistons will have to be installed.

11   Check the piston-to-bore clearance by measuring the bore (see Section 17) and the piston diameter. Make sure that the pistons and bores are correctly matched. Measure the piston across the skirt **(see illustration)**. Subtract the piston diameter from the bore diameter to obtain the clearance. If it is greater than specified, the block will have to be rebored and new pistons and rings installed. Check the piston-to-rod clearance by twisting the piston and rod in opposite directions. Any noticeable play indicates that there is excessive wear, which must be corrected. The piston/connecting rod assemblies should be taken to an automotive machine shop to have new piston pins installed and the pistons and connecting rods rebored.

19.11 Measure the piston diameter at a 90-degree angle to the piston pin

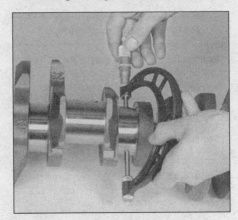

20.2 Measure the diameter of each crankshaft journal at several points to detect taper and out-of-round conditions

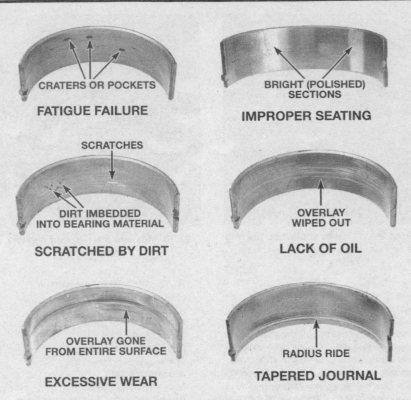

21.3 Typical bearing failures

12   If the pistons must be removed from the connecting rods, such as when new pistons must be installed, or if the piston pins have too much play in them, they should be taken to an automotive machine shop. While they are there, have the connecting rods checked for bend and twist, as automotive machine shops have special equipment for this purpose. Unless new pistons or connecting rods must be installed, do not disassemble the pistons from the connecting rods.

13   Check the connecting rods for cracks and other damage. Temporarily remove the rod caps, lift out the old bearing inserts, wipe the rod and cap bearing surfaces clean and inspect them for nicks, gouges or scratches. After checking the rods, replace the old bearings, slip the caps into place and tighten the nuts finger tight.

20   Crankshaft - inspection

Refer to illustration 20.2

1   Clean the crankshaft with solvent and dry it thoroughly. Be sure to clean the oil holes with a stiff brush and flush them with solvent. Check the main and connecting rod bearing journals for uneven wear, scoring, pitting or cracks. Check the remainder of the crankshaft for cracks and damage. Automotive machine shops are equipped with Magnaflux equipment to check the crankshaft for cracks that may not be visible to the eye.

2   Using a micrometer, measure the diameter of the main and connecting rod journals **(see illustration)** and compare the results to this Chapter's Specifications. By measuring the diameter at a number of points around the journal's circumference you will be able to determine whether or not the journal is out of round. Take the measurement at each end of the journal, near the crank counterweights, to determine whether the journal is tapered.

3   If the crankshaft journals are damaged, tapered, out-of-round or worn beyond the limits given in the Specifications, have the crankshaft reground by a reputable automotive machine shop. Be sure to use the correct undersize bearing inserts if the crankshaft is reconditioned.

21   Main and connecting rod bearings - inspection

Refer to illustration 21.3

1   Even though the main and connecting rod bearings should be replaced with new ones during the engine overhaul, the old bearings should be retained for close examination, as they may reveal valuable information about the condition of the engine.

2   Bearing failure occurs primarily because of lack of lubrication, the presence of dirt or other foreign particles, overloading the engine and corrosion. Regardless of the cause of bearing failure, it must be corrected before the engine is reassembled to prevent it from happening again.

3   When examining the bearings, remove them from the engine block, the main bearing caps, the connecting rods and the rod caps and lay them out on a clean surface in the same general position as their location in the engine. This will enable you to match any bearing problems with the corresponding crankshaft journal **(see illustration)**.

4   Dirt and other foreign particles get into the engine in a variety of ways. It may be left in the engine during assembly, or it may pass through filters or breathers. It may get into the oil, and from there into the bearings. Metal chips from machining operations and normal engine wear are often present. Abrasives are sometimes left in engine components after reconditioning, especially when parts are not thoroughly cleaned using the proper cleaning methods. Whatever the source, these foreign objects often end up embedded in the soft bearing material and are easily recognized. Large particles will not embed in the bearing and will score or gouge the bearing and shaft. The best prevention for this cause of bearing failure is to clean all parts thoroughly and keep everything spotlessly clean during engine assembly. Frequent and regular engine oil and filter changes are also recommended.

5   Lack of lubrication (or lubrication breakdown) has a number of interrelated causes.

23.3a Use the piston to square up the ring in the cylinder prior to checking the ring end gap

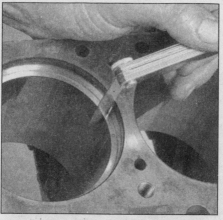

23.3b Measure the ring end gap with a feeler gauge

23.9a Install the spacer/expander in the oil control ring groove

Excessive heat (which thins the oil), overloading (which squeezes the oil from the bearing face) and oil leakage or throw-off (from excessive bearing clearances, worn oil pump or high engine speeds) all contribute to lubrication breakdown. Blocked oil passages, which usually are the result of misaligned oil holes in a bearing shell, will also oil-starve a bearing and destroy it. When lack of lubrication is the cause of bearing failure, the bearing material is wiped or extruded from the steel backing of the bearing. Temperatures may increase to the point where the steel backing turns blue from overheating.

6   Driving habits can have a definite effect on bearing life. Full-throttle, low-speed operation (or *lugging* the engine) puts very high loads on bearings, which tends to squeeze out the oil film. These loads cause the bearings to flex, which produces fine cracks in the bearing face (fatigue failure). Eventually the bearing material will loosen in pieces and tear away from the steel backing. Short-trip driving leads to corrosion of bearings because insufficient engine heat is produced to drive off the condensed water and corrosive gases. These products collect in the engine oil, forming acid and sludge. As the oil is carried to the engine bearings, the acid attacks and corrodes the bearing material.

7   Incorrect bearing installation during engine assembly will lead to bearing failure as well. Tight-fitting bearings leave insufficient bearing oil clearance and will result in oil starvation. Dirt or foreign particles trapped behind a bearing insert result in high spots on the bearing which can lead to failure.

22 Engine overhaul - reassembly sequence

1   Before beginning engine reassembly, make sure you have all the necessary new parts, gaskets and seals as well as the following items on hand:

Common hand tools
A 1/2-inch drive torque wrench
Piston ring installation tool
Piston ring compressor
Short lengths of rubber hose to fit over rod bolts
Plastigage
Feeler gauges
A fine-tooth file
New engine oil
Engine assembly lube or moly-base grease
RTV-type gasket sealant
Anaerobic-type gasket sealant
Thread locking compound

2   In order to save time and avoid problems, engine reassembly   must be done in the following order.

Rear main oil seal (two-piece seal only)
Crankshaft and main bearings
Piston rings
Piston/connecting rod assemblies
Oil pump
Oil pan
Camshaft (OHV only)
Timing chain/sprockets or gears (OHV only)
Timing chain/gear cover (OHV only)
Valve lifters (OHV only)
Cylinder head(s)
Camshaft and camshaft carrier assembly (OHC)
Camshaft sprocket and timing belt (OHC)
Pushrods and rocker arms (OHV only)
Intake and exhaust manifolds
Oil filter
Pre-oil the engine (2.8 and 3.1 liter V6 engines only - Section 26)
Valve covers
Fuel pump
Water pump
Rear main oil seal (one-piece seals)
Flywheel/driveplate
Carburetor/fuel injection components
Thermostat and housing cover
Distributor (if equipped), spark plug wires and spark plugs
Emissions control components
Alternator

23 Piston rings - installation

Refer to illustrations 23.3a, 23.3b, 23.9a, 23.9b and 23.12

1   Before installing the new piston rings, the ring end gaps must be checked. It is assumed that the piston ring groove clearance has been checked and verified correct (Section 18).

2   Lay out the piston/connecting rod assemblies and the new ring sets so the ring sets will be matched with the same piston and cylinder during the end gap measurement and engine assembly.

3   Insert the top ring into the cylinder and square it up with the cylinder walls by pushing it in with the top of the piston. To measure the end gap, slip a feeler gauge between the ends of the ring **(see illustrations)**. Compare the measurement to that listed in this Chapter's Specifications.

4   If the gap is larger or smaller than specified, double-check to make sure that you have the correct rings before proceeding.

5   If the gap is too small, it must be enlarged or the ring ends may come in contact with each other during engine operation, which can cause serious damage to the engine. The end gap can be increased by filing the ring ends very carefully with a fine file. Mount the file in a vise equipped with soft jaws, slip the ring over the file with the ends contacting the file face and slowly move the ring to remove material from the ends. When performing this operation, file only from the outside in.

6   Excess end gap is not critical unless it is greater than 0.040-inch. Again, double-check to make sure you have the correct rings for your engine.

7   Repeat the procedure for the rest of the rings. Remember to keep rings, pistons and cylinders matched up.

8   Once the ring end gaps have been checked, the rings can be installed on the pistons.

9   The oil control ring (lowest one on the piston) is installed first. It is composed of

23.9b Do not use a piston ring expander when installing the oil control rings, install them by-hand

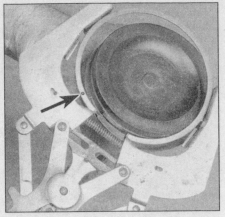

23.12 Install the compression rings with a ring expander - the mark (arrow) must face up

24.1 When correctly installed, the ends of the rope-type seal should extend beyond the surface of the block

three separate components. Slip the spacer/expander into the groove **(see illustration)**, then install the lower side rail **(see illustration)**. Do not use a piston ring installation tool on the oil ring side rails, as they may be damaged. Instead, place one end of the side rail into the groove between the spacer/expander and the ring land, hold it firmly in place and slide a finger around the piston while pushing the rail into the groove. Next, install the upper side rail in the same manner.

10   After the three oil ring components have been installed, check to make sure that both the upper and lower side rails can be turned smoothly in the ring groove.

11   The number two (middle) ring is installed next. It should be stamped with a mark so it can be readily distinguished from the top ring. **Note:** *Always follow the instructions printed on the ring package or box - different manufacturers may require different approaches.* Do not mix up the top and middle rings, as they have different cross sections.

12   Use a piston ring installation tool and make sure that the identification mark is facing the top of the piston, then slip the ring into the middle groove on the piston **(see illustration)**. Do not expand the ring any

more than is necessary to slide it over the piston.

13   Install the number one (top) ring in the same manner. Make sure the identifying mark is facing up.

14   Repeat the procedure for the remaining pistons and rings. Be careful not to confuse the number one and number two rings.

24 Crankshaft oil seals - installation

Rope-type seal

Refer to illustrations 24.1, 24.2, 24.3a, 24.3b, 24.4, 24.5a and 24.5b

1   Lay one seal section on edge in the seal groove in the block and push it into place with your thumbs. Both ends of the seal should extend out of the block slightly **(see illustration)**.

2   Seat it in the groove by rolling a large socket or piece of bar stock along the entire length of the seal **(see illustration)**. As an alternative, push the seal very carefully into place with a wooden hammer handle.

3   Once you are satisfied that the seal is completely seated in the groove, trim off the

24.2 Seat the seal in the groove, but do not depress it below the bearing surface (the seal must contact the crankshaft journal)

excess on the ends with a single-edge razor blade or razor knife. The seal ends must be flush with the block-to-cap mating surfaces **(see illustrations)**. Make sure that no seal fibers get caught between the block and cap.

4   Repeat the entire procedure to install the other half of the seal in the bearing cap.

24.3a Trim the ends flush with the block . . .

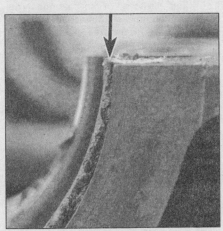

24.3b . . .but leave the inner edge (arrow) protruding slightly

24.4 Lubricate the seal with assembly lube or moly-base grease

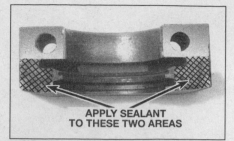

24.5a Apply anaerobic-type gasket sealant to the shaded areas of the rear main bearing cap

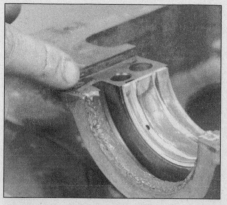

24.5b When applying the sealant, be sure it gets into the corner and onto the vertical cap-to-block mating surface or +oil leaks will result

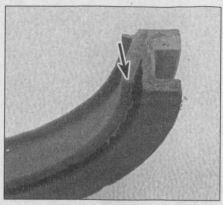

24.7 When installing the two-piece neoprene lip-type seal, apply RTV-type sealant to the area indicated

Apply a thin film of engine assembly lube to the edge of the seal where it contacts the crankshaft **(see illustration)**.

5   During final installation of the crankshaft, after the main bearing oil clearances have been checked with Plastigage as described in Section 25, apply a thin, even film of anaerobic-type gasket sealant to the areas of the rear main bearing cap.**(see illustrations). Caution:** *Do not get any sealant on the bearing or seal faces.*

Neoprene lip-type seal

Refer to illustration 24.7

6   Inspect the bearing cap and engine block mating surfaces and seal grooves for nicks, burrs and scratches. Remove any defects with a fine file or deburring tool.

7   Install one seal section in the block with the lip facing the front of the engine. Leave one end protruding from the block 3/8-inch and make sure it is completely seated. **Note:** *Apply a very thin coat of RTV type gasket sealant to the outer surface of the seal as shown in the accompanying illustration. Do not get any sealant on the seal lip* **(see illustration).**

8   Repeat the procedure to install the remaining seal half in the rear main bearing cap. In this case, leave the opposite end of the seal protruding from the cap the same distance the block seal is protruding from the block.

9   Prior to final installation of the crankshaft, lubricate the seal lips with moly-base grease or engine assembly lube.

One-piece seal

10   Later models are equipped with a one-piece, lip-type seal. The crankshaft must be in place and the main bearing caps installed before the seal is installed. See Part A, B or C (depending on which engine you have) for the procedure.

---

25   Crankshaft - installation and main bearing oil clearance check

Refer to illustrations 25.10, 25.14 and 25.20

1   Crankshaft installation is generally one of the first steps in engine reassembly. It is assumed at this point that the engine block

and crankshaft have been cleaned, inspected and repaired or reconditioned.

2   Position the engine with the bottom facing up.

3   Remove the main bearing cap bolts and lift out the caps. Lay them out in the proper order to help ensure that they are installed correctly.

4   If they are still in place, remove the old bearing inserts from the block and the main bearing caps. Wipe the main bearing surfaces of the block and caps with a clean, lint-free cloth. They must be kept spotlessly clean.

5   Clean the back sides of the new main bearing inserts and lay one bearing half in each main bearing saddle in the block. Lay the other bearing half from each bearing set in the corresponding main bearing cap. Make sure the tab on the bearing insert fits into the recess in the block or cap. Do not hammer the bearing into place and do not nick or gouge the bearing faces. No lubrication should be used at this time.

6   The flanged thrust bearing must be installed in the number three cap and saddle (V6 engines), or the number four cap and saddle (four-cylinder engines).

7   Clean the faces of the bearings in the block and the crankshaft main bearing journals with a clean, lint-free cloth. Check or clean the oil holes in the crankshaft, as any dirt here can go only one way - straight into the new bearings.

8   Once you are certain that the crankshaft is clean, carefully lay it in position (an assistant would be very helpful here) in the main bearings.

9   Before the crankshaft can be permanently installed, the main bearing oil clearance must be checked.

10   Trim several pieces of the appropriate size of Plastigage slightly shorter than the width of the main bearings and place one piece on each crankshaft main bearing journal, parallel with the journal axis **(see illustration)**.

11   Clean the faces of the bearings in caps and install the caps in their respective

positions (do not mix them up) with the arrows pointing toward the front of the engine. Do not disturb the Plastigage.

12   Starting with the center main and working out toward the ends, tighten the main bearing cap bolts, in three steps, to the torque listed in this Chapter's Specifications. Do not rotate the crankshaft at any time during this operation.

13   Remove the bolts and carefully lift off the main bearing caps. Keep them in order. Do not disturb the Plastigage or rotate the crankshaft. If any of the main bearing caps are difficult to remove, tap them gently from side-to-side with a soft-face hammer to loosen them.

14   Compare the width of the crushed Plastigage on each journal to the scale printed on the Plastigage container to obtain the main bearing oil clearance **(see illustration)**. Check your findings against those listed in this Chapter's Specifications to make sure it is correct.

15   If the clearance is not correct, double-check to make sure you have the right size bearing inserts. Also, make sure that no dirt or oil is between the bearing inserts and the

25.10 Lay the Plastigage strips on the main bearing journals, parallel to the crankshaft centerline

25.14 Compare the width of the crushed Plastigage to the scale on the envelope to determine the main bearing oil clearance (always take the measurement at the widest point of the Plastigage); be sure to use the correct scale - standard and metric ones are included

25.20 Fill the OHC rear main bearing cap side grooves with sealant

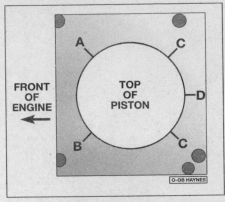

26.5 Before installing the pistons, position the ring end gaps as shown here

A   *Top compression ring gap*
B   *Second compression ring gap*
C   *Oil control ring gaps*
D   *Oil ring expander gap*

main bearing caps or the block when the clearance was measured.

16   Carefully scrape all traces of the Plastigage material off the main bearing journals and the bearing faces. Do not nick or scratch the bearing faces.

17   Carefully lift the crankshaft out of the engine. Clean the bearing faces in the block, then apply a thin, uniform layer of moly-base grease or engine assembly lube to each of the bearing surfaces. Be sure to coat the thrust flange faces as well as the journal face of the thrust bearing.

18   Lubricate the rear main bearing oil seal where it contacts the crankshaft with moly-base grease or engine assembly lube. Note that on all later model engines a 360 degree lip-type seal is utilized and is installed after the crankshaft is in place (refer to Parts A, B, or C of this Chapter).

19   If you are working on an engine with a two-piece seal, refer to Section 24 and apply anaerobic-type gasket sealant to the rear main bearing cap as described there. Make sure the crankshaft journals are clean, then lay the crankshaft back in place in the block. Clean the faces of the bearings in the caps, then apply a thin, uniform layer of assembly-lube or moly-base grease to each of the bearing faces.

20   Install the caps in their respective positions with the arrows pointing toward the front of the engine. Using a soft-faced hammer, gently tap the caps until they are fully seated against the block (do not use the bolts to pull the caps into position). On the OHC four cylinder engine, leave approximately 1/16-inch gap between the bottom of the rear main bearing cap and the block. Fill the side grooves with sealant, until the sealant is extruded out of the gap **(see illustration)**. Tap the cap into place and clean off the excess sealer.

21   Install the bolts and tighten them snugly. With a rubber mallet, strike both ends of the

crankshaft, rearward first, then forward to center the thrust bearing. Starting with the center main and working out toward the ends, tighten the bolts to the torque listed in this Chapter's Specifications.

22   Rotate the crankshaft a number of times by hand and check for any obvious binding.

23   Check the crankshaft endplay with a feeler gauge or a dial indicator as described in Section 15.

26   Piston/connecting rods - installation and rod bearing oil clearance check

Refer to illustrations 26.5, 26.8, 26.10, 26.12 and 26.14

1   Before installing the piston/connecting rod assemblies the cylinder walls must be perfectly clean, the top edge of each cylinder must be chamfered, and the crankshaft must be in place.

2   Remove the connecting rod cap from the end of the number one connecting rod. Remove the old bearing inserts and wipe the bearing surfaces of the connecting rod and cap with a clean, lint-free cloth (they must be kept spotlessly clean). Slip pieces of rubber hose over the connecting rod bolts to prevent crankshaft damage.

3   Clean the back side of the new upper bearing half, then lay it in place in the connecting rod. Make sure that the tab on the bearing fits into the recess in the rod. Do not hammer the bearing insert into place and be very careful not to nick or gouge the bearing face. Do not lubricate the bearing at this time.

4   Clean the back side of the other bearing insert and install it in the rod cap. Again, make sure the tab on the bearing fits into the recess in the cap, and do not apply any lubricant. It is critically important that the mating surfaces of the bearing and connecting rod are perfectly clean and oil-free when they are assembled.

5   Position the piston ring gaps as shown, **(see illustration)**, then slip a section of plas-

tic or rubber hose over the connecting rod cap bolts.

6   Lubricate the piston and rings with clean engine oil and attach a piston ring compressor to the piston. Leave the skirt protruding about 1/4-inch to guide the piston into the cylinder. The rings must be compressed as far as possible.

7   Rotate the crankshaft until the number one connecting rod journal is as far from the number one cylinder as possible (bottom dead center), and apply a coat of engine oil to the cylinder walls.

8   With the notch on top of the piston facing to the front of the engine **(see illustration)**, slip the piston/connecting rod assembly into the number one cylinder bore and rest the bottom edge of the ring compressor on the engine block. Tap the top edge of the ring compressor to make sure it is contacting the block around its entire circumference.

9   Clean the number one connecting rod journal on the crankshaft and the bearing faces in the rod.

26.8 The notch or arrow on each piston must face the front (drivebelt end) of the engine

26.10 If resistance is encountered when tapping the piston/connecting rod assembly into the block, stop immediately and make sure the rings carefully compressed

26.12 Position the Plastigage strip on the bearing journal, parallel to the journal axis

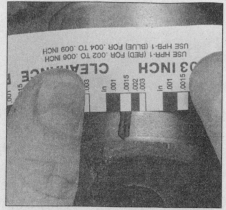

26.14 The crushed Plastigage is compared to the scale printed on the container to obtain the bearing oil clearance

10   Carefully tap on the top of the piston with the end of a wooden hammer handle **(see illustration)** while guiding the end of the connecting rod into place on the crankshaft journal. The piston rings may try to pop out of the ring compressor just before entering the cylinder bore, so keep some pressure on the ring compressor. Work slowly, and if any resistance is felt as the piston enters the cylinder, stop immediately. Find out what is hanging up and fix it before proceeding. Do not, for any reason, force the piston into the cylinder, as you will break a ring and/or the piston.

11   Once the piston/connecting rod assembly is installed, the connecting rod bearing oil clearance must be checked before the rod cap is permanently bolted in place.

12   Cut a piece of the appropriate size Plastigage slightly shorter than the width of the connecting rod bearing and lay it in place on the number one connecting rod journal, parallel with the journal axis. It must not cross the oil hole in the journal **(see illustration)**.

13   Clean the connecting rod cap bearing face, remove the protective hoses from the connecting rod bolts and install the rod cap in place. Make sure the mating mark on the cap is on the same side as the mark on the connecting rod. Install the nuts and tighten them to the torque listed in this Chapter's Specifications, working up to it in three steps. Do not rotate the crankshaft at any time during this operation.

14   Remove the rod cap, being careful not to disturb the Plastigage. Compare the width of the crushed Plastigage to the scale printed on the Plastigage container to obtain the oil clearance **(see illustration)**. Compare it to this Chapter's Specifications to make sure the clearance is correct. If the clearance is not correct, double-check to make sure that you have the correct-size bearing inserts. Also, recheck the crankshaft connecting rod journal diameter and make sure that no dirt or

oil was between the bearing inserts and the connecting rod or cap when the clearance was measured.

15   Carefully scrape all traces of the Plastigage material off the rod journal and bearing face. Be very careful not to scratch the bearing - use your fingernail or a piece of hardwood. Make sure the bearing faces are perfectly clean, then apply a uniform layer of moly-base grease or engine assembly lube to both of them. You will have to push the piston into the cylinder to expose the face of the bearing insert in the connecting rod. Be sure to slip the protective hoses over the rod bolts first.

16   Slide the connecting rod back into place on the journal, remove the protective hoses from the rod cap bolts, install the rod cap and tighten the nuts to the torque listed in this Chapter's Specifications. Again, work up to the torque in three steps.

17   Repeat the entire procedure for the remaining piston/connecting rod assemblies. Keep the back sides of the bearing inserts and the inside of the connecting rod and cap perfectly clean when assembling them. Make sure you have the correct piston for the cylinder and that the notch on the piston faces to the front of the engine when the piston is installed. Remember, use plenty of oil to lubricate the piston before installing the ring compressor. Also, when installing the rod caps for the final time, be sure to lubricate the bearing faces adequately.

18   After all the piston/connecting rod assemblies have been properly installed, rotate the crankshaft a number of times by hand and check for any obvious binding.

19   As a final step, the connecting rod endplay must be checked. Refer to Section 14 for this procedure. Compare the measured endplay to this Chapter's Specifications to make sure it is correct.

27   Initial start-up and break-in after overhaul

1   Once the engine has been properly installed in the vehicle, double check the

engine oil and coolant levels.

2   With the spark plugs out of the engine and the coil high-tension lead grounded to the engine block, crank the engine over until oil pressure registers on the gauge (if so equipped) or until the oil light goes off.

3   Install the spark plugs, hook up the plug wires and the coil high tension lead.

4   Make sure the carburetor choke plate is closed (if equipped), then start the engine. It may take a few moments for the gasoline to reach the carburetor or fuel injector(s), but the engine should start without a great deal of effort.

5   As soon as the engine starts it should be set at a fast idle to ensure proper oil circulation and allowed to warm up to normal operating temperature. While the engine is warming up, make a thorough check for oil and coolant leaks.

6   Shut the engine off and recheck the engine oil and coolant levels. Restart the engine and check the ignition timing and the engine idle speed (refer to Chapter 1). Make any necessary adjustments.

7   Drive the vehicle to an area with minimum traffic, accelerate from 30 to 50 mph, then allow the vehicle to slow to 30 mph with the throttle closed. Repeat the procedure 10 or 12 times. This will load the piston rings and cause them to seat properly against the cylinder walls. Check again for oil and coolant leaks.

8   Drive the vehicle gently for the first 500 miles (no sustained high speeds) and keep a constant check on the oil level. It is not unusual for an engine to use oil during the break-in period.

9   At approximately 500 to 600 miles, change the oil and filter, retorque the cylinder head bolts and recheck the valve clearances (if applicable).

10   For the next few hundred miles, drive the vehicle normally. Do not either pamper it or abuse it.

11   After 2000 miles, change the oil and filter again and consider the engine fully broken in.

Chapter 3
Cooling, heating and air conditioning systems

Contents

Specifications

General

Radiator cap pressure cap rating	15 psi
Thermostat rating	195-degrees F

Torque specifications

Ft-lbs (unless otherwise indicated)

Thermostat housing cover bolts/nuts (OHV engines only)	
Four cylinder engine	
1986 and earlier	20
1987 and later	89 in-lbs
V6 engine	20
Water pump mounting bolts	
Four-cylinder engines	18
V6 engine	89 in-lbs
Water pump pulley bolts (OHV engines)	18

1 General information

Engine cooling system

All vehicles covered by this manual employ a pressurized engine cooling system with thermostatically controlled coolant circulation. An impeller type water pump mounted on the front of the block pumps coolant through the engine. The coolant flows around each cylinder and toward the rear of the engine. Cast-in coolant passages direct coolant around the intake and exhaust ports, near the spark plug areas and in close proximity to the exhaust valve guide inserts.

During warm up, the closed thermostat prevents coolant from circulating through the radiator. When the engine reaches normal operating temperature, the thermostat opens and allows hot coolant to travel through the radiator, where it is cooled before returning to the engine.

The aluminum radiator is of the cross-flow type, with tanks on either side of the core.

The cooling system is sealed by a pressure type radiator cap. This raises the boiling point of the coolant and the higher boiling point of the coolant increases the cooling efficiency of the radiator. If the system pressure exceeds the cap pressure relief value, the excess pressure in the system forces the spring-loaded valve inside the cap off its seat and allows the coolant to escape through the overflow tube into a coolant reservoir. When the system cools, the excess coolant is automatically drawn from the reservoir back into the radiator.

The coolant reservoir serves as both the point at which coolant is added to the cooling system to maintain the proper fluid level and as a holding tank for overheated coolant.

This type of cooling system is known as a closed design because coolant that escapes past the pressure cap is saved and reused.

Heating system

The heating system consists of a blower fan and heater core located under the dashboard, the inlet and outlet hoses connecting the heater core to the engine cooling system and the heater/air conditioning control head on the dashboard. Hot engine coolant is circulated through the heater core at all times. When the heater mode is activated, a flap opens to expose the heater box to the passenger compartment. A fan switch on the control head activates the blower motor, which forces air through the core, heating the air.

Air conditioning system

The air conditioning system consists of a condenser mounted in front of the radiator, an evaporator mounted under the dash, a compressor mounted on the engine, a filter-drier (accumulator) which contains a high pressure relief valve and the plumbing connecting all of the above.

A blower fan forces the warmer air of the

Component location

1 Radiator
2 Cooling fan
3 Upper radiator hose
4 Thermostat housing and cap

5 Warning light temperature
   sending unit (bottom of
   thermostat housing)
6 Coolant reservoir

7 Blower motor
8 Heater assembly
9 Cooling fan relay

passenger compartment through the evaporator core (sort of a radiator-in-reverse), transferring the heat from the air to the refrigerant. The liquid refrigerant boils off into low pressure vapor, taking the heat with it when it leaves the evaporator.

2   Antifreeze – general information

Warning: *Do not allow antifreeze to come in contact with your skin or painted surfaces of the vehicle. Rinse off spills immediately with plenty of water. Antifreeze is highly toxic if ingested. Never leave antifreeze lying around in an open container or in puddles on the floor; children and pets are attracted by it's sweet smell and may drink it. Check with local authorities about disposing of used antifreeze. Many communities have collection centers which will see that antifreeze is disposed of safely.*

The cooling system should be filled with a water/ethylene glycol based antifreeze solution which will prevent freezing down to at least -20-degrees F. It also provides protection against corrosion and increases the coolant boiling point.

The cooling system should be drained, flushed and refilled at least every other year

(see Chapter 1). The use of antifreeze solutions for periods of longer than two years is likely to cause damage and encourage the formation of rust and scale in the system. If your tap water is "hard", use distilled water with the antifreeze.

Before adding antifreeze to the system, check all hose connections, because antifreeze tends to leak through very minute openings. Engines don't normally consume coolant, so if the level goes down, find the cause and correct it.

The exact mixture of antifreeze-to-water which you should use depends on the relative weather conditions. The mixture should contain at least 50-percent antifreeze, but should never contain more than 70-percent antifreeze. Consult the mixture ratio chart on the antifreeze container before adding coolant. Hydrometers are available at most auto parts stores to test the ratio of antifreeze to water.

3   Thermostat - check and replacement

Refer to illustrations 3.9, 3.10, 3.11, 3.12, 3.15, 3.16a, 3.16b and 3.17
Warning: *DO NOT remove the radiator cap,*

drain the coolant or replace the thermostat until the engine has cooled completely.
Caution 1: *The engine must be completely cool before beginning this procedure. Also, when working in the vicinity of the electric cooling fan, disconnect the negative battery cable from the battery to prevent the fan from coming on accidentally.*
Caution 2: *If the vehicle is equipped with a Delco Loc II audio system, make sure you have the correct activation code before disconnecting the battery. See the information at the front of this manual for the radio re-activation procedure.*

Check

1   Before assuming the thermostat is to blame for a cooling system problem, check the coolant level (see Chapter 1), drivebelt tension (see Chapter 1) and temperature gauge (or light) operation.
2   If the engine seems to be taking a long time to warm up (based on heater output or temperature gauge operation), the thermostat is probably stuck open. Replace the thermostat with a new one.
3   If the engine runs hot, use your hand to check the temperature of the upper radiator hose. If the hose isn't hot, but the engine is, the thermostat is probably stuck closed, pre-

3.9 V6 engine thermostat covers are secured by two fasteners (arrows)

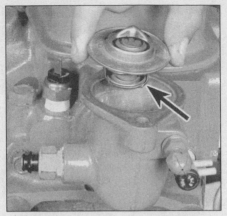

3.10 When installing the thermostat, make sure the spring end (arrow) is directed into the engine

3.11 Remove all traces of gasket material from the thermostat housing and cover

venting the coolant inside the engine from escaping to the radiator. Replace the thermostat. **Caution:** *Don't drive the vehicle without a thermostat. The computer may stay in open loop and emissions and fuel economy will suffer.*

4   If the upper radiator hose is hot, it means the coolant is flowing and the thermostat is open. Consult the *Troubleshooting* section at the front of this manual for cooling system diagnosis.

Replacement

5   Disconnect the negative battery cable and drain the cooling system (see Chapter 1). If the coolant is relatively new or in good condition, save it and reuse it.

6   Follow the upper radiator hose to the engine to locate the thermostat housing.

OHV four-cylinder and V6 engines

7   Loosen the hose clamp, then detach the hose from the fitting. If the hose sticks, grasp it near the end with a pair of large adjustable pliers and twist it to break the seal, then pull it off. If the hose is old or deteriorated, cut it off and install a new one.

8   If the outer surface of the large fitting that mates with the hose is severely deteriorated (corroded, pitted, etc.) it may be dam-

aged further by hose removal. If it is, the thermostat cover will have to be replaced.

9   Detach any hoses or electrical connectors that may interfere with removal of the thermostat cover. Remove the bolts/nuts and detach the thermostat cover **(see illustration)**. If the cover is stuck, tap it with a soft-face hammer to jar it loose. Be prepared for some coolant to spill as the gasket seal is broken.

10   Note how it's installed, then remove the thermostat **(see illustration)**.

11   Clean all gasket material from the mating surfaces of the thermostat housing and cover **(see illustration)**. Clean both mating surfaces with lacquer thinner or acetone.

12   Some models are equipped with a rubber gasket around the circumference of the thermostat **(see illustration)**. If the vehicle you are working on is equipped with this type of thermostat, replace the rubber gasket.

13   Install the new thermostat in the housing. Make sure the thermostat is installed the correct way - the spring end is normally directed into the engine.

14   If there was a gasket under the thermostat cover, install a new one. If the thermostat was equipped with a rubber gasket, apply a bead of RTV sealant to the mating flange of

3.12 Some models use a rubber gasket around the circumference of the thermostat

the cover. Install the cover and tighten the bolts to the torque listed in this Chapter's Specifications.

OHC four-cylinder engine

15   Remove the thermostat housing cap by pushing down and rotating it in a counter-clockwise direction **(see illustration)**.

16   Grasp the handle and pull the thermostat from the housing **(see illustrations)**.

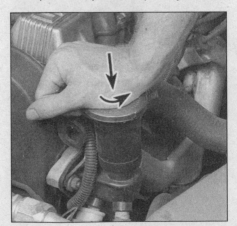

3.15 Push down while rotating (arrows) to remove the thermostat housing cap

3.16a With the cap removed, grasp the thermostat handle (arrow) . . .

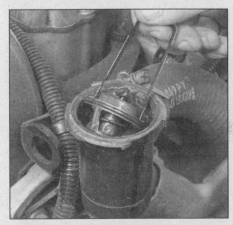

3.16b . . . and remove the thermostat from the housing

3.17 Whenever the thermostat is removed, make sure the O-ring (arrow) is not damaged

4.1 The fan motor can be tested by running fused jumper wires directly from the battery to the motor terminals

4.6 Remove the fan frame mounting bolts (arrows)

17   If the old thermostat is to be reinstalled, inspect the O-ring for cuts or damage **(see illustration)**. Insert the thermostat into the housing until it is fully seated and install the cap.

All models

18   The remaining steps are the reverse of removal.
19   Refill the cooling system (see Chapter 1).
20   Start the engine and allow it to reach normal operating temperature, then check for leaks and proper thermostat operation (as described in Step 3).

---

4   Engine cooling fan - check, removal and installation

Refer to illustrations 4.1 and 4.6
Caution: *When working in the vicinity of the electric fan, disconnect the negative battery cable from the battery to prevent the fan from coming on accidentally. If the vehicle is equipped with a Delco Loc II audio system, make sure you have the correct activation code before disconnecting the battery. See the information at the front of this manual for the radio re-activation procedure.*

Check

1   To test the fan motor, unplug the electrical connector at the motor and use jumper wires to connect the fan directly to the battery **(see illustration)**. If the fan still doesn't work, replace the motor.

1984 and earlier OHV models; 1986 and earlier OHC models

2   If the motor tested OK, the fault lies in the coolant fan switch, the relay or the wiring which connects the components. Plug in the electrical connector at the motor.
3   The coolant fan switch is usually mounted on the thermostat housing. Unplug the electrical connector from the switch and, using a jumper wire, connect it to a good ground (usually a green wire with a white stripe). If the fan now works, the coolant fan

switch is defective.
4   If it still doesn't work, the relay or the wiring that connects the components is defective. Carefully check all wiring and connections. If no obvious problems are found, further diagnosis should be done by a dealer service department or other repair shop.

1985 and later OHV models; 1987 and later models OHC models

5   The electric cooling fan on these models is controlled by the Electronic Control Module (ECM) and the coolant sensor. If the fan is inoperative, check to see if any trouble codes are stored in the computer. If a problem with the coolant temperature sensor is indicated, check the sensor and its circuit. If no trouble codes are stored, have the diagnosis performed by a dealer service department or other qualified repair shop.

Removal and installation

6   Remove the fan frame-to-radiator bolts **(see illustrations)**.
7   Lift the retaining tabs and unplug the fan connector.
8   Lift the fan assembly from the engine compartment.
9   If you're installing a new fan or fan motor, remove the nut that retains the fan to the motor. **Note:** *This nut may have left-hand threads. Check the hub of the fan for marks that indicate which way to loosen the nut.*
10   Installation is the reverse of removal.

---

5   Radiator - removal, servicing and installation

Refer to illustration 5.4, 5.6, 5.14a and 5.14b
Warning: *The engine must be completely cool before beginning this procedure. Also, when working in the vicinity of the electric fan, disconnect the negative battery cable from the battery to prevent the fan from coming on accidentally.*
Note: *Radiators used on later models are alu-*

minum and plastic (an aluminum core with plastic side tanks) The drain fitting is located on the lower part of one of the tanks and can be repaired. Radiator repairs should be performed by a dealer service department or radiator repair shop.

Removal

Warning: *Do not allow antifreeze to come in contact with your skin or painted surfaces of the vehicle. Rinse off spills immediately with plenty of water. Antifreeze is highly toxic if ingested. Never leave antifreeze lying around in an open container or in puddles on the floor; children and pets are attracted by it's sweet smell and may drink it. Check with local authorities about disposing of used antifreeze. Many communities have collection centers which will see that antifreeze is disposed of safely.*
1   Disconnect the cable from the negative battery terminal. **Caution:** *If the vehicle is equipped with a Delco Loc II audio system, make sure you have the correct activation code before disconnecting the battery. See the information at the front of this manual for the radio re-activation procedure.*
2   Drain the cooling system (see Chapter 1).
3   Disconnect the forward headlight harness from the frame and unplug the cooling fan electrical connector.
4   Remove the cooling fan assembly and shroud **(see illustration)**.
5   Scribe a line around the hood latch on the radiator support to mark its location, then remove the latch.
6   Detach the radiator hoses from the radiator, disconnect the coolant recovery hose, and on automatic transaxle models, disconnect and plug the fluid cooler lines **(see illustration)**.
7   On some models it may be necessary to remove the radiator air side baffle or air cleaner assembly that is adjacent to the radiator.
8   Remove the bolts from the radiator mounting panel (or on some models the radiator-to-radiator support bolts). Lean the top of the radiator rearward, then slide the radia-

5.4 Remove the fan and shroud as an assembly

5.6 Automatic transaxle cooler line fittings (arrows)

5.14a Inspect the lower radiator mount (arrow) for damage prior to installation

tor toward the right and lift the radiator from the engine compartment. **Note:** *On air-conditioned models it may be necessary to lift the driver's side of the radiator first, so the radiator neck will clear the compressor.*

Servicing

9   Carefully examine the radiator for evidence of leaks and damage. It is recommended that any necessary repairs be performed by a radiator repair shop.

10   With the radiator removed, brush accumulations of insects and leaves from the fins and examine and replace, if necessary, any hoses or clamps which have deteriorated.

11   The radiator can be flushed as described in Chapter 1.

12   Replace the radiator cap with a new one of the same rating, or if the cap is relatively new, have it tested by a service station.

Installation

13   If you are installing a new radiator, transfer the fittings from the old unit to the new one.

14   Installation is the reverse of removal. When setting the radiator in the chassis, make sure that it seats securely in the lower rubber mounting pads **(see illustrations)**.

15   After installing the radiator, refill it with the proper coolant mixture (see Chapter 1), then start the engine and check for leaks.

6   Water pump - check

Refer to illustration 6.3

1   A failure in the water pump can cause overheating and serious engine damage, as a defective pump will not circulate coolant through the engine.

2   There are two ways to check the operation of the water pump while it is installed on the engine. If the pump is defective, it should be replaced with a new or rebuilt unit.

3   Water pumps are equipped with weep or vent holes. If a pump seal failure occurs, coolant will leak from the weep holes. In most

5.14b The radiator should be securely inserted into the radiator mount (arrow)

cases it will be necessary to use a flashlight from under the vehicle to see evidence of leakage from this point on the pump body **(see illustration)**.

4   If the water pump shaft bearings fail, there may be a squealing sound emitted from the front of the engine while it is running. Shaft wear can be felt if the water pump pulley is forced up and down. Do not mistake drivebelt slippage, which also causes a squealing sound, for water pump failure.

7   Water pump - removal and installation

Warning: *The engine must be completely cool before beginning this procedure. Also, when working in the vicinity of the electric cooling fan, disconnect the negative battery cable from the battery to prevent the fan from coming on accidentally.*

Caution: *If the vehicle is equipped with a Delco Loc II audio system, make sure you have the correct activation code before disconnecting the battery. See the information at the front of this manual for the radio re-activation procedure.*

6.3 The water pump weep hole (arrow) will drip coolant when the seal or the pump shaft bearing fails

Removal

Refer to illustrations 7.5a and 7.5b

1   Drain the cooling system (see Chapter 1). **Warning:** *Do not allow antifreeze to come in contact with your skin or painted surfaces of the vehicle. Rinse off spills immediately with plenty of water. Antifreeze is highly toxic if ingested. Never leave antifreeze lying around in an open container or in puddles on the floor; children and pets are attracted by it's sweet smell and may drink it. Check with local authorities about disposing of used antifreeze. Many communities have collection centers which will see that antifreeze is disposed of safely.*

2   Remove the accessory drivebelt(s), alternator, air conditioning compressor and other components which could interfere with removal.

3   On OHV models remove the water pump pulley bolts and the pulley. Wedge a screwdriver between two bolts to prevent the pulley from turning as the bolts are loosened. Loosen all of the bolts before removing any of them.

4   On OHC engines, remove the timing belt front cover, timing belt and rear cover (Chap-

7.5a OHC four-cylinder engine water pump retaining bolts (arrows)

7.5b The mounting bolts are located around the perimeter of the pump (arrows) - V6 shown

7.6a Inspect the OHC engine O-ring groove (arrow) for nicks or damage

7.6b Check the OHC engine water pump cavity (arrow) for damage and corrosion

ter 2, Part B).

5   Remove the retaining bolts/nuts and lift the water pump from the engine **(see illustrations)**. If the pump is stuck, jar it loose with a soft-faced hammer or a block of wood. Don't pry between the pump and the engine, as damage to the sealing surfaces may result. On some models it may be necessary to unbolt the right side engine mount from the cradle (subframe) and raise the engine slightly to obtain enough clearance to remove the water pump.

Installation

Refer to illustrations 7.6a and 7.6b

Note: *If the water pump has a pressed-on pulley, take the pump to a dealer service department or other repair shop to have the pulley pressed off and transferred to the new pump. Don't pry or hammer on the pulley as damage may occur.*

6   On OHC engines, remove the O-ring from the water pump, inspect the seating surface of the groove for nicks, corrosion or damage and the O-ring for cuts **(see illustrations)**. Replace the O-ring with a new one if there is any doubt as to its sealing ability. Lubricate the groove with moly-based grease and install the O-ring.

7   Remove all traces of old gasket material and sealant from the water pump mating surface on the engine (and on the water pump if the same one is to be reinstalled).

8   On OHC engines, place the water pump in position with the adjusting tab up, install the mounting bolts finger tight. Install the timing belt rear cover, followed by the timing belt. Adjust the timing belt tension as described in Chapter 2, tighten the water pump mounting bolts to the torque listed in this Chapter's Specifications and install the timing belt cover.

9   On other models install a new gasket and position the water pump on the engine. Coat the threads of the retaining bolts with a thin film of RTV sealant to prevent leaks. Install the bolts and tighten them to the torque listed in this Chapter's Specifications. If you're working on a 1987 or later 2.8L or 3.1L V6 engine, be sure the locators on the pump and gasket are vertical.

10   Install the pulley and tighten the bolts to the torque listed in this Chapter's Specifications.

11   Connect the hoses to the water pump (where applicable) and tighten the hose clamps securely.

12   The remainder of installation is the reverse of the removal procedure. Refill the cooling system with the proper coolant mixture (see Chapter 1).

13   Connect the negative battery cable, start the engine and run it until normal operating temperature is reached, then check for leaks.

8   Coolant temperature sending unit - check and replacement

Refer to illustration 8.5a and 8.5b

Warning: *Since the ignition key will be in the On position for some of the diagnostic steps, be especially careful to stay clear of the electric cooling fan blades.*

1   The coolant temperature indicator system is composed of a light mounted in the instrument panel and a coolant temperature sending unit located in a water passage, usually in the cylinder head or engine block. If a temperature gauge is included in the instrument cluster, the temperature sending unit is replaced by a transducer.

2   If overheating occurs, check the coolant

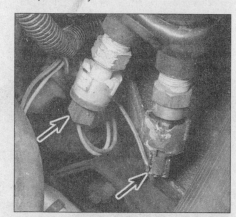

8.5a The coolant temperature sending units (arrows) are located in the thermostat housing on OHC engines

8.5b On V6 engines, the coolant temperature switch (arrow) is located adjacent to the EGR pipe - follow the wire back to the connector and disconnect it

10.1 Blower motor electrical connectors (arrows)

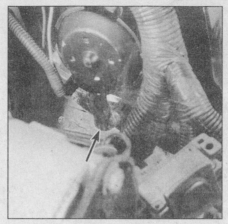

10.2 Remove the blower motor cooling tube (arrow)

10.3 Remove the blower motor and fan assembly from the housing

level in the system and then make sure that the wiring between the light or gauge and the sending unit is secure.

3   When the ignition switch is turned on and the starter motor is turning, the indicator light should be on (overheated engine indication). If the light is not on, the bulb may be burned out, the ignition switch may be faulty or the circuit may be open.

4   As soon as the engine starts, the light should go out and remain out unless the engine overheats. Failure of the light to go out may be due to grounded wiring between the light and the sending unit, a defective sending unit or a faulty ignition switch.

5   To test the circuit, unplug the electrical connector and, using a jumper wire, connect the wiring harness to a good ground **(see illustrations)**. **Caution:** *Some vehicles have more than one sending unit – the unit used for the indicator system has only one wire (usually solid green). DO NOT ground the Coolant Temperature Sensor (yellow and black wire) or damage to the computer may result.* With the ignition On, the indicator light should be glowing. If it does but the engine has been overheating and the light hasn't been coming on, replace the sending unit. If the light does not glow, there is a break in the wire or a burned-out bulb.

6   If the sending unit is to be replaced, it is simply unscrewed and a replacement installed. Wrap the threads of the new sending unit with Teflon tape. Make sure that the engine is cool before removing the defective sending unit there will be some coolant loss, so check the level after the replacement has been installed.

9   Heater and air conditioner blower motor and circuit check - check and switch replacement

Warning: *Since the ignition key will be in the On position for some of the diagnostic steps, be especially careful to stay clear of the electric cooling fan blades.*

1   If the blower motor speed does not correspond to the setting selected on the blower switch, or the blower motor does not operate at all, the problem could be a bad fuse, relay, switch, blower motor resistor, blower motor or blower motor circuit wiring.

2   Before checking the blower motor or circuit, always check the fuse and relay (if equipped) first (see Chapter 12). If the fuse and relay are good proceed as follows:

3   With the ignition key in the ON position, turn the blower switch to the faulty position(s) and, using a test light or voltmeter, check the voltage at the motor (purple wire). If the motor is receiving voltage but not operating, connect a jumper wire between the ground wire terminal on the blower motor and a good ground. If the motor operates, the ground circuit is bad. If the motor still doesn't operate the motor itself is faulty or the fan is binding. If you suspect the blower motor fan is binding, remove the blower motor (see Section 10) to check for free operation of the fan.

4   If there is no power to the blower motor (purple wire) locate the electrical connector for the blower motor resistor (see Section 10), usually attached to a heating/air conditioning duct or the blower motor case. Verify that the resistor is receiving voltage in all the blower speed positions.

5   If the resistor is receiving voltage but there is no power out to the blower relay or motor (usually a dark blue wire), replace the blower resistor assembly.

6   If there is no voltage reaching the resistor, unplug the electrical connector from the blower switch and check the continuity across the switch terminals with an ohmmeter. If the switch fails any of the continuity checks, replace it.

10   Heater and air conditioner blower motor - removal and installation

Refer to illustrations 10.1, 10.2, 10.3 and 10.4

1   Working in the engine compartment, disconnect the wires from the blower motor

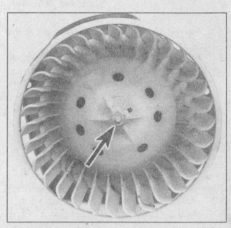

10.4 Remove the nut (arrow) and slip the fan off the motor shaft

(see illustration).

2   Detach the blower motor cooling tube **(see illustration)**.

3   Remove the screws and separate the motor/fan assembly from the housing **(see illustration)**. **Note:** *On some models it may be necessary to remove the power steering pump to provide clearance for blower removal.*

4   Remove the retaining nut and slide the fan off the motor shaft **(see illustration)**.

5   Before installing the blower motor, apply a strip of weather-strip caulking compound to the perimeter of the opening in the blower motor housing.

6   Installation is the reverse of removal. Be sure to attach the cooling hose to the motor.

11   Heater and air conditioner control assembly - removal and installation

Refer to illustrations 11.2, 11.3 and 11.4

1   Remove the trim panel around the heater and air conditioner control assembly (see Chapter 11).

11.2 Remove the heater and air conditioning control panel screws (arrows)

11.3 Unplug the electrical and vacuum connectors from the back of the back of the control panel. Be sure to unplug the entire vacuum connector - NOT the individual hoses

2   Remove the screws on each side of the control assembly **(see illustration)**.
3   Pull the control out of the dash then label and unplug the vacuum and electrical connectors **(see illustration)**. **Note:** *Do not disconnect the individual vacuum lines - disconnect the entire vacuum connector.*
4   Carefully pry the cable housing and cable retaining clips off with a small screwdriver **(see illustration)**.
5   Installation is the reverse of removal.

12   Heater core - removal and installation

Refer to illustration 12.2
Warning: *The engine must be completely cool before beginning this procedure.*
1   Disconnect the cable from the negative battery terminal. Drain the cooling system (see Chapter 1).
2   Raise the vehicle and support it securely on jackstands. Working underneath the vehicle, remove the drain tube from the heater case. Loosen the hose clamps and discon-

nect the heater hoses from the heater core tubes at the firewall. Plug the ends of the heater core tubes to prevent spillage when it is removed **(see illustration)**.
3   Lower the vehicle. Working inside the vehicle, remove the left and right side underdash panels.
4   Remove the heater floor outlet duct.
5   Remove the screws and clips that secure the heater core cover, then remove the cover.
6   Remove the heater core retaining straps and remove the heater core from the housing. Be careful not to spill any coolant as this is done.
7   Installation is the reverse of the removal procedure. Refill the cooling system with the proper coolant mixture (see Chapter 1). Run the engine and check for leaks.

13   Air conditioning system - check and maintenance

Warning: *The air conditioning system is under high pressure. Do not loosen any fit-*

tings or remove any components until after the system has been discharged. Air conditioning refrigerant should be properly discharged into an EPA-approved container at a dealer service department or an automotive air conditioning repair facility. Always wear eye protection when disconnecting air conditioning system fittings.
1   The following maintenance checks should be performed on a regular basis to ensure that the air conditioner continues to operate at peak efficiency. **Note:** *Long term non-use can cause hardening, and subsequent failure, of the seals.*

a) *Check the compressor drivebelt. If it's worn or deteriorated, replace it (see Chapter 1).*
b) *Check the drivebelt tension and, if necessary, adjust it (see Chapter 1).*
c) *Check the system hoses. Look for cracks, bubbles, hard spots and deterioration. Inspect the hoses and all fittings for oil bubbles and seepage. If there's any evidence of wear, damage or leaks, replace the hose(s).*
d) *Inspect the condenser fins for leaves, bugs and other debris. Use a "fin comb" or compressed air to clean the condenser.*
e) *Make sure the system has the correct refrigerant charge.*
f) *Check the evaporator housing drain tube for blockage.*

2   Because of the complexity of the air conditioning system and the special equipment necessary to service it, in-depth troubleshooting and repairs are not included in this manual. However, simple checks and component replacement procedures are provided in this Chapter. For more complete information on the air conditioning system, refer to the *Haynes Automotive Heating and Air Conditioning Manual.*
3   The most common cause of poor cooling is simply a low system refrigerant charge. If a noticeable drop in cool air output occurs, one of the following quick checks will help

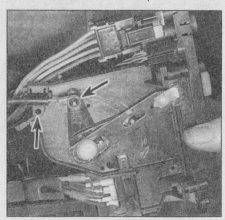

11.4 Two mounting clips (arrows) attach the temperature control cable and cable housing to the heater and air conditioning control assembly

12.2 Remove the heater hoses from the heater core tubes and plug the tubes (arrows)

15.3 Accumulator refrigerant line fittings (arrows)

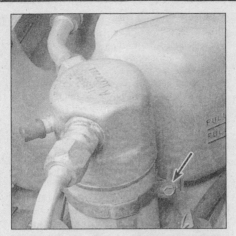

15.4 Remove the accumulator mounting bolt (arrow)

you determine if the refrigerant level is low.

4   Warm the engine up to normal operating temperature.

5   Place the air conditioning temperature selector at the coldest setting and put the blower at the highest setting. Open the doors (to make sure the air conditioning system doesn't cycle off as soon as it cools the passenger compartment).

6   When the compressor is engaged the clutch will make an audible click and the center of the clutch will rotate. Allow the system to operate at least five minutes.

7   With your hand, feel the temperature of the evaporator inlet pipe and the surface of the accumulator. If there's no perceptible temperature difference between the inlet pipe and the accumulator the system is properly charged. If there is a difference there's something wrong with the system. It might be a low charge - it might be something else. Take the vehicle to a dealer service department or other qualified repair shop for further diagnosis.

14 Air conditioning compressor - removal and installation

Warning: *The air conditioning system is under high pressure. Do not loosen any fittings or remove any components until after the system has been discharged. Air conditioning refrigerant should be properly discharged into an EPA-approved container at a dealer service department or an automotive air conditioning repair facility. Always wear eye protection when disconnecting air conditioning system fittings.*
Note: *The accumulator and expansion tube (Section 15 and 16) should be replaced whenever a new compressor is installed.*

Removal

1   Have the system discharged (see the Warning above).

2   Disconnect the negative cable from the battery. **Caution:** *If the vehicle is equipped*

with a Delco Loc II audio system, make sure you have the correct activation code before disconnecting the battery. See the information at the front of this manual for the radio re-activation procedure.

3   Set the parking brake and block the rear wheels. Raise the front of the vehicle and support it securely on jackstands.

4   Remove the right under-vehicle splash shield.

5   Remove the drivebelt (see Chapter 1). On some models it may also be necessary to remove the oil filter to provide clearance for compressor removal.

6   Disconnect the compressor clutch electrical connector.

7   Disconnect the refrigerant lines from the rear of the compressor. Plug the open fittings to prevent entry of dirt and moisture.

8   Unbolt the compressor from its mounting brackets and lower it from the vehicle.

Installation

9   If a new compressor is being installed, follow the directions with the new compressor regarding the draining of excess oil prior to installation.

10   The clutch may have to be transferred from the original to the new compressor.

11   Installation is the reverse of removal. Replace all O-rings with new ones made specifically for air conditioning system use and lubricate them with refrigerant oil.

12   Have the system evacuated, recharged and leak tested by the shop that discharged it.

15 Air conditioning accumulator - removal and installation

Refer to illustrations 15.3 and 15.4
Warning: *The air conditioning system is under high pressure. Do not loosen any fittings or remove any components until after the system has been discharged. Air conditioning refrigerant should be properly discharged into an EPA-approved container at a dealer service*

department or an automotive air conditioning repair facility. Always wear eye protection when disconnecting air conditioning system fittings.
Note: *Whenever the accumulator is replaced, the expansion tube should also be replaced (see Section 15).*

Removal

1   Have the system discharged (see the Warning above).

2   Disconnect the negative cable from the battery. **Caution:** *If the vehicle is equipped with a Delco Loc II audio system, make sure you have the correct activation code before disconnecting the battery. See the information at the front of this manual for the radio re-activation procedure.*

3   Disconnect the refrigerant lines from the accumulator **(see illustration)**. Use a back-up wrench to avoid twisting the tubing. Plug the open fittings to prevent the entry of dirt and moisture.

4   Loosen the mounting bracket bolts **(see illustration)** and remove the accumulator.

Installation

5   If a new accumulator is being installed, remove the Schrader valve and pour the oil out into a measuring cup, noting the amount. Add fresh refrigerant oil to the new accumulator equal to the amount removed from the old unit, plus one ounce.

6   The remainder of installation is the reverse of removal.

7   Have the system evacuated, recharged and leak tested by the shop that discharged it.

16 Air conditioning expansion tube - replacement

Warning: *The air conditioning system is under high pressure. Do not loosen any fittings or remove any components until after the system has been discharged. Air conditioning refrigerant should be properly discharged into an EPA-approved container at a dealer service department or an automotive air conditioning repair facility. Always wear eye protection when disconnecting air conditioning system fittings.*
Note: *If the expansion tube screen (orifice) experiences repeated plugging the accumulator should also be replaced (see Section 15).*

1   Have the system discharged (see the Warning above).

2   Disconnect the negative cable from the battery. **Caution:** *If the vehicle is equipped with a Delco Loc II audio system, make sure you have the correct activation code before disconnecting the battery. See the information at the front of this manual for the radio re-activation procedure.*

3   If you're working on a 1987 or earlier model, loosen the refrigerant line fitting at the evaporator inlet pipe. Separate the line from

the inlet pipe.

4 If you're working on a 1988 or later model, loosen the refrigerant line fitting at the condenser outlet pipe.

5 Using needle-nose pliers, carefully remove the expansion tube. If the expansion tube is plugged and difficult to remove, GM special tool no. J-26549 or equivalent may be needed to extract it.

6 Installation is the reverse of removal. Be sure to lube the O-ring with clean refrigerant oil and insert the expansion tube with the shorter screen end toward the evaporator.

7 Have the system evacuated, recharged and leak tested by the shop that discharged it.

17 Air conditioning condenser - removal and installation

Warning: *The air conditioning system is under high pressure. Do not loosen any fittings or remove any components until after the system has been discharged. Air conditioning refrigerant should be properly discharged into an EPA-approved container at a dealer service department or an automotive air conditioning repair facility. Always wear eye protection when disconnecting air conditioning system fittings.*

Removal

1 Have the system discharged (see the Warning above).

2 Disconnect the negative cable from the battery. **Caution:** *If the vehicle is equipped with a Delco Loc II audio system, make sure you have the correct activation code before disconnecting the battery. See the information at the front of this manual for the radio re-activation procedure.*

3 Disconnect the refrigerant lines from the condenser. Be sure to use a backup wrench on the condenser fittings to avoid twisting the line.

4 Depending on the model, remove the headlamp bezels and grille assembly or the front end filler panels to gain access to the condenser. Remove the hood latch release cable and the front end panel center support.

5 If equipped with retractable headlamps, manually open the headlamp doors by turning the headlamp door actuator knob. Remove the retaining bolts from the headlamp actuators and pull the actuator assemblies forward as far as possible.

6 Remove the condenser mounting bolts and lift out the condenser. Be careful not to bend the fins on either the radiator or condenser. If the original condenser is to be reinstalled, plug the line fittings to prevent dirt and moisture from entering.

Installation

7 If a new condenser is being installed, pour one ounce of refrigerant oil into it prior to installation.

8 Reinstall the components in the reverse order of removal. Be sure any rubber mounting pads that may have been present during removal are properly located.

9 Have the system evacuated, recharged and leak tested by the shop that discharged it.

18 Air conditioning evaporator core - removal and installation

Warning: *The air conditioning system is under high pressure. Do not loosen any fittings or remove any components until after the system has been discharged. Air conditioning refrigerant should be properly discharged into an EPA-approved container at a dealer service department or an automotive air conditioning repair facility. Always wear eye protection when disconnecting air conditioning system fittings.*

1 Have the system discharged (see the Warning above).

2 Disconnect the negative cable from the battery. **Caution:** *If the vehicle is equipped with a Delco Loc II audio system, make sure you have the correct activation code before disconnecting the battery. See the information at the front of this manual for the radio re-activation procedure.*

3 Drain the cooling system.

4 Remove the heater core (see Section 12).

5 Remove the screws retaining the defroster vacuum actuator to the heater case.

6 Remove the evaporator cover and carefully remove the evaporator core from the case. **(see illustration 12.2).**

7 Installation is the reverse of removal. If a new evaporator is being installed, add three ounces of refrigerant oil into it prior to installation.

8 Have the system evacuated, recharged and leak tested by the shop that discharged it.

Chapter 4
Fuel and exhaust systems

Contents

Specifications

General
Minimum idle speed adjustment (see Section 16) .... 600 +/- 25 rpm

Fuel pressure (at idle)
Carbureted engines .... 4 to 6 psi
Throttle Body Injection (TBI) .... 9 to 13 psi
Multi-Port Fuel Injection (MPFI) turbo
    Regulator vacuum hose connected .... Approximately 26 to 32 psi
    Regulator vacuum hose disconnected .... Pressure should increase by 5 to 10 psi
Multi-Port Fuel Injection (MPFI) non-turbo
    Regulator vacuum hose connected .... Approximately 41 to 47 psi
    Regulator vacuum hose disconnected .... Pressure should increase by 5 to 10 psi

Injector resistance
TBI injector .... 1.2 to 1.6 ohms
MPFI injectors .... 11.8 to 12.6 ohms

Torque specifications
	Ft-lbs (unless otherwise indicated)
Mechanical fuel pump mounting bolts/nuts	15 to 22
Carburetor mounting bolts/nuts	120 in-lbs
TBI unit mounting bolts/nuts	156 in-lbs
Exhaust pipe-to-manifold nuts	15 to 22
Throttle body (MPFI) mounting bolts/nuts	10 to 18
Air intake plenum mounting bolts/nuts	
2.2L engine	22
V6 engines	16
Injector retainer screws (2.2L four-cylinder engine)	31 in-lbs
Oil feed pipe-to-turbo	12
Oil feed pipe union	12
Oil feed pipe-to-block	12
Oil drain hose	35
Turbocharger throttle body	18
Turbocharger-to-exhaust manifold	18
Turbocharger outlet elbow-to-turbocharger	18
Turbocharger support bracket	
Lower bolt	37
Retaining nut	18

Component location

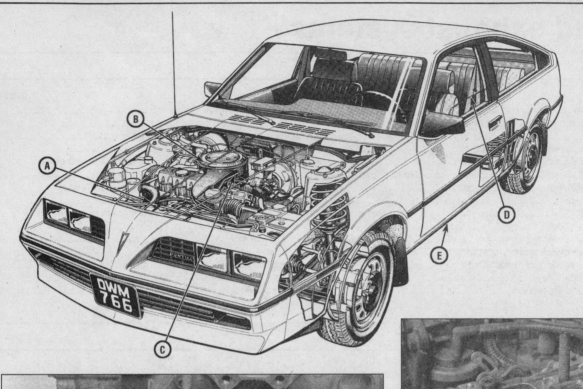

A Typical mechanical fuel pump used on carburetor models, typically located on the lower front side of the engine block

B Typical E2SE carburetor located under the air cleaner (carburetor models)

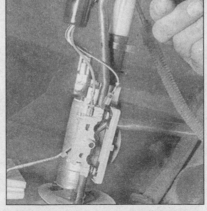

C The fuel injector are located under the air cleaner in the throttle body (throttle body models)

D Typical electric fuel pump located in the fuel tank (fuel injected models)

E The fuel filter is typically located in the rear of the car behind the fuel tank (fuel injected models)

1 General information

The fuel system consists of a fuel tank, a mechanical fuel pump (carbureted models) or an electric fuel pump and fuel pump relay (fuel-injected models), an air cleaner assembly and either a feedback carburetor system (E2SE), a Throttle Body Injection (TBI) system or a Multi Port Fuel Injection (MPFI) system. The basic difference between throttle body and port fuel injection systems is the number and location of the fuel injectors.

Carburetor systems

Early models are equipped with an E2SE feedback carburetor. The function of this system is to control the flow of fuel through the carburetor idle and main metering circuits. The components of the system are the mixture control (M/C) solenoid, coolant sensor, throttle position sensor (TPS), vehicle speed sensor (VSS), Manifold Absolute Pressure (MAP) sensor, barometric pressure sensor, Idle Speed Control (ISC) solenoid, the ECM (computer) and the oxygen sensor. **Note:** *The diagnostic procedures for many of these sensors and output actuators are covered in Chapter 6.*

Throttle Body Injection (TBI) system

The throttle body system utilizes a single injector, centrally mounted in a carburetor-like housing. The injector is an electrical solenoid, with fuel delivered to the injector at a constant pressure level. To maintain the fuel pressure at a constant level, excess fuel is returned to the fuel tank.

A signal from the ECM opens the solenoid, allowing fuel to spray through the injector into the throttle body. The amount of time the injector is held open by the ECM determines the fuel/air mixture ratio.

Multi Port Fuel Injection (MPFI) system

The port system utilizes injectors of a different type than the throttle body injection system. The fuel/air ratio is controlled in the same manner as the TBI system. Instead of an injector mounted in a centrally located throttle body, one injector is installed above each intake port. The throttle body on the MPFI system serves only to control the amount of air passing into the system. Because each cylinder is equipped with an injector mounted immediately adjacent to the intake valve, much better control of the fuel/air mixture ratio is possible.

Fuel pump and lines

Carbureted models utilize a mechanically operated fuel pump located on the side of the engine block. The pump lever is actuated by a camshaft lobe and fuel is drawn from the tank through a metal line extending from the fuel meter assembly to the fuel pump.

On fuel-injected engines, fuel is circulated from the fuel tank to the fuel injection system, and back to the fuel tank, through a pair of metal lines running along the underside of the vehicle. An electric fuel pump is attached to the fuel sending unit inside the fuel tank. A return system routes all vapors and excess fuel back to the fuel tank through separate return lines.

Exhaust system

The exhaust system includes an exhaust manifold fitted with an exhaust oxygen sensor, a catalytic converter, an exhaust pipe, and a muffler. The catalytic converter is an emission control device added to the exhaust system to reduce pollutants. A single-bed converter is used in combination with a three-way (reduction) catalyst. Refer to Chapter 6 for more information regarding the catalytic converter.

2 Fuel pressure relief procedure

Refer to illustration 2.4

Warning: *Gasoline is extremely flammable, so take extra precautions when you work on any part of the fuel system. Don't smoke or allow open flames or bare light bulbs near the work area, and don't work in a garage where a natural gas-type appliance (such as a water heater or a clothes dryer) with a pilot light is present. Since gasoline is carcinogenic, wear latex gloves when there's a possibility of being exposed to fuel, and, if you spill any fuel on your skin, rinse it off immediately with soap and water. Mop up any spills immediately and do not store fuel-soaked rags where they could ignite. The fuel system is under constant pressure, so, if any fuel lines are to be disconnected, the fuel pressure in the system must be relieved first. When you perform any kind of work on the fuel system, wear safety glasses and have a Class B type fire extinguisher on hand.*

Note: *After the fuel pressure has been relieved, it's a good idea to lay a shop towel over any fuel connection to be disassembled, to absorb the residual fuel that may leak out when servicing the fuel system.*

1   Before servicing any fuel system component on a fuel-injected vehicle, you must relieve the fuel pressure to minimize the risk of fire or personal injury.

2   Remove the fuel filler cap - this will relieve any pressure built up in the tank.

Throttle Body Injected (TBI) engines

Note: *Although some TBI units have an automatic internal bleed system, follow the procedure described below to relieve the fuel pressure on all TBI engines*

3   Remove the fuel pump fuse (see Chapter 12) and run the engine until it stalls, then crank the engine for three seconds. Disconnect the cable from the negative battery ter-

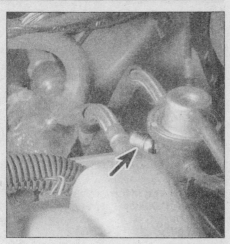

2.4 Remove the cap to gain access to the Schrader valve for connecting a fuel pressure gauge

minal. **Caution:** *If the vehicle is equipped with a Delco Loc II audio system, make sure you have the correct activation code before disconnecting the battery. See the information at the front of this manual for the radio re-activation procedure.*

Multi Port Fuel Injected (MPFI) engines

4   Use one of the two following methods:

a) Disconnect the fuel pump electrical connector at the fuel tank (lower the tank if necessary). Run the engine until it stops, then engage the starter again for another three seconds. With the ignition turned Off, reconnect the fuel tank electrical connector, then disconnect the cable from the negative terminal of the battery.

b) Loosen the fuel filler cap. Attach a fuel pressure gauge to the Schrader valve on the fuel rail **(see illustration)**. Place the gauge bleeder hose in an approved fuel container. Open the valve on the gauge to relieve pressure, then disconnect the cable from the negative terminal of the battery.

5   Unless this procedure is followed before servicing fuel lines or connections, fuel spray (and possible injury) may occur.

3 Fuel pump/fuel system pressure - check

Warning: *Gasoline is extremely flammable, so take extra precautions when you work on any part of the fuel system. Don't smoke or allow open flames or bare light bulbs near the work area, and don't work in a garage where a natural gas-type appliance (such as a water heater or a clothes dryer) with a pilot light is present. Since gasoline is carcinogenic, wear latex gloves when there's a possibility of being exposed to fuel, and, if you spill any fuel on your skin, rinse it off immediately with* soap and water. Mop up any spills immediately and do not store fuel-soaked rags where they could ignite. The fuel system is under constant pressure, so, if any fuel lines are to be disconnected, the fuel pressure in the system must be relieved first. When you perform any kind of work on the fuel system, wear safety glasses and have a Class B type fire extinguisher on hand.

Note: *The following checks assume the fuel filter is in good condition. If you doubt its condition, install a new one* (see Chapter 1).

1　Check that there is adequate fuel in the fuel tank. If you doubt the reading on the gauge, insert a long wooden dowel at the filler opening; it will serve as a dipstick.

Fuel pump output and pressure check

Carbureted models

2　If you suspect insufficient fuel delivery, first inspect all fuel lines to ensure that the problem is not simply a leak in a line.

3　If there are no leaks evident in the fuel lines, inspect the fuel pump itself. The following checks will tell you if the fuel pump is leaking and whether it is pumping fuel.

4　Remove the air cleaner housing.

5　Hook up a remote starter switch in accordance with the manufacturer's instructions. If you don't have a remote starter switch, you will need an assistant to help you with this and the following procedure.

6　Detach the fuel feed line at the carburetor **(see illustration 11.3)**.

7　Detach the wires from the primary terminals of the ignition coil (see Chapter 5).

8　Place a metal container under the open end of the fuel pump outlet line. If the line is metal and you can't get a can under the end of it, attach a length of fuel hose to the end of the line and place it in the can.

9　Direct the fuel pump outlet line into the container while cranking the engine for a few seconds with the remote starter (or while an assistant cranks the engine with the ignition key). If fuel is emitted in well defined spurts, the pump is operating satisfactorily (it should pump approximately one-pint in thirty seconds or less). If fuel dribbles or trickles out the hose, the pump is defective. Replace it (see Section 7).

10　Attach a pressure gauge to the end of the fuel hose. Crank the engine for a few seconds and note the reading of the gauge. If it is below the minimum fuel pressure listed in this Chapter's Specifications, replace the pump.

Multi Port Fuel Injection (MPFI) models

Refer to illustration 3.12

11　Install a fuel pressure gauge at the Schrader valve on the fuel rail **(see illustration 2.4)**. **Note:** *On models without a Schrader valve, install a fuel pressure gauge adapter between the fuel filter and fuel rail.*

12　Turn the ignition switch ON (engine not running) with the air conditioning off. The fuel

3.12 Apply battery voltage to the test connector located in the left rear corner of the engine compartment

pump should run for about two seconds - note the reading on the gauge. After the pump stops running the pressure should hold steady. It should be within the range listed in this Chapter's Specifications. **Note:** *If there is no response from the fuel pump, use a jumper wire attached to the positive terminal of the battery and apply battery voltage to the test terminal located on the driver's side of the engine compartment* **(see illustration)***. This procedure will bypass the fuel pump relay and allow voltage to flow directly to the fuel pump.*

13　Start the engine and let it idle at normal operating temperature. The pressure should be lower by 3 to 10 psi. If all the pressure readings are within the limits listed in this Chapter's Specifications, the system is operating properly.

14　If the pressure did not drop by 3 to 10 psi after starting the engine, apply 12 to 14 inches of vacuum to the pressure regulator. If the pressure drops, repair the vacuum source to the regulator. If the pressure does not drop, replace the regulator.

15　If the fuel pressure is not within specifications, check the following:

a) *If the pressure is higher than specified, check for a pinched or clogged fuel return hose or pipe. If the return line is OK, replace the regulator.*

b) *If the pressure is lower than specified, inspect the fuel filter - make sure it's not clogged. If the filter is good and there are no fuel leaks but the pressure is still low, pinch the fuel return line. If the pressure rises sharply, replace the regulator (see Section 18).*

c) *Check for leaking injectors.*

d) *Check the in-tank fuel pump check valve.*

16　After the testing is done, relieve the fuel pressure (see Section 2) and remove the fuel pressure gauge.

17　If there are no problems with any of the above-listed components, check the fuel pump electrical circuits (see below).

Throttle Body Injection (TBI) models

18　Relieve fuel system pressure (see Section 2).

19　Install a fuel pressure gauge between the fuel feed hose and the inlet fitting of the throttle body. The fuel hoses will be under high pressure during this check, so make your connections secure, with no possibility of leaks. **Note:** *If the fuel line fittings to adapt your fuel pressure gauge are not available, special adapters are available at auto parts stores or automotive specialty tool companies.*

20　With the ignition OFF, connect a fused jumper wire from the positive battery terminal to the fuel pump test terminal (red wire) **(see illustration 3.12)** and note the pressure reading.

21　If the pressure is within the limits listed in this Chapter's Specifications, no further testing is necessary.

22　If the pressure was higher than specified, check for a restricted fuel return line. If the line is OK, then replace the fuel meter cover, which contains the fuel pressure regulator (see Section 16).

23　If the pressure was less than specified, slowly pinch the hose between the gauge and the TBI unit and note the pressure. If the pressure rises above 9 psi, then replace the fuel meter cover. If there is no pressure, then check for a plugged fuel filter, plugged fuel pump inlet filter or a restricted fuel line.

24　After testing is completed, relieve the fuel pressure and remove the fuel pressure gauge.

25　If no problems are found with any of the above listed components, check the fuel pump electrical circuits (see below).

Fuel pump electrical circuit check (TBI and MPFI models)

26　If you suspect a problem with the fuel pump, verify the pump actually runs. Have an assistant turn the ignition switch to ON - you should hear a brief whirring noise as the pump comes on and pressurizes the system. Have the assistant start the engine. This time you should hear a constant whirring sound from the pump (but it's more difficult to hear with the engine running).

27　If the pump does not come on (makes no sound), proceed to the next Step.

28　Check the fuel pump fuse located in the passenger compartment **(see illustration 3.1 in Chapter 12, Section 3)**. If the fuse is blown, replace the fuse and see if the pump works. If the pump still does not work, go to the next step.

29　With the ignition OFF, apply 12 volts (battery voltage) to the fuel pump test terminal **(see illustration 3.12)** and listen for the fuel pump running.

30　If the pump runs, then check the fuel pump relay. If the pump does not run, check for an open circuit between the relay and the fuel pump. If the circuit is OK, disconnect the electrical connector(s) at the fuel pump. Con-

3.31a The fuel pump relay (arrow) is usually located together with the A/C relays (1993 Sunbird shown). Consult the underhood component location diagrams in Chapter 6 for additional information on other models

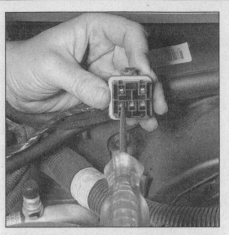

3.31b With the ignition key on (engine not running) check for battery voltage to the relay connector. Most models use a pink/black wire

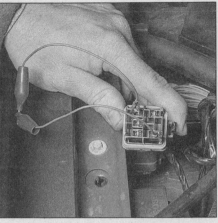

3.32a Jump the ignition wire to the fuel pump wire to activate the fuel pump. Be careful not to touch the wrong terminal and blow the fuel pump fuse

nect battery voltage to the gray wire terminal of the pump. Connect the black wire terminal to ground. If the fuel pump now runs, it's OK; check all connections and wiring again. If it does not run, it's faulty. Replace the fuel pump.

Fuel pump relay check

Refer to illustration 3.31a, 3.31b, 3.32a and 3.32b

31   To test the fuel pump relay, disconnect the fuel pump relay **(see illustration)** and connect a test light to the ignition wire and have an assistant turn the key ON (engine not running) **(see illustration)**. The test light should come on for two or three seconds and cycle itself off.

32   Use a jumper wire **(see illustration)** and connect the ignition wire to the fuel pump wire on the relay connector. The fuel pump should activate, making a distinct sound from the fuel tank area. **Note:** *Most of these models use a pink/black wire from the ignition key (B+) and a gray wire from the fuel pump. Double-check for the correct wire to the fuel pump by disconnecting the battery, install one test probe from an ohmmeter onto the test terminal* **(see illustration 3.12)** *and check for continuity at the fuel pump relay connector. The fuel pump circuit will be indicated by continuity on the ohmmeter* **(see illustration)**.

33   If the test results are correct, but the fuel pump relay does not come on (if it comes on, you should hear/feel a click at the relay when an assistant turns on the ignition key when

the relay is plugged in), replace the fuel pump relay with a new part. If there is no presence of voltage, check the ECM and the relating fuel pump circuits for a short or open circuit (see Chapter 12).

4   Fuel lines and fittings - repair and replacement

Refer to illustrations 4.10, 4.12 and 4.13
Warning: *Gasoline is extremely flammable, so take extra precautions when you work on any part of the fuel system. Don't smoke or allow open flames or bare light bulbs near the work area, and don't work in a garage where a natural gas-type appliance (such as a water heater or a clothes dryer) with a pilot light is present. Since gasoline is carcinogenic, wear latex gloves when there's a possibility of being exposed to fuel, and, if you spill any fuel on your skin, rinse it off immediately with soap and water. Mop up any spills immediately and do not store fuel-soaked rags where they could ignite. The fuel system is under constant pressure, so, if any fuel lines are to be disconnected, the fuel pressure in the system must be relieved first. When you perform any kind of work on the fuel system, wear safety glasses and have a Class B type fire extinguisher on hand.*

1   Always relieve the fuel pressure before servicing fuel lines or fittings on fuel-injected vehicles (see Section 2).

2   The fuel feed, return and vapor lines extend from the fuel tank to the engine compartment. The lines are secured to the underbody with clip and screw assemblies. These lines must be occasionally inspected for leaks, kinks and dents.

3   If evidence of dirt is found in the system or fuel filter during disassembly, the line should be disconnected and blown out. Check the fuel strainer on the fuel gauge sending unit (see Section 7) for damage and deterioration.

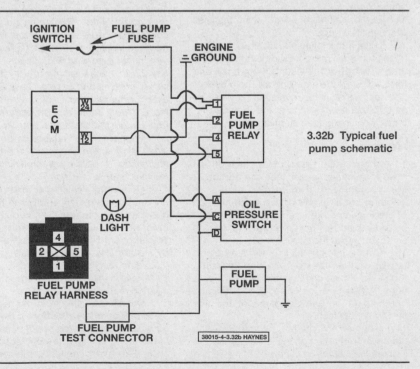

3.32b Typical fuel pump schematic

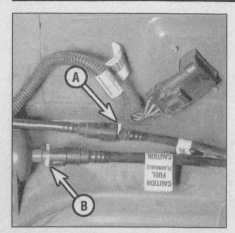

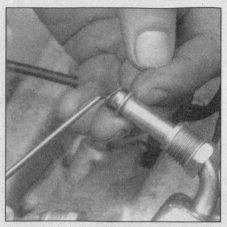

4.10 Some models are equipped with fuel lines that can be disconnected by pinching the tabs and separating each connector

    A   *Fuel return line*
    B   *Fuel feed line*

4.12 On quick connect fuel lines, use a special tool, available at most auto parts stores, and push them into the connector (arrows) to separate the fuel lines

4.13 Always replace the fuel line O-rings (if equipped)

Steel tubing

4   If replacement of a fuel line or emission line is called for, use welded steel tubing meeting GM specification 124-M or its equivalent.

5   Don't use copper or aluminum tubing to replace steel tubing. These materials cannot withstand normal vehicle vibration.

6   Because fuel lines used on fuel-injected vehicles are under high pressure, they require special consideration.

7   Most fuel lines have threaded fittings with O-rings. Any time the fittings are loosened to service or replace components:

  a) *Use a backup wrench while loosening and tightening the fittings.*
  b) *Check all O-rings for cuts, cracks and deterioration. Replace any that appear worn or damaged.*
  c) *If the lines are replaced, always use original equipment parts, or parts that meet the GM standards specified in this Section.*

Rubber hose

Warning: *On models equipped with multi port fuel injection, use only original equipment replacement hoses or their equivalent. Others may fail from the high pressures of this system.*

8   When rubber hose is used to replace a metal line, use reinforced, fuel resistant hose with the word *"Fluoroelastomer"* imprinted on it. Hose(s) not clearly marked like this could fail prematurely and could fail to meet Federal emission standards. Hose inside diameter must match line outside diameter.

9   Don't use rubber hose within four inches of any part of the exhaust system or within ten inches of the catalytic converter. Metal lines and rubber hoses must never be allowed to chafe against the frame. A minimum of 1/4-inch clearance must be main-

tained around a line or hose to prevent contact with the frame.

Removal and installation

Note: *The following procedure and accompanying illustrations are typical for vehicles covered by this manual. On quick-disconnect (non-threaded) fittings, clean off the fittings before disconnection to prevent dirt from getting in the fittings. After disconnection, clean the fittings with compressed air and apply a few drops of oil.*

10   Relieve the fuel pressure on fuel-injected models (see Section 2) and disconnect the fuel feed, return or vapor line at the fuel tank **(see illustration)**. **Note:** *Some fuel line connections may be threaded. Be sure to use a back-up wrench when separating the connections.*

11   Remove all fasteners attaching the lines to the vehicle body.

12   Detach the fitting(s) that attach the fuel hoses to the engine compartment metal lines **(see illustration)**. Twisting them back and forth will allow them to separate more easily.

13   Installation is the reverse of removal. Be sure to use new O-rings at the threaded fittings, if equipped **(see illustration)**.

Repair

14   In repairable areas, cut a piece of fuel hose four inches longer than the portion of the line removed. If more than a six inch length of line is removed, use a combination of steel line and hose so hose lengths won't be more than ten inches. Always follow the same routing as the original line.

15   Cut the ends of the line with a tube cutter. Using the first step of a double flaring tool, form a bead on the end of both line sections. If the line is too corroded to withstand bead operation without damage, the line should be replaced.

16   Use a screw type hose clamp. Slide the clamp onto the line and push the hose on. Tighten the clamps on each side of the repair.

17   Secure the lines properly to the frame to prevent chafing.

5   Fuel tank - removal and installation

Refer to illustration 5.8

Warning: *Gasoline is extremely flammable, so take extra precautions when you work on any part of the fuel system. Don't smoke or allow open flames or bare light bulbs near the work area, and don't work in a garage where a natural gas-type appliance (such as a water heater or a clothes dryer) with a pilot light is present. Since gasoline is carcinogenic, wear latex gloves when there's a possibility of being exposed to fuel, and, if you spill any fuel on your skin, rinse it off immediately with soap and water. Mop up any spills immediately and do not store fuel-soaked rags where they could ignite. The fuel system is under constant pressure, so, if any fuel lines are to be disconnected, the fuel pressure in the system must be relieved first. When you perform any kind of work on the fuel system, wear safety glasses and have a Class B type fire extinguisher on hand.*

Note: *Don't begin this procedure until the fuel gauge indicates the tank is empty or nearly empty. If the tank must be removed when it's full (for example, if the fuel pump malfunctions), siphon any remaining fuel from the tank prior to removal.*

1   Unless the vehicle has been driven far enough to completely empty the tank, it's a good idea to siphon the residual fuel out before removing the tank from the vehicle. **Warning:** *DO NOT start the siphoning action by mouth! Use a siphoning kit, available at most auto parts stores.*

2   Relieve the fuel system pressure on fuel-injected models (see Section 2).

3   Detach the cable from the negative terminal of the battery. **Caution:** *If the vehicle is equipped with a Delco Loc II audio system, make sure you have the correct activation code before disconnecting the battery. See*

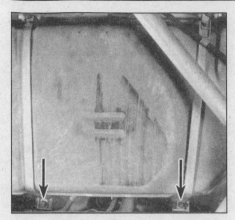

5.8 Remove the fuel tank strap retaining straps (arrows)

the information at the front of this manual for the radio re-activation procedure.

4   Raise the vehicle and place it securely on jackstands.

5   Locate the electrical connector for the electric fuel pump and fuel gauge sending unit in front of the tank, and unplug it. If the vehicle doesn't have a connector, see Step 9.

6   Disconnect the fuel feed and return lines, the vapor return line and the filler neck and vent tubes.

7   Support the fuel tank with a floor jack.

8   Disconnect both fuel tank retaining straps **(see illustration)**.

9   Lower the tank enough to disconnect the wires and ground strap from the fuel pump/fuel gauge sending unit, if you haven't already done so.

10   Remove the tank from the vehicle.

11   Installation is the reverse of removal.

6   Fuel tank cleaning and repair - general information

1   All repairs to the fuel tank or filler neck should be carried out by a professional who has experience in this critical and potentially

dangerous work. Even after cleaning and flushing of the fuel system, explosive fumes can remain and ignite during repair of the tank.

2   If the fuel tank is removed from the vehicle, it should not be placed in an area where sparks or open flames could ignite the fumes coming out of the tank. Be especially careful inside garages where a natural gas-type appliance is located, because the pilot light could cause an explosion.

7   Fuel pump - removal and installation

Warning: *Gasoline is extremely flammable, so take extra precautions when you work on any part of the fuel system. Don't smoke or allow open flames or bare light bulbs near the work area, and don't work in a garage where a natural gas-type appliance (such as a water heater or a clothes dryer) with a pilot light is present. Since gasoline is carcinogenic, wear latex gloves when there's a possibility of being exposed to fuel, and, if you spill any fuel on your skin, rinse it off immediately with soap and water. Mop up any spills immediately and do not store fuel-soaked rags where they could ignite. The fuel system is under constant pressure, so, if any fuel lines are to be disconnected, the fuel pressure in the system must be relieved first. When you perform any kind of work on the fuel system, wear safety glasses and have a Class B type fire extinguisher on hand.*

Mechanical pump (carbureted models)

Refer to illustration 7.3

1   The fuel pump is a sealed unit and cannot be rebuilt.

2   Disconnect the cable from the negative terminal of the battery.

3   Detach the fuel inlet hose, the outlet line and the vapor return hose (if equipped). Hold the fitting on the pump with a back-up

wrench as the outlet line is disconnected **(see illustration)**. Also, if possible, use a flare-nut wrench on the fuel line fitting.

4   Remove the two nuts from the mounting studs and remove the fuel pump by rotating the pump upward until it clears the studs.

5   Remove the gasket and mounting plate.

6   Remove all traces of old gasket and sealant with a scraper.

7   Clean the block mounting surface with lacquer thinner or acetone.

8   Position the new gasket, the mounting plate and the pump on the block, then install the nuts and tighten them to the torque listed in this Chapter's Specifications.

9   Reattach the inlet hose, the outlet line and the vapor return hose to the pump, if equipped. Be sure to tighten the fitting on the outlet line and the clamps on the hoses securely.

10   Start the engine and check for fuel leaks at the hose and line connections.

Electric pump (fuel-injected models)

Refer to illustrations 7.15, 7.16 and 7.18

11   Relieve the fuel system pressure (see Section 2).

12   Disconnect the cable from the negative battery terminal. **Caution:** *If the vehicle is equipped with a Delco Loc II audio system, make sure you have the correct activation code before disconnecting the battery. See the information at the front of this manual for the radio re-activation procedure.*

13   Remove the fuel tank (see Section 5).

14   The fuel pump/sending unit assembly is located inside the fuel tank. It is held in place by a cam lock ring mechanism consisting of an inner ring with three locking cams and an outer ring with three tangs. The outer ring is welded to the tank and can't be turned.

15   To unlock the fuel pump/sending unit assembly, turn the inner ring counterclockwise using a hammer and a BRASS punch or hardwood dowel until the locking cams are free of the tangs **(see illustration)**. **Warning:** *Do not use a steel punch to knock the lock*

7.3 When detaching the fuel line from the mechanical fuel pump, hold the inside fitting with one wrench while turning the outside fitting with another

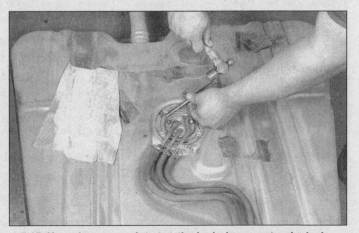

7.15 Use a brass punch to tap the lock ring counterclockwise until the tabs align with the recess areas of the fuel tank

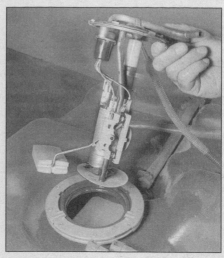

7.16 Lift the fuel pump assembly from the fuel tank

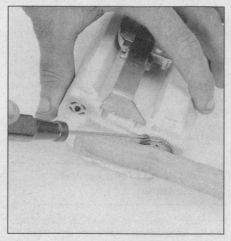

7.18 Inspect the fuel strainer for dirt; if too dirty to be cleaned carefully pry the fuel strainer from the inlet pipe

9   Air cleaner housing - removal and installation

1   Detach the cable from the negative terminal of the battery.
2   Remove the battery from the vehicle if necessary (see Chapter 5).

TBI engines

3   Remove the air cleaner element (see Chapter 1).
4   Unclamp the air intake duct from the air cleaner housing.
5   Unplug the electrical connector from the MAP sensor and remove any vacuum lines from the housing and detach any other fasteners retaining the air duct.
6   Remove the crankcase vent hose.
7   Disconnect the heated air inlet hose and lift the housing from the vehicle.
8   Installation is the reverse of removal.

MPFI engines

9   Remove the bolts that retain the air intake assembly to the front of the engine compartment.
10   Remove the bolt and the clamp from the engine brace and separate the air intake duct from the engine compartment.
11   Loosen the clamp from the throttle body/air intake duct.
12   Disconnect the Air Intake Temperature (AIT) sensor and lift the complete air cleaner housing from the engine compartment.
13   Installation is the reverse of removal.

rings loose - a spark could cause an explosion!
16   Lift the fuel pump/sending unit assembly from the fuel tank **(see illustration). Caution:** *The fuel level float and sending unit are delicate. Do not bump them against the tank during removal or the accuracy of the sending unit may be affected.*
17   Inspect the condition of the rubber gasket around the mouth of the lock ring mechanism. If it is dried, cracked or deteriorated, replace it.
18   Inspect the strainer on the lower end of the fuel pump **(see illustration)**. If it is dirty, remove it, clean it with a suitable solvent and blow it out with compressed air. If it is too dirty to be cleaned, replace it.
19   If it is necessary to separate the fuel pump and sending unit, disconnect the electrical connectors at the pump, noting their position. Remove the pump from the sending unit by pulling the fuel pump assembly into the rubber connector and sliding the pump away from the bottom support. Care should be taken to prevent damage to the rubber insulator and fuel strainer during removal. After the pump assembly is clear of the bottom support, pull it out of the rubber connector.
20   Reassemble the fuel pump to the sending unit and insert the assembly into the fuel tank.
21   Turn the inner lock ring clockwise until the locking cams are fully engaged with the retaining tangs. **Note:** *If you have installed a new O-ring type rubber gasket, it may be necessary to push down on the inner lock ring until the locking cams slide under the retaining tangs.*
22   Install the fuel tank (see Section 5).

8   Fuel level sending unit - check and replacement

Warning: *Gasoline is extremely flammable,*

so take extra precautions when you work on any part of the fuel system. Don't smoke or allow open flames or bare light bulbs near the work area, and don't work in a garage where a natural gas-type appliance (such as a water heater or a clothes dryer) with a pilot light is present. Since gasoline is carcinogenic, wear latex gloves when there's a possibility of being exposed to fuel, and, if you spill any fuel on your skin, rinse it off immediately with soap and water. Mop up any spills immediately and do not store fuel-soaked rags where they could ignite. The fuel system is under constant pressure, so, if any fuel lines are to be disconnected, the fuel pressure in the system must be relieved first. When you perform any kind of work on the fuel system, wear safety glasses and have a Class B type fire extinguisher on hand.*

Check

1   Raise the vehicle and support it securely on jackstands.
2   Disconnect the electrical connector for the fuel pump/fuel level sending unit. With the ignition key in the On position, the needle on the fuel level gauge should deflect to the maximum full position.
3   Using a jumper wire, ground the wire to the fuel level sending unit (it's usually the pink or purple wire). The needle on the gauge should now read empty.
4   If the gauge responds properly to these checks, the harness and gauge are OK. Replace the fuel level sending unit. If the gauge does not operate as described, the problem lies in the wiring harness to the gauge, or the gauge itself.

Replacement

5   Follow the procedure described in Section 7, beginning with Step 11, to remove the fuel level sending unit (and on fuel-injected models, the fuel pump). On fuel-injected models, transfer the fuel pump to the new sending unit.

10   Accelerator cable - removal and installation

Refer to illustrations 10.2, 10.6a and 10.6b

Removal

1   Detach the screws and the clip retaining the lower instrument panel trim and lower the trim (if necessary).
2   Detach the accelerator cable from the accelerator pedal **(see illustration)**.

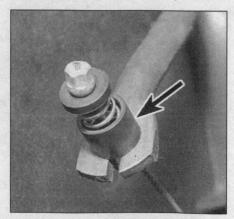

10.2 Move the cable end (arrow) away from the pedal arm and slide the cable out of the slot

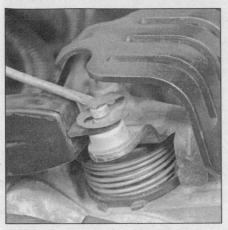

10.6a If your vehicle is equipped with a spring-clip retainer, use a screwdriver and pry the clip from the throttle arm

10.6b If your vehicle has the cable-snap type retainer, push the cable end forward and lift it up to detach it from the throttle lever arm

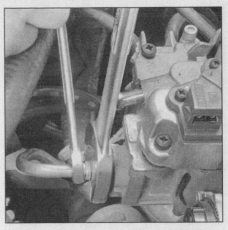

11.3 Be sure to use a back-up wrench on the inlet fitting when disconnecting the fuel line from the carburetor

3   Squeeze the accelerator cable cover tangs and push the cable through the firewall into the engine compartment.
4   Remove the cable clamp attaching screws and the cable clamp (if equipped).
5   Detach the routing clip (if equipped) and the accelerator cable.
6   Detach the accelerator cable-to-throttle lever retainer and detach the accelerator cable from the throttle body lever **(see illustrations)**.
7   Squeeze the accelerator cable retaining tangs and push the cable through the accelerator cable bracket.

Installation

8   Installation is the reverse of removal. **Note:** *To prevent possible interference, flexible components (hoses, wires, etc.) must not be routed within two inches of moving parts, unless routing is controlled.*
9   Operate the accelerator pedal and check for any binding condition by completely opening and closing the throttle.
10   At the engine compartment side of the firewall, apply sealant around the accelerator cable.

11   Carburetor - removal and installation

Refer to illustrations 11.3
Warning: *Gasoline is extremely flammable, so take extra precautions when you work on any part of the fuel system. Don't smoke or allow open flames or bare light bulbs near the work area, and don't work in a garage where a natural gas-type appliance (such as a water heater or a clothes dryer) with a pilot light is present. Since gasoline is carcinogenic, wear latex gloves when there's a possibility of being exposed to fuel, and, if you spill any fuel on your skin, rinse it off immediately with soap and water. Mop up any spills immediately and do not store fuel-soaked rags where they could ignite. When you perform any kind of work on the fuel system, wear safety*

glasses and have a Class B type fire extinguisher on hand.

Removal

1   Remove the fuel tank cap to relieve the pressure in the tank.
2   Detach the cable from the negative battery terminal, then remove the air cleaner.
Caution: *If the vehicle is equipped with a Delco Loc II audio system, make sure you have the correct activation code before disconnecting the battery. See the information at the front of this manual for the radio re-activation procedure.*
3   Mark and disconnect all hoses, vacuum lines and electrical connectors from the carburetor. Unscrew the fuel line from the carburetor inlet fitting, using a back-up wrench on the fitting to prevent the line from twisting **(see illustration)**.
4   Disconnect the accelerator linkage and cruise control linkage (if so equipped).
5   Disconnect the downshift cable (automatic transaxle models).
6   Remove the carburetor mounting nuts and/or bolts and separate the carburetor from the manifold .
7   Remove the gasket and/or Early Fuel Evaporation (EFE) heater and insulator. Check the EFE heater grids and the insulator for signs of overheating. Replace the EFE heater/insulator if any burned areas are noted.

Installation

8   Installation is the reverse of the removal procedure, but the following points should be noted:
   a) *By filling the carburetor bowl with fuel, the initial start-up will be easier and less drain on the battery.*
   b) *New gaskets should be used.*
   c) *Tighten the mounting bolts to the torque listed in this Chapter's Specifications.*
   c) *Idle speed and mixture settings should be checked and, if necessary, adjusted.*

12   Carburetor - diagnosis, overhaul and adjustment

Refer to illustrations 12.3, 12.6 and 12.7
Warning: *Gasoline is extremely flammable, so take extra precautions when you work on any part of the fuel system. Don't smoke or allow open flames or bare light bulbs near the work area, and don't work in a garage where a natural gas-type appliance (such as a water heater or a clothes dryer) with a pilot light is present. Since gasoline is carcinogenic, wear latex gloves when there's a possibility of being exposed to fuel, and, if you spill any fuel on your skin, rinse it off immediately with soap and water. Mop up any spills immediately and do not store fuel-soaked rags where they could ignite. When you perform any kind of work on the fuel system, wear safety glasses and have a Class B type fire extinguisher on hand.*

Diagnosis

1   A thorough road test and check of carburetor adjustments should be done before any major carburetor service work. Specifications for some adjustments are listed on the *Vehicle Emissions Control Information* (VECI) label found in the engine compartment.
2   Carburetor problems usually show up as flooding, hard starting, stalling, severe backfiring and poor acceleration. A carburetor that's leaking fuel and/or covered with wet looking deposits definitely needs attention.
3   Some performance complaints directed at the carburetor are actually a result of loose, out-of-adjustment or malfunctioning engine or electrical components. Others develop when vacuum hoses leak, are disconnected or are incorrectly routed. The proper approach to analyzing carburetor problems should include the following items:
   a) *Inspect all vacuum hoses and actuators for leaks and correct installation.*
   b) *Tighten the intake manifold and carburetor mounting bolts evenly and securely.*

12.3 The choke should be completely open at normal operating temperature (arrow)

12.7 Location of the carburetor identification (arrow)

c) Perform a cylinder compression test (see Chapter 2).

d) Clean or replace the spark plugs as necessary (see Chapter 1).

e) Check the spark plug wires (see Chapter 1).

f) Inspect the ignition primary wires.

g) Check the ignition timing (see Chapter 1).

h) Check the fuel pressure (see Section 3).

i) Check the thermo-sensor assembly in the air cleaner for proper operation (see Chapter 6).

j) Check/replace the air filter element (see Chapter 1).

k) Check the PCV system (see Chapters 1 and 6).

l) Check/replace the fuel filter (see Chapter 1). Also, the strainer in the tank could be restricted.

m) Check for a plugged exhaust system.

n) Check EGR valve operation (see Chapter 6).

o) Check the choke - it should be completely open at normal engine operating temperature **(see illustration).**

p) Check for fuel leaks and kinked or dented fuel lines.

q) Check accelerator pump operation with the engine off (remove the air cleaner cover and operate the throttle as you look into the carburetor throat - you should see a stream of gasoline enter the carburetor).

r) Check for incorrect fuel or bad gasoline.

s) Check the valve clearances (if applicable) and camshaft lobe lift (see Chapters 1 and 2).

t) Have a dealer service department or repair shop check the electronic engine and carburetor controls.

4   Diagnosing carburetor problems may require that the engine be started and run with the air cleaner off. While running the engine without the air cleaner, backfires are possible. This situation is likely to occur if the carburetor is malfunctioning, but just the removal of the air cleaner can lean the fuel/air mixture enough to produce an engine back-

fire. **Warning:** *Don't position any part of your body, especially your face, directly over the carburetor during inspection and servicing procedures. Wear eye protection!*

Overhaul

5   If you are going to overhaul the carburetor yourself, first obtain a good quality carburetor rebuild kit (which will include all necessary gaskets, internal parts, instructions and a parts list). You will also need some carburetor cleaner and a means of blowing out the internal passages of the carburetor with air.

6   Because carburetor designs are constantly modified by the manufacturer in order to meet emissions regulations, it isn't feasible for us to do a step-by-step overhaul of each type. You'll receive a detailed set of instructions with any quality carburetor overhaul kit. They will apply in a more specific manner to the carburetor on your vehicle. An exploded view of the carburetor used on the models covered by this manual is included in this Chapter **(see illustration).**

7   An alternative is to obtain a new or rebuilt carburetor. They are readily available from dealers and auto parts stores. Make sure the exchange carburetor is identical to the original. A number is cast into the side of the carburetor **(see illustration).** It will aid in determining the exact type of carburetor you have. When obtaining a rebuilt carburetor or a rebuild kit, take time to make sure that the kit or carburetor matches your application exactly. Seemingly insignificant differences can make a large difference in the performance of your engine.

8   If you choose to overhaul your own carburetor, allow enough time to disassemble the carburetor carefully, soak the necessary parts in the cleaning solvent (usually for at least one-half day or according to the instructions listed on the carburetor cleaner) and reassemble it, which will usually take much longer than disassembly. When disassembling the carburetor, match each part with the illustration in the carburetor kit and lay the parts out in order on a clean work surface.

Adjustments

9   Because there are a number of different configurations for Federal, California and Canadian carburetors and because a considerable number of special tools and tuning equipment is necessary to adjust these carburetors, it is impossible to include a detailed step-by-step procedure outlining every adjustment. Aside from idle speed adjustment and other adjustments shown in the carburetor overhaul kit, do not attempt to adjust the carburetor on your vehicle. If adjustments are needed other than those listed above, obtain a copy of the Haynes *Rochester Carburetor Manual* for detailed instructions.

13   Fuel injection systems - general information

Two types of fuel injection are used on models covered by this manual. Throttle Body Injection (TBI) and Multi-Port Fuel Injection (MPFI). Fuel injection provides optimum mixture ratios at all stages of combustion. Combined with its immediate response characteristics, fuel injection permits the engine to run on the leanest possible air/fuel mixture, which greatly reduces exhaust gas emissions.

The fuel injection system is controlled directly by the vehicle's Electronic Control Module (ECM), which automatically adjusts the air/fuel mixture in accordance with engine load and performance.

Throttle Body Injection (TBI)

The main component of the TBI system is the Throttle Body Injection (TBI) unit, which is mounted on the intake manifold just like a carburetor. The TBI unit is made up of two major assemblies: the throttle body and the fuel metering assembly.

The throttle body contains a single throttle valve, controlled by the accelerator pedal, similar to a carburetor. Attached to the exterior of the body are the Throttle Position Sensor (TPS), which sends throttle position information to the ECM, and the Idle Air Control (IAC) assembly, which is used by the ECM to maintain a constant idle speed during normal engine operation.

The fuel metering assembly contains the fuel pressure regulator and the single fuel injector. The regulator dampens the pulsations of the fuel pump and maintains a steady pressure at the injector. The fuel injector is controlled by the ECM through an electrically operated solenoid. The amount of fuel injected into the intake manifold is varied by the length of time the injector plunger is held open.

Multi-Port Fuel Injection (MPFI)

Multi-Port Fuel Injection (MPFI) consists of an air intake manifold, the throttle body,

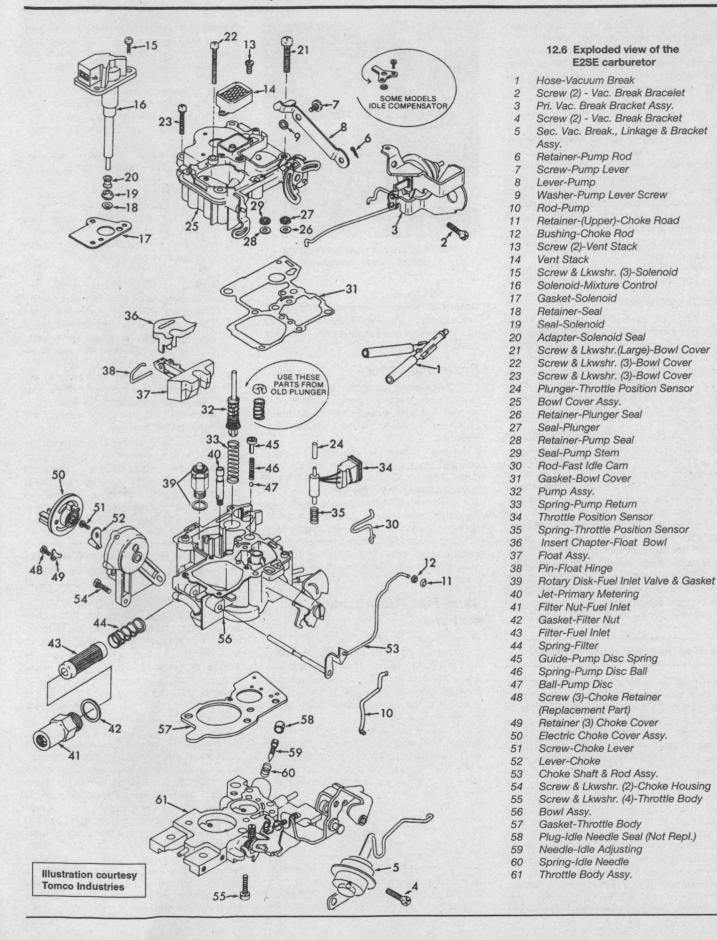

SOME MODELS
IDLE COMPENSATOR

USE THESE
PARTS FROM
OLD PLUNGER

Illustration courtesy
Tomco Industries

**12.6 Exploded view of the
E2SE carburetor**

1	Hose-Vacuum Break
2	Screw (2) - Vac. Break Bracelet
3	Pri. Vac. Break Bracket Assy.
4	Screw (2) - Vac. Break Bracket
5	Sec. Vac. Break., Linkage & Bracket Assy.
6	Retainer-Pump Rod
7	Screw-Pump Lever
8	Lever-Pump
9	Washer-Pump Lever Screw
10	Rod-Pump
11	Retainer-(Upper)-Choke Road
12	Bushing-Choke Rod
13	Screw (2)-Vent Stack
14	Vent Stack
15	Screw & Lkwshr. (3)-Solenoid
16	Solenoid-Mixture Control
17	Gasket-Solenoid
18	Retainer-Seal
19	Seal-Solenoid
20	Adapter-Solenoid Seal
21	Screw & Lkwshr.(Large)-Bowl Cover
22	Screw & Lkwshr. (3)-Bowl Cover
23	Screw & Lkwshr. (3)-Bowl Cover
24	Plunger-Throttle Position Sensor
25	Bowl Cover Assy.
26	Retainer-Plunger Seal
27	Seal-Plunger
28	Retainer-Pump Seal
29	Seal-Pump Stem
30	Rod-Fast Idle Cam
31	Gasket-Bowl Cover
32	Pump Assy.
33	Spring-Pump Return
34	Throttle Position Sensor
35	Spring-Throttle Position Sensor
36	Insert Chapter-Float Bowl
37	Float Assy.
38	Pin-Float Hinge
39	Rotary Disk-Fuel Inlet Valve & Gasket
40	Jet-Primary Metering
41	Filter Nut-Fuel Inlet
42	Gasket-Filter Nut
43	Filter-Fuel Inlet
44	Spring-Filter
45	Guide-Pump Disc Spring
46	Spring-Pump Disc Ball
47	Ball-Pump Disc
48	Screw (3)-Choke Retainer (Replacement Part)
49	Retainer (3) Choke Cover
50	Electric Choke Cover Assy.
51	Screw-Choke Lever
52	Lever-Choke
53	Choke Shaft & Rod Assy.
54	Screw & Lkwshr. (2)-Choke Housing
55	Screw & Lkwshr. (4)-Throttle Body
56	Bowl Assy.
57	Gasket-Throttle Body
58	Plug-Idle Needle Seal (Not Repl.)
59	Needle-Idle Adjusting
60	Spring-Idle Needle
61	Throttle Body Assy.

the injectors, the fuel rail assembly, an electric fuel pump and associated plumbing.

Air is drawn through the air cleaner and throttle body. A Mass Air Flow (MAF) sensor or a Manifold Absolute Pressure (MAP) sensor compensates for temperature and pressure variations.

While the engine is running, the fuel constantly circulates through the fuel rail, which removes vapors and keeps the fuel cool while maintaining sufficient pressure to the injectors under all running conditions.

As with TBI, the operation of the MPFI injection system is controlled by the ECM so that it works in conjunction with the rest of the vehicle functions to provide optimum driveability and emissions control.

Because the MPFI system meters fuel and air precisely, it is important to the proper operation of the vehicle that the fuel and air filters be changed at the specified intervals.

Both systems

The ECM controlling both types of fuel injection systems has a learning capability for certain performance conditions. If the battery is disconnected, part of the ECM memory is erased, which makes it necessary to "relearn" the computer. This is done by thoroughly warming up the engine and operating the vehicle at part throttle, stop and go and idle conditions.

A fuel pump relay is used to control the electric fuel pump operation. When the ignition is turned on, the fuel pump relay immediately supplies current to the fuel pump to pressurize the fuel system. If the engine doesn't start after two seconds, the fuel pump will automatically shut off. If the fuel pump relay fails, the fuel pump will still operate after the ECM receives pulses from the distributor or about four pounds of oil pressure has built up, depending on the model.

The throttle stop screw, used to regulate the minimum idle speed, is adjusted at the factory and sealed with a plug to discourage unnecessary adjustment.

14   Fuel injection system - check

Warning: *Gasoline is extremely flammable, so take extra precautions when you work on any part of the fuel system. Don't smoke or allow open flames or bare light bulbs near the work area, and don't work in a garage where a natural gas-type appliance (such as a water heater or a clothes dryer) with a pilot light is present. Since gasoline is carcinogenic, wear latex gloves when there's a possibility of being exposed to fuel, and, if you spill any fuel on your skin, rinse it off immediately with soap and water. Mop up any spills immediately and do not store fuel-soaked rags where they could ignite. The fuel system is under constant pressure, so, if any fuel lines are to be disconnected, the fuel pressure in the system must be relieved first. When you perform any kind of work on the fuel system, wear safety glasses and have a Class B type fire*

14.9 Measure the resistance of the injectors with an ohmmeter

extinguisher on hand.
Note: *The following procedure is based on the assumption that the fuel pump is working and the fuel pressure is adequate (see Section 3).*

Preliminary checks

1   Check all electrical connectors that are related to the system. Loose electrical connectors and poor grounds can cause many problems that resemble more serious malfunctions.
2   Check to see that the battery is fully charged, as the control unit and sensors depend on an accurate supply voltage in order to properly meter the fuel.
3   Check the air filter element - a dirty or partially blocked filter will severely impede performance and economy (see Chapter 1).
4   If a blown fuse is found, replace it and see if it blows again. If it does, search for a grounded wire in the harness to the fuel pump.

Multi-Port Fuel Injection systems

Refer to illustration 14.9
5   Check the air intake duct from the Mass Air Flow (MAF) sensor (if equipped) to the intake manifold for leaks, which will result in an excessively lean mixture. Also check the condition of the vacuum hoses connected to the intake manifold.
6   Remove the air intake duct from the throttle body and check for dirt, carbon or other residue build-up in the throttle body, particularly around the throttle plate. If it's dirty, clean it with carburetor cleaner and a toothbrush.
7   With the engine running, place a screwdriver (or stethoscope) against each injector, one at a time, and listen through the handle for a clicking sound, indicating operation.
8   If an injector isn't functioning (not clicking), purchase a special injector test light (sometimes called a "noid" light) and install it into the injector electrical connector. Start the engine and check to see if the noid light

flashes. If it does, the injector is receiving proper voltage. If it doesn't flash, further diagnosis should be performed by a dealer service department or other repair shop.
9   With the engine OFF and the fuel injector electrical connectors disconnected, measure the resistance of each injector **(see illustration)** and compare your findings with the values listed in this Chapter's Specifications.
10   The remainder of the system checks can be found in Section 4 and Chapter 6.

TBI systems

11   Set the parking brake, remove the air cleaner top plate and, with the engine idling in Park, observe the operating fuel injector. The spray pattern should be even and conical in shape. The spray should touch the throttle body bore.

    a) *If the spray is weak or uneven, the injector is clogged or faulty. Gasoline additives designed to clean fuel injectors can sometimes clear a clogged injector. If not, a dealer service department or other qualified shop has more effective cleaning equipment.*

    b) *If an injector is not operating at all, check its electrical connector. If the connection is good and the injector is receiving voltage, but the injector still doesn't work, the injector is faulty.*

12   Turn the engine off and observe the injector. There shouldn't be any leakage or dripping. If the injector does drip, either the injector seals are faulty or the injector itself is defective. Usually a problem like this will result in a hard-starting condition and/or a puff of smoke as the engine is started.

15   Throttle Body Injection (TBI) unit - removal and installation

Refer to illustration 15.4
Warning: *Gasoline is extremely flammable, so take extra precautions when you work on any part of the fuel system. Don't smoke or allow open flames or bare light bulbs near the work area, and don't work in a garage where a natural gas-type appliance (such as a water heater or a clothes dryer) with a pilot light is present. Since gasoline is carcinogenic, wear latex gloves when there's a possibility of being exposed to fuel, and, if you spill any fuel on your skin, rinse it off immediately with soap and water. Mop up any spills immediately and do not store fuel-soaked rags where they could ignite. The fuel system is under constant pressure, so, if any fuel lines are to be disconnected, the fuel pressure in the system must be relieved first. When you perform any kind of work on the fuel system, wear safety glasses and have a Class B type fire extinguisher on hand.*
Note: *The fuel injector, pressure regulator, throttle position sensor and the idle air control valve can be replaced without removing the throttle body assembly.*

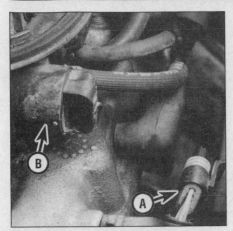

15.4 Unplug the electrical connector (A) from the Idle Air Control valve (B)

Removal

1   Relieve the fuel system pressure (see Section 2).
2   Disconnect the cable from the negative terminal of the battery. **Caution:** *If the vehicle is equipped with a Delco Loc II audio system, make sure you have the correct activation code before disconnecting the battery.*
3   Remove the air cleaner housing.
4   Unplug the electrical connectors from the idle air control valve **(see illustration)**, throttle position sensor and the fuel injector.
5   Remove the wiring harness and insulating grommet from the throttle body.
6   Disconnect the accelerator cable and return spring, transmission control and cruise control cables, if equipped.
7   Using pieces of numbered tape, mark all of the vacuum hoses to the throttle body and disconnect them.
8   Disconnect the fuel inlet and return lines. Use a backup wrench on the inlet and return fitting nuts to prevent damage to the throttle body and fuel lines. Remove the O-rings on the ends of the fuel lines and discard them (be sure to install new ones during

reassembly). Later models use quick-connect fuel lines - refer to Section 4 for the disconnection procedure.
9   Remove the TBI assembly mounting bolts/nuts and lift the unit from the intake manifold. It's a good idea to stuff a rag into the intake manifold opening to prevent foreign matter from falling in. Remove all old gasket material from the intake manifold and the underside of the throttle body unit.

Installation

•10   Installation is the reverse of the removal procedure. Be sure to install a new throttle body-to-intake manifold gasket, new fuel line O-rings and tighten the mounting bolts/nuts to the torque listed in this Chapter's Specifications.
11   Turn the ignition switch to the On position (don't start the engine) and check for fuel leaks.
12   Check to see if the accelerator pedal is free by depressing the pedal to the floor and releasing it with the ignition switch off.

---

16   Model 300 Throttle Body Injection (TBI) unit (1986 and earlier models) - component check and replacement

---

Warning: *Gasoline is extremely flammable, so take extra precautions when you work on any part of the fuel system. Don't smoke or allow open flames or bare light bulbs near the work area, and don't work in a garage where a natural gas-type appliance (such as a water heater or a clothes dryer) with a pilot light is present. Since gasoline is carcinogenic, wear latex gloves when there's a possibility of being exposed to fuel, and, if you spill any fuel on your skin, rinse it off immediately with soap and water. Mop up any spills immediately and do not store fuel-soaked rags where they could ignite. The fuel system is under constant pressure, so, if any fuel lines are to*

be disconnected, the fuel pressure in the system must be relieved first. When you perform any kind of work on the fuel system, wear safety glasses and have a Class B type fire extinguisher on hand.
Note: *Because of its relative simplicity, a throttle body assembly does not need to be removed from the intake manifold nor completely disassembled for component replacement. However, for the sake of clarity, the following procedures are shown with the TBI unit removed from the vehicle.*
1   Relieve the fuel system pressure (see Section 2).
2   Detach the cable from the negative terminal of the battery.
3   Remove the air cleaner housing assembly, adapter and gaskets.

Fuel meter cover and fuel injector

Refer to illustrations 16.6, 16.8, 16.9a, 16.9b, 16.11, 16.12, 16.18, 16.19 and 16.20

Check

4   Refer to Section 13 for the fuel injector checking procedure. Also check for stored trouble codes in the ECM (see Chapter 6).

Disassembly

5   Remove the injector electrical connector (on top of the TBI unit) by squeezing the two tabs together and pulling straight up.
6   Unscrew the five fuel meter cover retaining screws and lockwashers securing the fuel meter cover to the fuel meter body. Note the location of the two short screws **(see illustration)**.
7   Remove the fuel meter cover. **Caution:** *Do not immerse the fuel meter cover in solvent. It might damage the pressure regulator diaphragm and gasket.*
8   The fuel meter cover contains the fuel pressure regulator, which is pre-set and plugged at the factory. If a malfunction occurs, it cannot be serviced, and must be replaced as a complete assembly. **Warning:**

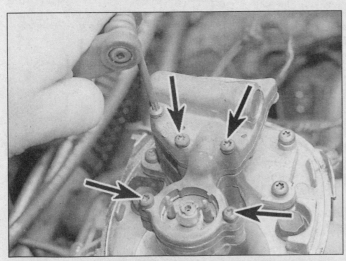

16.6 Fuel meter cover-to-fuel meter body screw locations

16.8 The fuel pressure regulator is installed in the fuel meter cover and pre-adjusted at the factory - don't remove the four retaining screws (arrows) or you may damage the regulator

16.9a The best way to remove the fuel injector is to pry on it with a screwdriver, using a second screwdriver as a fulcrum

16.9b Note the position of the terminals on top and the dowel pin on the bottom of the injector (arrow) in relation to the fuel meter body when you lift the injector out of the body

16.11 Carefully peel away the old fuel meter outlet passage gasket and fuel meter cover gasket with a razor blade

Do not remove the screws securing the pressure regulator to the fuel meter cover **(see illustration)**. *It has a large spring under heavy compression inside.*

9   With the old fuel meter cover gasket in place to prevent damage to the casting, carefully pry the injector from the fuel meter body with a screwdriver until it can be lifted free **(see illustrations). Caution:** *Use care in removing the injector to prevent damage to the electrical connector terminals, the injector fuel filter, the O-ring and the nozzle.*

10   The fuel meter body should be removed from the throttle body if it needs to be cleaned. To remove it, remove the fuel feed and return line fittings and the Torx screws that attach the fuel meter body to the throttle body **(see illustration 15.4a).**

11   Remove the old gasket from the fuel meter cover and discard it. Remove the large O-ring and steel back-up washer from the upper counterbore of the fuel meter body injector cavity **(see illustration)**. Clean the fuel meter body thoroughly in carburetor cleaner and blow it dry.

12   Remove the small O-ring from the nozzle end of the injector. Carefully rotate the

injector fuel filter back and forth and remove the filter from the base of the injector **(see illustration)**. Gently clean the filter in solvent and allow it to drip dry. It is too small and delicate to dry with compressed air. **Caution:** *The fuel injector itself is an electrical component. Do not immerse it in any type of cleaning solvent.*

13   The fuel injector is not serviceable. If it is malfunctioning, replace it as an assembly.

Reassembly

14   Install the clean fuel injector nozzle filter on the end of the fuel injector with the larger end of the filter facing the injector so that the filter covers the raised rib at the base of the injector. Use a twisting motion to position the filter against the base of the injector.

15   Lubricate a new small O-ring with automatic transmission fluid. Push the O-ring onto the nozzle end of the injector until it presses against the injector fuel filter.

16   Insert the steel back-up washer in the top of the fuel meter body injector cavity.

17   Lubricate a new large O-ring with auto-

matic transmission fluid and install it directly over the back-up washer. Be sure the O-ring is seated properly in the cavity and is flush with the top of the fuel meter body casting surface. **Caution:** *The back-up washer and large O-ring must be installed before the injector or improper seating of the large O-ring could cause fuel to leak.*

18   Install the injector in the cavity in the fuel meter body, aligning the raised lug on the injector base with the cast-in notch in the fuel meter body cavity. Push straight down on the injector with both thumbs **(see illustration)** until it is fully seated in the cavity. **Note:** *The electrical terminals of the injector should be approximately parallel to the throttle shaft.*

19   Install a new fuel outlet passage gasket on the fuel meter cover and a new fuel meter cover gasket on the fuel meter body **(see illustration)**.

20   Install a new dust seal into the recess on the fuel meter body **(see illustration)**.

21   Install the fuel meter cover onto the fuel meter body, making sure that the pressure regulator dust seal and cover gaskets are in place.

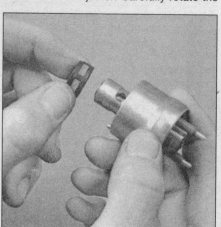

16.12 Gently rotate the fuel injector filter back and forth and pull it off the nozzle

16.18 Make sure that the lug is aligned with the groove in the bottom of the fuel injector cavity

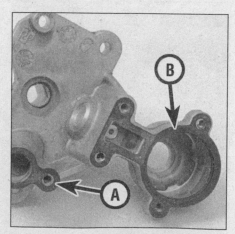

16.19 Position the fuel outlet passage gasket (A) and the fuel meter cover gasket (B) properly

16.20 Install a new dust seal into the recess of the fuel meter body

16.27 Carefully remove the IAC valve with a large wrench

body. Use the new gasket supplied with the assembly.

31   Plug in the electrical connector.

32   Install the air cleaner.

33   Start the engine and allow it to reach normal operating temperature. The Electronic Control Module (ECM) will reset the idle speed when the vehicle is driven above 35 mph.

Minimum idle speed adjustment

Refer to illustration 16.35

Note: *This adjustment should be performed only when the throttle body has been replaced or if the vehicle is experiencing a stalling problem at idle. The engine should be at normal operating temperature before making the adjustment.*

34   Remove the air cleaner housing. Connect a tachometer in accordance with the tool manufacturer's instructions.

35   Remove the plug covering the idle stop screw by piercing it with an awl, then applying leverage **(see illustration)**.

36   Plug any vacuum ports as required by the VECI label.

37   With the IAC valve connected, ground the diagnostic terminal of the ALDL connector (see Chapter 6). Turn the ignition to On but don't start the engine. Wait at least 30 seconds to allow the IAC valve pintle to extend and seat in the throttle body. Disconnect the IAC valve electrical connector. Remove the jumper wire from the ALDL connector and start the engine.

38   Adjust the idle stop screw to obtain the specified idle speed in Park.

39   Turn the ignition off and reconnect the IAC valve electrical connector.

40   Unplug any plugged vacuum ports and reconnect the hoses.

41   Install the air cleaner housing.

42   Disconnect the cable from the negative terminal of the battery for at least ten seconds. This will erase any stored trouble codes that may have been set by unplugging the IAC valve and running the engine. **Cau-**

22   Apply a thread locking compound to the threads of the fuel meter cover attaching screws. Install the screws (the two short screws go next to the injector) and tighten them securely. **Note:** *Service repair kits include a small vial of thread locking compound with directions for use. If this material is not available, use Loctite 262, GM part number 1052624, or equivalent. Do not use a higher strength locking compound than recommended, as this may prevent subsequent removal of the attaching screws or cause breakage of the screwhead if removal becomes necessary.*

23   Plug in the electrical connector to the injector.

24   Install the air cleaner.

Idle Air Control (IAC) valve

Refer to illustrations 16.27 and 16.28

Check

25   Refer to Chapter 6 and check for trouble codes stored in the ECM. If the IAC valve is malfunctioning, a trouble code indicating this condition would most likely have been set.

Removal

26   Unplug the electrical connector at the

IAC valve.

27   Remove the IAC valve with a wrench on the hex surface only **(see illustration)**.

Installation

28   Before installing a new IAC valve, measure the distance the valve is extended **(see illustration)**. The measurement should be made from the motor housing to the end of the cone. The distance should be no greater than 1-1/8 inch. If the cone is extended too far, damage may occur to the valve when it is installed.

29   Identify the replacement IAC valve as either a Type I (with a collar at the electrical connector end) or a Type II (without a collar). If the measured dimension "A" is greater than 1-1/8 inch, the distance must be reduced as follows:

Type I -Exert firm pressure on the valve to retract it (a slight side-to-side movement may be helpful).

Type II - Compress the retaining spring of the valve while turning the valve in a clockwise direction. Return the spring to its original position with the straight portion of the spring aligned with the flat surface of the valve.

30   Install the new IAC valve to the throttle

16.28 Distance A should be less than 1-1/8 inch for either type of Idle Air Control valve - if it isn't, determine which kind of valve you have and adjust it accordingly

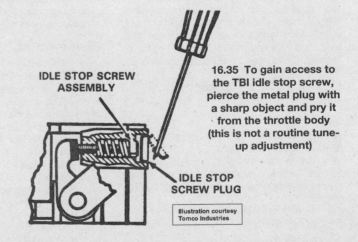

IDLE STOP SCREW ASSEMBLY

IDLE STOP SCREW PLUG

16.35 To gain access to the TBI idle stop screw, pierce the metal plug with a sharp object and pry it from the throttle body (this is not a routine tune-up adjustment)

Illustration courtesy Tomco Industries

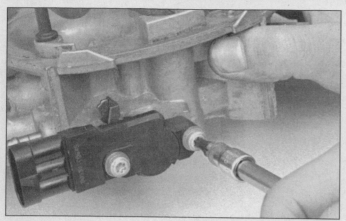

16.48 The Throttle Position Sensor (TPS) is mounted to the side of the TBI with two Torx screws

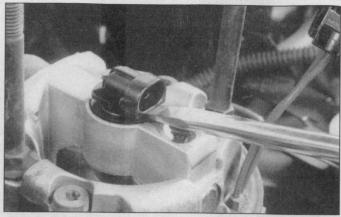

17.5 Pry the injector out of the fuel meter body using the bolt as a fulcrum (B) and a screwdriver as a lever (A)

tion: *If the vehicle is equipped with a Delco Loc II audio system, make sure you have the correct activation code before disconnecting the battery.*

Throttle Position Sensor (TPS)

Refer to illustration 16.48

General information and check

43   The Throttle Position Sensor (TPS) is connected to the throttle shaft on the TBI unit. As the throttle valve angle is changed (as the accelerator pedal is moved), the output of the TPS also changes. At a closed throttle position, the output of the TPS is below 1.25-volts. As the throttle valve opens, the output increases so that, at wide-open throttle, the output voltage is approximately 4.5-volts.

44   A broken or loose TPS can cause intermittent bursts of fuel from the injector and an unstable idle, because the ECM thinks the throttle is moving. If a problem with the TPS sensor or circuit develops, a trouble code most likely will be set (see Chapter 6).

45   Connect a digital voltmeter from the TPS electrical connector center terminal (dark blue wire) to outside terminal (black wire) (you'll have to backprobe the TPS connector very carefully to avoid damage to the harness wires).

46   With the ignition on (engine not running), TPS voltage should be between 0.45 and 1.25 volts (throttle closed). If it's more than specified, check and, if necessary, adjust the minimum idle speed before condemning the TPS.

47   The TPS is not adjustable. If the TPS malfunctions, it must be replaced as a unit.

Replacement

48   Unscrew the two Torx screws **(see illustration)** and remove the TPS.

49   Install the new TPS and tighten the screws securely. **Note:** *Make sure the tang on the lever is properly engaged with the stop on the TBI.*

50   Install the air cleaner assembly.

51   Attach the cable to the negative terminal of the battery.

17   Model 700 Throttle Body Injection (TBI) unit (1987 and later models) - component check and replacement

Warning: *Gasoline is extremely flammable, so take extra precautions when you work on any part of the fuel system. Don't smoke or allow open flames or bare light bulbs near the work area, and don't work in a garage where a natural gas-type appliance (such as a water heater or a clothes dryer) with a pilot light is present. Since gasoline is carcinogenic, wear latex gloves when there's a possibility of being exposed to fuel, and, if you spill any fuel on your skin, rinse it off immediately with soap and water. Mop up any spills immediately and do not store fuel-soaked rags where they could ignite. The fuel system is under constant pressure, so, if any fuel lines are to be disconnected, the fuel pressure in the system must be relieved first. When you perform any kind of work on the fuel system, wear safety glasses and have a Class B type fire extinguisher on hand.*

Fuel injector

Check

1   Refer to Section 14 for the fuel injector checking procedure. Also check for stored trouble codes in the ECM (see Chapter 6).

Replacement

Refer to illustration 17.5

2   Disconnect the negative battery cable. **Caution**: *If the vehicle is equipped with a Delco Loc II audio system, make sure you have the correct activation code before disconnecting the battery. See the information at the front of this manual for the radio re-activation procedure.*

3   Unplug the electrical connector from the fuel injector.

4   Remove the injector retainer screw and the retainer **(see illustration 15.4b)**.

5   Using one screwdriver as a fulcrum on the fuel meter body, place another screwdriver tip under the ridge on the fuel injector

opposite the electrical connector end and gently pry the injector out **(see illustration)**.

6   If the injector is to be reused, replace the upper and lower O-rings on the injector and in the fuel injector cavity. Install the upper O-ring in the groove on the injector and the lower O-ring flush against the filter element.

7   Install the injector assembly in the fuel meter body by pushing it straight down. Make sure the connector end is facing in the direction of the opening in the fuel meter body for the wire harness grommet.

8   Install the injector retainer and screw. Use a thread locking compound on the retainer screw (Loctite 262) available at most auto parts stores.

9   Reconnect the negative battery cable. Pressurize the fuel system by turning the ignition key to the On position, then inspect the area around the injector for leaks.

10   Plug the electrical connector into the injector and start the engine to check for correct operation.

Pressure regulator assembly

Check

11   Refer to Section 3 and perform the fuel pressure checks, which will diagnose a malfunctioning fuel pressure regulator.

Replacement

12   Underneath the pressure regulator cover assembly is a large spring which is highly compressed. Repairs to this component should be performed by a dealer service department or other repair shop due to the possibility of personal injury. Also, the tension on this spring affects fuel pressure and is set at the factory - any tampering with this component would be in violation of Federal law.

Idle Air Control valve

Check

13   Refer to Chapter 6 and check for trouble codes stored in the ECM. If the IAC valve is malfunctioning, a trouble code indicating this condition would most likely have been set.

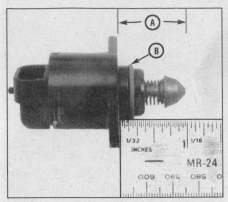

17.18a The Idle Air Control valve pintle must not extend more than 1-1/8 inch - also, replace the O-ring if it is brittle

A   *Distance of pintle extension*
B   *O-ring*

17.18b To reduce the IAC valve pintle extension, grasp the valve and depress the pintle using a slight side-to-side motion

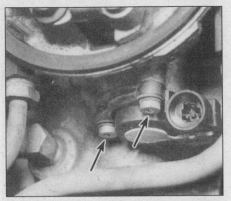

17.30 The Throttle Position Sensor mounts to the side of the throttle body and is not adjustable (arrows)

Replacement

Refer to illustrations 17.18a and 17.18b

14   Disconnect the negative battery cable. **Caution:** *If the vehicle is equipped with a Delco Loc II audio system, make sure you have the correct activation code before disconnecting the battery. See the information at the front of this manual for the radio re-activation procedure.*

15   Remove the air cleaner and unplug the electrical connector from the IAC valve.

16   Remove the two valve retaining screws and pull the valve out of the throttle body **(see illustration 15.4b)**.

17   If the same valve is to be reinstalled, be sure to use a new O-ring.

18   Before installing the valve, measure the distance from the end of the pintle to the mounting flange **(see illustration)**. If the distance exceeds 1-1/8 inch, reduce that distance by pushing the pintle into the valve assembly with a slight side-to-side motion **(see illustration)**. If this is not done, the valve will be damaged during installation.

19   Position the valve on the throttle body and install the screws. Plug in the electrical connector to the valve.

20   No adjustment of the IAC valve is necessary, as it is automatically reset by the ECM.

Minimum idle speed adjustment

21   Refer to Section 16, Steps 34 through 42 for this adjustment.

Throttle Position Sensor (TPS)

General information and check

22   The Throttle Position Sensor (TPS) is connected to the throttle shaft on the TBI unit. As the throttle valve angle is changed (as the accelerator pedal is moved), the output of the TPS also changes. At a closed throttle position, the output of the TPS is below 1.25-volts. As the throttle valve opens, the output increases so that, at wide-open throttle, the output voltage is approximately

4.5-volts.

23   A broken or loose TPS can cause intermittent bursts of fuel from the injector and an unstable idle, because the ECM thinks the throttle is moving. If a problem with the TPS sensor or circuit develops, a trouble code most likely will be set (see Chapter 6).

24   Connect a digital voltmeter from the TPS electrical connector center terminal (dark blue wire) to the side terminal (black wire) (you'll have to backprobe the TPS connector very carefully to avoid damaging the wire harness).

25   With the ignition on (engine not running), the TPS voltage should be between 0.45 and 1.25 volts (throttle closed). If it's more than specified, check and, if necessary, adjust the minimum idle speed before condemning the TPS.

26   The TPS is not adjustable. If the TPS malfunctions, it must be replaced as a unit.

Replacement

Refer to illustration 17.30

27   Disconnect the cable from the negative battery terminal. **Caution:** *If the vehicle is equipped with a Delco Loc II audio system, make sure you have the correct activation code before disconnecting the battery. See the information at the front of this manual for*

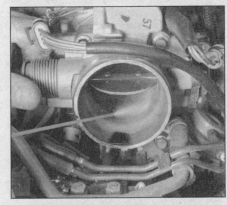

18.2 Clean the throttle body with carburetor cleaner to remove sludge deposits

the radio re-activation procedure.

28   Remove the air cleaner housing.

29   Unplug the electrical connector from the throttle position sensor.

30   Remove the two sensor mounting screws and pull the sensor from the throttle body **(see illustration)**.

31   To install the TPS, align the slot in the rear of the sensor with the throttle shaft and insert the sensor into the throttle body. Install the mounting screws and tighten them securely. This style TPS is not adjustable.

32   The remainder of installation is the reverse of the removal procedure.

18 Multi-Port Fuel Injection (MPFI) - component check, removal and installation

Warning: *Gasoline is extremely flammable, so take extra precautions when you work on any part of the fuel system. Don't smoke or allow open flames or bare light bulbs near the work area, and don't work in a garage where a natural gas-type appliance (such as a water heater or a clothes dryer) with a pilot light is present. Since gasoline is carcinogenic, wear latex gloves when there's a possibility of being exposed to fuel, and, if you spill any fuel on your skin, rinse it off immediately with soap and water. Mop up any spills immediately and do not store fuel-soaked rags where they could ignite. The fuel system is under constant pressure, so, if any fuel lines are to be disconnected, the fuel pressure in the system must be relieved first. When you perform any kind of work on the fuel system, wear safety glasses and have a Class B type fire extinguisher on hand.*

Throttle body

Check

Refer to illustration 18.2

1   Detach the air intake duct from the throttle body and move the duct out of the way.

2   Have an assistant depress the throttle pedal while you watch the throttle valve.

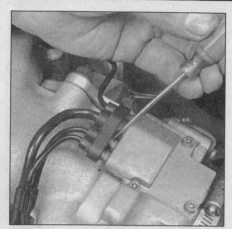

18.6 Using a small screwdriver, pry the vacuum harness connector from the throttle body

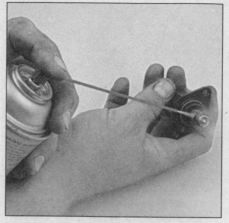

18.16a Clean the IAC valve pintle with carburetor spray to remove carbon deposits

18.16b Spray carburetor cleaner into the IAC valve housing and check for clogged air passages in the air intake plenum

Check that the throttle valve moves smoothly when the throttle is moved from closed (idle position) to fully open (wide open throttle). **Note:** *Spray carburetor cleaner into the throttle body, especially around the shaft area, to free-up any binding caused by the accumulation of carbon deposits or sludge buildup* **(see illustration).**

3   Wiggle the throttle lever while watching the throttle shaft inside the bore. If it appears worn (loose), replace the throttle body unit.

Removal

Refer to illustration 18.6

4   Disconnect the cable from the negative terminal of the battery. **Caution:** *If the vehicle is equipped with a Delco Loc II audio system, make sure you have the correct activation code before disconnecting the battery. See the information at the front of this manual for the radio re-activation procedure.*

5   Unplug the Idle Air Control (IAC) valve and the Throttle Position Sensor (TPS) electrical connectors.

6   Mark and disconnect any vacuum hoses connected to the throttle body **(see illustration).** Also detach the breather hose, if equipped.

7   Disconnect the accelerator cable from the throttle lever, then detach the cable housing from its bracket.

8   Loosen the clamps and disconnect the coolant hoses from the underside of the throttle body. Be prepared for some coolant spillage and plug the ends of the hoses. **Note:** *On some models you can't get to these hoses until after the throttle body has been unbolted from the plenum.*

9   Detach the air intake duct.

10   Remove the throttle body bolts and detach the throttle body.

Installation

11   Clean off all traces of old gasket material from the throttle body and the plenum.

12   Install the throttle body and a new gasket and tighten the bolts to the torque listed in this Chapter's Specifications.

13   The rest of the procedure is the reverse of removal. Be sure to check the coolant level (see Chapter 1) and add, if necessary.

Idle Air Control (IAC) valve
Check

Refer to illustrations 18.16a and 18.16b

14   The idle air control valve (IAC) controls the engine idle speed. This output actuator is mounted on the throttle body and is controlled by voltage pulses sent from the ECM (computer). The IAC valve pintle moves in or out allowing more or less intake air into the system according to the engine conditions. To increase idle speed, the ECM retracts the IAC valve pintle away from the seat and allows more air to bypass the throttle bore. To decrease idle speed, the ECM extends the IAC valve pintle towards the seat, reducing the air flow.

15   To check the IAC valve, unplug the electrical connector and, using an ohmmeter, measure the resistance across terminals A and B, then terminals C and D. Each resistance check should indicate 20 ohms or greater. If not, replace the IAC valve.

16   Next, remove the valve (see Step 17) and inspect it:

a)   *Check the pintle for excessive carbon deposits. If necessary, clean it with carburetor cleaner spray* **(see illustration).** *Also clean the IAC valve housing to remove any deposits* **(see illustration).**

b)   *Apply battery voltage to the IAC valve terminals (one at a time) while holding the valve against a good ground. Make sure the valve pintle extends and retracts with the voltage signal. If there is no movement from the valve, replace it with a new one.*

Removal

Refer to illustration 18.18

17   Unplug the electrical connector from the Idle Air Control (IAC) valve.

18   Unscrew the valve or remove the two IAC valve attaching screws and withdraw the

18.18 You'll need a Torx driver to remove the IAC valve retaining screw on some models (arrows)

valve **(see illustration).**

19   Check the condition of the rubber O-ring. If it's hardened or deteriorated, replace it. On models equipped with a gasket, remove the gasket.

20   Clean the sealing surface and the bore of the idle air/vacuum signal housing assembly to ensure a good seal. **Caution:** *The IAC valve itself is an electrical component and must not be soaked in any liquid cleaner, as damage may result.*

21   Before installing the IAC valve, the position of the pintle must be checked. If the pintle is extended too far, damage to the assembly may occur.

Installation

22   Measure the distance from the flange or gasket mounting surface of the IAC valve to the tip of the pintle **(see illustration 17.18a).**

23   If the distance is greater than 1-1/8 inch, reduce it by applying firm hand pressure on the pintle **(see illustration 17.18b)** to retract it (a slight side-to-side motion may help).

24   Position the new O-ring or gasket on the IAC valve. Lubricate the O-ring with a light film of engine oil. If the IAC valve is the

18.32 If you plan to install the same TPS, be sure to make an alignment mark between the TPS and the throttle body

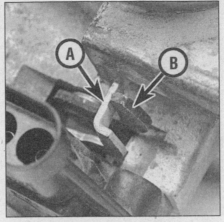

18.34 The TPS lever (A) must mate with the throttle body lever (B) when you attach the TPS to the throttle body

18.44 Location of the plenum mounting bolts (arrows) - 1987 and later 2.8L/3.1L V6 engines

screw-in type, apply a light film of RTV sealant to the threads of the valve.

25   Install the IAC valve and tighten the valve or the mounting screws securely.

26   Plug in the electrical connector at the IAC valve assembly. **Note:** *No adjustment is made to the IAC assembly after reinstallation. The IAC resetting is controlled by the ECM when the engine is started.*

Throttle Position Sensor (TPS)

Check

27   Check for stored trouble codes in the ECM (see Chapter 6).

28   To check the operation of the TPS, connect the positive probe of a high-impedance digital voltmeter to the center terminal of the TPS (dark blue wire) and the negative probe to the TPS ground wire, which will either be black or black with an orange stripe. Turn the ignition switch to the On position (don't start the engine). With the throttle in the closed (idle) position, the voltmeter should indicate approximately 0.45 to 1.25 volts. Now open the throttle completely and check the voltmeter - it should read approximately 4.5 volts.

29   If the TPS doesn't respond as described, replace it.

Replacement

Refer to illustrations 18.32 and 18.34

Note: *Only Throttle Position Sensors with slotted mounting holes are adjustable.*

30   Unplug the electrical connector from the TPS.

31   If the TPS is located on the underside of the throttle body, remove the throttle body as described in Steps 4 through 10.

32   If you intend to install the same TPS, scribe or paint an alignment mark between the TPS and the throttle body **(see illustration)**. If you're installing a new TPS, you'll have to set it with a voltmeter.

33   Remove the TPS screws and detach the TPS from the throttle body.

34   Installation is the reverse of removal. Be

sure to install the TPS onto the throttle body with the throttle valve in the closed position. Make sure the TPS lever lines up with the TPS drive lever on the throttle shaft **(see illustration)**. On models that don't have a lever, make sure the slot in the TPS aligns with the end of the throttle shaft.

35   Install the screws and retainers. Tighten the screws finger-tight at this time.

36   Plug in the electrical connector to the TPS and connect a high-impedance digital voltmeter as described in Step 28. Turn the ignition to the On position and, with the throttle shaft in the closed position, rotate the TPS to obtain a voltmeter reading of 0.55 +/- 0.05 volts. Tighten the TPS mounting screws and recheck the voltmeter reading to verify that the adjustment has not changed.

37   If the throttle body was removed, refer to Steps 11 through 13 to reinstall it.

Air intake plenum (2.2L, 2.8L and 3.1L engines only)

Refer to illustration 18.44

Note: *This component is sometimes referred to as the upper intake manifold.*

Removal

38   Disconnect the cable from the negative terminal of the battery. **Caution:** *If the vehicle is equipped with a Delco Loc II audio system, make sure you have the correct activation code before disconnecting the battery. See the information at the front of this manual for the radio re-activation procedure.*

39   Detach the air intake duct from the throttle body.

40   Disconnect the accelerator cable, transmission control cable and cruise control cable (if equipped) from the throttle lever. Unbolt the accelerator cable bracket and position the bracket and cables aside.

41   Detach any hoses and electrical connectors from the throttle body and plenum **(see illustration 18.6)**. If necessary, mark them with pieces of numbered tape to avoid confusion during reassembly.

42   On V6 models, remove the EGR valve (see Chapter 6). On 2.2L four-cylinder models, unscrew the EGR tube fitting.

43   If necessary, remove the bolts which secure the plastic spark plug wire shield and detach the shield.

44   Remove the plenum bolts and lift the plenum from the intake manifold **(see illustration)**. If the plenum sticks, use a block of wood and a hammer to dislodge it. Don't pry between the sealing flanges, as this will damage the machined surfaces and could cause vacuum leaks to develop.

45   Remove all traces of old gasket material from the plenum and intake manifold mating surfaces. It's a good idea to stuff rags into the intake manifold openings to prevent debris from falling in.

Installation

46   Install the new gasket(s) and set the plenum into position.

47   Install the plenum bolts and tighten them to the torque listed in this Chapter's Specifications in a criss-cross pattern.

48   The remainder of installation is the reverse or removal.

Fuel rail and injectors

Note: *Refer to Section 14 for the injector checking procedure.*

OHC four-cylinder and V6 engines

Refer to illustrations 18.51, 18.53, 18.54, 18.55, 18.56 and 18.57

Warning: *Before any work is performed on the fuel lines, fuel rail or injectors, the fuel system pressure must be relieved (see Section 2).*

49   Detach the negative battery cable from the battery. **Caution:** *If the vehicle is equipped with a Delco Loc II audio system, make sure you have the correct activation code before disconnecting the battery. See the information at the front of this manual for the radio re-activation procedure.*

50   Remove the plenum following the procedure described earlier in this Section (2.8L

18.51 Use a back-up wrench when disconnecting the fuel lines

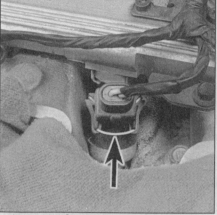

18.53 Before removing the injector electrical connectors (arrow), label the connectors according to cylinder number

18.54 To remove the fuel rail assembly, remove the retaining bolts (arrows) (1987 and later 2.8L/3.1L V6 shown)

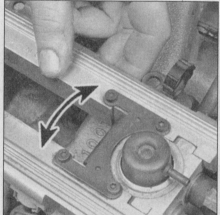

18.55 Use a gentle side-to-side rocking motion while pulling straight up to release the injectors from their bores in the intake manifold

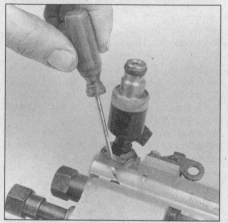

18.56 To remove an injector that is retained by a spring clip, simply pry off the clip with a small screwdriver, then pull the injector from the fuel rail

18.57 If you plan to use the same injectors, be sure to replace the O-rings with new ones

and 3.1L engines only).

51 Using a backup wrench, disconnect the fuel lines at the fuel rail **(see illustration)**. If you're working on a 1985 or 1986 2.8L V6 engine, disconnect the cold start valve tube from the fitting on the fuel rail.

52 Detach the vacuum line at the fuel pressure regulator.

53 Label and unplug the injector electrical connectors **(see illustration)**.

54 Remove the fuel rail retaining bolts **(see illustration)**.

55 Carefully remove the fuel rail with the injectors **(see illustration)**. **Caution:** *Use care when handling the fuel rail assembly to avoid damaging the injectors.* **Note:** *An identification number is stamped on the side of the fuel rail assembly. Refer to this number if servicing or parts replacement is required.*

56 To remove the fuel injectors on 1985 and 1986 2.8L engines, rotate the injector retaining clip and pull the injector from the fuel rail. On all other models spread open the end of the injector clip slightly and remove it from the fuel rail, then extract the injector **(see illustration)**.

57 Remove the injector O-ring seals **(see illustration)**.

58 Install the new O-ring seal(s), as required, on the injector(s) and lubricate them with a light film of engine oil.

59 Install the injectors on the fuel rail.

60 Secure the injectors with the retainer clips.

61 Installation is the reverse of the removal procedure.

2.2L four-cylinder engine

Warning: *Relieve the fuel system pressure before beginning this procedure.*

Note: *The fuel rail on this engine is integral with the lower intake manifold.*

62 Detach the negative battery cable from the battery. **Caution:** *If the vehicle is equipped with a Delco Loc II audio system, make sure you have the correct activation code before disconnecting the battery. See the information at the front of this manual for the radio re-activation procedure.*

63 Remove the air intake plenum (see Step 38).

64 Remove the fuel pressure regulator (see

the procedure beginning with Step 87). Be prepared for fuel spillage.

65 Remove the injector retainer screws and retainer. **Caution:** *Don't try to remove the injectors along with the retainer. Slide the retainer off the injectors far enough to completely disengage the injectors from the slots in the retainer.*

66 Disconnect the electrical connectors from the injectors.

67 Remove the injectors from the lower intake manifold. Be sure to check the injector mounting holes for O-rings that may have fallen off the injectors.

68 If the original injectors are being installed, be sure to use new O-rings.

69 Before installing the injectors, apply a light film of engine oil to the O-rings.

70 Install the injectors in their holes, using a twisting motion. Plug in the electrical connectors.

71 Install the injector retainer, making sure each injector properly fits into its retaining slot. Apply a non-hardening thread locking compound to the retainer screws and tighten the screws to the torque listed in this Chapter's Specifications.

18.79a A Torx driver is needed to remove the fuel pressure regulator mounting screws

18.79b Separate the fuel rail(s) from the regulator

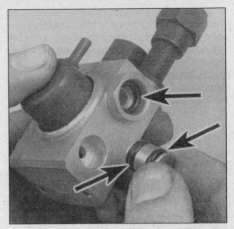

18.80 Always replace all O-rings when installing the regulator

72 The remainder of installation is the reverse of removal. Be sure to check for fuel leaks before returning the vehicle to normal service.

Fuel pressure regulator

Check

73 Refer to Section 3 for the fuel pressure checking procedure.

Replacement

OHC four-cylinder and V6 engines

Refer to illustrations 18.79a, 18.79b and 18.80

74 Relieve the fuel system pressure (see Section 2).
75 Disconnect the cable from the negative terminal of the battery. **Caution:** *If the vehicle is equipped with a Delco Loc II audio system, make sure you have the correct activation code before disconnecting the battery. See the information at the front of this manual for the radio re-activation procedure.*
76 Remove the fuel rail following the procedure described earlier in this Section.
77 **Note:** *According to the factory service manual, the fuel pressure regulator on 1985 and 1986 2.8L V6 engines is not serviceable, requiring replacement of the entire fuel rail if malfunctioning. However, regulator rebuild kits are now available and are much less costly than an entire fuel rail assembly.*
78 Unscrew the two fuel line fittings from the pressure regulator assembly.
79 Remove the pressure regulator mounting screws **(see illustration)** and separate the two fuel rails from the pressure regulator assembly **(see illustration).**
80 Reassembly is the reverse of disassembly. Be sure to replace all gaskets and seals **(see illustration)**, otherwise a dangerous fuel leak may develop. When installing the seals, lubricate them with a light film of engine oil.

2.2L four-cylinder engine

81 Relieve the fuel system pressure (see Section 2).

82 Disconnect the cable from the negative terminal of the battery. **Caution:** *If the vehicle is equipped with a Delco Loc II audio system, make sure you have the correct activation code before disconnecting the battery. See the information at the front of this manual for the radio re-activation procedure.*
83 Detach the vacuum hose from the regulator.
84 Detach the fuel return line from the bottom of the regulator. Be sure to hold the regulator with a wrench while unscrewing the fitting.
85 Remove the regulator securing screw and detach the regulator from the lower intake manifold.
86 Installation is the reverse of removal. Be sure to use new O-rings on the regulator and return line and lubricate them with a light film of engine oil. If the regulator is equipped with a filter screen, make sure it's clean.

Cold start valve (1985 and 1986 2.8L V6 engines only)

87 Relieve the fuel system pressure on fuel injected vehicles (see Section 2).
88 Disconnect the cable from the negative terminal of the battery. **Caution:** *If the vehicle is equipped with a Delco Loc II audio system, make sure you have the correct activation code before disconnecting the battery. See the information at the front of this manual for the radio re-activation procedure.*
89 Remove the air intake plenum by following the procedure earlier in this Section.
90 Remove the cold start valve retaining bolt.
91 Unscrew the cold start tube fitting from the fuel rail.
92 Remove the valve.
93 Remove the valve from the tube and body assembly by bending the tab back and unscrewing the valve.
94 If the same valve is to be reinstalled, be sure to install new O-rings on each end of the valve and also on the end of the tube that connects to the fuel rail.
95 Turn the cold start valve completely into

the tube and body assembly.
96 Turn the valve back one full turn, so the electrical connector is pointing up.
97 Bend the tang on the body forward to limit rotation of the valve.
98 Lubricate the O-rings with a light film of engine oil, then reinstall the valve by reversing the removal procedure.

19 Turbocharger - general information

The turbocharger increases power by using an exhaust gas-driven turbine to pressurize the fuel/air mixture before it enters the combustion chambers. The amount of boost (intake manifold pressure) is controlled by the wastegate (exhaust bypass valve). The wastegate is operated by a spring-loaded actuator assembly which controls the maximum boost level by allowing some of the exhaust gas to bypass the turbine. The wastegate is controlled by the Electronic Control Module (ECM).

The computerized fuel injection and emission control system is equipped with self-diagnosis capabilities that can access certain turbocharging system components. Refer to Chapter 6 for information pertaining to trouble codes and diagnosis.

20 Turbocharger - check

General checks

1 While it is a relatively simple device, the turbocharger is also a precision component which can be severely damaged by an interrupted oil or coolant supply or loose or damaged ducts.
2 Due to the special techniques and equipment required, checking and diagnosis of suspected problems dealing with the turbocharger should be left to a dealer service department. The home mechanic can, however, check the connections and linkages for security, damage and other obvious prob-

lems. Also, the home mechanic can check components that govern the turbocharger such as the wastegate solenoid, bypass valve and wastegate actuator. Refer to the checks later in this section.

3   Because each turbocharger has its own distinctive sound, a change in the noise level can be a sign of potential problems.

4   A high-pitched or whistling sound is a symptom of an inlet air or exhaust gas leak.

5   If an unusual sound comes from the vicinity of the turbine, the turbocharger can be removed and the turbine wheel inspected. **Warning:** *All checks must be made with the engine off and cool to the touch and the turbocharger stopped or personal injury could result. Operating the engine without all the turbocharger ducts and filters installed is also dangerous and can result in damage to the turbine wheel blades.*

6   With the engine turned off, reach inside the housing and turn the turbine wheel to make sure it spins freely. If it doesn't, it's possible the cooling oil has sludged or coked from overheating. Push in on the turbine wheel and check for binding. The turbine should rotate freely with no binding or rubbing on the housing. If it does the turbine bearing is worn out.

7   Check the exhaust manifold for cracks and loose connections.

8   Because the turbine wheel rotates at speeds up to 140,000 rpm, severe damage can result from the interruption of coolant or contamination of the oil supply to the turbine bearings. Check for leaks in the coolant and oil inlet lines and obstructions in the oil drainback line, as this can cause severe oil loss through the turbocharger seals. Burned oil on the turbine housing is a sign of this. **Caution:** *Whenever a major engine bearing such as a main, connecting rod or camshaft bearing is replaced, the turbocharger should be flushed with clean oil.*

Component checks

Wastegate actuator

9   Using a hand held vacuum pump, apply vacuum to the wastegate actuator and make sure the rod moves. **Note:** *Do not apply more than 5.0 psi or the diaphragm may be damaged.*

10   The rod should move 0.015 inches at 3.5 to 4.5 psi.

11   If the test results are incorrect, replace the wastegate actuator with a new part.

---

21   Turbocharger - removal and installation

Warning: *Wait until the engine is completely cool before beginning this procedure.*

Removal

1   Disconnect the cable from the negative terminal of the battery, raise the vehicle and support it securely on jackstands. **Caution:** *If the vehicle is equipped with a Delco Loc II audio system, make sure you have the correct activation code before disconnecting the battery. See the information at the front of this manual for the radio re-activation procedure.*

2   Drain the cooling system (see Chapter 1).

3   On models equipped with air conditioning, remove the rear bolt on the air conditioning compressor support bracket and loosen the remaining bolts (see Chapter 3).

4   Remove the exhaust pipe from the manifold.

5   Remove the rear turbocharger-to-engine support bolts.

6   Disconnect the oil drain hose from the turbocharger.

7   Lower the vehicle.

8   Disconnect the coolant recovery pipe and move it out of the way.

9   Remove the induction tube cooling fan (see Chapter 3) and oxygen sensor (see Chapter 6).

10   Disconnect the oil feed pipe at the union.

11   Disconnect the air intake duct and vacuum hose at the wastegate actuator.

12   Remove the oil feed pipe, exhaust elbow, support bracket, actuator assembly and turbocharger from the exhaust manifold.

Installation

13   Carefully clean the mating surfaces of the turbocharger and exhaust manifold.

14   Place the turbocharger in position and install the bolts.

15   Apply anti-seize compound to the studs and install the nuts. Tighten the nuts to the torque listed in this Chapter's Specifications.

16   If a new turbocharger was installed, install the turbocharger outlet and support bracket.

17   Install the cooling fan, induction tube and coolant recovery pipe.

18   Install the oil feed lines, oxygen sensor, air intake duct and wastegate actuator vacuum hose.

19   Raise the vehicle and support it on jackstands.

20   Install the rear turbocharger support bolt, air conditioning compressor support, oil drain hose, lower fan screw and exhaust pipe.

21   Lower the vehicle and connect the negative battery cable.

22   Change the engine oil (see Chapter 1).

22   Wastegate actuator - removal and installation

Warning: *Wait until the engine is completely cool before beginning this procedure*

Removal

1   Disconnect the negative battery cable. **Caution:** *If the vehicle is equipped with a Delco Loc II audio system, make sure you have the correct activation code before disconnecting the battery. See the information at the front of this manual for the radio re-activation procedure.*

2   Remove the induction tube.

3   Remove the actuator rod-to-wastegate clip and disconnect the vacuum hose.

4   Remove the retaining screws and lift the actuator assembly from the turbocharger.

Installation

5   Place the actuator assembly in position and install the retaining screws.

6   Connect the vacuum hose and install the rod clip and induction tube.

7   Connect the negative battery cable.

---

23   Exhaust system components - general information, removal and installation

Warning: *The vehicle's exhaust system generates very high temperatures and should be allowed to cool down completely before any of the components are touched. Be especially careful around the catalytic converter, where the highest temperatures are generated.*

1   Replacement of exhaust system components is basically a matter of removing the heat shields, disconnecting the component and installing a new one. The heat shields and exhaust system hangers must be reinstalled in the original locations or damage could result. Due to the high temperatures and exposed locations of the exhaust system components, rust and corrosion can seize parts together. Penetrating oils are available to help loosen frozen fasteners. However, in some cases it may be necessary to cut the pieces apart with a hacksaw or cutting torch. The latter method should be employed only by persons experienced in this work.

Crossover pipe

2   Remove the bolts or nuts securing the crossover pipe to the exhaust manifolds. Remove the crossover pipe.

3   Installation is the reverse of removal. Tighten the fasteners evenly and securely.

Chapter 5
Engine electrical systems

Contents

1 Ignition system - general information

Warning: *Because of the very high voltage generated by the ignition system, extreme care should be taken whenever an operation involving ignition components is performed. This not only includes the distributor, coil(s), module and spark plug wires, but related items that are connected to the systems as well, such as the plug connections, tachometer and testing equipment.*

Early models are equipped with High Energy Ignition (HEI) systems, consisting of an ignition switch, battery, coil, primary (low tension) and secondary (high tension) wiring circuits, a distributor and spark plugs. Later models are equipped with a distributorless ignition system (DIS).

High Energy Ignition (HEI) distributor

HEI equipped models use a special HEI distributor with Electronic Spark Timing (EST). Some HEI distributors combine all the ignition components into one unit with the ignition coil in the distributor cap. On other HEI distributors, the coil is mounted separately.

All spark timing changes in the HEI/EST distributor are carried out by the Electronic Control Module (ECM), which monitors data from various engine sensors, computes the desired spark timing and signals the distributor to change the timing accordingly. No vacuum or mechanical advance is used.

Electronic Spark Control (ESC)

Some engines are equipped with an Electronic Spark Control (ESC), which uses a knock sensor in conjunction with the ECM to control spark timing to allow the engine to have maximum spark advance without spark knock. This improves driveability and fuel economy.

Direct Ignition System (DIS)

All distributorless four-cylinder and V6 models use a distributorless ignition system called the Direct Ignition System (DIS). It use a "waste spark" method of spark distribution.

Each cylinder is paired with its opposing cylinder in the firing order (1-4, 2-3 on a four-cylinder, 1-4, 2-5, 3-6 on a V6) so that one cylinder on compression fires simultaneously with its opposing cylinder on exhaust stroke. Since the cylinder on exhaust stroke requires very little of the available voltage to fire its plug, most of the voltage is used to fire the cylinder on the compression stroke.

The DIS system includes a coil pack, an ignition module, a crankshaft reluctor ring, a magnetic crankshaft sensor and the ECM. The ignition module is located under the coil pack and is connected to the ECM.

The magnetic crankshaft sensor protrudes through the engine block, within about 0.050-inch of the crankshaft reluctor ring. The reluctor ring is a special disc cast into the crankshaft, which acts as a signal generator for the ignition timing.

The system uses Electronic Spark Timing (EST) and control wires from the ECM, just like conventional distributor systems. The ECM controls timing using crankshaft position, engine rpm, engine temperature and manifold absolute pressure (MAP) sensing.

Component location

A   Typical alternater location (four cylinder models)
B   Typical spark plug location location (four cylinder models)
C   Typical distributor location (four cylinder models)

D   The starter motor is located on the underside of the engine above the drivers side inner CV-joint (four cylinder models)

2   Battery - removal and installation

Refer to illustration 2.3
Warning: *Hydrogen gas is produced by the battery, so keep open flames and lighted cigarettes away from it at all times. Always wear eye protection when working around a battery. Rinse off spilled electrolyte immediately with large amounts of water.*

Removal

1   The battery is located at the left front of the engine compartment.
2   Detach the cables from the negative and positive terminals of the battery. **Caution 1:** *To prevent arcing, disconnect the negative (-) cable first, then remove the positive (+) cable.* **Caution 2**: *If the vehicle is equipped with a Delco Loc II audio system, make sure you have the correct activation code before disconnecting the battery. See the information at the front of this manual for the radio re-activation procedure.*
3   Remove the hold-down clamp bolt and the clamp from the battery carrier **(see illustration)**
4   Carefully lift the battery from the carrier. **Warning:** *Always keep the battery in an upright position to reduce the likelihood of electrolyte spillage. If you spill electrolyte on your skin, rinse it off immediately with large amounts of water.*

2.3 Remove the battery hold-down bolt (arrow) from the battery carrier

Installation

Note: *The battery carrier and hold-down clamp should be clean and free from corrosion before installing the battery. Make certain that there are no parts in the carrier before installing the battery.*
5   Set the battery in position in its carrier. Don't tilt it.
6   Install the hold-down clamp and bolt. The bolt should be snug, but overtightening it may damage the battery case.
7   Install both battery cables, positive first,

then the negative. **Note:** *The battery terminals and cable ends should be cleaned prior to connection* (see Chapter 1).

3   Battery - emergency jump starting

Refer to the *booster battery (jump) starting* procedure at the front of this manual.

4   Battery cables - check and replacement

1   Periodically inspect the entire length of each battery cable for damage, cracked or burned insulation and corrosion. Poor battery cable connections can cause starting problems and decreased engine performance.
2   Check the cable-to-terminal connections at the ends of the cables for cracks, loose wire strands and corrosion. The presence of white, fluffy deposits under the insulation at the cable terminal connection is a sign the cable is corroded and should be replaced. Check the terminals for distortion, missing mounting bolts or nuts and corrosion.
3   If only the positive cable is to be replaced, be sure to disconnect the negative cable from the battery first. **Caution:** *If the*

5.3 To use a calibrated ignition tester (available at most auto parts stores), simply disconnect a spark plug wire, attach the wire to the tester, clip the tester to a convenient ground (like a valve cover bolt) and operate the starter - if there's enough power to fire the plug, sparks will be visible between the electrode tip and the tester body

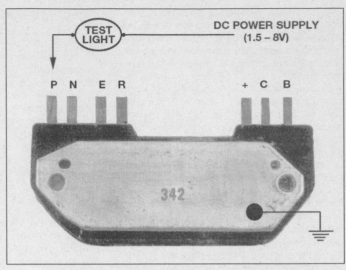

5.5 Typical ignition module terminal identification

vehicle is equipped with a Delco Loc II audio system, make sure you have the correct activation code before disconnecting the battery. See the information at the front of this manual for the radio re-activation procedure.

4   Disconnect and remove the cable. Make sure the replacement cable is the same length and diameter.

5   Clean the threads of the starter or ground connection with a wire brush to remove rust and corrosion. Apply a light coat of petroleum jelly to the threads to ease installation and prevent future corrosion.

6   Attach the cable to the starter or ground connection and tighten the mounting nut securely.

7   Before connecting the new cable to the battery, make sure it reaches the terminals without having to be stretched.

8   Connect the positive cable first, followed by the negative cable. Tighten the nuts and apply a thin coat of petroleum jelly to the terminal and cable connection.

5   Ignition system - check

Warning: *Because of the very high voltage generated by the ignition system, extreme care should be taken whenever an operation is performed involving ignition components. This not only includes the coils, control module and spark plug wires, but related items connected to the system as well, such as the plug connections, tachometer and any test equipment.*

General checks

Caution: *When handling secondary spark plug leads with engine running, insulated pliers must be used and care exercised to prevent a possible electrical shock.*

Refer to illustration 5.3

1   Check all ignition wiring connections for tightness, cuts corrosion or any other signs of a bad connection. A faulty or poor connection at a spark plug could also result in a misfire. Also check for carbon deposits inside the spark plug boots.

2   Remove the distributor cap (if equipped) and check the cap and rotor as described in Chapter 1. Remove the spark plugs, if necessary, and check for fouling.

3   Use a calibrated ignition tester to verify adequate available secondary voltage (25,000 volts) at the spark plug **(see illustration)**.

4   Using an ohmmeter, check the resistance of the spark plug wires. Each wire should measure less than 30,000 ohms.

High Energy Ignition (HEI) systems

Refer to illustration 5.5

Caution: *When handling secondary spark plug leads with engine running, insulated pliers must be used and care exercised to prevent a possible electrical shock.*

5   Use the terminal pin designations for testing the ignition module for the HEI ignition system **(see illustration)**. Perform a Diagnostic Circuit Check before proceeding with this test. (If a tachometer is connected to the Tach term., disconnect it before proceeding with the test).

6   **Test 1:** Two wires are checked to insure that an open is not present in a spark plug wire. If spark occurs with the four-terminal distributor connector disconnected, pick-up coil output is too low for the EST operation. Check for spark at the plug with a spark tester J-26792 or equivalent (ST-125) while cranking (if no spark on one wire, check a second wire) **Note**: A few sparks and then nothing is considered no spark. If spark is found, check for fuel, fuel pressure and the spark plugs, etc. (see Chapter 1.) If no park is found, see Step 7.

7   **Test 2:** A spark indicates that the prob-lem must be in the distributor cap or rotor. **Note:** *A few sparks followed by no spark is the same condition as a no spark at all.* Disconnect the 4 terminal distributor connector and check for spark. If spark is found replace the pick-up coil. If no spark is found, check for spark at the coil wire with a spark tester while cranking. If spark is found check the cap for water, cracks, etc. If OK, replace the distributor rotor. If no spark is found, see Step 7.

8   **Test 3:** Normally, there should be battery voltage at the "C" and "+" terminals. Low voltage indicates an open or high resistance circuit from the distributor to the coil or ignition switch. If the "C" terminal voltage is low, but the "+" terminal voltage is 10 volts or more, the circuit from "C" terminal to the ignition coil primary winding is open. Disconnect the distributor 2 terminal "C/+" connector. Turn the ignition switch to the "on" position, with the engine stopped. Check the volts at "+" and "C" terminal's of distributor harness connector. If the reading is under 10 volts at the "C" terminal only, check for an open op poor ground in the circuit from "C" terminal to the ignition coil. If circuit is OK, the fault is either the ignition coil or connection. If both terminal's are under 10 volts, repair the wire from module "+" terminal to the "B" terminal of black ignition coil connector or primary circuit to ignition switch. If both terminal are 10 volts or more, see Step 9.

9   **Test 4:** Checks for a shorted module or a ground circuit from the ignition coil to module. The distributor module should be turned off, so normal voltage should be about 12 volts. If the module is turned on, the voltage will be low, but above one volt. This could cause the ignition coil to fail from excessive heat. With an open ignition coil primary winding, a small amount of voltage will leak through the module from the "BAT" to the tach terminal.

10   Applying a voltage (1.5 to 8V) to module terminal "P" should turn the module on and

the tach terminal voltage should drop to about 7 to 9 volts. Reconnect the distributor 2 terminal connection and turn the ignition to the "on" position. Check the voltage from the tach. terminal to ground. Note: the terminal may be taped back in harness. If the voltmeter reading is 1 to 10 volts: Replace the module and check for spark from the coil, see Test B. If spark occurs the system is OK. If no spark occurs replace the ignition coil, it too is faulty and needs to be replaced. If the voltmeter reading is under 1 volt, repair the open tach. lead or connection and repeat Test D. If the voltmeter reading is over 10 volts, connect a test light from the tach. terminal to the ground and crank the engine while observing the light. If the light Blinks, replace the ignition coil and recheck for spark with a spark tester. If still no spark occurs, re-install the original coil and replace the distributor module. If the light is on steady see, Step 11.

11   **Test 5:** Will determine whether the module or coil is faulty or if the pick-up coil is not generating the proper signal to turn the module on. This test can be performed by using a DC battery with a rating of 1.5 to 8 volts. The use of the test light is to allow the "P" terminal to be probed more easily. Some digital multimeters can also be used to trigger the module by selecting ohms, usually the diode position. In this position, the meter may have a voltage across its terminals which can be used to trigger the module. The voltage in the ohms position can be checked by using a second meter or by checking the manufacturer's specifications for the tool being used. Disconnect the distributor 4 terminal connector, remove the distributor cap and disconnect pick-up coil connector from module. Connect a voltmeter from the tach. terminal to ground and turn the ignition to the "on" position. Insulate a test light probe to 1/4" from tip and note voltage, as test light is momentarily connected from a voltage source (1.5 to 8V) to module term. "P" **(see illustration 5.5)**. If the voltage doesn't drop, check the module ground. If the ground is OK replace the module. If the voltage drops see, Step 12.

12   **Test 6:** Should turn off the module and cause a spark. If no spark occurs, the fault is most likely in the ignition coil because most module problems would have been found before this point in the procedure. A GM HEI module tester can determine which is at fault. If you cannot obtain the module tester, take the vehicle to a dealer at this point. Check for spark from coil wire with spark tester as the test light is removed from module terminal. If spark occurs, check the pick-up coil or connections. (Coil resistance should be 500-1500 ohms and not grounded). If no spark occurs, replace the ignition coil and repeat Test E. If spark occurs the system is OK. If no spark occurs reinstall (good) coil and check the coil wire from the distributor cap. If the wire is OK, replace the distributor module. If a module tester is available; test the module and replace as necessary.

Direct Ignition System (DIS)

Caution: *When handling secondary spark plug leads with engine running, insulated pliers must be used and care exercised to prevent a possible electrical shock.*

13   If the engine misfires at idle or under load, with the engine idling at normal operating temp, disconnect IAC motor. Momentarily disconnect each spark plug lead, using insulated pliers, while observing engine RPM. See Caution* All plug lead(s) should result in an RPM drop when removed. If the RPM dropped See chapter 1 Compression checking. If the RPM didn't change see, Step 14

14   **Test 2:** Use a spark tester to verify adequate available secondary voltage (25,000 volts) at the spark plug. With the ignition in the "OFF" position, install a spark tester on plug lead(s) which did not result in RPM drop. The spark should jump the tester gap while cranking the engine. If it does check, for faulty, fouled, worn or cracked spark plug(s). If spark plugs check out ok, (see Chapter 2C Check compression). If no spark is occurs see, Step 15

15   **Test 3:** if the spark jumps the test gap after grounding the opposite plug wire, it indicates excessive resistance in the plug which was bypassed. A faulty or poor connection at that plug could also result in a misfire condition. Also check for carbon deposits inside the spark plug boot. Turn the Ignition to the "OFF" position and ground the opposite plug lead of the affected coil at the spark plug. A spark should jump the tester gap while cranking engine. If it does, replace that spark plug for the lead which was jumpered to ground. If the misfire is till present, start misfire test again, see Step 13. If no spark occurs, check the resistance of each plug wire of the coil which did not fire that spark tester. Plug wire resistance should be less than 30,000 OHMS each and wires should not be grounded. If wires are not OK replace the faulty wires. If the wires test OK see Step, 16.

16   **Test 4:** Remove coil retaining nuts and remove the coil(s). Check for carbon tracking on the coils. If the coil(s) have carbon tracking the coil(s) are faulty. Also check plug wire connection(s) and wire nipple(s) for carbon tracking. If there is no carbon tracking see Step 17.

17   **Test 5:** If a no spark condition disappears when the coil is switched for another coil, the original coil is faulty. If not, the ignition module is the cause of the no spark condition see Section 9. This test can also be performed by substituting a known good coil for the one causing the no spark condition.

18   If the engine misfires under a load, perform Test 6, see Step 12. Use a spark tester to verify adequate available secondary voltage (25,000 volts) at the spark plug. The spark should jump the test gap on all fours leads. This simulates a "load" condition.

19   **Test 7:** if the spark jumps the tester gap after grounding the opposite plug wire, it indicates excessive resistance in the plug which was bypassed. A faulty or poor condition at

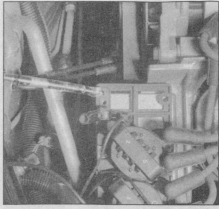

5.24 Connect a test light between the coil terminals on the ignition module and watch for a blinking light when the engine is cranked

the plug could also result in the miss condition. Also check for carbon deposits inside the spark plug boot.

20   **Test 8:** If carbon tracking is evident, replace the coil and be sure that the plug wires attached to that coil are clean and tight. Excessive wire resistance or faulty connections could damage the coil.

21   **Test 9:** If the no spark condition vanishes when the suspected coil is replaced by one of the other coils, that coil is faulty, If not, the ignition module is the reason there is no spark. This test could also be performed by substituting a known good coil for the one causing the no spark condition.

Module/coil assembly

Refer to illustration 5.24

22   **Test 1:** verifies the ability of the system to produce at least 25,000 volts.

23   **Test 2:** No spark on one cylinder may be caused by an open plug wire or secondary winding. Both wires related to a coil and the secondary winding resistance should therefore be checked. Resistance readings over the upper limit, but not infinite, will probably not cause a no start but may cause an engine miss under certain conditions.

24   **Test 3:** tests the triggering circuit in the ignition module **(see illustration)**. A blinking light indicates the module is triggering.

25   **Test 4:** A slowly blinking light, at this point, indicates the ECM is not seeing the crank sensor signal (see Chapter 6, Section 4).

26   **Test 5:** At this point, the crank sensor and its control circuits have proved to be good. The problem is in the combination sensor, sensor circuits or the ignition module.

27   Turn the ignition ON and listen for the fuel pump within the first two seconds. If the fuel pump runs, the fuse is okay.

28   Check to see if the problem is a grounded crank signal circuit **(see illustrations 7.22a, 7.22b and 7.22c)**.

29   The ignition module supplies the power to the sensor. Check to see if the problem is the module or the harness (see Section 7).

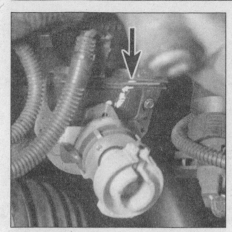

6.4 Mark the position of the rotor with respect to the distributor before removing the distributor - also mark the relationship of the distributor to the engine block

6.5 The distributor hold-down clamp and bolt must be removed before the distributor can be removed from the engine (four-cylinder engine shown)

7.4 To check the module for voltage, insert the voltmeter probe into the module positive terminal (arrow)

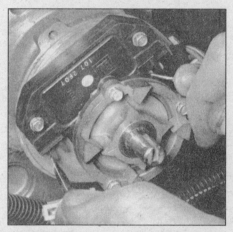

7.6 With a test light connected at terminal "P", check the voltage with the meter probe at the "C" terminal

6 HEI distributor - removal and installation

Removal

Refer to illustrations 6.4 and 6.5

1   Disconnect the cable from the negative battery terminal. **Caution:** *If the vehicle is equipped with a Delco Loc II audio system, make sure you have the correct activation code before disconnecting the battery. See the information at the front of this manual for the radio re-activation procedure.*

2   Remove the coil wire from the distributor cap.

3   Remove the distributor cap (see Chapter 1).

4   Note the position of the rotor and the distributor-to-block alignment. Make an alignment mark on the distributor to indicate the position of the rotor **(see illustration)**. Also make a mark to indicate distributor-to-block relationship.

5   Remove the distributor hold-down clamp bolt and clamp **(see illustration)**. Remove the distributor from the engine. **Caution:** *Do not turn the crankshaft while the distributor is removed from the engine. If the crankshaft is turned, the position of the rotor will be altered and the engine will have to be re-timed.*

Installation

6   Insert the distributor into the engine in exactly the same relation to the block in which it was removed. To mesh the gears, it may be necessary to turn the rotor slightly. At this point the distributor may not seat down against the block completely. This is due to the lower end of the distributor shaft not mating properly with the oil pump shaft. If this is the case, check again to make sure the distributor is aligned with the block in the same position it was in before removal and that the rotor is correctly aligned with the distributor body. The gear on the distributor shaft is

engaged with the gear on the camshaft, and this relationship cannot change as long as the distributor is not lifted from the engine. Use a socket and breaker bar on the crankshaft bolt to turn the engine over in the normal direction of rotation. The rotor will turn, but the oil pump shaft will not because the two shafts are not engaged. When the proper alignment is reached the distributor will drop down over the oil pump shaft, and the distributor body will seat properly against the block.

7   Install the hold-down clamp and tighten the bolt securely.

8   Install the distributor cap and coil wire.

9   Connect the cable to the negative terminal of the battery.

7 Ignition module and distributorless ignition system components - check and replacement

HEI (distributor) ignition system

Note: *It is not necessary to remove the distributor to check or replace the module.*

Check

Refer to illustrations 7.4, 7.6, and 7.11

1   Disconnect the tachometer (if so equipped) at the distributor.

2   Check for a spark at the coil and spark plug wires (see Section 5).

3   If there is no spark, remove the distributor cap. Remove the ignition module from the distributor but leave the connector plugged in.

4   With the ignition switch turned On, check for voltage at the module positive terminal **(see illustration)**.

5   If the reading is less than ten volts, there is a fault in the wire between the module positive (+) terminal and the ignition coil positive

connector or the ignition coil and primary circuit-to-ignition switch.

6   If the reading is ten volts or more, check the "C" terminal on the module **(see illustration)**.

7   If the reading is less than one volt, there is an open or grounded lead in the distributor-to-coil "C" terminal connection or ignition coil or an open primary circuit in the coil itself.

8   If the reading is one to ten volts, replace the module with a new one and check for a spark (Section 5). If there is a spark the module was faulty and the system is now operating properly. If there is no spark, there is a fault in the ignition coil.

9   If the reading in Step 4 is 10 volts or more, unplug the pick-up coil connector from the module. Check the "C" terminal voltage with the ignition switch On and watch the voltage reading as a test light is momentarily (five seconds or less) connected between the battery positive (+) terminal and the module "P" terminal **(see illustration 7.6)**.

10   If there is no drop in voltage, check the module ground and, if it is good, replace the module with a new one.

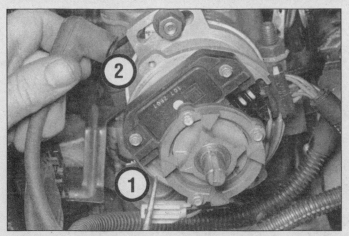

7.11 As the test light probe (1) is removed, check for a spark at the coil wire (2)

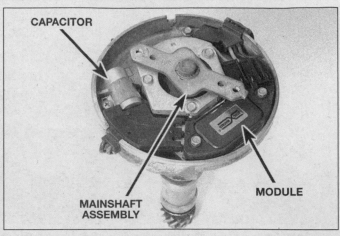

7.16 Silicone lubricant applied to the distributor base in the area under the ignition module dissipates heat and prevents module failure

11   If the voltage drops, check for spark at the coil wire as the test light is removed from the module terminal. If there is no spark, the module is faulty and should be replaced with a new one. If there is a spark, the pick-up coil or connections are faulty or not grounded **(see illustration)**.

Replacement
Refer to illustration 7.16
12   Detach the cable from the negative terminal of the battery. **Caution:** *If the vehicle is equipped with a Delco Loc II audio system, make sure you have the correct activation code before disconnecting the battery. See the information at the front of this manual for the radio re-activation procedure.*
13   Remove the distributor cap and rotor (see Chapter 1).
14   Remove both module attaching screws and lift the module up and away from the distributor.
15   Disconnect both electrical leads from the module. Note that the leads cannot be interchanged.
16   Do not wipe the grease from the module or the distributor base if the same module is to be reinstalled. If a new module is to be installed, a package of silicone grease will be included with it. Wipe the distributor base and the new module clean, then apply the silicone grease on the face of the module and on the distributor base where the module seats **(see illustration)**. This grease is necessary for heat dissipation.
17   Install the module and attach both electrical leads.
18   Install the distributor rotor and cap (see Chapter 1).
19   Attach the cable to the negative terminal of the battery.

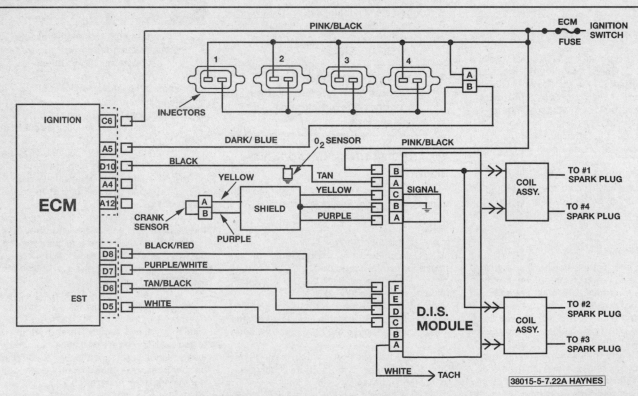

7.22a DIS schematic for the 2.0L and 2.2L OHV engines

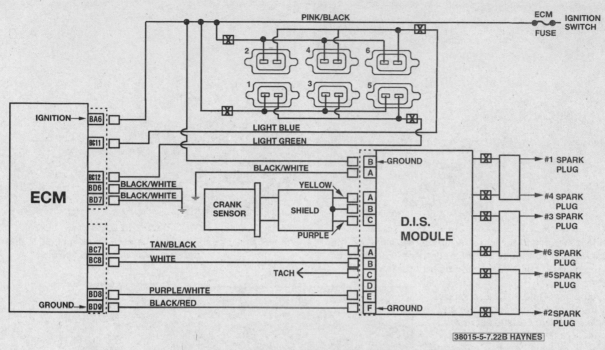

7.22b DIS schematic for the 2.8L and the 3.1L V6 engines

Distributorless ignition systems (DIS)

Check

Refer to illustrations 7.22a, 7.22b and 7.22c

20 First, perform the ignition system checks detailed in Section 5.

21 To check the ignition module, disconnect the electrical connectors from the ignition module.

22 With the ignition key ON (engine not running) check for battery voltage using a voltmeter at circuit 439 (pink/black wire) **(see illustrations)**. There should be battery voltage present.

23 Next, using an ohmmeter, check the resistance of the crankshaft sensor and circuit. On all except the 2.0L OHC engine, probe the crankshaft sensor terminals (yellow and purple wires) on the harness side of the module connector. It should read between

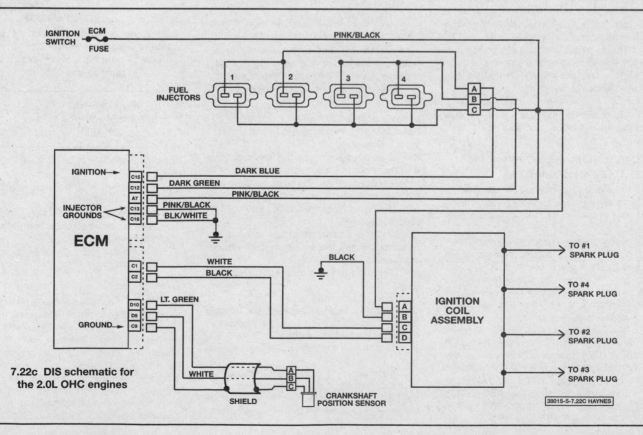

7.22c DIS schematic for the 2.0L OHC engines

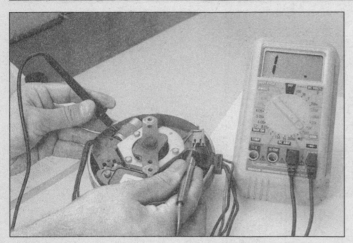

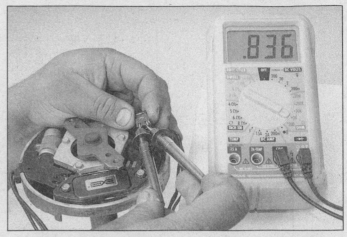

8.5 Connect the ohmmeter to a pick-up coil terminal and the distributor body. If continuity is indicated, there is a short from the pick-up coil wiring to the distributor body

8.6 Measure the resistance of the pick-up coil. It should be between 500 and 1,500 ohms

800 and 1,200 ohms. On 2.0L OHC engines, disconnect the ECM harness connector and probe terminals D10 and C9 **(see illustration 7.22c)** for the crankshaft position sensor resistance, it should fall between 480 and 680 ohms.

24   Finally, check the output voltage signal from the crankshaft sensor. With the probes attached to the same terminals (see Step 23), switch the meter to the volts scale (millivolts). Crank the engine over and confirm that the voltage output is greater than 0.1 volt (100 millivolts) on all except the 2.0L OHC engine, which should be greater than 0.3 volt (300 millivolts). Also, on the 2.0L OHC engine, check the ECM ignition control function by probing circuits 423 (white wire) and 485 (black wire) of the coil/module harness with the voltmeter. While cranking the engine the readings should be greater than one volt.

25   If all these tests are correct and there is no spark output at any of the coils, the ignition module is defective. In the event any of the system check findings are incorrect, diagnose the individual circuits and components.

Ignition module replacement (all except 2.0L OHC engines)

Note: *On the 2.0L OHC engine the ignition module is not serviced separately - circuitry is contained in the ignition coil assembly (see Section 9).*

26   Detach the cable from the negative terminal of the battery. **Caution:** *If the vehicle is equipped with a Delco Loc II audio system, make sure you have the correct activation code before disconnecting the battery. See the information at the front of this manual for the radio re-activation procedure.*

27   Clearly label, then disconnect, all spark plug wires from the DIS assembly. **Note:** *On 2.8L and 3.1L V6 engines, it may be necessary to remove the engine cooling fan and raise the vehicle to gain access to the DIS assembly, which is located on the front side of the engine.* **Warning:** *Always support the vehicle*

8.9a To remove the pick-up coil, mount the distributor shaft on a piece of wood, remove the coil spring securing the roll pin to the shaft and using a drift punch and hammer, knock out the roll pin

securely on jackstands when it's raised.

28   Unbolt or unplug the electrical connector at the module.

29   If equipped, detach the vacuum lines and the electrical connector from the EGR valve solenoid on the left end of the coil/module assembly.

30   Unbolt and remove the DIS and support bracket assembly.

31   Using a Torx screwdriver or bit (most models), remove the coil-to-module attaching screws.

32   Separate the coil and module assemblies.

33   Open the coil and module halves. Label, then detach, the wires between the module and the coil assemblies from the spade terminals on the underside of the coils.

34   Unbolt the module from the support bracket.

35   Installation is the reverse of removal. Be sure to attach the wires of the new module to the coil assembly spade terminals in exactly the same order in which they were removed.

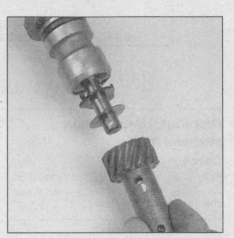

8.9b Remove the driven gear and spacer washers from the end of the shaft, making sure to note the order in which you remove any spacers

8   Ignition pick-up coil (HEI systems) - check and replacement

Refer to illustrations 8.5, 8.6, 8.9a, 8.9b, 8.10 and 8.11

1   Detach the cable from the negative terminal of the battery.

2   Remove the distributor cap and rotor.

3   Remove the distributor from the engine (see Section 6).

4   Detach the pick-up coil leads from the module.

Check

5   Connect one lead of an ohmmeter to the terminal of the pick-up coil lead and the other to ground as shown **(see illustration)**. Flex the leads by hand to check for intermittent opens. The ohmmeter should indicate infinite resistance at all times. If it doesn't, the pick-up coil is defective and must be replaced.

6   Connect the ohmmeter leads to both terminals of the pick-up coil lead as shown **(see illustration)**. Flex the leads by hand to

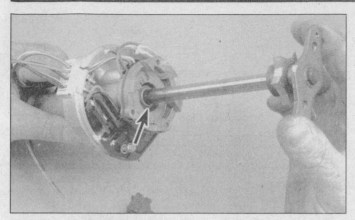

8.10 Remove the shaft from the distributor and on 1988 and later models remove the "E" clip (arrow)

8.11 To remove the pick-up coil from the HEI distributor, remove the retaining bolts from the pole piece and remove the pick-up coil

check for intermittent opens. The ohmmeter should read one steady value between 500 and 1500 ohms as the leads are flexed by hand. If it doesn't, the pick-up coil is defective and must be replaced.

Replacement

7   Remove the spring from the distributor shaft.

8   Mark the distributor tang drive and shaft so that they can be reassembled in the same position.

9   Carefully set the distributor on a piece of wood and, using a hammer and punch, remove the roll pin from the distributor shaft and gear **(see illustrations)**.

10   Remove the distributor shaft **(see illustration)**.

11   Lift the pick-up coil assembly straight up and remove it from the distributor **(see illustration)**. Note the order in which you remove the pieces.

12   Reassembly is the reverse of disassembly.

---

9   Ignition coil - check, removal and installation

High Energy Ignition (HEI) systems

Refer to illustration 9.2

1   Disconnect the cable from the negative terminal of the battery.

Check

2   Check the coil for opens and grounds by performing the following three tests with an ohmmeter **(see illustration)**.

3   Using the ohmmeter's high scale, hook up the ohmmeter leads as illustrated **(see test 1 in illustration 9.2)**. The ohmmeter should indicate a very high, or infinite, resistance value. If it doesn't, replace the coil.

4   Using the low scale, hook up the leads as illustrated **(see test 2 in illustration 9.2)**. The ohmmeter should indicate a very low, or zero, resistance value. If it doesn't, replace the coil.

5   Using the high scale, hook up the leads as illustrated **(see test 3 in illustration 9.2)**. The ohmmeter should not indicate an infinite resistance. If it does, replace the coil.

Removal

6   Unplug the coil high tension wire and both electrical leads from the coil.

7   Remove both mounting nuts and remove the coil from the engine.

Installation

8   Installation of the coil is the reverse of the removal procedure.

Distributorless Ignition System (DIS)

Check

Refer to illustrations 9.12 and 9.14

9   Refer to Section 6 and perform the ignition system checks.

Replacement

10   Detach the cable from the negative terminal of the battery.

11   Unplug the electrical connectors from

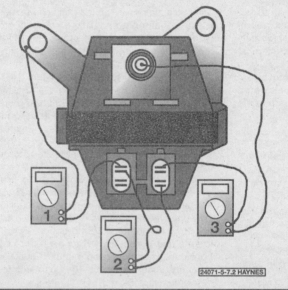

9.2 To check the ignition coil, use an ohmmeter to perform the following three checks

1   On high scale, the ohmmeter should read infinity

2   On low scale, the ohmmeter should read very low or zero

3   On high scale, the ohmmeter should not read infinite (if the coil fails any of these tests, replace it)

the module.

12   If the plug wires are not numbered, label them and detach the plug wires at the coil assembly **(see illustration)**.

13   Remove the module/coil assembly mounting bolts and lift the assembly from the vehicle (see Section 7).

14   On all except 2.0L OHC engines,

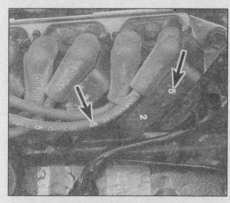

9.12 Original equipment coils and spark plug wires are numbered with their corresponding cylinder number

9.14 On all except the 2.0L OHC engine, the coils may be separated from the module

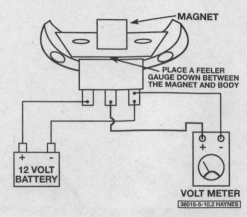

10.2 Hall effect switch test connections

remove the bolts attaching the coils to the module and separate them **(see illustration)**. The DIS assembly is not serviced separately on 2.0L OHC engines, the complete unit must be replaced if necessary.

15   Installation is the reverse of removal.

16   When installing the coils, make sure they are connected properly to the module and all plug wires are fully seated.

10   Hall effect switch (HEI systems) - check and replacement

Refer to illustration 10.2

1   Some HEI distributors are equipped with a Hall effect switch which is located above the pick-up coil assembly. The Hall effect switch is used in place of the R terminal of the HEI distributor to send engine RPM information to the ECM.

2   Test the switch by connecting a 12-volt power supply and voltmeter as shown **(see illustration)**. Check the polarity markings carefully before making any connections.

3   When the knife blade is not inserted as shown, the voltmeter should read less than 0.5 volts. If the reading is more, the Hall effect switch is faulty and must be replaced.

4   With the knife blade inserted, the voltmeter should read within 0.5 volts of battery voltage. Replace the switch with a new one if the reading is more.

5   Remove the Hall effect switch by unplugging the connector and removing the retaining screws.

6   Installation is the reverse of removal.

11   Charging system - general information and precautions

Caution: *If the vehicle is equipped with a Delco Loc II audio system, make sure you have the correct activation code before disconnecting the battery. See the information at the front of this manual for the radio re-activation procedure.*

The charging system consists of a belt-driven alternator with an integral voltage regulator and the battery. These components work together to supply electrical power for the ignition system, the lights and all accessories.

There are two types of alternators used. Earlier vehicles use the SI type and later models are equipped with the CS type. There are three types of CS alternators in use, the CS-130, CS-121 and the CS-144. All types use a conventional pulley and fan.

To determine which type of alternator is fitted to your vehicle, look at the fasteners employed to attach the two halves of the alternator housing. All CS models use rivets instead of screws. CS alternators are rebuildable once the rivets are drilled out. However, we don't recommend this practice. For all intents and purposes, CS types should be considered non-serviceable and, if found to be faulty, should be exchanged as cores for new or rebuilt units.

The purpose of the voltage regulator is to limit the alternator's voltage to a preset value. This prevents power surges, circuit overloads, etc., during peak voltage output. On all models with which this manual is concerned, the voltage regulator is contained within the alternator housing.

The charging system does not ordinarily require periodic maintenance. The drivebelts, electrical wiring and connections should, however, be inspected at the intervals suggested in Chapter 1.

Take extreme care when making circuit connections to a vehicle equipped with an alternator and note the following. When making connections to the alternator from a battery, always match correct polarity. Before using arc welding equipment to repair any part of the vehicle, disconnect the wires from the alternator and the battery terminal. Never start the engine with a battery charger connected. Always disconnect both battery leads before using a battery charger.

The charging indicator light on the dash lights when the ignition switch is turned on and goes out when the engine starts. If the light stays on or comes on once the engine is running, a charging system problem has occurred. See Section 12 for the proper diagnosis procedure for each type of alternator.

12   Charging system - check

Refer to illustration 12.5

1   If a malfunction occurs in the charging circuit, do not immediately assume that the alternator is causing the problem. First check the following items:

a) *Make sure the battery cable connections at the battery are clean and tight.*

b) *The battery electrolyte specific gravity (if possible). If it is low, charge the battery.*

c) *Check the external alternator wiring and connections. They must be in good condition.*

d) *Check the drivebelt condition and tension (Chapter 1).*

e) *Make sure the alternator mounting bolts are tight.*

f) *Run the engine and check the alternator for abnormal noise (may be caused by a loose drive pulley, loose mounting bolts, worn or dirty bearings, defective diode or defective stator).*

2   Using a voltmeter, check the battery voltage with the engine off. It should be approximately 12 volts.

3   Start the engine and check the battery voltage again. It should now be approximately 14 to 15 volts.

4   Locate the test hole in the back of the alternator. **Note:** *If there is no test hole, your vehicle is equipped with a newer CS type alternator. Further testing of this type of alternator must be done by a dealer or automotive electrical shop.*

5   Ground the tab that is located inside the hole by inserting a screwdriver blade into the hole and touching the tab and the case at the same time **(see illustration)**. **Caution:** *Do not run the engine with the tab grounded any longer than necessary to obtain a voltmeter reading. If the alternator is charging, it is running unregulated during the test. This condition may overload the electrical system and cause damage to the components.*

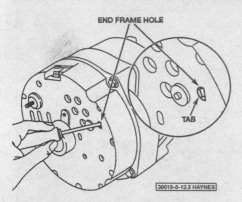

12.5 To full field the alternator, ground the tab located inside the test hole on the end frame (backside) of the alternator by inserting a screwdriver blade into the hole and touching the tab and the case at the same time

13.2 Remove the alternator electrical connectors

14.2 Mark the drive end frame and rectifier end frame assemblies with a scribe or paint before separating the two halves

6   The reading on the voltmeter should be 15 volts or higher with the tab grounded in the test hole.

7   If the voltmeter indicates low battery voltage, the alternator is faulty and should be replaced with a new one (see Section 15).

8   If the voltage reading is 15 volts or higher and a no charge condition is present, the regulator or field circuit is the problem. Remove the alternator (see Section 13) and have it checked further by an auto electric shop.

13 Alternator - removal and installation

Refer to illustration 13.2

1   Detach the cable from the negative terminal of the battery. **Caution:** *If the vehicle is equipped with a Delco Loc II audio system, make sure you have the correct activation code before disconnecting the battery. See the information at the front of this manual for the radio re-activation procedure.*

2   Clearly label, if necessary, then unplug and unbolt the electrical connectors from the alternator **(see illustration)**.

3   Remove the drivebelt (see Chapter 1).

4   Remove the alternator mounting bolts and remove the alternator.

5   Installation is the reverse of removal.

14 Alternator components - check and replacement

Note: *The following procedure applies only to SI type alternators. CS types have riveted housings and cannot be disassembled.*

Disassembly

Refer to illustrations 14.2, 14.3, 14.4, 14.5, 14.6 and 14.7

1   Remove the alternator from the vehicle

14.3 Using a hex wrench to hold the shaft, remove the pulley nut and pulley

14.5 After removing the nuts retaining the stator assembly to the rectifier bridge, remove the stator

(see Section 13).

2   Scribe or paint marks on the front and rear end frame housings of the alternator to facilitate reassembly **(see illustration)**.

3   Remove the nut retaining the fan pulley to the rotor shaft and remove the pulley **(see illustration)**.

4   Remove the four through-bolts holding

14.4 With the through bolts removed, carefully separate the drive end frame and the rectifier end frame

14.6 Remove the screws attaching the diode trio and resistor (if equipped) and remove the trio

the front and rear end frames together, then separate the drive end frame from the rectifier end frame **(see illustration)**.

5   Remove the nuts retaining the stator to the rectifier bridge and separate the stator from the end frame **(see illustration)**.

6   Remove the screws attaching the resistor (if equipped) and the diode trio and

14.7 Remove the screws that attach the brush holder and the regulator to the end frame, and remove the brush holder and regulator

14.9a Check for continuity between the two slip rings - if there's no continuity, the rotor is open and is defective

14.9b Check for continuity between each slip ring and the rotor shaft - if there's continuity, the rotor is grounded and is defective

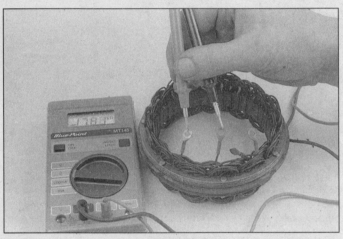

14.10a Check for continuity between the center stator terminal and each of the end terminals - if there's no continuity, there's an open in the windings and the stator is defective

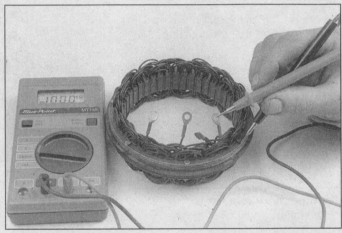

14.10b Check for continuity between each stator terminal and the frame - if there's continuity, the stator is grounded and is defective

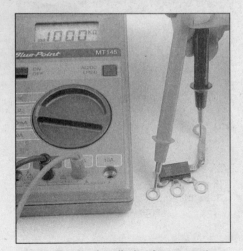

14.11 To check a diode trio, connect an ohmmeter as shown, then reverse the ohmmeter leads - one high and one low reading indicates a good diode, if the readings are the same the diode trio is defective (be sure to check all three diodes)

remove the trio **(see illustration).**

7   Remove the screws attaching the regulator and the brush holder to the end frame and remove the brush holder and regulator **(see illustration).**

8   Remove the capacitor lead from the rectifier bridge. Remove the screw and the nut retaining the rectifier bridge to the end frame and remove the rectifier bridge.

Component checks

Refer to illustrations 14.9a, 14.9b, 14.10a, 14.10b, 14.11 and 14.12

9   Remove the rotor from the end frame and check for an open between the two slip rings **(see illustration).** There should be 2 to 4 ohms resistance between the slip rings. Check for grounds between each slip ring and the rotor shaft **(see illustration).** There should be no continuity (infinite resistance) between the rotor shaft and either slip ring. If the rotor fails either test, or if the slip rings are excessively worn, the rotor is defective.

10   Check for opens between the center terminal and each end terminal of the stator windings **(see illustration).** If either reading is high (infinite resistance), the stator is defective. Check for a grounded stator winding between each stator terminal and the frame **(see illustration).** If there's continuity between any stator winding and the frame the stator is defective.

11   Check the diode trio by touching one probe of the ohmmeter on the single terminal and the other probe on one of the three terminals **(see illustration).** Then reverse the probes and check again. The diode should have continuity with the ohmmeter one way and no continuity when the probes are reversed. Check each of the three terminals in this manner. If any of the three diodes fail the test, the diode trio is defective.

12   To check the rectifier bridge, first bend each tab up slightly so the tabs are not touching each other and are not touching the center post. Check each diode in the rectifier by touching one probe of the ohmmeter to the tab and the other to the frame **(see illustration),** then reversing the probes. The diode should have continuity with the ohm-

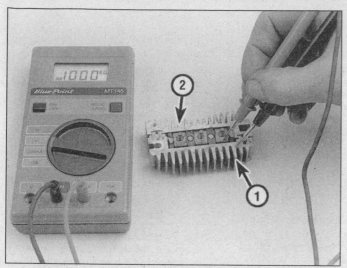

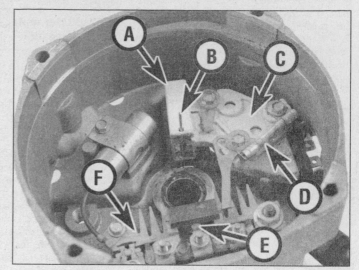

14.12 To check the rectifier bridge, bend up the metal tabs so they are not touching each other or the center post and connect an ohmmeter as shown (one lead to the frame and the other to a metal tab), then reverse the ohmmeter leads - you should get one high and one low reading, if the readings are the same the rectifier is defective - check the three diodes on one side of the rectifier (1) then check the three on the other side (2), make sure you reverse the ohmmeter leads on each of the diode checks

14.14a Inside a typical SI alternator

A *Brush holder*
B *Paper clip retaining brushes (for reassembly)*
C *Regulator (under brush holder)*
D *Resistor (not used on all models)*
E *Diode trio*
F *Rectifier bridge*

meter one way and no continuity when the probes are reversed. Check each diode on one side of the rectifier, then check the three on the other side. If any diode fails the test, the rectifier is defective.

Reassembly

Refer to illustrations 14.14a and 14.14b
13   Install the components in the reverse order of removal, noting the following:
14   Before installing the brush holder, push the brushes into the holder and slip a straightened paper clip or other suitable pin through the hole in the brush holder to hold the brushes in a retracted position. After the front and rear end frames have been bolted together remove the paper clip (**see illustrations**).

14.14b After the alternator is reassembled and the endframes bolted back together, pull-out the paper clip

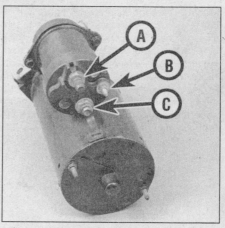

16.6 Typical starter solenoid terminals

A *Battery terminal*
B *Switch terminal (S)*
C *Motor terminal (M)*

15 Starting system - general information

Caution: *If the vehicle is equipped with a Delco Loc II audio system, make sure you have the correct activation code before disconnecting the battery. See the information at the front of this manual for the radio re-activation procedure.*

The function of the starting system is to crank the engine. The starting system is composed of a starting motor, solenoid and battery. The battery supplies the electrical energy to the solenoid, which then completes the circuit to the starting motor, which does the actual work of cranking the engine.

The solenoid and starting motor are mounted together at the lower front side of the engine. No periodic lubrication or mainte-

nance is required.

The electrical circuitry of the vehicle is arranged so that the starter motor can only be operated when the clutch pedal is depressed (manual transaxle) or the transaxle selector lever is in Park or Neutral (automatic transaxle).

Never operate the starter motor for more than 15 seconds at a time without pausing to allow it to cool for at least two minutes.

Excessive cranking can cause overheating, which can seriously damage the starter.

16 Starter motor - testing in vehicle

Refer to illustration 16.6

1   If the starter motor does not turn at all when the switch is operated, make sure that the shift lever is in Neutral or Park (automatic transaxle) or that the clutch pedal is depressed (manual transaxle).
2   Make sure that the battery is charged and that all cables, both at the battery and starter solenoid terminals, are secure.
3   If the starter motor spins but the engine is not cranking, the overrunning clutch in the starter motor is slipping and the motor must be removed from the engine for replacement.
4   If, when the switch is actuated, the starter motor does not operate at all but the solenoid clicks, then the problem lies with either the battery, the main solenoid contacts or the starter motor itself. **Note:** *Before diag-*

nosing starter problems, make sure the battery is fully charged.

5   If the solenoid plunger cannot be heard when the switch is actuated, the solenoid itself is defective or the solenoid circuit is open.

6   To check the solenoid, connect a jumper lead between the battery (+) and the "S" terminal on the solenoid **(see illustration)**. If the starter motor now operates, the solenoid is OK and the problem is in the ignition switch, neutral start switch or in the wiring.

7   If the starter motor still does not operate, remove the starter/solenoid assembly for disassembly, testing and repair.

8   If the starter motor cranks the engine at an abnormally slow speed, first make sure that the battery is charged and that all terminal connections are tight. If the engine is partially seized, or has the wrong viscosity oil in it, it will crank slowly.

9   Run the engine until normal operating temperature is reached, then stop the engine, disconnect the coil wire from the distributor cap and ground it on the engine.

10   Connect a voltmeter positive lead to the starter motor terminal of the solenoid and then connect the negative lead to ground.

11   Crank the engine and take the voltmeter readings as soon as a steady figure is indicated. Do not allow the starter motor to turn for more than 15 seconds at a time. A reading of 9 volts or more, with the starter motor turning at normal cranking speed, is normal. If the reading is 9 volts or more but the cranking speed is slow, the motor is faulty. If the reading is less than 9 volts and the cranking speed is slow, the solenoid contacts are probably burned.

17   Starter motor - removal and installation

1   Disconnect the negative battery cable. **Caution**: *If the vehicle is equipped with a Delco Loc II audio system, make sure you have the correct activation code before disconnecting the battery. See the information at the front of this manual for the radio re-activation procedure.*

2   Raise the front of the vehicle and support it securely on jackstands.

3   From under the vehicle, disconnect the solenoid wire and battery cable from the terminals on the solenoid.

4   Remove the starter motor bolts.

5   Remove the starter motor. Note the location of the spacer shim(s), if equipped.

6   Installation is the reverse of removal. Be sure to install the spacer shim(s) in exactly the same location, if equipped.

18   Starter solenoid - removal and installation

Removal

Refer to illustration 18.5

1   Disconnect the cable from the negative terminal of the battery. **Caution**: *If the vehicle is equipped with a Delco Loc II audio system, make sure you have the correct activation code before disconnecting the battery. See the information at the front of this manual for the radio re-activation procedure.*

2   Remove the starter motor (see Section 17).

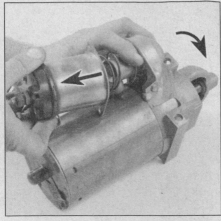

18.5 To remove the solenoid housing from the starter motor, remove the screws and turn it clockwise

3   Disconnect the strap from the solenoid to the starter motor terminal.

4   Remove the two screws which secure the solenoid to the starter motor.

5   Twist the solenoid in a clockwise direction to disengage the flange from the starter body **(see illustration)**.

Installation

6   To install, first make sure the return spring is in position on the plunger, then insert the solenoid body into the starter housing and turn the solenoid counterclockwise to engage the flange.

7   Install the two solenoid screws and connect the motor strap.

Chapter 6
Emissions and engine control systems

Contents

Component location

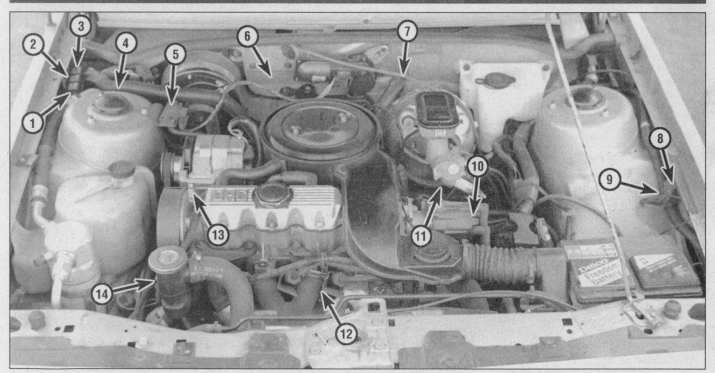

1.1a Emissions control system and related component locations - typical 1.8L/2.0L OHC TBI four-cylinder engine

1	Air conditioner control relay	7	Power steering cutout switch	11	EST four terminal electrical harness
2	Air conditioner constant run relay	8	Fan control relay		connector from distributor
3	Fuel pump relay	9	ECM pigtail connector on positive	12	Oxygen sensor (in exhaust manifold)
4	Air conditioner cycling switch		battery cable	13	Oil pressure switch
5	MAP sensor	10	TCC connector	14	Coolant sensor (in thermostat housing)
6	Blower motor relay (on cowl)				

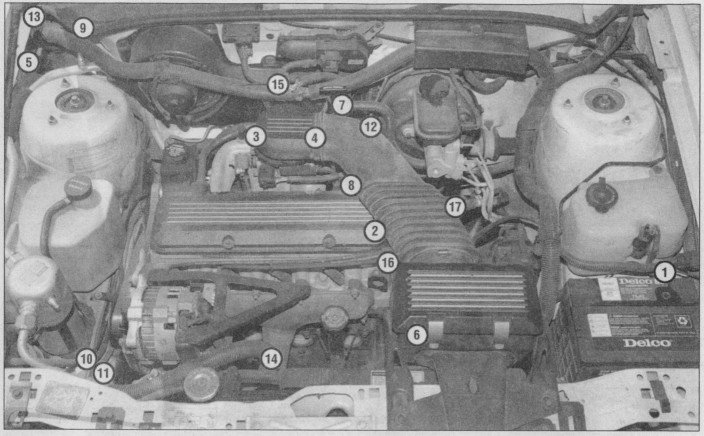

1.1b Emissions control system and related component locations - typical 2.0L OHV TBI four-cylinder engine

1	System power
2	System ground
3	Throttle body injection
4	Idle Air Control (IAC) valve
5	Fuel pump relay
6	Transmission Converter Clutch (TCC) connection

7	Electronic Spark Timing (EST) connector
8	EGR valve
9	EGR solenoid valve
10	Canister purge solenoid valve
11	Vapor canister
12	PULSAIR control

13	Manifold Absolute Pressure (MAP) sensor
14	Oxygen sensor
15	Throttle Position Sensor (TPS)
16	Coolant sensor
17	Fuel pump test connector

1 General information

Refer to illustrations 1.1a through 1.1e and 1.6

To prevent pollution of the atmosphere from burned and evaporating gases, a number of emissions control systems are incorporated on the vehicles covered by this manual. The combination of systems used depends on the year in which the0 vehicle was manufactured, the locality to which it was originally delivered and the engine type **(see illustrations)**. The major systems incorporated on the vehicles with which this manual is concerned include the:

*Air Injection Reaction (AIR)/PULSAIR or
 Air Management (AM) system
Fuel Control System
Electronic Spark Control (ESC) system
Electronic Spark Timing (EST) system
Early Fuel Evaporation (EFE) system
Exhaust Gas Recirculation (EGR) system
Evaporative Emissions Control (EECS)
 system*

*Transmission Converter Clutch (TCC)
Positive Crankcase Ventilation (PCV)
 system
Thermostatic Air Cleaner (THERMAC)
Catalytic converter*

All of these systems are linked, directly or indirectly, to the Computer Command Control System (CCCS).

The Sections in this Chapter include general descriptions, checking procedures (where possible) and component replacement procedures (where applicable) for each of the systems listed above.

Before assuming that an emissions control system is malfunctioning, check the fuel and ignition systems carefully. In some cases special tools and equipment, as well as specialized training, are required to accurately diagnose the causes of a rough running or difficult to start engine. If checking and servicing become too difficult, or if a procedure is beyond the scope of the home mechanic, consult your dealer service department. This does not necessarily mean, however, that the emissions control systems are particularly difficult to maintain and repair. You can

quickly and easily perform many checks and do most (if not all) of the regular maintenance at home with common tune-up and hand tools. **Note:** *The most frequent cause of emissions system problems is simply a loose or broken vacuum hose or wiring connection. Therefore, always check the hose and wiring connections first.*

Pay close attention to any special precautions outlined in this Chapter. It should be noted that the illustrations of the various systems may not exactly match the system installed on your particular vehicle due to changes made by the manufacturer during production or from year to year.

A *Vehicle Emissions Control Information (VECI)* label is located in the engine compartment of all vehicles with which this manual is concerned **(see illustration)**. This label contains important emissions specifications and setting procedures, as well as a vacuum hose schematic with emissions components identified. When servicing the engine or emissions systems, the VECI label in your particular vehicle should always be checked for up-to-date information. **Note:** *Because of a fed-*

1.1c Emissions control system and related component locations - OHV four-cylinder engine

1	System power	8	Thermo Air Cleaner	14	Oxygen sensor
2	System ground	9	Electronic Spark Timing (EST) connector	15	Throttle Position Sensor (TPS)
3	E2SE carburetor	10	Electronic Spark Control (ESC)	16	Coolant sensor connector
4	Idle air control (IAC) valve	11	Vapor canister	17	Manifold Air Temperature (MAT) sensor
5	Fuel pump relay	12	Positive Crankcase Ventilation Valve	18	P/N switch
6	Cooling fan relay	13	Manifold Absolute Pressure (MAP)	19	Knock sensor
7	Air conditioner control relay		sensor	20	Fuel pump test connector

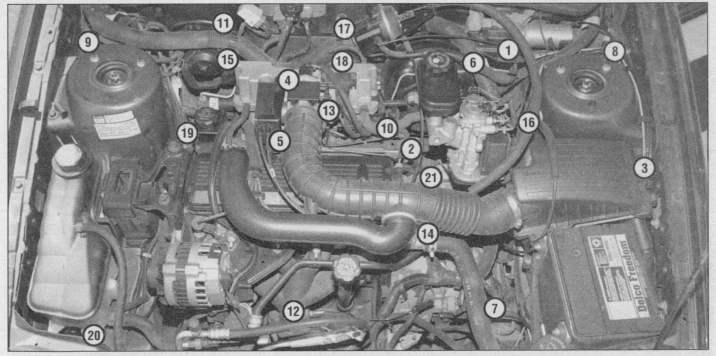

1.1d Emissions control system and related component locations - typical 2.2L OHV MPFI four-cylinder engine

1	ECM Power fuse	8	Cooling fan relay	15	Vehicle speed
2	ECM harness grounds	9	A/C compressor relay	16	P/N switch
3	Fuel pump test connector	10	Direct ignition system assembly	17	P/S pressure switch
4	Fuel injector solenoid	11	Manifold Pressure (MAP)	18	MAT sensor
5	Idle Air Control Valve	12	Exhaust oxygen	19	Crankcase vapor canister
6	Fuel pump relay	13	Throttle position	20	Fuel vapor canister
7	TCC solenoid connector	14	Coolant temperature	21	Exhaust recirculation valve

erally mandated extended warranty which covers the emission control system components (and any components which have a primary purpose other than emission control but have significant effects on emissions), check with your dealer about warranty coverage before working on any emission related systems.

Unless otherwise noted, procedures in this Chapter referring to carbureted models also apply to fuel-injected models. Because of their more precise fuel/air management, fuel-injected engines use simpler emissions systems which do not use all of the systems described previously.

The number of emissions control system components on later model fuel-injected vehicles has actually decreased due to the high efficiency of the new fuel injection and ignition systems. No longer needed are the AIR pump (most models), early fuel evaporation (EFE) system (except for TBI models), dual bed catalytic converter (although a single bed or monolithic converter is still used) and many of the confusing thermal vacuum switches, valves and hoses as installed on the carbureted engines.

2   Computer Command Control System (CCCS) and trouble codes

Refer to illustrations 2.7 and 2.16

General description

This electronically controlled emissions system is linked with as many as nine other related emissions systems. It consists mainly of sensors and an Electronic Control Module (ECM). Completing the system are various engine components which respond to commands from the ECM. **Note:** *1994 models are equipped with a Powertrain Control Module (PCM). This unit is essentially identical to the ECM in earlier vehicles. General Motors changed terminology to encompass the many functions of this computerized system.*

In many ways, this system can be compared to the central nervous system in the human body. The sensors (nerves) constantly gather information and send this data to the ECM (brain), which processes the data and, if necessary, sends out a command for some type of vehicle (body) change.

Here's a specific example of how one

1.1e Emissions control system and related component locations - typical 2.8L/3.1L MPFI V6 engine

1	ECM harness ground	17	Crankshaft sensor
2	Fuel pump test connector	18	Knock (ESC) sensor
3	Fuel pump/ECM fuse	19	MAT sensor
4	Fuel injector	20	P/N switch
5	Idle air control motor	21	P/S pressure switch
6	Fuel pump relay	22	A/C pressure fan switch
7	Trans, converter clutch connector	23	A/C low pressure switch (mounted in compressor)
8	Direct Ignition System (DIS)	24	A/C high pressure cut-out switch
9	Engine fan relay	25	Crankcase vent valve (PCV)
10	Exhaust gas recirculation valve	26	Engine temperature switch (telltale)
11	A/C compressor relay	27	Engine temperature sensor (gauge)
12	Fuel vapor canister solenoid	28	Oil pressure switch (telltale)
13	Manifold Pressure (MAP) sensor	29	Oil pressure sensor (gauge)
14	Exhaust oxygen sensor	30	Fuel pressure connector
15	Throttle position sensor	31	Vehicle speed sensor
16	Coolant temperature sensor		

portion of this system operates. An oxygen sensor, mounted in the exhaust manifold and protruding into the exhaust gas stream, constantly monitors the oxygen content of the exhaust gas as it travels through the exhaust pipe. If the percentage of oxygen in the exhaust gas is incorrect, an electrical signal is sent to the ECM. The ECM takes this information, processes it and then sends a command to the carburetor Mixture Control (M/C) solenoid or fuel injector(s) on a TBI or MPFI

system, telling it to change the fuel/air mixture. To be effective, all this happens in a fraction of a second, and it goes on continuously while the engine is running. The end result is a fuel/air mixture which is constantly kept at a predetermined ratio, regardless of driving conditions.

Testing

One might think that a system which uses exotic electrical sensors and is controlled by an on-board computer would be difficult to diagnose. This is not necessarily the case.

The Computer Command Control System has a built-in diagnostic system which indicates a problem by flashing a CHECK ENGINE light on the instrument panel. When this light comes on during normal vehicle operation, a fault has been detected.

Perhaps more importantly, the ECM will recognize this fault in a particular system monitored by one of the various information sensors and store it in its memory in the form

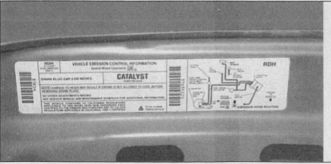

1.6 A Vehicle Emissions Control Information label will be found in the engine compartment of all vehicles - if it's missing, obtain a new one from a dealer parts department

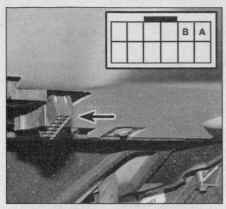

2.7 Typical diagnostic connector location (arrow)

of a trouble code. Although the trouble code cannot reveal the exact cause of the malfunction, it greatly facilitates diagnosis as you or a dealer mechanic can "tap into" the ECM's memory and be directed to the problem area.

To extract this information from the ECM memory, you must use a short jumper wire to connect terminals A and B on the Assembly Line Diagnostic Link (ALDL) **(see illustration)**. This terminal is part of an electrical connector located just behind the dashboard, next to the steering column. A small, rectangular plate is used to cover the connector and must be pried out of place to provide access to the terminals.

With the connector exposed to view, push one end of the jumper wire into the TEST terminal and the other end into the GROUND terminal. **Caution:** *Do not start the engine with the TEST terminal grounded.*

Turn the ignition to the On position (engine not running). The "CHECK ENGINE" or "SERVICE ENGINE SOON" light should flash Trouble Code 12, indicating that the diagnostic system is working. Code 12 will consist of one flash, followed by a short pause, and then two flashes in quick succession. After a longer pause, the code will repeat itself two more times .

If no other codes have been stored, Code 12 will continue to repeat itself until the jumper wire is disconnected. If additional

Trouble Codes have been stored, they will follow Code 12. Again, each Trouble Code will flash three times before moving on.

Once the code(s) have been noted, use the Trouble Code Identification information which follows to locate the source of the fault. **Note:** *Whenever the battery cable is disconnected, all stored Trouble Codes in the ECM are erased. Be aware of this before you disconnect the battery.* **Caution:** *If the vehicle is equipped with a Delco Loc II audio system, make sure you have the correct activation code before disconnecting the battery. See the information at the front of this manual for the radio re-activation procedure.*

It should be noted that the self-diagnosis feature built into this system does not detect all possible faults. If you suspect a problem with the Computer Command Control System, but the CHECK ENGINE or SERVICE ENGINE SOON light has not come on and no trouble codes have been stored, take the vehicle to a dealer service department or other repair shop for diagnosis.

Furthermore, when diagnosing an engine performance, fuel economy or exhaust emissions problem (which is not accompanied by a CHECK ENGINE or SERVICE ENGINE SOON light) do not automatically assume the fault lies in this system. Perform all standard troubleshooting procedures, as indicated elsewhere in this manual, before turning to the Computer Command Control System .

Finally, since this is an electronic system, you should have a basic knowledge of automotive electronics before attempting any diagnosis. Damage to the ECM, Programmable Read Only Memory (PROM) CAL-PAK or MEM-CAL calibration unit or related components can easily occur if care is not exercised.

Trouble Code Identification

Following is a list of the typical Trouble Codes which may be encountered while diagnosing the Computer Command Control System. Also included are simplified troubleshooting procedures. If the problem persists after these checks have been made, the vehicle must be diagnosed by a professional

2.16 Disconnect the ECM pigtail wire at the connector (arrow) to clear the ECM memory of all trouble codes

mechanic who can use specialized diagnostic tools and advanced troubleshooting methods to check the system. Procedures marked with an asterisk (*) indicate component replacements which may not cure the problem in all cases. For this reason, you may want to seek professional advice before purchasing replacement parts.

To clear the Trouble Code(s) from the ECM memory, unplug the ECM electrical pigtail at the positive (+) battery cable **(see illustration)**. If the vehicle you are working on does not have this connector, disconnect the cable from the negative terminal of the battery. **Caution:** *If the vehicle is equipped with a Delco Loc II audio system, make sure you have the correct activation code before disconnecting the battery. See the information at the front of this manual for the radio re-activation procedure.*

Disconnecting the power to the ECM to clear the memory can be an important diagnostic tool, especially on intermittent problems. On later models it is a simple matter to unplug the ECM harness positive battery cable pigtail for ten seconds to clear all the stored Trouble Codes. **Caution:** *To prevent damage to the ECM, the ignition switch must be off when disconnecting or connecting power to the ECM.*

Trouble Code	Circuit or system	Probable cause
12 (one flash, pause, two flashes)	No reference pulses to ECM	This code should flash whenever the Test terminal is grounded with the ignition On and the engine not running. If additional Trouble Codes are stored (indicating a problem), they will appear after this code has flashed three times. With the engine running, the appearance of this code indicates that no references from the distributor are reaching the ECM. Carefully check the four-terminal EST connector at the distributor.
13 (one flash, pause, three flashes)	Oxygen sensor circuit	Check the wiring and connectors from the oxygen sensor. Replace oxygen sensor (see Chapter 1).
14 (one flash, pause, four flashes)	Coolant sensor circuit	If the engine is experiencing overheating problems, the problem must be rectified before continuing (see Chapters 1 and 3). Check all wiring and connectors associated with the sensor. Replace the coolant sensor.*

Trouble Code	Circuit or system	Probable cause
15 (one flash, pause, five flashes)	Coolant sensor circuit (low temperature indicated)	See above. Also, check the thermostat for proper operation.
19 (one flash, pause, nine flashes)	Crankshaft position sensor reference signal intermittent	The reference signal from the crankshaft sensor is intermittent. Inspect PCM harness connector and crankshaft sensor wire harness for shorts or a damaged harness
21 (two flashes, pause, one flash)	TPS circuit (signal voltage high)	Check for sticking or misadjusted TPS. Check all wiring and connections at the TPS and at the ECM. Adjust or replace TPS* (see Chapter 4).
22 (two flashes, pause, two flashes)	TPS circuit (signal voltage low)	See above.
23 (two flashes, pause, three flashes)	Mixture Control (M/C) solenoid circuit (carbureted models only)	Check the electrical connections at the M/C solenoid (see Chapter 4). If OK, clear the ECM memory and recheck for code(s) after driving the vehicle. Check wiring connections at the ECM. Check wiring from M/C solenoid (Chapter 4).
23 (two flashes, pause, three flashes) (1986 through 1990 models)	Manifold Air Temperature (MAT) sensor circuit (low temperature)	Check the MAT sensor, wiring and connectors for an open. Replace the MAT sensor.*
23 (two flashes, pause, three flashes) (1991 and later models)	Intake Air Temperature (IAT) sensor circuit (low temperature)	See above.
24 (two flashes, pause, four flashes)	Vehicle Speed sensor (VSS) circuit	A fault in this circuit should be indicated only while the vehicle is in motion. Disregard code 24 if set when drive wheels are not turning. Check connections at the ECM Check the TPS setting (Chapter 4).
25 (two flashes, pause, five flashes) (1990 and earlier models)	Manifold Air Temperature (MAT) sensor (high temperature)	Check the resistance of the MAT sensor. Check the wiring and connectors to the sensor. Replace the MAT sensor.*
25 (two flashes, pause, five flashes) (1991 and later models)	Intake Air Temperature (IAT) sensor circuit (high temperature)	Check the resistance of the IAT sensor. Check the wiring and connections to the sensor. Replace the IAT sensor.*
26 (two flashes, pause, six flashes) (1994 2.2L models)	Quad-Driver Module (QDM) circuit	QDMs are switches within the PCM used to control various components such as: canister purge solenoid, EGR solenoid, cooling fan relay, etc. Due to the complexity of the system, it is suggested that diagnosis and repair of QDM malfunctions be left to a dealer service department or other authorized repair facility.
27/28 (two flashes, pause, seven or eight flashes) (1994 2.2L models)	QDM circuits	See above.
31 (three flashes, pause, one flash)	Wastegate actuator (turbocharged models only)	Possible sticking wastegate actuator or wastegate. Also check power to the ignition and/or a faulty ECM.
32 (three flashes, pause, two flashes)	No altitude compensator voltage (carbureted models only)	Check connections at altitude compensator. Check for an open circuit in the wiring from the sensor to the ECM. Replace the altitude compensator.*
32 (three flashes, pause, two flashes)	Exhaust Gas Recirculation (EGR) system failure	Check the vacuum source and all vacuum lines. Check the electrical connectors at the ECM and EGR valve. Replace the EGR valve or ECM as necessary.*
33 (three flashes, pause, three flashes)	Manifold Absolute Pressure (MAP) sensor or circuit	Check vacuum hose(s) from MAP sensor Check electrical connections at the ECM Replace MAP sensor.*
33 (three flashes, pause, three flashes)	MAF sensor or circuit	Excessive airflow indicated. Check terminal C on the MAF sensor: it should be about 0.5-volts at idle and 4.7-volts at wide open throttle. Trace the wire from terminal C and look for an open circuit condition. Replace the MAF sensor.*
34 (three flashes, pause, four flashes)	Vacuum sensor circuit (carbureted models only)	Check the wiring leading to terminals 20, 21 and 22 of the ECM) Check the connections at the ECM Check the vacuum sensor wiring and connections Replace vacuum sensor.*
34 (three flashes, pause, four flashes)	Mass Air Flow (MAF) sensor or circuit	Low airflow indicated. Check terminal C on the MAF sensor: it should be about 0.5-volts at idle and 4.7-volts at wide open throttle. Trace the wire from terminal C and look for a short to ground. Replace the MAF sensor.*
34 (three flashes, pause, four flashes)	Manifold Absolute Pressure (MAP) sensor circuit	Check for an Open or shorted to ground circuit. Check the MAP sensor. Replace it if malfunctioning.

*Component replacement may not cure the problem in all cases. For this reason, you may want to seek professional advice before purchasing replacement parts.

Trouble Code	Circuit or system	Probable cause
35 (three flashes, pause, five flashes)	Idle speed control circuit (IAC valve)	Idle RPM too low or too high. Check minimum idle speed (see Chapter 4), check fuel pressure, check for leaking injector and obstructions in the throttle body. Replace the IAC valve.*
41 (four flashes, pause, one flash)	No distributor reference signal to the ECM at specified vacuum (carbureted only)	Check all wires and connections at the distributor. Check distributor pick-up coil connections (see Chapter 5). Check vacuum sensor circuit (see above).
41 (four flashes, pause, one flash)	Cylinder select error	Remove the access cover on the ECM and check to see that the MEM-CAL, PROM or CALPAK is installed properly. Clear the trouble code and see if the code resets. If so, replace the MEM-CAL, PROM or CALPAK.*
42 (four flashes, pause, two flashes)	Electronic Spark Timing (EST) circuit	Check the wiring and connectors between the ignition module and the ECM. Replace the ignition module.* Replace the ECM.*
43 (four flashes, pause, three flashes)	Electronic Spark Control (ESC) circuit or Knock sensor (KS) circuit	Check wiring and connectors from the knock sensor to the ESC controller or ECM for an open or short to ground; if necessary, reroute the harness away from other wires such as spark plugs, etc. Replace the knock sensor.*
44 (four flashes, pause, four flashes)	Lean exhaust	Check the wiring and connectors from the oxygen sensor to the ECM. Check the ECM ground terminal. Check for a sticking M/C solenoid (Chapter 4). Check the fuel pressure (Chapter 4). Check for vacuum leaks at the carburetor base gasket, throttle body gasket, vacuum hoses or intake manifold gasket. Replace the oxygen sensor.*
45 (four flashes, pause, five flashes)	Rich exhaust	Check for a sticking M/C solenoid (Chapter 4). Check wiring at M/C solenoid connector. Check the evaporative charcoal canister and its components for the presence of fuel. Check for fuel contaminated oil. Check the fuel pressure regulator. Check for a leaking fuel injector. Check for a sticking EGR valve. Replace the oxygen sensor.*
51 (five flashes, pause, one flash)	PROM/EEPROM error	Faulty or incorrect PROM/EEPROM. Diagnosis should be performed by a dealer service department or other repair shop.
52 (five flashes, pause, two flashes)	CAL-PAK error	Faulty or incorrect CAL-PAK. Diagnosis should be performed by a dealer service department other repair shop.
53 (five flashes, pause, three flashes)	System over-voltage	Code 53 will set if the voltage at the ECM is greater than 17.1-volts or less than 10-volts. Check the charging system (see Chapter 5).
54 (five flashes, pause, four flashes)	Mixture control (M/C) solenoid (carbureted models only)	Check all M/C solenoid and ECM wires and connections Replace the M/C solenoid* (see Chapter 4).
54 (five flashes, pause, four flashes)	Fuel pump circuit	Check the fuel pump relay, circuit and connections. Check the oil pressure switch. Repair/replace faulty components.*
55 (five flashes, pause, five flashes)	ECM/PCM	Be sure the ECM/PCM ground connections are tight. If they are, replace the ECM/PCM.*
61 (six flashes, pause, one flash)	Contaminated oxygen sensor	Replace the oxygen sensor.* A contaminated sensor can be caused by fuel additives containing silicon or non-GM approved sealant or lubricants.
62 (six flashes, pause, two flashes)	Transaxle gear switch signal circuit	Check for an open circuit with a voltmeter at the TCC connector. Voltage should be about 12-volts. Further diagnosis is best left to a dealer service department or other repair facility with the proper diagnostic tools.
63 (six flashes, pause, three flashes)	Manifold Absolute Pressure (MAP) sensor circuit (low vacuum detected)	Check wiring and connections from the MAP sensor to the ECM. Check the vacuum hose to the sensor for leaks. Replace the MAP sensor.* Replace the ECM.*
64 (six flashes, pause, four flashes)	Manifold Absolute Pressure(MAP) sensor circuit (high vacuum detected)	Check the wiring and connections from the MAP sensor to the ECM. Replace the MAP sensor.* Replace the ECM.*
66 (six flashes, pause, six flashes)	A/C refrigerant pressure sensor circuit	Check the sensor electrical terminal connections and for a possible short to ground or open circuit in the sensor wiring. Replace the A/C refrigerant pressure sensor.*

*Component replacement may not cure the problem in all cases. For this reason, you may want to seek professional advice before purchasing replacement parts.

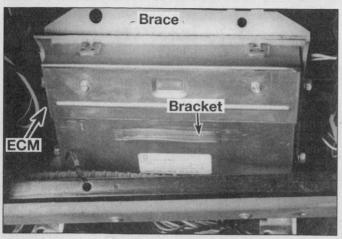

3.4a Typical Electronic Control Module (ECM) mounting details

3.4b To remove the Electronic Control Module (ECM) from the vehicle, remove the necessary interior panels to gain access to the mounting bolts (typical)

3   Electronic Control Module (ECM)/Powertrain Control Module (PCM) - replacement

ECM/PCM replacement

Refer to illustration 3.4a and 3.4b

Caution: *The ignition switch must be turned off when pulling out or plugging in the connectors to prevent damage to the ECM.*

Note: *1994 models are equipped with a Powertrain Control Module (PCM). This unit is essentially identical to the ECM. General Motors changed terminology to encompass the many functions of this computerized system.*

1   The Electronic Control Module (ECM) or Powertrain Control Module (PCM) is located in the passenger side of the passenger compartment, under the instrument panel.

2   Disconnect the cable from the negative battery terminal. **Caution:** *If the vehicle is equipped with a Delco Loc II audio system, make sure you have the correct activation code before disconnecting the battery. See the information at the front of this manual for*

the radio re-activation procedure.

3   Remove the right side under dash insulating panel and/or the glove box to gain access to the ECM/PCM.

4   Remove the retaining bolts **(see illustrations)** and carefully slide the ECM out far enough to unplug the electrical connectors.

5   Unplug the electrical connectors from the ECM.

6   Installation is the reverse of removal.

PROM, CALPAK or MEM-CAL replacement

Refer to illustration 3.8

Note: *1994 models are equipped with a Powertrain Control Module (PCM). The PCM is equipped with an Erasable Programmable Read Only Memory (EEPROM). The calibrations (parameters) are stored in the PCM within the EEPROM. If the PCM must be replaced, it is necessary to have the EEPROM programmed with a special scanning tool called TECH #1 available only at a dealership service department.*

7   To allow one model of ECM to be used for many different vehicles, a device called a

PROM (Programmable Read-Only Memory), CALPAK (calibration pack) or MEM-CAL (memory and calibration) is used. Some models use a combination of two of these. This device is located inside the ECM and contains information on the vehicle's weight, engine, transaxle, axle ratio, etc. One ECM part number can be used by many GM vehicles but the PROM, CALPAK or MEM-CAL is very specific and must be used only in the vehicle for which it was designed. For this reason, it's essential to check the latest parts book and Service Bulletin information for the correct part number when replacing one of these components. A replacement ECM doesn't come with a PROM, CALPAK or MEM-CAL. It (or they) must be carefully removed from the old ECM and installed in the new ECM.

8   Remove the access cover **(see illustration)**.

MEM-CAL

Refer to illustrations 3.9 and 3.10

9   To remove a MEM-CAL, push both retaining clips back away from the MEM-CAL **(see illustration)**. At the same time, grasp

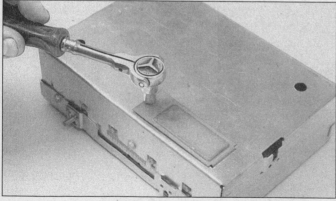

3.8 Remove the PROM cover bolts, then lift the cover off of the ECM

  1   *ECM assembly*
  2   *PROM, CALPAK or MEM-CAL unit*
  3   *Access cover*

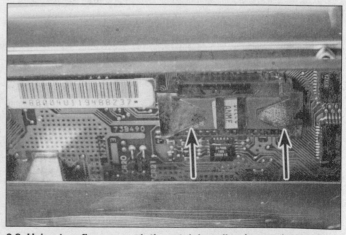

3.9 Using two fingers, push the retaining clips (arrows) away from the MEM-CAL and simultaneously grasp it at both ends and lift it up, out of the socket

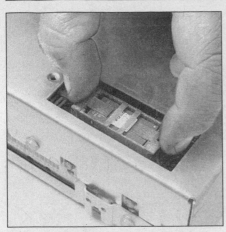

3.10 To install the MEM-CAL, press only on the ends (arrows) until the retaining clips snap into the ends of the MEM-CAL - make sure the notches in the MEM-CAL are aligned with the small notches in the socket

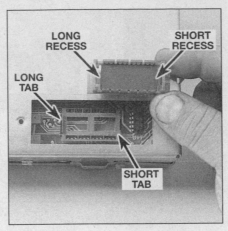

3.12 Make sure the locating tabs on the ECM coincide with the recess grooves in the PROM

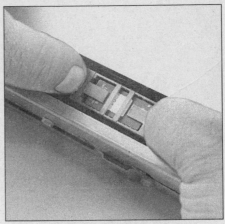

3.13 Press only on the ends of the carrier - pressure on the area in between could result in bent or broken pins or damage to the PROM

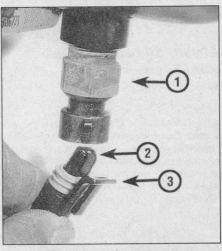

4.2 A typical engine coolant temperature sensor (1) electrical connector (2) has a locking tab (3) that must be released to unplug the connector

the unit at both ends and lift it up out of the socket. Don't remove the MEM-CAL cover itself. **Caution:** *Use of unapproved removal or installation methods may damage the MEM-CAL or socket.*

10   To install the MEM-CAL, press only on the ends. The small notches in the MEM-CAL must be aligned with the small notches in the MEM-CAL socket. Press on the ends of the MEM-CAL until the retaining clips snap into the ends of the MEM-CAL. Don't press on the middle of the MEM-CAL - press only on the ends **(see illustration)**.

PROM/CALPAK

Refer to illustrations 3.12 and 3.13

11   To remove a PROM or CALPAK, a special removal tool should be used. These usually are supplied when a replacement ECM/PCM is purchased. **Caution:** *Removal without this tool or with any other type of tool may cause damage. Grasp the PROM carrier at the narrow ends. Gently rock the carrier from end-to-end while carefully pulling up.*

12 Note the reference end of the PROM/CALPAK carrier **(see illustration)** before setting it aside.

13   Position the PROM or CALPAK and carrier assembly squarely over the socket with the small notched end of the carrier aligned with the small notch in the socket. Press on the carrier until it seats firmly in the socket **(see illustration)**. **Caution:** *Don't press on the PROM or CALPAK - press only on the carrier. Also, if the unit is installed backwards, it will be destroyed when the ignition switch is turned on.*

Final installation

14   The remainder of the installation is the reverse of removal.

15   Once the new MEM-CAL is installed in the old ECM/PCM (or the old unit is installed in the new ECM/PCM), check the installation to verify its been installed properly by doing

the following test:

a) *Turn the ignition switch on.*
b) *Enter the diagnostics mode at the ALDL (see Section 2).*
c) *Allow code 12 to flash four times to verify that no other codes are present. This indicates the PROM, CALPAK or MEM-CAL is properly installed and the ECM is functioning properly.*

16   If trouble codes 41, 42, 43, 51 or 52 occur, or if the "CHECK ENGINE" or "SERVICE ENGINE SOON" light is on constantly but isn't flashing any codes, the unit is either not completely seated or it's defective. If it's not seated, press firmly on the ends once again.

---

4   Information sensors

Note 1: *See the component location illustrations in Section 2 for the location of the following information sensors.*

Note 2: *After performing any checking procedure to any of the information sensors, be sure to clear the ECM of all trouble codes by disconnecting the cable from the negative terminal of the battery for at least ten seconds.*

Caution: *If the vehicle is equipped with a Delco Loc II audio system, make sure you have the correct activation code before disconnecting the battery. See the information at the front of this manual for the radio re-activation procedure.*

Engine coolant temperature sensor

Refer to illustrations 4.2 and 4.3

General description and check

1   The coolant sensor is a thermistor (a resistor which varies the value of its voltage output in accordance with temperature changes). A failure in the coolant sensor circuit should set either a Code 14 or a Code

15. These codes indicate a failure in the coolant temperature circuit, so the appropriate solution to the problem will be either repair of a wire or replacement of the sensor. The sensor can also be checked with an ohmmeter, by measuring its resistance when cold, then warming up the engine and taking another measurement. If the difference in resistance readings is not approximately 500 ohms or more, the sensor is probably bad.

Replacement

Warning: *Wait until the engine is completely cool before beginning this procedure.*

2   To remove the sensor, release the locking tab **(see illustration)**, unplug the electrical connector, then carefully unscrew the sensor. **Caution:** *Handle the coolant sensor with care. Damage to this sensor will affect the operation of the entire fuel injection system.*

3   Before installing the new sensor, wrap

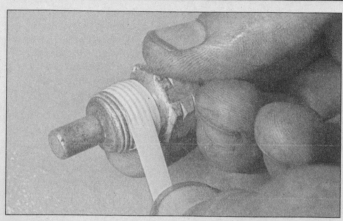

4.3 To prevent coolant leakage, be sure to wrap the temperature sensor threads with Teflon tape before installation

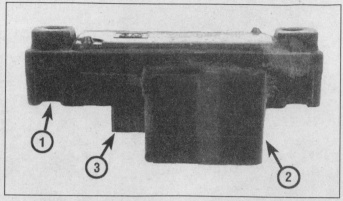

4.5 Typical Manifold Absolute Pressure (MAP) sensor

1   Sensor assembly   3   Manifold vacuum tube
2   Electrical connector

the threads with Teflon sealing tape to prevent leakage and thread corrosion **(see illustration)**.

4   Installation is the reverse of removal.

Manifold Absolute Pressure (MAP) sensor

Refer to illustrations 4.5 and 4.7

General description

5   The Manifold Absolute Pressure (MAP) sensor **(see illustration)** monitors the intake manifold pressure changes resulting from changes in engine load and speed and converts the information into a voltage output. The ECM uses the MAP sensor to control fuel delivery and ignition timing.

Check

6   A failure in the MAP sensor circuit should set a Code 33, 34, 63 or 64, but the operation of the sensor can also be checked using a high-impedance digital voltmeter. Unplug the electrical connector from the sensor and, using jumper wires, connect terminals A and C (the two outside terminals) to their corresponding terminals in the electrical connector. Connect the positive lead of the voltmeter to terminal B (the center terminal)

of the sensor and the negative lead to ground. With the ignition On (engine not running) the voltage reading should be about 4.5 to 5 volts. Start the engine and let it warm up. The reading should now be different from the original reading, and should fluctuate with changes in engine rpm. If it doesn't, check the vacuum hose for breaks or blockage. If the hose is OK, the sensor is probably bad.

Replacement

7   To replace the sensor, detach the vacuum hose, unplug the electrical connector and remove the mounting screws **(see illustration)**. Installation is the reverse of removal.

Manifold Air Temperature (MAT) sensor or Intake Air Temperature (IAT) sensor

Refer to illustration 4.10

General description

8   This sensor, located in the intake manifold air cleaner housing or air duct, is a thermistor (a resistor which changes the value of its voltage output as the temperature changes). The ECM uses the this signal to delay EGR until the manifold air temperature reaches 40-degrees F.

Check

9   A failure in the MAT/IAT sensor circuit should set either a Code 23 or Code 25. The sensor can also be checked with an ohmmeter, by measuring its resistance when cold, then warming it up (a hair dryer can be used for this) and taking another measurement. If the difference in resistance readings is not approximately 500 ohms or more, the sensor is probably bad.

Replacement

10   To remove a MAT/IAT sensor, unplug the electrical connector and remove the sensor with a wrench **(see illustration)**.

11   Installation is the reverse of removal.

Mass Air Flow (MAF) sensor

Refer to illustration 4.12

General description

12   The Mass Air Flow (MAF) sensor, which is located in a housing between the air cleaner housing and the intake duct **(see illustration)**, measures the amount of air entering the engine. The ECM uses this information to control fuel delivery. A large quantity of air indicates acceleration, while a small quantity indicates deceleration or idle.

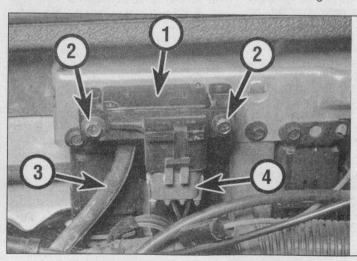

4.7 Typical MAP sensor installation details

1   MAP sensor assembly
2   Mounting screws
3   Vacuum line
4   Electrical connector

4.10 Remove the MAT sensor from the air cleaner housing (typical)

4.12 Typical Mass Air Flow (MAF) sensor installation details (arrow)

Check

13   If the sensor fails at a high frequency, a Code 33 should set and if it fails at a low frequency or power is lost to the sensor, a Code 34 should set. A Code 44 or 45 may also result if the MAF sensor is faulty. A quick check of the sensor can also be made by tapping the flat portion of the sensor body with a screwdriver handle as the engine is running. If the engine stumbles or dies, the sensor is faulty.

Replacement

14   To replace the MAF sensor, unplug the electrical connector, loosen the clamps and detach the sensor from the airducts.
15   Installation is the reverse of removal.

Oxygen sensor

General description

16   The oxygen sensor is mounted in the exhaust system where it can monitor the oxygen content of the exhaust gas stream. By monitoring the voltage output of the oxygen sensor, the ECM will know what fuel mixture command to give the mixture control solenoid (carbureted models) or fuel injector(s).
17   The oxygen sensor produces no voltage when it's below its normal operating temperature of about 600-degrees F. During this initial period before warm-up, the ECM operates in open loop mode.
18   If the engine reaches normal operating temperature and/or has been running for two or more minutes, and if the oxygen sensor is producing a steady signal voltage between 0.35 and 0.55-volt, even though the TPS indicates the engine isn't at idle, the ECM will set a Code 13.
19   A delay of two minutes or more between engine start-up and normal operation of the sensor, followed by a low voltage signal or a short in the sensor circuit, will cause the ECM to set a Code 44. If a high voltage signal occurs, The ECM will set a Code 45.
20   When any of the above codes occur, the ECM operates in the open loop mode - that is it controls fuel delivery in accordance with a

programmed default value instead of feedback information from the oxygen sensor.

Check

21   An open in the oxygen sensor circuit should set a Code 13. A low voltage in the circuit should set a Code 44. A high voltage in the circuit should set a Code 45. Codes 44 and 45 may also be set as a result of fuel system problems.
22   The sensor can also be checked with a high-impedance digital voltmeter. Warm up the engine to normal operating temperature, then turn the engine off. Unplug the oxygen sensor electrical connector and connect the positive probe of the voltmeter to the sensor side of the connector. **Caution:** *Don't let the sensor wire or the voltmeter lead touch the exhaust pipe or manifold. Ground the negative probe of the meter, turn the meter to the millivolt setting and start the engine.*
23   The reading on the voltmeter should fluctuate between 100 and 1,000 millivolts (0.1 and 1.0 volts). If the meter reading does not fluctuate, the sensor is probably bad (although a fuel system problem could be the cause).

Replacement

24   Refer to Chapter 1 for the oxygen sensor replacement procedure.

Throttle Position Sensor (TPS)

25   The Throttle Position Sensor (TPS) is located on the TBI unit or throttle body.
26   By monitoring the output voltage from the TPS, the ECM can determine fuel delivery based on throttle valve angle (driver demand). A broken or loose TPS can cause intermittent bursts of fuel from the injector and an unstable idle because the ECM thinks the throttle is moving.
27   A problem in any of the TPS circuits will set either a Code 21 or 28. Once a trouble code is set, the ECM will use an artificial default value for TPS and some vehicle performance will return.
28   Checking and replacement procedures for the TPS are contained in Chapter 4.

Park/Neutral (P/N) switch

29   The Park/Neutral (P/N) switch, located on the rear upper part of the automatic transaxle, indicates to the ECM when the transaxle is in Park or Neutral. This information is used for Transaxle Converter Clutch (TCC), Exhaust Gas Recirculation (EGR) and Idle Air Control (IAC) valve operation. **Caution:** *The vehicle should not be driven with the Park/Neutral switch disconnected because idle quality will be adversely affected.*
30   For more information regarding the P/N switch, which is part of the Neutral start and back-up light switch assembly, see Chapter 7B.

Air conditioning (A/C) On Signal

31   This signal tells the ECM the A/C selector switch is in the On position and the high

side low pressure switch is closed. The ECM uses this information to turn on the A/C and adjust the idle speed when the air conditioning system is working. If this signal isn't available to the ECM, idle may be rough, especially when the A/C compressor cycles.
32   Diagnosis of the circuit between the A/C On signal and the ECM requires expensive electrical diagnostic equipment and should be left to a dealer service department or other repair shop.

Vehicle Speed Sensor (VSS)

33   The Vehicle Speed Sensor (VSS) sends a pulsing voltage signal to the ECM, which the ECM converts to miles per hour. This sensor controls the operation of the Torque Converter Clutch (TCC) system.

Crankshaft position sensor

34   The crankshaft sensor is bolted to the rear of the engine block and sends a signal to the ECM to tell it both engine rpm and crankshaft position.
35   Unplug the electrical connector, remove the bolt and carefully lift the sensor from the engine block. Refer to Chapter 5 for the location of the crankshaft sensor in the 2.2L engine.
36   Installation is the reverse of removal.

Vacuum sensor (carbureted models only)

37   The function and operation of the vacuum sensor is similar to the MAP sensor. The vacuum sensor is located on a bracket mounted to the passenger side inner fender panel.

Altitude compensator (carbureted models only)

38   The altitude compensator detects ambient pressure changes that occur as the result of changes in the weather and/or the altitude of the vehicle. It then sends an electronic signal to the ECM that is used to adjust the air/fuel ratio and spark timing. The altitude compensator is located behind the glove box, taped to the ECM wiring harness.

---

5   Feedback carburetor systems

General description

1   The function of this system is to control the flow of fuel through the carburetor idle and main metering circuits. The components of the system are the mixture control (M/C) solenoid, coolant sensor, throttle position sensor (TPS), vehicle speed sensor ((VSS), vacuum sensor, altitude compensator, idle speed control (ISC) solenoid, the ECM (computer) and the oxygen sensor. **Note:** *The diagnostic procedures for many of these sensors are covered in Section 4.*
2   The M/C solenoid changes the fuel/air mixture by allowing more or less fuel to flow

through the carburetor. The M/C solenoid, located in the carburetor air horn, is in turn controlled by the Electronic Control Module (ECM), which provides a ground for the solenoid. When the solenoid is energized, the fuel flow through the carburetor is reduced, providing a leaner mixture. When the ECM removes the ground path, the solenoid de-energizes and allows more fuel flow.

3   The ECM determines the proper fuel mixture required by monitoring a signal sent by the oxygen sensor, located in the exhaust stream. When the mixture is too lean, the oxygen sensor voltage is low and the ECM commands a richer mixture. Conversely, when the mixture is rich, the oxygen sensor voltage is higher and the ECM commands a leaner mixture.

Feedback carburetor troubleshooting

4   The first step in diagnosing any feedback carburetor driveability problem is to use the self-diagnosis system and check for any codes that have been stored in the computer. This system is a big help for the home mechanic because it eliminates many tedious and involved testing procedures and "trial and error" methods of diagnosing a driveability problem.

5   The "CHECK ENGINE" light on the instrument panel will come on whenever a fault in the system has been detected, indicting that one or more codes pertaining to this fault are set in the Electronic Control Module (ECM). To retrieve the codes, you must use a short jumper wire to ground the diagnostic terminal. This terminal is part of an electrical connector known as the Assembly Line Diagnostic Link (ALDL) **(see illustration 2.7)**. On most models the ALDL is located under the dashboard on the driver's side. If the ALDL has a cover, slide it toward you to remove it. With the ignition key On, push one end of the jumper wire into the ALDL diagnostic terminal and the other into the ground terminal. **Caution:** *Don't crank the engine with the diagnostic terminal grounded - the ECM could be damaged.*

6   When the diagnostic terminal is grounded with the ignition On and the engine stopped, the system will enter Diagnostic Mode and the "CHECK ENGINE" light will display a Code 12 (one flash, pause, two flashes). The code will flash three times, display any stored codes, then flash three more times, continuing until the jumper is removed. Refer to Section 2 for a complete list of the diagnostic codes.

Idle Speed Control (ISC) motor
General description
Refer to illustration 5.7

7   The ISC motor is a more advanced version of a throttle positioner **(see illustration)**. The motor is under direct control of the computer, which has the desired idle speed programmed into its memory. The computer compares the actual idle speed from the

engine (taken from the distributor or crankshaft position sensor ignition impulses) to the desired rpm reference in memory. When the two do not match, the ISC plunger is moved in or out. This automatically adjusts the throttle to hold the idle speed, regardless of engine loads.

8   Many ISC motors have a throttle contact switch at the end of the plunger. The position of the switch determines whether or not the ISC should control idle speed. When the throttle lever is resting against the ISC plunger, the switch contacts are closed, at which time the computer moves the ISC motor to the programmed idle speed. When the throttle lever is not contacting the ISC plunger, the switch contacts are open and the ECM stops sending the idle speed commands and the driver controls engine speed.

Check

9   With the engine warmed to normal operating temperature, remove the air cleaner assembly and any other components that obscure your view of the ISC motor. Hook up a tachometer in accordance with the manufacturer's instructions and check the VECI label under the hood to determine what the correct idle rpm should be.

10   Have an assistant start the engine. Check that the engine rpm is correct. Have your assistant turn on the air conditioning (if equipped), headlights and any other electrical accessories. If the vehicle is equipped with power steering, have your assistant turn the steering wheel from side-to-side. Note the reading on the tachometer. The engine speed should remain stable at the correct idle speed. If the vehicle is equipped with an automatic transmission, block the wheels and have your assistant set the parking brake, place his/her foot firmly on the brake pedal and place the transmission in Drive. Again the engine rpm should remain stable at the correct speed. **Warning:** *Do not stand in front of the vehicle during this test.*

11   If the ISC motor is not functioning as it should, first check the condition of the wiring and electrical connector(s). Make sure the connector is securely attached and there is no corrosion at the terminals. Further diagno-

sis of this system requires expensive electrical diagnostic equipment, take the vehicle to a dealer service department or other qualified shop.

Mixture control (M/C) solenoid
General description

12   The mixture control (M/C) solenoid is a device that controls fuel flow from the bowl to the main well and at the same time controls the idle circuit air bleed.

13   The mixture control (M/C) solenoid is located in the float bowl in place of the power piston. It is equipped with a spring loaded plunger that moves up and down like a power piston but more rapidly. Certain areas on the plunger head contact the metering rods and an idle air bleed valve. Plunger movement controls both the metering rods and the idle air bleed valve simultaneously.

14   When the mixture control solenoid is energized it moves down causing the metering rods to move into the jets and restrict the flow of fuel into the main well. The idle air bleed plunger opens the air bleed and allows air into the idle circuit. Both these movements reduce fuel flow and thereby LEANS out the system.

15   When the plunger is de-energized, the M/C solenoid moves up, causing the metering rods to move out of the jets and allow more fuel to the main well, less idle air and increased fuel flow. Here the solenoid is in the RICH position.

16   The mixture control solenoid varies the air/fuel ratio based on the electrical input from the ECM. When the solenoid is ON, the fuel is restricted and the air is admitted. This gives a lean air/fuel ratio (approximately 18:1). When the solenoid is OFF, fuel is admitted and the air/fuel ratio is approximately 13:1. During closed loop operation, the ECM controls the M/C solenoid to approximately 14.7:1 by controlling the ON and OFF time of the solenoid.

17   For a more detailed description, diagnosis and repair procedures of the feedback carburetor system; see the *Haynes Rochester Carburetor Manual.*

6   Electronic Spark Timing (EST) system

1   Electronic Spark Timing is used on all engines with which this manual is concerned. The EST distributor contains no vacuum or centrifugal advance, depending on commands from the ECM instead. The ECM receives a reference pulse from the distributor, indicating both engine rpm and crankshaft position, determines the proper spark advance for the engine operating conditions and sends an EST pulse to the distributor. **Note:** *On distributorless ignition models, the ECM controls spark advance by receiving information from the crankshaft sensor and sending an EST pulse to the DIS module.*

2   Under normal operating conditions, the

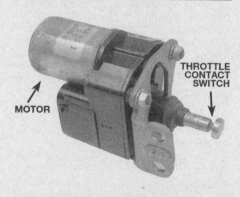

MOTOR

THROTTLE CONTACT SWITCH

5.7 A typical ISC motor

ECM will always control the spark advance. However, under certain conditions, such as cranking or setting base timing, the distributor can operate independent of ECM control. This condition is called Bypass mode and is determined by the bypass lead from the ECM to the distributor. When the bypass lead voltage is over two volts, the ECM will control the spark. Disconnecting the four terminal EST connector, or grounding the bypass lead, will cause the engine to operate in the bypass mode.

3   For further information (and checking and component replacement procedures) regarding the EST distributor, refer to Chapter 5.

7   Electronic Spark Control (ESC) system

Refer to illustration 7.3

General description

1   Irregular octane levels in modern gasoline can cause detonation in an engine. Detonation is sometimes referred to as "spark knock".

2   The Electronic Spark Control (ESC) system is designed to retard spark timing up to 20-degrees to reduce spark knock in the engine. This allows the engine to use maximum spark advance to improve driveability and fuel economy.

3   The ESC knock sensor, which is located on the engine block **(see illustration)**, sends a voltage signal of 8 to 10-volts to the ECM when no spark knock is occurring and the ECM provides normal advance. When the knock sensor detects abnormal vibration (spark knock), the ESC module turns off the circuit to the ECM and the voltage at the ECM drops to zero volts. The ECM then retards the timing until spark knock is eliminated.

4   Failure of the ESC knock sensor signal or loss of ground at the ESC module will

7.3 Typical Electronic Spark Control (ESC) knock sensor (arrow) located on the engine block

cause the signal to the ECM to remain high. This condition will result in the ECM controlling the EST as if no spark knock is occurring. Therefore, no retard will occur and spark knock may become severe under heavy engine load conditions. At this point, the ECM will set a Code 43.

5   Loss of the ESC signal to the ECM will cause the ECM to constantly retard EST. This will result in sluggish performance and cause the ECM to set a Code 43.

Check

6   Connect a timing light in accordance with the tool manufacturer's instructions. Start the engine and allow it to reach normal operating temperature.

7   With an assistant pointing the timing light at the timing marks, tap on the engine block with a hammer in the area of the ESC (knock) sensor. The ignition timing should retard noticeably each time the hammer strikes the block. If the timing retards, the system is operating properly.

8   If the timing does not retard, unplug the electrical connector from the sensor and, with the ignition On, check the voltage at the electrical connector using a high-impedance digital voltmeter. The meter should read between four and six volts. If there is no voltage present, trace the wire back and inspect it for an open circuit condition. If no problem is found, the ECM may be defective or the sensor may be malfunctioning.

9   If there is voltage present, check the resistance of the ESC sensor. Connect one lead of the ohmmeter to the sensor terminal and the other lead to ground. The resistance should be between 3300 and 4500 ohms. If it isn't, replace the sensor.

ESC sensor replacement

10   Disconnect the electrical connector from the ESC sensor.

11   Unscrew the ESC sensor from the block.

12   Installation is the reverse of the removal procedure.

8   Air Injection Reaction (AIR/PULSAIR) system

Refer to illustrations 8.22, 8.23, 8.29, 8.33 and 8.42

General description

Note: *If your engine is equipped with an air pump, your concern in this Section will be with the AIR system. If no air pump is present, refer to the procedures involving the PULSAIR system.*

AIR system

1   The AIR system helps reduce hydrocarbons and carbon monoxide levels in the exhaust by injecting air into the exhaust ports of each cylinder during cold engine operation, or directly into the catalytic converter

during normal operation. It also helps the catalytic converter reach proper operating temperature quickly during warm-up.

2   The AIR system uses an air pump to force the air into the exhaust stream. An air management valve, controlled by the vehicle's Electronic Control Module (ECM) directs the air to the correct location, depending on engine temperature and driving conditions. During certain situations, such as deceleration, the air is diverted to the air cleaner to prevent backfiring from too much oxygen in the exhaust stream. One-way check valves are also used in the AIR system's air lines to prevent exhaust gases from being forced back through the system.

3   The following components are utilized in the AIR system: an engine driven air pump; air control, switching and divert management valves; air flow and control hoses; check valves; and a dual bed catalytic converter.

PULSAIR system

4   This system performs some of the same functions as the AIR system, but utilizes exhaust pressure pulses to draw air into the exhaust system. Fresh air that is filtered by the air cleaner is supplied to the system on a command from the ECM.

5   Components utilized in the system include the PULSAIR valve and external tubes and hoses.

6   The PULSAIR system's operation begins with the engine's firing, creating a pulsating flow of exhaust gases which are of positive or negative pressure. The pressure or vacuum is transmitted through the external tubes to the PULSAIR valve, which reacts as follows:

7   If the pressure is positive, the disc in the valve is forced to the closed position and no exhaust gas is allowed to flow past the valve and into the air supply.

8   If there is negative pressure (vacuum) present in the exhaust system at the valve, the disc will open, allowing fresh air to mix with the exhaust gases.

9   The disc, due to the inertia of the system, ceases to follow the pressure pulsation at high engine rpm. At this point the disc remains closed, preventing any further flow of fresh air.

Check

AIR system

10   Because of the complexity of this system it is difficult for the home mechanic to make a proper diagnosis. If the system is suspected of not operating properly, individual components can be checked.

11   Begin any inspection by carefully checking all hoses, vacuum lines and wires. Be sure they are in good condition and that all connections are tight and clean. Also make sure the pump drivebelt is in good condition and properly adjusted.

12   To check the pump, allow the engine to reach normal operating temperature and run it at about 1500 rpm. Locate the hose running

8.22 The air pump pulley is retained by three bolts

8.23 Remove the AIR pump filter as shown - do not insert any tool behind the filter to pry it off, as damage to the pump may occur)

8.29 Loosen the clamp then remove the hose from the AIR system check valve

from the air pump and squeeze it to feel the pulsation. Have an assistant increase the engine speed and check for a parallel increase in airflow. If this is observed as described, the pump is functioning properly. If it is not operating in this manner, a faulty pump is indicated.

13   The check valve can be inspected by first removing it from the air line. Attempt to blow through it from both directions. Air should only pass through it in the direction of normal airflow. If it is either stuck open or stuck closed the valve should be replaced.

14   To check the air management valve disconnect the vacuum signal line at the valve. With the engine running see if vacuum is present in the line. If not, the line is clogged.

15   To check the deceleration valve plug the air cleaner vacuum source. With the engine running at the specified idle speed remove the small deceleration valve signal hose from the manifold vacuum source, then reconnect the signal hose and listen for airflow through the ventilation pipe and into the deceleration valve. There should also be a noticeable engine speed drop when the signal hose is reconnected. If the air flow does not continue for at least one second, or the engine speed does not drop noticeably, check the deceleration valve hoses for restrictions and leaks. If no restrictions or leaks are found replace the deceleration valve.

PULSAIR system

16   A simple, functional test of this system can be performed with the engine running. Disconnect the rubber hose from the air valve and hold a piece of paper over the valve's inlet hole. With the engine idling there should be a steady stream of air being sucked into the valve. Have an assistant apply throttle, and as the engine gains speed, see if the suction increases. If this does not occur, the lines are leaking or restricted or the check valves are sticking. Also make sure that air is not being blown out of the air valve, as this is also an indication that the check valves are sticking open. Service or replace the compo-

nents as necessary. If other PULSAIR problems are suspected, have a dealer or repair shop diagnose the problems, as they might relate to the ECM/Computer Command Control System.

Component replacement (AIR system)

Drivebelt

17   Loosen the pump mounting bolt and the pump adjustment bracket bolt.

18   Move the pump in until the belt can be removed.

19   Install the new belt and adjust it (see Chapter 1).

AIR pump pulley and filter

20   Compress the drivebelt to keep the pulley from turning and loosen the pulley bolts.

21   Remove the drivebelt as described above.

22   Remove the mounting bolts and lift off the pulley **(see illustration)**.

23   If the fan-like filter must be removed, grasp it firmly with needle-nose pliers and pull it from the pump **(see illustration)**. **Note:** *Do not insert a screwdriver between the filter and pump housing as the edge of the housing could be damaged.* The filter will usually be distorted when pulled off. Be sure no fragments fall into the air intake hose.

24   The new filter is installed by placing it in position on the pump, placing the pulley over it and tightening the pulley bolts evenly to draw the filter into the pump. Do not attempt to install a filter by pressing or hammering it into place. **Note:** *It is normal for the new filter to have an interference fit with the pump housing and upon initial operation it may squeal until worn in.*

25   Install the drivebelt and, while compressing the belt, tighten the pulley bolts securely.

26   Adjust the drivebelt tension (see Chapter 1).

Hoses and tubes

27   To replace any tube or hose always note how it is routed first, either with a sketch or with numbered pieces of tape.

28   Remove the defective hose or tube and replace it with a new one of the same material and size and tighten all connections.

Check valve

29   Disconnect the pump outlet hose at the check valve **(see illustration)**.

30   Remove the check valve from the pipe assembly, using a back-up wrench to hold the stationary fitting on the pipe to prevent twisting the assembly.

31   Install a new valve after making sure that it is a duplicate of the part removed, then tighten all connections.

Air management valve

32   Disconnect the cable from the negative battery terminal. **Caution:** *If the vehicle is equipped with a Delco Loc II audio system, make sure you have the correct activation code before disconnecting the battery. See the information at the front of this manual for the radio re-activation procedure.*

33   Disconnect the vacuum signal line from the valve. Also disconnect the air hoses **(see illustration)** and electrical connectors.

34   If the mounting bolts are retained by tabbed lock washers, bend the tabs back, then remove the mounting bolts and lift the valve off the adapter or bracket.

35   Installation is the reverse of the removal procedure. Be sure to use a new gasket when installing the valve.

Air pump

36   Remove the air management valve and adapter, if so equipped.

37   If the pulley must be removed from the pump, the bolts should be loosened prior to removing the drivebelt (see Step 20).

38   If the pulley is not being removed, remove the drivebelt.

39   Remove the pump mounting bolts and separate the pump from the engine.

40   Installation is the reverse of the removal

8.33 Remove the hoses from the AIR management valve

8.42 AIR system deceleration valve (arrow) (some V6 engines)

procedure. **Note:** *Do not tighten the pump mounting bolts until all components are installed.*
41   Following installation adjust the drivebelt tension as described in Chapter 1.

Deceleration valve

42   Disconnect the vacuum hoses from the valve **(see illustration)**.
43   Remove the screws retaining the valve to the engine bracket (if present) and remove the valve.
44   Install a new valve and reconnect all hoses.

Component replacement (PULSAIR system)

45   Remove the air cleaner and disconnect the negative cable from the battery. **Caution:** *If the vehicle is equipped with a Delco Loc II audio system, make sure you have the correct activation code before disconnecting the battery. See the information at the front of this manual for the radio re-activation procedure.*
46   Disconnect the hose from the PULSAIR valve.
47   Disconnect the support bracket.
48   Remove the PULSAIR solenoid and bracket from the PULSAIR unit.
49   Loosen the nuts that secure the air tubes to the cylinder head and remove the assembly. Due to the high temperature at this area, these connections may be difficult to loosen. Penetrating oil applied to the threads of the nuts may help.
50   Before installing, apply a light coat of oil to the ends of the air tubes and anti-seize compound to the threads of the attaching nuts.
51   Installation is the reverse of the removal procedure.

9   Early Fuel Evaporation (EFE) system

Refer to illustrations 9.6, 9.21 and 9.25

General description

Servo type

Note: *If your vehicle is equipped with vacuum*

servo-type EFE system, refer to Chapter 1 for a general description of the system.

Electrically heated type.

1   This unit provides rapid heat to the intake air supply on carbureted and some throttle body injection engines by means of a ceramic heater grid. The grid is integral with the carburetor/TBI base gasket and located under the primary bore.
2   The components involved in the EFE's operation include the heater grid, a relay, electrical wires and connectors and the ECM.
3   The EFE heater unit is controlled by the vehicle's Electronic Control Module (ECM) through a relay. The ECM senses the coolant temperature and applies voltage to the heater unit only when the engine temperature is below a predetermined point. At normal operating temperatures the heater unit is off.
4   If the EFE heater is not coming on, poor cold engine performance will be experienced. If the heater unit is not shutting off when the engine is warmed up the engine will run as if it is out of tune due to the constant flow of hot air through the carburetor or TBI unit.

PORT 1

VACUUM

PORT 2

9.6 A typical EFE/TVS switch employed in servo-type EFE systems, typically located in the intake manifold

Check

Servo type

5   To check the operation of the EFE/TVS (thermal vacuum switch), allow the engine temperature to fall below 80-degrees F.
6   Disconnect and label the vacuum hoses, then detach the hoses from the switch **(see illustration)**. Attach a length of vacuum hose to one of the ports.
7   Blow into the hose. Air should flow through the valve.
8   Warm up the engine to normal operating temperature.
9   Blow into the hose again. No air should flow through the valve.
10   If the condition in either Step 9 or 10 is not met, replace the valve with a new one.
11   For other checking procedures for the servo type EFE system, refer to Chapter 1.

Electrically heated type

12   If the EFE system is suspected of malfunctioning while the engine is cold, first check all electrical wires and connectors to be sure they are clean, tight and in good condition.
13   With the ignition switch in the On position, use a circuit tester or voltmeter to check that current is reaching the relay. If not, there is a problem in the wiring leading to the relay, in the ECM's thermo switch or the ECM itself.
14   With the engine cold and the ignition switch On, disconnect the heater unit electrical connector and use a test light or voltmeter to see if current is reaching the heater unit. If so, use an ohmmeter connected to the terminals of the electrical connector to check for continuity of the heater unit. If continuity exists, the system is probably operating correctly in the cold engine mode.
15   If current is not reaching the heater unit, but is reaching the relay, replace the relay.
16   To check that the system turns off at normal engine operating temperature, first allow the engine to warm up thoroughly. With the engine idling, disconnect the heater unit electrical connector and use a test light or voltmeter to check for current at the heater unit.
17   If current is reaching the heater unit, the

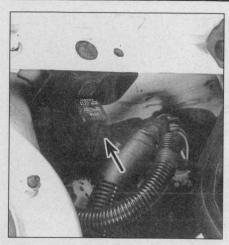

9.21 Typical EFE relay location (arrow)

9.25 Remove the EFE system heater element

relay is stuck closed or the ECM is faulty.

18   For confirmation of the ECM's condition, check for trouble codes (see Section 2) or have the system checked by a dealer service department or other repair shop.

Component replacement

Heater relay

19   Disconnect the cable from the negative battery terminal. **Caution:** *If the vehicle is equipped with a Delco Loc II audio system, make sure you have the correct activation code before disconnecting the battery. See the information at the front of this manual for the radio re-activation procedure.*

20   Remove the relay bracket from the inner fender panel.

21   Unplug the electrical connectors, remove the retaining bolts and lift the relay from the vehicle **(see illustration)**.

22   Installation is the reverse of removal.

Heater element

23   Remove the carburetor or TBI unit (see Chapter 4).

24   Unplug the EFE heater electrical connector.

25   Remove the EFE heater assembly **(see illustration)**.

26   Installation is the reverse of removal.

---

10   Exhaust Gas Recirculation (EGR) system

Non-digital EGR system

General description

1   An EGR system is used on all engines with which this manual is concerned. The system meters exhaust gases into the engine induction system through passages cast into the intake manifold. From there the exhaust gases pass into the fuel/air mixture for the purpose of lowering combustion temperatures, thereby reducing the amount of oxides of nitrogen (NOx) formed.

2   The amount of exhaust gas admitted is regulated by a vacuum or backpressure controlled (EGR) valve in response to engine operating conditions. The EGR valve, in turn, is under the control of the CCCS/ECM.

3   Common engine problems associated with the EGR system are rough idling or stalling at idle, rough engine performance during light throttle application and stalling during deceleration.

Check

Refer to illustration 10.6

4   Refer to Chapter 1 for EGR valve checking procedures.

5   If the EGR valve appears to be in proper operating condition, carefully check all hoses connected to the valve for breaks, leaks or kinks. Replace or repair the valve/hoses as necessary.

6   With the engine idling at normal operating temperature, disconnect the vacuum hose from the EGR valve and connect a vacuum pump. When vacuum is applied the engine should stumble or die, indicating the vacuum diaphragm is operating properly **(see illustration)**. **Note:** *Some models use a back-*

pressure-type EGR valve. On models so equipped, backpressure must be created in the exhaust system before the vacuum pump will actuate the valve. To create backpressure, have an assistant hold a thick, folded-up towel against the end of the exhaust pipe while you apply vacuum to the valve. **Warning:** *Be careful while doing this, since the exhaust gases will heat up the towel considerably. Don't restrict the exhaust system any longer than necessary to perform this test. Replace the EGR valve with a new one if the test does not affect the idle.*

7   Due to the interrelationship of the EGR system and the ECM, further checks of the system should be made by referring to Section 2 or having the system checked by a dealer service department or other repair shop.

Component replacement

Refer to illustrations 10.9 and 10.16

EGR valve

8   Disconnect the vacuum hose at the EGR valve.

9   Remove the nuts or bolts which secure the valve to the intake manifold or adapter **(see illustration)**.

10   Lift the EGR valve from the engine.

11   Clean the mounting surfaces of the EGR valve. Remove all traces of gasket material.

12   Place the new EGR valve, with a new gasket, on the intake manifold or adapter and tighten the attaching nuts or bolts.

13   Connect the vacuum signal hose.

TVS (some V6 engines)

Warning: *Wait until the engine is completely cool before beginning this procedure.*

14   Drain sufficient coolant from the radiator to bring the level below the bottom of the TVS. The TVS is usually located at the front of the intake manifold.

15   Remove the hoses from the valve, labeling them to ensure proper installation.

16   Prepare the new TVS by wrapping the threads with Teflon tape. Remove the TVS and replace it with the new one **(see illustration)**.

10.6 Check the EGR valve diaphragm using a vacuum pump

10.9 Remove the EGR valve from the manifold

10.16 Remove the EGR TVS (arrow) from the manifold (some V6 engines)

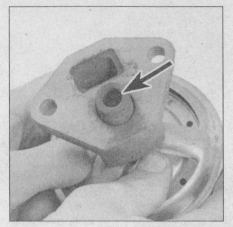

10.31 Check the EGR valve pintle where it extends into the exhaust passage for free movement and clean this area of deposits (arrow)

10.36 Typical digital EGR valve (arrow)

Cleaning

EGR valve

Refer to illustration 10.31

17   Some engines use an EGR valve which can be disassembled for cleaning at the specified intervals. This valve can be identified by two alignment punch marks and wrench slots on the pintle seat.

18   Clean the seat, base and threads and note the location of the punch marks for reassembly to the same position.

19   Measure and record the distance from the base surface to the shoulder of the seat as shown.

20   Place the valve securely in a vise and unscrew the seat. Because the pintle seat is staked in place, it may be necessary to work it back and forth to remove it. A suitable thread penetrant will also help ease removal.

21   With the valve in an upright position, use a pair of pliers to remove the pintle, taking care not to contact the sealing surface .

22   To clean the shaft opening, insert a suitable size drill into the opening in one inch increments, slowly turning it in a clockwise direction. The shaft depth is approximately two inches. Pull the drill bit directly out without turning it and repeat the procedure. The bit will bottom at a depth of about two inches. Tap the valve lightly to dislodge foreign material from the shaft opening.

23   Clean the hole in the pintle with a suitable size drill bit.

24   Clean the inside of the pintle with a suitable tool. Take care not to damage the snapring. Brush or use compressed air to blow out the particles. If compressed air is used, do not blow air directly into the shaft opening.

25   Place the pintle over the end of the shaft and force it down until the locking ring can be felt snapping into position.

26   Screw the seat into the base until the punch marks are aligned in their original positions and the base depth measurement made in Step 19 is reached.

27   Stake the seat in place at the three original staking locations.

28   On all other EGR valves, inspect the valve pintle for deposits.

29   Depress the valve diaphragm and check for deposits around the valve seating area.

30   Hold the valve securely and tap lightly on the round pintle with a plastic hammer, using a light snapping action, to remove any deposits from the valve seat. Make sure to empty any loose particles from the valve. Depress the valve diaphragm again and inspect the valve seating area, repeating the cleaning operation as necessary.

31   Use a wire brush to carefully clean deposits from the pintle **(see illustration)**.

32   Remove any deposits from the valve outlet using a screwdriver.

EGR passages

33   With the EGR valve removed, inspect the passages for excessive deposits.

34   It is a good idea to place a rag securely in the passage opening to keep debris from entering. Clean the passages by hand, using a drill bit.

Digital EGR valve system

General description

Refer to illustration 10.36

35   The digital EGR valve feeds small amounts of exhaust gas back into the intake manifold and then into the combustion chamber.

36   The digital EGR valve is designed to accurately supply EGR to the engine, independent of intake manifold vacuum. The valve controls EGR flow from the exhaust to the intake manifold through three orifices, which increment in size, to produce seven combinations. When a solenoid is energized, the armature, with attached shaft and swivel pintle, is lifted, opening the orifice. The flow accuracy is dependent on metering orifice size only, which results in improved control **(see illustration)**.

37   The digital EGR valve is opened by the ECM, grounding each solenoid circuit. This activates the solenoid, raises the pintle, and allows exhaust gas flow into the intake manifold. The exhaust gas then moves with the air/fuel mixture into the combustion chamber.

Check

38   Special electronic diagnostic equipment is needed to check this valve and should be left to a dealer service department or other repair shop.

Replacement

39   Disconnect the electrical connector from the EGR valve.

40   Remove the two mounting bolts and remove the EGR valve from the intake manifold.

41   Remove the EGR valve and gasket.

42   Clean the mounting surface of the EGR valve. Remove all traces of gasket material from the intake manifold and from the valve if it is to be reinstalled. Clean both mating surfaces with a cloth dipped in lacquer thinner or acetone.

43   Install a new gasket and the EGR valve and tighten the bolts securely.

44   Connect the electrical connector onto the EGR valve.

11   Evaporative Emissions Control System (EECS)

General description

1   This system is designed to trap and store fuel that evaporates from the carburetor (if equipped) and fuel tank which would normally enter the atmosphere and contribute to hydrocarbon (HC) emissions.

2   The system consists of a charcoal-filled canister and lines running to and from the canister. These lines include a vent line from the gas tank, a vent line from the carburetor float bowl or injection unit, an idle purge line into the vehicle's induction system and a vacuum line to the manifold. In addition, there is a purge valve in the canister. The CCCS/ECM controls the vacuum to the purge valve with an electrically operated solenoid. The fuel tank cap is also an integral part of the system.

3   An indication that the system is not operating properly is a strong fuel odor.

13.6 Vacuum applied to the vacuum motor should actuate the damper door

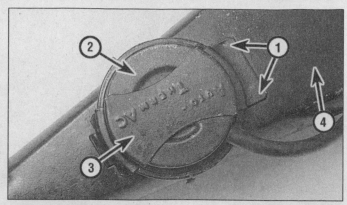

13.9a To replace the air cleaner vacuum motor, drill out the two spot welds which secure the motor retaining strap, remove the attaching strap, lift up the motor, then cock it to one side to unhook the linkage at the control damper assembly

1	Spot welds	3	Retaining strap
2	Motor assembly	4	Snorkle

Check

4   Maintenance and replacement of the charcoal canister filter is covered in Chapter 1.

5   Check all lines in and out of the canister for kinks, leaks and breaks along their entire lengths. Repair or replace as necessary.

6   Check the gasket in the gas cap for signs of drying, cracking or breaks. Replace the gas cap with a new one if defects are found.

7   Due to its interrelationship with the CCCS/ECM, other system checks should be made by referring to Section 2 or having the system checked by a dealer service department or other repair shop.

Component replacement

8   Replacement of the canister filter is covered in Chapter 1.

9   When replacing any line running to or from the canister, make sure the replacement line is a duplicate of the one you are replacing. These lines are often color coded to denote their particular usage.

12 Positive Crankcase Ventilation (PCV) system

General description

1   The positive crankcase ventilation system reduces hydrocarbon emissions by circulating fresh air through the crankcase to pick up blow-by gases, which are then rerouted through the carburetor to be burned in the engine.

2   The main components of this system are vacuum hoses and a PCV valve, which regulates the flow of gases according to engine speed and manifold vacuum.
Check and component replacement

3   Checking the system and PCV valve replacement are covered in Chapter 1.

13 Thermostatic Air Cleaner (THERMAC)

Refer to illustrations 13.6, 13.9a, 13.9b and 13.17

General description

1   The thermostatic air cleaner (THERMAC) system is provided to improve engine efficiency and reduce hydrocarbon emissions during the initial warm-up period by maintaining a controlled air temperature at the carburetor or TBI unit. This temperature control of the incoming air allows leaner fuel mixture calibrations.

2   The system uses a damper assembly, located in the snorkel of the air cleaner housing, to control the ratio of cold and warm air directed into the carburetor or TBI unit. This damper is controlled by a vacuum motor which is, in turn, modulated by a temperature sensor in the air cleaner **(see illustration 13.9b)**. On some engines a check valve is used in the sensor, which delays the opening of the damper flap when the engine is cold and the vacuum signal is low.

3   It is during the first few miles of driving, depending on outside temperature, that this system has its greatest effect on engine performance and emissions output. When the engine is cold, the damper flap blocks off the air cleaner inlet snorkel, allowing only warm air from around the exhaust manifold to enter the carburetor or TBI unit. Gradually, as the engine warms up, the flap opens the snorkel passage, increasing the amount of cold air allowed in. Once the engine reaches normal operating temperature, the flap opens completely, allowing only cold, fresh air to enter.

4   Because of this cold engine-only function, it is important to periodically check this system to prevent poor engine performance when cold or overheating of the fuel mixture once the engine has reached operating temperatures. If the air cleaner valve sticks in the

no-heat position, the engine will run poorly, stall and waste gas until it has warmed up on its own. A valve sticking in the heat position causes the engine to run as if it is out of tune due to the constant flow of hot air to the carburetor or TBI unit.

Check

5   Refer to Chapter 1 for maintenance and checking procedures for this system. If problems were encountered in the system's performance while performing the routine maintenance checks, refer to the procedures which follow.

6   If the damper door did not close off snorkel air when the cold engine was first started, disconnect the vacuum hose at the snorkel vacuum motor and place your thumb over the hose end, checking for vacuum. If there is vacuum going to the motor, check that the damper door and link are not frozen or binding within the air cleaner snorkel. If a vacuum pump is available, disconnect the vacuum hose and apply vacuum to the motor to make sure the damper door actuates **(see illustration)**. Replace the vacuum motor if the application of vacuum does not open the door and the hose routing is correct but the damper door moves freely.

7   If there was no vacuum going to the motor in the above test, check the hoses for cracks, crimps and proper connection. If the hoses are clear and in good condition, replace the temperature sensor inside the air cleaner housing.

Component replacement

Air cleaner vacuum motor

8   Remove the air cleaner assembly from the engine and disconnect the vacuum hose from the motor.

9   Drill out the two spot welds which secure the vacuum motor retaining strap to the snorkel tube **(see illustrations)**.

10   Remove the motor attaching strap.

11   Lift up the motor, cocking it to one side

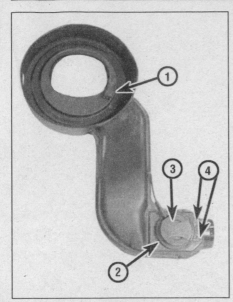

13.9b Components involved in removing the THERMAC vacuum motor on a typical TBI-equipped model

1 Spot welds
2 Motor assembly
3 Retaining strap
4 Sensor

to unhook the motor linkage at the control damper assembly.

12 To install the new motor, drill a 7/64-inch hole in the snorkel tube at the center of the retaining strap.

13 Insert the vacuum motor linkage into the control damper assembly.

14 Using the sheet metal screw supplied with the motor service kit, attach the motor and retaining strap to the snorkel. Make sure the sheet metal screw does not interfere with the operation of the damper door. Shorten the screw if necessary.

15 Connect the vacuum hose to the motor and install the air cleaner assembly .

Air cleaner temperature sensor

16 Remove the air cleaner from the engine and disconnect the vacuum hoses at the sensor.

13.17 Carefully note the position of the sensor before removing the retaining clip (arrow)

17 Carefully note the position of the sensor. The new sensor must be installed in exactly the same position **(see illustration)**.

18 Pry up the tabs on the sensor retaining clip and remove the sensor and clip from the air cleaner.

19 Install the new sensor with a new gasket in the same position as the old one.

20 Press the retaining clip onto the sensor. Do not damage the control mechanism in the center of the sensor.

21 Connect the vacuum hoses and attach the air cleaner to the engine.

14 Transmission Converter Clutch (TCC)

1 Toward optimizing the efficiency of the emissions control network, the ECM controls an electric solenoid mounted in the automatic transaxle of vehicles so equipped. When the vehicle reaches a specified speed, the ECM energizes the solenoid and allows the torque converter to lock-up and mechanically couple the engine to the transmission, under which conditions emissions are at their minimum. However, because of other operating condition demands (deceleration, passing, idle, etc.), the transmission must also func-

tion in its normal, fluid-coupled mode. When such latter conditions exist, the solenoid de-energizes, returning the torque converter to normal operation. The converter also returns to normal operation whenever the brake pedal is depressed.

2 Due to the requirement of special diagnostic equipment for the testing of this system, and the possible requirement for dismantling of the automatic transmission to replace components of this system, checking and replacing of the components should be handled by a dealer service department or other repair shop.

15 Catalytic converter

General description

1 The catalytic converter is an emission control device added to the exhaust system to reduce pollutants from the exhaust gas stream. There are two types of converters used. One converter contains pellets coated with the three way catalysts while the monolithic converter contains a honeycomb mesh which is also coated with three catalysts. The coating on the three way catalyst contains platinum and rhodium, which lowers the levels of oxides of nitrogen (NOx) as well as hydrocarbons (HC) and carbon monoxide (CO) emissions.

Check

2 The test equipment for a catalytic converter is expensive and highly sophisticated. If you suspect the converter is malfunctioning, take it to a dealer service department or authorized emissions inspection facility for diagnosis and repair.

3 Whenever the vehicle is raised for service of underbody components, check the converter for leaks, corrosion and other damage. If damage is discovered, the converter should be replaced.

4 Because the converter is welded to the exhaust system, converter replacement requires removal of the exhaust pipe assembly (see Chapter 4). Take the vehicle, or the exhaust system, to a dealer service department or a muffler shop.

Notes

Chapter 7 Part A
Manual transaxle

Contents

Specifications

Torque specifications
Ft-lbs (unless otherwise indicated)

Clutch cover housing bolts	10
Suspension support bolts	75
Transaxle mount	
Mount-to-transaxle bolts	40
Mount-to-side frame	
Bolts	40
Nuts	23
Mount through-bolt	95 to 118
Transaxle strut	
Strut bracket-to-transaxle bolts	35
Strut bracket mounting stud nut	30
Strut bolts	30
Transaxle-to-engine bolts	55

1 General information

The manual transaxle combines the transmission and differential assemblies into one compact unit. These models are equipped with either four or five-speed transaxles which are very similar in design.

Shifting is accomplished by a floor-mounted shifter, which is connected to the transaxle shift levers by cable assemblies.

2 Shift cables - removal and installation

Removal

1 Disconnect the battery negative cable. **Caution:** *If the vehicle is equipped with a Delco Loc II audio system, make sure you have the correct activation code before disconnecting the battery. See the information at the front of this manual for the radio re-activation procedure.*

2 Remove the C-clips, detach the cable housings, remove the cotter pins and disconnect the forward cable ends from the transaxle.

3 Remove the shift lever knob, boot and console (see Chapter 11).

4 Disconnect the cables from the shift lever assembly.

5 Remove the sill plate, pull back the car-

pet from the center tunnel far enough to gain access to the cables and trace the cables to the cable cover in the floorpan.

6   Remove the screws from the cable cover and remove the cover, grommet and cable assembly from the vehicle.

Installation

7   Route the cables into position and install the cable grommet, cover and attaching screws.

8   Place the carpet in position and install the sill plate.

9   From under the vehicle, route the cables to the transaxle.

10   In the engine compartment, connect the cables and retainers to the transaxle levers.

11   In the passenger compartment, connect the cables to the shift lever and install the console and shifter boot.

12   If the vehicle has a 4-speed transaxle or a 1982 through 1987 5-speed transaxle, adjust the linkage (see Section 4).

13   Connect the negative battery cable.

---

3   Shift lever - removal and installation

Removal

1   Disconnect the negative battery cable. **Caution:** *If the vehicle is equipped with a Delco Loc II audio system, make sure you have the correct activation code before disconnecting the battery. See the information at the front of this manual for the radio re-activation procedure.*

2   Remove the shift lever knob and boot.

3   Remove the console (see Chapter 12).

4   Remove the cotter pins and disconnect the shift cable ends from the shift lever pin studs (see Section 2). Pry the C-clips from the shift lever base and detach the shift cable housings from the base.

5   Unbolt and remove the shift lever.

Installation

6   Place the shift lever assembly in position, install the attaching nuts and tighten them securely.

7   Connect the cable ends to the shift lever pin studs and install the cotter pins. Connect the cable housings to the shift lever base and install the C-clips.

8   Install the console, boot and shift lever knob.

9   If the vehicle has a 4-speed transaxle or a 1982 through 1987 5-speed transaxle, adjust the linkage (see Section 4).

10   Connect the negative battery cable.

---

4   Transaxle shift linkage - adjustment

Note: *This procedure doesn't apply to 1988 or later 5-speeds.*

1   Disconnect the negative battery cable.

4.16 The shift mechanism is held in alignment during adjustment by inserting a drill bit (arrow) as shown

Caution: *If the vehicle is equipped with a Delco Loc II audio system, make sure you have the correct activation code before disconnecting the battery. See the information at the front of this manual for the radio re-activation procedure.*

4-speeds

2   Place the transaxle in first gear.

3   Remove the console trim plate, slide the shifter boot up the handle and then remove the console.

4   With the shifter pulled to the left and held against the stop (first gear position), insert a yoke clip or suitable shim so that it is snug enough to hold the lever from moving.

5   Insert a 5/32 inch or No. 22 drill bit into the alignment hole at the side of the shifter assembly.

6   Install a yoke clip or suitable shim between the tower and carrier.

7   To remove any lash from the transaxle, rotate shifter to the driver's side while tightening the nut.

8   Remove the drill bit and yoke clip from the shifter assembly and install the shifter boot and retainer.

9   Lubricate the moving parts of the shift mechanism with lithium-base grease, using a stiff bristle brush.

10   Connect the negative battery cable and road test the vehicle to check the shifting operation. It may be necessary to repeat the adjustment procedure to completely remove looseness or misalignment from the linkage.

1982 through 1987 5-speeds

Refer to illustration 4.16

11   Shift the transaxle into third gear.

12   Remove the locking pin H and install it tapered side down to lock the transaxle in third gear.

13   Loosen the shift cable attaching nuts at the transaxle levers G and F.

14   Remove the console trim plate, slide the shifter boot up the lever and remove the console (see Chapter 11).

15   Insert a 5/32-inch drill bit into the align-

ment hole next to the shifter assembly.

16   Align the slot in the shift lever with the slot in the shifter plate and insert a 3/16-inch drill bit **(see illustration)**.

17   Tighten all three lever nuts.

18   Remove the drill bit used for alignment and install the locking pin with the tapered side up.

19   Install the console, shifter boot and trim plate and connect the negative battery cable.

20   Lubricate the shift mechanism moving parts with white lithium-base grease using a stiff-bristled brush.

21   Road test the vehicle and check the shifting operation. It may be necessary to repeat the adjustment procedure to eliminate all looseness or misalignment from the shift mechanism.

---

5   Back-up light switch - check and replacement

Check

1   When the shift lever is placed in the Reverse position, the back-up light switch closes the circuit for the back-up lights and the lights are activated. On 4-speeds, the switch is located to the left of the shift lever base; to get at the switch on these vehicles, remove the shift lever knob, the boot and the console (see Chapter 11). On 5-speeds, the switch is located on the front left corner of the transaxle itself.

2   To check the switch, start the engine, turn on the lights and verify that the back-up lights come on when you put the shift lever in Reverse.

3   If the back-up lights don't come on, check the fuse (see Chapter 12) for the back-up light circuit (it shares a fuse with the turn-signal light circuit).

4   If the fuse is bad, replace it and recheck the circuit. If the fuse is okay, use a test light to verify that there's voltage available at the back-up light switch.

5   If the back-up light switch is getting voltage, use the test light to verify that the switch passes voltage when the shift lever is placed in Reverse.

6   If the switch doesn't pass voltage when the shift lever is placed in Reverse, replace the switch. If the switch passes voltage, inspect the back-up light bulb filaments, the wire harness and all connectors in the back-up light circuit. Replace or repair as necessary.

Replacement

4-speeds

7   If the switch is on the shift lever base, remove the shift lever knob, the boot and the console (see Chapter 11), if you haven't already done so.

8   Unplug the connector and detach the switch from the shift lever base.

9   Installation is the reverse of removal.

5-speeds

10   Unplug the connector from the switch (located on the front left corner of the transaxle).

11   Unscrew and remove the switch.

12   Wrap the threads of the new switch with pipe sealant or Teflon tape.

13   Installation is otherwise the reverse of removal.

6   Transaxle mounts - check and replacement

Caution: *On early models, a suitable size (1/4 x 4-inches) alignment bolt or punch must be inserted in the right front engine mount whenever a transmission mount is removed to prevent damage to the driveaxle CV joints.*

Check

1   Watch the mount as an assistant pulls up and pushes down on the transaxle. If the rubber separates from the plate or the case moves up but not down, indicating the mount is bottomed out, replace the mount with a new one.

Replacement

Refer to illustration 6.4

2   Disconnect the negative battery cable.

3   Support the transaxle with a jack.

Mount

4   Remove the transaxle mount through-bolt **(see illustration)**.

5   Remove the retaining bolts and remove the mount.

6   Place the new mount in position and install the mount-to-side frame bolts.

7   Install the through-bolt and tighten the nut to the torque listed in this Chapter's Specifications.

8   Loosen the two nuts at the top of the mount and lower the jack supporting the transaxle so the weight will center the mount. Tighten the nuts to the torque listed in this Chapter's Specifications.

9   Remove the alignment bolt, lower the vehicle and connect the negative battery

cable.

Strut

10   Disconnect the strut from the cross-member and from the bracket on the transaxle.

11   Install the new strut and tighten all fasteners to the torque listed in this Chapter's Specifications.

12   Lower the vehicle and connect the negative battery cable.

7   Transaxle - removal and installation

Removal

1   Disconnect the negative battery cable.

Caution: *If the vehicle is equipped with a Delco Loc II audio system, make sure you have the correct activation code before disconnecting the battery. See the information at the front of this manual for the radio re-activation procedure.*

2   Raise the vehicle to provide sufficient clearance for lowering the transaxle and support it securely on jackstands.

3   Support the engine weight with a suitable lifting device. Alternatively, a jack under the engine can be used, although this must be placed in a position where it won't affect access while working underneath.

4   On early models, insert a suitable size alignment bolt (1/4 x 4-inches) or pin into the front engine mount (see illustration 6.4a) to prevent damage to the driveaxle CV joints or boots caused by driveline misalignment when the transaxle mount is removed.

5   Remove the transaxle mount attachment bolts.

6   Disconnect the shift cables and clutch linkage. Remove the push- rod from the hydraulic clutch master cylinder, then unbolt the slave cylinder and lay aside.

7   Disconnect the ground cables and the back-up light connector from the transaxle.

8   On 4-speed models, remove the heater hose clamp at the transaxle mount bracket and remove the horn assembly.

9   If so equipped, remove the air manage-

ment valve attaching bolts to provide clearance to the right upper transaxle-to-engine bolt.

10   Drain the transaxle lubricant into a suitable container.

11   Remove the left front wheel and the inner splash shield.

12   Remove the transaxle strut and strut bracket from the transaxle.

13   Remove the clutch housing cover.

14   Disconnect the speedometer cable from the transaxle.

15   Disconnect the stabilizer bar from the control arm.

16   Disconnect the inner CV joints from the transaxle (see Chapter 8).

17   Remove the brake caliper, hang it out of the way using a piece of wire, and remove the brake disc (see Chapter 9).

18   Place a jack under the left front suspension assembly. **Caution:** *Care must be taken not to overextend the CV joints and boots whenever the suspension is disconnected.*

19   Remove the six suspension support attaching bolts and lower the support, suspension and driveaxle from the vehicle as an assembly (see Chapter 10).

20   Remove the transaxle-to-engine mounting bolts.

21   Slide the transaxle away from the engine until it is clear and then lower it from the vehicle.

Installation

22   Raise the transaxle into position and carefully guide the right-hand driveaxle into the bore.

23   With the transaxle in position, install two four-inch long bolts with the same threads as the mounting bolts in the top transaxle-to-engine bolt holes to use as guide pins when drawing the transaxle into place. Insert the input shaft and slide the transaxle toward the engine. If it does not move easily, have an assistant turn the engine over using a socket on the front pulley bolt as the transaxle is moved into position.

24   Install the transaxle-to-engine mounting bolts, tightening to the torque listed in this Chapter's Specifications.

25   Install the transaxle mount, bracket and bolts.

26   Install the left hand driveaxle into its bore and seat both driveaxles (see Chapter 8).

27   Place the suspension support in position and install the attaching bolts, tightening them to the torque listed in this Chapter's Specifications.

28   Install the brake disc and caliper.

29   Connect the sway bar to the suspension support and control arm.

30   Connect the speedometer cable.

31   Install the clutch housing cover.

32   Install the strut bracket and strut assembly, tightening to the torque listed in this Chapter's Specifications.

33   Install the inner splash shield and the wheel and lower the vehicle.

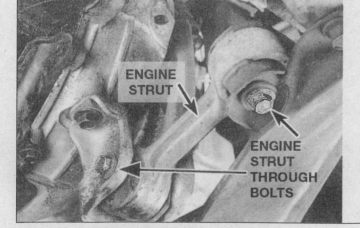

ENGINE STRUT

ENGINE STRUT THROUGH BOLTS

6.4 Typical transaxle/engine strut layout

34   Install the air management valve attaching bolts (if so equipped).
35   Connect the ground cables and back-up light connector to the transaxle.
36   Install the transaxle mount bracket and connect the clutch cable to the release lever and the bracket. Install the hydraulic clutch slave cylinder and the master cylinder pushrod.
37   Install the transaxle mount to the side frame.
38   Tighten the mount-to-transaxle bracket bolts to the torque listed in this Chapter's Specifications. Before tightening the bolts, check the alignment bolt or pin in the engine mount to make sure excessive effort is not required to remove it. If there is, re-align the drivetrain. Remove the bolt.
39   Install the hose clamp and install the horn.
40   Remove the engine supports or jack, connect the negative battery cable and refill the transaxle with the specified fluid.
41   Adjust the shift linkage (see Section 4).

8   Transaxle overhaul - general information

1   Overhauling a manual transaxle is a difficult job for the do-it-yourselfer. It involves the disassembly and reassembly of many small parts. Numerous clearances must be precisely measured and, if necessary, changed with select fit spacers and snap-rings. As a result, if transaxle problems arise, it can be removed and installed by a competent do-it-yourselfer, but overhaul should be left to a transmission repair shop. Rebuilt transaxles may be available - check with your dealer parts department and auto parts stores. At any rate, the time and money involved in an overhaul is almost sure to exceed the cost of a rebuilt unit.
2   Nevertheless, it's not impossible for an inexperienced mechanic to rebuild a transaxle if the special tools are available and the job is done in a deliberate step-by-step manner so nothing is overlooked.
3   The tools necessary for an overhaul include internal and external snap-ring pliers, a bearing puller, a slide hammer, a set of pin punches, a dial indicator and possibly a hydraulic press. In addition, a large, sturdy workbench and a vise or transaxle stand will be required.
4   During disassembly of the transaxle, make careful notes of how each piece comes off, where it fits in relation to other pieces and what holds it in place. Noting how the parts are installed when you remove them will make it much easier to get the transaxle back together.
5   Before taking the transaxle apart for repair, it will help if you have some idea what area of the transaxle is malfunctioning. Certain problems can be closely tied to specific areas in the transaxle, which can make component examination and replacement easier. Refer to the *Troubleshooting* section at the front of this manual for information regarding possible sources of trouble.

Chapter 7 Part B
Automatic transaxle

Contents

Specifications

Torque specifications

	Ft-lbs
Transaxle-to-engine bolts	55

1 General information

Due to the complexity of the clutches and the hydraulic control system, and because of the special tools and expertise required to perform an automatic transmission overhaul, it should not be undertaken by the home mechanic. Therefore, the procedures in this Chapter are limited to general diagnosis, routine maintenance and adjustment and transmission removal and installation.

If the transmission requires major repair work it should be left to a dealer service department or an automotive or transmission repair shop. You can, however, remove and install the transmission yourself and save the expense, even if the repair work is done by a transmission specialist.

Adjustments that the home mechanic may perform include those involving the throttle valve cable, the shift linkage and the neutral safety switch. **Caution:** *Never tow a disabled vehicle equipped with an automatic transaxle at speeds greater than 30 mph or distances over 50 miles unless the front wheels are off the ground. Failure to observe this precaution may result in severe transmission damage caused by lack of lubrication.*

2 Diagnosis - general

Note 1: *Automatic transaxle malfunctions may be caused by five general conditions: poor engine performance, improper adjustments, hydraulic malfunctions, mechanical malfunctions or malfunctions in the computer or its signal network. Diagnosis of these problems should always begin with a check of the easily repaired items: fluid level and condition (see Chapter 1), shift linkage adjustment (see Section 3) and throttle linkage adjustment (see Section 5). Next, perform a road test to determine if the problem has been corrected or if more diagnosis is necessary. If the problem persists after the preliminary tests and corrections are completed, additional diagnosis should be done by a dealer service department or transmission repair shop. Refer to the Troubleshooting section at the front of this manual for transaxle problem diagnosis.*
Note 2: *A common problem on TCC-equipped models is the engine stalling after cruising. For more information, see Troubleshooting at the front of this manual, under the heading Engine stalls.*

Preliminary checks

1 Drive the vehicle to warm the transaxle to normal operating temperature.

2 Check the fluid level as described in Chapter 1:

a) *If the fluid level is unusually low, add enough fluid to bring the level within the designated area of the dipstick, then check for external leaks.*

b) *If the fluid level is abnormally high, drain off the excess, then check the drained fluid for contamination by coolant. The presence of engine coolant in the automatic transmission fluid indicates that a failure has occurred in the internal radiator walls that separate the coolant from the transmission fluid (see Chapter 3).*

c) *If the fluid is foaming, drain it and refill the transaxle, then check for coolant in the fluid or a high fluid level.*

3 Check the engine idle speed. **Note:** *If the engine is malfunctioning, do not proceed with the preliminary checks until it has been repaired and runs normally.*

4 Check the Throttle Valve (TV) cable for freedom of movement. Adjust it if necessary (see Section 5). **Note:** *The TV cable may function properly when the engine is shut off and cold, but it may malfunction once the engine is hot. Check it cold and at normal engine operating temperature.*

5 Inspect the shift control cable (see Section 3). Make sure that it's properly adjusted and that the linkage operates smoothly.

Fluid leak diagnosis

6 Most fluid leaks are easy to locate visually. Repair usually consists of replacing a seal or gasket. If a leak is difficult to find, the following procedure may help.

7 Identify the fluid. Make sure it's transmission fluid and not engine oil or brake fluid (automatic transmission fluid is a deep red color).

8 Try to pinpoint the source of the leak. Drive the vehicle several miles, then park it over a large sheet of cardboard. After a minute or two, you should be able to locate the leak by determining the source of the fluid dripping onto the cardboard.

9 Make a careful visual inspection of the suspected component and the area immediately around it. Pay particular attention to gasket mating surfaces. A mirror is often helpful for finding leaks in areas that are hard to see.

10 If the leak still cannot be found, clean the suspected area thoroughly with a degreaser or solvent, then dry it.

11 Drive the vehicle for several miles at normal operating temperature and varying speeds. After driving the vehicle, visually inspect the suspected component again.

12 Once the leak has been located, the cause must be determined before it can be properly repaired. If a gasket is replaced but the sealing flange is bent, the new gasket will not stop the leak. The bent flange must be straightened.

3.3 Remove the cotter pin (arrow) and disconnect the cable

13 Before attempting to repair a leak, check to make sure that the following conditions are corrected or they may cause another leak. **Note:** *Some of the following conditions cannot be fixed without highly specialized tools and expertise. Such problems must be referred to a transmission shop or a dealer service department.*

Gasket leaks

14 Check the pan periodically. Make sure the bolts are tight, no bolts are missing, the gasket is in good condition and the pan is flat (dents in the pan may indicate damage to the valve body inside).

15 If the pan gasket is leaking, the fluid level or the fluid pressure may be too high, the vent may be plugged, the pan bolts may be too tight, the pan sealing flange may be warped, the sealing surface of the transaxle housing may be damaged, the gasket may be damaged or the transaxle casting may be cracked or porous. If sealant instead of gasket material has been used to form a seal between the pan and the transaxle housing, it may be the wrong sealant.

Seal leaks

16 If a transaxle seal is leaking, the fluid level or pressure may be too high, the vent may be plugged, the seal bore may be damaged,
the seal itself may be damaged or improperly installed, the surface of the shaft protruding through the seal may be damaged or a loose bearing may be causing excessive shaft movement.

17 Make sure the dipstick tube seal is in good condition and the tube is properly seated. Periodically check the area around the speedometer gear or sensor for leakage. If transmission fluid is evident, check the O-ring for damage. Also inspect the side gear shaft oil seals for leakage.

Case leaks

18 If the case itself appears to be leaking, the casting is porous and will have to be repaired or replaced.

19 Make sure the oil cooler hose fittings are tight and in good condition.

Fluid comes out vent pipe or fill tube

20 If this condition occurs, the transaxle is overfilled, there is coolant in the fluid, the case is porous, the dipstick is incorrect, the vent is plugged or the drain back holes are plugged.

3   Shift cable - replacement and adjustment

Replacement

Refer to illustration 3.3

1 Disconnect the negative battery cable. **Caution:** *If the vehicle is equipped with a Delco Loc II audio system, make sure you have the correct activation code before disconnecting the battery. See the information at the front of this manual for the radio re-activation procedure.*

2 Remove the shift lever knob, the shift lever boot and the console (see Chapter 11).

3 Remove the cotter pin and disconnect the shift cable from the shift lever (**see illustration**).

4 Pry off the C-clip and remove the cable housing from the bracket at the front of the shift lever base.

5 In the engine compartment, remove the nut and disconnect the shift cable from the transaxle shift lever.

6 Remove the sill plate, pull up the carpet and trace the cable to the cable cover (the point at which it goes through the firewall). Remove the cover bolts, pull back the cover and pry the grommet out of its hole. Pull the cable through the hole and remove it.

7 Installation is the reverse of removal. When you're done installing the new cable, adjust it.

Adjustment

8 The shift linkage must be maintained in

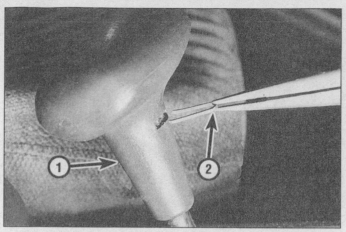

4.2 Remove the shift lever knob retaining clip and remove the knob

1   Shift lever knob
2   Shift lever knob retaining clip

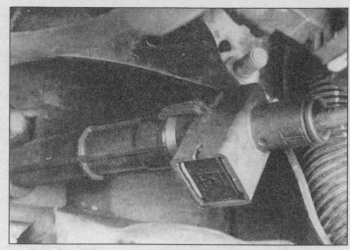

5.3 Adjustment details of a typical Throttle Valve (TV) cable

proper adjustment so that the shifter detents always correspond with the transaxle detents. If the linkage is not kept in adjustment, an internal leak in the transaxle could result, causing slippage.

9   Apply the parking brake and block the wheels to prevent the vehicle from rolling.
10   If equipped, loosen the nut retaining the shift cable to the transaxle shift lever. If there's no nut, pry the cable off the lever.
11   Place the console shift lever in Neutral.
12   Place the transaxle lever in the Neutral position. This is accomplished by rotating the lever clockwise from the Park position, through Park, Reverse and into Neutral.
13   If equipped, tighten the attaching nut securely. The shift lever must be held out of the Park position during tightening.
14   If there is not an attaching nut (later models), hold the transaxle shift lever in position, re-attach the cable and push the locking tab on the shift cable to automatically adjust the cable. An assistant may be necessary.
15   Make sure the engine will start in the Park and Neutral positions only.
16   If the engine can be started in any of the drive positions, as indicated by the shifter inside the vehicle, see Section 7 for the neutral safety switch adjustment procedure or have the vehicle examined by a dealer service department or other repair shop.

4   Shift lever - removal and installation

Refer to illustration 4.2

1   Disconnect the negative battery cable. **Caution:** *If the vehicle is equipped with a Delco Loc II audio system, make sure you have the correct activation code before disconnecting the battery. See the information at the front of this manual for the radio re-activation procedure.*
2   Remove the shift lever knob **(see illustration)**, the shift lever boot and the console

(see Chapter 11).
3   Disconnect the shift cable from the shift lever (see Section 3).
4   Remove the retaining nuts **(see illustration 4.2)** and remove the shift lever assembly.
5   Place the shift lever in position on the mounting studs and install the nuts. Tighten the nuts securely.
6   Connect the shift cables (see Section 3).
7   Install the console (see Chapter 11), dust boot and shift lever knob.
8   Connect the negative battery cable.

5   Throttle Valve (TV) cable - adjustment and replacement

1   The Throttle Valve cable controls the transaxle line pressure and consequently the shift feel and timing, as well as the part throttle and detent downshifts.
2   The TV cable is attached to the link at the throttle lever and bracket at the transaxle and to the throttle lever on the carburetor or throttle body on the engine.

Adjustment

Refer to illustrations 5.3 and 5.7

3   Whenever the TV cable has been disconnected from the carburetor/throttle body, it must be adjusted after installation **(see illustration)**.
4   The freeness of the TV cable can be checked by pulling the upper end of the cable. The cable should travel a short distance with light resistance due to the small coiled return spring. Pull the cable farther out to move the lever into contact with the plunger, thus compressing the heavier TV spring. When released, the cable should return to the closed position, verifying that the cable, TV lever and bracket and the TV plunger are moving freely.
5   The engine must be off during adjustment.
6   Remove the air cleaner, labeling all

5.7 To adjust the TV cable, press down on the readjust tab, move the slider back against the fitting until it stops, release the readjust tab and rotate the throttle lever toward the wide-open position until you hear a click

hoses as they are removed to simplify installation (see Chapter 4 if necessary).
7   Depress and hold-down the metal readjusting tab at the engine end of the TV cable **(see illustration)**.
8   While holding the tab down, move the slider until it stops against the fitting.
9   Release the readjustment tab.
10   Rotate the throttle lever to the maximum travel stop position. The cable will ratchet through the slider and automatically readjust itself.
11   Road test the vehicle. If delayed or only full-throttle shifts still occur, have the vehicle checked by a dealer service department or transmission shop.

Replacement

Refer to illustrations 5.13, 5.15 and 5.16
12   Disconnect the TV cable from the throttle lever at the carburetor or throttle body.

5.13 Use needle-nose pliers to compress the TV cable tangs, then push the housing back through the bracket

5.15 Remove the TV cable bolt (arrow) and pull up on the cable until it's out of the transaxle

5.16 Hold the transaxle TV link with needle-nose pliers and slide the cable link off the pin

13   Disconnect the TV cable housing from the bracket by compressing the tangs and pushing the housing back through the bracket **(see illustration).**

14   Disconnect any clips or straps retaining the cable to the transaxle.

15   Remove the bolt retaining the cable housing to the transaxle **(see illustration).**

16   Pull up on the cover until the end of the cable can be seen, then disconnect it from the transaxle TV link **(see illustration).** Remove the cable from the vehicle.

17   To install the cable, connect it to the transaxle TV link and install the bolt. Tighten the bolt securely and push the cover securely over the cable. Route the cable to the top of the engine, push the housing through the bracket until it clicks into place, then connect the TV cable to the throttle lever. Adjust the cable (see above).

6   Park/lock cable - removal and installation

Removal

1   Disconnect the negative cable at the battery. **Caution:** *If the vehicle is equipped with a Delco Loc II audio system, make sure you have the correct activation code before disconnecting the battery. See the information at the front of this manual for the radio re-activation procedure.*

2   Remove the console (see Chapter 11).

3   Place the transaxle shift lever in Park and the ignition key switch in the Run position.

4   Insert a screwdriver blade into the slot in the ignition switch inhibitor, depress the cable latch and detach the cable.

5   Push the cable connector lock button located at the shift control base to the up position and detach the cable from the park lock lever pin. Depress the two cable connector latches and remove the cable from the shift control base.

6   Remove the cable clips.

Installation

7   Make sure the cable lock button is in the up position and the shift lever is in Park. Snap the cable connector into the shift control base.

8   With the ignition key in the Run position (this is very important), snap the cable into the inhibitor housing.

9   Turn the ignition key to the Lock position.

10   Snap the end of the cable onto the shifter park/lock pin.

11   Push the nose of the cable connector forward to remove the slack.

12   With no load on the connector nose, snap the cable connector lock button on.

13   Check the operation of the park/lock cable as follows:

  a) *With the shift lever in Park and the key in Lock, make sure the shifter lever cannot be moved to another position and the key can be removed.*

  b) *With the key in Run and the shift lever in Neutral, make sure the key cannot be turned to Lock.*

14   If it operates as described above, the park/lock cable system is properly adjusted. Proceed to Step 16.

15   If the park/lock system does not operate as described, return the cable connector lock to the up position and repeat the adjustment procedure. Push the cable connector down and recheck the operation.

16   If the key cannot be removed in the Park position, snap the lock button to the up position and move the nose of the cable connector rearward until the key can be removed from the ignition switch.

17   Install the cable into the retaining clips.

7   Neutral start and back-up light switch - replacement and adjustment

1   Disconnect the negative cable from the battery. **Caution:** *If the vehicle is equipped*

7.6 If the neutral start switch is on the transaxle (1985 and later models), trace the wires from the switch to the connector (arrow) and unplug it

with a Delco Loc II audio system, be sure you have the correct code before disconnecting the battery. See the information at the front of this manual for the radio re-activation procedure.

2   Set the parking brake firmly and shift the transaxle into Neutral.

3   On 1984 and earlier models, the switch is mounted on the base of the shift lever. To get at it, remove the shift lever knob and the boot (see Section 4) and remove the console (see Chapter 11).

4   On 1985 and later models, the switch is mounted at the transaxle shift lever. Disconnect the shift cable from the transaxle shift lever (see Section 3).

Replacement

Refer to illustrations 7.6, 7.7a and 7.7b

5   On 1984 and earlier models, disconnect the electrical connector at the switch.

6   On 1985 and later models, trace the wire harness from the neutral start switch to the connector **(see illustration)** and unplug it.

7   Remove the screws or bolts **(see illus-**

7.7a Remove the neutral start switch bolts (arrows) (1985 and later models)

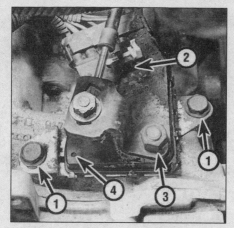

7.7b Typical on-transaxle-type neutral start switch installation details - note that on some on-transaxle types, the adjustment hole is located just beneath the transaxle shift lever

1 Switch retaining bolts
2 Switch
3 Transaxle shift lever shaft
4 Adjustment hole

8.4 The rubber-type driveaxle oil seal (arrow) can be pried out of the transaxle housing with a screwdriver; be careful not to damage the splines of the axleshaft (transaxle removed for clarity)

trations) and detach the switch.
8   On 1984 and earlier models, align the carrier tang on the new switch with the tang slot (see illustration 7.5), set the switch loosely in place and loosely install the screws. Adjust the switch (see below). The remainder of installation is the reverse of removal.
9   On 1985 and later models, line up the flats on the shift shaft with the flats in the new switch and lower the switch onto the shaft. If the switch is new and the shaft hasn't moved, tighten the bolts. If the switch requires adjustment, leave the bolts loose and follow the procedure below. The remainder of installation is the reverse of removal.

Adjustment

10   Loosen the switch mounting bolts, then insert a 3/32-inch drill bit into the adjustment hole in the switch.
11   On 1984 and earlier models, rotate the switch until the adjustment hole on the switch is aligned with the carrier tang hole. The drill bit should slide in to a depth of about 5/8-inch.
12   On 1985 and later models, rotate the switch until the drill bit can be felt dropping into the switch, indicating that it's now in the Neutral position. Tighten the switch bolts.
13   The remainder of installation is the reverse of removal. Connect the negative battery cable and verify that the engine will start only in Neutral or Park.

8   Oil seal replacement

1   Oil leaks frequently occur due to wear of the driveaxle oil seals. Replacement of these seals is relatively easy, since the repairs can usually be performed without removing the transaxle from the vehicle.

Driveaxle oil seals

Refer to illustrations 8.4 and 8.5
2   The driveaxle oil seals are located in the

sides of the transaxle, where the driveaxles are attached. If leakage at the seal is suspected, raise the vehicle and support it securely on jackstands. If the seal is leaking, fluid will be found on the sides of the transaxle.
3   Remove the driveaxles (see Chapter 8).
4   On rubber-type seals, use a screwdriver or prybar to carefully pry the oil seal out of the transaxle bore. Be careful not to damage the splines on the output shaft (see illustration). If the oil seal cannot be removed with a screwdriver or prybar, a special oil seal removal tool (available at auto parts stores) will be required.
5   On metal-type seals, use a hammer and chisel to pry up the outer lip of the seal to dislodge it so it can be pried out of the housing (see illustration).

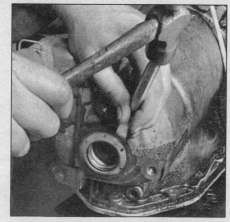

8.5 Dislodge the metal-type driveaxle oil seal by working around the outer circumference with a chisel and hammer (transaxle removed for clarity)

6   Compare the old seal to the new one to be sure it's the correct one.
7   Coat the outside and inside diameters of the new seal with a small amount of transmission fluid.
8   Using a large section of pipe or a large deep socket as a drift, install the new oil seal. Drive it into the bore squarely and make sure it's completely seated.
9   Install the driveaxle(s). Be careful not to damage the lip of the new seal.

Speedometer gear seal

10   Disconnect the speedometer cable, if equipped, from the transaxle (see Chapter 10). Note: Some later models may use a vehicle speed sensor and an electric speedometer instead of a conventional mechanical speedometer, so there is no cable. However, the drive gear assembly - and the seals themselves - are similar to a conventional mechanical speedometer drive gear assembly and its seals.
11   On models with a mechanical speedometer, remove the retainer clip that secures the speedometer cable, remove the speedometer driven gear and sleeve assembly and discard the O-ring.
12   On models with an electric speedometer, unplug the VSS connector, remove the governor cover or (on some models) the speed sensor housing, and discard the O-ring.
13   Installation is the reverse of removal. Be sure to dip the new O-ring into clean automatic transmission fluid before installing it.

9   Transaxle - removal and Installation

Removal

Refer to illustrations 9.8, 9.21 and 9.23
1   Disconnect the negative battery cable.

9.8 Support the engine with an engine hoist before removing any transaxle mounting bracket or transaxle-to-engine fasteners

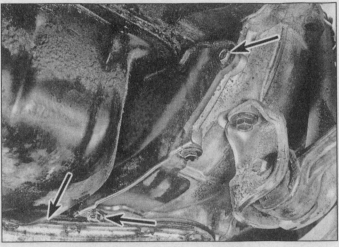

9.21 Torque converter shield mounting bolts (arrows)

Caution: *If the vehicle is equipped with a Delco Loc II audio system, make sure you have the correct activation code before disconnecting the battery. See the information at the front of this manual for the radio re-activation procedure.*

2   On early models, insert a 1/4 X 2-inch bolt into the right front engine mount to maintain mount alignment during the transaxle removal.

3   Remove the air cleaner assembly (see Chapter 4), tagging all hoses for ease of installation.

4   Disconnect the TV cable from the carburetor or throttle body, remove the TV cable-to-transaxle bolt, pull up on the cable cover until the cable is visible, then disconnect the cable from the transaxle (see Section 5).

5   Disconnect the vacuum hoses at the Thermal Vacuum Switch (TVS) (if equipped).

6   On TCC-equipped models, disconnect the connector at the transaxle and the coolant sensor connector at the water outlet.

7   Remove the horn assembly.

8   Attach a suitable lifting device to the engine **(see illustration)** and raise the engine sufficiently to remove the weight from the engine mounts.

9   Remove the transaxle mount and bracket assembly.

10   Remove the air management valve (if equipped) attaching bolts for access to the upper right transaxle-to-engine bolts.

11   Remove the upper transaxle-to-engine mounting bolts and loosen, but do not remove, the transaxle-to-engine bolt near the starter.

12   With the steering column unlocked, raise the vehicle and support it securely on jackstands.

13   Remove the left front wheel.

14   Remove the lower left balljoint cotter pin and nut, then separate the balljoint (see Chapter 10).

15   Disconnect the stabilizer bar from the lower control arm (see Chapter 10).

16   Remove the six bolts attaching the left suspension support assembly (see Chapter 10).

17   Remove the left driveaxle (see Chapter 8) and plug the transaxle bore.

18   Remove the control cable bracket-to-transaxle nut, followed by the engine-to-transaxle stud.

19   Disconnect the speedometer cable from the transaxle (see Chapter 12).

20   Disconnect the transaxle strut at the transaxle.

21   Remove the torque converter shield **(see illustration)**.

22   Mark the relative position of the torque converter and driveplate and remove the retaining bolts.

23   Disconnect and plug the transaxle cooler lines **(see illustration)**.

24   On air conditioning-equipped models, remove the compressor brace attachment bolt from the right side of the transaxle (see Chap-ter 3).

25   Support the transaxle with a jack and remove the remaining transaxle-to-engine bolts.

26   Remove the transaxle from the engine by sliding it toward the left side of the vehicle. The right driveaxle will come out of the transaxle bore at this point and must be supported.

Installation

27   Installation is the reverse of removal,

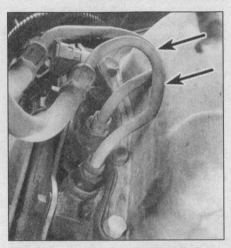

9.23 Transaxle cooler line installation details - Note: *The pipes (arrows) should touch transaxle cover before tightening the lines*

with attention paid to the following points:

a) *Be sure to tighten the transaxle-to-engine bolts to the torque listed in this Chapter's Specifications.*

b) *Guide the right hand axle into the transaxle at the time of installation as it cannot be inserted later.*

c) *Follow the front suspension support assembly bolt tightening sequence described in Chapter 10.*

d) *The suspension alignment should be checked by a dealer or suitably equipped shop.*

e) *Adjust the TV cable (see Section 5).*

f) *Check the transaxle fluid level (see Chapter 1).*

Chapter 8
Clutch and driveaxles

Contents

Specifications

Clutch

Fluid type	See Chapter 1
Disc runout	0.020 inch maximum
Slave cylinder pushrod travel	3/8-inch minimum

Driveaxles

Collapsed CV joint boot dimension	
Tri-pot design	5-1/16 inches
Double-offset design	5-7/32 inches

Torque specifications

Ft-lbs (unless otherwise indicated)

Clutch pressure plate-to-flywheel bolts	15
Clutch master cylinder mounting nuts	15
Clutch slave cylinder mounting nuts	16
Driveaxle/hub nut	
Initial	70
Final	
1982 through 1991	185
1992 on	192
Intermediate shaft bracket bolts (turbo models)	35
Wheel lug nuts	See Chapter 1

1   General information

The information in this Chapter deals with the components from the rear of the engine to the drive wheels, except for the transaxle, which is covered in the previous Chapter. For the purposes of this Chapter, these components are grouped into two categories: clutch and driveaxles. Separate sections within this Chapter offer general descriptions and checking procedures for each of these groups.

Since many of the procedures covered in this Chapter involve working under the vehicle, make sure it is firmly supported on sturdy jackstands or on a hoist where the vehicle can easily be raised and lowered.

2.1 Exploded view of the clutch components

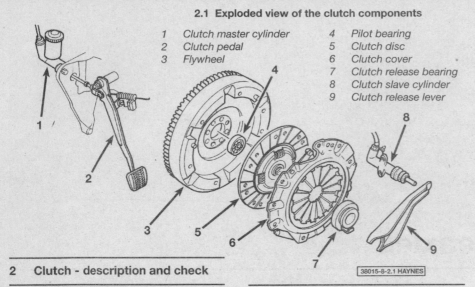

1	*Clutch master cylinder*	4	*Pilot bearing*
2	*Clutch pedal*	5	*Clutch disc*
3	*Flywheel*	6	*Clutch cover*
		7	*Clutch release bearing*
		8	*Clutch slave cylinder*
		9	*Clutch release lever*

38015-8-2.1 HAYNES

2   Clutch - description and check

Refer to illustration 2.1

1   All models with a manual transaxle use a single dry plate, diaphragm spring type clutch **(see illustration)**. The clutch disc has a splined hub which allows it to slide along the splines of the transaxle input shaft. The clutch disc and flywheel are held in contact by pressure exerted by the diaphragm spring in the pressure plate.

2   The clutch release system is operated by hydraulic pressure on 1985 and later models; a mechanical system is used on earlier models. The hydraulic release system consists of the clutch pedal, a master cylinder, the hydraulic line, a slave cylinder which actuates the clutch release lever and the clutch release (or throwout) bearing. The mechanical release system includes the clutch pedal with adjuster mechanism, a clutch cable which actuates the clutch release lever and the release bearing.

3   When pressure is applied to the clutch pedal to release the clutch, hydraulic or mechanical pressure is exerted against the outer end of the clutch release lever. As the lever pivots, the shaft fingers push against the release bearing. The bearing pushes against the fingers of the diaphragm spring of the pressure plate assembly, which in turn releases the clutch plate.

4   Other than to replace components with obvious damage, some preliminary checks should be performed to diagnose a clutch system failure.

   a)   *The first check should be of the fluid level in the clutch master cylinder. If the fluid level is low, add fluid as necessary and inspect the hydraulic clutch system for leaks. If the master cylinder reservoir has run dry, bleed the system as described in Section 4 and re-test the clutch operation.*

   b)   *To check "clutch spin down time," run the engine at normal idle speed with the transaxle in Neutral (clutch pedal up - engaged). Disengage the clutch (pedal down), wait nine seconds and shift the transaxle into Reverse. No grinding noise should be heard. A grinding noise would most likely indicate a problem in the pressure plate or the clutch disc.*

   c)   *To check for complete clutch release, run the engine (with the parking brake on to prevent movement) and hold the clutch pedal approximately 1/2-inch from the floor. Shift the transaxle between 1st gear and Reverse several times. If the shift is not smooth, component failure is indicated. On vehicles with a hydraulic release system, measure the slave cylinder pushrod travel. With the clutch pedal depressed completely the slave cylinder pushrod should extend 7/16-inch minimum. If the pushrod doesn't meet this requirement, check the fluid level in the clutch master cylinder.*

   d)   *Visually inspect the clutch pedal bushing at the top of the clutch pedal to make sure there is no sticking or excessive wear.*

   e)   *On vehicles with mechanical release systems, a clutch pedal that is difficult to operate is most likely caused by a faulty clutch cable. Check the cable where it enters the casing for fraying, rust or other signs of corrosion. If it looks good, lubricate the cable with penetrating oil. If pedal operation improves, the cable is worn out and should be replaced.*

3   Clutch hydraulic release system - removal and installation

Note: *The hydraulic clutch release system is serviced as a complete unit and has been bled of air from the factory, as individual components are not available separately. Other than replacing the entire system, bleeding the system of air is the only service procedure that may become necessary. There are no provisions for adjustment of clutch pedal height or freeplay.*

Removal

Four-cylinder engine

1   Disconnect the cable from the negative battery terminal.

2   Remove the left side under-dash panel.

3   Remove the clutch master cylinder pushrod retaining clip and slide the pushrod off of the pedal pin.

4   If the system is equipped with a remote fluid reservoir, disconnect the hose at the clutch master cylinder and plug it. Remove the two master cylinder mounting nuts.

5   Remove the clutch slave cylinder mounting nuts and detach the slave cylinder, the hydraulic line and the master cylinder from the vehicle as a unit.

V6 engine

6   Remove the air intake duct from the air cleaner.

7   Disconnect the battery cables from the battery, negative cable first.

8   Remove the left fender brace above the battery.

9   Remove the battery from the vehicle (see Chapter 5).

10   Using pieces of numbered tape, mark the electrical connectors at the air cleaner and the Mass Air Flow sensor then disconnect the connectors.

11   Remove the PCV pipe clamp from the air intake duct and the air intake duct clamp at the throttle body.

12   Remove the Mass Air Flow sensor mounting bolt (if equipped) and the air cleaner bracket mounting bolts then remove the air cleaner, the Mass Air Flow sensor and the air intake duct as an assembly.

13   Remove the two bolts retaining the windshield washer bottle to the left inner fenderwell then remove the bottle.

14   If your vehicle is equipped with cruise control, unbolt the servo bracket nuts from the left strut tower and reposition the servo assembly.

15   Remove the left side under-dash panel.

16   Remove the clutch master cylinder pushrod retaining clip and slide the pushrod off of the pedal pin.

17   If the system is equipped with a remote fluid reservoir, disconnect the hose at the clutch master cylinder and plug it. Remove the two master cylinder mounting nuts **(see illustration 3.4)**.

18   Remove the clutch slave cylinder mounting nuts and detach the slave cylinder, the hydraulic line and the master cylinder from the vehicle as a unit.

Installation (all models)

19   Install the new slave cylinder into the support bracket and insert the pushrod into the cup on the clutch release lever. Tighten the nuts evenly, a little at a time, to the torque listed in this Chapter's Specifications. **Note:** *Do not remove the plastic strap that holds the pushrod in position. It is designed to break off the first time the clutch pedal is depressed.*

20   Mount the clutch master cylinder to the

N

6.4 Before removing the release bearing from the transaxle, index the bearing pad to the clutch release fork (arrow)

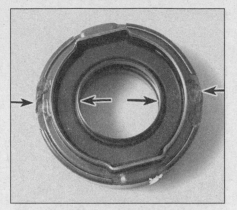

6.5 Inspect the inner and outer contact surfaces of the clutch release bearing for damage, wear and cracks at the areas shown (arrows)

6.6 A small brush makes it easier to lubricate the fork ends

firewall and install the nuts. Tighten the nuts evenly, a little at a time, to the torque listed in this Chapter's Specifications. If the vehicle is equipped with a remote fluid reservoir, reconnect the hose to the clutch master cylinder.

21   Remove the plastic pedal restrictor from the master cylinder pushrod. Coat the inside of the pushrod bushing with multi-purpose grease, connect the pushrod to the brake pedal pin and install the retaining clip. If the vehicle is equipped with cruise control, check to see that the disengage switch on the clutch pedal bracket is in contact with the clutch pedal when the pedal is at rest. If it is not, adjust it accordingly.

22   Pump the clutch pedal several times to break the slave cylinder retaining strap. Leave the remaining plastic button under the pushrod in place.

23   The remainder of the installation is the reverse of the removal procedure.

4   Clutch hydraulic release system - bleeding

1   If it becomes necessary to bleed the hydraulic release system, clean and remove the reservoir cap and fill the reservoir with the recommended fluid. Open the bleed screw on the slave cylinder body and allow the fluid to drip into a container (do not depress the clutch pedal). When it is apparent that there are no more bubbles at the bleed screw opening and a steady stream of fluid is flowing out, close the bleed screw. Re-check the fluid reservoir, topping it up if necessary. The system should now be free of air.

2   To confirm this, depress the clutch pedal and shift into Reverse. There should be no grinding sounds as the gears mesh. If the gears do grind, the system still contains air the bleeding operation should be repeated. Another way to verify that the system is free of air is to measure the slave cylinder pushrod travel as described in Section 2 (if there's air in the system, the pushrod won't protrude fully from the slave cylinder when the pedal is depressed).

5   Clutch cable - removal, installation and adjustment

Removal

1   Pull the clutch pedal rearward and support it against the bumper stop so that the adjuster pawl is released.

2   Disconnect the clutch cable from the release lever at the transaxle, taking care not to let it snap rearward, which could damage the adjusting mechanism.

3   Remove the left side under-dash panel.

4   Disconnect the clutch cable from the tangs of the detent, lift the locking pawl away from the detent and carefully slide the cable forward between the detent and pawl.

5   Remove the windshield washer reservoir.

6   In the engine compartment, pull the clutch cable out to disengage it from the firewall. Be prepared to retrieve the insulators, dampener and washers, which may separate during removal.

7   Disconnect the cable from the mounting bracket on the transaxle and remove it from the vehicle.

8   Inspect the cable and replace it if it's frayed, worn, damaged or kinked.

Installation and adjustment

9   Connect the cable into both of the insulators and the damper and washers. Lubricating the rear insulator with a small amount of light oil will ease the installation into the pedal mounting bracket.

10   Inside the passenger compartment, route the cable casing into the rubber isolator on the pedal bracket and then attach the cable end to the detent. Make sure the cable is routed underneath the pawl and into the detent cable groove.

11   Install the under-dash panel.

12   Hold the clutch pedal up against the bumper stop to release the pawl from the detent and install the other end of the cable to the release lever and transaxle mount bracket.

13   Install the windshield washer reservoir.

14   Lift the clutch pedal up several times to allow the mechanism to adjust the cable length, then depress it several times to mesh the pawl with the detent teeth.

6   Clutch release bearing - removal and installation

Removal

Refer to illustrations 6.4 and 6.5

1   Disconnect the negative cable from the battery.

2   On vehicles with hydraulic release systems, remove the under-dash panel and disconnect the clutch master cylinder pushrod from the clutch pedal pin.

3   Remove the transaxle (see Chapter 7A).

4   Remove the clutch release bearing from the clutch fork. Place a mark on the release bearing pad and the release fork so the bearing can be returned to its original position if it is to be re-used (see illustration). Remove the bearing retaining spring from the release fork holes and remove the bearing.

5   Hold the center of the bearing and spin the outer portion. If the bearing doesn't turn smoothly or if it's noisy, replace it with a new one. Wipe the bearing with a clean rag and inspect it for damage, wear or cracks (see illustration). Do not immerse the bearing in solvent - it is sealed for life and to do so would ruin it.

Installation

Refer to illustration 6.6

6   Lubricate the clutch fork ends where they contact the bearing lightly with white lithium-base grease (see illustration). Pack the inner diameter of the bearing with this grease.

7   Install the release bearing on the transaxle retainer so that both of the fork tangs fit into the outer diameter of the bearing groove. Be sure the bearing pads are resting on the fork ends with the previously inscribed marks aligned, then install the retaining spring. The spring must be fully seated in the retaining groove and both ends

7.4 A clutch alignment tool in position to hold the disc during removal or to center the disc during installation

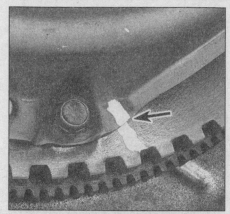

7.5 If you're going to re-use the same pressure plate, mark its relationship to the flywheel (arrow)

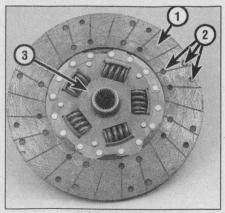

7.9 Typical clutch disc

1   *Lining - wears down in use*
2   *Rivets - secure the lining and can damage the flywheel or pressure plate if allowed to contact the surfaces*
3   *Markings - "Flywheel side" or similar*

secured in the clutch fork holes **(see illustration 6.4)**.

8   Install the transaxle, making sure that the clutch lever does not move toward the flywheel until the transaxle is bolted to the engine.

9   On models with hydraulic release systems, reconnect the clutch master cylinder pushrod and install the under-dash cover.

10   Check the clutch operation. Adjust the clutch cable and depress the pedal slowly several times to mesh the pawl with the detent teeth (mechanically actuated systems).

7   Clutch components - removal, inspection and installation

Warning: *Dust produced by clutch wear and deposited on clutch components may contain asbestos, which is hazardous to your health. DO NOT blow it out with compressed air and DO NOT inhale it. DO NOT use gasoline or petroleum-based solvents to remove the dust. Brake system cleaner should be used to flush the dust into a drain pan. After the clutch components are wiped clean with a rag, dispose of the contaminated rags and cleaner in a covered container.*

Removal

Refer to illustrations 7.4 and 7.5

1   Access to the clutch components is normally accomplished by removing the transaxle, leaving the engine in the vehicle. If, of course, the engine is being removed for major overhaul, then the opportunity should always be taken to check the clutch for wear and replace worn components as necessary. The following procedures assume that the engine will stay in place.

2   Remove the left side under-dash panel and disconnect the clutch master cylinder pushrod from the clutch pedal (hydraulic release systems).

3   Referring to Chapter 7 Part A, remove the transaxle from the vehicle. Remove the release bearing (see Section 6).

4   To support the clutch disc during removal, install a clutch alignment tool through the middle of the clutch **(see illustration)**.

5   If the pressure plate is to be re-used, mark the relationship of the pressure plate-to-flywheel so it can be installed in the same position **(see illustration)**.

6   Turning each bolt a little at a time, loosen the pressure plate-to-flywheel bolts. Work in a criss-cross pattern, again, loosening only a little at a time until all spring pres-

sure is relieved. Support the pressure plate and completely remove the bolts, followed by the pressure plate and clutch disc.

Inspection

Refer to illustrations 7.9, 7.11a and 7.11b

7   Ordinarily, when a fault is found in the clutch system, it can be attributed to wear of the clutch driven plate assembly (clutch disc). However, all components should be inspected at this time.

8   Inspect the flywheel for cracks, heat checking, grooves or other signs of obvious defects. If the imperfections are slight, a machine shop can machine the surface flat and smooth, which is highly recommended regardless of the surface appearance. Refer to Chapter 2 for the flywheel removal and installation procedure.

9   Inspect the lining on the clutch disc. There should be at least 1/16-inch of lining above the rivet heads. Check for loose rivets, distortion, cracks, broken springs or any other obvious damage **(see illustration)**. As mentioned above, ordinarily the disc is replaced as a matter of course, so if in doubt about the quality, replace it with a new one.

NORMAL FINGER WEAR

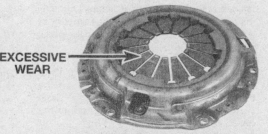

EXCESSIVE WEAR

EXCESSIVE FINGER WEAR

BROKEN OR BENT FINGERS

7.11a Replace the pressure plate if excessive wear is noted

7.11b Examine the pressure plate friction surface for score marks, cracks and evidence of overheating

10 Ordinarily, the release bearing is also replaced along with the clutch disc (see Section 6).

11 Check the machined surfaces of the pressure plate **(see illustrations)**. If the surface is grooved or otherwise damaged, take it to a machine shop for possible machining or replacement. Also check for obvious damage, distortion, cracking, etc. Light glazing can be removed with sandpaper or emery cloth. If a new pressure plate is indicated, new or factory-rebuilt units are available.

Installation

12 Before installation, carefully wipe clean the flywheel and pressure plate machined surfaces. It is important that no oil or grease is on these surfaces or the lining of the clutch disc. Handle these parts only with clean hands.

13 Position the clutch disc and pressure plate with the clutch disc held in place with an alignment tool **(see illustration 7.4)**. Make sure the disc is installed properly (most replacement discs will be marked "flywheel side" or similar. If not marked, install the disc with the damper springs toward the transaxle).

14 Tighten the pressure plate-to-flywheel bolts only finger tight, working around the pressure plate.

15 Center the clutch disc by inserting the alignment tool through the splined hub and into the bore in the end of the crankshaft (if not already done). Wiggle the tool up, down, or side-to-side, as necessary, to center the disc. Tighten the pressure plate-to-flywheel bolts a little at a time, working in a criss-cross pattern to prevent distorting the cover. After all of the bolts are snug, tighten them to the torque listed in this Chapter's Specifications. Remove the alignment tool.

16 Using high temperature grease, lubricate the inner groove of the release bearing (see Section 6). Also place grease on the fork fingers.

17 Install the clutch release bearing as described in Section 6.

18 Install the transaxle and all components that were removed previously.

19 Adjust the shift linkage as outlined in Chapter 7 Part A.

8 Clutch pedal - removal and installation

Cable-actuated clutch

Removal

1 Pull back on the clutch pedal and support it in the raised position. Disconnect the clutch cable from the release lever at the transaxle.

2 Remove the left side under-dash panel then remove the starter safety switch from the pedal and bracket (see Section 9).

3 Disconnect the clutch cable from the tangs of the detent, lift the pawl away and slide the cable between the detent and pawl.

4 Remove the pivot bolt. Remove the spring, pawl and spacer from the pedal assembly.

5 Remove the detent spacer, bushings, spring and pawl.

6 Clean the parts and inspect for wear or damage. Replace both the pawl and detent if the teeth on either are damaged or worn.

Installation

7 Position the detent spring in the side of the detent and install the detent into the clutch pedal opening, hooking the spring onto the pedal.

8 Install the bushings onto the pedal assembly.

9 Install the pawl, spring, spacer and pivot mounting bolt and tighten the bolt securely.

10 Attach the clutch pedal to the mounting bracket and install the pivot bolt and nut. Both the pivot and pawl bolts must be installed as shown as one unit.

11 Check the pawl and detent for proper operation to make sure the pawl disengages when pulled to the upper position and the detent rotates freely in both directions.

12 Attach the cable end to the pawl, making sure to route the cable underneath the pawl and into the detent cable groove.

13 Install the starter safety switch.

14 Hold the clutch pedal up against the bumper stop and release the pawl from the detent.

15 Check the clutch pedal mechanism for proper operation and adjust the cable length by lifting the pedal. Depress the pedal slowly several times so the pawl meshes properly with the detent teeth.

16 Install the under-dash panel.

Hydraulically actuated clutch

Removal

17 Remove the left side under-dash panel.

18 Remove the starter safety switch from the pedal and bracket (see Section 9).

19 Remove the clutch master cylinder pushrod retaining clip and slide the pushrod off of the pedal pin.

20 Remove the clutch pedal pivot bolt and

pull the pedal from the mounting bracket. Extract the bushings and spacer and inspect them for wear, replacing them as necessary.

Installation

21 Lubricate the spacer and bushings with multi-purpose grease and install them on the clutch pedal. Position the pedal in the bracket and install the pivot bolt.

22 Lubricate the master cylinder pushrod bushing with multi-purpose grease, slide it onto the pedal pin and install the retaining clip.

23 Install and adjust the starter safety switch (see Section 9).

24 Install the under-dash panel.

9 Starter safety switch - check and replacement

Check

1 The starter safety switch is mounted on the clutch pedal support and allows the vehicle to be started only with the clutch pedal fully depressed. Place the shift lever in Neutral, depress the clutch pedal and turn the ignition key to the start position. The engine should only crank over when the pedal is depressed.

2 Remove the under-dash panel and unplug the electrical connector from the starter safety switch. Connect the leads of an ohmmeter to the terminals on the switch. There should only be continuity through the switch when the pedal is pushed down. If the switch doesn't operate as described, replace it.

Replacement

3 Disconnect the negative cable at the battery.

4 Remove the left side under-dash panel to gain access to the top of the clutch pedal.

5 At the top of the clutch pedal is a small rod which passes through the pedal. Remove the clip from the end of this rod.

6 Remove the screw which secures the starter safety switch to the clutch pedal support bracket.

7 Unplug the electrical connector from the switch and remove the switch.

8 Install the new switch in the reverse order of removal. Test to be sure that the vehicle can be started only when the clutch pedal is fully depressed. Be sure to perform this test with the shift lever placed in Neutral.

10 Driveaxles - general information

Refer to illustrations 10.1a and 10.1b

Power is transmitted from the transaxle to the front wheels by two driveaxles, which consist of splined solid axles with constant velocity (CV) joints at each end. There are two types of inner CV joints used. On certain models a double-offset design using ball

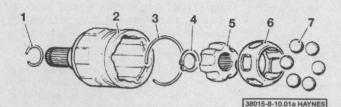

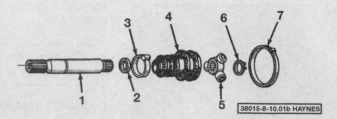

10.1a An exploded view of a typical "double-offset" (or "ball-and-cage") constant velocity (CV) joint

1 Circlip	*5 Inner bearing race*
2 CV joint housing or race	*6 Bearing cage*
3 Large circlip	*7 Ball bearings*
4 Snap ring (if equipped)	

10.1b An exploded view of a typical "tri-pot" constant velocity (CV) joint

1 Axle shaft	*5 Tri-pot assembly*
2 spacer (if equipped)	*6 Snap ring*
3 Boot clamp	*7 Boot clamp*
4 CV boot	

11.2 A screwdriver inserted through the caliper and into a disc cooling vane will hold the hub stationary while loosening the hub nut

11.4 Support the driveaxle with a piece of wire after it has been freed from the hub (letting it hang could damage the inner CV joint)

11.5 A two-jaw puller works well for pushing the driveaxle from the hub

11.6 Use a large prybar as shown to "pop" the inner CV joint from the transaxle - it may be necessary to tap the prybar with a hammer if difficulty is encountered

bearings with an inner and outer race is used to allow angular movement. The other CV joint used is a tri-pot design, using a spider bearing assembly and tri-pot housing to allow angular movement **(see illustrations)**. To determine which CV joint is used on your vehicle, look at the housing while it is still installed on the vehicle and compare it to the accompanying illustrations, noting that the tri-pot housing will have three major indenta-

tions in it and a very thin retaining clamp holding the boot in position. All outer CV joints are the double-offset design.

The CV joints are protected by rubber boots, which are retained by clamps so that the joints are not contaminated by water or dirt. The boots should be inspected periodically for damage, leaking lubricant or cuts (see Chapter 1). Damaged CV joint boots must be replaced immediately or the joints can be damaged. Boot replacement involves removing the driveaxles (see Section 11). It is advisable to disassemble, clean, inspect and repack the CV joint whenever replacing a CV joint boot to ensure that the joint is not contaminated with moisture or dirt, which would cause premature failure of the CV joint.

The most common symptom of worn or damaged CV joints, besides lubricant leaks, are a clicking noise in turns, a clunk when accelerating from a coasting condition or vibration at highway speeds.

11   Driveaxles - removal and installation

Removal

Refer to illustrations 11.2, 11.4, 11.5 and 11.6

1   Remove the wheel cover and break loose the driveaxle/hub nut. Loosen the

wheel lug nuts, raise the front of the vehicle and support it securely on jackstands. Remove the front wheel.

2   Remove the driveaxle/hub nut. To prevent the hub from turning, insert a screwdriver through the caliper and into a disc cooling vane, then remove the nut **(see illustration)**.

3   Separate the control arm from the steering knuckle (see Chapter 10).

4   Push the driveaxle from the hub. If the driveaxle is stuck in the splines, tap on the end of it with a soft-faced hammer. Support the outer end of the driveaxle with a piece of wire to prevent damage to the inner CV joint **(see illustration)**.

5   If it's still stuck, remove the brake caliper and disc and support the caliper out of the way with a piece of wire (see Chapter 9). Push the driveaxle from the hub with a puller **(see illustration)**.

6   Carefully pry the inner end of the axle from the transaxle, using a large prybar positioned between the transaxle housing and the CV joint housing **(see illustration)**.

7   Support the CV joints and carefully remove the driveaxle from the vehicle.

Installation

Refer to illustration 11.8

8   Lubricate the differential seal with multipurpose grease, raise the driveaxle into position while supporting the CV joints and insert

11.8 A large punch or screwdriver, positioned in the groove on the CV joint housing, can be used to seat the joint into the transaxle

12.4 Snap-ring pliers should be used to remove both the inner and outer retaining rings

12.10 Before installing the CV joint boot, wrap the axle splines with tape to prevent damage to the boot

the splined end of the inner CV joint into the differential side gear. Seat the shaft into the side gear by inserting a screwdriver into the groove in the CV joint and tapping it into position with a hammer **(see illustration)**.

9 Grasp the inner CV joint housing (not the driveaxle) and pull out to make sure it has seated securely in the transaxle.

10 Apply a light coat of multi-purpose grease to the outer CV joint splines, pull out on the strut/steering knuckle assembly and install the stub axle into the hub.

11 Connect the control arm to the steering knuckle (see Chapter 10).

12 Install the brake disc and caliper, if removed (see Chapter 9 if necessary).

13 Install the hub nut. Lock the disc so that it cannot turn, using a screwdriver or punch inserted through the caliper into a disc cooling vane, and tighten the hub nut to the initial torque listed in this Chapter's Specifications.

14 Install the wheel and lower the vehicle.

15 Tighten the hub nut to the final torque listed in this Chapter's Specifications. Tighten the lug nuts to the torque listed in the Chapter 1 Specifications.

12 Driveaxle boot replacement and constant velocity (CV) joint overhaul

Note: *If the CV joints exhibit signs of wear indicating need for an overhaul (usually due to torn boots), explore all options before beginning the job. Complete rebuilt driveaxles are available on an exchange basis, which eliminates much time and work. Whichever route you choose to take, check on the cost and availability of parts before disassembling your vehicle.*

1 Remove the driveaxle (see Section 11).

2 Place the driveaxle in a vise lined with rags so as not to mar the shaft.

Inner CV joint

Tri-pot design

Refer to illustrations 12.4, 12.10, 12.11 and 12.13

3 Cut off the boot retaining clamps and slide the boot towards the center of the driveaxle. Mark the tri-pot housing to the driveaxle so it can be returned to its original position, then slide the housing off of the spider assembly.

4 Remove the spider assembly from the axle by first removing the inner retaining ring **(see illustration)** and sliding the spider assembly back to expose the front retaining

ring. Remove the front retaining ring and slide the joint off the driveaxle.

5 Use tape or a cloth wrapped around the spider bearing assembly to retain the bearings during removal and installation.

6 Remove the spider assembly from the axle.

7 Slide the boot off the axle.

8 Clean old grease from the housing and spider assembly. Carefully disassemble each section of the spider assembly, one at a time, and clean the needle bearings with solvent. Inspect the rollers, spider cross, bearings and housing for scoring, pitting or other signs of abnormal wear. Apply a coat of CV joint grease to the inner bearing surfaces to hold the needle bearings in place when reassembling the spider assembly.

9 Pack the housing with half of the grease furnished with the new boot and place the remainder in the boot.

10 Wrap the driveaxle splines with tape to avoid damaging the boot, then slide the boot onto the axle **(see illustration)**.

11 Install the spider bearing with the recess in the counterbore facing the end of the driveaxle **(see illustration)**.

12 Install the tri-pot housing over the spider.

13 Seat the boot in the housing and axle seal grooves, and adjust the collapsed dimension of the joint **(see illustration)**. Install the retaining clamps then install the driveaxle as described in Section 11.

12.11 When installing the spider assembly onto the driveaxle, make sure the recess in the counterbore is facing the end of the driveaxle

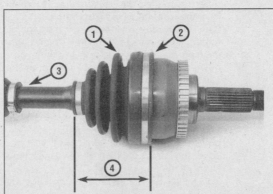

12.13 The collapsed dimension of all inner CV joints must be adjusted before the large boot clamp is tightened

1 *Boot*
2 *Clamp*
3 *Axleshaft*
4 *Adjust the collapsed length of the joint, from the small end of the boot to the groove on the outer race, to 5-1/16 inches (tri-pot) or 5-7/32 inches (double-offset)*

12.15 Carefully tap around the circumference of the retaining ring to remove it from the housing

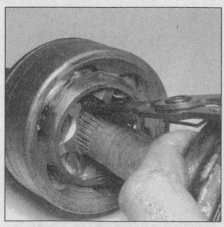

12.17 Use snap-ring pliers to remove the inner retaining ring

12.20 Gently tap the inner race with a brass punch to tilt it enough to allow ball bearing removal

12.21 Using a dull-bladed screwdriver, carefully pry the balls from the cage

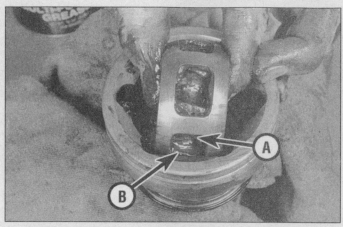

12.22 Tilt the inner race and cage 90 degrees, then align the windows in the cage (A) with the lands (B) and rotate the inner race up and out of the outer race

Double offset design

14   Refer to the procedure outlined in Steps 15 through 33, but take note that the cage and inner race assembly is retained in the outer race by a ball retaining ring, which is removed after the driveaxle is withdrawn from the CV joint. Also, the inner race and cage must be marked in relation to each other, as the cage is not symmetrical. Refer to Step 13 when adjusting CV joint collapsed dimension.

Outer CV joint

Refer to illustrations 12.15, 12.17, 12.20, 12.21, 12.22, 12.23, 12.24a, 12.24b, 12.27, 12.28 and 12.32

15   Tap lightly around the outer circumference of the seal retainer with a hammer and drift to dislodge and remove it. Take care not to deform the retainer, as this would destroy its ability to seal properly **(see illustration)**.
16   Cut off the band retaining the boot to the shaft.
17   Remove the snap-ring and slide the joint assembly off **(see illustration)**.
18   Slide the old boot off the driveaxle.
19   Place marks on the inner race and cage

so that they both face out when reassembling the joint.
20   Press down on the inner race far enough to allow a ball bearing to be removed. If it's difficult to tilt, tap the inner race with a brass drift and a hammer **(see illustration)**.
21   Pry the balls from the cage, one at a time, with a blunt screwdriver or wooden tool **(see illustration)**.
22   With all of the balls removed from the cage and the cage/inner race assembly tilted 90-degrees, align the cage windows with the outer race lands and remove the assembly from the outer race **(see illustration)**.
23   Remove the inner race from the cage by turning the inner race 90-degrees in the cage, aligning the inner lands with the cage windows and rotating the inner race out of the cage **(see illustration)**.
24   Clean the components with solvent to remove all traces of grease. Inspect the cage and races for pitting, score marks, cracks and other signs of wear and damage. Shiny, polished spots are normal and will not adversely affect CV joint performance **(see illustrations)**.
25   Install the inner race in the cage by

reversing the technique described in Step 22.
26   Install the inner race and cage assembly in the outer race by reversing the removal method used in Step 21. The marks that were previously applied to the inner race and cage must both be visible after the assembly is installed in the outer race.
27   Press the balls into the cage windows **(see illustration)**.
28   Pack the CV joint assembly with lubricant through the inner splined hole. Force the grease into the bearing by inserting a wooden dowel through the splined hole and pushing it to the bottom of the joint. Repeat this procedure until the bearing is completely packed **(see illustration)**.
29   Install the boot on the driveaxle as described in Step 10. Apply a liberal amount of grease to the inside of the boot.
30   Position the CV joint assembly on the driveaxle, aligning the splines. Using a brass or plastic tipped hammer, drive the CV joint onto the driveaxle until the retaining ring is seated in its groove.
31   Seat the inner end of the boot in the seal groove and install the retaining clamp.
32   Install the seal retainer securely by tap-

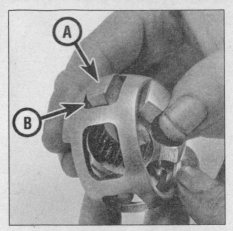

12.23 Align the inner race lands (A) with the cage windows (B) and rotate the inner race out of the cage

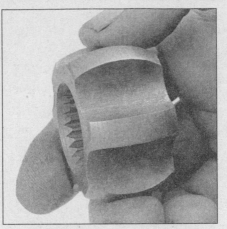

12.24a Inspect the inner race lands and grooves for pitting and scoring marks

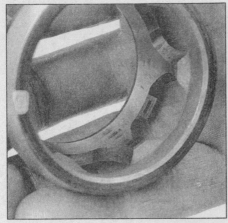

12.24b Inspect the cage for cracks, pitting and scoring marks - shiny spots are normal, and don't affect operation

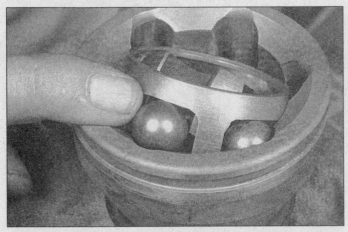

12.27 Align the cage windows and the inner and outer race grooves, then tilt the cage and inner race to insert the balls

12.28 Apply grease through the splined hole, then insert a wood dowel through the splined hole and push down - the dowel will force the grease into the joint

ping evenly around the outer circumference with a hammer and punch **(see illustration)**.

33 Install the driveaxle as described in Section 11.

---

13 Intermediate shaft (turbo models only)- removal and installation

---

Removal

Refer to illustration 13.5

1 Loosen the right front wheel lug nuts, raise the front of the vehicle and support it securely on jackstands. Apply the parking brake and block the rear wheels to keep the vehicle from rolling off the jackstands. Remove the right wheel.

2 Support the engine with a floor jack underneath the oil pan. Place a wood block on the jack-head to act as a cushion. **Caution:** *The pickup for the oil pump is very close to the bottom of the oil pan. Be careful not to distort the oil pan or damage to the pickup tube could occur.*

3 Remove the right driveaxle (see Section 11).

4 Detach the stabilizer bar from the right control arm (see Chapter 10).

5 Remove the three bolts retaining the rear engine mount and intermediate shaft bracket to the block.

6 Place a drain pan under the transaxle just in case transaxle lubricant starts to leak out when the intermediate shaft is removed. Pull the intermediate shaft assembly out of the transaxle.

7 Turn the shaft and listen carefully to the bearing. If the bearing is rough or noisy, take the intermediate shaft assembly to an automotive machine shop and have the old bearing removed and the new bearing installed. This procedure is beyond the scope of the home mechanic.

Installation

8 Lubricate the lips of the differential seal with multi-purpose grease and slide the intermediate shaft into the transaxle.

9 The remainder of installation is the reverse of removal. Be sure to tighten the bracket bolts to the torque listed in this Chapter's Specifications.

12.32 Carefully tap around the circumference of the retaining ring to install it on the housing

Notes

Chapter 9 Brakes

Contents

Specifications

Front disc brakes
Minimum (discard) thickness	Cast into disc
Disc runout (maximum)	0.004 inch
Disc thickness variation (maximum)	0.0005 inch

Rear drum brakes
Maximum (discard) diameter	Cast into drum
Drum taper (maximum)	0.003 inch
Out-of-round (maximum)	0.002 inch

Torque specifications
	Ft-lbs (unless otherwise indicated)
Power brake booster-to-pedal bracket nuts	15 to 20
Brake hose-to-caliper banjo bolt	33
Caliper mounting bolts	35 to 38
Master cylinder-to-brake booster mounting nuts	20
Proportioner valve caps	40 to 140 in-lbs
Wheel lug nuts	See Chapter 1

1 General information

Conventional (non-ABS) system

All vehicles covered by this manual are equipped with hydraulically operated front and rear brake systems. All front brake systems are disc type, while the rear brakes are drum type.

All brakes are self-adjusting. The front and rear disc brakes automatically compensate for pad wear, while the rear drum brakes incorporate an adjustment mechanism which is activated as the brakes are applied when the vehicle is driven in reverse.

The hydraulic system consists of two separate circuits and, on most models, is diagonally split. (The hydraulic system on ABS models is split front-to-rear.) The master cylinder has separate reservoirs for the two circuits, and in the event of a leak or failure in one hydraulic circuit, the other circuit will remain operative. A visual warning of circuit failure, air in the system, or other pressure differential conditions in the brake system is given by a warning light activated by a failure warning switch in the master cylinder. 1986 and earlier models use a pressure differential warning switch. 1987 and later models are equipped with a fluid level sensor.

The proportioner valves are designed to provide better front-to-rear braking balance with heavy brake application. These valves allow more pressure to be applied to the front brakes (under certain braking operations) due to the fact the rear of the vehicle is lighter and does not require as much braking force.

The parking brake mechanically operates the rear brakes only. It is activated by a lever mounted between the two front seats.

The power brake booster, located in the engine compartment on the firewall, uses engine manifold vacuum and atmospheric pressure to provide assistance to the hydraulically operated brakes. Some models are equipped with an electric auxiliary vacuum pump mounted under the battery tray. This pump supplements the brake booster when the vacuum level is low.

After completing any operation involving the disassembly of any part of the brake system, always test drive the vehicle to check for proper braking performance before resuming normal driving. Test the brakes while driving on a clean, dry, flat surface. Conditions other than these can lead to inaccurate test results. Test the brakes at various speeds with both light and heavy pedal pressure. The vehicle

Component location

Typical front disc brake assembly

1   Front disc
2   Caliper
3   Outer brake pad
4   Brake line

Typical rear brake drum assembly

1   Primary shoe
2   Secondary shoe
3   Return spring
4   Actuating link
5   Actuating lever
6   Hold down spring
7   Return spring
8   Adjusting screw
9   Hold down spring
10 Return spring

2.5 A large C-clamp can be used to compress the piston into the caliper for removal

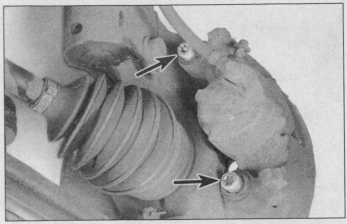

2.6a Remove the brake caliper mounting bolts (arrows) (some early models may have Allen bolts; later models use Torx head bolts)

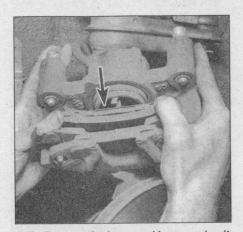

2.6b Remove the inner pad by snapping it out of the piston in the direction indicated by the arrow

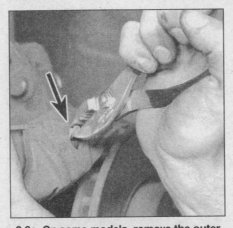

2.6c On some models, remove the outer pad by bending the tabs (arrow) straight out with pliers . . .

2.6d . . . then dislodge the pad from the caliper with a hammer

should stop evenly without pulling to one side or the other. Avoid locking the brakes because this slides the tires and diminishes braking efficiency and control.

Tires, vehicle load and front end alignment are factors which also affect braking performance.

Torque values given in the Specifications section are for dry, unlubricated fasteners.

Anti-lock Brake System (ABS)

This system is available as an option on 1992 and later models. It is designed to prevent the loss of traction while braking. The system is similar to the non-ABS system except for the controller (computer) and related wiring, speed sensors and the hydraulic actuator which replaces the master cylinder and power brake booster.

Anti-lock braking occurs only when a wheel is about to lock up (lose traction). Input signals from the wheel speed sensors to the computer are used to determine when a wheel is about to lose traction during braking. Hydraulic pressure will be limited or reduced for the wheel about to lose traction. Diagnosis of this system is beyond the scope of the home mechanic. **Note:** *The ABS system is*

equipped with a self-diagnosis system similar to the engine codes. However, it is necessary to use a Tech 1 Diagnostic Computer (#94-00101A) linked into the ALDL for access to these codes. Any failures in the ABS system should be repaired by a dealer service department or other repair shop. For more information regarding the ABS system, refer to Section 14.*

2 Disc brake pads – replacement

Refer to illustrations 2.5 and 2.6a through 2.6l

Warning: *Disc brake pads must be replaced on both front wheels at the same time - never replace the pads on only one wheel. Also, the dust created by the brake system may contain asbestos, which is harmful to your health. Never blow it out with compressed air and do not inhale any of it. An approved filtering mask should be worn whenever servicing the brake system. Do not, under any circumstances, use petroleum-based solvents to clean brake parts. Use brake system cleaner only.*

1   Remove the cover from the brake fluid reservoir, siphon off about half of the fluid into a container and discard it.
2   Loosen the wheel lug nuts, raise the vehicle and support it securely on jackstands.
3   Remove the front wheel, then reinstall three wheel lug nuts (flat side toward the disc) to hold the disc in place. Work on one brake assembly at a time, using the assembled brake for reference if necessary.
4   Inspect the disc carefully as outlined in Section 4. If machining is necessary, follow the information in that Section to remove the disc, at which time the pads can be removed from the calipers as well.
5   Push the piston back into its bore, using a large C-clamp **(see illustration)**. As the piston is depressed to the bottom of the caliper bore, the fluid in the master cylinder will rise. Make sure it does not overflow. If necessary, siphon off more of the fluid as directed in Step 1.
6   Follow the accompanying illustrations, beginning with 2.6a, for the actual pad replacement procedure. Be sure to stay in order and read the caption under each illustration.
7   When reinstalling the caliper, be sure to

2.6e On some models, pry the ends of the retaining clip out of the holes in the caliper

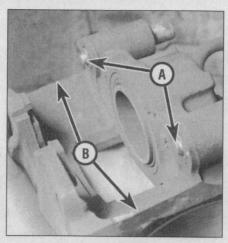

2.6f Inspect the caliper bolts and bushings (A) for damage and the contact surfaces (B) for corrosion

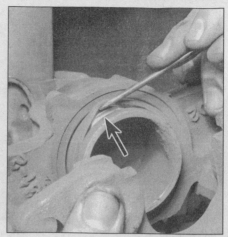

2.6g Carefully peel back the edge of the piston boot and check for corrosion and leaking fluid

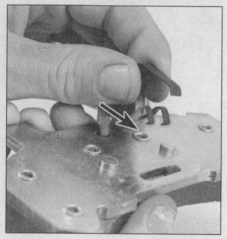

2.6h Snap the inner pad retainer spring into the new pad in the direction shown (arrow)

2.6i Lightly lubricate the lower steering knuckle contact surfaces with high-temperature grease

2.6j Also apply a light coat of high-temperature grease to the upper steering knuckle contact surface

2.6k Place the pads in position and snap the inner pad into place in the piston (arrow)

2.6l After installing the caliper, tighten the bolts to the torque listed in this Chapter's Specifications. On models with tabs that protrude through the caliper frame, insert a large screwdriver between the outer pad flange and the disc hat to seat the pad, then bend the tabs over with a hammer - on other models, make sure the ends of the retaining clip on the outer pad fit into the holes in the caliper frame

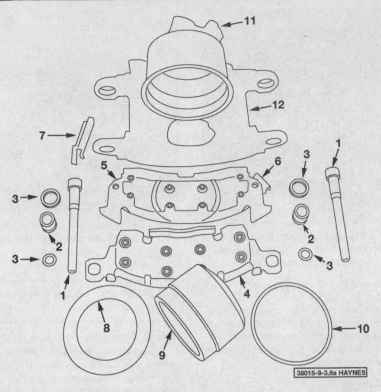

3.8a An exploded view of a typical disc brake caliper assembly

1	Mounting bolt	5	Inner pad	9	Piston
2	Sleeve	6	Wear sensor	10	Piston seal
3	Bushing	7	Pad retainer	11	Bleeder screw
4	Outer pad	8	Dust boot	12	Caliper housing

3.8b With the caliper padded to catch the piston, use compressed air to force the piston out of its bore (make sure your fingers aren't between the piston and the caliper!)

Overhaul

Refer to illustrations 3.8a, 3.8b, 3.9, 3.10, 3.14, 3.15, 3.16 and 3.17

Note: *If an overhaul is indicated (usually because of fluid leakage) explore all options before beginning the job. New and factory rebuilt calipers are available on an exchange basis, which makes this job quite easy. If you decide to rebuild the calipers, make sure rebuild kits are available before proceeding.*

7　Clean the exterior of the brake caliper with brake system cleaner. Never use gasoline, kerosene or petroleum-based solvents. Place the caliper on a clean workbench.

8　Place a wooden block or shop rag in the caliper as a cushion, then use compressed air to remove the piston from the caliper **(see illustrations)**. Use only enough air pressure to ease the piston out of the bore. If the piston is blown out, even with the cushion in place, it may be damaged. **Warning:** *Never place your fingers in front of the piston in an attempt to catch or protect it when applying compressed air, as serious injury could occur.*

9　Carefully pry the dust boot out of the caliper bore **(see illustration)**.

10　Using a wood or plastic tool, remove the piston seal from the groove in the caliper bore **(see illustration)**. Metal tools may

tighten the mounting bolts to the torque listed in this Chapter's Specifications. After the job has been completed, firmly depress the brake pedal a few times to bring the pads into contact with the disc. Test the brakes to confirm proper operation before driving vehicle in traffic.

3　Disc brake caliper - removal, overhaul and installation

Warning: *The dust created by the brake system may contain asbestos, which is harmful to your health. Never blow it out with compressed air and do not inhale any of it. An approved filtering mask should be worn whenever servicing the brake system. Do not, under any circumstances, use petroleum-based solvents to clean brake parts. Use brake system cleaner only.*

Removal

1　Remove the cover from the brake fluid reservoir and siphon off two thirds of the fluid into a container and discard it.

2　Loosen the wheel lug nuts, raise the front of the vehicle and support it securely on jackstands. Remove the front wheels.

3　Reinstall two lug nuts, flat side against the disc, to hold the disc in place.

4　Bottom the piston in the caliper bore.

This is accomplished by pushing on the caliper, although it may be necessary to carefully use a prybar or a C-clamp **(see illustration 2.5)**.

5　If the caliper is to be removed from the vehicle, remove the brake hose inlet fitting bolt and disconnect the fitting.

6　Remove the two mounting bolts **(see illustration 2.6a)** and detach the caliper from the steering knuckle. If the caliper is not to be removed from the vehicle, hang it out of the way with a piece of wire so the brake hose will not be damaged.

3.9 Carefully pry the dust boot out of the caliper, taking care not to scratch the bore

3.10 To remove the seal from the caliper bore, use a plastic or wooden tool, such as a pencil

3.14 When you position the seal in the caliper bore, make sure it isn't twisted

3.15 Install the new dust boot in the piston groove with the folds facing the open end of the piston

3.16 Install the piston squarely in the caliper bore

cause bore damage.

11 Remove the caliper bleeder valve, then remove the sleeves and bushings from the caliper ears. Discard all rubber parts.

12 Clean the remaining parts with brake system cleaner.

13 Carefully examine the piston for nicks and burrs and loss of plating. If surface defects are present, parts must be replaced. Check the caliper bore in a similar way, but light polishing with crocus cloth is permissible to remove light corrosion and stains. Discard the mounting bolts if they are corroded or damaged.

14 When assembling, lubricate the piston bore and seal with clean brake fluid. Position the seal in the caliper bore groove **(see illustration)**.

15 Lubricate the piston with clean brake fluid, then install a new boot in the piston groove with the fold toward the open end of the piston **(see illustration)**.

16 Insert the piston squarely into the caliper bore, then apply force to bottom the piston in the bore **(see illustration)**.

17 Position the dust boot in the caliper counterbore, then use a seal driver to drive it into position **(see illustration)**. Make sure the

boot is seated evenly below the caliper face.

18 Install the bleeder valve.

19 The remainder of the installation procedure is the reverse of the removal procedure. Always use new sealing washers when connecting the brake hose and bleed the system as described in Section 12.

Installation

Refer to illustration 3.22

20 Inspect the mounting bolts for excessive corrosion.

21 Place the caliper in position over the disc and mounting bracket, install the bolts and tighten them to the torque listed in this Chapter's Specifications.

22 Check to make sure the clearance between the caliper and the bracket stops is between 0.005 and 0.012 inch **(see illustration)**.

23 Connect the inlet fitting (if removed) and install the bolt (using new sealing washers), tightening it to the torque listed in this Chapter's Specifications. It will be necessary to bleed the brakes (see Section 12) if the fitting was disconnected.

24 Install the wheels and lower the vehicle.

4   Brake disc - inspection, removal and installation

Refer to illustrations 4.4, 4.5a, 4.5b and 4.6

1 Loosen the wheel lug nuts, raise the vehicle and place it securely on jackstands.

2 Remove the wheel and reinstall three lug nuts, flat side against the disc, to retain the disc to the hub.

3 Remove the brake caliper assembly (see Section 3). **Note:** *It is not necessary to disconnect the brake hose. After removing the caliper mounting bolts, hang the caliper out of the way on a piece of wire. Never hang the caliper by the brake hose because damage to the hose will occur.*

4 Inspect the disc surfaces **(see illustration)**. Light scoring or grooving is normal, but deep grooves or severe erosion is not. If pulsating has been noticed during application of the brakes, suspect disc runout.

5 Attach a dial indicator to the caliper mounting bracket, turn the disc and note the amount of runout **(see illustration)**. Check

3.17 Use a hammer and seal driver to seat the boot into the caliper bore

3.22 Measure the clearance between the caliper and bracket stops

4.4 The brake pads on this vehicle were obviously neglected, as they wore down to the rivets and cut deep grooves into the disc - wear this severe means the disc must be replaced

4.5a To check disc runout, mount a dial indicator as shown and rotate the disc

4.5b Using a swirling motion, remove the glaze from the disc with sandpaper or emery cloth

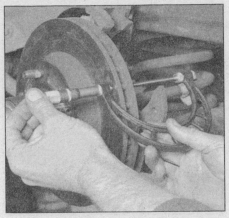

4.6 Use a micrometer to measure the thickness of the brake disc

5.5a Typical rear drum brake assembly

1   Primary shoe
2   Secondary shoe
3   Return spring
4   Actuating link
5   Actuating lever
6   Hold down spring
7   Return spring
8   Adjusting screw
9   Hold down spring
10 Return spring

5.5b Remove the brake drum and clean the brake assembly with brake system cleaner - DO NOT use compressed air to blow the dust from the brake assembly

the inner and outer surfaces. If the runout is more than the maximum allowable, the disc must be removed from the vehicle and taken to an automotive machine shop for resurfacing. **Note:** *The discs should be resurfaced, regardless of the dial indicator reading, to impart a smooth finish and ensure perfectly flat brake pad surfaces which will eliminate pedal pulsations. At the very least, if you don't have the discs resurfaced, remove the glaze with sandpaper or emery cloth using a swirling motion* **(see illustration).**

6   Using a micrometer, measure the thickness of the disc **(see illustration)**. If it is less than the minimum thickness cast into the disc, replace the disc with a new one. Also measure the thickness at several points to determine variations in the surface. Any variation over 0.0005-inch may cause pedal pulsations during brake application. If this condition exists and the thickness is not below the minimum, the disc can be removed and taken to an automotive machine shop for resurfacing.

7   To remove the disc, remove the lug nuts that were installed in Step 2, then slide the disc off the hub.

8   Installation is the reverse of removal.

5   Drum brake shoes - replacement

Refer to illustrations 5.5a through 5.5x and 5.6

Warning: *Drum brake shoes must be replaced on both wheels at the same time - never replace the shoes on only one wheel. Also, the dust created by the brake system may contain asbestos, which is harmful to your health. Never blow it out with compressed air and do not inhale any of it. An approved filtering mask should be worn whenever servicing the brake system. Do not, under any circumstances, use petroleum-based solvents to clean brake parts. Use brake system cleaner only.*

Caution: *Whenever the brake shoes are replaced, the retractor and hold-down springs should also be replaced. Due to the continuous heating/cooling cycle that the springs are subjected to, they lose their tension over a period of time and may allow the shoes to drag on the drum and wear at a much faster rate than normal.*

1   Loosen the wheel lug nuts.
2   Raise the vehicle and support it securely on jackstands.

5.5c Remove the return springs using brake spring pliers

3   Release the parking brake handle.
4   Remove the wheel and mark the relationship of the brake drum to the wheel flange. **Note:** *All four rear shoes must be replaced at the same time, but to avoid mixing up parts, work on only one brake assembly at a time.*

5   Refer to the accompanying illustrations, beginning with **illustration 5.5a**, to perform

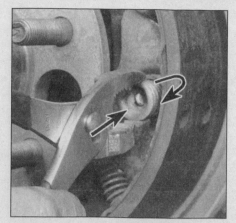

5.5d Remove the hold-down springs and pins by pushing in with pliers (or a brake hold-down spring tool) and turning them 90-degrees

5.5e Lift up on the actuator lever and remove the actuating link from the anchor pin pivot along with the actuator lever and return spring

5.5f Spread the shoes apart and remove the parking brake strut

5.5g With the shoe assembly spread to clear the hub flange, lift it from the backing plate

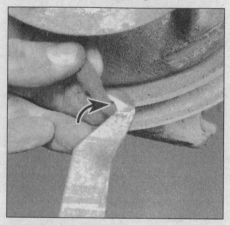

5.5h Disconnect the parking brake lever from the cable in the direction shown (arrow) and remove the shoe assembly

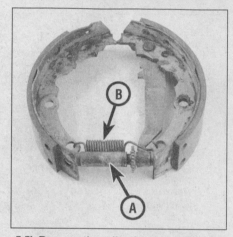

5.5i Remove the adjusting screw (A) and spring (B) from the shoe assembly, making sure to note the direction in which they're installed

the brake shoe replacement procedure **(see illustrations)**. Be sure to stay in order and read the caption under each illustration. **Note:** *If the brake drum cannot be easily pulled off the axle and shoe assembly, make sure that the parking brake is completely*

released, then squirt some penetrating oil around the center hub area. Allow the oil to soak in and try to pull the drum off. If the drum still cannot be pulled off, the brake shoes will have to be retracted. This is accomplished by first removing the lanced

cutout in the brake drum with a hammer and chisel. With the cutout removed, disengage the lever from the adjusting screw wheel with one small screwdriver while turning the adjusting wheel with another small screwdriver, moving the shoes away from the drum.

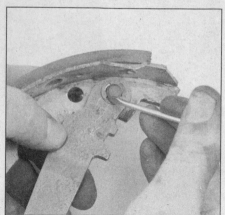

5.5j Remove the parking brake lever by prying off the C-clip

5.5k Install the parking brake lever on the new brake shoes by pressing the C-clip into place with needle-nose pliers

5.5l Lubricate the contact surfaces of the backing plate with high-temperature grease

5.5m Lubricate the adjuster screw threads and end with high-temperature grease prior to installation

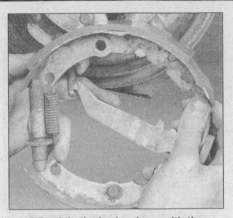

5.5n Join the brake shoes with the adjuster screw spring, install the adjuster screw (with the long end pointing to the front of the vehicle), then connect the parking brake lever to the cable

5.5o Spread the brake assembly apart sufficiently to clear the hub flange and raise it into position

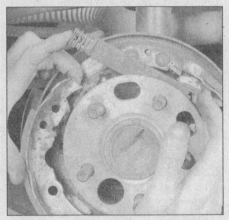

5.5p Install the parking brake strut

5.5q Make sure the parking brake strut is positioned in the shoes properly (arrows)

5.5r Install the hold-down pin and spring on the primary brake shoe

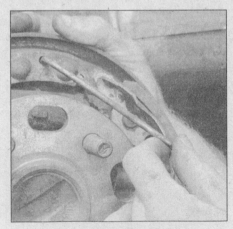

5.5s Install the actuating link

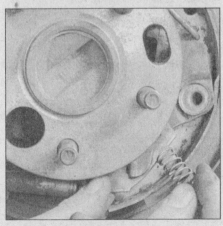

5.5t Install the actuator pivot, lever and return spring

5.5u Install the hold-down spring assembly on the secondary shoe

The drum may now be pulled off.

6   Before reinstalling the drum it should be checked for cracks, score marks, deep scratches and hard spots, which will appear as small discolored areas. If the hard spots cannot be removed with emery cloth or sandpaper or if any of the other conditions listed above exist, the drum must be taken to an automotive machine shop to have it resurfaced. If the drum will not "clean up" before the maximum drum diameter is reached in the machining operation, the drum will have to be replaced with a new one. **Note:** *The maximum diameter is cast into the brake drum* **(see illustration)**.

7   Install the brake drum.

8   Mount the wheel, install the lug nuts, then lower the vehicle. Tighten the lug nuts to the torque listed in the Chapter 1 Specifications.

9   Make a number of forward and reverse stops to adjust the brakes until a satisfactory pedal action is obtained.

5.5v Install the return springs - the special brake spring pliers shown make this step much easier and safer (they're available at most auto parts stores)

5.5w Center the brake shoe assembly so the drum will slide over it

5.5x Adjust the star wheel so the shoes just barely drag on the drum, then back it off a few clicks until the drum turns freely

5.6 The drum has a maximum permissible diameter cast into it which must not be exceeded when removing scoring or other service imperfections in the friction surface

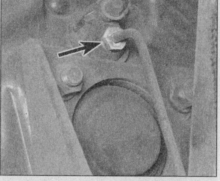

6.4 A flare-nut wrench should be used to disconnect the brake line

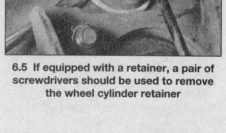

6.5 If equipped with a retainer, a pair of screwdrivers should be used to remove the wheel cylinder retainer

6   Wheel cylinder - removal, overhaul and installation

Removal

Refer to illustrations 6.4 and 6.5

1   Raise the rear of the vehicle and support it securely on jackstands.

2   Remove the brake shoe assembly (see Section 5).

3   Carefully clean all dirt and foreign material from around the wheel cylinder.

4   Unscrew the brake fluid inlet fitting **(see illustration)**. Don't pull the line away from the wheel cylinder.

5   Remove the wheel cylinder bolts or retainer. If equipped with a retainer, remove the retainer by using a pair of screwdrivers to pry off the clip **(see illustration)**. Immediately plug the brake line to prevent fluid loss and contamination.

6   Remove the wheel cylinder from the brake backing plate and place it on a clean workbench.

Overhaul

Refer t illustration 6.7

7   Remove the bleeder screw, seals, pistons, boots and spring assembly from the cylinder body **(see illustration)**.

8   Clean the wheel cylinder with brake system cleaner. Do not, under any circumstances, use petroleum-based solvents to clean brake parts.

9   Use unlubricated compressed air to remove excess fluid from the wheel cylinder and to blow out the passages.

10   Check the cylinder bore for corrosion and scoring. Crocus cloth may be used to remove light corrosion and stains, but the cylinder must be replaced with a new one if the defects can't be removed easily, or if the bore is scored.

11   Lubricate the pistons, the cylinder bore and the new seals with brake fluid.

12   Assemble the brake cylinder, making sure the seal lips face each other (inward) and the boots are properly seated.

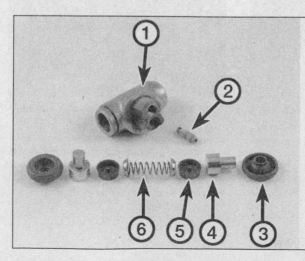

6.7 Typical wheel cylinder components

1   *Wheel cylinder body*
2   *Bleeder screw*
3   *Boot*
4   *Piston*
5   *Seal*
6   *Spring*

6.13 A wood block should be used to hold the wheel cylinder in position

Installation

Refer to illustration 6.13

13   Place the wheel cylinder in position and use a wooden block wedged against the axle flange to hold it in place **(see illustration)**.
14   If equipped with a retainer, install the retainer over the wheel cylinder using a 1-1/8 inch 12 point socket to press it into place. If equipped with bolts, install the bolts and tighten them securely.
15   Connect the brake line, tightening the fitting securely. Install the brake shoe assembly (see Section 5).

7   Master cylinder - removal, overhaul and installation

Note 1: *Before deciding to overhaul the master cylinder, check on the availability and cost of a new or factory rebuilt unit and the availability of a rebuild kit.*
Note 2: *This procedure does not apply to vehicles with ABS.*
1   A master cylinder overhaul kit should be purchased before beginning this procedure. The kit will include all the replacement parts necessary for the overhaul procedure. The

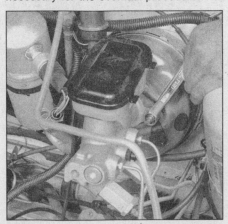

7.4 Remove the master cylinder mounting nuts (the passenger-side nut isn't visible in this photo)

7.2 Unplug the electrical connector for the brake warning switch (or fluid level sensor) (it's down on the master cylinder on 1982 through 1986 units, as shown here, and up on the reservoir on 1987 and later units)

rubber replacement parts, particularly the seals, are the key to fluid control within the master cylinder. As such, it is very important that they be installed securely and facing in the proper direction. Be careful during the rebuild procedure that no grease or petroleum-based solvents come in contact with the rubber parts.

Removal

Refer to illustrations 7.2, 7.3 and 7.4
Caution: *Completely cover the front fender and cowling area of the vehicle, as brake fluid can ruin painted surfaces.*
2   Unplug the electrical connector from the brake warning switch **(see illustration)**.
3   Remove as much fluid as possible from the master cylinder reservoir. Disconnect the brake line connections at the master cylinder, using a flare nut wrench, if available **(see illustration)**. Rags or newspapers should be placed under the master cylinder to soak up the fluid that will drain out.
4   Remove the two master cylinder mounting nuts **(see illustration)**, move the bracket

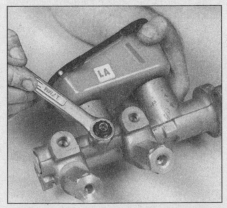

7.6 On 1982 through 1986 models, the pressure differential warning switch is located in the master cylinder body - to remove it, simply unscrew it

7.3 Unscrew the threaded fittings for the brake lines from the master cylinder with a flare nut wrench so the corners of the fittings won't be rounded off

retaining the combination valve forward slightly (if equipped), taking care not to bend the hydraulic lines running to the combination valve. Remove the master cylinder from the vehicle.

Overhaul

Refer to illustrations 7.6, 7.7a, 7.7b, 7.7c, 7.12, 7.13, 7.15, 7.16, 7.28, 7.30, 7.32, 7.33a, 7.33b, 7.33c, 7.33d, 7.33e, 7.33f, 7.34, 7.35a, 7.35b, 7.35c, 7.35d, 7.35e and 7.37
5   Remove the reservoir cover or cap and reservoir diaphragm, then discard any remaining fluid in the reservoir. Clamp the master cylinder flange in a vise. Don't apply pressure to the master cylinder body.
6   1986 and earlier models are equipped with a pressure differential warning switch mounted to the side of the master cylinder. If so, unscrew it **(see illustration)**. If you're working on a 1987 or later model, remove the brake fluid level sensor. Use needle-nose pliers to compress the locking tabs at the inner side of the master cylinder.
7   On 1982 through 1986 models, remove the proportioner valves and the switch piston

7.7a On 1982 through 1986 models, remove the proportioner valves . . .

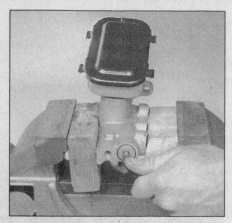

7.7b ... remove the switch
piston plug ...

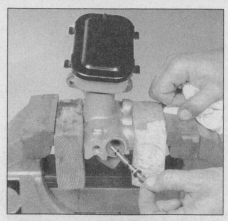

7.7c ... and remove the switch
piston assembly

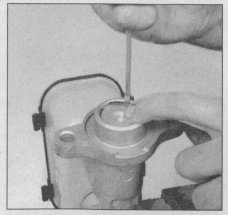

7.12 Press down on the piston and
remove the lock ring

7.13 Remove the primary piston assembly

7.15 Pry the plastic reservoir from the
cylinder body

7.16 Remove the reservoir grommets

(see illustrations). It may be necessary to lightly tap the master cylinder to remove the piston.

8   On 1987 and later models, remove the proportioner valve caps, O-rings and springs. You may have to use needle-nose pliers to remove the proportioner valve pistons - be careful not to scratch or damage the piston stems.

9   On 1987 and later models, drive out the spring pins with a 1/8-inch punch. Be careful not to damage the reservoir or master cylinder body when driving out the pins.

10   Remove the proportioner valve seals.

11   Inspect the proportioner valve pistons for corrosion and deformation and replace them if necessary.

12   Remove the primary piston lock ring by depressing the piston and prying the ring out with a screwdriver (see illustration).

13   Remove the primary piston assembly (see illustration). Be sure to note the installed direction of the old seal lips so the new seals can be installed the same way. The primary piston assembly is serviced as an assembly, while the secondary piston seals can be serviced separately.

14   Remove the secondary piston assembly. It may be necessary to remove the cylinder from the vise, invert it and tap it against a

wood block.

15   Place the master cylinder in a vise and pry the reservoir from the cylinder body with a prybar (see illustration). On 1987 and later model master cylinders, remove the reservoir by pulling it straight up (it won't come off if you forgot to remove those spring pins in Step 9).

16   Remove the reservoir grommets or O-rings from the master cylinder body (see illustration).

17   Inspect the reservoir for cracks and distortion. Replace it if damage is noted.

18   Do not attempt to remove the quick take-up valve from the cylinder body, as this valve is not serviceable.

19   Clean all parts with denatured alcohol and dry them with unlubricated compressed air.

20   Inspect the cylinder bore for corrosion and damage. If any corrosion or damage is found, replace the master cylinder body with a new one, as abrasives cannot be used on the (aluminum) bore.

21   Lubricate all rubber parts with clean brake fluid to ease reassembly.

22   Lubricate the new O-rings, proportioner valve seals and proportioner valve pistons with silicone grease supplied in the repair kit.

23   On 1987 and later models, install the

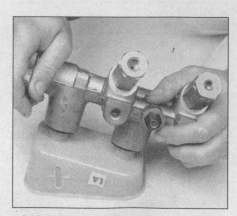

7.28 Using a rocking motion, press the
reservoir into the master cylinder

new seals on the proportioner valve pistons with the seal lips facing up, towards the cap assembly.

24   Install the proportioner valve pistons and seals in the master cylinder body.

25   Install the springs in the master cylinder body.

26   Install new O-rings in the grooves of the proportioner valve caps and install the caps in the master cylinder. Tighten the caps to the torque listed in this Chapter's Specifications.

27   Lubricate the new reservoir grommets

7.30 The secondary piston seals must be installed with the lips facing out

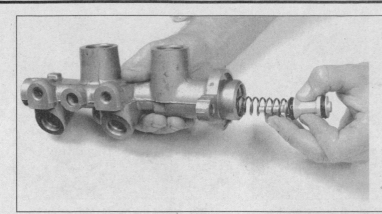

7.32 Install the secondary piston assembly

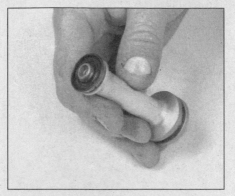

7.33a The primary piston seal must be installed with the lip facing away from the piston

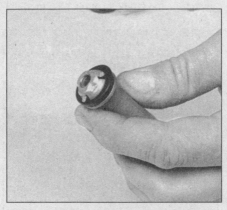

7.33b Install the seal guard over the seal

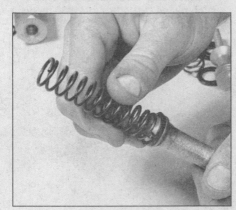

7.33c Place the primary piston spring in position

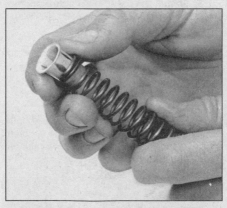

7.33d Insert the spring retainer into the spring

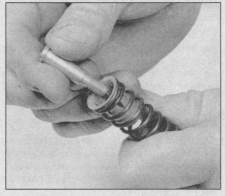

7.33e Insert the spring retaining bolt through the retainer and spring and thread it into the piston, tightening it securely

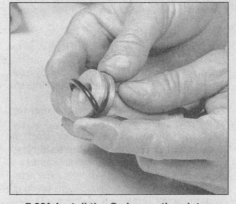

7.33f Install the O-ring on the piston

(or O-rings) with silicone grease and press the grommets into the master cylinder body, making sure they are properly seated. If you don't have any silicone grease, use clean brake fluid.

28   Lay the reservoir on a hard surface and press the master cylinder body onto the reservoir, either by using a rocking motion or by pressing it straight down onto the master cylinder body (see illustration).

29   Drive in the spring pins to retain the reservoir, using care not to damage the reservoir or master cylinder body (1987 and later models).

30   Remove the old seals from the secondary piston assembly and install the new seals so the cups face out (away from each other) (see illustration).

31   Attach the spring retainer to the secondary piston assembly.

32   Lubricate the cylinder bore and secondary piston assembly with clean brake fluid and install the spring and secondary piston assembly into the cylinder (see illustration).

33   Disassemble the primary piston assembly, noting the position of the parts, then lubricate the new seals with clean brake fluid and install them on the piston (see illustrations).

34   Lubricate the primary piston assembly and install it in the cylinder bore. Depress it and install the lock ring (see illustration).

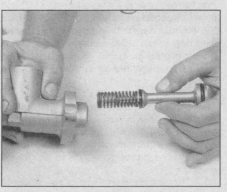

7.34 Install the primary piston assembly in the body

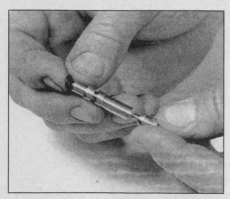

7.35a Install the small O-ring on the switch piston (1982 through 1986 models)

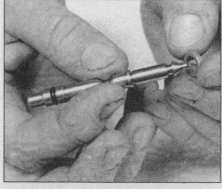

7.35b Install the metal retainer on the switch piston (1982 through 1986 models)

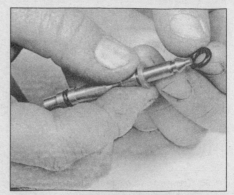

7.35c Install the large O-ring on the switch piston (1982 through 1986 models)

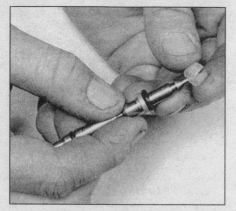

7.35d Install the plastic retainer on the switch piston (1982 through 1986 models)

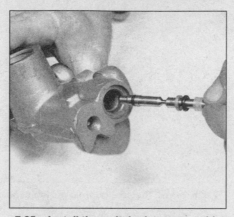

7.35e Install the switch piston assembly into the cylinder body (1982 through 1986 models)

7.37 Install the reservoir diaphragm into the cover (1982 through 1986 models)

35   On 1986 and earlier models, install the new O-rings on the switch piston, lubricate the piston with brake fluid and carefully insert it back into the master cylinder **(see illustrations)**.

36   Install a new O-ring on the piston plug and install the plug.

37   On 1986 and earlier models, attach the diaphragm to the cover **(see illustration)**.

38   **Note:** *Whenever the master cylinder is removed, the complete hydraulic system must be bled.* The time required to bleed the system can be reduced if the master cylinder is filled with fluid and bench bled before the master cylinder is installed on the vehicle. Insert threaded plugs of the correct size into the cylinder outlet holes and fill the reservoir with brake fluid. The master cylinder should be supported in such a manner that brake fluid will not spill during the bench bleeding procedure.

39   Loosen one plug at a time and push the piston assembly into the bore to force air from the master cylinder. To prevent air from being drawn back into the cylinder, the appropriate plug must be replaced before allowing the piston to return to its original position.

40   Stroke the piston three or four times for each outlet to ensure that all air has been expelled.

41   Refill the master cylinder reservoirs and

install the cap or diaphragm and cover assembly. **Note:** *The reservoirs should only be filled to the top of the reservoir divider to prevent overflowing when the cover is installed.*

Installation

42   Install the master cylinder by reversing the removal steps. Be sure to tighten the master cylinder-to-brake booster mounting nuts to the torque listed in this Chapter's Specifications.

43   Bleed the brake system (see Section 12).

44   Test the brakes carefully before driving the vehicle in traffic.

8   Brake hoses and lines - inspection and replacement

1   Every six months, with the vehicle raised and placed securely on jackstands, the flexible hoses which connect the steel brake lines with the front and rear brake assemblies should be inspected for cracks, chafing of the outer cover, leaks, blisters and other damage. These are important and vulnerable parts of the brake system and inspection should be complete. A light and mirror will prove helpful for a thorough check. If a hose

exhibits any of the above conditions, replace it with a new one.

Front brake hose

Refer to illustration 8.2

2   Using a back-up wrench, disconnect the brake line from the hose fitting, being careful not to bend the frame bracket or brake line **(see illustration)**.

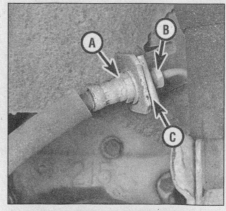

8.2 Using a back-up wrench on the flexible hose side of the fitting (A), loosen the tube nut (B) with a flare nut wrench, then remove the U-clip (C) from the hose fitting

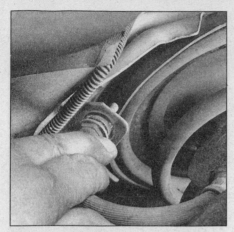

8.14 Insert the ends of the hose into the frame bracket, without twisting the line

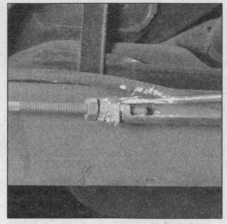

9.3 Lubricate the threads of the parking brake equalizer before adjusting the cable

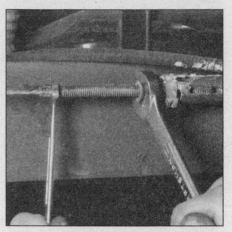

9.4 To adjust the parking brake cable, use two wrenches - one to prevent the threaded rod from turning and one to turn the equalizer nut; turn the adjusting nut until the right rear wheel can just be turned in a rearward direction but not in the forward direction

3   Use pliers to remove the U-clip from the female fitting at the bracket, then remove the hose from the bracket.

4   At the caliper end of the hose, remove the bolt from the fitting block, then remove the hose and the sealing washers on either side of the fitting block.

5   When installing the hose, always use new sealing washers on either side of the fitting block and lubricate all bolt threads with clean brake fluid before installation.

6   With the fitting flange engaged with the caliper locating ledge, attach the hose to the caliper. Tighten the fitting bolt to the torque listed in this Chapter's Specifications.

7   Without twisting the hose, install the female fitting in the hose bracket. It will fit the bracket in only one position.

8   Install the U-clip retaining the female fitting to the frame bracket.

9   Using a back-up wrench, attach the brake line to the hose fitting.

10   When the brake hose installation is complete, there should be no kinks in the hose. Make sure the hose does not contact any part of the suspension. Check this by turning the wheels to the extreme left and right positions. If the hose makes contact, remove the hose and correct the installation as necessary.

Rear brake hose

Refer to illustration 8.14

11   Using a back-up wrench, disconnect the hose at both ends, being careful not to bend the bracket or steel lines.

12   Remove the two U-clips with pliers and separate the female fittings from the brackets.

13   Unbolt the hose retaining clip and remove the hose.

14   Without twisting the hose, install the female ends of the hose in the frame brackets. It will fit the bracket in only one position **(see illustration)**.

15   Install the U-clips retaining the female end to the bracket.

16   Using a back-up wrench, attach the

steel line fittings to the female fittings. Again, be careful not to bend the bracket or steel line.

17   Check that the hose installation did not loosen the frame bracket. Tighten the bracket if necessary.

18   Fill the master cylinder reservoir and bleed the system (see Section 12).

Steel brake lines

19   When replacing brake lines be sure to use the correct parts. Never substitute copper tubing because copper is subject to fatigue cracking and corrosion. The outside diameter of the tubing is used for sizing.

20   Prefabricated brake line, with the tube ends already flared and fittings installed, is available at auto parts stores and dealer parts departments. These lines are also bent to the proper shapes.

21   When installing the new brake line, make sure it's securely supported in the brackets and has plenty of clearance from moving or hot components.

22   After installation, check the master cylinder fluid level and add fluid as necessary (see Chapter 1). Bleed the brake system (see Section 12) and test the brakes carefully before driving the vehicle in traffic.

9   Parking brake - adjustment

Refer to illustrations 9.3 and 9.4

1   Apply the parking brake lever four ratchet clicks.

2   Raise the rear of the vehicle and support it securely on jackstands. Block the front wheels.

3   Before adjusting, make sure the threads of the parking brake equalizer are lubricated with multi-purpose grease **(see illustration)**.

4   Tighten the adjusting nut until the right rear wheel can just be turned rearward with two hands, but locks when forward motion is attempted **(see illustration)**.

5   Release the parking brake pedal and check to make sure the rear wheels turn

freely in both directions with no drag.

6   Lower the vehicle.

10   Parking brake cable - replacement

Front cable

1   Remove the rear console trim to gain access to the parking brake handle mechanism (refer to Chapter 11).

2   Remove the cable nut from the cable at the handbrake lever and push the cable and casing assembly through the floorpan.

3   Raise the rear of the vehicle and support it securely on jackstands.

4   Pull the cable casing from the L-shaped guide just above the rear of the exhaust pipe heat shield.

5   Maneuver the cable out of the wire bracket at the left rear suspension pivot.

6   Slide the cable casing out of the equalizer and disconnect the cable from the cable joiner.

7   Installation is the reverse of the removal procedure. Refer to Section 9 for the cable adjustment procedure.

Left cable

Refer to illustration 10.12

8   Raise the vehicle and support it securely on jackstands.

9   Loosen the equalizer adjusting screw and disconnect the left cable from the equalizer.

10   Disconnect the cable casing at the frame mounting bracket by depressing the tangs on the retainer with a pair of pliers.

11   Remove the brake drum and brake shoes as described in Section 5.

Disconnect the parking brake cable from the parking brake lever.

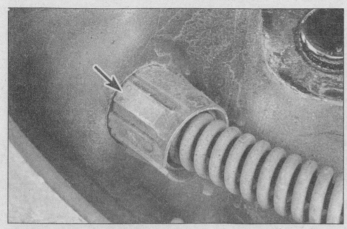

10.12 Depress the tangs on the cable casing retainer and push it through the backing plate

11.10 Remove the brake booster mounting nuts (arrows)

12   Using a pair of pliers, depress the tangs on the cable casing retainer and push the cable and casing out through the backing plate **(see illustration)**.

13   Installation is the reverse of the removal procedure. Be sure to adjust the cable as described in Section 9.

Right cable

14   Raise the rear of the vehicle and support it securely on jackstands.

15   Remove enough tension at the equalizer to enable the cable to be removed from the cable joiner.

16   Disconnect the cable casing at the frame mounting bracket by depressing the tangs on the retainer with a pair of pliers.

17   Remove the brake drum and brake shoes (see Section 5) Disconnect the parking brake cable from the parking brake lever.

18   Using a pair of pliers, depress the tangs on the cable casing retainer and push the cable and casing out through the backing plate **(see illustration 10.12)**.

19   Installation is the reverse of the removal procedure. Be sure to adjust the cable as described in Section 9.

---

11   Power brake booster - check, removal and installation

---

1   The power brake unit requires no special maintenance apart from periodic inspection of the hoses and inspection of the air filter beneath the boot at the pedal pushrod end.

2   Dismantling of the power brake unit requires special tools. If a problem develops, it is recommended that a new or factory-exchange unit be installed rather than trying to overhaul the original booster.

Operating check

3   Depress the brake pedal several times with the engine off and make sure there's no change in the pedal reserve distance.

4   Depress the pedal and start the engine.

If the pedal goes down slightly, operation is normal.

Airtightness check

5   Start the engine and turn it off after one or two minutes. Depress the brake pedal slowly several times. If pedal resistance increases each time (gets harder to push down), the booster is airtight.

6   Depress the brake pedal while the engine is running, then stop the engine with the pedal depressed. If there's no change in the pedal reserve travel after holding the pedal for 30 seconds, the booster is airtight.

Removal and installation

Refer to illustration 11.10

7   Remove the mounting nuts which hold the master cylinder to the power brake unit. Position the master cylinder out of the way, being careful not to strain the lines leading to the master cylinder. If there is any doubt as to the flexibility of the lines, disconnect them at the cylinder and plug the ends.

8   Disconnect the vacuum hose leading to the front of the power brake booster. Cover the end of the hose.

9   Inside the vehicle, disconnect the power brake pushrod from the brake pedal. Do not force the pushrod to the side when disconnecting it.

10   Remove the four booster mounting nuts and carefully lift the unit out of the engine compartment **(see illustration)**.

11   When installing, loosely install the four mounting nuts and connect the pushrod to the brake pedal. Tighten the nuts to the torque listed in this Chapter's Specifications and reconnect the vacuum hose and master cylinder. If the hydraulic brake lines were disconnected, the entire brake system must be bled to eliminate any air which has entered the system (see Section 12).

---

12   Hydraulic system - bleeding

Note: *Check the fluid level often during the*

bleeding procedure and make sure there is adequate fluid present. If the level drops too low, air could be sucked into the hydraulic system.

1   Bleeding the hydraulic system is necessary to remove air whenever it is introduced into the brake system.

2   It may be necessary to bleed the system at all four brakes if air as entered the system due to low fluid level, or if the brake lines have been disconnected at the master cylinder.

3   If a brake line was disconnected only at one wheel, then only that wheel cylinder or caliper must be bled.

4   If a brake line is disconnected at a fitting located between the master cylinder and any of the brakes, that part of the system served by the disconnected line must be bled.

Conventional brake system

Refer to illustration 12.19

5   If the master cylinder has been removed from the vehicle or is suspected of having air in the bore, the master cylinder must be bled before any wheel cylinder or caliper is bled. Follow Steps 6 through 15 to bleed the master cylinder while it is installed on the vehicle.

6   Remove the vacuum reserve from the brake power booster by applying the brake several times with the engine off.

7   Remove the master cylinder reservoir cover and fill the reservoir with brake fluid. Keep checking the fluid level often during the bleeding operation, adding fluid as necessary to keep the reservoir full. Reinstall the cover.

8   Disconnect the forward brake line connection at the master cylinder.

9   Fill the master cylinder with brake fluid until it begins to flow from the forward line connector port. Have a container and shop rags handy to catch and clean up spilled fluid.

10   Reconnect the forward brake line to the master cylinder.

11   Have an assistant depress the brake pedal very slowly, one time only, and hold it down.

12.19 When bleeding the brakes, a hose is connected to the bleed screw at the caliper or wheel cylinder and then submerged in brake fluid - air will be seen as bubbles in the tube and container (all air must be expelled before moving to the next wheel)

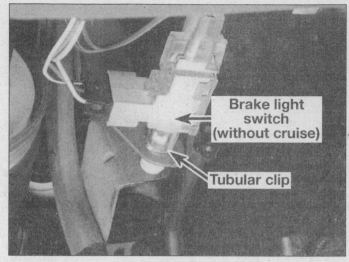

13.3 Typical brake light switch details

12 Loosen the forward brake line at the master cylinder to purge the air from the bore, retighten the connection, then have the brake pedal released slowly.

13 Wait 15 seconds (this is important).

14 Repeat the sequence, including the 15 second wait, until all air is removed from the bore.

15 After the forward port has been completely purged of air, bleed the rear port in the same manner.

16 To bleed the individual wheel cylinders or calipers, first refer to Steps 6 and 7.

17 Have an assistant on hand, as well as a supply of new brake fluid, an empty clear plastic container, a length of 3/16-inch plastic, rubber or vinyl tubing to fit over the bleeder valve and a wrench to open and close the bleeder valve. The vehicle may have to be raised and placed on jackstands for clearance.

18 Beginning at the right rear wheel, loosen the bleeder valve slightly, then tighten it to a point where it is snug but can still be loosened quickly and easily.

19 Place one end of the tubing over the bleeder valve and submerge the other end in brake fluid in the container **(see illustration)**.

20 Have the assistant pump the brakes a few times to get pressure in the system, then hold the pedal firmly depressed.

21 While the pedal is held depressed, open the bleeder valve just enough to allow a flow of fluid to leave the valve. Watch for air bubbles to exit the submerged end of the tube. When the fluid flow slows after a couple of seconds, close the valve again and have your assistant release the pedal.

22 Repeat Steps 20 and 21 until no more air is seen leaving the tube, then tighten the bleeder valve and proceed to the left front wheel, the left rear wheel and the right front wheel, in that order, and perform the same procedure. Be sure to check the fluid in the master cylinder reservoir frequently.

23 Never use old brake fluid because it absorbs moisture which will deteriorate the brake system components and could cause the fluid to boil, which could render the brake system inoperative.

24 Refill the master cylinder with fluid at the end of the operation. Check the operation of the brakes. The pedal should feel solid when depressed, with no sponginess. **Warning:** *Do not operate the vehicle if you are in doubt about the effectiveness of the brake system.*

Anti-lock Brake System (ABS)

25 The brakes on models equipped with ABS require a slightly different bleeding procedure.

26 Start the engine and let it run for at least ten seconds. During this time, don't depress the brake pedal. Also, watch the ABS warning light on the dash - if the light comes on and stays on after the ten second period, the vehicle will have to be towed to a dealer service department or other repair shop for ABS malfunction diagnosis.

27 If the light comes on for approximately three seconds then turns off and stays off, turn the ignition switch Off. Repeat Step 26 one more time, then proceed the step 28.

28 Connect a length of clear tubing to the rear bleeder screw on the hydraulic modulator and submerge the other end in a container partially filled with clean brake fluid. Slowly open the the bleeder screw approximately 1/2-turn. Have an assistant depress the brake pedal and hold it in that position until fluid flows from the hose, then close the bleeder screw and have the assistant slowly let up on the pedal.

29 Repeat Step 28 until no air bubbles flow from the the bleeder screw.

30 Repeat Steps 28 and 29 on the front bleeder screw on the hydraulic modulator.

31 Bleed the brakes at the wheels by following Steps 17 through 22, but note that the order for bleeding them is:

right rear
left rear
right front
left front

32 Check the fluid level in the master cylinder and add some, if necessary, to bring it to the appropriate level.

33 Repeat Steps 28 through 30.

34 Refill the master cylinder with fluid at the end of the operation. Never use old brake fluid because it absorbs moisture which will deteriorate the brake system components and could cause the fluid to boil, which could render the brake system inoperative.

35 Check the operation of the brakes. The pedal should feel solid when depressed, with no sponginess. **Warning:** *Do not operate the vehicle if you are in doubt about the effectiveness of the brake system.*

13 Brake light switch - check and replacement

Refer to illustration 13.3

1 The switch is located on a flange or bracket protruding from the brake pedal support.

2 With the brake pedal in the fully released position. the plunger on the body of the switch should be completely pressed in. When the pedal is pushed in, the plunger releases and sends electrical current to the brake lights.

3 If the brake lights are inoperative and it has been determined that the bulbs are not burned out, push the brake light switch into the tubular clip, noting that audible clicks can be heard as the threaded portion of the switch is pushed through the clip toward the brake pedal **(see illustration)**.

4 Pull the brake pedal all the way to the rear against the pedal stop until no further clicks can be heard. This will seat the switch in the tubular clip and provide the correct adjustment.

5   Release the brake pedal and repeat Step 4 to ensure that no further clicks can be heard.
6   Make sure the brake lights are working.
7   If the lights are not working, disconnect the electrical connectors at the brake light switch and remove the switch from the clip.
8   Install a new switch and adjust it by performing Steps 3 through 6.

14   Vacuum pump - removal and installation

1   Raise the front of the vehicle and support it securely on jackstands.
2   Remove the left side splash shield.
3   Disconnect the vacuum hoses and electrical connector from the vacuum pump.
4   Remove the retaining nuts and lower the pump from the vehicle.
5   Installation is the reverse of removal.

15   Anti-lock Brake System (ABS) - general information

Some 1992 and later models are equipped with an anti-lock brake system (ABS) which provides optimal deceleration while maintaining directional stability and vehicle steerability, even under severe braking conditions on less-than-ideal road surfaces. It accomplishes this task by monitoring the rotational speed of the front and rear wheels and controls the brake line hydraulic pressure to all four wheels during braking.

Components

A hydraulic brake modulator is attached to the side of the brake master cylinder and controls pressure generated by the brake master cylinder. It proportions this pressure to each wheel based on the input from the input control module.

Wheel speed sensors

A speed sensor and a toothed ring are installed at each wheel. The sensor generates electrical signals, indicating wheel rotational speed, and sends these signals to the control module.

Electronic Brake Control Module (EBCM)

The control module is located under the dash panel. The function of the control module is to accept and process information received from the wheel speed sensors and send electrical signals to the modulator on the master cylinder. This controls hydraulic line pressure to all four wheels to prevent wheel lock-up. The control module also constantly monitors the ABS system, even under driving conditions, to find faults within the system.

When the control module finds a fault, a diagnostic code will be stored in the control unit which, when retrieved by a dealer service technician, will indicate the problem area or component.

ABS warning light (amber)

The electronic control unit monitors itself and all other ABS components. If there's a problem in any portion of the system, but it doesn't affect ABS braking ability, the ABS warning light will flash on and off, alerting the driver to the problem and reminding him that repairs should be made as soon as possible. If the ABS light comes on and stays on (i.e. doesn't flash), there's a serious problem in the system and NO anti-lock braking is available (but the system will continue to function in the normal, non-ABS mode). If this condition occurs, repairs should be made immediately.

Diagnosis and repair

If the ABS light comes on and flashes, or stays on, while the vehicle is in operation, the ABS system requires attention. Although troubleshooting the ABS system is beyond the scope of the home mechanic, you can perform a few preliminary checks before taking the vehicle to a dealer service department for diagnosis.

a)   *Check the hydraulic brake fluid level in the master cylinder reservoir, adding fluid if necessary (see Chapter 1).*
b)   *Verify that the electronic brake control module unit electrical connector is securely connected and is free of corrosion.*
c)   *Inspect the electrical connectors at each speed sensor, modulator and all connection locations. Make sure each electrical connector is securely connected and is free of corrosion.*
d)   *Check the system fuses, replacing them as necessary. If the above preliminary checks don't rectify the problem, the vehicle should be diagnosed by a dealer service department. Due to the rather complex nature of this system, and the high operating pressures involved, all actual repair work must be done by a dealer service department.*

Chapter 10
Suspension and steering systems

Contents

Specifications

General

Power steering fluid type	See Chapter 1

Torque Specifications

Ft-lbs (unless otherwise indicated)

Front suspension

Balljoint stud-to-steering knuckle nut	55
Control arm pivot bolt nuts	67
Driveaxle/hub nut	See Chapter 8
Hub-to-steering knuckle bolts	
1982 through 1986	40 to 60
1987 on	70
Stabilizer bar (front)	
Link nuts	15
Bushing clamp nuts	18
Strut assembly	
Piston rod locknut	15
Upper mounting nuts	20
Strut-to-steering knuckle nuts	140
Suspension support-to-chassis bolts	63

Torque Specifications   Ft-lbs (unless otherwise indicated)

Rear suspension

Hub-to-rear axle bolt/nut	37
Rear axle control arm-to-body bracket bolt	68
Shock absorber	
Upper mounting nut	13
Lower mounting bolt/nut	35
Stabilizer bar	
Bushing clamp nuts	10
U-bolt nuts	13

Steering system

Coupling-to-stub shaft pinch bolt	37
Coupling-to-steering column pinch bolt	30
Steering gear mounting clamp nuts	28
Steering wheel-to-steering column nut	30
Tie-rods	
Inner tie-rod-to-steering gear bolts	65
Tie-rod pinch bolts	25
Tie-rod end-to-steering knuckle nut	35
Tie-rod end-to-strut steering arm nut	35

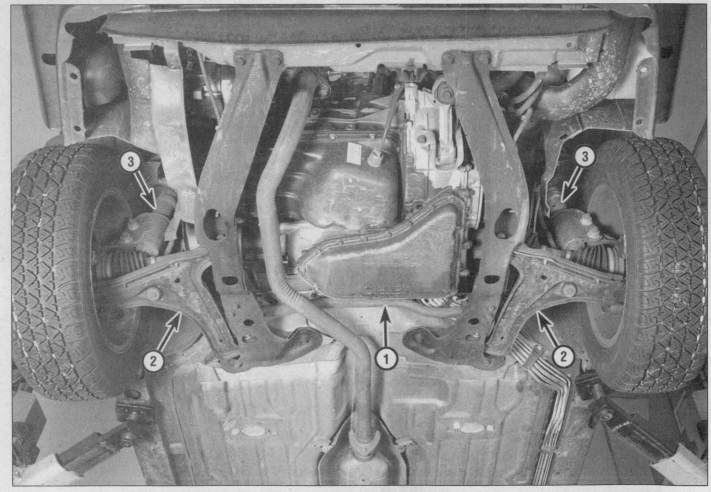

1.1 Front suspension components

1 Stabilizer bar	*2 Control arm*	*3 Strut assembly*

1 Suspension system - general information

Refer to illustrations 1.1 and 1.3
Warning: *Whenever any of the suspension or steering fasteners or removed, they must be inspected and, if necessary, replaced with new ones of the same part number or of original equipment quality and design. Torque specifications must be followed for proper reassembly and component retention. Never attempt to heat or straighten any suspension or steering components. Instead, replace any bent or damaged part with a new one.*
Note: *These vehicles have a combination of standard and metric fasteners on the various suspension and steering components, so it would be a good idea to have both types of tools available when beginning work.*

1   The vehicles covered by this manual feature an independent front suspension which uses a combination strut and spring design attached between the body and the steering knuckles. The inner ends of the control arms pivot from the suspension support;

their outer ends are attached to the steering knuckles by balljoints **(see illustration)**.
2   To minimize the transmission of vibration to the body, rubber bushings are used in the control arm pivots in the engine cradle. The cradle also uses rubber bushings for isolation from the body. The upper end of the strut is isolated by a rubber mount which contains a bearing that allows it to pivot as the wheels are turned.
3   The rear suspension **(see illustration)** is a semi-independent design consisting of a rear axle assembly with two trailing arms welded to a twisting cross beam, two coil springs, two shock absorbers and, on some models, a stabilizer bar. The configuration of the axle assembly maintains the proper geometric relationship of the wheels to the body during acceleration, braking and cornering.
4   The two coil springs support the weight of the vehicle in the rear. Each spring is positioned between a seat in the underbody and another seat welded to the top of the control arm portion of the rear axle. A rubber insulator isolates the underbody seat from the upper end of the spring; a combination com-

pression bumper/spring insulator does the same thing at the lower end of the spring.
5   The two shock absorbers are conventional sealed hydraulic units. They are non-adjustable, non-refillable and cannot be disassembled. If they lose their resistance, are damaged or leak, replace them. The lower ends of the shocks are attached to the axle assembly; the upper ends are attached to the body.
6   The one-piece rear hub and bearing assemblies are bolted to the ends of the rear axle. These are sealed units; the bearing is not replaceable as a separate unit.

2 Strut assembly - removal and installation

Refer to illustrations 2.1 and 2.5
Caution: *Whenever the front suspension is disconnected use care to avoid damaging the driveaxle CV joint boots.*
1   Loosen the front wheel lug nuts. In the engine compartment, remove the upper

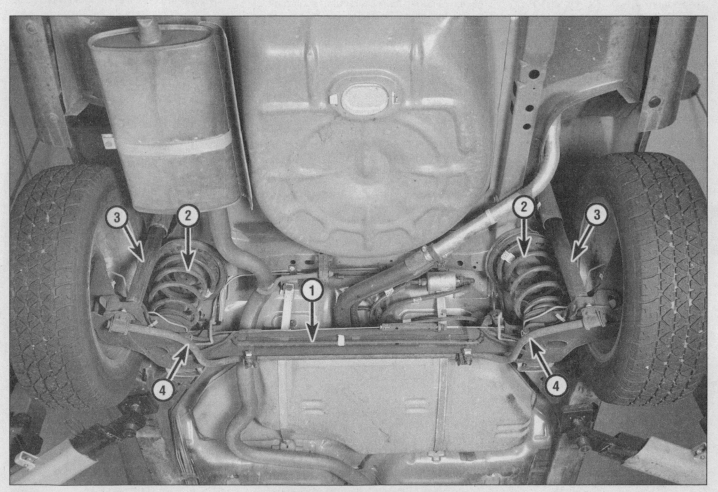

1.3 Rear suspension components

1	Rear axle assembly	3	Shock absorber
2	Coil spring	4	Stabilizer bar

2.1 The strut-to-body nuts (arrows) are accessible from the engine compartment

2.5 Be sure to make an alignment mark with a scribe across the strut flange and the steering knuckle to insure proper realignment during reassembly, then remove the strut-to-knuckle nuts (arrows) and bolts

3.4 A spring compressor must be used to disassemble the strut

strut-to-body nuts **(see illustration)**.
2   Raise the front of the vehicle, support it securely on jackstands and allow the suspension to hang free.
3   Remove the wheel(s).
4   Disconnect the tie-rod from the strut (see Section 17).
5   Loosen the strut-to-knuckle bolts until they are flush with the end of the nut **(see illustration)**. Using a brass hammer, drive the bolts, which are splined, out of the knuckle. Remove the nuts, extract the bolts, lower the assembly and remove the strut from the vehicle. **Caution:** *Don't allow the steering knuckle to fall outwards, as this could damage the brake hose and also allow the inner CV joint to become overextended. If necessary, secure the steering knuckle with a piece of wire.*
6   Installation is the reverse of removal, making sure to tighten the nuts and bolts to the torque listed in this Chapter's Specifications. **Note:** *When inserting the strut-to-knuckle bolts, place the flats of the bolt heads in the horizontal position.*

3   Strut/coil spring - replacement

Refer to illustrations 3.4 and 3.6
Warning: *Disassembling a strut is a potentially dangerous job. Be very careful and follow the instructions exactly or serious injury may result. Use only a high quality spring compressor and carefully follow the manufacturer's instructions furnished with the tool. After removing the coil spring from the strut assembly, set it aside in a safe, isolated area.*
1   The spring on the strut is under considerable pressure, requiring that a spring compressor be used to compress the spring and disengage its components. Do not attempt to disassemble the strut without a compressor, as serious injury can occur.
2   A spring compressor can either be rented on a daily basis from an equipment rental agency, or one can be purchased at a tool supply house or some auto parts stores.
3   Hold the strut in a vise, using wood

blocks to cushion the jaws, preventing damage to the strut body.
4   Follow the manufacturer's instructions for the particular spring compressor being used. Slightly compress the spring, making sure that the jaws of the compressor are firmly seated around the coils and cannot slip off **(see illustration)**.
5   Tighten the compressor from side to side, a little at a time, until the spring seat is clear of the uppermost coil. This can be confirmed by wiggling the spring.
6   With the spring firmly compressed and clear of its seat, remove the top locknut and washer **(see illustration)**.
7   Pull the mount off the top of the shock absorber assembly.
8   Remove the spring seat, bumper, shield and insulator.
9   Remove the spring from the strut unit. Depending on the type of spring compressor used, you may have to loosen the compressor until the tension on the spring is relieved, then lift the spring from the strut. Although some compressors allow you to lift the spring off the shock absorber in its compressed state, this could prove dangerous should the compressor and spring be jostled and accidentally disengaged from each other. **Warning:** *Always keep your head away from the ends of the spring.*
10   The spring should be checked for cracking or deformation of any kind. If the vehicle was sagging in the front, this is an indication that the springs are in need of replacement.
11   To test the strut damper unit after the coil spring has been removed, hold it in an upright position and work the piston rod up and down its full length of travel. If you can feel a strong resistance because of hydraulic pressure, the strut damper is functioning properly. If you feel no substantial resistance, or there is sudden free movement in travel, the strut should be replaced. If there is fluid leakage evident on the outside of the strut,

replace the strut.
12   If the spring compressor was removed from the spring, reinstall it and compress the spring. With the strut mounted in a vise lined with protective wood blocks, install the spring.
13   Install the insulator, shield and bumper to the shock body.
14   Install the spring seat, with the flat portion of the seat facing the flange at the bottom of the strut **(see illustration 3.6)**.
15   Install the mount assembly.
16   Install the lockwasher and locknut to the top of the piston rod, tightening the nut to the torque listed in this Chapter's Specifications.
17   Carefully relieve tension on the spring by loosening the compressor from side to side, a little at a time. Check to be sure the top of the spring is raised properly into its seat.

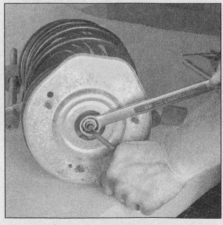

3.6 With the spring compressed, remove the upper retaining nut

4.2 To disconnect the stabilizer bar from the control arms, remove the link nut (upper arrow, nut not visible in this photo) and pull the link bolt (lower arrow) through the control arm; after you've removed the link assembly bushings, spacers and washers, inspect them for damage and wear and replace as necessary before reassembling

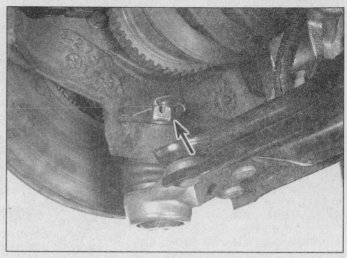

5.3 Remove the cotter pin and loosen - but don't remove - the castellated nut (arrow) from the balljoint stud

4 Stabilizer bar (front) - removal and installation

Removal

Refer to illustration 4.2

1   Loosen the front wheel lug nuts. Raise the front of the vehicle and support it securely on jackstands so that the lower control arms hang free. Remove the front wheels.
2   Disconnect the stabilizer bar links from the lower control arms **(see illustration)**.
3   The stabilizer bar is attached to the upper side of the rear support with two clamps; the bolts for these clamps are installed through the support from underneath. Remove these clamp bolts and remove the stabilizer bar assembly.
4   Inspect the stabilizer bar clamp bushings for cracks, tears and deterioration. If they're worn, replace them.

Installation

5   Install the stabilizer bar with the split in the insulator facing forward.
6   Install the bolts loosely and center the bar from side to side. The two ends of the stabilizer bar should be canted up at a 55-degree angle in order to install the link assemblies.
7   Reassemble the links as shown **(see illustration 4.2)** and tighten the link nuts to the torque listed in this Chapter's Specifications.
8   Tighten the stabilizer bar clamp bolts to the torque listed in this Chapter's Specifications.
9   The remainder of installation is the reverse of removal.

5 Control arm - removal and installation

Removal

Refer to illustrations 5.3, 5.4, 5.5, 5.6a and 5.6b

1   Loosen the wheel lug nuts, raise the front of the vehicle and support it securely on jackstands. Apply the parking brake and block the rear wheels to keep the vehicle from rolling off the jackstands. Remove the wheel(s).
2   Disconnect the stabilizer bar from the control arm being removed (see Section 2). (If only one control arm is being removed, disconnect only that end of the stabilizer bar; if both control arms are being removed, disconnect both ends.)
3   Remove the balljoint stud-to-steering knuckle castellated nut and cotter pin **(see illustration)**.
4   Using a hammer, strike the ballstud boss on the steering knuckle **(see illustration)**. until the ballstud pops loose from the knuckle. If the ballstud is frozen in the knuckle, you may have to use a special balljoint separator (J-38892, or equivalent), or a picklefork tool. Keep in mind that a picklefork will damage or destroy the boot, so it should be used only as a last resort.
5   Using a large pry bar positioned between the control arm and steering knuck-

5.4 Pop the balljoint out of the steering knuckle by striking the knuckle ballstud boss sharply with a hammer as shown

5.5 Once the ballstud is loose in its hole in the knuckle boss, separate the control arm from the steering knuckle by prying the ballstud out of the hole with a large prybar as shown

le, separate the ballstud from the knuckle **(see illustration)**. **Caution:** *When removing the balljoint from the knuckle, be careful not to overextend the inner CV joint or it may be damaged.*

6   Remove the front control arm pivot bolt and the rear vertical bushing bolt **(see illustrations)** and detach the control arm.

7   The control arm bushings are replaceable, but special tools and expertise are necessary to do the job. Carefully inspect the bushings for hardening, excessive wear and cracks. If they appear to be worn or deteriorated, take the control arm to a dealer service department or repair shop.

Installation

8   Position the control arm in the suspension crossmember and install the front pivot bolt and the rear vertical bushing bolt. Do not tighten them completely at this time.

9   Insert the balljoint stud into the steering knuckle boss, install the castellated nut and tighten it to the torque listed in this Chapter's Specifications. If necessary, tighten the nut a little more (up to, but not beyond, the specified maximum listed in the Specifications) if the cotter pin hole doesn't line up with an opening on the nut. Install a new cotter pin.

10   Install the stabilizer bar-to-control arm link bolt, bushings, spacers and washers (see Section 2) and tighten the link nut to the torque listed in this Chapter's Specifications.

11   Install the wheel and lower the vehicle. Tighten the lug nuts to the specified torque.

12   With the weight of the vehicle on the suspension, tighten the control arm pivot bolt and the rear vertical bushing bolt to the torque listed in this Chapter's Specifications. **Caution:** *If the bolts aren't tightened with the weight of the vehicle on the suspension, control arm bushing damage may occur.*

13   Drive the vehicle to a dealer service department or an alignment shop to have the front wheel alignment checked and, if necessary, adjusted.

---

6   Balljoints - check and replacement

Check

1   Raise the front of the vehicle and support the chassis securely on jackstands.

2   Grasp the top and bottom of the wheel and move it in and out. If there is any horizontal movement of the steering knuckle in relation to the lower control arm, the balljoint is worn and should be replaced with a new one.

3   To check the ballstud when it is disconnected, grasp it and try to move it or twist it in the socket. If there is any movement, replace the balljoint.

Replacement

4   Remove the control arm (see Section 5).

5   The balljoint is riveted to the control arm, so first determine if there is a counter-

5.6a   The front control arm pivot bolt (arrow) is accessed from the front of the suspension crossmember

sunk pilot hole in the center of the rivets. If there is not, carefully mark the rivet centers with a suitable punch.

6   Drill a pilot hole in the rivets with a 1/8-inch drill and then drill the rivet out with a 1/2-inch drill.

7   Remove the balljoint from the control arm.

8   Place the new balljoint in position and install the nuts and bolts, tightening the nuts to the torque listed in the specifications provided with the instructions included in the kit.

9   Install the control arm (see Section 5).

10   After installation, have the front end alignment checked by a dealer or a properly equipped shop.

---

7   Front suspension support assembly - removal and installation

---

Removal

1   Raise the front of the vehicle, support it securely on jackstands and remove the front wheel.

2   Remove the control arm inner pivot bolts (see Section 5).

3   Support the control arm, steering knuckle and strut damper assembly with a jack and move it away from the support assembly.

4   Remove the front suspension support assembly attaching bolts **(see illustration 5.4)** and lower the assembly from the vehicle.

Installation

5   Raise the support assembly into position and loosely install the center bolt **(A in illustration 5.4)**.

6   Loosely install the tie bar bolt **(B in illustration 5.4)** into the outboard hole.

7   Install both rear bolts **(C in illustration 5.4)** and tighten to the torque listed in this Chapter's Specifications.

8   Install the bolt into the center hole **(D in**

5.6b   To separate the rear part of the control arm from the suspension crossmember, remove the vertical bushing bolt (arrow)

illustration 5.4) and tighten to the torque listed in this Chapter's Specifications.

9   Tighten bolt A to the torque listed in this Chapter's Specifications.

10   Install the bolt into hole E and tighten to the torque listed in this Chapter's Specifications.

11   Tighten the bolt in hole B to the torque listed in this Chapter's Specifications.

12   Move the lower control arm back into position, install the pivot bolts and tighten to the torque listed in this Chapter's Specifications.

13   Install the wheel and lower the vehicle.

---

8   Hub and bearing assembly (front) - removal and installation

---

Refer to illustrations 8.6, 8.9a and 8.9b

1   Break loose the driveaxle/hub nut.

2   Raise the front of the vehicle and support it securely on jackstands.

3   Remove the front wheel. Insert a punch through the caliper and into the disc to allow removal of the hub nut (see Chapter 8, if necessary).

4   Remove the brake caliper as described in Chapter 9. **Note:** *It is not necessary to disconnect the brake line.* Support the caliper out of the way with a piece of wire - don't let it hang by the brake hose.

5   Remove the brake disc.

6   Remove the hub and bearing assembly attaching bolts **(see illustration)**. If the old assembly is to be reinstalled, mark the attaching bolts so they can be installed in the same holes from which they were removed.

7   Using a two-jaw puller, remove the hub and bearing assembly from the driveaxle (see Chapter 8, if necessary).

8   Spin the bearing with your finger and check for any roughness or noise. Check the bearing mating surfaces and steering knuckle bore for dirt or nicks. This assembly is a sealed unit and if the bearing needs replacing, the entire hub and bearing assembly

8.6 Remove the front hub and bearing retaining bolts

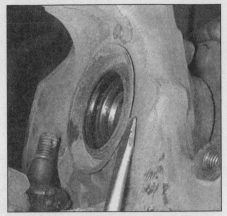

8.9a Pry the seal out of the knuckle with a screwdriver

8.9b Using a large socket, drive the new seal into place

must be replaced.

9   If the hub and bearing assembly is being replaced, a new steering knuckle dust seal must be installed in the steering knuckle prior to installation of the hub and bearing assembly. Remove the driveaxle assembly (see Chapter 8), pry the old seal out of the knuckle with a screwdriver **(see illustration)** and, using a large socket, drive the new seal into place **(see illustration)**. Install the driveaxle.

10   Install the hub and bearing assembly onto the driveaxle. Install the hub nut onto the driveaxle and tighten it until the hub and bearing assembly is seated.

11   Install the shield and hub assembly attaching bolts. Tighten the hub attaching bolts to the torque listed in this Chapter's Specifications.

12   Install the brake disc and caliper (see Chapter 9).

13   Install the wheel and lower the car to the ground.

14   Tighten the hub nut to the torque listed in the Chapter 8 Specifications. Tighten the wheel lug nuts to the torque listed in the Chapter 1 Specifications.

9   Steering knuckle - removal and installation

Removal

1   Raise the front of the vehicle and support it securely on jackstands.

2   Remove the front wheel.

3   Loosen the front hub nut. This can be accomplished by inserting a screwdriver or similar tool through the caliper into the brake disc cooling vanes to lock the disc.

4   Remove the brake caliper and disc (see Chapter 9)

5   Disconnect the driveaxle from the hub (see Chapter 8).

6   Disconnect the lower balljoint (see Section 6).

7   Remove the strut-to-knuckle bolts (see Section 2) and lift the steering knuckle from the vehicle.

Installation

8   Place the steering knuckle in position and install the attaching bolts finger tight.

9   Connect the knuckle to the balljoint, install the nut and tighten the nut to the torque listed in this Chapter's Specifications. Use a new cotter pin.

10   Tighten the strut-to-knuckle bolts to the torque listed in this Chapter's Specifications.

11   Connect the driveaxle and install the hub nut.

12   Install the brake rotor and caliper.

13   Install the front wheel, lower the vehicle and tighten the hub nut to the torque listed in the Chapter 8 Specifications. Tighten the wheel lug nuts to the torque listed in the Chapter 1 Specifications.

10   Rear shock absorbers - removal, inspection and installation

Removal

Refer to illustrations 10.1a, 10.1b and 10.3

1   Open the trunk or hatch, remove any trim which would interfere with access and remove the cover and upper shock absorber nut **(see illustrations)**. If both shock absor-

bers are to be replaced, complete one replacement procedure before starting the other to avoid damage to the brake lines and hoses (the shock absorbers limit the downward travel of the suspension).

2   Raise the vehicle and support it securely on jackstands. If the vehicle is being raised by the chassis, support the rear axle with a jack or jackstands.

3   Remove the lower shock absorber attaching bolt **(see illustration)** and remove the shock absorber from the vehicle.

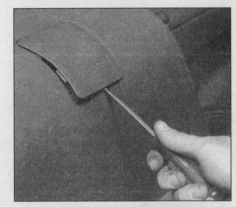

10.1a Pry off the access cover . . .

10.1b . . . then hold the shock absorber shaft with the smaller wrench and remove the shock retaining nut with the larger one

10.3 To disconnect the shock absorber from the rear axle assembly, remove this bolt (arrow)

11.2 Support the axle assembly control arms with floor jacks and blocks of wood as shown, then carefully lower the axle to remove the spring; after the new spring is installed, raise the axle assembly high enough to install the shock absorber-to-axle bolts and nuts

Installation

4   Place the shock absorber in position on the axle and install the bolt finger tight. Make sure the bushings and washers are installed in the correct order.
5   Lower the vehicle or raise the axle sufficiently to feed the upper stud of the shock absorber through the body opening and install the nut loosely.
6   Tighten the lower shock absorber bolt to the torque listed in this Chapter's Specifications.
7   Remove the axle support, lower the vehicle weight onto the suspension and tighten the upper nut to the torque listed in this Chapter's Specifications.
8   Replace the cover and trim.

---

11   Coil springs and insulators - removal and installation

Removal

Refer to illustration 11.2
1   Raise the vehicle by the chassis and support it securely on jackstands.
2   Support the rear control arms securely on two floor jacks. Place blocks of wood between the jack heads and the control arm **(see illustration).**
3   Remove the rear wheels.
4   Disconnect the brake line brackets by removing the retaining screws.
5   Remove the shock absorber lower attaching bolts (see Section 10).
6   Lower the rear axle with the jacks until the spring and insulator assemblies can be removed. Keep the springs separate so they are reinstalled in their original locations.

13.3 If a Torx bit isn't available, hold the hub bolts with a pair of locking pliers while loosening the nuts

Installation

7   With the help of an assistant, place the insulator, spring and compression bumper in position and slowly raise the control arms with the jacks, guiding the springs into place. The jacks must be placed under the control arms below the shock absorber mount to obtain the leverage needed to raise the arms evenly.
8   Install the shock absorber bolts and tighten them to the torque listed in this Chapter's Specifications.
9   Connect the brake line brackets, install the wheels and lower the vehicle.

---

12   Stabilizer bar (rear) - removal and installation

Removal

1   Raise the rear of the vehicle, support it on jackstands and remove the rear wheels.
2   Remove the retaining nuts from the clamps that attach the ends of the stabilizer bar to the control arms and from the U-bolts that attach the bar to the axle beam. Remove the stabilizer bar assembly from the vehicle.

Installation

3   Install the U-bolts, upper clamps, spacers and insulators on the axle beam and install the stabilizer bar with the lower clamp nuts finger tight. Make sure the spacers between the U-bolt nuts and the axle beam are in firm contact with the axle beam after the nuts are installed.
4   Connect the stabilizer bar to the control arms, install the retaining nuts and tighten them to torque listed in this Chapter's Specifications.
5   Tighten the stabilizer bar-to-axle U-bolt nuts to the torque listed in this Chapter's Specifications.
6   Install the wheels and lower the vehicle.

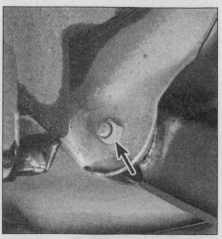

14.8 To disconnect the rear axle assembly from the vehicle, remove the pivot bolts (arrow) that attach the axle control arms to the body (left side shown)

---

13   Hub and bearing assembly (rear) - removal and installation

Refer to illustration 13.3
1   Raise the rear of the vehicle and support it securely on jackstands.
2   Remove the brake assembly (see Chapter 9).
3   Remove the four retaining nuts. The bolts have Torx heads and a special tool to hold the heads of the bolts will be necessary. Alternatively, locking pliers can be used to hold the bolts while the nuts are removed **(see illustration).**
4   After removing the last bolt, be prepared to support the weight of hub and bearing assembly and lower it from the vehicle.

Installation

5   Place the hub and bearing assembly in position on the axle, install the bolts and nuts and tighten them to the torque listed in this Chapter's Specifications.
6   Install the brake assembly.

---

14   Rear axle assembly - removal and installation

Removal

Refer to illustration 14.8
1   Loosen the rear wheel lug nuts. Raise the rear of the vehicle, support it securely on jackstands placed under the frame and remove the rear wheels.
2   Support the control arms with floor jacks **(see illustration 11.2).**
3   Remove the stabilizer bar (if equipped) (see Section 12).
4   Disconnect the shock absorber lower ends from the control arms (see Section 10).
5   Disconnect the parking brake cable (see Chapter 9).

16.2 Typical steering wheel installation

16.3 Mark the relationship of the steering wheel to the steering shaft before pulling off the wheel

16.5 Use a steering wheel puller to detach the steering wheel from the steering shaft

6   Disconnect and plug the brake line at the axle assembly bracket (see Chapter 9).
7   Remove the rear springs and insulators (see Section 11).
8   Remove the bolts attaching the control arms to the chassis **(see illustration)** and lower the axle from the vehicle.

Installation

9   Install the stabilizer bar to the axle (see Section 12).
10   Raise the axle into position with a jack.
11   Install the control arm-to-chassis bolts but don't tighten them at this time.
12   Connect the brake line and parking brake cable (see Chapter 9).
13   Install the spring and insulator assemblies (see Section 11) and tighten the shock absorber nuts to the torque listed in this Chapter's Specifications.
14   Install the wheels, connect the parking brake cable to the guide hook and adjust the parking brake (see Chapter 9).
15   Bleed the brake system (see Chapter 9).
16   Lower the vehicle weight onto the suspension and tighten the control arm-to-chassis bolts to the torque listed in this Chapter's Specifications.

15 Steering system - general information

Warning: *Whenever any of the steering fasteners are removed, they must be inspected and, if necessary, replaced with new ones of the same part number or of original equipment quality and design. Torque specifications must be followed for proper reassembly and component retention. Never attempt to heat or straighten any suspension or steering components. Instead, replace any bent or damaged part with a new one.*

1   All models covered by this manual use a rack-and-pinion steering system. The components making up the system are the steering wheel, steering column, intermediate shaft, rack-and-pinion steering gear assembly, tie-rods, struts and steering knuckles. The power steering system uses a belt-driven pump to provide hydraulic pressure.
2   In a manual system, the motion of turning the steering wheel is transferred through the column and intermediate shaft to the pinion shaft in the rack-and-pinion assembly. Teeth on the pinion shaft are meshed with teeth on the rack, so when the shaft is turned, the rack is moved left or right in the housing. The inner ends of the tie-rods are attached to the middle of the rack; their outer ends are attached to the struts, which are bolted to the steering knuckles. This left and right movement of the rack is the direct force which turns the wheels.
3   The power steering system operates in essentially the same way as the manual system, except that the power rack-and-pinion system uses hydraulic pressure to boost the manual steering force. A rotary control valve in the rack-and-pinion assembly directs hydraulic fluid from the power steering pump to either side of the integral rack piston, which is attached to the rack. Depending on which side of the piston this hydraulic pressure is applied to, the rack will be forced either left or right, which moves the tie-rods, etc.
4   If the power steering system loses its hydraulic pressure it will still function manually, though with increased effort.
5   The steering column is of the collapsible, energy-absorbing type, designed to compress in the event of a front end collision to minimize injury to the driver. The column also houses the ignition switch lock, key warning buzzer, turn signal controls, headlight dimmer control and windshield wiper controls. The ignition and steering wheel can both be locked to inhibit theft while the car is parked.
6   Due to the column's collapsible design, it is important that only original equipment screws, bolts and nuts be used as designated and that they be tightened to the specified torque values. Other precautions partic-
ular to this design are noted in appropriate Sections.
7   In addition to the standard steering column, optional tilt and key release versions are also offered. The tilt model can be set in various positions, while with the key release model the ignition key is locked in the column until a lever is depressed to extract it.
8   Because disassembly of the steering column is more often performed to repair a switch or other electrical part than to correct a problem in the steering functioning, the steering column disassembly and reassembly procedure is included in Chapter 12.

16 Steering wheel - removal and installation

Removal

Refer to illustrations 16.2, 16.3 and 16.5

1   Disconnect the negative battery cable. **Caution:** *If the vehicle is equipped with a Delco Loc II audio system, make sure you have the correct activation code before disconnecting the battery. See the information at the front of this manual for the radio re-activation procedure.*
2   Remove the horn pad **(see illustration)**.
3   Mark the relative position of the steering wheel and shaft for installation in the same position **(see illustration)**.
4   Remove the retaining nut.
5   Use a steering wheel puller to remove the steering wheel from the shaft **(see illustration)**. **Caution:** *Don't beat on the shaft with a hammer in an attempt to remove the wheel - this will damage the steering column.*

Installation

6   Place the steering wheel in position, aligning the marks made during removal.
7   Install the nut and tighten to the torque listed in this Chapter's Specifications
8   Install the horn pad and connect the battery negative cable.

17.2 Before disconnecting the tie-rod end from the steering arm, loosen the pinch bolt (arrow)

17 Tie-rod end - removal and installation

Removal

Refer to illustrations 17.2, 17.3 and 17.4

1   Loosen the wheel lug nuts, raise the vehicle and support it securely on jackstands. Remove the wheel.

2   Loosen the tie-rod end pinch bolt **(see illustration)**.

3   Disconnect the tie-rod end from the steering knuckle or strut arm with a puller **(see illustration)**.

4   Mark the relationship of the tie-rod end to the threaded adjuster **(see illustration)**. This will ensure that the toe-in setting is restored when reassembled.

5   Unscrew the tie-rod end from the inner tie-rod. **Caution:** *Do NOT loosen the inner tie-rod pinch bolt and remove the threaded adjuster. Removing the adjuster is unnecessary for this procedure, and removal of the adjuster will make it even more difficult to maintain the correct toe-in adjustment.*

18.3 Roll back the boot at the bottom of the steering column and you'll find the steering coupler assembly - remove the upper steering coupler pinch bolt (arrow)

17.3 A two-jaw puller works well for separating the tie-rod end from the steering arm - if the tapered stud hangs up in the bore, it's okay to rap the steering arm to free it up, but DON'T POUND ON THE STUD!

Installation

6   Thread the tie-rod end onto the adjuster to the marked position. Connect the tie-rod end to the steering arm. Install the castellated nut and tighten it to the torque listed in this Chapter's Specifications. Install a new cotter pin. If necessary, tighten the nut a little more to insert the cotter pin - never loosen the nut to allow cotter pin installation.

7   Install the pinch bolt and tighten it to the torque listed in this Chapter's Specifications. Install the wheel and lug nuts. Lower the vehicle and tighten the lug nuts to the torque listed in the Chapter 1 Specifications.

8   Have the front end alignment checked by a dealer service department or an alignment shop.

18 Steering gear - removal and installation

Removal

Refer to illustrations 18.3 and 18.10

Note: *If the steering gear on your vehicle is a manual unit, disregard any Steps which refer to a power unit.*

1   Disconnect the cable from the negative battery terminal. **Caution:** *If the vehicle is equipped with a Delco Loc II audio system, make sure you have the correct activation code before disconnecting the battery. See the information at the front of this manual for the radio re-activation procedure.*

2   Remove the left (driver's side) under-dash panel.

3   Peel back the boot at the bottom of the steering column to expose the flange and steering coupler assembly. Mark the coupler to the steering column shaft and remove the upper pinch bolt **(see illustration)**.

4   Remove the two left (driver's side) steer-

17.4 Mark the relationship of the tie-rod end to the tie-rod

ing gear-to-firewall clamp nuts and the right (passenger's side) upper clamp nut.

5   Remove the pressure hose retainer from the support bracket at the center of the rack.

6   Place a drain pan or tray under the vehicle, positioned beneath the left side of the steering gear. Using a flare nut wrench, disconnect the pressure and return lines from the steering gear (the two lines closest to the firewall, angled toward the left side of the vehicle). Plug the lines to prevent excessive fluid loss.

7   Loosen the front wheel lug nuts, raise the vehicle and support it securely on jackstands. Remove both front wheels.

8   Remove the lower right (passenger's side) steering gear clamp nut.

9   Separate the tie-rod ends from the steering arms (see Section 17).

10   Move the steering gear forward and remove the lower pinch bolt **(see illustration)** from the coupler. Slide the coupler off the pinion shaft.

11   Support the steering gear and carefully maneuver the entire assembly out through the left (driver's side) wheel opening.

18.10 The lower steering column coupler pinch bolt (arrow)

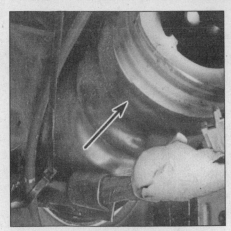

18.15a After you reattach the coupler between the steering gear and the steering column, make sure you install the seal correctly to protect the coupler from dirt and water (arrow)

18.15b Make sure the steering gear clamps are installed with the "TOP" markings facing up

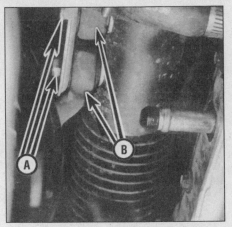

19.2 Remove the inner tie-rod bolts (A) and detach the inner tie-rods from the steering gear (B)

Installation

Refer to illustrations 18.15a and 18.15b

12   If any of the mounting studs came out with the clamps, apply a thread locking compound to the firewall side of the threads and install them snugly into the firewall.

13   Pass the steering gear assembly through the left (driver's side) wheel opening into approximate position.

14   Install the coupler and tighten the lower pinch bolt securely.

15   Center the steering gear, ensuring that the dash seal is installed properly **(see illustration)**. Have an assistant guide the coupler onto the steering column shaft, with the previously applied marks aligned. Position the right (passenger's side) clamp and install the lower clamp nut, tightening it to the torque listed in this Chapter's Specifications. **Note:** *Make sure the clamps are installed with the "TOP" markings facing up* **(see illustration)**.

16   Connect the tie-rod ends to the steering arms and tighten the nuts to the torque listed in this Chapter's Specifications. Install new cotter pins.

17   Install the front wheels, lower the vehicle and tighten the lug nuts to the torque listed in the Chapter 1 Specifications.

18   Install the pressure and return lines to the steering gear. Connect the line retainer to the support bracket.

19   Install the left (driver's side) clamp and nuts and the upper right (passenger's side) clamp nut, tightening them to the torque listed in this Chapter's Specifications.

20   Install the upper pinch bolt in the coupler and tighten it to the torque listed in this Chapter's Specifications.

21   Install the under-dash panel.

22   Reconnect the negative battery cable.

23   Fill the power steering pump with the recommended fluid, bleed the system of air (see Section 21) and recheck the fluid level. Check for leaks.

24   Have the front end alignment checked by a dealer service department or an alignment shop.

19   Steering gear boot - replacement

Refer to illustration 19.2

1   Remove the steering gear from the vehicle (see Section 18).

2   Detach the inner tie-rods from the steering gear **(see illustration)**.

3   Using a flare nut wrench, remove the hydraulic cylinder lines from the steering gear assembly. **Note:** *Use new O-rings when you reconnect the lines.*

4   Remove the right mounting grommet from the rack housing.

5   Cut off both boot clamps and discard them.

6   Slide the cylinder end (right end) of the boot toward the center of the steering gear, enough to expose the boot groove. Place a rubber band in the groove to occupy the space then slide the boot off of the steering gear.

7   Install a new clamp on the left end of the boot and insert the boot retaining bushing into the end of the boot. Apply multi-purpose grease to the inside diameter of the bushing and slide the boot onto the steering gear housing.

8   Press the center housing cover washers into the center housing cover.

9   Align the center housing bolt holes with the rack guide assembly and install the two tie-rod bolts. This will ensure proper alignment of the center housing, rack and rack guide.

10   Tighten the left side boot clamp.

11   Slide the right end of the boot onto the housing, remove the rubber band and seat the boot into the boot groove. Install the clamp and tighten it.

12   Install the hydraulic cylinder lines.

13   Install the inner tie-rods as shown in illustration 19.2 and tighten the bolts to the torque listed in this Chapter's Specifications.

14   Install the mounting grommet.

15   Install the steering gear assembly.

20   Power steering pump - removal and installation

Removal

1   Disconnect the negative battery cable.

2   Remove the air cleaner assembly.

3   Disconnect the pressure line from the pump and remove the clip which secures the line to the pump.

4   Loosen the adjustment and pivot bolts and remove the drivebelt.

5   Remove the pump-to-bracket bolts and lift the pump from the engine.

Installation

6   Place the pump in position on the bracket, install the retaining bolts and tighten them securely.

7   Fasten the pressure line to the pump with the clip but do not connect it.

8   Connect the reservoir-to-pump hose.

9   Add the specified power steering fluid to the reservoir until the fluid can be seen at the pressure line port.

10   Connect the pressure line and secure the clip.

11   Install and adjust the drivebelt.

12   Install the air cleaner and connect the negative battery cable.

13   Bleed the system (see Section 21).

21   Power steering system - bleeding

1   Following any operation in which the power steering fluid lines have been disconnected, the power steering system must be bled of air to obtain proper steering performance.

2   With the front wheels turned all the way to the left, check the power steering fluid level and, if low, add fluid until it reaches the

METRIC TIRE SIZES
P 185 / 80 R 13

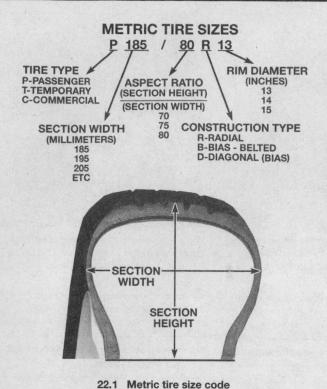

TIRE TYPE
P-PASSENGER
T-TEMPORARY
C-COMMERCIAL

ASPECT RATIO
(SECTION HEIGHT)
―――――――――――
(SECTION WIDTH)
70
75
80

RIM DIAMETER
(INCHES)
13
14
15

SECTION WIDTH
(MILLIMETERS)
185
195
205
ETC

CONSTRUCTION TYPE
R-RADIAL
B-BIAS - BELTED
D-DIAGONAL (BIAS)

SECTION WIDTH

SECTION HEIGHT

22.1 Metric tire size code

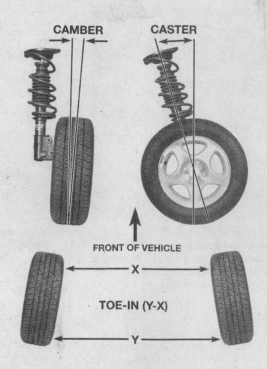

CAMBER   CASTER

FRONT OF VEHICLE

X

TOE-IN (Y-X)

Y

23.1 Camber, caster and toe-in angles

Cold mark on the dipstick.

3 Start the engine and allow it to run at fast idle. Recheck the fluid level and add more if necessary to reach the Cold mark on the dipstick.

4 Bled the system by turning the wheels from side to side, without hitting the stops. This will work the air out of the system. Be careful that the reservoir does not run empty of fluid.

5 When the air is worked out of the system, return the wheels to the straight ahead position and leave the car running for several more minutes before shutting it off.

6 Road test the car to be sure the steering system is functioning normally and is free from noise.

7 Recheck the fluid level to be sure it is up to the Hot mark on the dipstick while the engine is at normal operating temperature. Add fluid if necessary.

22 Wheels and tires - general information

Refer to illustration 22.1

All vehicles covered by this manual are equipped with metric-sized radial tires **(see illustration)**. Use of other size or type of tires may affect the ride and handling of the vehicle. Don't mix different types of tires, such as radials and bias belted, on the same vehicle as handling may be seriously affected. It's recommended that tires be replaced in pairs on the same axle, but if only one tire is being replaced, be sure it's the same size, structure

and tread design as the other.

Because tire pressure has a substantial effect on handling and wear, the pressure on all tires should be checked at least once a month or before any extended trips (see Chapter 1).

Wheels must be replaced if they are bent, dented, leak air, have elongated bolt holes, are heavily rusted, out of vertical symmetry or if the lug nuts won't stay tight. Wheel repairs that use welding or peening are not recommended.

Tire and wheel balance is important to the overall handling, braking and performance of the vehicle. Unbalanced wheels can adversely affect handling and ride characteristics as well as tire life. Whenever a tire is installed on a wheel, the tire and wheel should be balanced by a shop with the proper equipment.

23 Front end alignment - general information

Refer to illustration 23.1

A front end alignment refers to the adjustments made to the front wheels so they are in proper angular relationship to the suspension and the ground. Front wheels that are out of proper alignment not only affect steering control, but also increase tire wear **(see illustration)**.

Getting the proper front wheel alignment is a very exacting process, one in which complicated and expensive machines are necessary to perform the job properly. Because of

this, you should have a technician with the proper equipment perform these tasks. We will, however, use this space to give you a basic idea of what is involved with front end alignment so you can better understand the process and deal intelligently with the shop that does the work.

Toe-in is the turning in of the front wheels. The purpose of a toe specification is to ensure parallel rolling of the front wheels. In a vehicle with zero toe-in, the distance between the front edges of the wheels will be the same as the distance between the rear edges of the wheels. The actual amount of toe-in is normally only a fraction of an inch. Toe-in adjustment is controlled by the tie-rod end position on the tie-rod. Incorrect toe-in will cause the tires to wear improperly by making them scrub against the road surface.

Camber is the tilting of the front wheels from the vertical when viewed from the front of the vehicle. When the wheels tilt out at the top, the camber is said to be positive (+). When the wheels tilt in at the top the camber is negative (-). The amount of tilt is measured in degrees from the vertical and this measurement is called the camber angle. This angle affects the amount of tire tread which contacts the road and compensates for changes in the suspension geometry when the vehicle is cornering or traveling over an undulating surface.

Caster is the tilting of the top of the front steering axis from the vertical. A tilt toward the rear is positive caster and a tilt toward the front is negative caster.

Chapter 11 Body

Contents

1 General information

Caution: *If the vehicle is equipped with a Delco Loc II audio system, make sure you have the correct activation code before disconnecting the battery. See the information at the front of this manual for the radio re-activation procedure.*

The vehicles covered by this manual are available in four models: Two-door coupe, two-door hatchback, four-door sedan and a four-door wagon. Differences between the various models are noted where appropriate in the service procedures within this Chapter.

These vehicles are of unitized construction, in which the body is designed to provide vehicle rigidity so that a separate frame is not necessary. Front and rear frame side rails, integral with the body, support the front end sheet metal, front and rear suspension systems and other mechanical components. Due to this type of construction, it is very important that, in the event of collision damage, the underbody be thoroughly checked by a facility with the proper equipment to do so.

Only general body maintenance practices and body panel repair procedures within the scope of the do-it-yourselfer are included in this Chapter.

2 Body - maintenance

1   The condition of your vehicle's body is very important, the resale value depends a great deal on it. It is much more difficult to repair a neglected or damaged body than it is to repair mechanical components. The hidden areas of the body, such as the wheel wells, the frame and the engine compartment, are equally important, although obviously do not require as frequent attention as the rest of the body.

2   Once a year, or every 12,000 miles, it is a good idea to have the underside of the body and the frame steam cleaned. All traces of dirt and oil will be removed and the underside can then be inspected carefully for rust, damaged brake lines, frayed electrical wiring, damaged cables, and other problems. The front suspension components should be greased after completion of this job.

3   At the same time, clean the engine and the engine compartment using either a steam cleaner or a water soluble degreaser.

4   The wheel wells should be given particular attention, as undercoating can peel away and stones and dirt thrown up by the tires can cause the paint to chip and flake, allowing rust to set in. If rust is found, clean down to the bare metal and apply an anti-rust paint.

5   The body should be washed once a week (or when dirty). Wet the vehicle thoroughly to soften the dirt, then wash it down with a soft sponge and plenty of clean, soapy water. If the surplus dirt is not washed off very carefully, it will in time wear down the paint.

6   Spots of tar or asphalt coating thrown up from the road should be removed with a cloth soaked in solvent.

7   Once every six months, give the body and chrome trim a thorough waxing. If a chrome cleaner is used to remove rust from any of the vehicle's plated parts, remember that the cleaner also removes part of the chrome, so use it sparingly.

3 Upholstery and carpets - maintenance

1   Every three months remove the carpets or mats and clean the interior of the vehicle (more frequently if necessary). Vacuum the upholstery and carpets to remove loose dirt and dust.

2   If the upholstery is soiled, apply upholstery cleaner with a damp sponge and wipe it off with a clean, dry cloth.

3   Leather upholstery requires special care. Stains should be removed with warm water and a very mild soap solution. Use a clean, damp cloth to remove the soap, then wipe again with a dry cloth. Never use gasoline, nail polish remover or thinner to clean leather upholstery.

4   In areas where the interior of the vehicle is subject to bright sunlight, cover leather seats with a sheet if the vehicle is to be left out for any length of time.

4   Vinyl trim - maintenance

Vinyl trim should not be cleaned with detergents, caustic soaps or petroleum-based cleaners. Plain soap and water or a mild vinyl cleaner is best for stains. Test a small area for color fastness. Bubbles under the vinyl can be corrected by piercing them with a pin and then working the air out.

5   Hinges and locks - maintenance

Every 3000 miles or three months, the door, hood and trunk/liftgate hinges and locks should be lubricated with a few drops of oil. The door, trunk and liftgate striker plates should also be given a thin coat of grease to reduce wear and ensure free movement.

6   Body repair - minor damage

See photo sequence

Repair of minor scratches

1   If the scratch is very superficial and does not penetrate to the metal of the body, repair is very simple. Lightly rub the scratched area with a fine rubbing compound to remove loose paint and built-up wax. Rinse the area with clean water.

2   Apply touch-up paint to the scratch, using a small brush. Continue to apply thin layers of paint until the surface of the paint in the scratch is level with the surrounding paint. Allow the new paint at least two weeks to harden, then blend it into the surrounding paint by rubbing with a very fine rubbing compound. Finally, apply a coat of wax to the scratch area.

3   If the scratch has penetrated the paint and exposed the metal of the body, causing the metal to rust, a different repair technique is required. Remove all loose rust from the bottom of the scratch with a pocket knife, then apply rust inhibiting paint to prevent the formation of rust in the future. Using a rubber or nylon applicator, coat the scratched area with glaze-type filler. If required, the filler can be mixed with thinner to provide a very thin paste, which is ideal for filling narrow scratches. Before the glaze filler in the scratch hardens, wrap a piece of smooth cotton cloth around the tip of a finger. Dip the

cloth in thinner and then quickly wipe it along the surface of the scratch. This will ensure that the surface of the filler is slightly hollow. The scratch can now be painted over as described earlier in this section.

Repair of dents

4   When repairing dents, the first job is to pull the dent out until the affected area is as close as possible to its original shape. There is no point in trying to restore the original shape completely as the metal in the damaged area will have stretched on impact and cannot be restored to its original contours. It is better to bring the level of the dent up to a point which is about 1/8-inch below the level of the surrounding metal. In cases where the dent is very shallow, it is not worth trying to pull it out at all.

5   If the back side of the dent is accessible, it can be hammered out gently from behind using a soft-face hammer. While doing this, hold a block of wood firmly against the opposite side of the metal to absorb the hammer blows and prevent the metal from being stretched.

6   If the dent is in a section of the body which has double layers, or some other factor that makes it inaccessible from behind, a different technique is required. Drill several small holes through the metal inside the damaged area, particularly in the deeper sections. Screw long, self-tapping screws into the holes just enough for them to get a good grip in the metal. Now the dent can be pulled out by pulling on the protruding heads of the screws with locking pliers.

7   The next stage of repair is the removal of paint from the damaged area and from an inch or so of the surrounding metal. This is easily done with a wire brush or sanding disk in a drill motor, although it can be done just as effectively by hand with sandpaper. To complete the preparation for filling, score the surface of the bare metal with a screwdriver or the tang of a file (or drill small holes in the affected area). This will provide a good grip for the filler material. To complete the repair, see the Section on *filling and painting*.

Repair of rust holes or gashes

8   Remove all paint from the affected area and from an inch or so of the surrounding metal, using a sanding disk or wire brush mounted in a drill motor. If these are not available, a few sheets of sandpaper will do the job just as effectively.

9   With the paint removed you will be able to determine the severity of the corrosion and decide whether to replace the whole panel, if possible, or repair the affected area. New body panels are not as expensive as most people think and it is often quicker to install a new panel than to repair large areas of rust.

10   Remove all trim pieces from the affected area except those which will act as a guide to the original shape of the damaged body, such as headlight shells, etc. Using metal snips or a hacksaw blade, remove all loose

metal and any other metal that is badly affected by rust. Hammer the edges of the hole in to create a slight depression for the filler material.

11   Wire brush the affected area to remove the powdery rust from the surface of the metal. If the back of the rusted area is accessible, treat it with rust inhibiting paint.

12   Before filling is done, block the hole in some way. This can be done with sheet metal riveted or screwed into place, or by stuffing the hole with wire mesh.

13   Once the hole is blocked off, the affected area can be filled and painted.

Filling and painting

14   Many types of body fillers are available, but generally speaking, body repair kits which contain filler paste and a tube of resin hardener are best for this type of repair work. A wide, flexible plastic or nylon applicator will be necessary for imparting a smooth and contoured finish to the surface of the filler material. Mix up a small amount of filler on a clean piece of wood or cardboard (use the hardener sparingly). Follow the manufacturer's instructions on the package, otherwise the filler will set incorrectly.

15   Using the applicator, apply the filler paste to the prepared area. Draw the applicator across the surface of the filler to achieve the desired contour and to level the filler surface. As soon as a contour that approximates the original one is achieved, stop working the paste. If you continue, the paste will begin to stick to the applicator. Continue to add thin layers of paste at 20-minute intervals until the level of the filler is just above the surrounding metal.

16   Once the filler has hardened, the excess can be removed with a body file. From then on, progressively finer grades of sandpaper should be used, starting with a 180-grit paper and finishing with 600-grit wet-or-dry paper. Always wrap the sandpaper around a flat rubber or wooden block, otherwise the surface of the filler will not be completely flat. During the sanding of the filler surface, the wet-or-dry paper should be periodically rinsed in water. This will ensure that a very smooth finish is produced in the final stage.

17   At this point the repair area should be surrounded by a ring of bare metal, which in turn should be encircled by the finely feathered edge of good paint. Rinse the repair area with clean water until all of the dust produced by the sanding operation is gone.

18   Spray the entire area with a light coat of primer. This will reveal any imperfections in the surface of the filler. Repair the imperfections with fresh filler paste or glaze filler and once more smooth the surface with sandpaper. Repeat this spray-and-repair procedure until you are satisfied that the surface of the filler and the feathered edge of the paint are perfect. Rinse the area with clean water and allow it to dry completely.

19   The repair area is now ready for painting. Spray painting must be carried out in a warm, dry, windless and dust free atmo-

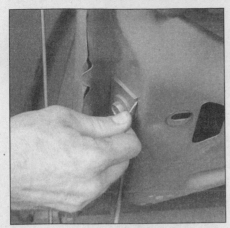

9.1 Scribe or draw a line around both hinge plates

10.1 Disconnect the latch release cable while holding the bracket with needle-nose pliers

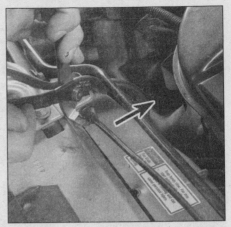

10.2 Grasp the cable securely with pliers and detach it from the bracket as shown

sphere. These conditions can be created if you have access to a large indoor work area, but if you are forced to work in the open, you will have to pick the day very carefully. If you are working indoors, dousing the floor in the work area with water will help settle the dust which would otherwise be in the air.

20   If the repair area is confined to one body panel, mask off the surrounding panels. This will help minimize the effects of a slight mismatch in paint color. Trim pieces such as chrome strips, door handles, etc., will also need to be masked off or removed. Use masking tape and several thicknesses of newspaper for the masking operations.

21   Before spraying, shake the paint can thoroughly, then spray a test area until the spray painting technique is mastered. Cover the repair area with a thick coat of primer. The thickness should be built up using several thin layers of primer, rather than one thick one. Using 600-grit wet-or-dry sandpaper, rub down the surface of the primer until it is very smooth. While doing this, the work area should be thoroughly rinsed with water and the wet-or-dry sandpaper periodically rinsed as well. Allow the primer to dry before spraying additional coats.

22   Spray on the top coat, again building up the thickness by using several thin layers of paint. Begin spraying in the center of the repair area and then, using a circular motion, work out until the whole repair area and about two inches of the surrounding original paint is covered. Remove all masking material 10 to 15 minutes after spraying on the final coat of paint. Allow the new paint at least two weeks to harden, then use a very fine rubbing compound to blend the edges of the new paint into the existing paint. Finally, apply a coat of wax.

7   Body repair - major damage

1   Major damage must be repaired by an auto body shop specifically equipped to perform unibody repairs. These shops have

available the specialized equipment required to do the job properly.

2   If the damage is extensive, the underbody must be checked for proper alignment or the vehicle's handling characteristics may be adversely affected and other components may wear at an accelerated rate.

3   Due to the fact that all of the major body components (hood, fenders, etc.) are separate and replaceable units, any seriously damaged components should be replaced rather than repaired. Sometimes these components can be found in a wrecking yard that specializes in used vehicle components, often at considerable savings over the cost of new parts.

8   Windshield and fixed glass - replacement

Replacement of the windshield and fixed glass requires the use of special fast-setting adhesive/caulk materials and some specialized tools and techniques. These operations should be left to a dealer service department or a shop specializing in glass work.

9   Hood – removal, installation and adjustment

Refer to illustration 9.1
Note: *The hood is heavy and somewhat awkward to remove and install – at least two people should perform this procedure.*

Removal and installation

1   Make marks around the bolt heads and mounting brackets to ensure proper alignment during installation **(see illustration)**.

2   Use blankets or pads to cover the cowl area of the body and fenders. This will protect the body and paint as the hood is lifted off.

3   Disconnect any cables or wires that will interfere with removal.

4   Have an assistant support the hood. Remove the hinge-to-hood bolts.

5   Lift off the hood.

6   Installation is the reverse of removal.

Adjustment

7   Fore-and-aft and side-to-side adjustment of the hood is done by moving the hinge plate slot after loosening the bolts.

8   Scribe or draw a line around the bolt heads and the entire hinge plate so you can judge the amount of movement **(see illustration 9.1)**.

9   Loosen the bolts and move the hood into correct alignment. Move it only a little at a time. Tighten the hinge bolts or nuts and carefully lower the hood to check the position.

10   If necessary after installation, the entire hood latch assembly can be adjusted up-and-down as well as from side-to-side on the radiator support so the hood closes securely, flush with the fenders. To make the adjustment, scribe a line around the hood latch mounting bolts to provide a reference point, then loosen them and reposition the latch assembly, as necessary . Following adjustment, retighten the mounting bolts.

11   Finally, adjust the hood bumpers on the radiator support so the hood, when closed, is flush with the fenders.

12   The hood latch assembly, as well as the hinges, should be periodically lubricated with lithium-base grease to prevent binding and wear.

10   Hood latch release cable - replacement

Refer to illustrations 10.1, 10.2, 10.3 and 10.4

1   In the engine compartment, disconnect the release cable from the latch mechanism **(see illustration)**.

2   Detach the cable from the retaining bracket with pliers **(see illustration)**.

These photos illustrate a method of repairing simple dents. They are intended to supplement *Body repair - minor damage* in this Chapter and should not be used as the sole instructions for body repair on these vehicles.

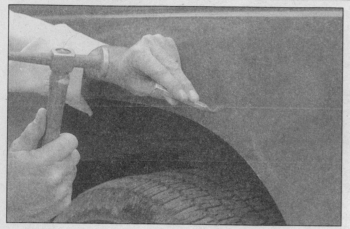

1   If you can't access the backside of the body panel to hammer out the dent, pull it out with a slide-hammer-type dent puller. In the deepest portion of the dent or along the crease line, drill or punch hole(s) at least one inch apart . . .

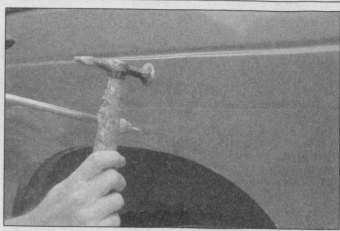

2   . . . then screw the slide-hammer into the hole and operate it. Tap with a hammer near the edge of the dent to help 'pop' the metal back to its original shape. When you're finished, the dent area should be close to its original contour and about 1/8-inch below the surface of the surrounding metal

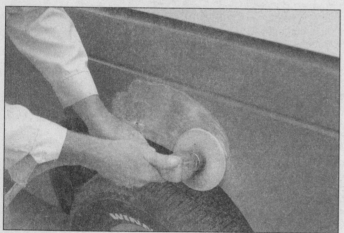

3   Using coarse-grit sandpaper, remove the paint down to the bare metal. Hand sanding works fine, but the disc sander shown here makes the job faster. Use finer (about 320-grit) sandpaper to feather-edge the paint at least one inch around the dent area

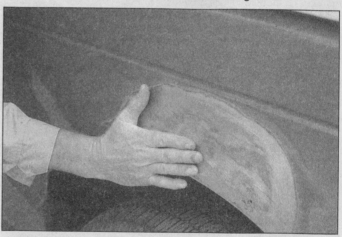

4   When the paint is removed, touch will probably be more helpful than sight for telling if the metal is straight. Hammer down the high spots or raise the low spots as necessary. Clean the repair area with wax/silicone remover

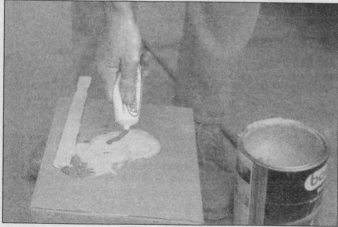

5   Following label instructions, mix up a batch of plastic filler and hardener. The ratio of filler to hardener is critical, and, if you mix it incorrectly, it will either not cure properly or cure too quickly (you won't have time to file and sand it into shape)

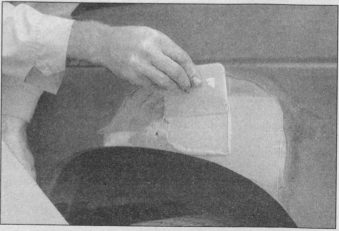

6   Working quickly so the filler doesn't harden, use a plastic applicator to press the body filler firmly into the metal, assuring it bonds completely. Work the filler until it matches the original contour and is slightly above the surrounding metal

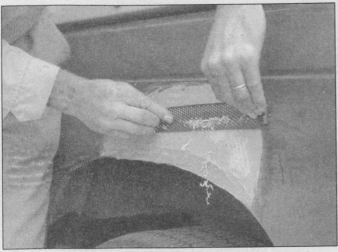

7   Let the filler harden until you can just dent it with your fingernail. Use a body file or Surform tool (shown here) to rough-shape the filler

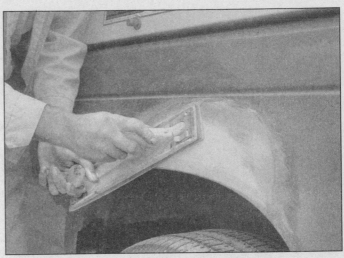

8   Use coarse-grit sandpaper and a sanding board or block to work the filler down until it's smooth and even. Work down to finer grits of sandpaper - always using a board or block - ending up with 360 or 400 grit

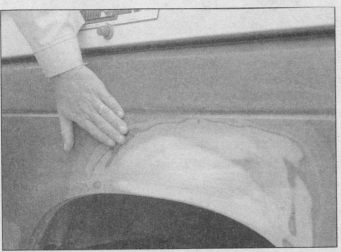

9   You shouldn't be able to feel any ridge at the transition from the filler to the bare metal or from the bare metal to the old paint. As soon as the repair is flat and uniform, remove the dust and mask off the adjacent panels or trim pieces

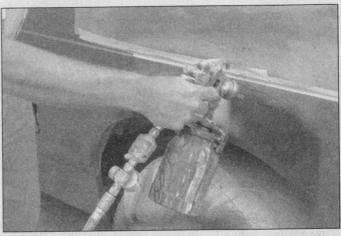

10   Apply several layers of primer to the area. Don't spray the primer on too heavy, so it sags or runs, and make sure each coat is dry before you spray on the next one. A professional-type spray gun is being used here, but aerosol spray primer is available inexpensively from auto parts stores

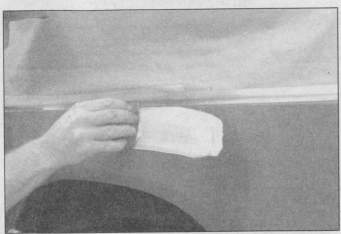

11   The primer will help reveal imperfections or scratches. Fill these with glazing compound. Follow the label instructions and sand it with 360 or 400-grit sandpaper until it's smooth. Repeat the glazing, sanding and respraying until the primer reveals a perfectly smooth surface

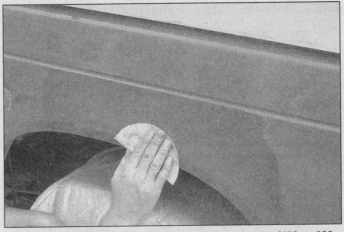

12   Finish sand the primer with very fine sandpaper (400 or 600-grit) to remove the primer overspray. Clean the area with water and allow it to dry. Use a tack rag to remove any dust, then apply the finish coat. Don't attempt to rub out or wax the repair area until the paint has dried completely (at least two weeks)

10.3 The parking brake handle is retained by screws, on this early model a Torx-head tool is required for removal

10.4 Use snap-ring or needle-nose pliers to unscrew the cable retainer

11.2a On later models, use a screwdriver to pry the upper retainer from the support

3   In the passenger compartment, remove the bolt holding the T-handle to its bracket **(see illustration)**.
4   Use needle-nose or snap-ring pliers to unscrew the cable retainer **(see illustration)**.
5   Connect string or thin wire to the end of the cable and remove the cable by pulling it through into the passenger compartment.
6   Installation is the reverse of removal after connecting the string or wire to the new cable and pulling it into position.

11 Liftgate supports - removal and installation

Refer to illustrations 11.2a, 11.2b and 11.2c
1   Support the liftgate in the fully open position.

Hatchback

2   On earlier models the upper ends of the supports can simply be pried free **(see illustration)**. On later models, use a screwdriver to remove the clips, then detach the support **(see illustration)**. The lower end of the supports are retained by bolts **(see illustration)**.

Station wagon

3   On these models, the struts are retained by clips at both ends.
4   Installation is the reverse of removal, taking care to replace the supports with ones of the correct length and capacity.

12 Liftgate - removal and installation

Removal

1   Open the liftgate and support it with a prop rod.
2   Place protective pads along the edges of the liftgate opening to prevent damage to the painted surfaces while work is being performed.

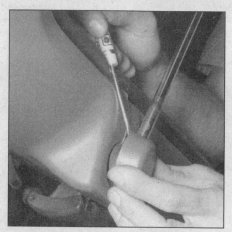

11.2b Pry off the lower strut cover . . .

3   Detach the liftgate supports from the liftgate (see Section 11) and support the liftgate in the fully open position.
4   Disconnect any cables or wire harness connectors attached to the liftgate that would interfere with removal.

Hatchback models

5   Make alignment marks around the hinge mounting flange.
6   Detach the headliner for access and remove the retaining nuts. While an assistant supports the liftgate, remove the nuts on both sides and lift it off.
7   Installation is the reverse of removal.
Note: *When reinstalling the liftgate, align the lid-to-hinge bolts with the marks made during removal.*
8   After installation, close the liftgate and make sure it's in proper alignment with the surrounding body.
9   Forward-or-backward and side-to-side adjustments are made by detaching the headliner, loosening the hinge to liftgate nuts and gently moving the liftgate into correct alignment.
10   The liftgate latch can be adjusted up-and-down as well as from side-to-side. To make the adjustment, scribe a line around the

11.2c . . . for access to the lower strut Torx-head bolt (arrow)

mounting bolts to provide a reference point, then loosen them and reposition the latch assembly, as necessary. Following adjustment, retighten the mounting bolts.

Station wagon models

11   If equipped, detach the trim panel covering the liftgate-to-body pins.
12   Place a 3/16-inch metal rod on the pointed end of the hinge pin. Strike the rod sharply with a hammer to shear off the retaining clip tabs and drive the pin out of the hinge. With the help of an assistant, remove the liftgate from the vehicle.
13   Installation is the reverse of removal, but new retaining clips must be installed with their tabs toward the head of the pins before the pins are driven into place.

13 Front fender - removal and installation

1   Loosen the wheel lug nuts. Raise the vehicle, support it securely on jackstands and remove the front wheel.
2   Disconnect the antenna and all light bulb electrical connectors and other compo-

15.2 Remove the three cowl vent retaining screws (arrows) and raise the cowl to gain access to the remaining mounting screws under the cowl

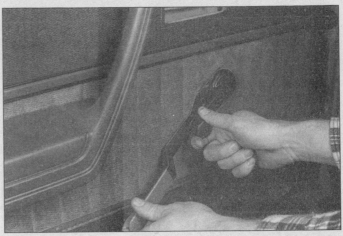

16.2 A special tool (available at most auto parts stores) can be used to remove the window crank

16.3 Disconnect the lock knob by detaching the locking rod with a small screwdriver inserted behind the leading edge

16.4 A trim panel removal tool can be used to pry the door panel off, but a putty knife or screwdriver will also work

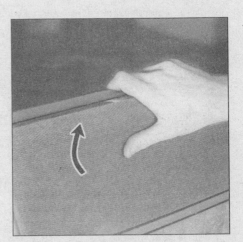

16.5 Detach the panel by lifting it up and off the top of the door

nents that would interfere with fender removal.
3   Remove the front bumper (see Section 17).
4   Remove the splash shield and fender mounting bolts.
5   Detach the fender. It is a good idea to have an assistant support the fender while it's being moved away from the vehicle to prevent damage to the surrounding body panels.
6   Installation is the reverse of removal. Tighten all nuts, bolts and screws securely.

14   Bumpers - removal and installation

1   Disconnect any wiring, bumper cover (if equipped) or other components that would interfere with bumper removal.
2   Support the bumper with a jack or jackstand. Alternatively, have an assistant support the bumper as the bolts are removed.

3   Installation is the reverse of removal. Tighten the retaining bolts securely.

15   Cowl vent panel – removal and installation

Refer to illustration 15.2
1   Remove the windshield wiper arms.
2   Remove the screws, detach the cowl vent panel and remove it from the vehicle (see illustration).
3   Installation is the reverse of removal.

16   Door trim panel – removal and installation

Refer to illustrations 16.2, 16.3, 16.4, 16.5 and 16.6
1   Disconnect the negative cable from the battery. Caution: If the vehicle is equipped with a Delco Loc II audio system, make sure you have the correct activation code before

disconnecting the battery. See the information at the front of this manual for the radio re-activation procedure.
2   Remove the window crank by detaching the retaining clip. A special tool, available at most auto parts stores, makes this job easier (see illustration). If this isn't available, working a cloth back-and-forth behind the handle will also dislodge the retainer. With the clip removed, pull off the handle.
3   Remove any door trim panel retaining screws and door pull/armrest assemblies (see illustration). Remove the speaker panels and the speaker assemblies.
4   Insert a trim panel removal tool or a wide putty knife or thin prybar between the trim panel and door to disengage the retaining clips (see illustration). Work around the outer edge until the panel is free.
5   Once all of the clips are disengaged, detach the trim panel, unplug any electrical connectors and remove the trim panel from the vehicle by gently pulling it up and out (see illustration).
6   For access to the inner door, peel back

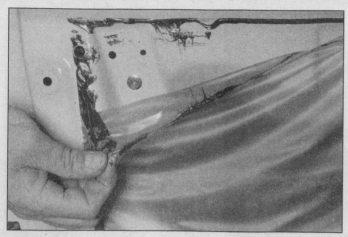

16.6 Peel the water deflector carefully away from the door, taking care not to tear or distort it

17.4 Use two small screwdrivers to spread the legs of the clip at the base of the pin (arrows) apart, then tap the pin out

the plastic water deflector or insulator, taking care not to tear it **(see illustration)**. To install the trim panel, first press the water deflector into place.

7   Prior to installation of the door panel, be sure to reinstall any clips in the panel which may have come out during the removal procedure and stayed in the door.

8   Plug in any electrical connectors and place the panel in position. Press it into place until the clips are seated and install any retaining screws and armrest/door pulls. Install the manual regulator window crank.

---

17   Door – removal and installation

Refer to illustration 17.4

1   Remove the door trim panel (see Section 16) and disconnect any electrical connectors and push them through the door opening so they won't interfere with removal.

2   Position a floor jack under the door or have an assistant on hand to support the door when the hinge pins are removed. **Note:** *If a jack is used, place a rag between it and the door to protect the door's paint.*

3   Detach the door return spring.

4   Remove the clips from the door hinge pins by using two small screwdrivers to spread the legs apart to move them toward the pointed end of the pin **(see illustration)**.

5   While an assistant grasps the lower end of the pin with pliers, use a plastic hammer to carefully tap the pin out. The clip will fall free as the pin is removed. Tap the upper pin out and remove the door from the vehicle.

6   Installation is the reverse of removal, taking care to reinstall the clips in the pins before installation.

---

18   Trunk lid - removal, installation and adjustment

1   Open the trunk lid and cover the edges of the trunk compartment with pads or cloths

to protect the painted surfaces when the lid is removed

2   Disconnect any cables or electrical connectors attached to the trunk lid that would interfere with removal.

3   Use a marking pen to make alignment marks around the hinge bolts.

4   While an assistant supports it's weight, remove the hinge bolts on both sides and lift the trunk lid off.

5   Installation is the reverse of the removal procedure. When reinstalling the lid, align the heads of the bolts with the marks made during removal.

6   After installation, close the lid and make sure it's in proper alignment with the surrounding body panels. Fore-and-aft and up-and-down adjustments of the lid are controlled by the position of the bolts in the hinge arms. To adjust it, loosen the hinge bolts, reposition the lid and retighten the bolts.

7   Side-to-side movement of the lid is adjusted by loosening the hinge-to-body nuts under the rear package shelf, moving the lid and then tightening the nuts.

8   The height of the lid in relation to the body can be adjusted by loosening the latch striker, repositioning the striker and retightening the bolts.

---

19   Door lock cylinder, latch and handle - removal and installation

Refer to illustration 19.3

1   Raise the window, remove the trim panel (see Section 16) and peel back the water deflector sufficiently to gain access to the components.

Lock cylinder

2   Disconnect the lock cylinder actuating rod from the cylinder.

3   Use a screwdriver to slide the lock cylinder retainer forward until it is disengaged and the lock cylinder can be removed **(see illustration)**.

19.3 To detach the lock cylinder from the door, insert a large screwdriver through the small hole above the lock cylinder and pry off this retainer

4   Installation is the reverse of removal, making sure the gasket is correctly installed.

Latch

5   Remove the retaining screws in the end of the door, lower the latch assembly, the disengage the lock rod and lower the assembly from the door **(see illustration 19.3)**.

6   Installation is the reverse of removal. Tighten the retaining screws securely.

Handle

7   Remove the two attaching nuts from the handle studs **(see illustration 19.3)**.

8   Remove the handle by sliding it forward while rotating it up to disengage it from the attaching nut holes.

9   Installation is the reverse of removal.

---

20   Console - removal and installation

1   Disconnect the negative cable at the battery. **Caution:** *If the vehicle is equipped*

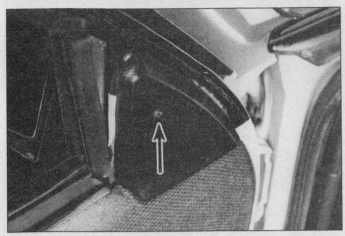

23.1 Remove the trim panel retaining screw (arrow)

23.2 Remove the mirror retaining screws

with a Delco Loc II audio system, make sure you have the correct activation code before disconnecting the battery. See the information at the front of this manual for the radio re-activation procedure.

2   Remove the shift knob. On earlier models they are held in place by an Allen head screw, while on later models a clip is used.

3   Remove the ash trays, trim plate and, on later models, the heater control assembly.

4   Remove the retaining bolts and screws, lift the console up for access and unplug the electrical connector(s).

5   Pull the parking brake lever up about three quarters of its travel and remove the console by lifting it over the lever.

21   Instrument cluster bezel – removal and installation

1   Disconnect the negative cable from the battery. **Caution:** *If the vehicle is equipped with a Delco Loc II audio system, make sure you have the correct activation code before disconnecting the battery. See the information at the front of this manual for the radio re-activation procedure.*

2   Remove the steering column trim panel.

3   Remove the screws, grasp the bezel and pull it straight back to disengage any clips, then remove it.

4   Installation is the reverse of the removal procedure.

22   Door window glass - removal and installation

Caution: *On 1993 and later power window equipped models with the Express Down fea-*

ture, the glass will drop quickly when operated which could cause personal injury. On these models the power window switch must be disconnected whenever working inside the driver's door.

1   Remove the door trim panel and water shield (see Section 16).

2   With the glass in the full up position, work through the rear access hole, remove the front glass retainer and bolts through the rear access hole.

3   Lower the glass about to about three inches above the opening, then rotate it forward to disengage the regulator roller from the sash channel.

4   Lower the glass into the door and disengage the rear guide on the glass from the rear channel.

5   Lift the glass straight up carefully while tilting it forward and remove it from the door inboard of the window frame.

6   Installation is the reverse of removal.

23   Exterior mirror - removal and installation

Refer to illustrations 23.1 and 23.2

1   Remove the trim panel or bezel **(see illustration)**. On some models it may be necessary to remove the door trim panel and peel the water deflector back for access to the retaining nuts.

2   Remove the retaining screws or nuts and lift the mirror from the vehicle **(see illustration)**. On remote control mirrors, detach the cable clip and remove the mirror and cable as an assembly.

3   Install the mirror, making sure the mirror gasket is properly aligned.

4   Installation is the reverse of the removal procedure.

24   Headlight door and actuator assembly - removal and installation

1   Disconnect the cable from the negative terminal of the battery. **Caution:** *If the vehicle is equipped with a Delco Loc II audio system, make sure you have the correct activation code before disconnecting the battery. See the information at the front of this manual for the radio re-activation procedure.*

Headlight door

2   Turn the knob on the actuator to partially raise the headlight door.

3   Remove the nuts and screws attaching the door to the actuator assembly. Lift the door from the actuator.

4   Installation is the reverse of removal.

Actuator assembly

5   Remove the radiator support filler panel.

6   Turn the knob on the actuator to open the headlight door.

7   Remove the headlight lower trim.

8   Remove the four headlight actuator fasteners.

9   Apply masking tape or place rags around the opening of the headlight assembly to protect the paint. Carefully pull the assembly out far enough to unplug the electrical connectors, then remove it from the vehicle.

10   If it's necessary to remove the actuator motor, remove the shaft-to-actuator nut and the three mounting bolts, then separate the actuator from the motor from the rest of the assembly.

11   Installation is the reverse of the removal procedure.

Notes

Chapter 12
Chassis electrical system

Contents

1 General information

The electrical system is a 12-volt, negative ground type. Power for the lights and all electrical accessories is supplied by a lead/acid-type battery which is charged by the alternator. This chapter covers repair and service procedures for the various electrical components not associated with the engine. Information on the battery, alternator, distributor and starter motor can be found in Chapter 5.

It should be noted that whenever portions of the electrical system are worked on, the negative battery cable should be disconnected to prevent electrical shorts and/or fires. **Caution:** *If the vehicle is equipped with a Delco Loc II audio system, make sure you have the correct activation code before disconnecting the battery. See the information at the front of this manual for the radio re-activation procedure.*

2 Electrical troubleshooting - general information

A typical electrical circuit consists of an electrical component, any switches, relays, motors, fuses, fusible links or circuit breakers related to that component and the wiring and electrical connectors that link the component to both the battery and the chassis. To help you pinpoint an electrical circuit problem, wiring diagrams are included at the end of this book.

Before tackling any troublesome electrical circuit, first study the appropriate wiring diagrams to get a complete understanding of what makes up that individual circuit. Trouble spots, for instance, can often be narrowed down by noting if other components related to the circuit are operating properly. If several components or circuits fail at one time, chances are the problem is in a fuse or ground connection, because several circuits are often routed through the same fuse and ground connections.

Electrical problems usually stem from simple causes, such as loose or corroded connections, a blown fuse, a melted fusible link or a bad relay. Visually inspect the condition of all fuses, wires and connections in a problem circuit before troubleshooting it.

If testing instruments are going to be utilized, use the diagrams to plan ahead of time where you will make the necessary connections in order to accurately pinpoint the trouble spot.

The basic tools needed for electrical troubleshooting include a circuit tester or voltmeter (a 12-volt bulb with a set of test leads can also be used), a continuity tester, which includes a bulb, battery and set of test leads, and a jumper wire, preferably with a circuit breaker incorporated, which can be used to bypass electrical components. Before attempting to locate a problem with test instruments, use the wiring diagram(s) to decide where to make the connections.

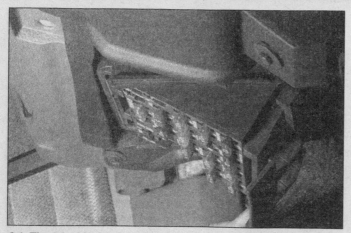

3.1 The fuse block is located under the left side of the instrument panel - early models swing down - on later models it's under a cover

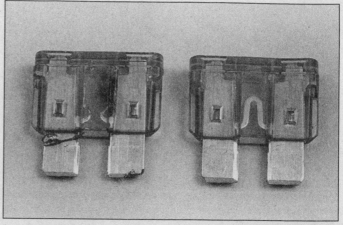

3.3 To check for a blown fuse, pull it out and inspect it visually - the fuse on the left is blown - the one on the right is good

Voltage checks

Voltage checks should be performed if a circuit is not functioning properly. Connect one lead of a circuit tester to either the negative battery terminal or a known good ground. Connect the other lead to a electrical connector in the circuit being tested, preferably nearest to the battery or fuse. If the bulb of the tester lights, voltage is present, which means that the part of the circuit between the electrical connector and the battery is problem free. Continue checking the rest of the circuit in the same fashion. When you reach a point at which no voltage is present, the problem lies between that point and the last test point with voltage. Most of the time the problem can be traced to a loose connection. **Note:** *Keep in mind that some circuits receive voltage only when the ignition key is in the Accessory or Run position.*

Finding a short

One method of finding shorts in a circuit is to remove the fuse and connect a test light or voltmeter in its place to the fuse terminals. There should be no voltage present in the circuit. Move the wiring harness from side to side while watching the test light. If the bulb goes on, there is a short to ground somewhere in that area, probably where the insulation has rubbed through. The same test can be performed on each component in the circuit, even a switch.

Ground check

Perform a ground test to check whether a component is properly grounded. Disconnect the battery and connect one lead of a self-powered test light, known as a continuity tester, to a known good ground. Connect the other lead to the wire or ground connection being tested. If the bulb goes on, the ground is good. If the bulb does not go on, the ground is not good.

Continuity check

A continuity check is done to determine if there are any breaks in a circuit - if it is passing electricity properly. With the circuit off (no power in the circuit), a self-powered continuity tester can be used to check the circuit. Connect the test leads to both ends of the circuit (or to the "power" end and a good ground), and if the test light comes on the circuit is passing current properly. If the light doesn't come on, there is a break somewhere in the circuit. The same procedure can be used to test a switch, by connecting the continuity tester to the power in and power out sides of the switch. With the switch turned On, the test light should come on.

Finding an open circuit

When diagnosing for possible open circuits, it is often difficult to locate them by sight because oxidation or terminal misalignment are hidden by the electrical connectors. Merely wiggling an electrical connector on a sensor or in the wiring harness may correct the open circuit condition. Remember this when an open circuit is indicated when troubleshooting a circuit. Intermittent problems may also be caused by oxidized or loose connections.

Electrical troubleshooting is simple if you keep in mind that all electrical circuits are basically electricity running from the battery, through the wires, switches, relays, fuses and fusible links to each electrical component (light bulb, motor, etc.) and to ground, from which it is passed back to the battery.

3   Fuses - general information

Refer to illustrations 3.1 and 3.3

The electrical circuits of the vehicle are protected by a combination of fuses, circuit breakers and fusible links. The fuse block is located on the underside of the instrument panel on the driver's side. On earlier models, the fuses are accessible after pulling the fuse block down on earlier models or under a cover on later models **(see illustration)**. A convenience center containing related components is located under the instrument panel above the fuse block on earlier models.

Each of the fuses is designed to protect a specific circuit, and the various circuits are identified on the fuse panel itself. Miniaturized fuses are employed in the fuse block. These compact fuses, with blade terminal design, allow fingertip removal and replacement.

If an electrical component fails, your first check should be the fuse. A fuse which has blown is easily identified by inspecting the element inside the clear plastic body **(see illustration)**. Also, the blade terminal tips are exposed in the fuse body, allowing for continuity checks.

It is important that the correct fuse be installed. The different electrical circuits need varying amounts of protection, indicated by the amperage rating molded in bold, color coded numbers on the fuse body. If the replacement fuse immediately fails, do not replace it again until the cause of the problem is isolated and corrected. In most cases, this will be a short circuit in the wiring caused by a broken or deteriorated wire.

4   Fusible links - general information

In addition to fuses, the wiring is protected by fusible links. These links are used in circuits which are not ordinarily fused, such as the ignition circuit. Some later models use a maxi-fuse, which looks like a version on a standard fuse and performs the same function, to act as a fusible link on some circuits

Although the fusible links appear to be a heavier gauge than the wire they are protecting, the appearance is due to the thick insulation. All fusible links are several wire gauges smaller than the wire they are designed to protect. The location of the fusible links on your particular vehicle may be determined by referring to the wiring diagrams at the end of this book.

8.3 Screwdrivers can be used to remove the lock plate cover

8.4 After relieving the tension on the locking ring, screwdrivers can be used to remove it

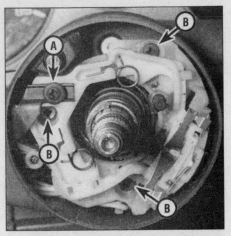

8.7a Remove the retaining screw (A) from the turn signal lever, then the turn signal switch retaining screws (B)

8.7b Use a small Phillips screwdriver to remove the hazard flasher knob

The fusible links cannot be repaired, but a new link of the same size wire can be put in its place. The procedure is as follows:

a) *Disconnect the negative cable at the battery.*
b) *Disconnect the fusible link from the starter solenoid.*
c) *Cut the damaged fusible link out of the wiring just behind the connector.*
d) *Strip the insulation approximately 1/2-inch.*
e) *Position the connector on the new fusible link and crimp it into place.*
f) *Use rosin core solder at each end of the new link to obtain a good solder joint.*
g) *Use plenty of electrical tape around the soldered joint. No wires should be exposed.*
h) *Connect the fusible link at the starter solenoid. Connect the battery ground cable. Test the circuit for proper operation.*

5 Circuit breakers - general information

A circuit breaker is used to protect the headlight wiring and is located in the light switch. An electrical overload in the system will cause the lights to go on and off, or in some cases to remain off. If this happens, check the entire headlight circuit immediately. Once the overload condition is corrected, the circuit breaker will function normally. Circuit breakers are also used with accessories such as power windows, power door locks and the rear window defogger.

6 Relays - general information

Several electrical accessories in the vehicle use relays to transmit the electrical signal to the component. If the relay is defective, that component will not operate properly.

The various relays are grouped together in the fuse block on most models, as well as in other locations.

If a faulty relay is suspected, it can be removed and tested by a dealer service department or a repair shop. Defective relays must be replaced as a unit.

7 Turn signal and hazard flashers - check and replacement

1   Small canister-shaped flasher units are incorporated into the electrical circuits for the directional signals and hazard warning lights.
2   When the units are functioning properly, an audible click can be heard with the circuit in operation. If the turn signals fail on one side only and the flasher unit cannot be heard, a faulty bulb is indicated.
3   If the turn signal fails on both sides, the problem many be due to a blown fuse, faulty flasher unit or switch, or a broken or loose connection. If the fuse has blown, check the wiring for a short before installing a new fuse.
4   The hazard warning lights are checked the same way.
5   The hazard warning flasher is located in the convenience center adjacent to the fuse block.
6   The turn signal flasher is retained by a spring clip and mounted near the convenience center or next to the steering column.
7   When replacing either of the flasher units, be sure to buy a replacement of the same capacity. Compare the new flasher to the old one before installing it.

8 Steering column switches and ignition key lock cylinder - removal and installation

1   Disconnect the negative cable at the battery. **Caution:** *If the vehicle is equipped with a Delco Loc II audio system, make sure*
you have the correct activation code before disconnecting the battery. See the information at the front of this manual for the radio re-activation procedure.

1982 through 1990 models

Turn signal switch

Refer to illustrations 8.3, 8.4, 8.7a, 8.7b, 8.9 and 8.11

2   Remove the steering wheel (see Chapter 10).
3   Pry the lock plate cover off, using two screwdrivers **(see illustration)**.
4   Push the lock ring in sufficiently to allow removal of the ring retainer with two screwdrivers **(see illustration)**.
5   Remove the lock plate.
6   Remove the retaining screw and remove the turn signal lever. On later models without a retaining screw, firmly pull the lever straight out.
7   Remove the three retaining screws and the hazard switch button **(see illustrations)**.
8   Remove the trim panel from beneath the steering column to gain access to the turn signal switch harness.

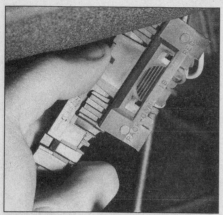

8.9 The turn signal electrical connector can be unplugged after removal of the trim panel

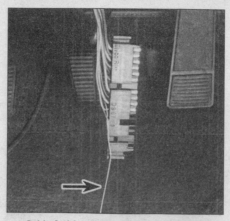

8.11 A thin piece of wire should be fastened to the connector to aid in the installation of the new harness

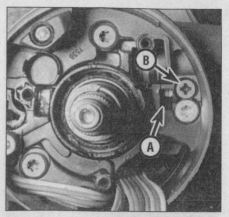

8.15 Needle-nose pliers can be used to remove the warning buzzer switch (A), then remove the ignition lock cylinder retaining screw (B)

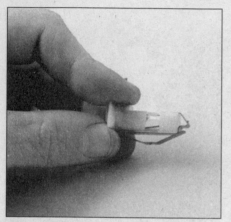

8.17 The warning buzzer switch and spring looks like this when assembled

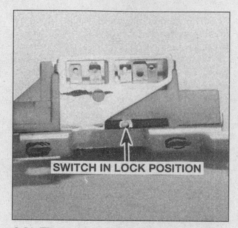

8.21 The ignition switch should be placed in the lock position (A) prior to installation

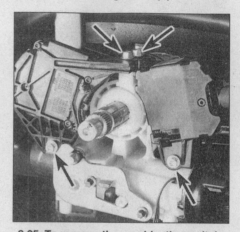

8.25 To remove the combination switch, remove the indicated screws (upper arrows and lower left arrow); to remove the windshield wiper/washer switch, remove the combination switch and remove the windshield wiper/washer switch mounting screw (lower right arrow)

9   Unplug the switch electrical connector **(see illustration)**.
10   Remove the steering column retaining bracket bolts and nuts, then lower the bracket.
11   Remove the switch assembly and harness, carefully guiding the harness and connector out of the column. For ease of reassembly, tie a string or fasten a thin wire to the harness connector to use in pulling the connector back through the narrow confines of the steering column **(see illustration)**.
12   Installation is the reverse of removal.

Ignition key lock cylinder

Refer to illustrations 8.15 and 8.17

13   Perform Steps 1 through 9 and pull the turn signal switch up sufficiently to provide access to the lock cylinder.
14   With the key in the On position, remove the ignition warning buzzer switch contacts with needle-nose pliers. Don't lose the spring.
15   Remove the switch retaining screw **(see illustration)**.
16   Withdraw the switch from the steering column.
17   Installation is the reverse of removal, paying attention to the following points:

a) *Assemble the ignition warning buzzer switch and spring before inserting them* **(see illustration)**.
b) *When installing the turn signal actuator arm, make sure it is securely engaged in the lever mechanism before tightening the screw.*

Ignition switch

Refer to illustration 8.21

18   Unbolt the steering column bracket from the dash (see Chapter 10) and lower the column.
19   Unplug the electrical connector from the switch.
20   Turn the ignition key to the LOCK position. Remove the two screws securing the switch to the steering column and remove the switch.
21   To install the switch, reverse the removal procedure, but make sure the new switch is set in the Lock position **(see illustration)**. This can be determined by inserting a small screwdriver in the actuating rod slot and then moving the switch slide all the way to the left, then back one detent. **Caution:** *Use only the original screws or genuine factory replacements. Longer or thicker screws*

could cause the collapsible design of the steering column to become impaired.

1991 through 1994 models

Caution: *If the vehicle is equipped with a Delco Loc II or Theftlock audio system, make sure you have the correct activation code before disconnecting the battery.*

Combination switch

Refer to illustrations 8.25 and 8.26

22   Detach the cable from the negative battery terminal.
23   Remove the steering wheel (see Chapter 10).
24   Remove the steering column covers (see Chapter 11).
25   Remove the combination switch mounting screws **(see illustration)**.
26   Detach the combination switch from the steering column housing and unplug the electrical connector **(see illustration)**.
27   Installation is the reverse of removal.

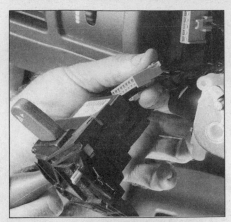

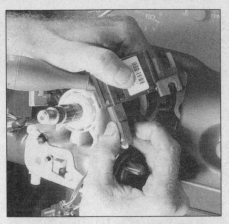

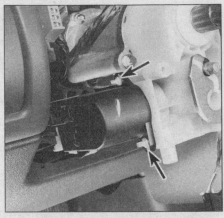

8.26 Detach the combination switch from the steering column housing and unplug the electrical connector

8.33 Detach the windshield wiper/washer switch from the steering column housing and unplug the electrical connector

8.37 To remove the ignition switch from the steering column housing, remove these two screws (arrows)

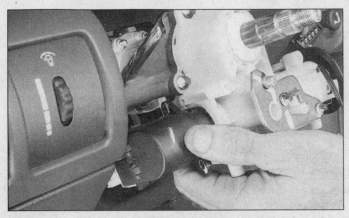

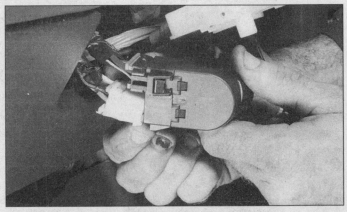

8.38a Move the ignition switch to the left to detach it from the steering column housing . . .

8.38b . . . then pull it back and down and unplug the electrical connectors

Windshield wiper/washer switch

Refer to illustration 8.33

28   Detach the cable from the negative battery terminal.
29   Remove the steering wheel (see Chapter 10).
30   Remove the upper and lower steering column covers (see Chapter 11).
31   Remove the combination switch (see Steps 22 through 26).
32   Remove the windshield wiper/washer switch mounting screws **(see illustration 8.25)**.
33   Detach the windshield wiper/washer switch from the steering column housing and unplug the electrical connector **(see illustration)**.
34   Installation is the reverse of removal.

Ignition switch and key lock cylinder

35   Detach the cable from the negative terminal of the battery.
36   Remove the tilt lever, if equipped. Remove the upper and lower steering column covers (see Chapter 11).

Ignition switch

Refer to illustrations 8.37, 8.38a and 8.38b

37   Remove the ignition switch retaining

screws **(see illustration)**.
38   Detach the ignition switch from the steering column housing and unplug the electrical connectors **(see illustrations)**.
39   Installation is the reverse of removal.

Key lock cylinder

Refer to illustration 8.41

40   Turn the key to the Run position.
41   Depress the lock button **(see illustration)** and remove the key lock cylinder.
42   To install the key lock cylinder, turn the key to the Run position, depress the lock button and, rotating the key counterclockwise about five degrees, gently push the lock cylinder into place.
43   Installation is otherwise the reverse of removal.

---

9   Headlight - removal and installation

Refer to illustrations 9.3, 9.4 and 9.8

Sealed beam headlights

Removal

1   When replacing the headlight, do not

turn the spring-loaded adjusting screws or the headlight aim will be changed.
2   Remove the bezel.
3   Remove the four screws which secure each retaining ring and withdraw the ring

8.41 To remove the key lock cylinder, turn the ignition key to the Run position, depress the lock button with a screwdriver or other suitable tool, then pull out the lock cylinder

9.3 Remove the retaining screws (arrows) to change a headlight

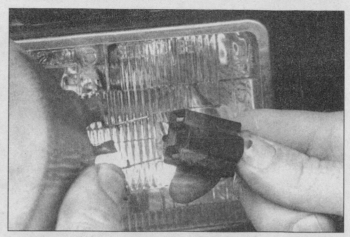

9.4 Support the headlight while unplugging the connector

9.8 Rotate the bulb assembly counterclockwise and pull it out of the housing

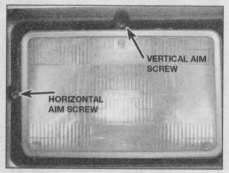

10.1 Sealed beam headlight adjustment screw locations

VERTICAL AIM SCREW

HORIZONTAL AIM SCREW

(see illustration). Support the light as this is done.

4   Pull the light away, unplug the connector and remove it from the vehicle **(see illustration)**.

Installation

5   Position the new unit close enough to connect the wires. Make sure the numbers molded into the lens are at the top.

6   Install the retaining ring and mounting screws.

7   Install the bezel and check for proper operation. If the adjusting screws were not turned, the headlight should not require adjustment.

Composite headlights

Caution: *The composite headlights have halogen bulbs which contain a gas under pressure. Handling a bulb improperly could cause it to shatter into flying glass fragments. To help avoid personal injury, be sure to turn off the headlights and allow the bulb to cool before changing bulbs. Leave the headlights off until the bulb change is complete. Always wear eye protection when changing a halo-*

gen bulb. Handle the bulb only by its base. Avoid touching the glass. if you do touch the glass, clean it off with rubbing alcohol. Do not drop or scratch the glass. Keep moisture away. Place the used bulb in the new bulb carton and dispose of it properly. Keep halogen bulbs out of the reach of children.

8   Turn the bulb assembly on the back of the headlight housing counterclockwise and with a vertical rocking motion, pull the bulb to the rear **(see illustration)**.

9   With one hand, grip the wire harness end of the bulb. Do not grip the wires. With the other hand, grip the base of the bulb. Do not grip the bulb glass. Lift the plastic locking tab and pull the bulb and base apart. **Note**: *The bulbs for high and low beams are the same and have two separate filaments. Instead of using a new bulb for a burned out light, low and high beam bulbs can be interchanged.*

10   Installation is the reverse of removal.

---

10   Headlights - adjustment

Refer to illustrations 10.1 and 10.3

Caution: *The headlights must be aimed correctly. If adjusted incorrectly they could blind the driver of an oncoming vehicle and cause a serious accident or seriously reduce your ability to see the road. The headlights should*

be checked for proper aim every 12 months and any time a new headlight is installed or front end body work is performed. It should be emphasized that the following procedure is only an interim step which will provide temporary adjustment until the headlights can be adjusted by a properly equipped shop.

1   Headlights have two spring loaded adjusting screws, one on the top controlling up-and-down movement and one on the side controlling left-and-right movement **(see illustration)**.

2   There are several methods of adjusting the headlights. The simplest method requires a blank wall 25 feet in front of the vehicle and a level floor.

3   Position masking tape vertically on the wall in reference to the vehicle centerline and the centerlines of both headlights **(see illustration)**.

4   Position a horizontal tape line in reference to the centerline of all the headlights. **Note:** *It may be easier to position the tape on the wall with the vehicle parked only a few inches away.*

5   Adjustment should be made with the vehicle sitting level, the gas tank half-full and no unusually heavy load in the vehicle.

6   Starting with the low beam adjustment, position the high intensity zone so it is two inches below the horizontal line and two inches to the side of the headlight vertical line, away from oncoming traffic. Adjustment is made by turning the top adjusting screw clockwise to raise the beam and counterclockwise to lower the beam. The adjusting screw on the side should be used in the same manner to move the beam left or right.

7   With the high beams on, the high intensity zone should be vertically centered with the exact center just below the horizontal line. **Note:** *It may not be possible to position the headlight aim exactly for both high and low beams. If a compromise must be made, keep in mind that the low beams are the most used and have the greatest effect on safety.*

8   Have the headlights adjusted by a dealer service department or service station at the earliest opportunity.

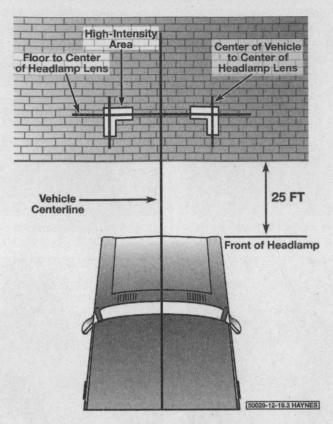

10.3 Headlight aiming details

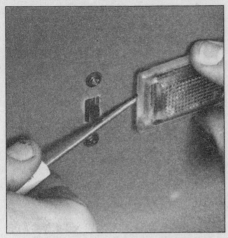

11.12 Use a screwdriver to pry the rear compartment courtesy light housing out for access to the bulb

Instrument panel lights

4   Most instrument panel bulbs can be replaced after removal of the instrument cluster (see Section 14). If a bulb is located in a recess and cannot be grasped with the fingers, push a suitable piece of tubing, such as vacuum hose, over the bulb and pull straight out to remove it.

Ashtray light

5   Remove the ashtray and console cover for access to the bulb.

Glovebox light

6   Open the glove box and remove the striker assembly for access to the bulb.

Heater and air conditioner control panel light

7   Remove the right side trim panel and instrument panel trim cover. Remove the screws retaining the control to the instrument panel.
8   Pull the control out sufficiently to gain access to the bulb socket and remove it. Remove the bulb from the socket.

Radio bulb

9   Remove the radio.
10   Remove the top cover from the radio, grasp the bulb and pull straight out.

Console

11   Remove the console cover retaining screws and pull the cover up sufficiently to gain access to the bulb socket. Twist the socket counterclockwise to remove it and then remove the bulb.

Rear end

Courtesy light

12   The rear compartment courtesy light bulb is contained in a plastic housing. Use a screwdriver to pry the housing out of the panel for access to the bulb (see illustration).

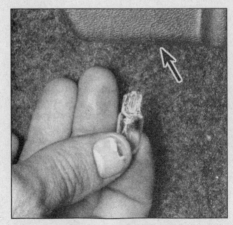

11.2 Reach up behind the trim panel for access to the lower courtesy light bulbs

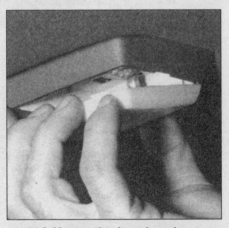

11.3 Unsnap the dome lamp lens - remove the bulb by grasping it and pulling it straight out

11   Bulb replacement

Refer to illustrations 11.2, 11.3, 11.12, 11.13a and 11.13b

Front end

Parking and turn signal and side marker lights

1   The front parking, turn signal and side marker light bulb can be replaced from inside the engine compartment after removing the four screws and detaching the fascia panel. The side marker bulb is located between the front end panel and radiator support. Turn the bulbs to remove them from the housings.

Interior

Courtesy lights

2   The lower courtesy light bulbs are replaced by grasping them and pulling them directly out of the socket (see illustration).

Dome light

3   Detach the lens with a small screwdriver and remove the bulb by grasping it securely and pulling straight down (see illustration).

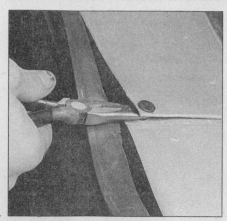

11.13a Use needle-nose pliers to remove the trim panel retainers to gain access to the tail light housing on early models

11.13b Install the bulb by pushing it in, then turning it counterclockwise

12.3 Radio retaining bolt locations (arrows)

Tail and back-up lights

13   On early hatchback models, detach the interior panel to gain access **(see illustration)**. On other remove the four plastic wing nuts and remove the tail light assembly. Turn the bulb socket to remove, then push the bulb in and turn it counterclockwise to release it **(see illustration)**.

Side marker lights

14   Remove the two plastic screws retaining the speaker cover trim panel in the rear compartment. Pull the carpet back and swing the speaker and cover assembly into the rear compartment for access to the bulb.

License plate light

15   Access to the license plate lamp is gained by removing the two screws and removing the lamp assembly. Turn and pull the bulb to remove it.

---

12   Radio and speakers - removal and installation

Radio

Refer to illustrations 12.3, 12.6a and 12.6b
1   Disconnect the negative cable at the battery. **Caution:** *If the vehicle is equipped with a Delco Loc II audio system, make sure you have the correct activation code before disconnecting the battery. See the information at the front of this manual for the radio re-activation procedure.*
2   Remove the instrument cluster bezel and panel trim plate (see Chapter 11).
3   Remove the radio retaining screws **(see illustration)**.
4   Pull the radio out sufficiently for access to the antenna cable.
5   Unplug the antenna cable from the back of the radio.
6   Unplug the electrical connectors from the radio by depressing the tabs **(see illustrations)**.
7   Lift the radio from the dash.
8   Installation is the reverse of removal.

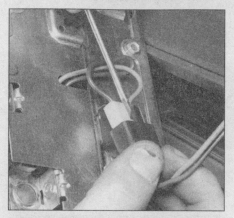

12.6a Lift the tab with a screwdriver and unplug the connector

Speakers

Front

9   Remove the attaching screws, disconnect the clips and detach the speaker grille from the instrument panel.
10   Remove the two screws attaching the speaker to the instrument panel and lift the speaker sufficiently to disconnect the wiring .
11   Remove the speaker.
12   Installation is the reverse of removal.

Rear

Hatchback

13   On hatchback models, remove the two plastic retaining screws and detach the speaker, cover trim panel.
14   Pull the carpet back sufficiently for clearance and swing the speaker and cover assembly into the rear compartment.
15   Disconnect the wires and remove the speaker.
16   Installation is the reverse of removal.

Sedan

17   The speakers are accessible after opening the trunk. Remove the nut and speaker cover, then unplug the electrical connector from the speaker.
18   Disengage the speaker retaining clip and remove the speaker.
19   Installation is the reverse of removal.

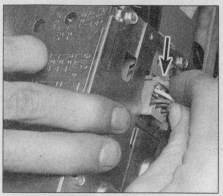

12.6b Press the tab in (arrow) and separate the connector from the radio

---

13   Radio antenna - removal and installation

Refer to illustration 13.2
1   The antenna mast can be removed by simply using a small wrench to unscrew it from its base.
2   The antenna body and cable assembly can be removed after the mast has been removed by unbolting it from the fender **(see illustration)**.

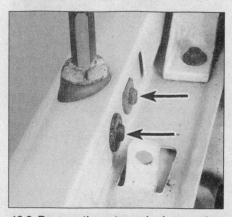

13.2 Remove the antenna body mounting bolts (arrows)

14.3 Remove the cluster mounting screws (arrows)

3   Installation is the reverse of removal, taking care to locate the studs securely in the fender.

14   Instrument cluster - removal and installation

Refer to illustration 14.3

1   Disconnect the negative cable at the battery. **Caution:** *If the vehicle is equipped with a Delco Loc II audio system, make sure you have the correct activation code before disconnecting the battery. See the information at the front of this manual for the radio re-activation procedure.*
2   Remove the cluster bezel left side trim panels (Chapter 11).
3   Remove the four cluster retaining screws **(see illustration)**.
4   Pull the cluster out, disconnect the speedometer cable and electrical connectors and remove it from the instrument panel.
5   Installation is the reverse of removal.

15   Speedometer cable - replacement

Refer to illustrations 15.5

1   Disconnect the cable from the negative battery terminal. **Caution:** *If the vehicle is equipped with a Delco Loc II audio system, make sure you have the correct activation code before disconnecting the battery. See the information at the front of this manual for the radio re-activation procedure.*
2   Remove the steering column trim plate.
3   Remove the instrument cluster trim plate and pad.
4   After removing the cluster retaining screws, pull the cluster out carefully so as not to disconnect the cluster wiring until there is sufficient clearance to reach the speedometer cable retaining collar.
5   Press the clip directly back toward the cluster to disconnect it **(see illustration)**.
6   Disconnect the cable at the transaxle or cruise control transducer.
7   Slide the old cable out from the upper

end of the casing, or, if broken, from both ends of the casing.
8   If the speedometer operation has been noisy, but the speedometer cable appears to be in good condition, take a short piece of speedometer cable with a tip to fit the speedometer and insert it in the speedometer socket. Spin the piece of cable between your fingers. If binding is noted, the speedometer is faulty and should be repaired or replaced with a new one.
9   Inspect the speedometer cable casing for sharp bends and breaks, especially at the transaxle end. If breaks are noted, replace the casing with a new one.
10   When installing the cable, perform the following steps to ensure quiet operation.
11   Wipe the cable clean with a lint-free cloth.
12   Flush the bore of the casing with solvent and blow it dry with compressed air.
13   Place some speedometer cable lubricant in the palm of one hand.
14   Feed the cable through the lubricant and into the casing until lubricant has been applied to the lower two-thirds of the cable. Do not over-lubricate.
15   Seat the upper cable tip in the speedometer and snap the retainer onto the housing.
16   The remaining installation steps are the reverse of removal.

15.5 Press the lever (arrow) to release the cable from the speedometer

16   Headlight switch - removal and installation

1   Disconnect the negative cable from the battery. **Caution:** *If the vehicle is equipped with a Delco Loc II audio system, make sure you have the correct activation code before disconnecting the battery. See the information at the front of this manual for the radio re-activation procedure.*
2   Remove the left side instrument panel trim.
3   Remove the retaining screws and lift the switch from the instrument panel. Unplug the electrical connector.
4   Installation is the reverse of removal.

17   Rear window washer/wiper and rear window defogger switches - removal and installation

1   Disconnect the negative cable at the battery. **Caution:** *If the vehicle is equipped with a Delco Loc II audio system, make sure you have the correct activation code before disconnecting the battery. See the information at the front of this manual for the radio re-activation procedure.*
2   Remove the center instrument panel trim cover.
3   Remove the retaining screws and lift the appropriate switch from the trim cover. Unplug the electrical connector.
4   Installation is the reverse of removal.

18   Wiper motor - removal and installation

1   Disconnect the negative cable at the battery.

Windshield wiper motor

2   Remove the wiper arms.
3   Remove the cowl panel (see Chapter 11).
4   Loosen, but don't remove the motor crank arm to the wiper transmission drive link bolts and detach the link.
5   Disconnect the wiring and washer hoses from the wiper motor.
6   Remove the three motor-to-body attaching screws and carefully remove the wiper motor from the vehicle.
7   Installation is the reverse of the removal procedure, noting that the drive link bolts should be tightened securely.

Rear window wiper motor

8   Remove the rear wiper arm.
9   Remove the wiper shaft nut and washers.
10   Open the liftgate.
11   Remove the liftgate trim panel.
12   Unplug the electrical connector, then remove the bolts/nuts and detach the wiper motor assembly.
13   Installation is the reverse of removal.

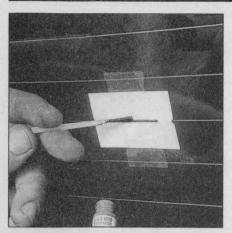

19.11 Applying repair material to a broken rear defogger grid

19   Rear window defogger - check and repair

Refer to illustration 19.11

1   This option consists of a rear window with a number of horizontal elements baked into the glass surface during the glass forming operation.
2   Small breaks in the element can be successfully repaired without removing the rear window.
3   To test the grids for proper operation, turn on the system.
4   Ground one lead of a test light and carefully touch the other lead to each element line.
5   The brilliance of the test light should increase as the lead is moved across the element from right to left. If the test light glows brightly at both ends of the lines, check for a loose ground wire. All of the lines should be checked in at least two places.
6   To repair a break in a line, it is recommended that a repair kit specifically for this purpose be purchased from a GM dealer parts department or auto parts store. Included in the repair kit will be a decal, a container of silver plastic and hardener, a mixing stick and instructions.
7   To repair a break, first turn off the system and allow it to de-energize for a few minutes.
8   Lightly buff the element area with fine steel wool then clean it thoroughly with rubbing alcohol.
9   Use the decal supplied in the repair kit or apply strips of electrician's tape above and below the area to be repaired. The space between the pieces of tape should be the same width as the existing lines. This can be checked from outside the vehicle. Press the

tape tightly against the glass to prevent seepage.
10   Mix the hardener and silver plastic thoroughly.
11   Using the wood spatula, apply the silver plastic mixture between the pieces of tape, overlapping the undamaged area slightly on either end **(see illustration)**.
12   Carefully remove the decal or tape and apply a constant stream of hot air directly to the repaired area. A heat gun set at 500 to 700-degrees F is recommended. Hold the gun one inch from the glass for two minutes.
13   If the new element appears off color, tincture of iodine can be used to clean the repair and bring it back to the proper color. This mixture should not remain on the repair for more than 30 seconds.
14   Although the defogger is now fully operational, the repaired area should not be disturbed for at least 24 hours.

20   Power door lock system - description and check

The power door lock system operates the door lock actuators mounted in each door. The system consists of the switches, actuators and associated electrical wiring.

Diagnosis can usually be limited to simple checks of the wiring connections and actuators for minor faults which can be easily repaired. These include:

a) *Checking the system fuse and/or circuit breaker.*
b) *Checking the switch wiring for damage or loose connections.*
c) *Checking the switches for continuity.*
d) *Removing the door panel(s) and checking the actuator electrical connections for looseness or damage. Inspect the actuator rods to make sure they are not bent, damaged or binding. The actuator can be checked by applying battery power momentarily. A solid click indicates the solenoid is operating properly.*

21   Power window system - description and check

The power window system operates the electric motors mounted in the doors which lower and raise the windows. The system consists of the control switches, the motors, glass mechanisms (regulators) and associated wiring.

Diagnosis can usually be limited to simple checks of the electrical connections and

motors for minor faults which can be easily repaired. These include:

a) *Inspecting the power window actuating switches and wiring for broken wires or loose connections.*
b) *Checking the power window fuse and/or circuit breaker.*
c) *Removing the door panel(s) and checking the power window motor electrical connections for looseness and damage, and inspecting the glass mechanisms for damage which could cause binding.*

22   Cruise control - description and check

The cruise control system maintains vehicle speed with a vacuum actuated servo motor located in the engine compartment, which is connected to the throttle linkage by a cable. The system consists of the servo motor, clutch switch, brake switch, transducer (early models) control switches, a relay and associated vacuum hoses.

Diagnosis can usually be limited to simple checks of the wiring and vacuum connections for minor faults which can be easily repaired. These include:

a) *Inspect the cruise control actuating switches for broken wires and loose connections.*
b) *Check the cruise control fuse.*
c) *The cruise control system is operated by vacuum so it's critical that all vacuum switches, hoses and connections are secure. Check the hoses in the engine compartment and under the dash at the vacuum release switch for tight connections, cracks and obvious vacuum leaks.*

23   Wiring diagrams - general information

Since it isn't possible to include all wiring diagrams for every year covered by this manual, the following diagrams are those that are typical and most commonly needed.

Prior to troubleshooting any circuits, check the fuse and circuit breakers (if equipped) to make sure they're in good condition. Make sure the battery is properly charged and check the cable connections (see Chapter 1).

When checking a circuit, make sure that all connectors are clean, with no broken or loose terminals. When unplugging a connector, do not pull on the wires. Pull only on the connector housings themselves.

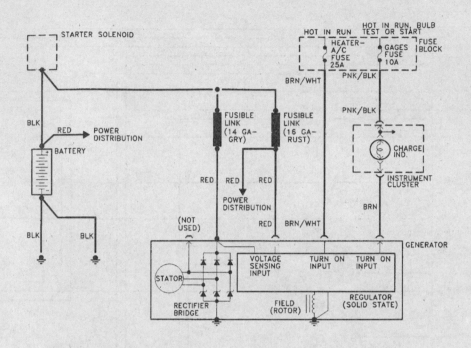

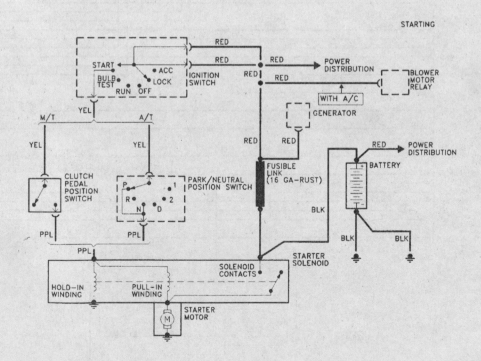

Typical starting, charging and ignition system

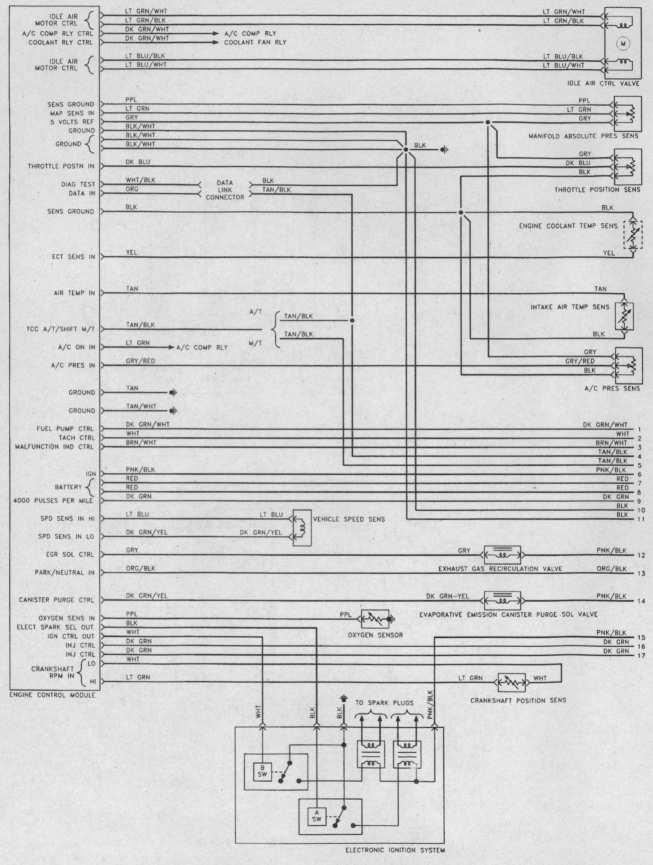

Typical 2.0 L engine control systems (1 of 2)

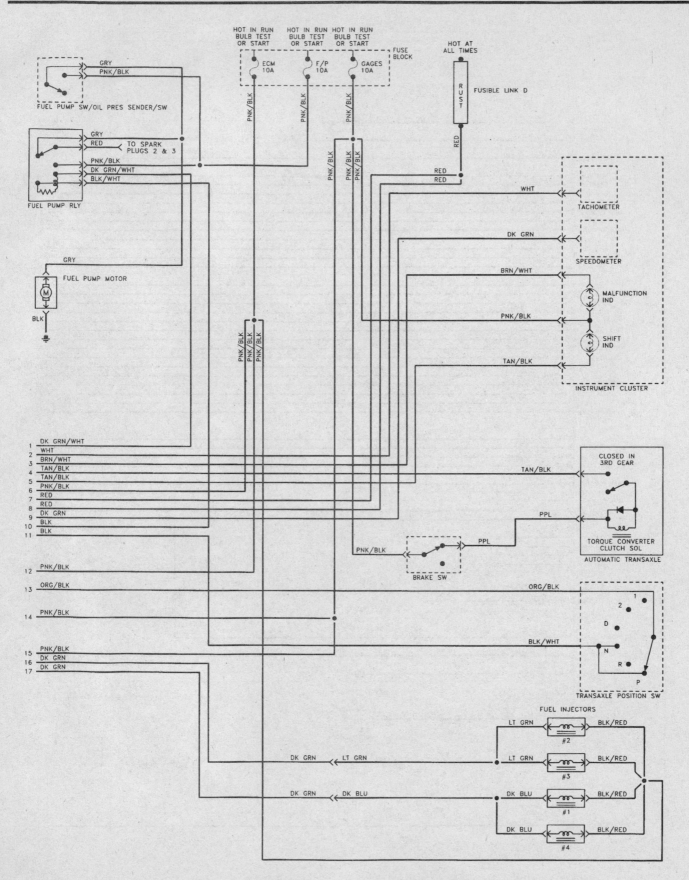

Typical 2.0 L engine control systems (2 of 2)

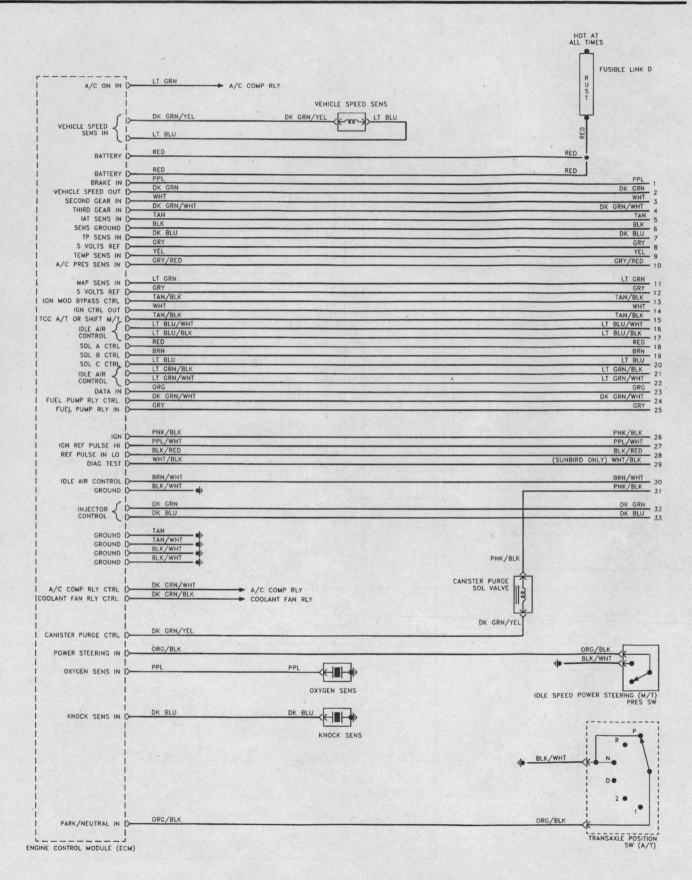

Typical 3.1 L engine control systems (1 of 3)

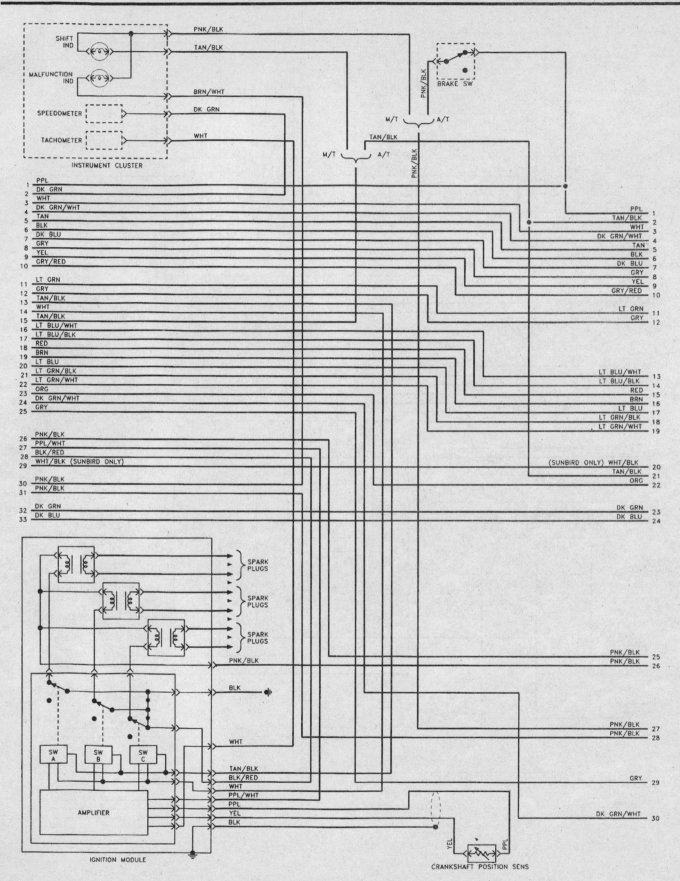

Typical 3.1 L engine control systems (2 of 3)

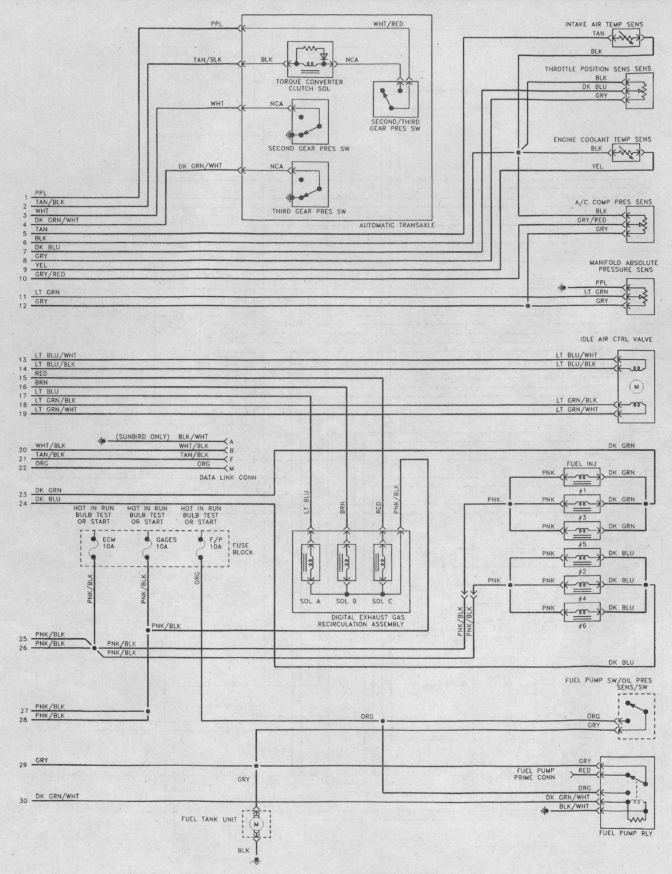

Typical 3.1 L engine control systems (3 of 3)

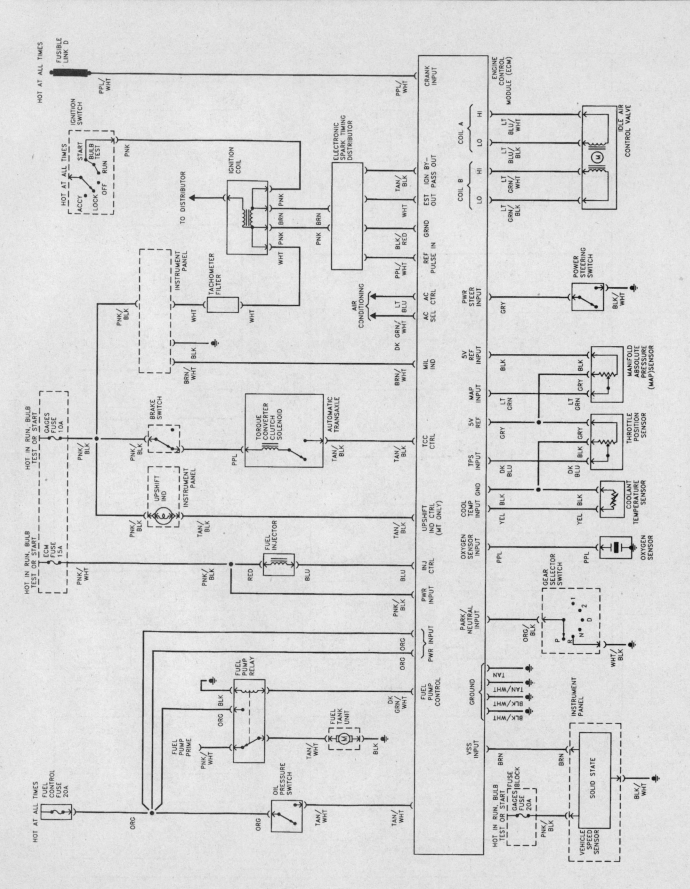
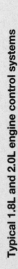

Typical 1.8L and 2.0L engine control systems

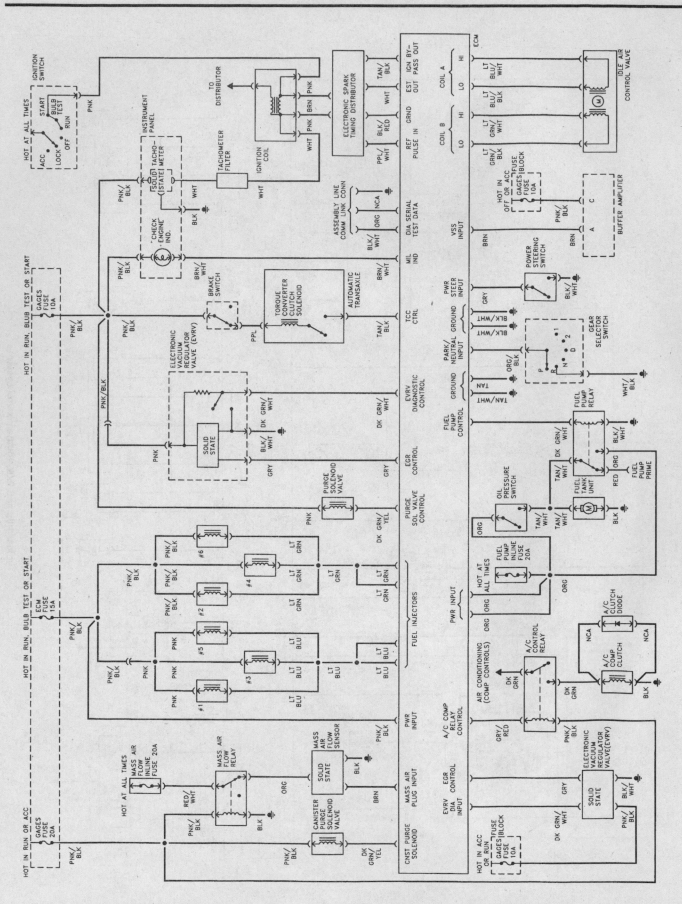

Typical Multiport fuel injection engine controls

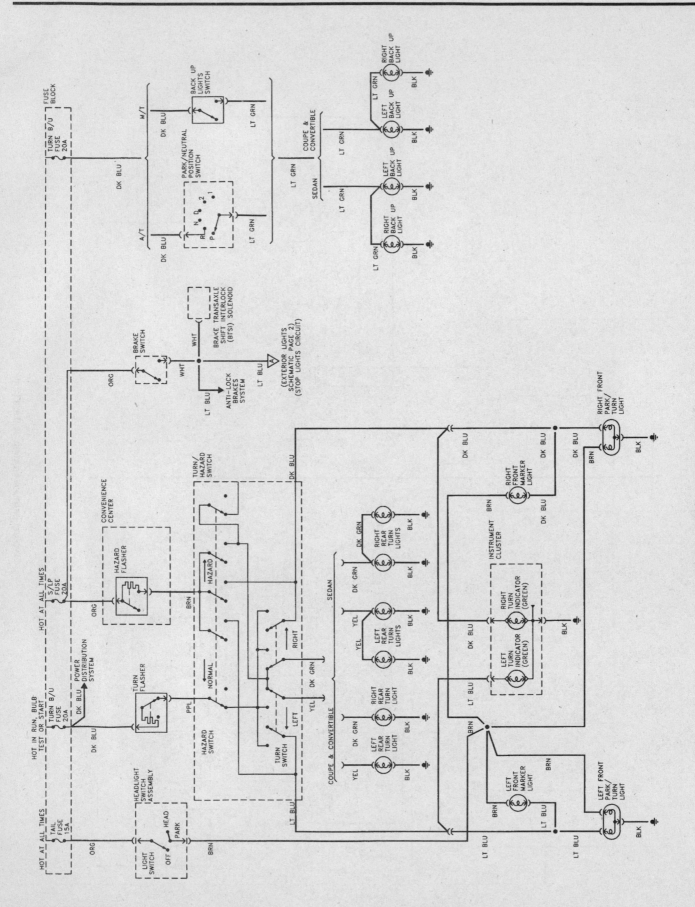

Typical exterior lighting system (1 of 2)

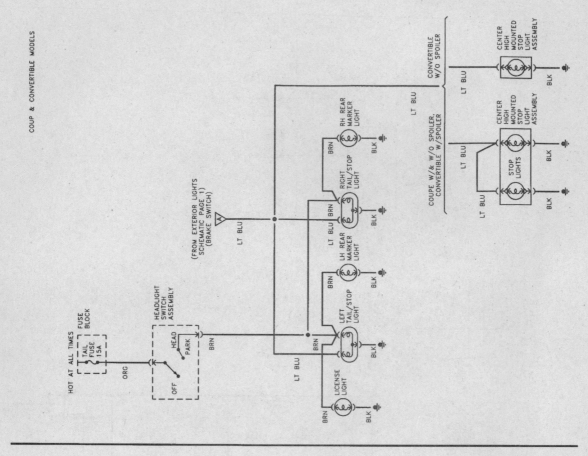

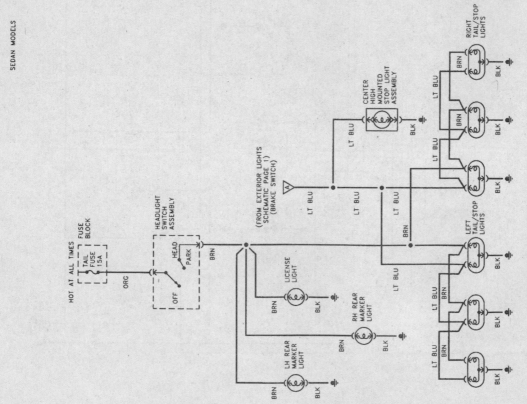

Typical exterior lighting system (2 of 2)

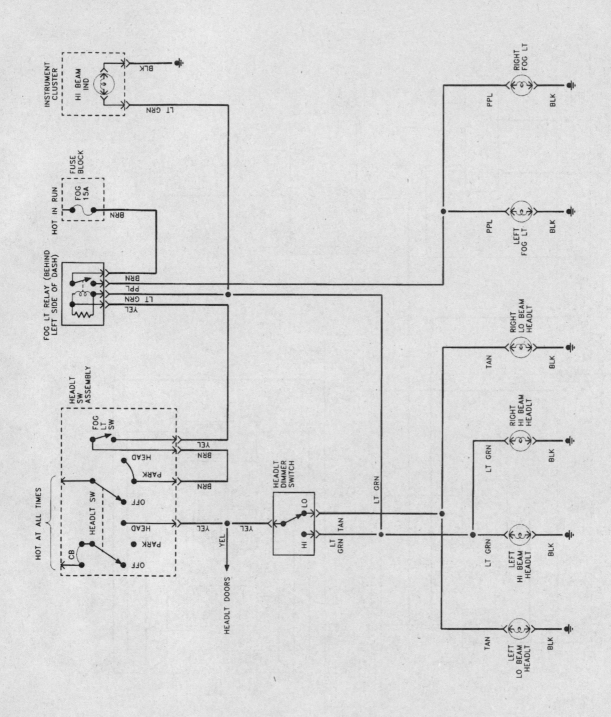

Typical headlight system

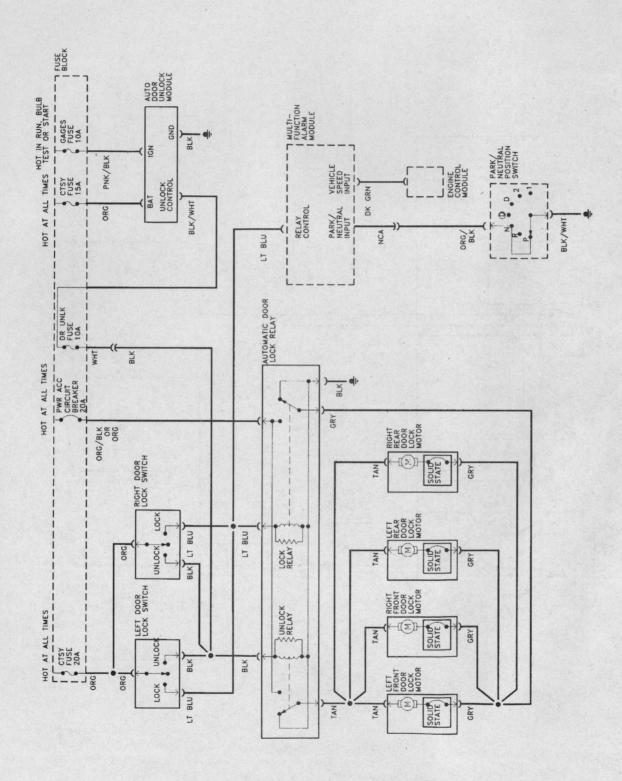

Typical power door lock system

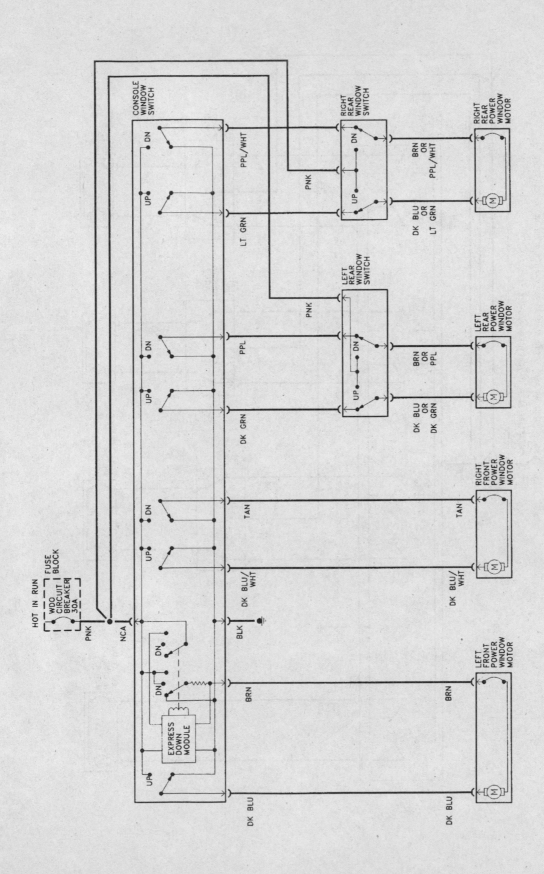

Typical 1993 and later power window system

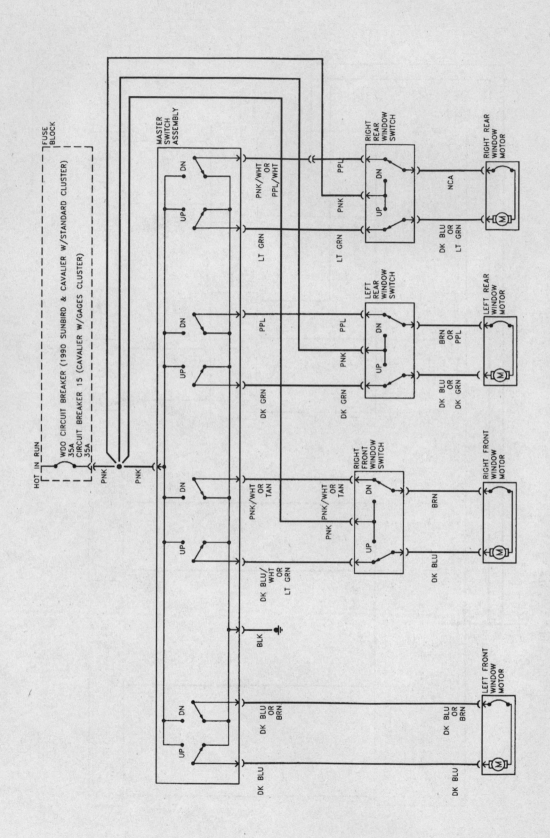

Typical 1992 and earlier power window system

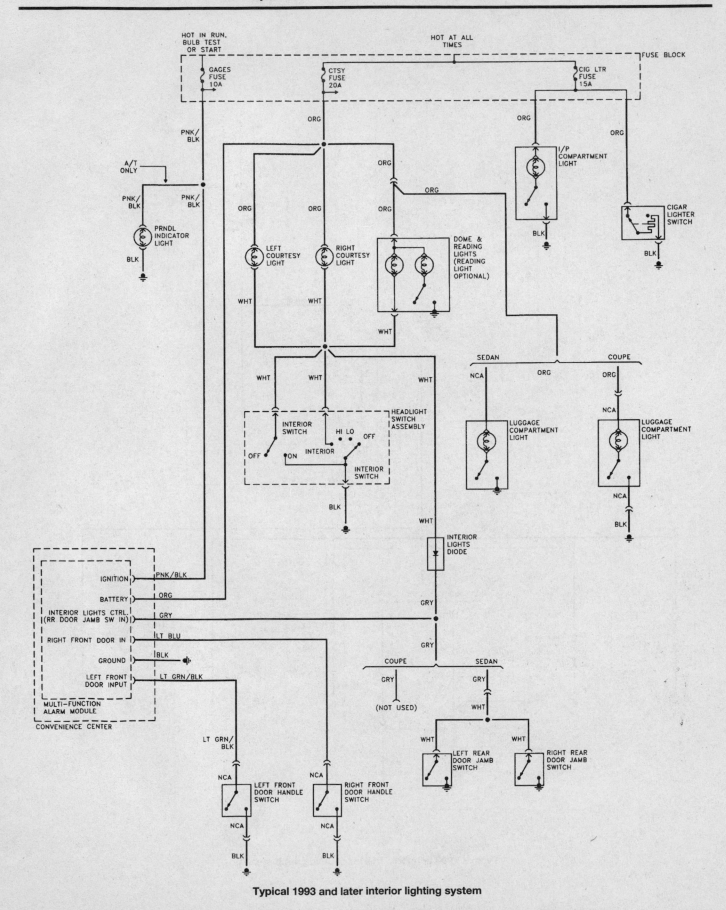

Typical 1993 and later interior lighting system

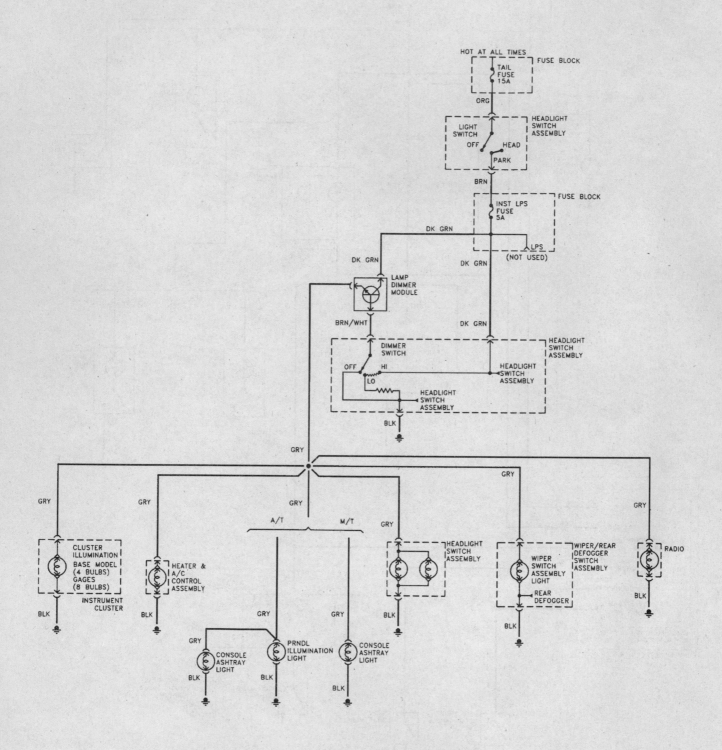

Typical 1993 and later interior dimming lamp system

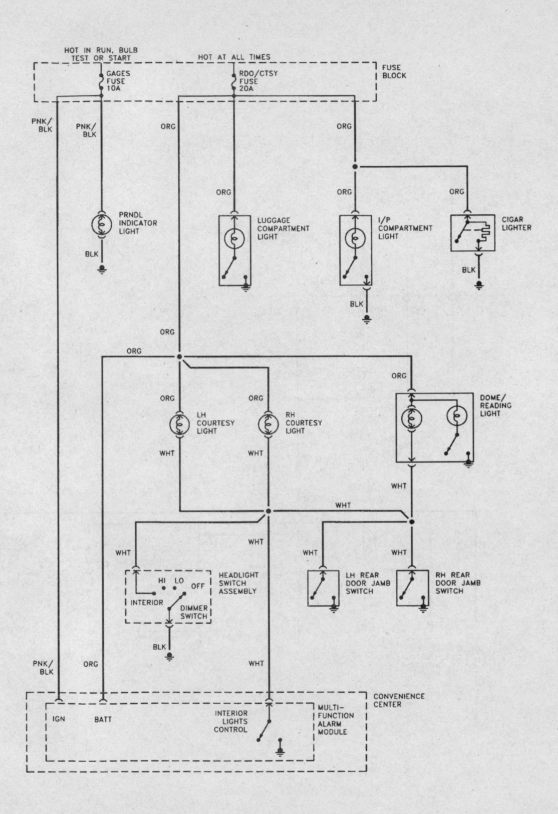

Typical 1989 thru 1992 interior lighting system

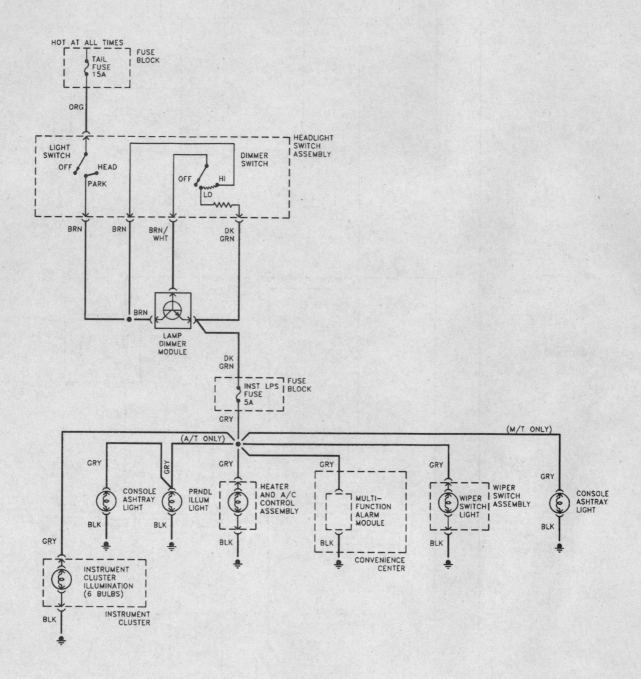

Typical 1989 thru 1992 interior dimming lamp system

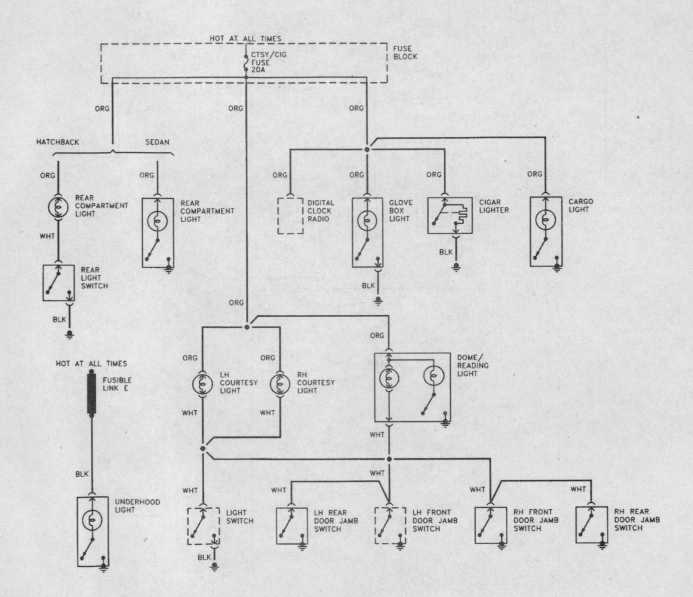

Typical 1986 and earlier interior lighting system

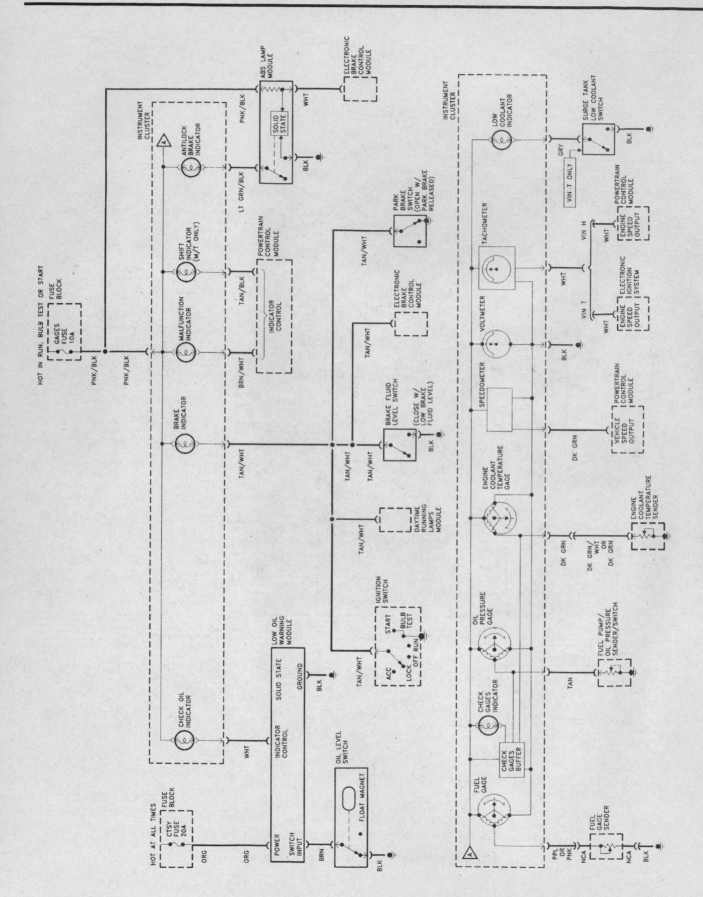

Typical gauges, indicators and warning system

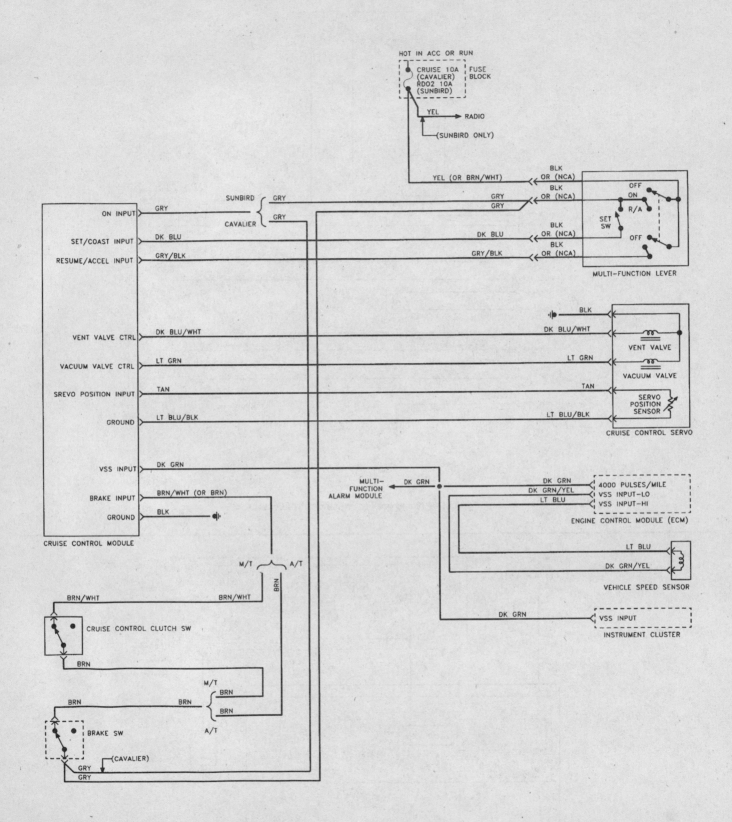

Typical 1993 and later cruise control system

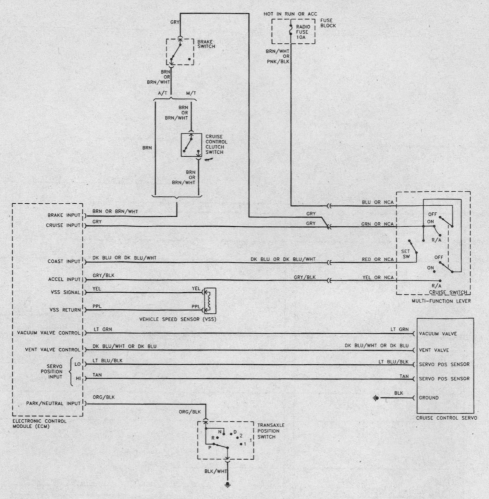

Typical 1992 and earlier cruise control system

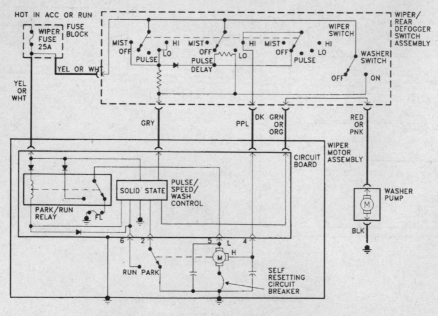

Typical windshield wiper/washer system

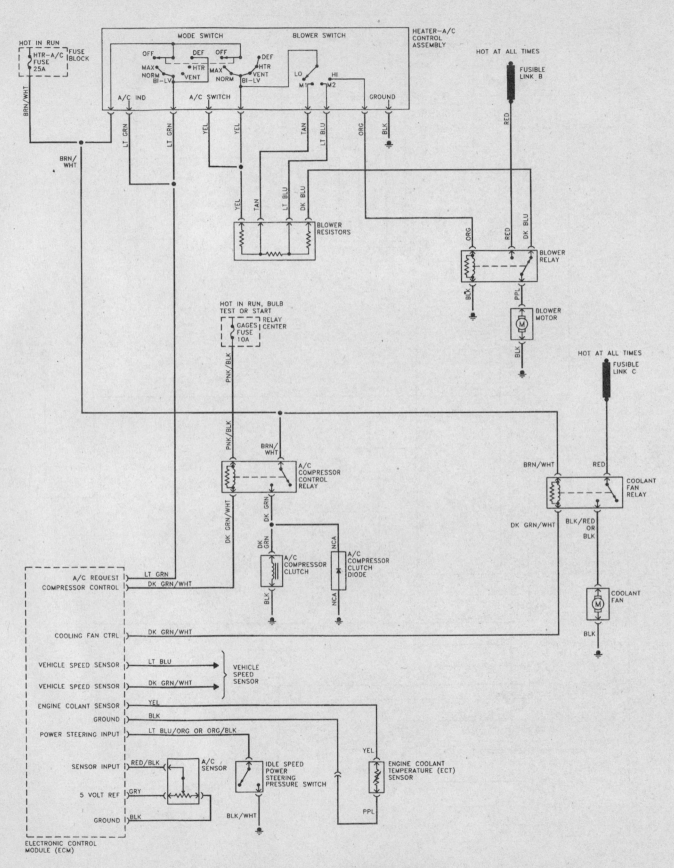

Typical 1993 and later air conditioning system

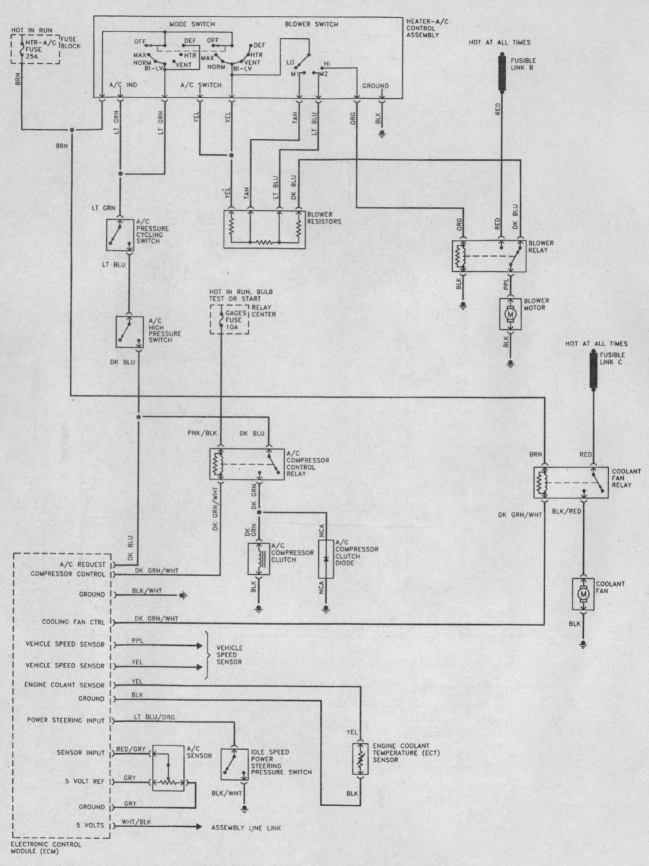

Typical 1987 thru 1992 air conditioning system

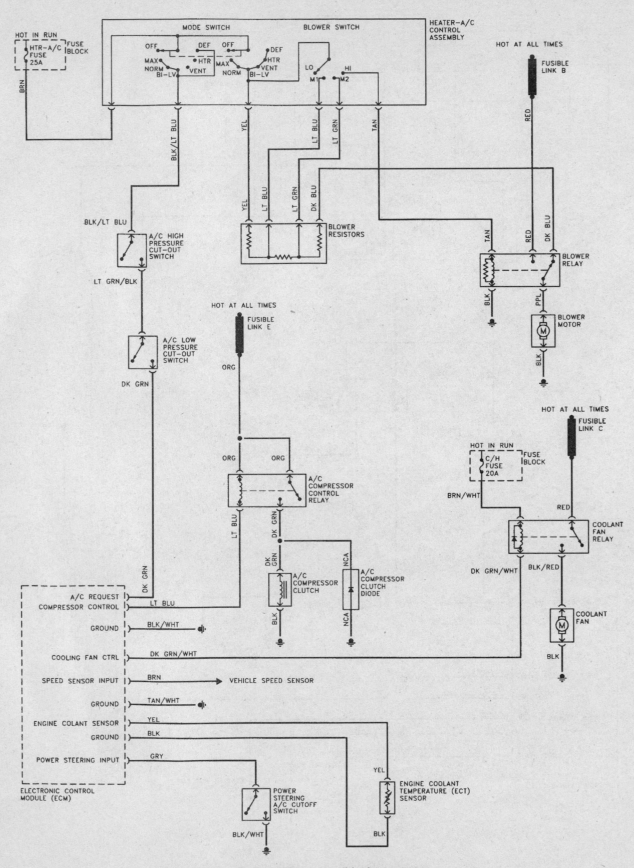

Typical 1986 air conditioning system

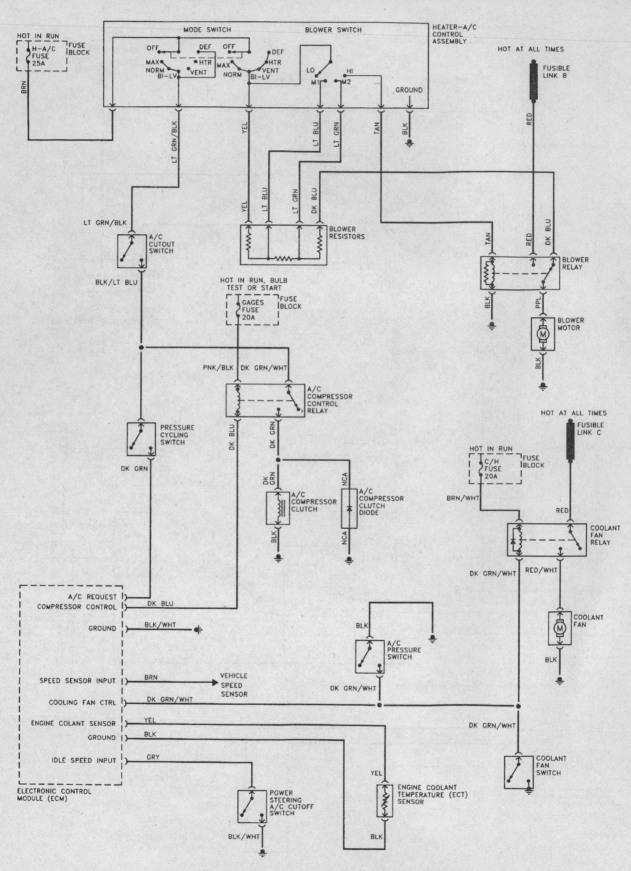

Typical 1986 (Sunbird models only) air conditioning system

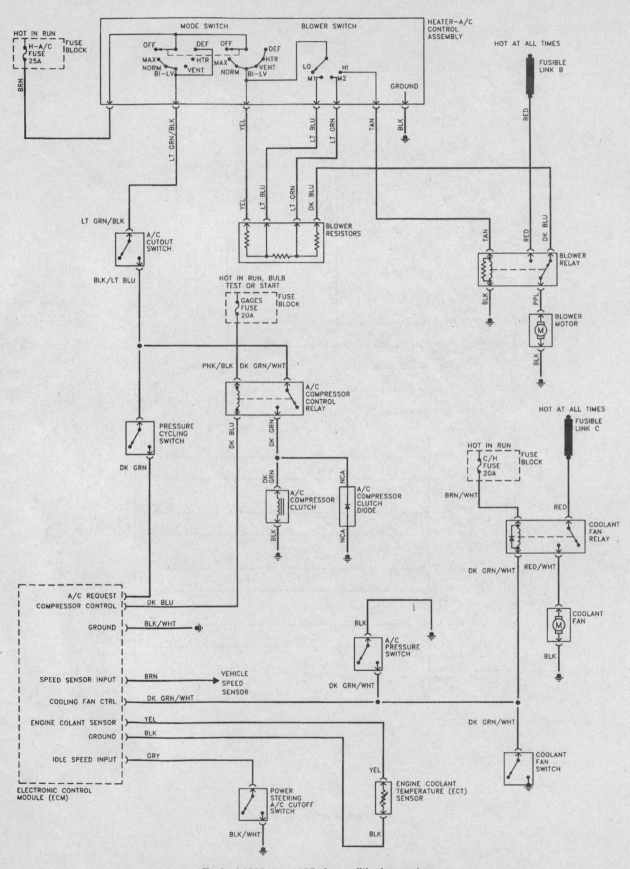

Typical 1982 thru 1985 air conditioning system

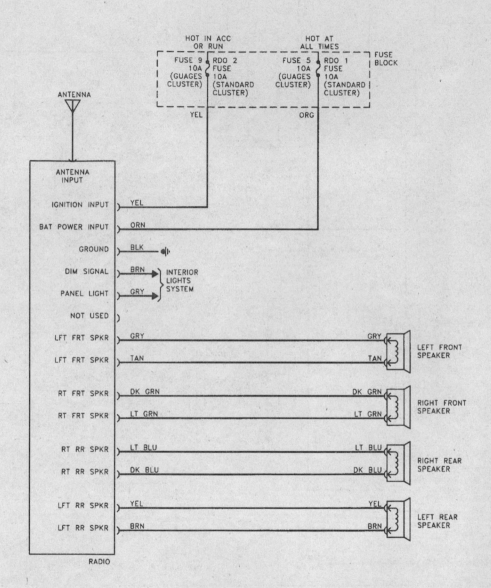

Typical audio system

Index

A

B

Haynes Automotive Manuals

NOTE: New manuals are added to this list on a periodic basis. If you do not see a listing for your vehicle, consult your local Haynes dealer for the latest product information.

ACURA
12020 Integra '86 thru '89 & Legend '86 thru '90
12021 Integra '90 thru '93 & Legend '91 thru '95

AMC
Jeep CJ - see JEEP (50020)
14020 Mid-size models '70 thru '83
14025 (Renault) Alliance & Encore '83 thru '87

AUDI
15020 4000 all models '80 thru '87
15025 5000 all models '77 thru '83
15026 5000 all models '84 thru '88

AUSTIN-HEALEY
Sprite - see MG Midget (66015)

BMW
*18020 3/5 Series not including diesel or all-wheel drive models '82 thru '92
18021 3-Series incl. Z3 models '92 thru '98
18025 320i all 4 cyl models '75 thru '83
18050 1500 thru 2002 except Turbo '59 thru '77

BUICK
*19010 Buick Century '97 thru '02
Century (front-wheel drive) - see GM (38005)
*19020 Buick, Oldsmobile & Pontiac Full-size (Front-wheel drive) '85 thru '02
Buick Electra, LeSabre and Park Avenue;
Oldsmobile Delta 88 Royale, Ninety Eight and Regency; Pontiac Bonneville
19025 Buick Oldsmobile & Pontiac Full-size (Rear wheel drive)
Buick Estate '70 thru '90, Electra '70 thru '84, LeSabre '70 thru '85, Limited '74 thru '79
Oldsmobile Custom Cruiser '70 thru '90, Delta 88 '70 thru '85, Ninety-eight '70 thru '84
Pontiac Bonneville '70 thru '81, Catalina '70 thru '81, Grandville '70 thru '75, Parisienne '83 thru '86
19030 Mid-size Regal & Century all rear-drive models with V6, V8 and Turbo '74 thru '87
Regal - see GENERAL MOTORS (38010)
Riviera - see GENERAL MOTORS (38030)
Roadmaster - see CHEVROLET (24046)
Skyhawk - see GENERAL MOTORS (38015)
Skylark - see GM (38020, 38025)
Somerset - see GENERAL MOTORS (38025)

CADILLAC
21030 Cadillac Rear Wheel Drive
all gasoline models '70 thru '93
Cimarron - see GENERAL MOTORS (38015)
DeVille - see GM (38031 & 38032)
Eldorado - see GM (38030 & 38031)
Fleetwood - see GM (38031)
Seville - see GM (38030, 38031 & 38032)

CHEVROLET
*24010 Astro & GMC Safari Mini-vans '85 thru '02
24015 Camaro V8 all models '70 thru '81
24016 Camaro all models '82 thru '92
24017 Camaro & Firebird '93 thru '02
Cavalier - see GENERAL MOTORS (38016)
Celebrity - see GENERAL MOTORS (38005)
24020 Chevelle, Malibu & El Camino '69 thru '87
24024 Chevette & Pontiac T1000 '76 thru '87
Citation - see GENERAL MOTORS (38020)
24032 Corsica/Beretta all models '87 thru '96
24040 Corvette all V8 models '68 thru '82
24041 Corvette all models '84 thru '96
10305 Chevrolet Engine Overhaul Manual
24045 Full-size Sedans Caprice, Impala, Biscayne, Bel Air & Wagons '69 thru '90
24046 Impala SS & Caprice and Buick Roadmaster '91 thru '96
Impala - see LUMINA (24048)
Lumina '90 thru '94 - see GM (38010)
*24048 Lumina & Monte Carlo '95 thru '01
Lumina APV - see GM (38035)
24050 Luv Pick-up all 2WD & 4WD '72 thru '82
Malibu '97 thru '00 - see GM (38026)
24055 Monte Carlo all models '70 thru '88
Monte Carlo '95 thru '01 - see LUMINA (24048)

24059 Nova all V8 models '69 thru '79
24060 Nova and Geo Prizm '85 thru '92
24064 Pick-ups '67 thru '87 - Chevrolet & GMC, all V8 & in-line 6 cyl, 2WD & 4WD '67 thru '87; Suburbans, Blazers & Jimmys '67 thru '91
24065 Pick-ups '88 thru '98 - Chevrolet & GMC, full-size pick-ups '88 thru '98, C/K Classic '99 & '00, Blazer & Jimmy '92 thru '94; Suburban '92 thru '99; Tahoe & Yukon '95 thru '99
*24066 Pick-ups '99 thru '03 - Chevrolet Silverado & GMC Sierra full-size pick-ups '99 thru '02, Suburban/Tahoe/Yukon/Yukon XL '00 thru '02
24070 S-10 & S-15 Pick-ups '82 thru '93, Blazer & Jimmy '83 thru '94,
*24071 S-10 & S-15 Pick-ups '94 thru '01, Blazer & Jimmy '95 thru '01, Hombre '96 thru '01
*24072 Chevrolet TrailBlazer & TrailBlazer EXT, GMC Envoy & Envoy XL, Oldsmobile Bravada '02 and '03
24075 Sprint '85 thru '88 & Geo Metro '89 thru '01
24080 Vans - Chevrolet & GMC '68 thru '96

CHRYSLER
25015 Chrysler Cirrus, Dodge Stratus, Plymouth Breeze '95 thru '00
10310 Chrysler Engine Overhaul Manual
25020 Full-size Front-Wheel Drive '88 thru '93
K-Cars - see DODGE (30008)
Laser - see DODGE Daytona (30030)
25025 Chrysler LHS, Concorde, New Yorker, Dodge Intrepid, Eagle Vision, '93 thru '97
*25026 Chrysler LHS, Concorde, 300M, Dodge Intrepid, '98 thru '03
25030 Chrysler & Plymouth Mid-size front wheel drive '82 thru '95
Rear-wheel Drive - see Dodge (30050)
*25035 PT Cruiser all models '01 thru '03
*25040 Chrysler Sebring, Dodge Avenger '95 thru '02

DATSUN
28005 200SX all models '80 thru '83
28007 B-210 all models '73 thru '78
28009 210 all models '79 thru '82
28012 240Z, 260Z & 280Z Coupe '70 thru '78
28014 280ZX Coupe & 2+2 '79 thru '83
300ZX - see NISSAN (72010)
28016 310 all models '78 thru '82
28018 510 & PL521 Pick-up '68 thru '73
28020 510 all models '78 thru '81
28022 620 Series Pick-up all models '73 thru '79
720 Series Pick-up - see NISSAN (72030)
28025 810/Maxima all gasoline models, '77 thru '84

DODGE
400 & 600 - see CHRYSLER (25030)
30008 Aries & Plymouth Reliant '81 thru '89
30010 Caravan & Plymouth Voyager '84 thru '95
*30011 Caravan & Plymouth Voyager '96 thru '02
30012 Challenger/Plymouth Saporro '78 thru '83
30016 Colt & Plymouth Champ '78 thru '87
30020 Dakota Pick-ups all models '87 thru '96
*30021 Durango '98 & '99, Dakota '97 thru '99
30025 Dart, Demon, Plymouth Barracuda, Duster & Valiant 6 cyl models '67 thru '76
30030 Daytona & Chrysler Laser '84 thru '89
Intrepid - see CHRYSLER (25025, 25026)
*30034 Neon all models '95 thru '99
30035 Omni & Plymouth Horizon '78 thru '90
30040 Pick-ups all full-size models '74 thru '93
*30041 Pick-ups all full-size models '94 thru '01
30045 Ram 50/D50 Pick-ups & Raider and Plymouth Arrow Pick-ups '79 thru '93
30050 Dodge/Plymouth/Chrysler RWD '71 thru '89
30055 Shadow & Plymouth Sundance '87 thru '94
30060 Spirit & Plymouth Acclaim '89 thru '95
*30065 Vans - Dodge & Plymouth '71 thru '03

EAGLE
Talon - see MITSUBISHI (68030, 68031)
Vision - see CHRYSLER (25025)

FIAT
34010 124 Sport Coupe & Spider '68 thru '78
34025 X1/9 all models '74 thru '80

FORD
10355 Ford Automatic Transmission Overhaul
36004 Aerostar Mini-vans all models '86 thru '97
36006 Contour & Mercury Mystique '95 thru '00
36008 Courier Pick-up all models '72 thru '82
*36012 Crown Victoria & Mercury Grand Marquis '88 thru '00
10320 Ford Engine Overhaul Manual
36016 Escort/Mercury Lynx all models '81 thru '90
36020 Escort/Mercury Tracer '91 thru '00
36022 Ford Escape & Mazda Tribute '01 thru '03
36024 Explorer & Mazda Navajo '91 thru '01
36025 Ford Explorer & Mercury Mountaineer '02 and '03
36028 Fairmont & Mercury Zephyr '78 thru '83
36030 Festiva & Aspire '88 thru '97
36032 Fiesta all models '77 thru '80
*36034 Focus all models '00 and '01
36036 Ford & Mercury Full-size '75 thru '87
36044 Ford & Mercury Mid-size '75 thru '86
36048 Mustang V8 all models '64-1/2 thru '73
36049 Mustang II 4 cyl, V6 & V8 models '74 thru '78
36050 Mustang & Mercury Capri all models Mustang, '79 thru '93; Capri, '79 thru '86
*36051 Mustang all models '94 thru '03
36054 Pick-ups & Bronco '73 thru '79
36058 Pick-ups & Bronco '80 thru '96
*36059 F-150 & Expedition '97 thru '02, F-250 '97 thru '99 & Lincoln Navigator '98 thru '02
*36060 Super Duty Pick-ups, Excursion '97 thru '02
36062 Pinto & Mercury Bobcat '75 thru '80
36066 Probe all models '89 thru '92
36070 Ranger/Bronco II gasoline models '83 thru '92
*36071 Ranger '93 thru '00 & Mazda Pick-ups '94 thru '00
36074 Taurus & Mercury Sable '86 thru '95
*36075 Taurus & Mercury Sable '96 thru '01
36078 Tempo & Mercury Topaz '84 thru '94
36082 Thunderbird/Mercury Cougar '83 thru '88
36086 Thunderbird/Mercury Cougar '89 and '97
36090 Vans all V8 Econoline models '69 thru '91
*36094 Vans full size '92 thru '01
*36097 Windstar Mini-van '95 thru '03

GENERAL MOTORS
10360 GM Automatic Transmission Overhaul
38005 Buick Century, Chevrolet Celebrity, Oldsmobile Cutlass Ciera & Pontiac 6000 all models '82 thru '96
*38010 Buick Regal, Chevrolet Lumina, Oldsmobile Cutlass Supreme & Pontiac Grand Prix (FWD) '88 thru '02
38015 Buick Skyhawk, Cadillac Cimarron, Chevrolet Cavalier, Oldsmobile Firenza & Pontiac J-2000 & Sunbird '82 thru '94
*38016 Chevrolet Cavalier & Pontiac Sunfire '95 thru '01
38020 Buick Skylark, Chevrolet Citation, Olds Omega, Pontiac Phoenix '80 thru '85
38025 Buick Skylark & Somerset, Oldsmobile Achieva & Calais and Pontiac Grand Am all models '85 thru '98
*38026 Chevrolet Malibu, Olds Alero & Cutlass, Pontiac Grand Am '97 thru '00
38030 Cadillac Eldorado '71 thru '85, Seville '80 thru '85, Oldsmobile Toronado '71 thru '85, Buick Riviera '79 thru '85
*38031 Cadillac Eldorado & Seville '86 thru '91, DeVille '86 thru '93, Fleetwood & Olds Toronado '86 thru '92, Buick Riviera '86 thru '93
38032 Cadillac DeVille '94 thru '02 & Seville - '92 thru '02
38035 Chevrolet Lumina APV, Olds Silhouette & Pontiac Trans Sport all models '90 thru '96
*38036 Chevrolet Venture, Olds Silhouette, Pontiac Trans Sport & Montana '97 thru '01
General Motors Full-size Rear-wheel Drive - see BUICK (19025)

GEO
Metro - see CHEVROLET Sprint (24075)
Prizm - '85 thru '92 see CHEVY (24060), '93 thru '02 see TOYOTA Corolla (92036)

(Continued on other side)

---

* Listings shown with an asterisk (*) indicate model coverage as of this printing. These titles will be periodically updated to include later model years - consult your Haynes dealer for more information.

Haynes North America, Inc., 861 Lawrence Drive, Newbury Park, CA 91320-1514 • (805) 498-6703

Haynes Automotive Manuals (continued)

NOTE: New manuals are added to this list on a periodic basis. If you do not see a listing for your vehicle, consult your local Haynes dealer for the latest product information.

40030   Storm all models '90 thru '93
        Tracker - see SUZUKI Samurai (90010)

GMC
        Vans & Pick-ups - see CHEVROLET

HONDA
42010   Accord CVCC all models '76 thru '83
42011   Accord all models '84 thru '89
42012   Accord all models '90 thru '93
42013   Accord all models '94 thru '97
*42014 Accord all models '98 and '99
42020   Civic 1200 all models '73 thru '79
42021   Civic 1300 & 1500 CVCC '80 thru '83
42022   Civic 1500 CVCC all models '75 thru '79
42023   Civic all models '84 thru '91
42024   Civic & del Sol '92 thru '95
*42025 Civic '96 thru '00, CR-V '97 thru '00,
        Acura Integra '94 thru '00
42040   Prelude CVCC all models '79 thru '89

HYUNDAI
*43010 Elantra all models '96 thru '01
43015   Excel & Accent all models '86 thru '98

ISUZU
        Hombre - see CHEVROLET S-10 (24071)
*47017 Rodeo '91 thru '02; Amigo '89 thru '94 and
        '98 thru '02; Honda Passport '95 thru '02
47020   Trooper & Pick-up '81 thru '93

JAGUAR
49010   XJ6 all 6 cyl models '68 thru '86
49011   XJ6 all models '88 thru '94
49015   XJ12 & XJS all 12 cyl models '72 thru '85

JEEP
50010   Cherokee, Comanche & Wagoneer Limited
        all models '84 thru '00
50020   CJ all models '49 thru '86
*50025 Grand Cherokee all models '93 thru '00
50029   Grand Wagoneer & Pick-up '72 thru '91
        Grand Wagoneer '84 thru '91, Cherokee &
        Wagoneer '72 thru '83, Pick-up '72 thru '88
*50030 Wrangler all models '87 thru '00

LEXUS
        ES 300 - see TOYOTA Camry (92007)

LINCOLN
        Navigator - see FORD Pick-up (36059)
*59010 Rear-Wheel Drive all models '70 thru '01

MAZDA
61010   GLC Hatchback (rear-wheel drive) '77 thru '83
61011   GLC (front-wheel drive) '81 thru '85
61015   323 & Protegé '90 thru '00
*61016 MX-5 Miata '90 thru '97
61020   MPV all models '89 thru '94
        Navajo - see Ford Explorer (36024)
61030   Pick-ups '72 thru '93
        Pick-ups '94 thru '00 - see Ford Ranger (36071)
61035   RX-7 all models '79 thru '85
61036   RX-7 all models '86 thru '91
61040   626 (rear-wheel drive) all models '79 thru '82
61041   626/MX-6 (front-wheel drive) '83 thru '91
61042   626 '93 thru '01, MX-6/Ford Probe '93 thru '97

MERCEDES-BENZ
63012   123 Series Diesel '76 thru '85
63015   190 Series four-cyl gas models, '84 thru '88
63020   230/250/280 6 cyl sohc models '68 thru '72
63025   280 123 Series gasoline models '77 thru '81
63030   350 & 450 all models '71 thru '80

MERCURY
64200   Villager & Nissan Quest '93 thru '01
        All other titles, see FORD Listing.

MG
66010   MGB Roadster & GT Coupe '62 thru '80
66015   MG Midget, Austin Healey Sprite '58 thru '80

MITSUBISHI
68020   Cordia, Tredia, Galant, Precis &
        Mirage '83 thru '93
68030   Eclipse, Eagle Talon & Ply. Laser '90 thru '94
*68031 Eclipse '95 thru '01, Eagle Talon '95 thru '98
68035   Mitsubishi Galant '94 thru '03
68040   Pick-up '83 thru '96 & Montero '83 thru '93

NISSAN
72010   300ZX all models including Turbo '84 thru '89
72015   Altima all models '93 thru '01
72020   Maxima all models '85 thru '92
*72021 Maxima all models '93 thru '01
72030   Pick-ups '80 thru '97 Pathfinder '87 thru '95
*72031 Frontier Pick-up '98 thru '01, Xterra '00 & '01,
        Pathfinder '96 thru '01
72040   Pulsar all models '83 thru '86
        Quest - see MERCURY Villager (64200)
72050   Sentra all models '82 thru '94
72051   Sentra & 200SX all models '95 thru '99
72060   Stanza all models '82 thru '90

OLDSMOBILE
73015   Cutlass V6 & V8 gas models '74 thru '88
        For other OLDSMOBILE titles, see BUICK,
        CHEVROLET or GENERAL MOTORS listing.

PLYMOUTH
        For PLYMOUTH titles, see DODGE listing.

PONTIAC
79008   Fiero all models '84 thru '88
79018   Firebird V8 models except Turbo '70 thru '81
79019   Firebird all models '82 thru '92
79040   Mid-size Rear-wheel Drive '70 thru '87
        For other PONTIAC titles, see BUICK,
        CHEVROLET or GENERAL MOTORS listing.

PORSCHE
80020   911 except Turbo & Carrera 4 '65 thru '89
80025   914 all 4 cyl models '69 thru '76
80030   924 all models including Turbo '76 thru '82
80035   944 all models including Turbo '83 thru '89

RENAULT
        Alliance & Encore - see AMC (14020)

SAAB
*84010 900 all models including Turbo '79 thru '88

SATURN
*87010 Saturn all models '91 thru '02
87020   Saturn all L-series models '00 thru '04

SUBARU
89002   1100, 1300, 1400 & 1600 '71 thru '79
89003   1600 & 1800 2WD & 4WD '80 thru '94

SUZUKI
90010   Samurai/Sidekick & Geo Tracker '86 thru '01

TOYOTA
92005   Camry all models '83 thru '91
92006   Camry all models '92 thru '96
*92007 Camry, Avalon, Solara, Lexus ES 300 '97 thru '01
92015   Celica Rear Wheel Drive '71 thru '85
92020   Celica Front Wheel Drive '86 thru '99
92025   Celica Supra all models '79 thru '92
92030   Corolla all models '75 thru '79
92032   Corolla all rear wheel drive models '80 thru '87
92035   Corolla all front wheel drive models '84 thru '92
92036   Corolla & Geo Prizm '93 thru '02
92040   Corolla Tercel all models '80 thru '82
92045   Corona all models '74 thru '82
92050   Cressida all models '78 thru '82
92055   Land Cruiser FJ40, 43, 45, 55 '68 thru '82
92056   Land Cruiser FJ60, 62, 80, FZJ80 '80 thru '96
92065   MR2 all models '85 thru '87
92070   Pick-up all models '69 thru '78
92075   Pick-up all models '79 thru '95
*92076 Tacoma '95 thru '00, 4Runner '96 thru '00,
        & T100 '93 thru '98
*92078 Tundra '00 thru '02 & Sequoia '01 thru '02
92080   Previa all models '91 thru '95

*92082 RAV4 all models '96 thru '02
92085   Tercel all models '87 thru '94

TRIUMPH
94007   Spitfire all models '62 thru '81
94010   TR7 all models '75 thru '81

VW
96008   Beetle & Karmann Ghia '54 thru '79
*96009 New Beetle '98 thru '00
96016   Rabbit, Jetta, Scirocco & Pick-up gas
        models '74 thru '91 & Convertible '80 thru '92
96017   Golf, GTI & Jetta '93 thru '98
        & Cabrio '95 thru '98
*96018 Golf, GTI, Jetta & Cabrio '99 thru '02
96020   Rabbit, Jetta & Pick-up diesel '77 thru '84
96023   Passat '98 thru '01, Audi A4 '96 thru '01
96030   Transporter 1600 all models '68 thru '79
96035   Transporter 1700, 1800 & 2000 '72 thru '79
96040   Type 3 1500 & 1600 all models '63 thru '73
96045   Vanagon all air-cooled models '80 thru '83

VOLVO
97010   120, 130 Series & 1800 Sports '61 thru '73
97015   140 Series all models '66 thru '74
97020   240 Series all models '76 thru '93
97040   740 & 760 Series all models '82 thru '88
97050   850 Series all models '93 thru '97

TECHBOOK MANUALS
10205   Automotive Computer Codes
10210   Automotive Emissions Control Manual
10215   Fuel Injection Manual, 1978 thru 1985
10220   Fuel Injection Manual, 1986 thru 1999
10225   Holley Carburetor Manual
10230   Rochester Carburetor Manual
10240   Weber/Zenith/Stromberg/SU Carburetors
10305   Chevrolet Engine Overhaul Manual
10310   Chrysler Engine Overhaul Manual
10320   Ford Engine Overhaul Manual
10330   GM and Ford Diesel Engine Repair Manual
10340   Small Engine Repair Manual, 5 HP & Less
10341   Small Engine Repair Manual, 5.5 - 20 HP
10345   Suspension, Steering & Driveline Manual
10355   Ford Automatic Transmission Overhaul
10360   GM Automatic Transmission Overhaul
10405   Automotive Body Repair & Painting
10410   Automotive Brake Manual
10411   Automotive Anti-lock Brake (ABS) Systems
10415   Automotive Detailing Manual
10420   Automotive Eelectrical Manual
10425   Automotive Heating & Air Conditioning
10430   Automotive Reference Manual & Dictionary
10435   Automotive Tools Manual
10440   Used Car Buying Guide
10445   Welding Manual
10450   ATV Basics

SPANISH MANUALS
98903   Reparación de Carrocería & Pintura
98905   Códigos Automotrices de la Computadora
98910   Frenos Automotriz
98915   Inyección de Combustible 1986 al 1999
99040   Chevrolet & GMC Camionetas '67 al '87
        Incluye Suburban, Blazer & Jimmy '67 al '91
99041   Chevrolet & GMC Camionetas '88 al '98
        Incluye Suburban '92 al '98, Blazer &
        Jimmy '92 al '94, Tahoe y Yukon '95 al '98
99042   Chevrolet & GMC Camionetas
        Cerradas '68 al '95
99055   Dodge Caravan & Plymouth Voyager '84 al '95
99075   Ford Camionetas y Bronco '80 al '94
99077   Ford Camionetas Cerradas '69 al '91
99088   Ford Modelos de Tamaño Mediano '75 al '86
99091   Ford Taurus & Mercury Sable '86 al '95
99095   GM Modelos de Tamaño Grande '70 al '90
99100   GM Modelos de Tamaño Mediano '70 al '88
99110   Nissan Camioneta '80 al '96, Pathfinder '87 al '95
99118   Nissan Sentra '82 al '94
99125   Toyota Camionetas y 4Runner '79 al '95

Over 100 Haynes
motorcycle manuals
also available

9-04

* Listings shown with an asterisk (*) indicate model coverage as of this printing. These titles will be periodically
updated to include later model years - consult your Haynes dealer for more information.

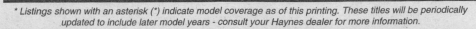

Haynes North America, Inc., 861 Lawrence Drive, Newbury Park, CA 91320-1514 • (805) 498-6703